D0070517

FOREST FIRE
Control and Use

McGraw Hill Series in Forest Resources

Henry J. Vaux, Consulting Editor

WALTER MULFORD WAS CONSULTING EDITOR OF THIS SERIES FROM ITS INCEPTION IN
1931 UNTIL JANUARY 1, 1952.

FOREST FIRE
Control and Use

Second Edition

Arthur A. Brown
Former Director of Forest Fire Research
for the United States Forest Service

Kenneth P. Davis
Professor of Forest Land Use
School of Forestry and
Environmental Studies
Yale University

McGraw-Hill Book Company

New York   St. Louis   San Francisco   Düsseldorf   Johannesburg
Kuala Lumpur   London   Mexico   Montreal   New Delhi   Panama
Rio de Janeiro   Singapore   Sydney   Toronto

FOREST FIRE: Control and Use

1 2 3 4 5 6 7 8 9 0 K P K P 7 9 8 7 6 5 4 3

Library of Congress Cataloging in Publication Data

Brown, Arthur Allen, 1900-
Forest fire.

(McGraw-Hill series in forest resources)
A revision of the 1959 ed. by K. P. Davis.
Bibliography: p.
1. Forest fires. I. Davis, Kenneth Pickett, 1906-
Forest fire: control and use. II. Title.
SD421.B76 1973   634.9′6′18   72-8655
ISBN 0-07-008205-7

This book was set in Times Roman by Black Dot, Inc. The editors were William P. Orr, Norma Frankel, and Shelly Langman; the production supervisor was John A. Sabella. The drawings were done by John Cordes, J & R Technical Services, Inc.
The printer and binder was Kingsport Press, Inc.

To the small but highly dedicated group of fire fighters, leaders, planners, and researchers who have built and who maintain national defense against destructive fires on our wild lands.

CONTENTS

PREFACE

Since the first publication of this book in 1959, much has happened in wild-land resource management which makes its revision timely. New progress in understanding wildfire behavior has taken place, new methods of fire fighting have been developed, and better means of using fire productively in wild-land management have been found. This has changed the perspective. At the same time growing public concern with ecology and with maintaining the environment has greatly enhanced the importance of such information.

Fire has long been a part of most wild-land ecology and has the demonstrated capacity to profoundly change the environment. Those who aspire to preserve and maintain the natural environment or to bring about ecological changes favorable to their purpose need first to understand the behavior of fire, its capacity for either constructive or destructive effects, and how such effects can be controlled. The primary purpose of this book is to provide essential information about these matters and about techniques to accomplish such purposes.

In preparing this second edition, Arthur A. Brown entered as senior author, undertaking the brunt of the revision job. He initiated the chapter revision, with the junior author giving detailed critical review, and there was free and vigorous give and take. Final decision was, however, left to the senior author, who assumes prime responsibility.

This book is intended to serve as a college text at both the undergraduate and graduate levels, to have reference value to the practitioner, and to be of interest to the general reader. Advanced students may need to supplement it with additional references in specialized areas of fire science. The practitioner will find this book a useful guide in developing fire plans and in training fire control personnel. For all readers, the comprehensive bibliography opens doors to further study. The index brings together subject-matter groupings that do not fit into the chapter organization. This organization has been revised to give better continuity, yet individual chapters have sufficient autonomy to be read separately and in different sequences without confusion.

As in the previous edition, subject treatment centers mostly on the United States with its early leadership in the fire field and its wide diversity of topography, climate, and forest cover. Treatment has been broadened, however, by drawing on the experience and literature of other areas—Canada and Australia in particular.

Acknowledgment is made to many people who have contributed to this edition. Although separate authorship of three chapters in the first edition by George M. Byram, long with the Forest Service, and William R. Krumm of the U.S. Weather Bureau has been discontinued, these men have collaborated generously in the revision of these chapters. Charles C. Buck, a veteran expert in Forest Service fire research, has critically reviewed several chapters.

Others to whom we are particularly indebted include Dever Colson and R. C. Elvander of the Weather Bureau; Merle Lowden, John Keetch, Dee Taylor, Hal E. Anderson, Richard Rothermel, Malcolm Hardy, E. W. Zimmerman, Kenneth Parker, J. B. Hilman, Clark Row, and Ellis Williams, all of the U.S. Forest Service; also W. R. Moore of the Forest Service, Missoula, Montana, Brian M. Ainsley, Michigan Department of Natural Resources of Lansing, Michigan, and W. G. Cleavely, Ontario Department of Lands and Forests of Toronto, Canada, who accepted responsibility for contacting authors and for updating organization descriptions for the first three case accounts of fire-control practice in Chapter 16. David E. Williams, Director of the Forest Fire Research Institute of Canada, and Alan G. McArthur, Director, Forest Research Institute of Australia, each gave valuable counsel and references.

The text and both authors owe much to the wife of the senior author, Marie Sicher Brown, who helped with the revision throughout.

Arthur A. Brown
Kenneth P. Davis

Part One

Fire in the Forests

The purpose of Part One is to help the reader develop an understanding of fire as it occurs in forests and other wild lands. This begins with the ancient association between man and fire and the role of fire in American forests. It continues with the effects fire creates and the fuels and weather that affect its behavior. The nature of the combustion process and why fires behave in certain ways in wild-land areas is then considered. The final chapter integrates much of this information in an analysis of the problem of rating and forecasting fire danger.

Chapter 1

Man, Fire, and Forests

Fire, particularly the wood fire, has been intimately associated with mankind from the beginnings of civilization. The anthropologist sees the discovery of fire and its uses as one of the basic factors that permitted man to live and thrive in the temperate zone. Man had, in effect, leapfrogged a few million years of the evolutionary adaptations he would otherwise have needed to survive a cold winter. Instead, he suddenly realized his capacity for modifying the environment to meet his needs. From this beginning fire has continued to play an intimate role in all cultures. To the early Greek philosophers fire ranked with air, earth, and water as one of the four basic elements. If the concept is broadened to include both combustion and the thermal energy produced, the Greeks were not far wrong.

In spite of this long and basic human association, the wood fire, including fire in all plant materials, has continued to hold much of its mystery. Other kinds of combustion are much better understood. These mostly concern liquid and gaseous fuels whose chemical and physical makeup, rate of fuel feed, and rate of mixing with oxygen can be subjected to precise control. The internal combustion engine is a good example of the application of what is known about such fires. The combustion process in wood fires is much less subject to precise control. Because wood is a solid fuel, it must first be converted to a gaseous state before it can ignite. The gases, in turn, vary in chemical and physical properties at different stages of the generating process. These variations depend on time, temperature, and access to oxygen. The rate of mixing with oxygen, though subject to control in the laboratory, cannot be paced to produce a precise result. So a free-burning fire, which typifies the behavior of a forest fire, is further removed from the known and predictable. It increases its energy with time; it determines its own rate of fuel feed; and it interacts with its local environment to create a highly variable phenomenon.

For these reasons scientific understanding of the wood fire, and especially the forest fire out of control, is still much less complete than that of atomic fission, for example. For the same reason wildfire has a challenge and a fascination for the student, the scientist, and the administrator as well as for the fire fighter.

Since World War II, the free-burning fire has been receiving increased attention from scientists. This has come about through the active sponsorship and coordination of basic research in this field among all agencies by the Committee on Fire Research of the National Academy of Sciences–National Research Council and also through increased emphasis by the U.S. Forest Service and its cooperators on research in the natural laws underlying fire behavior. This is providing new insights into formerly mysterious aspects of fire behavior, as will be detailed in later chapters. It is also bringing about changes in concepts in the use and control of fire. Such changes augur well for rapid progress in this field in the next few decades. But the translation of laboratory findings into new and improved methods and techniques takes time and will not be completed in the foreseeable future. Any treatment of forest fires must deal with both control and use of fire as a science and as an art. In following chapters, what has been learned from practice and from empirical methods is presented and evaluated along with what has been learned scientifically. This is done in an effort to integrate what is known in terms of the "what," the "why," and the "how much" of each phase of this complex field.

FIRE AS A NATURAL PHENOMENON

It is natural that fire should have a basic relationship to forestry and that it should be of vital concern to the forester. Commercial forestry is directly concerned with the production of usable wood fiber and with creating and maintaining a living plant cover. All forestry consists of the management of the creative force of photosynthesis. This is the chemical process on which all life depends, by which carbon dioxide, water, and the sun's energy are combined to produce cellulose and other carbohydrates. It moves slowly, like a tide powered by the sun, in all green plants.

Fire suddenly reverses the process and releases the heat energy stored by photosynthesis. It is easy to visualize this basic relationship if the comparison is written as a general formula,[1] thus:

Photosynthesis

$$CO_2 + H_2O + \text{solar energy} \rightarrow (C_6H_{10}O_5)_n + O$$

Combustion

$$(C_6H_{10}O_5)_n + O + \text{kindling temperature} \rightarrow CO_2 + H_2O + \text{heat}$$

When these two formulas are compared it is apparent they are nearly identical but reversed in direction. In photosynthesis, energy is being fixed slowly; in combustion, it is being released rapidly. The kindling temperature entered as the third element in the combustion formula may be regarded as only the trigger action or catalyst to start and maintain the process. At lower temperatures oxidation can and does take place with the same end products.

A third formula could represent wood decay by simply removing the kindling-temperature term from the combustion formula. Most decay takes place with fungi, bacteria, and insects acting as intermediaries. This introduces biological processes with complex intermediate products; nevertheless the end products are identical to those from combustion. The essential difference between combustion and decay is again in the speed of the process. At best decay proceeds slowly. Usually the heat of oxidation is not noticeable, and inorganic materials are released gradually. Each of these basic processes can be utilized by the forester, but each requires control in any plan of forest land management.

The management of tree growth is the underlying purpose of silviculture. This entails management of photosynthesis through selection and maintenance of the trees that are to be involved in the process. It is a constructive undertaking.

Potentially, fire is totally destructive, since it can disrupt plans of

---

[1] The formula used is for cellulose. That for lignin is similar. Photosynthesis also involves the synthesis of other complex organic compounds which include inorganic salts. These may affect fire behavior to a degree but have no significance for the present purpose.

forest management by injuring or killing trees of all ages, by consuming or downgrading merchantable timber products, by quickly consuming litter and all organic matter, and by suddenly altering the forest environment in ways that may expose it to deterioration through erosion, leaching, insect attacks, etc. Yet not all the effects are destructive. Speeding the deterioration of accumulated dead material and the elimination of existing living cover may at times and places fit the needs of management. This is so where there is a need to wipe the slate clean, as it were, so that more complete control and a favorable environment can be ensured for a new crop. Selection of the area and control of the combustion process to attain the effects desired are the prerequisites.

The natural processes of decay operate to clear the way for the living. These processes are as essential as is photosynthesis in the endless natural cycle of growth and decay. In this sense they are constructive. But associated with heart-rot fungi, they are highly destructive of forest products. In the virgin forest, decay is presumed to be in equilibrium with growth. In the forest managed for timber production, minimum depletion through decay is sought.

Of more direct concern from a fire control standpoint is the annual accumulation of litter and annual vegetation under a forest stand. The rate of decay determines the depth of the duff layer and is a strong factor in determining the stand's susceptibility to fire and how it will burn. Intervention in the decay process is direct only in the measures used to dispose of logging slash following timber harvest and in prescribed burning where the chief objective is reduction of fire hazard. These aspects are developed in later chapters.

FIRE AND PROFESSIONAL FORESTRY

Systematic control and use of fire is relatively new in professional forestry in spite of the basic relationships described. There are several reasons for this. The first is the absence of professional involvement with the fire problem in European forestry and the consequent absence of early technical literature on the subject. This precedent has strongly influenced academic recognition of the fire problem in North American forestry. Professional forestry training in this country began in the European tradition, with forest fire control treated as something of an innovation peculiar to North America and the less developed countries. This pattern has tended to persist.

A closely related reason for the newness of this approach is that constructive professional treatment of fire in the forest depends on the development of an adequate forest fire literature. This takes time. Though handicaps in this respect are being overcome, much remains to be done to unify and to give perspective to this field.

A third important reason is the tendency to focus on the physical tasks in fire fighting and to regard the whole subject as vocational in nature and to be learned on the job.

A fourth reason is a belief by some that the threat of fire is transient and is important only in the pioneering phases of forestry. In North America, fire control as a major forestry activity has been associated with the pioneering stage of forest land management. In Australia, Siberia, and, in fact, wherever extensive forest management is practiced, conflagrations continue to occur periodically. This suggests that extensive management and conflagrations tend to go together, particularly in temperate regions. In Europe, the more intensive the silviculture practiced, the less the fire losses, so that fire control activities tend to become incidental. The most important reason for this is the intensive utilization. This results in a clean forest floor with all dead and down material removed. Even dead branches are often lopped from standing trees. Added to this is the complete and uniform accessibility developed, the creation of numerous barriers to fire, a generally mesophytic climate, and the presence of nearby manpower and facilities that make it easy to control fires before they gain headway. Though the differences in climate and in economics make comparisons difficult, a reduced fire threat does seem a reasonable expectation for forest areas where intensive management is practiced. But since close utilization is a prerequisite, there is a long way to go before this kind of "built-in" solution to the fire problem can be relied upon in North America.

This is well illustrated by data in the U.S. Forest Service's *Forest Resources Report* no. 17 of 1965. In this report the status of protection of the 759 million acres of forest land in the United States, including Alaska, is reviewed. Four categories of adequacy are distinguished:

Class 4: Unprotected
Class 3: Protection adequate only for the easy year with some failures likely in the average year
Class 2: Protection adequate for the average year but failures likely in the periodic drought year
Class 1: Protection adequate to meet the fire situation in bad years and under serious peak loads

Under this classification only 18 percent of the forest land in federal holdings and 34 percent of that in state, county, and municipal ownership was credited with Class 1 protection. This was in spite of the fact that only in Alaska is there any significant unprotected area and all National Forest and National Park lands are protected by a fire control system thought to be adequate for at least the average year. The reasons for a continuing conflagration threat in critical years in so much of the forest area are lack of access, the large amount of unutilized dead material in unmanaged stands, and the often hazardous condition of cutover stands even where classed as in productive condition from a silvicultural standpoint. The tendency is strong in partially cutover areas to depend on the fire control organization to hold down losses rather than to invest substantially in reducing the fire potential through hazard reduction and other fire prevention measures.

On the great areas of forest land on which only extensive forest management for wood products will be practiced and on most of the forest lands dedicated to special nontimber objectives, such as wilderness areas, parks, wildlife preserves, and city watersheds, the fire problem cannot be expected to abate. Forest fuels will remain abundant and are likely to be exposed to increasing risk of fire as human use of the area increases. Such relationships are developed further in the later discussion of fire prevention. It is sufficient to note here that the forest fire problem in all forest regions of North America will remain a challenge to land managers for the foreseeable future.

KINDS OF FOREST FIRES

What constitutes a forest fire? From the point of view of the land manager it is "Any wild-land fire not prescribed for the area by an authorized plan."[2] A more descriptive definition is uncontained and freely spreading combustion which consumes the natural fuels of a forest, that is, duff, litter, grass, dead branch wood, snags, logs, stumps, weeds, brush, foliage, and, to a limited degree, green trees. This is the most useful definition. The essential characteristic of a forest fire is that it is unconfined and free to spread. A very useful synonym coming into increasing use is "free-burning." A "free-burning fire" is a fire free to respond to its environment. Due to chance combinations of natural fuels, weather, and topography, a free-burning fire may long remain only a smoldering spot or it may quickly develop into a young tornado. In both cases it is responding freely to its local environment. These responses are analyzed in the chapter on fire behavior.

---

[2] U.S. Forest Service, *Glossary of Terms Used in Forest Fire Control*, U.S. Department of Agriculture Handbook no. 104, 1956.

The term *forest fire* as defined above is a generalized term for any wild-land fire burning in natural fuels. Among forest protection agencies, however, fires are often differentiated according to the prevailing natural fuels in which they are burning. A convenient differentiation is *grass, brush,* and *timber* fires. Where grass is the primary fuel over large areas, the grass fire is sufficiently distinctive as a fire control problem to merit separate treatment in both planning and action. This attention has not always been accorded to it by foresters.

In reporting forest fires for the statistical record, fire control organizations make various technical distinctions. Though organizational in nature, these provide a further vantage point from which to define a forest fire. For example, a statistical fire is commonly defined as one which occurred on the area the agency protects or which threatened that area and on which some expenditure of dollars or man-hours chargeable to fire funds was made. If, for example, a slash burning fire escapes but is put under control again without the expenditure of fire funds, it would not be included in the statistical record.

A useful and long accepted classification of fires is based on the degree to which fuels from mineral soil upward to treetops were involved in combustion. This is in effect a fire behavior classification. This classifies all fires as ground, surface, or crown fires.

Ground Fire

A ground fire consumes the organic material beneath the surface litter of the forest floor. In many forest types, particularly in northern latitudes, at higher elevations, and in bog areas in all locations, a mantle of organic material accumulates on top of the mineral soil. It may be identified as duff, muck, or peat. A fire spreading in and consuming such material is a ground fire. With very deep organic material, as in muck soil and in peat beds or bogs, under drought conditions the fire may penetrate several feet below the surface and travel entirely underground. A ground fire may and often does follow a surface fire, depending on the moisture content of the organic layer. A true ground fire spreads within rather than on top of the organic mantle. It is characterized by a slowly smoldering edge with no flame and little smoke. Ground fires are often hard to detect and are the least spectacular and slowest moving. But acre for acre they are usually the most destructive of all fires. Per unit of perimeter they are usually, too, the most difficult to control. Such fires create distinctive problems in forest fire fighting that must enter into the policy and practices of all fire control agencies.

Figure 1.1 Mild surface fires in hardwood leaf litter. *(U.S. Forest Service photo.)*

Surface Fire

A surface fire is "A fire that burns surface litter, other loose debris of the forest floor and small vegetation (Figure 1.1).[3] This is the most common type of fire in timber stands of all species. It may be a mild, low-energy fire in sparse grass and pine needle litter, or it may be a very hot, fast-moving fire where slash, flammable understory shrubs, or other abundant fuel prevails. A surface fire may and often does burn up into the taller vegetation and tree crowns as it progresses. This is called "crowning out," but so long as it is sporadic in nature, the fire remains in the category of a surface fire.

[3] Ibid.

Crown Fire

A crown fire is "A fire that advances from top to top of trees or shrubs more or less independently of the surface fire.[4] In dense conifer stands on steep slopes or on level ground, with a brisk wind, the crown fire may race ahead of the supporting surface fire. This is the most spectacular kind of forest fire. Since it is over the heads of ground forces it is uncontrollable until it again drops to the ground, and since it is usually fast-moving it poses grave danger to fire fighters and wildlife in its path. It is the most common cause of fire fighters becoming trapped and burned. A fire moving through the crowns of shrubs is also a crown fire. Such fires are common in chaparral cover in California and certain other Western states. A crown fire does not necessarily run ahead of the surface fire. In some situations, and always in chaparral cover, it remains coupled to the surface fire. To distinguish the degree of independence from the surface fire, crown fires are often classed as "running" or "dependent." Figure 1.2A and B pictures a dependent crown fire in a mixed conifer stand and in California chaparral.

Fire Combinations

In actual fire situations, these three kinds of fire may occur simultaneously and in all kinds of combinations. Surface fires are by far the most common, and nearly all fires start as such. A surface fire may spread into the crowns and develop into a sweeping crown fire. A crown fire may drop to the ground and become a surface fire. Similarly, a surface fire may develop into a stubborn ground fire that may plague control forces for days or weeks. On a hot, dry, and windy afternoon, a rather innocuous-appearing ground fire may be fanned into a surface or crown fire. This has happened many times. Figure 1.3 illustrates the basic nature of these three kinds of forest fires.

THE FIELD OF FIRE CONTROL

Because fire itself has a long-standing association with man, attempts to control fire are also very old. But control of forest fires was limited at first to defense of improved property. The systematic development of forest fire control to protect forest values is a relatively young science which is still evolving. The various aspects of this evolution are the subject of the chapters which follow.

[4] Ibid.

Figure 1.2 Dependent crown fire. *(U.S. Forest Service photos.)* *A.* In stand of mixed conifers. *B.* In California chaparral.

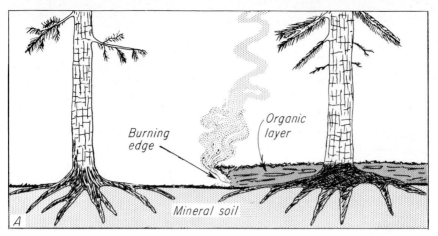

Figure 1.3 Kinds of forest fire. *A.* Ground fire. *B.* Surface fire. *C.* Crown fire.

As in most fields, an active research program has furnished much of the stimulus to progress in the United States. The bibliography well illustrates this relationship between forest fire control and fire research activities. Starting in 1925, forest fire research in the United States has expanded, and since World War II it has grown into a strong program in both basic and applied research drawing from many disciplines (Brown, 1964; Barrows, 1971).

Fire as a field of professional interest concerns the physical and biological sciences and the social sciences as well. It draws heavily on the applied fields of meteorology, engineering, and administration and it repeatedly tests the operating skill of the man on the ground.

Chapter 2

Fire in
North American Forests

A critical review of how forest fires relate to virgin North American forests and to land settlement and development in the United States will help to establish basic relationships. It is also essential to an understanding of the present status of fire control activity and can help to answer the "why" of fire control before the "how," "when," and "where" are examined in more detail.

FIRE IN THE VIRGIN FOREST

There is ample evidence that fire had been a factor in shaping North American forests long before the advent of the white man. Plummer (1912) presents definite evidence of great conflagrations previous to any written record. Fire scars on California's *Sequoia gigantea* show that destructive fires occurred in those stands in 245, 1441, 1580, and 1797. Similar evidence in Colorado reveals that extensive fires burned there in 1676, 1707, 1722, 1753, and 1781. In the region south of Mount Katahdin, Maine, there is evidence of an extensive fire or fires in 1795.

In the Southwest, in the Douglas-fir region, in the northern Rocky Mountain region and throughout the South, similar evidence has been found.

Plummer compiled a tabulation of "dark days" produced by drift smoke from extensive fires. The first of these was recorded as May 12, 1706, in New England, and the darkest day from smoke palls, known as Black Friday, was on May 19, 1780.

Many of the early travelers and explorers mentioned forest fires in their accounts. Often they referred to them as "acts of God," though others credited them to the Indians.

Probably, in the wilderness state, fire tended to follow weather cycles, with great conflagrations in drought periods leading to the creation of extensive open grass and brush areas. In the long intervals that followed, grass and brush would gradually be replaced by the prevalent forest types. In the high-lightning zones, many small areas must have burned annually.

The part played by Indian tribes in causing forest fires has often been debated, particularly in California. It is known that Indians at times set fires to drive game and that they also used fire in fighting an enemy. So they no doubt contributed to some degree to forest fire history. However, the firsthand testimony of old Indians of Western tribes indicates that they had great fear of conflagrations and a high respect for fire's destructiveness. Certainly the Indian camp and signal fire was always smaller and more carefully guarded than the fire used by the white man, and they did not have matches. It is at least a fair assumption that no habitual or systematic burning was carried out by the Indians.

But lightning set fires without any human intervention, and this, along with tornadoes, hurricanes, and insect epidemics, must have kept much of the so-called virgin forest in a state of flux. These agents were often large-scale harvesters of timber.

During the nineteenth century, the movement of settlers into the area now encompassed by the United States broke like a wave over the Alleghenies into the great heartland of the Middle West and on to the West Coast. The settlers continually encountered the forest as an obstacle to permanent land use. Except for the Great Plains, almost the entire area needed for agricultural settlement had to be hewn from a seemingly never-ending forest. The great hardwood forests of the Ohio River Valley were almost annihilated as the area was transformed into one of the great agricultural and industrial regions of the world. Land clearing was a major need for generations, and fire was the principal force available to the settler for freeing the land from forest growth. In pioneer days the smoke from "settler fires" was regarded as an encouraging sign of progress.

As a consequence of the extensive land clearing that accompanied settlement and development in forest regions, certain concepts about forests and forest fires naturally developed. One was that of forest inexhaustibility; that there was plenty of timber for everyone. Another was that most of the land in settlement areas was destined for agricultural use, and the sooner cleared the better. Still another was that forest fires, except as they threatened personal property or specific stands of accessible timber, did not cause important damage. These ideas added up to a general indifference to forest fire. It has taken a series of holocausts, a threatened timber shortage, and decades of agitation to combat and substantially overcome them.

THE BEGINNINGS AND GROWTH OF FOREST PROTECTION

The period during which farms were carved out of the wilderness and forest land was considered primarily useful for agriculture continued until settlement began to move into the Prairie states around 1850.

The next 50 years was a period of rapid exploitation of forest resources. Production of lumber went from 1 billion feet in 1840 to 35 billion in 1869 and up to 46 billion in 1906 and 1907. There was no longer any compelling need to use fire in the forests. Nevertheless, indifference to forest destruction persisted. It was during this period that many of the famous forest fires of American history occurred.

However, a gradually changing attitude began to be manifest. The Timber Culture Act passed by Congress in 1873 reflected this change. It was intended to ensure wood supplies for the settler of the Western states. In the same year a committee was appointed by the American Association for the Advancement of Science "to memorialize Congress and the state legislatures upon the importance of promoting the cultivation of timber and the preservation of forests and to recommend proper legislation for securing these objects." The American Forestry Association was organized two years later, in 1875. In 1876, in response to this awakened public interest, a forestry agent was appointed in the Department of Agriculture to study the forest situation and to make recommendations. The impact of publicity attending the spectacularly destructive series of conflagrations in the Lake states gave impetus to this change. In 1891, the President was empowered to create timber reserves out of the public domain. Finally, in 1897, Congress provided for administration of the timber reserves. This was a reversal of the traditional policy of moving land into private ownership as rapidly as possible. For the first time too, responsibility for control of fires was assumed by a public agency.

These changes were the direct result of a new consciousness of the waste and destruction of natural resources that was arising from federal land policies. Leadership in the movement to reverse this trend was assumed by Gifford Pinchot who, in 1898, became chief of the new Division of Forestry in the Department of Agriculture. It had grown out of the forestry activity initiated in 1876, and in 1901 it became the Bureau of Forestry. In 1905 the Forest Reserves were transferred from the Department of Interior to the Department of Agriculture to be administered by the Bureau of Forestry, which was then renamed the Forest Service, and in 1907 the Forest Reserves became National Forests.

The first big task in the administration of these extensive public lands was protection of their resources from trespass and fire. The former was naturally not a very popular undertaking, but all could agree on the need to do something about fire. Even so, only the strong emotional zeal for conservation awakened by Pinchot and others and given vigorous implementation by Theodore Roosevelt as President made it possible to reverse the trend and initiate a positive policy of protection of forest resources.

Such efforts were not limited to federal action. As early as 1885 four states had commissions to deal with problems of forest and watershed protection. These were California, Colorado, Ohio, and New York. The New York organization was the only one which has continued without interruption, due in part to the early acquisition of state forest lands. Pennsylvania acquired forest land in 1898 and Minnesota in 1899. So both began early to assume responsibility for protecting them from fire. In 1885 both Colorado and New York passed laws which created a statewide forest warden force and introduced the principle of centralized supervision. The importance of such actions by individual states is in the precedents they set and the patterns of protection organization they helped to create.

The Weeks law of 1911 and the Clark McNary law of 1924 gave federal support to state forest protection and helped to set standards of performance. But most of all it gave legal sanction to the thesis that regardless of land ownership, the public interest is involved when forest fires are not controlled.

Highlights of the story of protection of forest resources in the United States for the period 1926 to 1969 are reflected by the statistical data contained in Figure 2.1A and B.[1]

The forest area under organized protection from fire kept increasing

---

[1] These data were generously computed by the Division of Cooperative Forest Fire Control of the U.S. Forest Service in response to a request by the senior author.

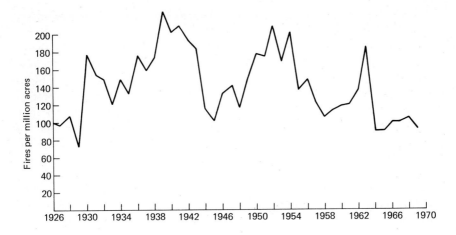

Figure 2.1 *A*. Graph showing number of fires per million acres protected for the United States between 1926 and 1969. *B*. Graph showing number of acres burned per million acres protected for the United States between 1926 and 1969.

during the period. Consequently, the number of fires per million acres and acres burned per million acres protected are more significant than annual totals. But in referring to these data, the constantly changing land base from which they come and the rapid changes in access, use, and tributary populations must also be kept in mind.

Both graphs show fluctuations in number of fires and area burned that are characteristic of forest fire statistics. These are similar to fluctuations in the occurrence of many other natural phenomena. Both graphs reflect periodic variations in fire weather, particularly variations in precipitation during the critical fire season. However, area burned per million acres reflects wet and dry years more closely than does the number of fires, particularly for forest backcountry in the western United States. It reached a peak in 1930 and 1931, which were drought years in the Northwest, at 14,555 and 15,983 acres per million, even though the number of fires per million acres protected was about average for the subsequent 10-year period. Peaks and low points in both graphs are exaggerated by coincidence in above- or below-average fire activity in two or more forest regions.

When viewed as a whole, both graphs show encouraging progress in wildfire control in the United States, even though this is not immediately apparent from Figure 2.1A. In the period of 1926 to 1969 there was constantly increased access, increasing population, and greatly increased recreational use in the areas protected. The fact that the number of fires per million acres protected was less in 1969 than in 1926 meant that good progress in fire prevention had been made. The favorable decreasing trend in area burned per million acres in Figure 2.1B is more obvious.

LARGE FOREST FIRES OF THE PAST

Though large forest fires occurred before the coming of the white man, their size, intensity, and frequency were greatly increased by settlement and logging. Great continuous areas of heavy fuels were created by logging. These were exposed to new and frequent sources of ignition. So whenever weather conditions created a situation now known as extreme fire danger, the stage was set for a conflagration.

To appreciate the destructive potentiality of forest fires and the tremendous forces they may unleash, it will be helpful to review some of the forest conflagrations of the past, emphasizing particularly the conditions that brought them about and the lessons still to be learned from them. Attention is concentrated on the United States, which offers abundant examples. The experience of Australia closely parallels that of the United States. With variations, the story can be repeated for many other countries of the world.

Information about ten major fires or groups of fires that may be classed as conflagrations and that have made history is given in Table 2.1.

Figure 2.2 Conflagration fire in progress. Sleeping Child fire in western Montana, 1961. *(U.S. Forest Service photo.)*

Much of this information is drawn from *Burning an Empire*, by Stewart Holbrook (1943), which gives a full and vivid account of most of these fires. Many other big fires, recent as well as old, could well have been included; there are many nominations for this hall of notorious fame. Those listed were selected to include some of the largest, most destructive, and best known. They are also representative, though not completely so, of conditions under which large fires can and have occurred. They are not representative of forest fires in general, most of which are small and not spectacular. It must also be recognized that large forest fires of the past have made news and linger in memory largely in proportion to loss of

Table 2.1 Ten Forest Conflagrations of the Past

Name	Date	Location	Area, acres	Lives lost
Miramichi and Maine fires	Oct. 7, 1825	New Brunswick and Maine. A series of large fires, the Miramichi the best known.	3,000,000 (830,000 in Maine)	Undetermined
Peshtigo (Wisconsin) and Michigan	Oct. 8, 1871	Eastern Wisconsin and central Michigan. A series of large fires, the Peshtigo best known from loss of life.	Peshtigo 1,280,000 Michigan 2,500,000	1,500 Undetermined
Michigan	Sept. 1–5, 1881	Eastern Michigan in Thumb area. A series of large fires.	1,000,000	169
Hinckley, Minnesota	Sept. 1, 1894	East-Central Minnesota. A series of large fires.	Undetermined	418
Wisconsin	Summer, 1894 (mostly Sept.)	Northwestern Wisconsin.	Undetermined but covered several million acres	Undetermined but few
Far West (Yacoult fire)	Sept. 12–13, 1902 (period of greatest spread)	Western Washington and Oregon. A series of 110 or more large fires.	Undetermined but probably over 1 million acres	38

Sources of Ignition	Weather conditions before and during fire	Forest type and fuels
Developed from many small settler and logging fires burning at the time.	Extremely unusual and severe summer drought and probably strong winds at time of fire.	Spruce-fir and some pine type, mostly uncut. Largest fire of all time in eastern North America.
Many uncontrolled settler and logging fires.	Long and severe drought throughout spring and summer. Hot weather. Strong wind, the same that drove the Great Chicago fire occurring on the same date.	Mostly red and white pine types with some spruce-fir and mixed hardwoods and hemlock. Large areas of logging slash. Burned both cut and uncut stands.
Many uncontrolled settler and logging fires, plus some lightning fires set on Aug. 31.	Extremely hot and dry summer. No rain for months. Hot days with only moderate winds at time of fire.	Red and white pine types with mixed hemlock and hardwoods, much of it killed in 1871 fire. Large areas of slash from logging and land clearing.
Many uncontrolled settler and logging fires burning through July and August.	Protracted spring and summer drought. Hot weather, moderate winds, and low humidity at time of fire.	Red and white pine types, with some spruce and mixed hardwoods. Large areas of slash from logging and land clearing. Both cut and uncut areas burned. Heavy timber damage.
Many uncontrolled settler and logging fires.	An extremely hot and dry summer. Most area burned Sept. 1 under same conditions as nearby Hinckley fire.	Red and white pine types, with some spruce and mixed hardwoods. Large areas of slash from logging and land clearing. Both cut and uncut areas burned. Heavy timber damage.
Many uncontrolled settler and logging fires.	Extremely dry summer. Low humidity and moderate to strong winds at time of fire.	Douglas-fir type. Heavy fuels. Burned mostly uncut timber but started in slashings.

Table 2.1   Ten Forest Conflagrations of the Past (Continued)

Name	Date	Location	Area, acres	Lives lost
Adirondack	Apr. 20–June 8, 1903	Northern New York in and around Adirondack Park. A series of fires.	637,000	None
Great Idaho	Aug. 10–21, 1910	Northern Idaho and northwestern Montana.	3,000,000	85
Tillamook	Aug. 14–25, 1933	Northwestern Oregon.	311,000 (270,000 Aug. 24–25)	1
Maine	Oct. 21–25, 1947	Maine.	205,678 (179,342 forested)	16

human life and property destroyed and only secondarily because of acreage covered or natural resources damaged. There have been many large forest fires, before and since the advent of permanent settlement, which have remained unrecorded except by scars and other evidence in the forests.

From a study of the fires given in Table 2.1 as well as others of similar scope, a few generalizations of significance can be drawn on the control of forest fires. They are here discussed in terms of sources of ignition, weather, fuels, and control.

Sources of ignition	Weather conditions before and during fire	Forest type and fuels
A multiplicity of causes; locomotives (started at least half); logging, smoking, and campfires; incendiaries.	Scanty snowfall and extremely dry spring. Precipitation from Apr. 16–June 7 only 0.2 in. Strong winds May 28–June 3 when most of spread occurred.	Spruce-fir with mixed hardwoods. Both cutover and uncut timber burned.
Many uncontrolled fires starting from lightning, also some from logging, land clearing, and railroads. Estimated 1,736 fires burning at time on National Forests of area alone.	Winter drought, extremely dry, hot, and windy spring and summer. Strong wind on Aug. 20 and 21 when many fires "blew up."	Western white pine type mostly uncut. About 6 billion bd. ft. of timber killed by fire. A whole cycle of subsequent fires in 1919, 1926, 1929, etc., were engendered by the 1910 fire.
Friction from power log skidding plus one incendiary fire.	Dry summer with hot weather. Low humidity and moderate winds during fire.	Douglas-fir type, mostly old growth. Fire killed about 12 billion bd ft of saw timber.
A number of untended and uncontrolled fires burning at the time plus a general feeling that the fire season was over.	Prolonged summer and fall drought with high temperatures and low humidity. Unusually warm fall. No rain since 0.62 in. on Sept. 22. Strong winds Oct. 21–25, worst on Oct. 23 when major break occurred. No rain until Nov. 8.	Second growth hardwoods and conifers with considerable logging slash on ground. Stands broken and intermixed in many places with fields and residential development. Heavy property damage.

Sources of Ignition

Except for the Tillamook fire, the monotonously recurrent pattern of causes for this group of fires was the existence of a large number of untended and uncontrolled fires at the time blowup burning conditions occurred. When the right combination of wind and related atmospheric conditions came about, existing fires were fanned into conflagrations. These big fires were nearly always in reality a series of fires in a general area, some merging and some separate, that went on a rampage at about the same time. For most of the fires listed, there is uncertainty as to which was the cause or even *the* fire.

The big fires included in Table 2.1 were mostly man-caused. The only exceptions were a few lightning-caused fires in connection with the Michigan fires of 1881 and a series of such fires which merged to produce most of the Great Idaho burn of 1910. In general, this situation reflected the public indifference to forest fires that had persisted for so many years and still lingers on to some degree. The Maine fires of 1947 were a sobering reminder in this respect. They occurred at a time when fire danger measurement was well understood and means for mass public dissemination of this information were well developed. Responsible officials were aware of the mounting fire danger. Nonetheless, some fifty fires are reported to have been burning in Maine at the time the major break occurred on October 23. A contributing circumstance was the general feeling that, as it was late October, the fire season was over.

The Tillamook fire of Oregon is an exception to the above general pattern of causes on two significant counts. First, the causes were specific and are known. The main fire was caused by friction in power log skidding. A companion fire was of incendiary origin. Second, these causes did not reflect general public carelessness and indifference. The logging fire represented a specific ill-advised act in a generally fire-conscious environment. The other fire represented individual malice.

Weather Conditions

As might be expected, all conflagration-size forest fires have occurred during extreme burning conditions. Protracted drought, accompanied by high air temperature and low relative humidity, set the stage for most bad fires by reducing the moisture content of all classes of forest fuels to abnormally low levels. High air temperatures and low relative humidity usually continued during the fire, aggravated at times by wind and associated atmospheric turbulence. While some big fires have been driven by strong surface winds, moderate but turbulent air circulation was more common.

Large fires often create violent atmospheric turbulence. The strong and gusty winds invariably associated with conflagrations and always mentioned by eyewitness accounts are usually caused by the fire itself. In an analysis of weather data available at the time of the Michigan, Hinckley, Far West, and Great Idaho fires, Beals (1914) found that, apart from the immediate vicinity of the fires, surface winds averaged between only 10 and 14 miles per hour during the worst burning days, with

Figure 2.3 Aftermath of conflagration fire. *(U.S. Forest Service photo.)* Tillamook burn 11 years later, after much material was salvaged.

maximums of 20 to 25 miles. Blowup fire conditions consequently may develop with only moderate surface winds (Chapters 7 and 16).

While the most severe burning conditions normally occur during the heat of sunny days, adverse burning conditions may continue around the clock. Some fires have reached their greatest intensity during the evening and night; in fact, most really bad fires have not observed daylight hours. Some fires have made their major spread when neither temperature nor humidity were particularly extreme. The same divergence from "normal" applies to season of the year. Some major fires have occurred outside of what is considered the normal fire season because of abnormal weather conditions.

Fuels

An outstanding fact about major forest conflagrations is that most of them have developed in dominantly conifer types. In California, however, some of the most powerful and savage of forest fires develop in mountain brush types. While there is plenty of heat energy in natural hardwood fuels, no really large forest fires have occurred in them. It is the flashier and more combustible fuels of conifers or flammable mountain brush that have powered most of the big fires. It should also be noted that all the fires listed in Table 2.1 occurred north of the 42d parallel, roughly across the northern quarter of the United States. The northern conifer forests tend to be dense; decay is slow, permitting accumulation of snags, slash, and duff; they support crown fires; and occasional periods of extreme and protracted summer drought occur.

More acres have burned in the southern pine region than in any other part of North America, and many individual fires, or groups of fires occurring at the same time, have severely burned very large areas. None, however, have equaled the major northern fires in total destructiveness.

This reflects the generally more open nature of southern pine stands and the lower total fuel volumes, which are the natural result of a rapid rate of decay of dead material and the more frequent reduction of fuels by winter fires. A generally moist climate also enters into the equation. Nevertheless, "flashy" fuels abound, particularly in the lower coastal plain, in which fire spreads rapidly even under moist conditions. Such fuels support rates of fire spread equaled only by that of grass fires in the West. The special problems of this region are discussed in later chapters.

It is highly significant that every one of the fires listed started in slash or other debris resulting from logging and land clearing and gained initial momentum from such fuels.

Control

While in active progress, a really large forest conflagration is beyond human control by any means yet known. The pertinent question about control consequently centers on whether these conflagrations of the past could have been checked in their early stages or during subsequent lull periods. Under conditions at the time, with the possible exception of the Tillamook and Maine fires, the answer is definitely no. All these earlier fires occurred before the existence of effective fire control organizations.

Weather and fuel conditions provided the powder keg. All that was needed was a spark. This was amply provided by numerous logging and settler fires and some lightning fires. The rest was inevitable. No fire control organization could hope to deal with the explosive combination of weather, fuel, and extant fires at the time blowup conditions occurred. It should also be noted that most of these fires made their major spread in a relatively short period of time, mostly 24 hours or less. When burning conditions are right, (Chapter 7), large fires can spread with phenomenal speed, much faster than any control organization can hope to move in dealing with them.

The Tillamook fire is an outstanding example of the potentiality of single hit-and-run fires. The logging fire got away, despite the presence of men at the scene when it started. Probably it *could* have been stopped; this is one of those agonizing "ifs" of history. The incendiary fire in logging slash had more of a head start before control forces reached it. The Maine fires had each been worked on and were thought to be under control prior to the first breakaway on October 21. Clearly they could have been entirely extinguished at that time, though not after the major spread occurred. Among the reasons they were not checked are, first, the failure to completely extinguish a fire after controlling its spread and, second, the failure to organize to meet the problems of a large fire situation until after it occurred. This was the natural outcome of dependence on the local and largely autonomous town fire warden system. Obviously such a system must have been reasonably adequate under average conditions.

Future Outlook

This review leads to a key question: Are large fires still possible? The answer is yes, but their occurrence can be made extremely rare.

Adverse burning conditions will occur in the future as they have in the past. There is no reason to suppose that weather in the future will be any more favorable or easier to control. It may be worse in that the foreseeable extremes of drought conditions have not been encountered since the advent of organized control (Show, 1955).

As a result of past wildfires, heavy fuel accumulations on many large areas have been removed and the areas now offer less total fire hazard. For example, large areas of relatively low-hazard aspen replaced former conifer types in the Lake states. This situation is, however, largely transitory, and conifers are coming back. Large old growth and heavy fuel areas in the West have been replaced by young and less hazardous fuel types as a result of wildfires.

Application of effective fire control and increasingly intensive practice of forest management have both plus and minus aspects in their effect on fuel volumes to support large fires. On the plus side, cutting and close utilization break up continuous forest areas and reduce total fuel volumes. Well-managed forests are relatively young and do not support large fuel volumes. In the South, partial cutting practices plus fire control are encouraging a greater proportion of less flammable but ecologically more persistent hardwoods in relation to pines in some areas.

On the minus side, the proportion of conifers to hardwoods is increasing. Large acreages have been planted to pines in many parts of the country, and better management and fire control are being practiced. The net result is more total forest-fuel volume. Despite closer utilization, the volume of slash fuels is being increased in some areas of the West. In ponderosa and mixed pine types especially, cutting practices and grazing, both with and without fire, are often followed by invasion of highly flammable cheat grass and by flammable brush types. Increasingly effective fire control in the lower coastal plain of the South is permitting much accumulation of highly flammable surface fuels.

The overall conclusion seems to be that while slash and other high-hazard fuels may become less prevalent, the basic fuels to support conflagrations, once started, will continue to be available in probably increasing volume. The obvious need is to prevent potentially dangerous fires from starting and gaining momentum.

While two basic ingredients for large fires—that is, suitable weather conditions and available fuels—will continue to be present, the sources of fire risk and effectiveness of fire fighting efforts are subject to more favorable change. The many existing fires that in the past touched off conflagrations, once weather conditions were right, can either be prevented or stamped out by an alert fire control organization supported by a prevention-conscious public. These risks need not and should not be tolerated.

There remains the menace of an occasional accidental (or lightning) fire set at a crucial time and place and the grim possibility of incendiary fires. It is possible to provide for the recognition and accurate gauging of potential blowup fire conditions and for well-equipped organizations that are strongly coordinated, aggressive, and quickly able to bring strong control force to bear at critical places. This is increasingly being done. Large fires have been successfully fought, and facilities to cope with them continue to improve. This offers great hope that the occasional breakaway fire, the one that gets into the several-thousand-acre class, can be controlled and a possible major conflagration averted. It is nonetheless both easy and dangerous to let this very real hope lull one into believing that big fires cannot occur again. They can, and one should never forget it. This is well borne out by the several costly blowup fires in northern Idaho in 1967, fires which laid waste over 100,000 acres of timberland and otherwise assumed the characteristics of the Great Idaho fires of 1910 (Anderson, 1968).

Fire weather, fuels, fire risk, fire behavior, and control methods are discussed at length later in this book. Perhaps the central point is the fact that big forest fires, the ones that cause most of the damage and also cost the most, develop from a combination, fortunately rather rare, of simultaneously adverse circumstances of weather, fuels, fire-starting agents, and control facilities.

FIRE AND FOREST TYPES

As already discussed, fire is no stranger in the forest. Forest fires—large or small, intense or light—have had a profound influence on forests and wild lands generally throughout the world, in the tropical, temperate, and arctic zones. In temperate regions, all forest types have been affected to some degree by fire. The preceding discussion has indicated the widespread occurrence of fires on forest lands in a general way but has not brought out their longer-term impact in shaping the character and composition of forest types found on them. More specific and shorter-term effects are presented in Chapter 3.

First, it will be useful to review what is meant by *forest type*. This concept is used to group forest stands of similar character. The designation of a particular type is based on its composition and development, which arise from ecological factors and give it its unique, recognizable character. A type may be temporary if its character is due to a passing influence, such as fire, or it may be climax if it is the ultimate stage of a succession of temporary types. Usually a type is named for the most prevalent or important species, but types may be pure or mixed. A pure type, like many ponderosa pine stands, has a single species, while a mixed type, such as the western white pine, may have as little as 10 percent of the species for which it is named. However, the term *cover type* refers only to the vegetative type that is occupying the ground and may have no other implications. Fuel types, which are discussed in Chapter 4, are based on fuels rather than species.

Wild-land fire ecology is in itself a most interesting but complex subject. Complete treatment would require a voluminous treatise. The discussion here is limited to a brief survey of the effects of fire in shaping the major forest types in the United States and Canada. It will serve to bring out the range of effects of a recurring fire regime. Some of these effects relate to adaptation of the species itself through evolutionary processes.

Forest compositions that occur naturally give clues to the role played by fire in the past. The key is the degree to which climax types of timber cover are represented. A climax forest type is capable of maintaining itself indefinitely in balance against competition of other plant cover so long as climatic and soil conditions remain unchanged. It is the final stage of a succession which may take several hundred years to attain. Few of the intolerant species could persist in a true climax type. Aspen is perhaps the outstanding example of an intolerant species which occurs over a very wide range of territory yet is regarded by dendrologists as a transitory species everywhere in its range. Many intermediate combinations occur as well. In fact, they predominate, so that pure climax types are relatively rare. Most of the more valuable commercial timber types are subclimax. This is of particular significance to the forest manager.

Ponderosa Pine

Ponderosa pine, though an intolerant species, forms a stable type over a large part of its range in western North America. Most of this range is in zones of low rainfall, 25 inches or less, and in areas where lightning fires are frequent. The role of fire in maintaining the type is important, but not all interrelationships have yet become clearly established. It occurs extensively in pure stands but forms mixed types as well, particularly with Rocky Mountain Douglas-fir. A part of the pure type and the mixed type may be classed as subclimax, but relationships can best be examined separately for each of these categories.

Examples of the pure or nearly pure type are the extensive stands on the Coconino Plateau of the Southwest, in California east of the Sierras, in central Washington and Oregon, in southern Idaho, and in the Black Hills of South Dakota. The virgin stands were mostly open and parklike with uneven age classes. In most of these areas ponderosa pine has no closely competing tree species but does compete with grass and various shrub species for dominance. In the Southwest, the periodic coincidence of a good seed year and a favorable moisture regime in the year following result in dense stands of reproduction at long intervals of 30 to 50 years. The periodicity of good seed years is typical of ponderosa pine. It gives a degree of periodicity to age classes even in areas such as the Black Hills of South Dakota, where summer rains are normally sufficient for new seedlings to survive. The joint operation of these two factors imitates or accentuates the effect of large fires in creating stands or understories of a single age class.

These stands are very susceptible to fire during their first 20 to 40 years. Where it is kept out, the dense young stands greatly increase the volume of hazardous fuel, and when they do burn a complete kill of both young growth and mature trees is likely. Where fire intervenes before reproduction adds substantially to the fuels, the mature trees remain mostly undamaged but only an occasional seedling survives. Admirers of the open, parklike stands advocate frequent burning to keep down young growth and shrub cover. Tests of burning, uncontrolled except for timing, indicate that fire under such conditions is too unselective to produce net silvicultural benefits. Where forage, game production, or recreational values outrank potential timber value, benefits from use of fire may be more easily realized.

In mixed types, ponderosa pine occurs in association with a number of conifers, principally Douglas-fir, the true firs, lodgepole pine, and incense cedar. This type carries heavier volumes of fuel and fires tend to be more severe. The fire history of the area is reflected by the age and proportion of pine. Following a fire, ponderosa pine—and lodgepole pine too when present—are favored by the seed-bed conditions of the burn. Ponderosa pine seed trees are also likely to survive the burn because of their occurrence on more open southern and western slopes and their fire resistance, which is greater than that of the associated species.

In both pure and mixed types, fire affects type boundaries. In general, the pure ponderosa pine type lies between grasslands at lower elevations, and mixed conifers at higher elevations. At its lower limit, fire causes frequent shifts of the boundary between grass and forest. In general, pines gradually invade the grasslands between fires; grass invades former forest areas following severe fires. In the Sand Hills of Nebraska and in parts of eastern Montana and South Dakota, considerable areas of potential ponderosa pine type are treeless, probably because fires were too frequent for this species to reproduce itself successfully. The boundary between the pine and mixed types fluctuates also in response to fire. For the reasons cited, a severe burn favors pine reproduction, which may completely replace a former mixed stand. Occasional light fires, where a few veteran pines survive, eliminate reproduction of the competing more tolerant species and produce a similar result.

Douglas-fir in the Pacific Northwest

The Douglas-fir forests on the coastal slopes of western Oregon, Washington, and southern British Columbia are some of the most productive and valuable in the world. They too represent a subclimax type. The principal associates of Douglas-fir are western hemlock, silver, noble and grand firs, and western red cedar. While the rainfall is well over 50 inches annually in most parts of the region, the summers and early fall are dry, sometimes extremely so. This plus the great volume of fuels, both living and dead, and the occasional dry east winds dreaded by fire fighters, all combine at times to produce high-energy fires that become uncontrollable even in early stages, as was brought out in discussion of the Tillamook fire.

Whether caused by lightning, Indians, or by the white man, fire has always been an active factor in the Douglas-fir country. Surface and ground fires are by far the most common, and under natural conditions individual fires are, on the average, fairly small in area and kill only part of the stand. Under particularly adverse weather conditions, extensive surface and crown fires occur, sweeping large areas. While the tree kill is often complete over large areas, bold topography and variable air currents commonly permit some trees, either isolated or in patches or groups, to survive even the most severe fires. The significance of this is that under natural conditions, a nearby seed source almost always remains after a stand has been opened up by fire. The Tillamook fire was the exception.

Douglas-fir is an abundant seed producer, regenerates readily on fire-prepared seedbeds, and makes its most rapid growth in the open. The net effect of fires, and especially the most severe ones, in breaking up old-growth stands is to favor reestablishment of pure Douglas-fir at the expense of its more tolerant but less aggressive associates. The processes of natural ecological succession in most of the region are toward development of a forest dominated by western hemlock, western red cedar, and the true firs. Fires interrupt and partially reverse this natural trend and maintain the high proportion of Douglas-fir in the even-aged stands that characterize the region. The facts that large fires in a specific locality occur only at intervals, often spanning several human generations, and that the cumulative effects of small fires are often hard to see, tend to obscure the total effect of fire in the region. The presence in Washington and Oregon of about $4\frac{1}{2}$ million acres of stands 20 to 120 years of age that are known to have originated following fires (McArdle, Meyer, and Bruce, 1949) gives statistical weight to the importance of fire. It is hard to find a natural stand of any extent that did not originate following fire. So the Douglas-fir type, as commonly found and defined, is ecologically a subclimax, or intermediate, stage in succession. It is a fire type.

Widespread application of clear cutting in old-growth stands, followed by extensive use of fire to reduce the resultant slash hazard and clear the ground for reproduction, is an effort to simulate nature's method of regenerating Douglas-fir and maintaining a high proportion of it in relation to other species. But results are mixed. Severe and repeated fires, aggravated by logging and permanent settlement, have created many unproductive areas which do not regenerate to Douglas-fir or to any other commercial tree species. Wildfires have caused many difficult problems of regeneration, utilization, and protection in keeping forest lands productive. Fire—past, present, and potential—colors and affects almost every phase of management in the region. It created the Douglas-fir type in the first place, and wildfire certainly can play havoc with its management.

Western White Pine

The western white pine type is also a subclimax forest. So most of what has been said about Douglas-fir can be applied to the western white pine type of northern Idaho, eastern Washington, and western Montana.

Fire, disease, insects, wind, and snow all play a part in the slow march toward the climax, operating in an irregular and haphazard manner that often obscures the successional trend. At almost any stage, partial or complete destruction of the forest may cause a partial or complete repetition of successional development. In fact, few stands ever reach the climax stage; the western white pine type is essentially a transition type of scarcely subclimax stability, perpetuated largely by fire (Haig, Davis, and Weidman, 1941).

As suggested by this statement, the western white pine is a less pure and a somewhat less stable type than the Douglas-fir. It is in competition with larch, the Rocky Mountain form of Douglas-fir, hemlock, and the true firs. The two former compete more strongly at later stages.

The size and severity of the burn affects the forest composition that emerges. In small burns that must have been typical of lightning fires in average years, all the associated species reseed and compete at an early age. Lacking a head start, the highly intolerant larch is at some disadvantage in such situations. Rocky Mountain Douglas-fir too survives chiefly on south and west exposures, which reproduce slowly. White pine may start as 10 percent or less of the reproduction, but in most of its range it is faster-growing and more aggressive than its associates, so it may progressively increase its proportion to 50 or 75 percent or more at early maturity. With overmaturity this trend reverses.

In very large burned areas few white pine seed trees survive, since the individual mature tree is much less resistant to fire than veteran ponderosa pines, Douglas-fir, or larch. A further handicap to white pine reproduction is the very heavy volume of dead fuel following a severe burn in green timber. In the huge burns of 1910 in northern Idaho, reburns in subsequent years seemed inevitable. Those of 1919 were particularly damaging since, over large areas, they eliminated all reproduction from the seed of nearby fire-killed trees, and living seed trees were too far away to reseed the area. The light-seeded larch has a tremendous advantage in such situations and usually appears as the pioneer species. Lodgepole pine also gains dominance near every seed source.

Though the succession in the very large burns in northern Idaho is obscured by planting programs, it is clear that extensive nonforested brush and grass areas would have persisted over a very long period in the natural state. Since such areas were of negligible extent prior to the start of logging, it would appear that the huge areas burned and reburned in 1910 and in the next three decades were not nature's usual fire regime and may even be regarded as an abnormal situation, perhaps because much more dead fuel from logging was available to trigger and to feed a conflagration.

In the management of white pine, the use of fire prior to planting or natural seeding simulates the natural conditions under which it reproduced most successfully. However, management of this species is now greatly complicated by the presence of white pine blister rust. It is a new factor in the dynamics of this type. Studies by Moss and Wellner (1953) show that fire can be both an aid and a hindrance in the control of this disease.

Lodgepole Pine and Jack Pine

The lodgepole pine is a widely distributed western conifer, being found in the northern and central Rocky Mountain and Pacific Coast regions from the Yukon to the central Rockies and southern California. It is also a subclimax species over most of its range. As a type, lodgepole pine characteristically occurs in pure, even-aged stands. It is found in two major situations: as a climax or near-climax type and as a temporary type. The former is characterized by the nearly pure lodgepole pine forests found at the higher elevations in the northern and central Rockies. Here, pine follows pine, with an assist from fire.

As stands become old, they become less resistant to damage, by insects particularly. They open up, fuels accumulate, and the forests become increasingly susceptible to fire. Under natural conditions, an insect epidemic often adds to the fuels. Lightning sooner or later supplies the torch. Then a very hot fire sweeps the area and a new pine stand starts. This accounts for the pattern of irregularly distributed but usually fairly extensive even-aged stands so characteristic of these forests. As with pure ponderosa pine, there is considerable question as to how much of the present pure type would continue with permanent fire exclusion; spruce, true firs, and sometimes the Rocky Mountain form of Douglas-fir are climax species over much of the area. Nevertheless, lodgepole does form a stable type over large areas.

As a more temporary type, in fringe areas lodgepole pine and its West Coast subspecies assume a different role. Lodgepole pine is frequently found in mixture with several other Rocky Mountain and some Northern coastal species as a result of fire, giving way after a single rotation to other species. Lodgepole is often the first tree species to establish itself after burns. It acts as nature's nurse crop to help bring in the permanent components of the climax forest, components which develop as an understory and eventually grow up through the comparatively short-lived lodgepole.

The capacity of lodgepole pine to establish itself promptly after fires is due to two outstanding characteristics of the species. The first is the closed cone (serotinous) habit of this species. A part of the seed remains sealed in the cones, which adhere to the tree for many years. This results in an accumulation of viable seed on the tree sometimes amounting to ten times the annual production. Following fire, by which lodgepole is very easily killed, the cones open up and shower a nicely prepared seedbed with this abundant stored seed. The second characteristic of lodgepole that ensures its initial dominance is the exceptional hardiness and rapid initial growth of seedlings. This combination of a good local seed source plus the capacity of seedlings to survive and grow rapidly in open burns accounts for the frequently prompt and abundant establishment of lodgepole as the initially dominant species following fire, even when it formed a relatively small proportion of the parent stand.

Essentially the same story can be told for the equally widely distributed and closely related jack pine of the Lake states and Canada.

Fire has had more influence than any other factor on distribution of jack pine in the original and in the present forests of the Lake States and Canada. It was mainly due to fire that jack pine, although a shorter-lived smaller species than red pine and eastern white pine, nevertheless maintained a position of importance in the dense virgin forests of the region. Fire running through mature uncut stands of jack pine, or of jack pine mixed with red pine and other trees, encourages reproduction of jack pine at the expense of associated species because of the former's peculiar seeding habits. Like lodgepole pine but unlike most other forest trees, jack pine does not shed much of its seed at the time of seed ripening. By far the greater part remains sealed in the closed cones, which persist on the branches for many years. . . . Although a fire sweeping through a jack pine stand kills nearly all the vegetation, the insulation afforded by the thick cone scales preserve much of the seed unharmed. The heat of the flames . . . opens the scales and releases the seed onto soil that is practically bare. The fire thus simultaneously prepares a favorable seedbed, reduces plant competition, and releases an immense number of seed. [Eyre and LeBarron, 1944]

Aspen in the Lake States and Canada

Aspen is a highly intolerant species, and the aspen forest type is regarded as transient except in localized areas in the Great Basin and western Colorado. Nevertheless the aspen type predominates over a very large portion of the northern Lake states and eastern Canada. This is entirely the result of past fires, mostly resulting from logging and land clearing. The cycle of fires that swept the northern Lake states in 1871, 1881, and in subsequent years brought in the millions of acres of "popple" now so characteristic of the region. Both the trembling and the bigtooth aspen are outstanding examples of species that literally thrive on forest fires. The reason does not stem from any resistance of the tree itself—it is easily killed by fire—but from its reproductive habits. These habits are totally different from those of jack pine, its fire companion of the region, but are also highly effective.

No doubt a sprinkling of aspen occurred naturally over much, if not all, of the area it now occupies as a type. These trees were of no interest to the early loggers, and hence they were seldom mentioned. Following widespread and repeated fire, aspen multiplied rapidly, spreading from these scattered parent clones. Aspen has a habit of sending out long lateral roots, often extending 60 or more feet from the parent tree. These roots come near the surface at intervals and produce root suckers. The roots are not killed by fire. Repeated fires merely stimulate more root suckering and more aspen. Study of existing stands indicates that most of them are of root-sucker origin.

Although regeneration is usually vegetative, seedling origin can also be important. Aspen produces seeds frequently and in prodigious numbers. The seeds are exceedingly light, borne in tufts of cottony down which can be disseminated for long distances by air currents. They require moist, bare ground for germination and favorable conditions of moisture and temperature for subsequent survival. Although suitable seedbed and climatic conditions are infrequent, they probably coincided at times following large fires of the past, and this may account in part for the rapid spread of aspen in this region.

The many millions of acres of aspen that replaced former coniferous forests in the Lake states and eastern Canada have had varied effects.

Aspen is a valuable nurse crop to tolerant species in natural succession and is functioning in that respect in parts of its range. It has very low fire hazard and has been a controlling factor in preventing repetitions of the conflagrations of the past. It has acquired surprising commercial value on some sites. Management to maintain stands of aspen and to take full advantage of such assets must take account of the role played by fire. But any use of fire is conditioned by the long-term destructive effects of uncontrolled fire that still prevail in this region.

Red and Eastern White Pine

The red and eastern white pine types of the Lake states, the Northeast, and southeastern Canada illustrate situations in which fire is extremely important but in which its specific effects are highly complex and variable. Under "natural" conditions—that is, before the white man—the two species, and especially red pine, occurred in fairly pure types. They were associated to some extent and also found separately in association with various northern hardwoods. Neither species is a major component of climax types occurring within their ranges. As a generality, the relative abundance of these species as found in natural stands over extensive areas is basically due to forest fires of the past. Yet neither commonly forms a fire type that can as clearly be identified as can the western white pine and Douglas-fir types. Nevertheless, the best natural stands of each species (that is, from a forester's standpoint) almost invariably originated after extensive fires. Red pine especially reproduces best under open conditions and often occurs naturally in fairly open stands, much like ponderosa pine, which the species closely resembles. The fire history of the Itasca Lake region in Minnesota, as unraveled by Spurr (1954), shows that there were repeated and extensive fires over as long a period (about 200 years) as information could be obtained from tree scars and reports of early explorers. The present patchwork pattern of forest types in the area, including extensive red pine and jack pine types, is a direct result of these fires.

With severe and repeated fires in the northern forests, both red pine and white pine tend to give way to aspen and jack pine, which definitely are fire types. With few or light fires, the natural trend is toward northern hardwood and in some areas spruce-fir types as climaxes. The relative position of white pine in the forest as affected by fire is somewhat different in the southerly extension of the species in the hardwood associations of the Appalachian Mountains. Here, white pine is able to maintain itself without fire and in fact often seems to be encouraged by fire exclusion.

Longleaf Pine

Longleaf, once king of the southern pines, is an outstanding illustration of a species perpetuated because of the outstanding capacity of the tree to endure fire. Key species components of other forest types so far discussed, with the partial exception of ponderosa and red pine, owe their preponderance under natural conditions to their regenerative ability following fire. Longleaf is an example of a species constituting an important forest type that wins out primarily because of the ability of the tree to withstand fire. It is not a particularly abundant seeder and has no advantage in regeneration.

As found by the white man, the longleaf forests extended from the southern edge of Virginia to east Texas, characteristically occurring in open, parklike, and nearly pure stands. Since time immemorial, fires have periodically covered the area. Before the advent of fire control, extensive areas burned over at two- to four-year intervals. "Lightning must have been the principal causes of fire in the piney woods before the Indians came. . . . Subsequently, both Indians and white settlers engaged in frequent woods burning" (Wahlenberg, 1946). Fires are mostly of the surface type, consuming or charring the forest litter and killing much of the low vegetative cover. A few fires are more severe, going into the crowns and killing many trees.

Longleaf pine is the only North American species that has appreciable resistance to fire in the juvenile stage. Under normal conditions, longleaf seedlings have a habit of staying down in the grass and delaying height growth from $2^{1}/_{2}$ to $3^{1}/_{2}$ years. If the seedling is smothered by grass or afflicted with the brown-spot disease, it may survive in this grass stage for 10 or as many as 20 years. After about a year, during which the seedling is vulnerable to fire, the thick terminal bud of the seedling, which is protected by an insulating layer of fringed corky cells and a thick tuft of long needles, is able to survive the average surface fire occurring in the region. A period of rapid initial height growth follows the grass stage, the seedling rising like a large and very hairy candle out of the grass. This lasts for three or four years until the tree is 8 to 10 feet tall. During this period longleaf is relatively vulnerable to fire during the growing season, even though most trees will survive a light surface fire at other times. Larger trees are increasingly resistant to fire because of development of a thick, fire-resistant bark, those about 10 inches in diameter or larger being able to withstand all but the more severe fires. Longleaf is one of few conifer species that can survive almost complete defoliation by fire, probably due to its well-insulated buds. This resistance of the individual tree is augmented by the usually open nature of longleaf stands, which tends to prevent the development of crown fires.

Although wildfire has been responsible for perpetuation of the type under natural conditions, it also is the source of a great deal of damage from a management and utilization standpoint. It is a contributing cause of the generally low average stocking characteristic of unmanaged stands. Logging, fire control, and hogs (in some areas) have greatly reduced the area of the longleaf pine type. Slash pine and loblolly pine have spread into much of the area, and low-grade hardwood species have become more abundant, dominating some areas.

Regeneration, control of brown-spot disease, and control of low-value hardwoods, each of which are essential steps in producing longleaf pine, are all made more effective by judicious use of fire.

Bottomland Hardwoods

The bottomland hardwoods of the Mississippi Delta and other river bottoms of the lower South are as totally different from the piney woods of the longleaf region as any two forest types could be, yet they occur side by side in the same geographic region. Since they are dense and luxuriant and normally under water part of the year and wet for much of the rest, a natural reaction is to assume that these forests are unaffected by fire. Such is not the case.

Fire in bottomland hardwoods is a very real problem, and all too often insufficient attention is given it. Fire in the bottomlands does not rage through the tree crowns and bad fire seasons do not occur every year. Nevertheless, every five to eight years a serious fire season occurs when ground and surface fires cause very great damage.

"Fire in the bottomlands usually moves rapidly along the surface, consuming the abundant shrub and weed growth and killing all tree reproduction under about ten years of age. It also scorches the highly sensitive bark of the younger trees, causing wounds that later develop into catfaces and points of entry for rot, stain, and insects. Under extreme conditions, large saw-timber trees may be killed. A fire once every ten years over a given area eliminates any possibility of the practice of forestry. For this reason, it is emphasized without qualification that an effective fire protection system is a prerequisite to management. . . . With the rare exception of a dry early spring, fall is the fire season. The dangerous years are those in which the usual summer drought extends into autumn and early winter. The later the drought continues, the more fallen leaves and frost-killed vegetation are added to the fuel" (Putnam, 1951).

Much the same story about fire can be told for the commercial hardwood forests of the eastern United States and Canada. Wildfires are seldom spectacular or frequent, and, because of partial killing, rapid decay, and quick vegetative regrowth following burning, they are often overlooked and unappreciated. A forester accustomed to the obvious and often stark effect of fire in conifers finds it difficult to see the results of fire in hardwood forests. While fire seldom causes sweeping changes in hardwood types, wildfires are a major factor in reducing lumber yield and quality. Hedgcock (1937) estimated that 90 percent of the butt rots in hardwoods in the eastern United States enter through fire wounds. Often mature hardwood stands are reduced to stands of worthless "cripples" which must be removed before a new stand can be established. This kind of fire damage is often greater than the more obvious direct damage to coniferous stands. Fires often greatly affect stocking and species composition in hardwoods as well. On the positive side, they at times favor reproduction of yellow birch and tulip poplar. The cumulative importance of fire in hardwoods should not be underestimated, as is too often the case.

Swamp and Bog Fires

Because of the wet conditions normally present in swamps and bogs of various sorts, it is commonly assumed that they are not affected by or subjected to forest fires. As in the case of bottomland hardwoods, the facts indicate otherwise. While infrequent, some of the most destructive and stubborn fires burn in swamp areas. Potential fuels—ground, surface, and aerial—are usually abundant in swamps and become available to burn when the water table recedes. No job in fire control compares with the brute effort required to trench a deep-burning ground fire in a peat bog. Destructive crown fires can sweep over conifer and grassland swamps even when the surface is covered with water. Under natural conditions, fire is a major factor in the establishment and perpetuation of a number of swamp types. Southern white cedar and pond pine are good Southern examples. Spruce and tamarack (larch) bogs of the North are others.

The valuable, characteristically dense, and even-aged white cedar occurring in swampy areas of the East Coast from southern New Jersey to western Florida mostly in freshwater bogs is essentially a fairly well-stabilized fire type (Wells, 1942). Fires are not only extremely destructive in such stands, especially after logging when they burn furiously right over the water, but they also can create conditions favoring prompt and abundant natural regeneration. Seed usually accumulates in the surface layers of the peat. When this is too wet to burn and the fire is followed by a few dry seasons, reducing surface moisture to a level permitting seed germination and subsequent seedling survival, abundant white cedar regeneration occurs. If the surface peat is destroyed by fire, pond pine, slash pine, or swamp hardwoods commonly result.

The effects of fire in swampy areas are exceedingly varied and complex and cannot be further explored here. The essential point of emphasis is that fires do occur in such areas and are exceedingly important.

Forest Fires and Forest Types in Summary

The preceding review of forest-fire relationships and impacts in some major forest types is decidedly incomplete. Almost every forest type in North America has a fire history of some sort, usually important. This includes the California redwoods. The forest types selected have, however, given an indication of the scope, importance, and complexity of fire and emphasized the fact that it is no stranger to the forest.

The following are some general conclusions and statements regarding fire in the forests that can be drawn from this analysis:

1 Wildfires of past centuries have established and maintained over long periods of time a number of extensive subclimax fire types. Douglas-fir, western white pine, longleaf pine, and parts of the ponderosa pine and lodgepole pine types are outstanding examples. In fact, the most valuable conifer types of the United States are fire types to a greater or lesser degree. This is particularly true of the pines. The role of fire in these types is to maintain a subclimax condition.

2 Type composition may be completely changed as a result of man's misuse of fire. Examples of this may be found around the world. In this country, the extensive aspen and jack pine types in the Lake states are excellent forest examples. Here, fire has brought about extensive occurrence of forest types not found under natural conditions.

3 Along with insects, disease, and other biological and physical factors, fire is also a factor in the regeneration of several climax types. Examples are pure ponderosa and lodgepole pine where classed as climax. Other examples are Engelmann spruce and alpine fir types of the Rockies, growing on sites where no other tree species can compete successfully. These are not fire types, and fire ordinarily does not change the type, but it *is* a major factor in reproducing it. Under certain circumstances, as in the case of light surface fires in the Douglas-fir, western white pine, red pine, and eastern white pine types, fire may hasten the development of a climax from a subclimax type by constituting a form of partial cutting.

4 Fire causes tremendous forest damage from man's standpoint. This scarcely needs to be emphasized; control of wildfires is necessary for the practice of forestry of any kind, and most of this book is on how to do this. The very long list of destructive things that fire does need not be elaborated here.

5   Fire types usually breed fire control problems. Without exception, fire control is a major need and problem in natural fire types. The Douglas-fir, western white pine, and California chaparral types are good examples of very difficult fire control situations. Fire is a problem in longleaf pine, but there it is not inherently as difficult to control as in some western fire types. Fire control is relatively easy in aspen which, however, in its present extent, is not considered a natural type since its prevalence is the direct and recent result of man's actions.

6   Many present-day management problems stem from past fires. To a very large degree, present-day problems of maintaining desirable species composition in pine types are a direct outgrowth of their fire history. For example, the increasing prevalence of low-value hardwoods in pine types of the South, rated as a major management problem, is a direct result of fire control and of partial cutting where wildfires previously kept the hardwoods in check. Perpetuation of Douglas-fir and western white pine as major components of their respective types in the absence of wildfire gives rise to difficult silvicultural, economic, and protection problems that naturally follow from their long and close association with fire. The prevalence of the aspen and jack pine types also engenders a series of management problems directly related to their fire origin.

Study of fire in the forest—its effects, control, and use—should be approached with balance and full realization of its role, past, present, and potential. Fire control is not an end in itself but a means of accomplishing definite objectives in wild-land management.

Chapter 3

Fire Effects

It is important to fully understand the effects of fire in the forest. Such knowledge provides the economic basis for fire control and is a key consideration in both public and private forest policy, forest practices, and overall forest management. It is also the essential prerequisite to beneficial use of fire for land-management purposes.

Though highly important, fire effects are also inherently complex. This can be visualized by first considering briefly the vagaries of fire behavior, which are dealt with in more detail in Chapter 7. Fires respond to fuels, weather, and topography, with so many variables operating that it is nearly impossible to exactly duplicate fires in outdoor test plots, even where measured samples give assurance of reasonably uniform fuels and the weather conditions and topography are carefully selected. The fire research man sets himself a very difficult task, as has been repeatedly demonstrated, when he undertakes to obtain precise information on fire behavior by this method. Secondly, even if fire itself were uniform in its physical entity, it operates in an inherently complex environment of living things. It is simple to place a market value on a merchantable product consumed by the fire but much more difficult to evaluate also the various effects on future growth and composition of the stand or on the soil and site. The result, then, of a highly variable phenomenon operating in a complex living environment is endless variation in the specific effects of fire. For such reasons few generalizations are valid, and any can be misleading if standing alone. Recognition of this inherent complexity is the first essential in approaching this subject. Failure to do so has led to much controversy in the past.

A forest fire does several specific things. First, and perhaps most obviously, it consumes woody material. Aside from physical removal of material from the forest, as in logging, fire is the only means of quickly removing large quantities of woody and other vegetative material. The use of fire in slash burning and in land clearing generally is a direct application of combustion as a quick means of physically freeing the ground of large quantities of forest debris. Second, it creates heat effects, as a result of which living vegetation and animal life are killed or damaged and the soil may be altered. In most fires, much more is killed, injured, or changed through heat effects than is consumed. Third, it produces residual mineral products that may cause chemical effects, which are mostly important in relation to the soil.

A wide range of effects may result from these actions of fire. Some may be immediate and readily apparent, and some may be delayed and difficult to detect. Physical, biological, and chemical changes in the forest environment are always involved.

Fire effects are here grouped by effects on trees, lesser vegetation, forest microclimate, and soil, with full appreciation that there are many interrelationships and that any such grouping is unsatisfactory in some respects.

EFFECTS ON TREES

Any tree can be killed by a fire of sufficient duration and intensity. In forest fires of high heat intensity and considerable duration, killing practically all trees, differences in fire resistance between individual trees and species become unimportant. With fires of lower heat intensity in which only a part of the forest stand is killed, relative differences between trees in heat resistance and susceptibility to injury become important both in wildfire control and in the prescribed use of fire in forest land management. Fires causing only partial kill are much more common.

Lethal Temperatures

What directly injures or kills a tree is the raising of the internal temperature of living cells at critical positions in the tree, most commonly in the bole near its base, to a lethal level. The phloem and cambium are injured first because they are nearer the outside of the tree. Even if not initially injured, the outer living portion of the xylem cannot continue to function if the cambium is killed.

Precise information is lacking on internal temperatures necessary to kill living tissues in trees and shrubs. "There is no evidence that the protoplasm of one species of vascular plants has a higher thermal tolerance than that of another when the protoplasm is well hydrated and in an actively functional state" (Baker, 1950). In other words, differences in heat tolerance are accounted for chiefly by differences in the degree of insulation from heat sources. Lethal temperatures of tree tissues have been mostly studied in connection with injury to seedling stems occurring just above the ground line during the first year (Baker, 1929; Haig, 1936).

Both the temperature and its duration are important. Killing of tissues begins at about 120°F if exposure at this temperature is prolonged for approximately an hour. At around 130°F killing is sure and accomplished in a few minutes. This figure is a good average for minimum but definitely lethal temperatures. A test of needles of four southern pines by the water-bath method showed no significant differences between the species tested (Nelson, 1952). As shown in Figure 3.1, taken from this study, at 130°F killing occurred in about six minutes, at 140°F in half a minute, and almost instantaneously at 147°, all species averaged together. The 140°F point is a very useful level to keep in mind. It is a critical point in the curve, and in field studies it has been found to be a common lethal point for seedlings.

Studies of heat injury to plant tissues consistently show the zone of minimum critical temperatures to be rather narrow for a given time of exposure. Below the critical temperature, no injury is apparent unless the duration is long. At the critical point, damage appears suddenly; and at higher temperatures, the speed of killing multiplies rapidly. A 10°F temperature increase may decrease the time necessary for lethal damage 25 or more times. This comparatively narrow critical zone and rapidly increasing speed of killing with higher temperatures is often of key importance in fire control and use of fire, since a moving fire front in forest litter commonly exposes living stems to high heat for only a brief period of a few minutes or seconds. Two fires may seem much the same superficially, and yet one may result in much more killing and injury than the other because of relatively small differences in the duration and intensity of heat applied.

The above temperatures are internal; that is, they apply to the protoplasm of living cells. Much higher temperatures obviously can be sustained at the surface of the plant, at least for a period. Resistance of trees to heat injury in a specific situation depends primarily on the

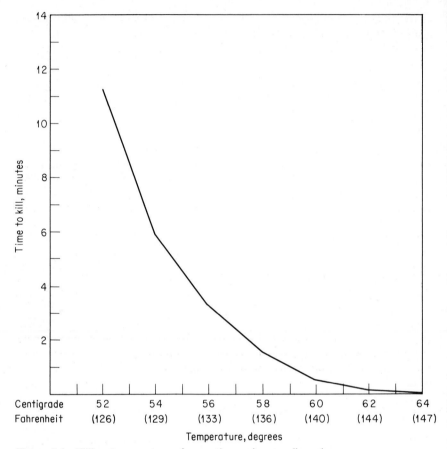

Figure 3.1 Killing temperatures for southern pine needles when immersed in a water bath. Average of four species. *(After Nelson, 1952.)*

protection afforded by their bark layer, their bulk, and their internal temperature at the time. Several factors contribute to the end result.

Factors Affecting Susceptibility to Damage

A number of things may affect the susceptibility of trees and forests to heat damage under natural field conditions.

   1   Initial temperature of the vegetation. Foliage temperatures of over 100°F may occur naturally, and 70 to 80°F is common. The higher the initial temperature, the less additional heat is necessary to bring about lethal temperatures and the more quickly they can develop. This point is of importance in prescribed use of fire, since initial temperatures can be controlled by selecting the time of burning.

2   The size of the critical tree portion exposed and its morphology. Young trees, leaves, and small branches are easily killed because they can quickly be heated to a lethal temperature. Buds are particularly important, and their resistance to heat damage is directly related to size. The larger the bud, especially if it is protected by hairs and clustered leaves, the more heat it takes to produce killing temperatures in the bud cells (Byram, 1948).

3   The thickness and character of the bark. Of all the protective mechanisms of the tree, the bark is the most important. This is especially true near the ground surface where most fires occur. Bark is an excellent insulating material; "bark structure, in general, is a natural design for insulation board" (Chang, 1954). The insulating capacity of the bark layer depends on its structure, composition, density, moisture content, and thickness. It is known that these things vary widely by species, growth habitat, and possibly by seasons to some degree, but complete information is not available. Bark thickness is the most easily determined and undoubtedly the most important single factor. It is known that differences between trees in resistance to heat damage are directly related to total bark thickness. The precise effect of fissures, cracks, and other inequalities of the bark upon its insulating capacity is not known. Fritz (1932) describes the formation of fire scars in redwood between heavy bark ridges where the bark covering is soft, succulent, and thin. It is known that trees with thick bark near the base can withstand hot fires of considerable duration with no penetration of lethal temperatures to the living phloem and cambium. Where several species are associated, bark thickness is the most important and measurable single index of relative resistance.

With most species, bark thickness is strongly related to age: The older the tree the thicker the bark, and consequently the more resistant the tree to fire. The rate of bark thickening with age is especially significant. The bark of longleaf pine, for example, is not much thicker than that of the other southern pines at ages exceeding about a hundred years. But bark thickening occurs sooner. This difference is significant in giving longleaf an advantage over the other pines in resisting ground fires in the sapling and pole ages.

4   Branching and growth habit. Other things being equal, trees that self-prune readily and develop high and open crowns are more successful in escaping fire damage because they are less susceptible to crown fires and they accumulate less litter close to the stem. So the intensity and duration of fire immediately around individual stems are reduced. Conversely, trees with low, dense crowns, especially if festooned with flammable mosses and lichens, are more susceptible to damage. Persistence of dead limbs, especially if they tend to be draped with dead needles, increases the flammability of some conifers.

5   Rooting habit. Roots have thin cortical covering and, if near the

surface, are easily damaged by fire. Shallow-rooted species, like the spruces and most of the true firs, are frequently damaged by ground fires through root injury, even though the stem and crown are not affected.

6 Organic material covering the mineral soil. The depth and character of the organic mantle on the ground may largely control damage by surface fires to the roots, especially of the more shallow-rooted trees. If the mantle is fairly thick and the lower part does not burn, its high insulating ability will protect roots from damage. If, however, the organic mantle burns, it becomes a source of heat rather than of protection, and damaging soil temperatures are likely to result. Fires in swampy areas during drought periods are very destructive for these reasons.

7 Flammability of foliage. Evergreens as a group, and conifers especially, are more flammable than deciduous hardwoods. There are significant differences between conifer species, though these are not of critical importance in damage susceptibility. There are wider differences within hardwoods, particularly as between deciduous and evergreen species. The differences are least in times of severe drought, and at such times some species of both groups, mostly occurring in scrub or brush types, will burn furiously. In general, however, green hardwood foliage will not carry a forest fire except when abnormally dry.

8 Stand habit. Because of their greater liability to crown fires, coniferous trees that grow in dense stands or are commonly associated with abundant subordinate vegetation are more subject to fire damage than those occurring in sparsely canopied open stands with scanty subordinate ground cover. Canopy density is of little importance in hardwoods because the foliage is relatively nonflammable. Damage is controlled mostly by the flammability of subordinate vegetation and surface fuels. The volume and vertical distribution of available fuels, affecting crown-fire incidence, and the duration and intensity of the fire are closely related to stand habit.

9 Season and growth cycle. The seasonal stage of growth affects net damage in three ways. First, it greatly affects the total moisture content of the crown, which in turn affects its flammability. Second, succulent growth is much more susceptible to fire damage. So growing tips and cambium are more easily damaged during the active growing stage than during the dormant state. Third, the ability of the tree to recover is affected by the food reserves in the roots, which fluctuate with the season. Fortunately, the rapid growing stage, when food reserves are low, is also the period of lowest susceptibility to crown fires. The distinction between damage due simply to higher internal temperatures discussed under 1 above and that due to growth stage are difficult to separate. Both are important.

All nine factors above are important, as they affect the likelihood of the tree's critical plant tissues reaching lethal temperatures. Interrelations combine to vary the resulting damage all the way from minor injury to complete kill from the same fire.

The best summary to date of what has been learned about heat effects on trees is contained in the reference given (Hare, 1961).

Relative Resistance of Tree Species to Fire Damage

Some tree species are notoriously susceptible to fire injury, and a few are astonishingly resistant. While unimportant in severe fires, natural differences between species and individual trees become of practical importance in appraising the effects of the less intense fires that cause only partial kill. Relative resistance is important both in forest management and in the natural development of forest types. Even small differences between trees may be highly significant. A consideration of relative tree resistance is an excellent means of bringing out the combined influence of the various factors affecting tree susceptibility to fire. Discussion here is limited to the actual resistance of trees themselves in their normal forest environment and does not include their capacity to persist in a forest subjected to periodic fires. Aspen, for example, is easily killed by fire but promptly and abundantly regenerates after fire because of its habit of sending up root suckers. The individual tree is highly susceptible, but the aspen type is extremely fire-resistant. It should also be emphasized that resistance is relative only; trees of all species can be and commonly are injured or killed by fire.

As would be expected, no precise rating of relative fire resistance is possible. Many interacting factors are involved, and information available is mostly of an empirical nature. Comparative information on a number of selected eastern and western species is given in Tables 3.1 and 3.2. Much of this information has been gathered by Starker (1934), but it has been supplemented from other sources.

Considering the western trees first, an old-growth redwood is undoubtedly the most fire-resistant because of its particularly thick and nonresinous bark, often exceeding 12 inches near the base of old trees. Redwood resistance is enhanced by the great size attained by the species plus the fact that it grows in a moist region only occasionally subject to fire. Even so, basal fire wounds on large trees are common and much damage results (Fritz, 1932). Young redwoods are easily damaged and killed by fire; immature stands are no more resistant than several of the pines. Consequently, it may be a mistake to consider redwood as the most resistant western conifer; only the big veterans are.

At ages from about 100 to perhaps 250 years, western larch is undoubtedly the most fire-resistant tree in North America. This is primar-

Table 3.1 Relative Fire Resistance of Selected Conifers of the Western United States[*]

Species	Basal bark thickness of mature trees	Character of tree crown	Character of stands	Rooting habit	Associated lichen growth
Extremely resistant (old trees only):					
Redwood (*Sequoia sempervirens*)	Extremely thick	High and moderately open	Dense	Deep	Not a factor
Western larch (*Larix occidentalis*)	Very thick	High and very open	Moderately open	Deep	Medium
Highly resistant:					
Ponderosa pine (*Pinus ponderosa*)	Very thick	Moderately high and open	Open	Deep	Light
Douglas-fir (*Pseudotsuga menziesii*)	Very thick	Moderately high and dense	Dense	Deep	Heavy
Moderately resistant:					
White and grand fir (*Abies concolor* and *grandis*)	Thick	Low and dense	Dense	Moderately shallow	Heavy
White pine and sugar pine (*Pinus monticola* and *lambertiana*)	Medium	Moderately high and dense	Dense	Medium	Medium
Lodgepole pine (*Pinus contorta*)	Very thin	Moderately high and open	Open	Deep	Medium
Low resistance:					
Western red cedar (*Thuja plicata*)	Thin	Low and dense	Dense	Shallow	Moderate to heavy
Western hemlock (*Tsuga heterophylla*)	Medium	Low and dense	Dense	Shallow	Heavy
Engelmann spruce (*Picea engelmannii*)	Thin	Low and dense	Dense	Shallow	Heavy
Sitka spruce (*Picea sitchensis*)	Thin	Moderately high and dense	Dense	Shallow	Heavy
Very low resistance:					
Alpine fir (*Abies lasiocarpa*)	Very thin	Very low and dense	Dense	Shallow	Heavy

[*] After Starker (1934) and Flint (1925).

Table 3.2 Relative Fire Resistance of Selected Tree Species of the Eastern United States*

Species and resistance group	Basal bark thickness of mature trees	Character of tree crown†	Character of stands	Rooting habit
Highly resistant:				
Longleaf pine (*Pinus palustris*)	Thick	High and open	Open	Very deep
Resistant:				
Pitch pine (*Pinus rigida*)	Medium	Moderately high and open	Moderately open	Medium deep
Pond pine (*Pinus serotina*)	Medium	Moderately high and open	Moderately open	Medium
Red pine (*Pinus resinosa*)	Medium	Moderately high and dense	Moderately open	Deep
Slash pine (*Pinus elliottii*)	Medium	Moderately high and open	Moderately open	Medium deep
Shortleaf pine (*Pinus echinata*)	Medium	Moderately high and open	Moderately open	Medium deep
Loblolly pine (*Pinus taeda*)	Medium	Medium height and density	Moderately dense	Medium
Moderately resistant:				
Chestnut oak (*Quercus montana*)	Thick		Moderately dense	Medium
Yellow poplar (*Liriodendron tulipifera*)	Medium		Moderately dense	Medium
Black and post oak (*Quercus velutina, stellata*)	Medium		Moderately open	Medium
Eastern white pine (*Pinus strobus*)	Medium	Medium height and density	Medium dense	Medium
Jack pine (*Pinus banksiana*)	Medium	Medium height and density	Moderately open	Medium
Of intermediate resistance:				
Red oak (*Quercus rubra*)	Medium		Medium	Medium
Hickory (*Carya* spp.)	Medium		Moderately dense	Medium
Sweetgum (*Liquidambar styraciflua*)	Moderately thin		Moderately dense	Medium
White oak (*Quercus alba*)	Moderately thin		Moderately dense	Medium
Of low resistance:				
Sugar maple (*Acer saccharum*)	Moderately thin		Dense	Medium
Scarlet oak (*Quercus coccinea*)	Thin		Dense	Medium
Yellow birch (*Betula lutea*)	Moderately thin		Dense	Medium
Black cherry (*Prunus serotina*)	Moderately thin		Dense	Medium
Spruces (*Picea* spp.)	Thin	Low and dense	Dense	Shallow
Aspens (*Populus tremuloides* and *grandidentata*)	Thin	High and open	Medium	Medium
Cedars (*Thuja* and *Juniperus* spp.)	Thin	Medium height and density	Dense	Shallow
Firs (*Abies* spp.)	Very thin	Low and dense	Dense	Shallow

* After Starker (1934) and others.

† Not considered significant for hardwoods since fires seldom burn in crowns.

ily because of the unusually thick bark of high insulating capacity that develops near the base of the tree (see Figure 3.2) and also because larch trees have high and open crowns of low flammability and usually grow in fairly open stands. Furthermore, the roots are deep and there is seldom much brush or surface litter near the base of the larger trees. The net result is that larch is amazingly fire-resistant; in western Montana and northern Idaho, it is common to see a few veteran larch trees as the sole survivors after fire.

Ponderosa pine and Douglas-fir are two other western species of relatively high fire resistance. The resistance of ponderosa pine is highly variable because of the variety of associated fuels in its wide geographic range. But it develops moderate resistance over most of its range at 40 to 100 years due to a combination of thick bark and a natural habit of open stand growth. Douglas-fir derives its resistance almost entirely from a thick, corky bark (on the older trees) of high insulating capacity. However it is quite susceptible to crown fires.

The white and grand firs, white pines, and lodgepole pine are a moderately resistant group, their relative order depending mostly on habitat. The grand fir, for example, when growing in upland situations and in open stands, is fairly deep-rooted, thick-barked, and moderately fire-resistant, probably more so than western white pine on the average. Many trees will survive an average surface fire, and ground fires are scarce because of lack of litter accumulation. But in the moister lowlands it succumbs readily to a creeping surface fire and particularly to a ground fire; duff accumulations are often heavy in the flats and bottoms. Mature lodgepole pine possibly can be considered as moderately fire-resistant because of the open stands, lack of limbs near the ground, and low flammability of the ground cover characteristic of most lodgepole forests. The tree is rather thin-barked, and the younger trees are easily killed by anything hotter than a light surface fire. Nonetheless, old lodgepole pines are found that have survived several surface fires, as attested by butt scars. Western red cedar is easily injured, but it is tenacious in clinging to life despite severe basal wounding.

Western hemlock, the spruces, and alpine fir compose a very susceptible group. Fire-scorched trees are scarce; they seldom survive any fire, and Table 3.1 shows why. They are thin-barked, shallow-rooted trees with low, dense crowns. They are also frequently festooned with long streamers of lichen growth. A lighted match touched to one of these streamers on a hot, dry afternoon can ignite the tree crown with almost the explosive speed of a firecracker.

It should be emphasized that none of the western conifers of less than pole size has significant fire resistance. Also, as a generality, the

Figure 3.2 Conifer tree forms as related to fire resistance. *(U.S. Forest Service photos.) A.* Mature ponderosa pine; thick bark near base of tree, high crowns and open stands, sparse ground cover. *B.* Very thick bark at base of western larch. *C.* Mature western hemlock; dense stands, deep crowns, and much debris on forest floor. *D.* Longleaf pine; thickish-barked trees with sparse crowns growing in open stands. Surface fire in amount of fuels shown would damage little of this stand.

55

older and larger the tree, the more resistant it is, because the bark is thicker and there is usually less litter to burn near the base of the tree.

The eastern tree species, selectively represented in Table 3.2, form a more diverse group including both conifers and hardwoods, which are hard to compare as to fire resistance. The longleaf pine is unquestionably the most resistant, but for larger than pole-sized trees it probably does not equal the larch of the West in fire resistance. Habitat conditions are so diverse that it is hard to make direct comparisons. Longleaf has a high and fairly open branching habit and under natural conditions (before the advent of fire control) occurred in open stands with light fuels on the ground. It develops a thickish bark near the ground at ages of 15 to 20 years, and hence even pole-sized trees exhibit considerable fire resistance; trees of saw-timber size survive all but the more severe fires normally occurring in the area. Longleaf also has the unique characteristic of relatively high fire resistance in the juvenile or grass stage because of the corky scales and the needles that protect the bud (Chapter 2).

Following the longleaf, the slash, shortleaf, and loblolly pines of the South, pitch pine and pond pine of the Eastern seaboard, and red pine of the Lake states form a relatively resistant group, and it is difficult to differentiate between them. They differ considerably in regenerative capacity after fire and hence in their resistance as continuing type components, but trees of comparable size subjected to about the same fire intensity do not differ much by species.

Some of the oaks, notably chestnut oak, which has the thickest bark, and black and post oak, are moderately resistant, particularly as fairly large trees. Perhaps some of them are as resistant as the hard pines; opinions differ, largely because burning conditions are seldom comparable. In general, they are more susceptible to basal wounding than the pines but are more tenacious in clinging to life despite damage. This is what makes fire injury so serious in both conifers and hardwoods from a management standpoint; the tree may survive but its merchantable value may be seriously reduced.

The spruces, cedars, true firs, and aspens are the least resistant species. It is for this reason that prescribed burning in established stands is never practicable with these species. Fire may, however, be employed after clear-cutting to reduce slash and aid in regeneration.

Fire Injury to Trees

The foregoing has dealt with the relative total capacity of different species to withstand fire. Considered here are the more specific effects of fire on a living tree. As has been pointed out, the fact that a tree is relatively fire-resistant does not mean that it is not susceptible to damage. Specific fire effects on trees consist of (1) physical damage to the tree, which includes wounding of the bole—mostly near the base, root injury, defoliation, branch damage, and any other injury that may result directly from the fire; and (2) damage by disease and insects induced by fire injury.

Physical Damage   Trees with basal scars of all sorts and sizes are a common sight in the woods. Most frequently, these scars are the result of fire. Living trees are often found with the base completely hollowed out, sometimes by a series of fires. Figure 3.3 shows some common types of bole injury. Root injury resulting from surface but more especially ground fires is common but hard to identify unless the tree is killed. The size and character of basal tree wounds are directly related to the extent and severity of the burning. If the fire was just hot enough to kill the living tissues, the affected bark will slough off, leaving the woody stem exposed. Callus tissues will form at the edge of the killed area. If the wound is not too large, it will heal over and the tree may eventually show little if any surface indication of the injury. With large wounds, and especially if the wood itself was charred and burned into, open catfaces result that never heal over. Initial injury to the bole by mechanical means, as in logging, may be followed and aggravated by subsequent fire, especially in the case of species exuding considerable resin, which increases flammability. Trees chipped to produce resin are very vulnerable on this account.

From a physical standpoint, the major damage suffered from fire wounds is reduction in the usable volume of the tree through various wood defects resulting from the scars. This may be substantial; cull reductions of 10 to 20 percent of total bole volume directly chargeable to fire scars are common. Reduction in rate of growth from basal wounding may be significant for a few years after damage is sustained, but it seldom persists. Jemison (1944), in a careful study of basal wounding in southern Appalachian hardwoods, found that "even severe basal wounding does not retard the rate of diameter growth of white oak and yellow poplar trees and that only occasionally does it influence the growth of scarlet oaks. . . ." This is generally true of both hardwoods and conifers; if the tree is not killed outright, even a fairly narrow band of conducting tissue, often less than 25 percent of the tree circumference, seems to be enough to sustain the tree with only temporary reduction in growth. The ability of many tree species to survive almost complete ax girdling is indicative in this respect.

Scorching of the foliage and resultant defoliation and branch injury will substantially reduce growth for a period and may cause permanent injury to the crown. The specific effects are, of course, highly variable by

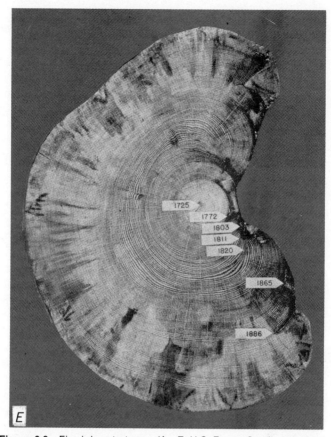

Figure 3.3 Fire injury to trees. *(A—E, U.S. Forest Service photos.)* A. A southern red oak immediately after a hot fall fire. *B.* Same tree two years after the fire. *C.* Same tree three years after the fire. Decay has progressed far enough for breakage to occur. *D.* Basal fire damage to southern red oak about 15 years after a fire. Rot now extends up through all of the first log. *E.* Cross section of an 18-inch red pine, 227 years old, showing scars of six different fires. Stasca State Park, Minnesota. *(Photo by S. H. Spurr.)*

species and fire intensity. Defoliation by fire is important mostly in pole-sized or smaller trees. When the crowns of larger trees are scorched, the fire is usually also hot enough to kill the tree, in which case degree of scorching is of little practical significance. In general, hardwood foliage is considerably less susceptible to damage than that of conifers because the foliage is less flammable (when green) and the species tend to replace killed buds and twigs more readily.

Of the conifers, the pitch, pond, longleaf, slash, loblolly, and short-leaf pines are the most able to endure fire defoliation. Pitch and pond pine sprout readily after fire. Small, healthy longleaf pine trees can survive complete defoliation by a winter fire. Even larger trees may withstand almost complete defoliation. The other southern pines, especially slash, can also endure considerable scorching. The effect of fire defoliation on growth seems to be in fairly direct proportion to the degree of scorch, as brought out by Wahlenberg (1946) for longleaf pine and Gruschow (1952) and McCulley (1950) for slash pine. None of the northern and western conifers equal these Eastern seaboard and southern pines in enduring fire defoliation and in making subsequent recovery.

Disease and Insect Relations   The most serious aspect of fire injury to living trees is that it so frequently increases susceptibility to disease and insect attack. These relationships are exceedingly widespread, common, and also complex. Some effects are felt more or less immediately after the fire and some develop over a period of years, reflecting both direct physical injury to the tree and changes in forest environment resulting from the fire. In the case of disease, the most frequent and damaging result is the increased incidence of root and butt rots, which is, of course, a long-time and cumulative effect. Stickel (1940) studied these effects, and the rate of healing of fire scars, in the Northeast. Hepting and Hedgcock (1937), working in southern Appalachian hardwoods, found that 94 percent of butt defect occurred in trees with basal wounds and estimated that 97 percent of these wounds were caused by fire. Hedgcock (1927), in considering eastern hardwoods generally, estimated that more than 90 percent of butt rots entered through fire scars at that time. There is no such thing as an accurate overall figure, but these studies are indicative of the magnitude of hardwood damage indirectly caused by fire. From coast to coast, incidence of butt rot in conifers is known to be large and fire is a major predisposing factor. The significant point from a fire-control standpoint is to recognize that fire is a principal contributor to rot-caused defect in standing timber, defect which in its cumulative effect may outweigh in importance the more obvious tree mortality.

The situation with insects is equally complex and cannot be explored here. Much insect attack, both endemic and epidemic, is aided or induced by fire. For example, "both the Black Hills beetle, *Dendroctonus ponderosae,* and the mountain pine beetle, *D. monticolae,* are species that frequently build up to outbreak proportions in fire-killed or wind-thrown materials" (Graham, 1952). The same can be true of the southern pine beetle *(D. frontalis)* or several species of ips in the South.

The usual difference between fire-induced diseases and insects is that the heart rots usually lead to deterioration or partial loss of merchant-able volume of living trees, whereas insect infestation is more often fatal and consequently results in loss of the entire tree.

EFFECTS ON FOREST MICROCLIMATE AND VEGETATION

Effects of fire on trees, as presented in the preceding section, and on the origin, composition, and continuance of forest types (Chapter 2) are of obvious and practical importance to the forester. But trees are not the only products of forests, and they are only a part, albeit a dominant part, of the vegetative association as a whole. Partial or complete destruction of an existing forest and related vegetative cover type may profoundly change the entire forest environment and induce a series of related effects of far-reaching importance. Detailed consideration of the complex short- and long-range relationships existing between vegetation, microclimate, water, and soil affected by fire or other forest disturbance is beyond the scope of this book. These subjects are a part of the general field of forest influences. Much of this literature has been brought together by Shantz (1947), Kittredge (1948), Sampson (1952), and Colman (1953). Only the importance and general nature of these relationships can be considered here.

The pronounced influence of a forest cover on the microclimate is well known. Air temperature is strongly affected. Many studies have emphasized the capacity of a forest to reduce maximum and increase minimum air temperatures within and under the canopy and especially near the ground. Since maximums are usually decreased more than minimums are increased, the net effect of a forest is to decrease mean temperatures as compared with open conditions. No forest visitor can escape noticing the cooling effect of a forest cover on a hot summer day. Average changes of only a few degrees may be highly significant. Following partial or complete removal of the forest canopy, a heavy duff layer may largely disappear in a few years primarily because of increased fungal and other biotic activity induced by higher air temperatures at the ground level. Regeneration of trees and other forest vegetation is strongly affected by light, temperature, and soil moisture, all of which are closely associated with forest cover. On exposed sites, surface temperatures may reach a lethal level and prevent seedling establishment. Subsequent growth is affected by temperature and soil moisture.

Air movement is markedly affected by a forest cover, as has been repeatedly demonstrated. Under a full canopy of a mature forest, air movement will seldom exceed 3 to 4 miles per hour within 2 feet of the ground, almost irrespective of wind velocities above the canopy. Air movements in a stand, in relation to open conditions, increase as a function of height above ground and stand density.

Relative humidity is almost always higher under a forest canopy than outside; in general, the more dense and complete the forest cover the greater the difference. This is a combined result of reduced air temperature and movement and the transpiration of vegetation. Fuels consequently dry more slowly under a forest canopy.

Microclimatic changes caused by fire or other forest disturbances are naturally important in fire control since they materially affect local fuel and burning conditions. But, more broadly, they affect the whole fauna and flora of an area in many and complex ways. As pointed out in Chapter 2, fire, especially if recurrent, can convert a high forest area into semipermanent or permanent woodland, brush type, or grassland.

As a powerful molder of forest environment, fire exerts profound total effects on wildlife. Fire can and does kill birds and animals and destroy their natural habitat. Lye leaching from the ashes of larger fires can kill whole fish populations. Yet fire, by opening up forest stands and creating more forest margin area, often increases food production and desirable habitat, and hence it also increases the wildlife population. This is especially true in coniferous forests; large positive as well as negative effects must be considered and balanced. Use of fire for wildlife purposes is briefly considered in Chapter 17.

Through changes induced in microclimate and vegetation, fire has major effects in the interception, evaporation, transpiration, storage, and movement of water in forest stands and soils. Destruction of forest cover on relatively small areas of less than a thousand acres may, with unstable soil conditions and high-intensity rainfall, permit serious flood damage. The relation of forest cover to water is a major field of study in itself. The only points that can be made here are that the subject is important and that water resources alone are a major, and in many areas a primary, consideration requiring control of wildfires.

EFFECTS ON SOIL

Because of the continuing and fundamental importance of the soil, concern over the possible effects of forest fires on it is natural. In what way and to what extent can physical and chemical soil properties be affected by fire? Is the continued burning of some forest areas gradually reducing their productivity because of soil deterioration? To what degree and in what respect can changes in the soil brought about by fire aid or impede the reestablishment of desirable forest cover? The need for answers to these and related questions has stimulated interest and research on the effects of forest fires on soils.

At the outset, it must be recognized clearly that the subject is complex and that few specific answers are possible. Soil effects are, to a considerable degree, a by-product of the more direct effects of fire on the vegetation and microclimate. It is often difficult to separate soil effects from total site effects. Soils, topography, fuels, and burning conditions are often highly variable from area to area, and results on the forest and soil beneath can vary accordingly. In fact, fire can cause almost any effect on the soil, good or bad depending on viewpoint, that can be induced by other means in the vegetative cover of wild lands. There is little that is peculiar to fire alone. Logging, agricultural use, grazing, storm, and flood can have similar results.

It should also be recognized that the effect of fire on the forest environment is often considered in an atmosphere charged with strong feeling and sometimes prejudice. Wildfire has been painted, and rightly, as an archdemon and enemy of the forest; it has been a long and often uphill battle to develop public awareness of and support for wildfire control. Since wildfire is bad, it is easy to assume that all fire is bad and to direct research to finding out only how bad it can be. Soil effects, in particular, have been the subject of much misunderstanding, largely because some effects are clearly undesirable and because specific information is difficult to obtain. Most attention has been directed to extremes; to comparison of frequent fires with no fires and with single severe fires. Much less attention has been given to fires of moderate to low intensity and of infrequent occurrence. Effects may vary widely within a particular fire. The need is to gain a balanced understanding.

Factors Controlling the Effects of Fire on Soil

A first step in appraising what forest fires can do to the soil is to identify the key variables. The words *fire* and *soil* are in themselves general terms with no specific meaning. Both the kind of fire and the kind of soil must be identified.

Following are four primary, controlling variable factors of fire and soil that must be specified before possible effects can be considered. It is completely useless to talk about fire-induced soil effects, which may range all the way from beneficial to highly detrimental, unless these factors are all carefully defined.

Frequency of Fire It is one thing to talk about fires in the piney woods of the lower South, another to consider the occasional though severe fires characteristic of the Douglas-fir and western white pine country which have created and maintained these types, and still another to talk about the cycle of severe fires which accompanied and followed early logging in the Lake states. The effects were and are different in these regional situations, and the frequency of burning has much to do with it. In piney woods of the South, visitation by fire is characteristically frequent; a given acre may be burned over annually, every few years, or every decade, but until rather recently it will seldom have escaped fire much longer. In the western Douglas-fir and white pine types, fire usually covers a particular acre infrequently, often at intervals of over a hundred years. Infrequent fires are often severe and normally result in the establishment of a new stand. Severe and repeated fires in the Lake states wrecked the original forest types over millions of acres, bringing in aspen and jack pine over large areas and reducing others to brush and semibarren sand plains. Early-day logging and repeated fires in the South also destroyed the seed source and prevented natural regeneration over large areas.

The frequency of burns is highly important. The effects are cumulative in varying degree. A single fire may have little effect on the soil. A sequence of two or more fires in fairly close succession may induce substantial soil effects. Consequently, the effect of a single fire must be appraised in relation to the fires that have preceded or may follow it. Two fires of similar intensity in the same area may cause widely differing results; in the case of so-called double burns in the West, the second is more damaging to the soil. For these reasons, the periodicity and timing of fire must be carefully identified in appraising soil effects.

Heat Intensity and Duration   Forest fires range from light grass fires with low heat intensity and a duration of only a few minutes in a particular spot to fires of several hours' duration in heavy slash and ground fuels that develop high heat intensities. Fires of low heat intensity but long duration also occur as ground fires in duff and peat. In fine but abundant flash fuels like dry conifer slash, the fire may be of short duration but hot while it lasts. Effects on the soil may vary according to the joint effect of intensity and duration.

Forest Floor   The presence or absence of duff, humus, and other unincorporated organic material on the forest floor and the amount of it consumed are of key importance in appraising soil effects. In fact, much confusion and misunderstanding about the effect of fire on soil stems from failure to be specific about the character of the organic mantle overlying the mineral soil and what a particular fire does to it. In many forest types, conifer especially, partially decayed vegetative material forms a layer that is sometimes a foot or more in depth. A surface fire skimming over the top of this layer will have no direct effect on the soil, although indirect effects may develop from the killing of some trees and consequent changing of the forest environment. A ground fire over the same area consumes this organic mantle and exposes the mineral soil, thus producing direct and substantial soil effects. Changes in the organic layer also affect the chemical materials that infiltrate the mineral soil.

Soil Characteristics   The physical characteristics of the soil below the duff layer strongly influence the effects of fire. These include particle size, texture, and structure, which in turn are modified in their effect by the moisture content and the organic content of the soil. Sandy soils and clay soils differ widely in texture, structure, moisture content, and in their physical and chemical characteristics, such as thermal conductivity and colloidal structure. The effects of fire as a causal agent in creating changed conditions are correspondingly dissimilar. Mull soils will retain much of their permeability even if the humus layer on the surface is removed; other kinds of soils will not. Failure to be clear about the kind of soil is another prime source of confusion about fire effects. It seems rather obvious that a specific knowledge of forest soils is prerequisite to an appraisal of what fire can do to them.

Soil Heating by Fires

Surface soil is quite susceptible to change through heating. This is because of its soil organisms, its organic content, and, where present, its colloidal structure. For that reason heating of the soil even to the lethal point for living protoplasm is often important.

The heat of combustion from a fire is transmitted by convection, radiation, and conduction. Convection, which accounts for 70 to 80 percent of the heat released, rapidly dissipates heat upward. Consequently, the heat transmitted downward to the soil surface under and around a fire is transmitted primarily by radiation and conduction. This limits the rate and intensity of soil heating. Above the surface, temperatures may approach 2000°F from convected and radiated heat in hot fires. Temperature of the soil surface may reach 400°F or higher from the radiated heat. Temperatures below the surface depend on conducted heat and decrease rapidly with depth.

The temperatures reached and the temperature profile downward depend on several factors. The intensity and duration of the fire, a function of the fuels consumed, is obviously a controlling factor. Whenever an organic soil mantle enters into the combustion, this intensifies the effect. Two fires consuming an equal quantity of fuel—one burning down through an established and compacted organic mantle, which is a poor heat conductor, and the other burning in loose fuels piled directly on bare mineral soil—will differ widely in their effect on soil temperatures even though the total heat released may be about the same. The thermal conductivity of the soil itself is also important.

Studies by Beadle (1940) on sandy soils in a eucalyptus forest in Australia give some specific information illustrative of the nature of the problem. Natural fires in the area spread rapidly and are of short duration. Maximum soil temperatures were determined at 1- and 3-inch depths by burying a series of glass vials containing chemical compounds of known melting temperatures. These are not so precise as recording thermocouples because a range rather than a specific temperature is recorded, but since the compounds take a little time to melt, they are probably more representative than thermocouple control of temperature effects on organic materials. Temperatures below 3 inches were obtained by thermometers. Beadle simulated three forest conditions: (1) A "natural" fire in an area not burned for six years with no fuel added. (2) Maximal temperatures possible in natural fires. For this test, fuels from 9 square feet were concentrated into a pile 2 feet in diameter on top of the natural forest floor. (3) Maximum intensity of fires burning heavy fuels obtained by concentrating the dry-timber equivalent of trees along with the natural dead fuels and undergrowth of an area.

The results of Beadle's tests (averaged) are given in Table 3.3. As might be expected, there was considerable variation between individual tests. Varying amounts of dead plant material on the ground were a major reason. The general picture given by the tests is, however, fairly clear.

Table 3.3   Maximum Soil Temperatures, in Degrees Fahrenheit, during Forest Fires*†

Depth, in.	"Natural" fires in light fuels burning 3/4 hr	Maximum-intensity "natural" fires in light fuels burning 2 hr	Maximum-intensity fires burning in heavy fuels	
			Burning 2 hr	Burning 8 hr (stoked)
Surface	290	480	‡	‡
1	130	235	350	480
3	. . .	145	210	430
6	. . .	95	147	185
9	. . .	59	104	136
12	. . .	54	70	116

* After Beadle (1940).

† Temperatures from a number of tests averaged. Those obtained at 1- and 3-inch depths from chemical-compound melting points averaged to nearest 5°.

‡ Not determined.

With natural fires, soil heating might cause lethal damage to soil organ-isms to a 1-inch depth. With the maximum-intensity natural fires, some damage might occur down to 3 inches. The prolonged fires in heavy fuels probably caused lethal heating 6 to 9 inches down. In sandy soils, the principal effect of these temperatures is probably on soil organisms. No actual combustion of organic matter even at the 1-inch level could take place from the natural fire. The effect of burning on the productivity of the soil cannot be determined from these tests.

Studies of damage to three types of soil from the burning of heavy logging slash in the Douglas-fir type near Corvallis, Oregon, were carried out in 1957. These identified the severely burned spots under log piles as the areas of significant damage to properties of clay and silt soils. Such areas, however, comprised only 8 percent of the region. Subsequent studies have shown that these severely burned spots return to full productivity after a varying period of years.

Heyward (1938), working in fine sandy soils of the longleaf type, studied soil temperatures by thermocouple at a depth of $1/8$ to $1/4$ inch. Test fires were set in areas that had been unburned from 1 to 15 years and that had varying volumes of fuel on the ground. Maximum temperatures $1/8$ to $1/4$ inch below the surface were as follows:

Type of area	Degrees Fahrenheit
15-year rough*	175
Heavy 5-year rough	190
Very heavy 5-year rough	190
Heavy 4-year rough	210
Light 2-year rough	210
Unburned for 1 year	210

*The term *rough* applies to the accumulation of all living and dead herbaceous vegetation. A "15-year rough" means a 15-year accumulation since last burning.

Burning was done with fires spreading with and against the wind. The latter tended to heat the soil more, probably because of slower spread and consequently longer fire duration at a particular spot. Temperatures reached a maximum from four to six minutes after ignition, stayed at or near the maximum for two to four minutes, and then declined rapidly. As shown, the highest temperatures were attained on the one- to four-year roughs, the lowest on the fifteen-year rough. The fires were hotter in the heavier fuels, hotter than in average fires, with flames 12 to 14 feet high. But the protective mat of vegetative matter on the soil surface was effective in insulating the soil. Heyward concluded that "at a soil depth of only $1/8$ to $1/4$ inch, the heat generated even by hot fires in the longleaf pine region is insufficient to destroy organic matter."

Sampson and Craddock (Sampson, 1944) measured temperatures

during fires in chaparral types in California. They employed a pyrometer recording from thermocouples placed $1/2$-inch deep in the duff and litter and at varying depths up to 3 inches in the mineral soil. Data from their studies are summarized in Table 3.4. These data show, as would be expected, that temperatures are highest in the duff and progressively less at greater soil depths. They also show wide variation in the relationship between duff and soil temperatures both as regards the time it took to reach maximum temperature and the duration of temperatures over 150°F.

The three preceding soil-temperature studies, in which temperature measurements were taken, illustrate the nature of resulting data to be expected and the problems introduced by the many variables.

The general pattern of soil heating can be predicted fairly well from what is known of the physical properties of soils. In general, soil is a poor conductor of heat.

> It appears that the thermal conductivity of dry mineral soil material varies but little from one soil to another. Factors such as the content of organic matter, the texture, volume weight, and porosity are more important than the composition of the mineral material. [Lutz and Chandler, 1946]

Thermal conductivity is decreased as organic content and porosity increase. Partially decomposed organic matter is a very poor conductor, primarily because of its porosity, as witnessed by the high insulating capacity of a duff layer. Air is one of the best insulating materials; its thermal conductivity is extremely low. Rocky and sandy soils heat more readily than clays, largely because rock is a better conductor of heat. Agriculturally, these soils are always characterized as "warm" in relation to the clays. Moisture increases the thermal conductivity of soils, but the net effect on soil temperature is more than offset by the fact that the specific heat of water and of its vaporization is much higher than that of mineral soil. This means that while moist soils can transmit heat more quickly, it takes much more energy to heat them up to the high temperatures necessary for organic disintegration. Moist soils are, in general, cool soils.

Effects on Unincorporated Organic Material

Much of the effect of fire on soil depends on the character and amount of the mantle of unincorporated organic material that may be present overlying the mineral soil and on what a particular fire does to it.

This mantle is especially important in relation to soil effects, since it usually represents an accumulation of many years and frequently aggre-

Table 3.4 Litter and Soil Temperatures in California Chaparral Types during Burning*

Vegetation	Depth of thermocouples, in.	Maximum temperatures, °F	Minutes to reach maximum temperature	Minutes temperature remained over 150°F
Chamise, fairly dense grasses and weeds	On soil surface	635	9	3
	3/4 in. in soil	320	9	12
	1 1/2 in. in soil	230	16	17
Mixed chaparral of blue oak, dwarf interior live oak, wedgeleaf ceanothus, with scattered herbs	1/2 in. in duff	840	4	40
	1/2 in. in soil	410	7	61
	1 1/2 in. in soil	235	14	74
Wedgeleaf ceanothus with scattered grasses	1/2 in. in litter	300	5	11
	1/2 in. in soil	200	1	5
	1 1/2 in. in soil	†		
Common manzanita, scattered grasses and weeds	1/2 in. in litter	960	8	34
	1 1/2 in. in soil	215	16	17

*After Sampson (1944).
†Below 150°F. Instrument does not record below this temperature, and hence no reading.

gates much more in total organic content than the more conspicuous forest fuels above it. It also may constitute a major part of the total combustible fuel volume and certainly is that part of it closest to the mineral soil. Where this organic material is heavy and dry enough to burn, the total effect of the fire on the soil may be very damaging. This is especially true if the underlying mineral-soil layer is thin. For example, a duff and muck layer a foot or more thick may slowly accumulate on very thin soils in spruce-fir types. A fire in this type, under conditions dry enough for the whole organic layer to burn, may leave virtually nothing but bare rocks with a skin of mineral soil. Such a fire is extremely damaging to the site and may prevent full reestablishment and normal growth of a forest cover for centuries. Similar effects occur in several other forest types.

As was pointed out in Chapter 1, fires in swamps are very destructive due to the heavy accumulation of organic material. There is a tendency to think that swampy areas do not burn. Since they are normally wet, this is naturally true most of the time. There are times, however, even though only once in a decade or even a human generation, when they dry out sufficiently to permit the occurrence of extremely damaging fires. Such a situation occurred rather generally in the South in 1955 (Figure 3.4). Swamps and "bays," which normally can be counted on to serve as barriers to fire spread, became flammable and burned extensively and destructively. Canals and drainage ditches also cause abnormal drying out of swamps and often lead to this kind of damage. What swamp fires lack in frequency of occurrence they make up for in destructiveness. A deep layer of accumulated organic material may be consumed, the forest completely destroyed, and growing conditions for trees seriously impaired for many years.

The combustion of large organic accumulations does not necessarily result in soil damage, although it commonly does in the situations cited above. In the western white pine type of northern Idaho (Chapter 1), fairly heavy accumulations of duff are common under old timber stands. For the most part, the underlying soils are fairly deep. With a single burn, that is, a fire in an area of green timber that has not burned over for many years, only a part of this duff is ordinarily consumed; the soil and lower layers of duff are usually moist. Only under extreme drought conditions will most of the duff be consumed. It is astonishing how hard it is to burn all the organic mantle in a single burn. Following what may seem to be a very hot fire, blackening everything in sight, a substantial proportion of the area will still have unburned duff covering the mineral soil. In such a situation, increased erosion and other direct physical effects on the mineral soil are slight. Even if the duff burns, this may not hinder the

Figure 3.4 Deep burning of organic soil during drought conditions. Hand shows normal level of water table. *(U.S. Forest Service photo.)*

reestablishment of a new forest cover. Indeed, it is a common observation that tree seedlings and other vegetation grow especially well on burned-over areas. It must be remembered that, since time immemorial, vigorous stands of western white pine and associated species have become reestablished following severe wildfires.

A second fire following the first in a few years or even a decade or two is much more damaging. With more open and consequently drier conditions and an abundance of fire-killed timber, the summer fire hazard is usually higher than before the first fire. If a second fire occurs in such a situation, it is hotter than the first and will ordinarily kill all young growth that started after the burn as well as the seed trees from which the new growth came. It also consumes all organic material down to bare mineral soil. Following this second fire, or double burn, as such a condition is commonly termed (and triple burns have also occurred), damage to the soil often results. This is usually immediately apparent through increased erosion. Much of the concern over the effects of fire on the soil in this forest type centers on the results of multiple burns. In northern Idaho, unpublished studies showed that much of the accelerated erosion set in motion by the conflagrations of 1910 and 1919 had not yet stabilized after 40 years.

As illustrated by the above situations, consumption of the organic mantle on the soil by fire can range all the way from none to complete with equally varied resultant effects on the soil and on forest growth.

Effects on Mineral Soil

As previously pointed out, a number of factors jointly control the effects of fire on the soil. From the standpoint of specifically defining what a fire can do, they may be summarized as (1) soil heating, (2) release of mineral residual products of combustion present in the ashes, and (3) environmental changes wrought by the partial or complete destruction of the forest vegetation. Soil heating is, of course, an immediate and direct result of a fire, but, as has been shown, the direct heating of soils is usually a minor consideration. It can become important only in fires of considerable duration and intensity, usually in heavy fuels and especially when concentrated, as in slash piles. The leaching of mineral products from ashes into the soil is less immediate. While most of the effects of leaching occur within a year or two, they may be significant for several years. The effects of environmental changes may be both immediate and exceedingly long-range in character. Complex interaction of short- and long-range effects make appraisal of the effect of fire on soil difficult. The problem is further compounded by the soil which is a very variable and complex biological as well as physical entity.

Keeping these points in mind, physical, chemical, and biological aspects of fire effects on the mineral soil are discussed.

Physical Exposure of the soil surface through destruction of the vegetative cover, especially following repeated fires, may permit severe erosion and accelerated surface water runoff. (Figure 3.5) This is frequently the most serious and long-lasting result of fire, and the subject would make a book in itself. All that can be said here is that wildfire is a major cause of erosion and excessive surface runoff. Unwise agricultural practices and timber cutting which expose bare soil on sloping terrain can produce similar results.

With the heavier soils, surface compaction may result from the effect of repeated fires in exposing the mineral soil. Muddy water soon seals the surface layer and reduces infiltration capacity. Sandy soils are but little affected in this respect.

Soil heating from fires of long duration may, in the heavier soils

Figure 3.5 Severe erosion following intense burn on San Dimas Experimental Forest in southern California. *(U.S. Forest Service photo.)*

particularly, bake particles into larger aggregates and change the colloidal structure unfavorably. It is common to observe that seedlings and other vegetation often do not become established for several years where large slash piles have been burned. A profusion of vegetation may fringe the area, but the center may be bare. The reasons seem to be physical as well as biological and chemical.

Burning can significantly increase surface-soil temperatures directly through the blackening of the surface and consequent increase in heat absorption and indirectly through exposure of the site through removal of shade. Charcoal, which is black, durable, and high in heat-absorptive capacity, is often left on the surface following fire and increases surface temperatures. The general effect of charcoal is otherwise favorable to the soil, and whether the effects of increased surface-soil temperatures are desirable or not depends on whether surface-soil temperatures in a particular situation are or are not critical in the establishment of natural reproduction. The increase in surface-soil temperature because of blackening has been shown by research to be critical in certain situations. However, its overall importance is less than the general and sustained increase in surface and soil temperature and dryness due to partial or complete destruction of the living cover. This increased exposure to sun and wind may be of long duration following fires in heavy coniferous stands of the North or of only a season or two following light surface fires in the South. In the latter area, higher soil temperatures in the spring following winter fires promote early seedling and tree growth. Rapid growth of grass and forbs protects new seedlings by late spring and summer. The same effect can occur in any area of rapid vegetative growth.

The effect of fire on soil moisture content is extremely variable, as would be expected (Sampson, 1952). The immediate effect of soil exposure following fire is to reduce soil moisture, especially near the surface. In general, frequently burned-over soils are drier near the surface than comparable unburned soils. This relationship can, however, be upset by the countereffect of removing shallow-rooted vegetation that uses water. Soil moisture may actually increase following burning as a combined result of a loose surface mulch and reduced vegetative transpiration. If the vegetation killed by fire is mostly of the deeper-rooted shrubs and trees and is followed by shallow-rooted annuals, soil moisture content at the lower levels may increase following burning. This increase can substantially affect underground water storage, water table, and stream flow.

Chemical   Fire produces chemical effects on the soil in two ways: (1) through minerals released in the process of combustion and left in the ash, and (2) through changed microclimatic conditions following burning. These effects include a general reduction in soil acidity and warming of the soil resulting from exposed conditions. This accelerates decomposition of remaining organic materials and enables establishment of a different vegetative cover, as a deciduous cover replacing conifers, or grass and weeds replacing shrubs as subordinate vegetation.

The most immediate chemical effect of burning is the release of mineral elements that leach down into the soil. Most studies show an increase in available plant nutrients following burning. Replaceable calcium, potash, phosphoric acid, and other substances are more abundant for a while following burning and stimulate growth provided they are not leached out or eroded away before plants can utilize them. Loss from leaching may be very rapid in sandy soils, and the increase in available nutrients immediately following burning may be of little consequence in plant growth. In heavier soils, if there is very little runoff from precipitation, the increased supply may persist for several years.

Less immediate but important chemical effects may be brought about by changes in the vegetative cover. In the South, for example, fire-stimulated chemical changes in the top 6 inches of the soil seem to be largely due to alterations in the ground cover. Increased growth of grass and weeds following burning contributes more organic material and biological activity to the soil than accumulations of pine needles do.

Nitrogen in organically bound form is lost into the air from combustion of organic material. This does not mean, however, that the quantity available to plants is decreased, because most of the nitrogen lost from burning organic material would be lost without burning through slow decomposition of the same material. Studies show that available nitrogen in the soil is usually increased following burning. Soil and vegetative conditions favoring nitrification seem to be the major reason.

Soil acidity is decreased by burning, especially near the surface. The change may be enough to stimulate nitrification and growth of subordinate vegetation. Most mature forest trees do not seem to be significantly affected by the change in soil acidity brought about by fire.

Although stimulated tree and plant growth following fire is often noted in the field and, as stated above, studies usually show improved mineral nutrient conditions resulting from fire, one should not jump to the conclusion that the chemical effects of fire on the mineral soil are always good.

The fertilizing effect and lowering of the pH balance may be very valuable in establishing a new stand of seedlings or in preparing a plantation site. For such purposes some permanent loss of soluble nutrients through leaching and some loss of both soil and nutrients through erosion can be accepted as long as the total for the period between burns conforms closely to what might be expected from normal geological processes or as long as any deficiency can be remedied by available means such as artificial fertilizing. But even keeping within such limits requires careful control of the size, frequency, and intensity of the burn. Severe and repeated fires are so destructive of living things that they produce long-term damage effects that are difficult to compensate. Fire affects the availability of chemicals already in or drawn from the soil, but it never adds anything new. Each time it burns, it induces new liabilities for some permanent loss of soluble nutrients.

Biological Since soil heating by fires is seldom at a lethal level except very close to the surface, biological effects are mostly bound in with the environmental and chemical changes following fire. As with other fire relationships, effects are highly variable. Repeated fires, as in the South, may reduce the number of soil organisms near the surface. Increased average soil temperatures following burning can increase the number of organisms present. Chemical effects may also stimulate biological activity. In general, the total effects of burning on soil bacteria are of secondary importance.

Soil Effects in Summary

From a fire control and use standpoint, the following conclusions regarding effects of fire on soil merit emphasis:

1 Specific effects are extremely variable, making generalizations difficult and often misleading. The frequency, duration, and intensity of the fire, the presence or absence of an organic mantle and the amount of it consumed, and the character of the mineral soil all must be considered. Each situation must be individually and specifically appraised.

2 Direct heating effects are relatively minor in most situations. Soils are hard to heat, and only in extreme conditions is direct heating important.

3 The depth of the organic mantle on the mineral soil and the amount consumed are extremely important. Where the organic layer is heavy and dry enough to burn, the effect on the underlying soil and on the site in general may be very destructive. Peat and swamp fires or situations in which the mineral soil layer is thin are examples.

4 Changes in microclimate and vegetation following burning have significant soil effects, often more important and usually of longer duration than the immediate heat and chemical effects of burning.

5 Physical soil effects, especially from repeated fires, are generally unfavorable. Erosion in hilly or mountainous areas of unstable soils is usually the most serious result.

6 Chemical effects tend to be favorable but not strongly so; they are seldom a justification for burning.

7 There is a tendency to overemphasize the unfavorable effects of fire on mineral soil by stressing extreme situations in frequency and intensity of burning. There should be no minimizing of the destructive and undesirable results of wildfires, and this applies both to occasional severe fires and to the cumulative deteriorating effect of frequent moderate fires. But it must also be recognized that many fires have little total effect on the soil one way or another and some are beneficial. This fact permits a fairly wide range of choice in using fire in particular situations as a tool in forest management without risking significant soil damage (Hare, 1962).

EFFECTS ON THE ECOLOGY

From the foregoing, it is obvious that fire must have some effect on all uses of forest land, since it has the potential for drastically changing the forest environment. Besides its effect on trees, it has a profound effect on annual and perennial herbaceous vegetation and on the many species of shrubs that occur as understory vegetation in forest types or as the dominant cover on extensive nonforest areas.

Effects on Grass, Brush, and Woodlands

The physical effects of fire in stimulating herbaceous vegetation are of two kinds: removal of overhead shade and removal of heavy ground litter. The removal of shade stimulates growth of sun-loving plants and increases soil temperatures. The removal of litter exposes mineral soil to the sun, reduces its acidity, and stimulates germination of stored seed of all kinds. For at least some years, a severe timber fire produces some offsetting benefits in the form of greatly increased production of forage and browse for domestic livestock or game. This is, of course, accentuated by the chemical effects when heavy volumes of forest fuel are consumed. Natural plant succession—with its trend from annuals to perennials, to shrubs, to tree cover—gradually changes the environment back to forest again. However, this process may be slow and it may be interrupted or arrested.

In woodland areas, range and browse plants are often of more economic value than tree growth. This is usually because of limitations imposed by soil or climate or both. In such areas use of fire to help maintain a dominant cover of shrubs and grass finds a legitimate place in land management.

Though most forms of herbaceous vegetation are stimulated by fire, other forms of soil disturbance are almost equally effective and can usually be made more selective in encouraging desired species of forest cover. Cost is usually the deciding factor.

The ecology of brushland species, an interesting and challenging subject in itself, can only be touched on here.

The *Ceanothus*, manzanita, chamise, and scrub oak species that predominate in the brushlands of California and the Southwest are generally regarded as fire species. Collectively they are referred to as *chaparral.* They are well adapted to quick reestablishment after a fire through vigorous sprouting from the root crowns or by production of long-lived, hard-shelled seed which remains dormant in the surface litter and soil until the seed coat is cracked by heat. Then the seed germinates profusely. Without fire, such species reproduce very poorly and the type changes in composition to so-called mixed chaparral, woodland, or forest. With frequent fires, chaparral types expand; with infrequent burns, they shrink. Though costly, the use of fire and herbicides can be combined to bring about the conversion of chaparral to grass, woodland or timber as subclimax or even as climax types (Bentley, 1967).

Rather drastic changes in cover type of this nature naturally have a profound effect on other flora and on the fauna of the area. In northern

California, severe fires in the pine type destroy bitter brush, the most important browse shrub for deer. But in the brush type, fire greatly increases the amount of available browse from other species for a few years. Small animals, particularly mice and the rabbit population, are strongly affected by the drastic changes in environment induced by fire.

Such changes also affect the bird population. In Alaska, late spring fires in the nesting grounds of wild ducks and geese are often very destructive. Game managers report that spring fires often occur in the nesting season of wild turkeys in the South, resulting in loss of eggs and young birds. However, winter burns at sufficient intervals to maintain an open cover are considered desirable in maintaining a favorable habitat for this bird.

Game managers of quail and pheasant populations favor the use of fire to create grassy openings in the cover. What is sought is the maximum amount of "edge," consisting of shrub or timber cover, around such openings. Only very rarely do wildfires create such patterns in abundance. To bring about the desired patchy effect of this nature, carefully controlled burning at considerable cost is necessary (Chapters 17 and 18).

General Fire Effects

In summary, a few generalizations are justified in a still quite controversial field:

1   Fire induces many changes in habitat for both plants and animals, affecting food, cover, and microclimate. As a large-scale conflagration, it may be highly destructive of existing flora and fauna. In the form of small-scale prescribed burns, it may become an effective instrument in successful wild-land management.

2   A burn, whether by a wildfire or by a carefully controlled fire, always produces certain sorts of damage and certain benefits. It is the purpose of a prescribed fire to produce maximum *net* benefits.

3   Usually fire effects are regarded as beneficial as long as the intended purpose of a burn is accomplished. Offsetting damages are often disregarded or unforeseen.

4   Fire effects in the form of long-term or continuing deterioration in the productivity of the soil and site are difficult to measure but are naturally of primary concern to the public.

5   Short-term fire effects which affect only the current forest crop are easier to recognize and to appraise. These are normally the primary concern of the landowner.

Chapter 4

Forest Fuels

The nature of combustion in woody fuels has been briefly considered in Chapter 1. The demonstrated potential of this phenomenon in terms of large forest fires of the past has been reviewed in Chapter 2, and the more specific effects of fire have been considered in Chapter 3.

The ignition, buildup, and behavior of fire depends on fuels more than any other single factor. It is the fuel that burns, that generates the energy with which the fire fighter must cope, and that largely determines the rate and level of intensity of that energy. Other factors that are important to fire behavior (that is, moisture, wind, etc.) must always be considered in relation to fuels. In short, no fuel, no fire!

Discussion of fuels is significant only in relation to fire, yet the makeup of forest fuel complexes must be understood before the interactions between fire and its environment can be examined constructively. To achieve this, the student must be able to appraise forests and wild lands in general from the point of view of their fire potential. In figurative terms, it is like viewing the forest through a different pair of glasses, the kind worn constantly by skilled fire control men. The vegetative cover, living and dead, is then perceived as potential fuel, capable of being ignited and burned under certain conditions. Conditions that affect the ease of ignition and combustion, namely weather and topography, will be examined in the following chapter, again through the same glasses. Though fire behavior cannot be entirely excluded from these discussions, the focus is first placed on fuels. In Chapter 5 it is on weather and topography in relation to fuels. This may simplify the understanding of why free-burning fires behave as they do in wild-land environments.

SOURCES OF FUELS

As discussed in Chapter 1, combustible materials, composed chiefly of lignin and cellulose, are continually being built up by the process of photosynthesis in growing plants. Starting with a young pine plantation on bare ground, there is soon a mixture of green and dead material. First, grass and dead weeds at the end of the growing season create a cover through which fire could spread under certain conditions. Then, as the young trees grow to produce a closed crown canopy, the lower branches die, as do the grass and weeds underneath, and needles are shed. This is a very dangerous stage in the development of a coniferous plantation because of the very high prevalence of "flash" fuels, that is, fuels that ignite easily and burn rapidly. This is accentuated by the distribution of such fuels, as both vertically and horizontally no significant breaks in the fuel occur. After a period of years the situation changes. The dead branches drop, the remnants of ground vegetation disappear, and an increasing gap between surface litter and tree crowns develops. Usually too, decay in the surface litter increases to a point where it balances the rate of addition.

In deciduous hardwood stands, vertical distribution of flammable fuels does not develop and there is less tendency for dangerous fuels to accumulate, but annual leaf fall in great volume produces hazardous surface fuels during the dormant season. Cyclic changes of this kind, both seasonal and long-term, are prevalent in growing forests. The natural result is a constantly changing fuel complex with both seasonal and longer-term fluctuations.

Besides these fuels that may be regarded as the result of a natural lag between the production of dead material and its decay, forest disturbances of all kinds may suddenly bring about an increase in the volume of dead fuels. Woods operations such as logging, thinning, and pruning create a large volume of branch wood and tops on the ground. Unless disposed of by special measures, this logging or thinning slash may remain a high-hazard fuel for long periods.

Tornadoes and high winds at times blow down timber over considerable areas. These "blowdowns" create extreme fuel hazards and aggravate the fire-control problem by making access to the area very difficult.

Attacks by bark beetles and other epidemic insects at times kill whole stands of coniferous timber. These too create high fuel hazards over large areas. In the absence of salvage or hazard-reduction measures, such areas go through a cycle. Usually fire hazards are extreme for the first few years and then, as needles and twigs drop from the dead trees and disintegrate, fuel hazards reduce to a lower level until decay and blowdown create an area of half-decayed snags and down timber to mingle with surface fuels.

Crown fires in dense stands of coniferous timber commonly create severe fire hazards, so that one fire breeds another. Material removed by the first fire is only a small percentage of the wood volume on the ground, even though fine fuels have been removed temporarily. In the absence of salvage of the fire-killed timber, it eventually blows down to form jackstrawlike piles intermingled with standing dead snags. This is a combination dreaded by fire fighters. In northern Idaho, the huge fire-killed areas of 1910 were the scene of uncontrollable fires in subsequent drought years (notably 1919) and on to 1930, until only remnants of the 1910 burns had escaped reburning.

As reflected by the situations described, fuel hazards are closely linked to the kind of land management practiced. They can be controlled in commercial timber areas, particularly where close utilization is feasible. In wilderness and other inaccessible areas, high fuel hazards will continue to be the natural consequence of each disturbance in forest conditions. However, as will be discussed in Chapter 18, fuel hazards can be controlled through use of fire in some areas.

KINDS OF FUELS

Since natural forest fuels vary widely in their distribution, their physical characteristics, and their effect on fire behavior, some means of classification is needed for systematic analysis. Fuels are here classified into three groups, based on vertical distribution and general properties: (1) ground fuels, (2) surface fuels, and (3) aerial fuels (Figure 4.1).

Ground Fuels

This includes all burnable material below the loose surface litter. The principal materials are duff, tree roots, punky wood, muck, and peat. Sawdust also belongs in this category. All these fuels support glowing

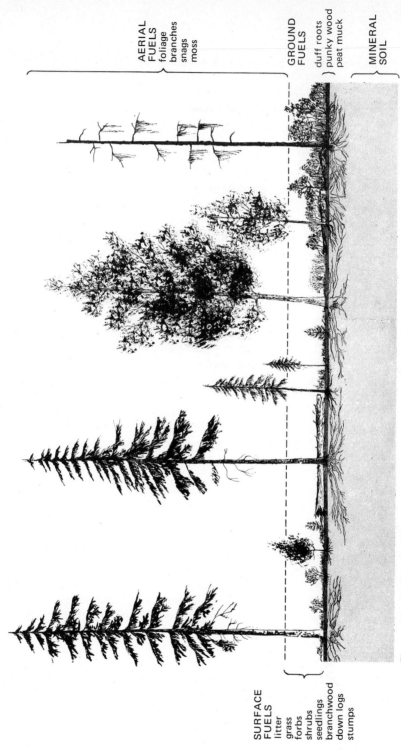

AERIAL FUELS
foliage
branches
snags
moss

GROUND FUELS
duff roots
punky wood
peat muck

MINERAL SOIL

SURFACE FUELS
litter
grass
forbs
shrubs
seedlings
branchwood
down logs
stumps

Figure 4.1 Profile of a forest showing location and classification of fuels.

combustion rather than flame. They normally retain higher moisture contents than surface or aerial fuels, and fire will not ignite in them until their moisture content is below 20 percent. However, once ignited, combustion is very persistent. Exothermic reactions are induced, which can generate heat below the kindling point; combustion needs little or no outside oxygen to proceed; and the materials themselves provide such good insulation that very little of the heat of combustion is lost. At very low moisture contents all these materials develop a water repellent character and resist wetting. Together, these factors cause long and tedious mop-up operations and require special techniques in use of water for complete extinguishment.

Though fire in these fuels plays very little part in the initial spread of a fire, ground fires in deep duff or muck soils are very destructive.

Roots   Like duff, roots are not an important factor in rate of spread because greatly restricted air supply prevents rapid combustion. Fire will long persist and travel in dead roots, especially in large, partially decayed laterals extending from snags. Many fires have escaped control through fire in roots, either by following root tunnels under the control line or by long-delayed ignition of materials still unburned inside the line after mop-up is thought to be complete. When these fires reach the surface, they often start fires outside the line.

Surface Fuels

Surface fuels include the loose surface litter on the forest floor, normally consisting of fallen leaves or needles, twigs, bark, cones, and small branches that have not yet decayed sufficiently to lose their identity.

It also includes grasses, low shrubs, seedlings, and forbs interspersed with or partially replacing the litter. Shrubs over 4 feet in height are classed as understory fuels. The heavier branchwood, down logs, and stumps are also included.

Tree Leaves and Fine Litter   Dead leaves or needles and other loose litter on the ground constitute a highly flammable surface layer. It is the most common fuel in which surface fires spread in forest areas. Flammability depends on the physical characteristics of the fuel and on its arrangement and quantity rather than on differences in chemical composition. Among hardwood leaves, for example, oak leaves are especially flammable. There are several reasons: they are shed late, they curl tightly so have minimum contact with the soil, they resist wetting for a considerable period so are slow to weather, and they do not mat down readily. This results in high exposure of aerated edge and surface. However, oak leaves seldom carry over as flash fuel into the second growing season.

Conifer needles persist much longer in the litter. On sandy soils and dry sites an undecomposed mat of ten years or more of needle fall is common. Pine needles are shed in the two- to five-needle clusters in which they grow. Thus pines produce a looser, more persistent, and more flammable litter than do other conifers that drop their needles singly. Because of their greater length and diameter and their resistance to decay, the needles of hard pines tend to develop deep, well-aerated mats of litter and therefore more dangerous fuel hazards. In contrast, spruce or Douglas-fir needles, while equally flammable intrinsically, shed their needles singly. Hence they come in close contact with the ground and are less persistent, forming a rather compact mat which ignites and burns slowly, more like a ground than a surface fuel.

The importance of these physical characteristics and relationships was illustrated by unpublished experiments, carried out in California some years ago, which compared the burning rate of lodgepole pine and ponderosa pine needle mats. As expected, a tray of ponderosa pine needles burned much faster than the same quantity of lodgepole pine needles. When cut to equal the average length of the lodgepole pine needles, the burning rate was reduced to that of the lodgepole pine. When the cut needles were separated rather than left in their bundles, the burning rate was reduced even further.

Dead needles or leaves attached to the branches are particularly flammable because they are fully exposed to the air and usually are not in direct contact with more moist materials on the ground. This is the major reason why logging slash with the leaves or needles still attached is so dangerous; the needles supply a highly combustible kindling material for ignition of coarser fuels.

Grasses and Forbs   Grass, weeds, bracken ferns, and other small herbaceous plants constitute the major seasonal fuel variable in coniferous stands. They are fine fuels, well exposed to the air. When dry and continuous, they will support the fastest rate of spread of any surface fuel. Their flammability essentially follows the season. During the growing period, they are green and succulent and act as fire barriers rather than carriers. As the season advances, they cure; and when fully mature or killed by frost, they no longer take up moisture through their roots. They may cure weeks earlier than normal when subjected to a severe summer drought, and they may suddenly be transformed, after a hard killing frost, from a fire barrier to a dangerous carrier. The moisture content of these fuels, once dead, closely follows daily weather. In other words, these fuels are extremely sensitive to changes in wind, temperature, and atmospheric moisture.

Open Grass Open grass types are everywhere an important fuel for the reasons described and because of their greater continuity and their complete exposure to sun and wind. Many species of grass and associated herbage are involved. All produce similar, fast-moving fires, with intensity in direct proportion to the volume of dry fuel per acre. Some of the more important problem grass types that have a critical effect on the success of forest fire control are wild oat mixtures in the central valleys of California, cheatgrass and bunchgrasses throughout the Rocky Mountain regions (Figure 4.3*E*, page 103), desert stipa and cheatgrass in the Southwest and the Great Basin, broom sedge in the Central and Southern states (Figure 4.4*C*) and wire grass in southern pine (Figure 4.4*B*, page 106), marsh grasses and cattails in the Lake states, and mixed hay and pasture grasses in the Northeast. In the high plains west of the Mississippi River, the native buffalo and other grass cover fueled intense prairie fires which were common prior to settlement and cultivation. Grain and stubble fires continue as a problem, though they seldom threaten forest areas.

Low Brush and Tree Reproduction Low brush, tree seedlings, and saplings less than 4 feet in height are classified as surface fuels because they are either continuous to or intermixed with grass, weeds, and litter which are close to the ground. There are hundreds of perennial "brush" species, and their growth, abundance, and flammability vary widely in different parts of the country. Some are deciduous and some are not. This understory vegetation may either accelerate or slow the rate of fire spread depending on how green it is and how much admixture of dead material it contains. Amount and flammability of some brush fuel follows a seasonal pattern, like grass and weeds though less pronounced.

Fine Branches and Other Deadwood Fine deadwood may accumulate in considerable volume as debris from the upper crowns, particularly in dense coniferous stands. It consists of twigs, small branches, bark, and other decaying material less than 2 inches in diameter. In dense stands, it may provide the principal kindling fuel to coarser fuels and to the crowns, but it is seldom in heavy volume except as a result of sudden additions through cutting operations or fallen trees. Though less flashy than grass and needles, it is a fast-burning, high-energy fuel. Its flammability depends closely on its moisture content, which in turn varies with the weather and degree of exposure to the sun. Normally its moisture content is very low long before grass and other succulent vegetation becomes flammable.

Dry, punky wood is usually present in surface fuels and is more likely to be exposed than in ground fuels. It burns slowly, without flame, as described for the ground fuels. But it can be ignited by a single spark, which it incubates until heat is sufficient to kindle other fuels. Wherever exposed, it is a primary medium for establishment of spot fires ahead of the main fire. It is important among aerial fuels too, as will be discussed. It usually consists of very fine particles lightly compacted and partially exposed to the air.

Large Limbs, Down Logs, and Stumps   Large limbs, down logs, and stumps constitute the coarse, or, as frequently termed, the "heavy" ground fuels. Their amount is, of course, highly variable. In general, concentrations are of relatively short duration in hardwood types (three to five years mostly) and in southern pine types because of rapid decay. In contrast, such fuels persist and accumulate for many years in northern and western conifers. Coarse fuels require long periods of hot, dry weather before they become highly flammable. But when they do become dry, a concentration of them can support extremely hot and long-lasting fires that are very difficult to approach and control. Individual logs and stumps, however, seldom burn intensely unless the fire is supported by accumulations of fine deadwood. Pitchy pine logs and stumps are an exception.

The rate of fire spread is paced by the finer fuels as long as the fire stays on the ground. Large volumes of coarse fuels are important in fire behavior because of the very high thermal energy they yield. However, only that part of it emanated during "residence time"[1] affects the spread of the fire. The remainder may be given off at a decreasing rate for many hours or days afterward. The burning of such fuels often results in deep heating of the soil and deep fire wounds in the bases of any nearby trees. Often considerable mop-up time is expended in extinguishing fire in such fuels.

Aerial Fuels

Aerial fuels include all burnable material, live or dead, located in the understory and in the upper forest canopy and separated from the ground by more than 4 feet. The main aerial fuels are branches and foliage of

---

[1] Residence time is the time required to complete the flaming stage. This is the time it takes for forward spread of the flame front to travel a distance equivalent to the depth of the flame front.

trees and shrubs, dead standing trees (snags), mosses, lichens, and epiphytic plants.

Tree Branches and Foliage Being both well-aerated and flammable, the live needles and twigs on coniferous trees constitute an abundant source of fine fuels that can support a fast-spreading crown fire. In total volume, crown fuels usually exceed all others. The moisture content and consequent flammability of needles and leaves vary significantly with the phenology of growth and with drought conditions. This has been established for brush species. A diurnal fluctuation in moisture content of up to 30 percent has also been demonstrated in green ponderosa pine needles (Philpot, 1965). Dead needles, twigs, and branches on trees are important aerial fuels. Concentrations of such fuels, as found in insect- or disease-killed stands, may carry fire from tree to tree. An abundance of dead branches extending from near the ground to the crowns, so often found in older coniferous plantations, provides an escalator for surface fires to mount into the crowns.

Live leaves of hardwood high-forest tree species ordinarily will not carry fire. Foliage of some deciduous and nondeciduous scrub oak and high-brush species will, however, burn furiously at times, under protracted drought conditions and when there is a mixture of dry branches and leaves. As with conifers, precise information is lacking on seasonal moisture-content gradients of the principal hardwood tree species. Some of the most rapid-spreading and vicious fires in the country occur in California high chaparral types.

Understory Trees and Shrubs In most forest types, various species of shrubs occur. They vary widely in their effect on the spread of fire. Some, such as the low, fine-leaved huckleberry which is commonly found under lodgepole pine in the Rocky Mountain region, serve as definite retardants to fire; others, such as the gallberry, the palmetto, and the yaupon *(Ilex vomitoria)* of the South commonly act as incendiary materials. Only those that provide fuels or affect flammability more than 4 feet above the surface are included in aerial fuels.

In general, evergreen shrubs are much more flammable than deciduous species. Usually evergreen foliage contains volatile oils, and its moisture content remains generally lower than that of deciduous leaves.

In western timber types, *Ceanothus inergermis,* often known as buck brush, is a typical fire species. It comes in following fires and persists as a flammable element until finally suppressed by dense overhead shade. One or more species of understory character aggravate the fire control problem in every timber type. Dense reproduction often increases the fire control problem in the same way. The most significant threat from these understory fuels that merits separate discussion is their effect on vertical distribution of fuels between the ground and crown canopy. Hot surface fuels plus abundant understory fuels result quickly in crown fires in coniferous stands and in high rates of kill and of fire wounding in all cases. In southern pine types and in ponderosa pine in the West, much of the justification for using prescribed fire rests on the potential benefit of keeping down these dangerous understory fuels.

Single-story Brush Stands   In California there are 11 million acres of brush cover often referred to as *chaparral.* Large areas of brush types occur as well in the other West Coast states and in the Southwest. In other Western states, sagebrush, low-growing juniper, and other shrub species dominate large areas.

Brush species have special significance as fuels and have a special set of requirements for successful fire control. The fuels in dense brush cover are principally in the crowns, and a fire in California brush is invariably a crown fire. Though such fuels may be close to the ground, they are logically included in aerial fuels. Typically very little surface litter is accumulated under the brush except in old stands of heavy mixed chaparral (Table 4.3, page 95). In chaparral stands, there seem to be no mild fires. When fire will spread, it burns fiercely. Though the green foliage and twigs burn, dead twigs, leaves, and branch wood provide the kindling fuels. Until such fuels have accumulated to a critical proportion, fire will not spread in the brush cover. With age, with drought years, or with damage by disease or insects, flammability increases. The kindling-fuel balance is illustrated too by seasons. During the period of rapid growth of the brush species, new lush growing tips increase the percentage of moisture in the crowns sufficiently to prevent development of brush fires for a varying period of several weeks.

Snags   Standing dead trees or snags are an important and dangerous fuel, as can be vouched for by experienced fire fighters. Standing dead timber maintains a low moisture content. As the bark and sapwood gradually decay, shaggy bark and punky surfaces are exposed which ignite readily from flying sparks or embers and from lightning strikes. Once ignited, the snag becomes a prolific source of flying embers which may start spot fires at considerable distances and may ignite adjoining snags during all active burning. Or the fire may smolder in the punky wood on the surface or inside a hollow tree until finally some of the top breaks off, scattering firebrands onto surface fuels below. The susceptibility of a snag to ignition increases with age and varies somewhat by species. Smooth, solid snags, mostly free of bark and branches (western larch is typical) are not easily ignited. In contrast, a broken-topped, shaggy-barked, rotten hemlock is a virtual firetrap and firebrand generator. Studies of the natural history of fire-killed Douglas-fir snags in the Northwest showed that they decay from the top down. With age they decrease in height until finally they are overtopped at about 70 years by the young stand which followed the burn. At this point they decrease rapidly in importance. Because their moisture content remains higher, they decay more rapidly, and their decreased exposure reduces their proclivity for igniting and for scattering firebrands.

Mosses, Lichens, and Epiphytic Plants Various species of such genera, popularly called *moss*, often festoon trees and are the lightest and flashiest of all aerial fuels. They are very important in Alaska and are often present on northern conifers, especially at higher elevations, and on both conifer and hardwood trees in the lower coastal plain of the South. Hanging streamers of the material ignite readily when dry and act as fuses in carrying a surface fire into the tree crowns. A lighted match can convert a moss-draped tree into a giant torch in a matter of seconds. Hanks of burning Spanish moss, often enclosing needles, twigs, or pieces of bark, are the principal embers responsible for long-distance spotting in the deep South.

FUEL CONTINUITY

The continuity of fuels is a primary factor in the behavior of fires and in the difficulty of bringing them under control. This is because the transfer of heat by radiation, conduction, and convection, as discussed in Chapter 7, operates over a quite limited though variable radius.

The critical relationship of the vertical continuity of fuels to the development of crown fires has already been discussed. Because of the upward convection of heat, breaks in vertical continuity need to be greater than in the horizontal plane for the same degree of effectiveness. For the same reason, fire can cross wider breaks going up a steep slope than on level ground. The critical spacing required between surface and aerial fuels to prevent a surface fire from becoming a crown fire varies with the rate of heat-energy production in surface fuels. Critical limits have not yet been established, but experienced fire control men learn to make reliable predictions in a specific fuel complex.

Continuity is a relative term, both vertically and horizontally. Always the degree of continuity is important, but at just what point fuels cease to be continuous depends on the burning conditions and heat energy produced in each situation.

Horizontal continuity is often confused by the tendency of fires to spot. Since a different fuel characteristic and a different mechanism enter into spotting, it is usually excluded in considering the continuity of fuels.

Patches of logging slash surrounded by green grass and other lush vegetation lack horizontal continuity and are regarded as relatively safe, since it is easy to confine a fire in them to a small area. If the grass and other vegetation cures to create a continuous kindling or flash fuel, the slash patches then become dangerous areas in which fire can build up momentum to become a threatening conflagration. Firebreaks, roads, cultivated areas, and recently burned areas all create breaks in the continuity of fuels and may interrupt the spread of a fire in them.

Continuity of fuels on a small plot scale is also very important. If surface litter is patchy, flash fuels—when ignited—may not build up enough heat to ignite the lower-flammability fringe areas. When this is so, a running fire does not develop, and such areas too are relatively safe from fire.

If the potential for spot fires is taken into account, continuity on a much larger scale becomes significant. If the patches of logging slash described in the first instance also have standing dead snags, fire may spot from one nearby patch to the next even though continuous spread does not occur in surface fuels. Similarly, even sparse distribution of fire-brand-producing and firebrand-susceptible fuels can cancel out the effect of both natural and artificial firebreaks in restricting the spread of a fire.

Experienced fire control men are usually more concerned about the continuity of fuels and their location in relation to other fuels than they are about the flammability of the fuel in a specific area. However, it needs to be emphasized that even small areas supporting large volumes of fast-burning fuels become very dangerous when extreme burning conditions occur. Such fuels may quickly generate an intense fire, subject to erratic behavior. Often the result is long-distance spotting or explosive behavior which generates fire whirls capable of overrunning all ordinary fire barriers. Observation of the behavior of fire in a variety of forest fuels and under a range of burning conditions is a necessary supplement in developing sound judgment on the significance of all aspects of fuel continuity.

FUEL QUANTITY

From the foregoing discussions, it should be obvious that the quantity of fuel is very important but also highly variable. It is also very difficult to classify and to measure in a meaningful way. Fine, well-aerated, dry fuels such as pine needle litter, loose hardwood leaves, and standing dead grass can be sampled and classed quite significantly on the basis of tons of dry weight per acre. But when a part of the grass is still green, for example, the number of tons of dry weight measures only the potential. Similarly, the weight of heavy limb wood and logs can measure only the potential fuel and the potential thermal energy it contains. The same is often true of closely compacted fine fuels. The fuel available for combustion in a moving fire front, or that will enter into combustion in a given time, depends more on the amount of surface exposed to the air and so to heat than it does on the weight of material present.

Since both surface area and compactness are involved, the relationship becomes complex. Fons (1946) gave emphasis to the ratio between the surface area and the volume occupied and found this significant in explaining the rate of spread of field fires. More detailed examination of this ratio has been undertaken more recently in the laboratory (Anderson et al., 1966).

The fuel available for combustion at a given time depends also on the moisture content of the various elements in the fuel complex. Because of their differential drying rate, some of the fuel in mixed fuel types is nearly always too moist to burn. So the quantity of fuel available for combustion in a given situation may depend not only on the amount of exposed fuel surface but also on the vegetative stage of all living plant material and the moisture content of all dead plant materials.

Though living tree crowns become available fuels only under conditions favorable to the development of crown fires, their volume becomes highly important when timber-cutting operations convert them to surface fuels, often referred to as slash fuels.

Volume, weight, and surface area of the leaves of living forest trees has been studied by Kittredge (1944, 1948) and by Rothacher, Blow, and Potts (1954). These studies did not include branch wood. A study of crown characteristics of 211 rather uniform and mostly young and dominant trees of 11 coniferous species was made by Storey, Fons, and Sauer (1955). They investigated relationships between weight of crown, branch wood, foliage, and main-stem diameter. For the species studied, they found a high correlation to exist between the product of length and dry weight of crown and stem diameter at the base of live crown. The relationship was found to be linear in logarithms and can be expressed by a regression equation of the form

$$WL = aD_s^b$$

where W = weight of dry crown in pounds

L = length of live crown in feet from tip to base of major live crown (straggling lower branches excepted)

a = coefficient of intercept distance on vertical axis

D_s = stem diameter in inches inside bark at base of crown

b = coefficient of slope of the regression line

Since length of crown and stem diameter can be estimated or measured in the field, the dry weight of the crown can be determined from the equation by solving for W. Equations of the same form and of approximately similar accuracy were separately determined for branch wood and for foliage components. There were substantial differences between the a regression coefficients both between species and within species for different growth locations, indicating important average differences between species and locations. The b, or slope, coefficients varied within a rather narrow range, indicating that the diameter-crown length-weight relationship is fairly constant regardless of species and location.

Tree-foliage volumes are of particular significance in relation to slash created by logging and have been studied mostly in this connection. Olson and Fahnestock (1955) undertook intensive studies of logging slash of coniferous species in the northern Rocky Mountains. The following is taken from their work. Utilizing the general approach of Storey, Fons, and Sauer (1955), Fahnestock[2] found that, for the species studied, dry weight of crown could directly be estimated from the product of length of live crown and diameter at breast height (dbh) with little loss in accuracy. A regression equation was employed of the form

$$W = a(LD_{bh})^b$$

where W = weight of dry crown in pounds

a = coefficient of intercept distance on vertical axis

L = length of live crown in feet from tip to base of major live crown (straggling lower branches excepted)

D_{bh} = diameter in inches breast-high outside bark

b = coefficient of slope of regression line

The results of this analysis, based on 96 trees of 8 species, are given in Figure 4.2. As shown, ponderosa pine has the heaviest crowns, largely because of a tendency toward large branches. The tolerant spruce, grand fir, and western hemlock come next because of their tendency to carry much foliage, though their branch wood is much lighter. The trends are strongly linear because the b coefficients are close to 1. Since dbh and crown length can be determined in the field fairly readily, dry crown weights can be estimated from the curves. For example, if the tree diameter is 20 inches and the crown length 80 feet, the product is 1,600.

---

[2] Unpublished manuscript.

For this combination, Figure 4.2 indicates about 200 and 740 pounds of dry crown for western white pine and ponderosa pine, respectively. A 30-inch white pine with a crown length of 53 feet (a somewhat unusual but possible tree) should also have about 200 pounds of dry crown. These data apply to fairly evenly shaped trees; the relationships would be different for irregular and abnormal crowns. They also should not be extrapolated beyond the observed ranges.

Differences between species are increased when crown volume is related to commercial timber volume. For lack of better means, the amount of slash in practice is commonly estimated by the volume cut in thousand board feet, a very crude and unsatisfactory measure. To illustrate the point, a 16-inch white pine and hemlock tree have a scale of about 370 and 160 board feet, respectively. From Figure 4.2, and assuming a crown length of 70 feet for each (a product of 16 × 70, or 1,120), the crown weights are 140 and 320 pounds. Combining the difference in board-foot scale with crown weight indicates that hemlock produces about five times as much slash per board foot as does white pine for a 16-inch tree of the same crown length.

The cubic volume of a given amount of slash varies widely with

Figure 4.2 Dry crown weight of selected conifers in relation to the product of tree diameter and crown length.

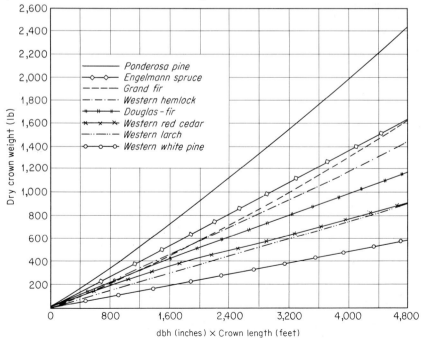

degree of compaction, as would be expected. Some general relationships, as determined from 25 western white pine trees about 80 years old, averaging 14.6 inches dbh, are illustrated by the following (Olson, 1953a):

Type of slash	Cubic feet per tree
Fresh untreated "jumble" slash	1,050
Freshly lopped slash	631
Lopped slash after 1 year	473
Freshly piled slash	72
Chipped slash	19
Solid content of slash	7

Another measure of significance in combustion is surface area. It has been estimated (Olson and Fahnestock, 1955) that "the average pound of Douglas-fir slash has a surface area of about 25 sq. ft." The surface of a cube of the same weight is approximately 0.6 square foot.

Combining weight and volume in pounds per cubic foot gives a measure of density related to rate of burning. The nature of these relationships is illustrated by data obtained in a study of logging slash at the Priest River Experimental Forest, Idaho. Fresh slash of branches, nearly all 2 inches or less in diameter, from each of nine western commercial species was scattered as evenly as possible on a series of small plots at the rate of 7.5, 20, and 32.5 tons per acre dry weight. This gave weights of dry fuel per square foot of 0.34, 0.92, and 1.5 pounds, respectively. The depth of slash was measured on these plots when the slash was first scattered and after one year to determine the cubic volume.

As might be expected, compaction increased with increasing tons per acre and with overwinter snow effects. Data were not adequate to define species differences, but the average pounds per cubic foot for the nine species was as follows:

Table 4.1   Dry Weight of Lopped Slash per Cubic Foot

Type	7.5 tons	20 tons	32.5 tons
Fresh	1.06	1.23	1.51
One year old	1.14	1.51	1.85

Compaction due to increasing weight per square foot ranged up to 42 percent; that due to overwinter snow effects ranged from 7 to 23 percent. In succeeding years weathering more strongly affected the slash at low volumes per acre than at the heavier volumes, due no doubt to differences in soil temperatures.

Information is more scanty on the amount of fuel occurring in grass and brush. Table 4.2 indicates approximate air-dry weights of materials

Table 4.2   Average Fuel Weights Occurring in the Longleaf–Slash Pine Type of Florida, in Tons per Acre*

Fuel cover type	Open stands, with age of rough:			Dense stands, with age of rough:		
	1 year	2 years	10–15 years	1 year	2 years	10–15 years
Palmetto and gallberry	2.5	7.5	8.4	6.8	8.9	10.5
Palmetto only	3.7	6.3	7.2	6.3	8.3	20.8
No palmetto or gallberry (mostly grass)	1.5	3.3	6.9	7.5	4.4	10.5

* After Bruce (1951).

less than 1 inch in diameter normally consumed by fires in the roughs developing under longleaf–slash pine stands in Florida. The highest and lowest average weights in the table, 20.8 and 1.5 tons, respectively, agree well with other measurements which indicate maximum fuel accumulations of 25 tons per acre in dense stands, and grass growth in the open adding as much as 1 to $1\frac{1}{2}$ tons per acre per year (Bruce, 1951). It was also estimated that from 50 to 90 percent of the total weight of fuel in open stands was composed of rapid-drying flash fuels.

Data on the dry weight and composition of some southern California grass and brush types are given in Table 4.3. Fuel weight of tall grass goes up to 3.4 tons per slope acre and on typical plots was nearly 2 tons. Heavy

Table 4.3   Weight of Vegetation in Southern California Grass and Brush Types*

Cover type and species	Average height, ft	Dry weight, tons/slope acre			
		Total fuel	Green	Dead	Duff and litter
Grass (15 plots): *Avena fatua, Festuca myuros*	3	1.97† (3.40)‡	1.28 (2.02)	0	0.69 (2.33)
Light brush (11 plots): *Artemesia californica, Lotus scoparius*	4	13.21 (17.09)	3.72 (8.64)	2.84 (4.49)	6.65 (9.38)
Chamise (12 plots): *Adenostoma fasiculatum, Ceanothus cuneatus, Lotus scoparius*	4	13.68 (32.54)	3.81 (20.08)	4.56 (8.95)	5.31 (6.08)
Heavy chaparral (12 plots): *Quercus dumosa, Photinia arbutifolia*	7	26.28 (46.84)	15.13 (34.00)	5.20 (6.51)	5.95 (21.67)

* Anonymous (1955).
† Figures are weight for typical plot. The total column gives the sum of green, dead, and litter components.
‡ Figures in parentheses are maximum weight observed. The total is not the sum of the components given since upper limits observed are not averages but extremes.

chaparral contained up to 47 tons of fuel per acre and typically ran about 26 tons. The green, dead, duff, and litter components are of considerable significance in combustion in this type.

In a comprehensive study of the distinctive forest fuels in the coastal plain of North Carolina (Wendel, Storey, Byram, 1962), 14 fuel types were distinguished and total dry weight for an average acre was determined for each. Most of these types illustrate the distinction between total fuel and available fuel. Most of the time a large proportion of the total fuel is green, but during drought periods available fuels increase rapidly. Much of the terrain is in distinctive bog areas known as pocosins. Fuel weights by types are shown in Table 4.4 in ascending order of tons per acre. The high reed type in particular, known as switch cane, supports fearsome fires at times.

In the Lake states, studies of crown fuels in plantations of red and jack pine by Lloyd Lamois and James K. Brown (Brown, 1965) showed up to 30 tons per acre. Brown also developed criteria for estimating fuel weights.

The above data and discussion accent the importance and complexity of the problem of forest fuels. The fire problem exists because forest fuels exist. But they exist in endless combinations. Always the natural fuel bed or fuel type is a complex of fuel elements. Each fuel element affects the ease of ignition and rate of burning of the whole. At the same time both are affected by small changes in the environment. This makes it very difficult to obtain measurements or to develop reliable predictions of the exact effect of the fuel complex on fire behavior. Basic research in fire

Table 4.4 Average Fuel Dry Weights in Pocosin Types of Eastern North Carolina, in Tons per Acre

Fuel types	Total fuel	Vegetation	Litter
Wire grass	4.46	1.54	2.92
Low pocosin (open shrubs)	5.68	2.06	3.62
Grass—low brush	6.44	2.89	3.55
Low reeds—grass	6.48	3.91	2.57
Dense—low Pocosin	8.45	4.00	4.45
Brush—sand ridge	8.55	4.14	4.41
Medium reeds—brush	8.75	4.70	4.05
Low brush—grass, sand ridge	8.84	2.90	5.94
Medium brush—grass	9.37	4.78	4.59
High reeds	10.07	6.06	4.01
Very high reeds	13.18	8.48	4.70
High pocosin	15.00	5.95	9.05
High brush	17.34	11.98	5.36
High brush—swamp	21.00	15.64	5.36

physics and in combustion under controlled conditions is increasing the understanding of the role of the physical characteristics of each fuel element in fire behavior. But such information requires careful interpretation and integration of all factors before it can be properly applied to the fuel complex. This process gives much future promise but is of necessity slow. In the meantime the forest and other wild-land managers must make daily decisions based on more subjective evaluations of existing and prospective fire hazards.

FUEL TYPES AND FUEL CLASSIFICATION

City fire departments always have a considerable range in fire potential in the areas of their responsibility. For example, the warehouse district, the poor residential, the good residential, and the downtown business district each may be expected to present a distinctive set of fire problems. To take account of these differences, municipal areas are commonly classified and planning and action by the fire department are varied accordingly.

A similar need exists in protecting large forest areas. The fire potential varies widely, and the more closely the fire organization and its daily operations can be adapted to these variations, the more efficient it will be.

Some of the earliest work in fire control planning was aimed at this objective. Show and Kotok (1919) initiated correlation of fire behavior and fire fighting requirements with cover type, which was formulated by 1930 into so-called "hour control" zones for California (Show and Kotok, 1930). The term *hour control* meant "the estimated or probable time that will elapse between the origin of the fire at any given point or locality and the arrival of the first man or men of a given fire suppression force, distributed according to the prearranged fire plan."

These zones were based on statistical studies of how quickly attack *must* be made on a fire after its start in order to attain an acceptable *success* score. This was usually defined as less than 15 percent of fires of Class C size (10–100 acres). This definition resulted in a range of maximum time limits by cover types from one-half hour to four hours. This provided the basis for the planned fire organization. Cover types classed as in the half-hour control zone required twice the intensity of organization needed in the one-hour zone, etc. This constituted a broad though crude fuel-type classification.

In California, the native cover types reflected the successive life zones associated with elevation and exposure of the topography, particularly along the front of the Sierra Nevada Mountains. The use of fire statistics identified by cover types had the virtue also of systematically taking account of past experience. Together they provided a degree of insurance against major error and have enabled early fire plans to retain a surprising degree of validity. However, most boundaries of hour-control zones were lines on a map which disregarded changes in fuel due to current logging or recent fires and were otherwise quite arbitrary.

Because of these faults and because silvicultural types in the Northwest had very little significance in identifying forest fuels, a system designed to focus on fuels and their condition rather than on tree species was devised by Lloyd G. Hornby of the Northern Rocky Mountain Region (Region One) of the U.S. Forest Service in the early 1930s. (Hornby, 1936). This system was applied first in that region, then was extended to most other Forest Service regions with slight modifications during the next ten years. Since it has had considerable influence on thinking and planning by fire control men and since it is still the only systematic field method of classifying fuels on a map, it will be considered in some detail here.

Rate of Spread and Resistance to Control

Hornby's approach to fuel types was very much that now utilized by "operations research." Effort was made to convert each important but unmeasured factor to a valid numerical basis, to develop models on which to base standards, and to devise a systematic method of application.

Essentially, the answers to two questions were sought for any given fuel complex. If a fire starts here, how fast will it spread and what will it take to stop it? These two queries were identified as *rate of spread* and *resistance to control.*

The rate of spread model was a small fire spreading from the source of ignition in surface fuels. It was making definite forward spread so had a differential rate of spread at its rear, at its flanks, and at its head. This was summed up as *rate of perimeter increase.* The total perimeter at any stage was expected to represent the size of the fire control job. The perimeter was expected to vary by fuel type and with time. To avoid the further variation due to burning conditions, a fixed condition termed *average worst* was adopted. This was intended to represent the burning conditions typical of the worst part of the average fire season. To provide numerical values for rate of perimeter increase, statistical analyses of computed rates of spread from individual fire reports were made. By graphic means the range was divided up into four categories, later expanded to five. Descriptive terms were assigned to each of these—low, medium, high, extreme. Later studies (Barrows, 1951) added a fifth class, flash, to give more identity to cheatgrass and similar nonforest fuels that seemed to be in a special category. With rate-of-spread classes established and numerical values assigned to each, the next step was the identification of fuels on the ground with these classes. Preliminary surveys to accomplish this resulted in the development of guidelines and keys for classifying and mapping fuels on the ground.

At best, the rate-of-spread classification would forecast the perimeter of the fire after any given time interval. From this, the amount of fire control line that would be needed for control could also be estimated. But the kind of fuel, the terrain, the cover, and the kind of soil each affect the amount of work necessary to establish the control line. To provide for this variable the term *resistance to control* was adopted.

The resistance-to-control factor was also designed for model treatment. By trial, data were obtained on the rate at which fire crews could construct a fire trail down to mineral soil in different fuel types. Data was also obtained from analysis of fire reports. Together, this established the range. It was divided into four descriptive categories as was rate of spread: low, medium, high, extreme. Numerical values based on the number of chains of fire line that could be built per hour were then assigned to each. However, one difficulty was almost immediately apparent. What about the instances where the fire is too hot for the fire line to stop it, so that strenuous work to cool the fire down or to build new line is necessary for control? This objection was met by going to the concept of *held line.* This satisfied one objection. The man-hours or machine-hours necessary to control a fire can logically be charged to the number of chains of final control line. But it created a new area of uncertainty. The number of chains of fire line constructed per man-hour in a particular fuel type can be measured and predicted quite closely. But the number of chains of *held* line was a much more elusive quantity.

In a similar fashion, aerial fuels were troublesome. In the model it was assumed that crown fires and rapid spread by spotting would not occur in the period before first attack. But in other forest regions this assumption was found not to be tenable. This was covered in fuel-type classifications in one region by using the letter C as a numerator to the fuel rating; e.g., C/HH[1] was used wherever it was judged that a free burning fire would start to crown in one hour or less from the time of origin.

In spite of these troublesome questions, rate of spread and resistance to control did at least provide a logical approach to the two questions: How big will the fire be when the fire crew arrives, and how much effort will it take to control it? These are critical questions to the fire control officer.

Perhaps the most important accomplishment of the fuel classifica-

---

[1] This would be in a fuel type rated as high rate of spread, high resistance to control. The C rating often occurred where one or both factors were rated E, extreme, and on occasion where one factor was only rated M, medium or moderate.

tion was the emphasis it gave to recognition of *fuel type* independent of the status of the land, its geography, or of its cover type. It was valuable too, wherever applied, because fuel-type mapping demanded a careful preliminary evaluation and analysis of local fuel combinations and their effect on fire behavior. This led to a rather rigorous examination of past fire experience as recorded in fire reports.

In rate-of-spread evaluations, it soon becomes apparent that mixed fuels constitute most forest fuel types. Several or sometimes all of the ground, surface, and aerial fuels previously described may be present. Ignition and combustion proceeds as a chain-reaction process. Ignition from a weak firebrand, such as a match or cigarette butt, can ignite only dry punky wood, exposed dry duff, or fine flashy fuels. In punky wood or duff, a slow-spreading, smoldering, but persistent fire will result; in grass, dead needles, and other fine litter a flaming, fast-spreading, but transient fire will burn. If both fuels are abundant, both kinds of combustion develop quickly. Whether the fire keeps on spreading depends on the continuity of the flash fuels and on the amount of heat energy generated. The critical importance of these two primary ignition fuels is their ability to hold fire, to carry fire, and to act as kindling to heavier hot-burning fuels. The fire in dead grass and needles will soon kindle a hot fire in slash and in the branch wood of fallen trees. Where there is vertical continuity, the fire may quickly become a crown fire.

The development of fuel-type maps must take into account all these potentials of the fuel combinations on the ground. Usually the delineation of boundaries is facilitated by using a topographic map as a base with cover types, timber sale areas, etc., delineated in advance.

The first project for mapping fuels was undertaken by Hornby in Montana and northern Idaho. It covered some 70 fuel conditions considered typical of that region. Experienced fire control men were specially trained for the job, which was completed in the early 1930s. Samples of the range and nature of the fuel types concerned are given in Figure 4.3.

Adaptation of fuel-type mapping to the Lake States Region by the U.S. Forest Service resulted in identification of some 38 typical fuel combinations in that region. Separate ratings for spring and summer conditions were assigned to each because of the strong influence of deciduous trees and plants. From this, average rates of spread for low, moderate, high, and extreme fuel classes in relation to the Lake states burning index were estimated and are quoted in Table 4.5. The data are crude and based on limited information, but they do give an indication of the wide variation in perimeter spread that may be encountered.

Jemison and Keetch (1942) applied much the same system to the forests of the Eastern mountains and seaboard. Fourteen general fuel

Figure 4.3

Figure 4.3 Sample fuel types chiefly in Idaho and Montana classified by rate of spread and resistance to control. *(U.S. Forest Service photos.)* *A.* H-H. Cutover area with residual stand killed by fire. Many broken-topped, loose-barked snags. Much windfall and debris on ground. *B.* H-E. Two-year-old logging slash in old growth of Douglas-fir where no hazard reduction measures have been applied. Heavy volume of both fine and coarse fuels. Willamette National Forest. *C.* H-M. Cutover ponderosa pine with patches of heavy logging debris. Grass moderate, snags few. *D.* M-H. Fire-killed stand with much windfall but moderate volume of fine fuels on the ground. *E.* H-L. Heavy stand of ungrazed bunchgrass. *F.* L-L. Cutover area double-burned. Snags and windfalls charred and scattered. Grass and weed ground cover.

Table 4.5 Rate of Spread in Northern Lake States Fuels by Fuel Classification, Burning Index*, and a Wind Velocity of 8 to 12 Miles per Hour

Burning index	Fuel rate of spread, in chains perimeter per hour, classified as:			
	Low	Moderate	High	Extreme
10	8	16	31	62
20	10	21	41	83
30	12	24	47	94
40	13	26	51	103
50	14	27	55	109
60	14	29	57	115
70	15	30	60	119

*A number in an arithmetic scale determined from fuel-moisture content, wind speed, and other selected factors that affect burning conditions and from which ease of ignition of fires and their probable behavior may be estimated.

types were recognized, based essentially on broad forest cover types that could be readily identified in the field. Rate of spread and resistance to control were studied on 3,200 fires burning in the seven Eastern National Forests for the period 1930 to 1941. Results for selected fuel types are given in Table 4.6. These data represent broad averages. There is much variation by individual fires within fuel types, and averages do not always

Table 4.6 Rate of Spread and Resistance to Control of Selected Eastern Fuel Types

Fuel type	Rate of spread			Resistance to control	
	Classification	Average	Fastest 25%	Classification	Rate of held-line construction, chains per man-hour*
Northern conifers, 4 in. +	L	12.1	21.7	M	1.8
Northern conifers, cutover, duff, no slash	H	30.2	86.7	H	1.3
Northern and Appalachian hardwoods, 3 in. +	M	20.7	47.4	M	2.1
Southern pine, 6 in. +	M	22.7	53.0	L	2.8
Conifer slash, fresh	L	15.8	35.8	E	0.4
Hardwood and southern pine slash	M	25.4	60.9	M	1.8
Grass, ferns, and weeds	H	26.8	58.8	L	3.2
Scrub oak	E	35.6	85.2	M	1.9

* Rate of spread and resistance to control classified as L = low, M = medium, H = high, E = extreme.

consistently follow the type rating. The general trend is, however, highly significant and brings out the wide range between fuel types in spread and resistance categories. A few sample fuel types of the southeastern United States are shown in Figure 4.4.

Working in the northern Rocky Mountain regions, Barrows (1951) and others extended Hornby's (1936) rate-of-spread ratings, developed a classification key, and related the types to perimeter increase observed on a large number of actual fires. Barrows divided fuel types occurring in the region into seven major groups:

> Grass and range land
> Brush and reproduction
> Dense coniferous forests
> Open coniferous forests
> Subalpine and spruce forests
> Logging slash
> Cutover forests with slash disposal work completed

For each group, a key was prepared relating the spread classification to a number of fuel factors including stand density, duff conditions, character of slash and other surface fuels, snags and down timber, moss and other flash fuels, and fuel continuity. Based on a statistical study of 2,955 wildfires burning in Region One of the U.S. Forest Service 1936 to 1944 (Barrows, 1951), Table 4.7 gives the fuel characteristics and rates of spread for the five spread classification groups recognized. Aspect, elevation, and slope were not taken into account. The wide range in rates of perimeter increase by fuel classes is highly significant in planning control action.

Appraisal of Fuel-type Classifications

Despite the obvious importance of fuels and the stimulus of Hornby's classification work in the 1930s, fuel-type mapping has not been extensive, being largely limited to work by the U.S. Forest Service in a few forest regions. It is also true that specific fuel-type classifications have not been generally employed in day-to-day fire control operations. An analysis of the reasons may help to put the problem of fuels and their classification in perspective.

1 Accuracy. Besides being expensive to develop and maintain, fuel-type maps by the Hornby system could not be detailed beyond the nearest 10-acre tract, and in most surveys to the nearest 40 acres. This was adequate for planning fire control systems on an area basis, and has

Figure 4.4 Southeastern United States fuel types. *A.* Extremely heavy 20-year "rough" of palmetto, gallberry, and needle accumulation in lower coastal plain of Georgia. *(Georgia Forestery Commission photo.) B.* Highly flammable four-year wire-grass rough in Piedmont. *(U.S. Forest Service photo.) C.* Fine, flashy broomsedge and grass. De Soto National Forest, Mississippi. *(U.S. Forest Service photo.) D.* Heavy 10-year needle and grass rough in coastal plain. The backfire shown will not kill larger trees but may kill longleaf in the grass (arrow). *(U.S. Forest Service photo.) E.* Shortleaf-loblolly pine reproduction under fairly dense overwood. A fire would kill most of this reproduction. *(U.S. Forest Service photo.)*

Table 4.7 Rate of Spread in Perimeter of Fuel-type Classes in the Northern Rocky Mountains*

Rate-of-spread classification	Av. initial rate of spread, chains†	Max. rate of spread for 85% of fires, chains‡	Fuel characteristics
Low	4.5	8	Sparse, fine, dead ground fuels. Generally protected from sun and wind. Very few snags. Type usually found in dense timber.
Medium	6.0	10	Moderate amounts of fine dead ground fuels. Generally protected from sun and wind. Occasional concentration of down logs and limbs. Few snags. Tree moss may be present. Crown fires likely. Type usually found in dense timber or reproduction.
High	13.0	28	Large amounts of fine dead ground fuels only partially protected from wind and sun. Many shaggy-barked snags often present. Type may be found in open ponderosa pine forests, single burns in heavily timbered forests, brush fields containing many dead stems, insect-killed forests, heavy windthrow areas, and sparsely covered cured grass fields.
Extreme	18.0	35	Very heavy concentration of fine dead ground fuels largely exposed to wind and sun. Very large numbers of shaggy-barked snags may be present. Type usually found in heavy logging slash, the worst single burns, and moderate stands of cured grass.
Flash	33.0	65	Type generally confined to dense stands of cured cheatgrass and bunchgrass or heavy logging slash with dry needles remaining on limbs.

*Evaluated for a burning index of 70 as given by northern Rocky Mountain meter model 6.
†Perimeter increase from discovery to first attack. This rate of spread may be anticipated during the first 4

been the most productive use of such maps. But it was not accurate
enough to be of much value in dispatching fire fighters to small reported
fires. Efforts to refine these maps for the fire dispatcher have proved
largely unsuccessful.

2   Obsolescence. Fuel types do not remain static, particularly in
forest areas under active management. Drastic changes due to logging,
fire, insect and disease attack, blowdowns, and other forms of disturbance
demand careful revision of fuel-type maps every year if they are to be
kept current. This proved burdensome in practice. Even where drastic
changes do not occur, significant changes due to fluctuations in the
weather may occur. Above-average precipitation may result in several
times the average production of grass and forbs and a much greater
fine-fuel hazard in the cured stage. Conversely, wet seasons sometimes
maintain green grass through normally dangerous periods. Drought periods and especially a series of drought years produce increased proportions of fine dead fuels due to dieback in trees and shrubs and reduced
rates of decay. Such changes are not always apparent but lead to fire
behavior inconsistent with the formal rating of the fuels in which it is
burning.

3   Fixed Burning Condition (Average Worst). A closely related
factor is the falseness of assumptions regarding the fixed burning conditions, assumptions which are used to make the ratings. The amount and
kind of available fuels change not only by season and from year to year
but currently by moisture content as well. When fuels are too wet to burn;
they cease to be available fuels. In a mixed fuel type this does not change
on a smooth curve but in stairs-step fashion as different thresholds are
approached. Consequently, broad assumptions with uncertain limits are
made regarding burning conditions, and these are often based on different
fuels than those which actually burn.

A closely related aspect is the tendency for fire in all fuels to spread
at nearly the same rate under extreme burning conditions. This, too,
reduced confidence in the reality and validity of the fixed burning condition.

4   "Initial" Rate of Spread. The fuel-type ratings were of most
potential value in evaluating the threat from large fires. But they were
designed primarily to reflect the early period surface spread of a small
fire. For that reason fuels that would generate fires too hot for direct
attack, or fires that would crown or spot badly in less than an hour after
ignition, could be described only by assigning high resistance to control
ratings. For that reason, large-fire behavior was often quite different from
that expected of small fires in the fuel ratings. Statistically, predictions of
the initial spread of the small fire have the most validity. Unfortunately,
80 to 90 percent of the damage is done by the 5 to 10 percent that spread
as large fires.

5   Inadequacy of Quantitative Data on Resistance to Control. The

model on which the system was based was two-dimensional, while control work on large or high-intensity fires must be three-dimensional. In the model, a fire is visualized as increasing its perimeter at a certain rate; also a small fire crew with hand tools can build fire line at a certain rate. If the crew can build fire line faster than the fire perimeter increases, they can control the fire. The only question then is how long it will take. In other words the problem and solution are both in two dimensions only, like a problem in plane geometry. Small fires in surface litter conform well to this concept. But as soon as a fire develops too much heat for direct attack to be successful, it must be dealt with as a three-dimensional phenomenon. The actual resistance to control is then reflected much more accurately by the rate at which thermal energy is being generated than by the perimeter of the fire. It is possible for a fire of less than $1/4$ acre to be a young tornado in its violence.

This lack in the resistance-to-control concept was basic. Efforts to correct it by adopting held line (rather than constructed line) and other devices only confused the issue.

A further difficulty was introduced by the use of mechanical equipment to build fire line and by the use of water and chemicals by both ground and aerial equipment. Obstacles to building line by machine were not identical to those in building hand line, and man-hours were not readily converted to equivalent accomplishment in machine-hours. These difficulties were accentuated by the great variety of equipment, fuels, terrain, and environment throughout the United States.

6   Recognition of Fuel Potential. Ability to recognize the potential of various fuel combinations to power fires and ability to discriminate between the various critical fire-behavior attributes of forest fuels has more value than the physical existence of fuel maps. Attention to fuels and to their proper classification had the important virtue of developing such abilities among a wide-ranging group of participants.

7   Basic Needs. The scheme of fuel classification was no doubt too ambitious, and it is not likely that it can be replaced on an equally comprehensive basis. Nevertheless, identification of important fuel attributes and of fuel potential are critical to the success of all fire control activities. Continued emphasis on the rate of spread of fire in different fuel types is needed. It can and should be divorced from resistance to control and can become much more meaningful if potential fuels, available fuels, and probable rate of energy release can also be measured and classified. The requirement of simplicity for field use imposes rather exacting but not impossible restraints.

Chapter 5

Fire Weather

Although forest fuels determine fire's potential to spread, to do damage, and to resist control efforts, weather conditions determine the current level of that potential. This is significant to the practitioner. He can control fuels to varying degrees but has very little control of any of the weather elements. Similarly, most significant changes in natural fuels move slowly with the seasonal cycle, while marked changes in weather may take place from hour to hour.

So action plans to cope with the impact of fire weather must have a different focus than plans for managing fuels. Such plans are discussed in Chapters 8 and 10. The basic requirements are a good understanding of the complex effects of weather on fire behavior and the ability to anticipate changes.

To clarify such generalizations, it is well to consider how much knowledge of meteorology the forester needs in order to successfully plan and execute the fire control job. In terms of geographic scope or scale, meteorology may be separated into three categories: micro-, meso-, and macrometeorology. The forester is primarily concerned with micrometeorology, a scale that can represent the weather environment of a single $1/4$-acre fire. He is also concerned with weather phenomena on the mesoscale, such as interpretation of the weather patterns for one of the 14 logical forecast regions for the continental United States (Schroeder, 1964), but weather on the macro scale concerns him only incidentally.

This chapter has been formulated with these needs in mind. Its purpose is to give a balanced introduction. A good working knowledge of the specialized meteorology a forester needs requires supplemental field observations, reading, and study.

Fire weather is defined as weather conditions which influence fire starts, fire behavior, or fire control. Although this is the area of primary interest, a background of general meteorology must form the foundation from which to develop a working concept of fire weather. Byers (1959) and Petterssen (1941, 1956) are suggested as general meteorological references. The current *Glossary of Meteorology* sponsored by the American Meteorological Society is also very helpful. Micrometeorology and its interactions with forest cover and topography are best developed in *Fire Weather,* Agriculture Handbook no. 360 (Shroeder and Buck, 1970), representing a joint effort by meteorologists and foresters. This is the primary reference for this chapter.

CLIMATE AND FIRE SEASONS

Climate is the weather at a given place or area over a period of time. It is expressed in averages, totals, extremes, and frequencies to give a picture of the weather which has occurred and may recur. Regional climatological descriptions consist of such averages, totals, and extremes for a specific area of interest. Climatological data is very valuable in developing advance plans for the organization and financing of fire control forces. It is often used to define the expected fire season and to determine the normal strength and scheduling of fire control forces.

A fire season is defined as "the period or periods of the year during which fires are likely to occur, spread and do sufficient damage to warrant organized fire control" (U.S. Forest Service, 1956). The pattern, duration, and intensity of these seasons in a particular area are primarily functions of climate but are strongly influenced by the nature of forest fuels (Chapter 4). A given set of weather conditions may not bring about the same severity of burning conditions in different areas. For example, a summer relative humidity of 30 percent is not regarded as particularly dangerous in interior California or the northern Rocky Mountains, but in western Washington and Oregon it is considered sufficiently dangerous to suspend logging operations. The difference is due to the larger volumes of kindling fuels, many of them "flashy," that are characteristic of this area.

Statistical analysis of fire occurrence is usually depended on to define the fire season. However, occurrence alone may be misleading unless the variable potential of fires to spread and to do damage is also evaluated. In the Southwest, for example, summer lightning fires reach their peak of occurrence in June and July and occasionally continue at a high level into August. But in normal seasons for that region, summer rains begin in early July, and "greening up" of grass and other vegetation abruptly reduces the potential spread of any fires ignited. With these limitations in mind, attention is called to Table 5.1, which shows the average percentage of the year's fires that occurred in each month in different regions of the United States over a five-year period. Although the exact percentages will vary from year to year, seasonal trends remain relatively stable. This can be demonstrated by plotting the regional percentages in Table 5.1 on a curve, then plotting current records for the same region in relation to them. The controlling influence of weather and climate on fire seasons is evident.

Several distinctive types of fire season can be identified from Table 5.1.

1   A single period and normally short fire season. This is well illustrated by the pattern of occurrence for the Pacific Northwest and for the northern Rocky Mountain regions. Both show a strong July–August peak, reflecting the very dry summers that are so characteristic of these regions.

2   The spring and fall or two-period fire season. This reflects both weather and fuels and is characteristic of deciduous broadleaf forests. After the leaves fall in autumn, flammable surface fuels are much more abundant and are more exposed to sun and wind due to the drastic change in the forest canopy. Flash fuels reach maximum volume at this time, and the potential for severe fire damage is high during drought periods. Fall rains or snow usually limit both the duration and severity of this period. In the spring after snow is gone but before new grass and other lush surface vegetation create new microclimates and new barriers to the spread of fire, fires again threaten. Usually the spring fire season persists longer than the fall season, but fires tend to be less severe. The fire occurrence for the more mountainous areas of New Jersey (Table 5.1) illustrates the pattern.

3   Year-long seasons with short intermittent safe periods and with peak periods corresponding to numbers 1 and 2 above. This is well illustrated by the pattern shown for Florida, with some fires in all months but with a decided winter and early spring peak season in its southern pine forests. In other parts of the Southeast a higher proportion of fires occurs in October and November. California is also a good example of fires in all

Table 5.1   Monthly Percentage of Forest Fire Occurrence by Regions*

Month	Southeast (Florida)	Middle Atlantic Mountainous		Level topography	
		(New Jersey)	(New York)	(New Jersey)	(New Yc
January	16.1	1.7	0.3	2.1	0.8
February	18.0	0.6	0.2	2.6	1.4
March	27.3	14.5	1.1	20.1	9.2
April	11.8	43.5	18.7	28.2	37.9
May	6.6	17.0	26.2	21.4	19.3
June	2.2	0.9	9.8	5.9	3.2
July	1.1	0.6	12.6	5.2	6.2
August	0.7	0.6	14.5	2.5	3.5
September	0.2	0.3	5.5	1.4	2.4
October	1.5	4.9	7.3	2.6	7.9
November	3.7	12.8	3.1	6.6	5.6
December	10.8	2.6	0.7	1.4	2.6

*These occurrence percentages are illustrative only of the trends by regions and are mostly for a five-year period between 1929 and 1936.

but one month of the year but with a strong July–October peaking of occurrence corresponding to that of other Western regions with dry summers. Statistics for southern California alone would accentuate the year-long character and late-season peak period of occurrence.

CRITICAL FIRE WEATHER PATTERNS

The long dry seasons of California are caused by the summer and fall location of the Pacific high-pressure system which often centers over the Colorado plateau. Dry, subsiding air from that high-pressure system then moves westward over California in successive surges. The states bordering California are affected by this dry air also, but not to the same degree. East of the Rockies, moist air from the Gulf of Mexico and cool air from Canada or the North Pacific Ocean alternately move across the United States, accounting for the pattern of rainy and clear days. On occasion, a migratory high-pressure system may stagnate over an area east of the Continental Divide and the area affected will experience a period of severe fire weather.

A variety of synoptic patterns affect fire weather over the continent. However, studies carried out by fire weather forecasters under leadership of Mark J. Shroeder, which were published in 1964, concluded that only a few of these patterns are associated with critical fire weather. The following is quoted from their conclusions:

Lake states (Minnesota)	Pacific Northwest (Oregon)	South-west (Arizona, New Mexico)	Cali-fornia	Northern Rockies (Idaho, Montana)
. . .	. . .	. . .	0.1	
. . .	. . .	. . .	1.4	
22.4	. . .	1.6	2.0	1.6
25.9	5.6	7.0	4.9	7.9
4.5	8.1	30.8	9.8	9.0
14.5	24.4	43.2	23.7	33.6
18.9	37.6	12.1	25.5	34.4
5.8	13.5	2.2	14.4	8.2
7.8	10.8	3.1	15.1	4.5
0.2	. . .	. . .	2.6	0.8
. . .	. . .	. . .	0.5	

From the Rocky Mountains eastward most of the high fire danger occurs in the periphery of high pressure areas, particularly in the prefrontal and postfrontal areas. Along the eastern slopes of the Rockies, weather patterns producing Chinook winds are the most important. In the mountain and intermountain areas high fire danger is associated either with the presence of the jet stream overhead and the short-wave troughs moving along the jet stream or with the surface dry front passages. In the Far West patterns resulting in heat waves and patterns producing an offshore flow or foehn wind are important.

Throughout the West the conditions described as associated with high fire danger are frequently aggravated by the occurrence of dry thunderstorms of air-mass origin.

Besides the annual, recurrent, seasonal patterns reflecting both fuels and weather, severe fire seasons are also associated with periodic drought and tend to occur in cycles. In much of California, as already discussed, a protracted rainless period in late season with severe burning conditions is normal. In other parts of the West severe drought occurs at irregular intervals. It is not uncommon in Western regions for each 10-year period to show three critical fire years, spaced at irregular intervals, marking the drought years of the period. Though there seems to be some cyclic trend to the recurrence of severe droughts, they are due to large-scale fluctuations in the circulation of the earth's atmosphere which are not yet well understood.

BASIC FACTS OF ATMOSPHERE AND EARTH CLIMATE

Changeability of the earth's weather is caused by two major factors: (1) the rotation of the earth and its movement about the sun with its axis of rotation inclined to the plane of its orbit, and (2) variation in the pattern and elevation of land and water on the earth's surface. These factors interact to cause wide variation in the amount of solar energy absorbed at the earth's surface.

First is the diurnal change with each rotation of the earth. This sets up the daily cycle of daylight and darkness, with associated changes in temperature, humidity, and air movement. Superimposed on the diurnal is the seasonal change. The earth makes a rotation from west to east on its axis once each 24 hours at the rate of 15° of longitude each hour, which is about equal to the distance from Pittsburgh to Omaha at that latitude. The earth's axis of rotation is tilted at an angle of $23^1/_2°$ from a perpendicular to the plane of the earth's orbit about the sun. The earth moves about the sun once each approximately $365^1/_4$ days. This movement of the tilted earth is responsible for the apparent movement of the sun northward each spring and southward each fall, thus accounting for the seasons of the year.

Evaporation occurs from both land and water surfaces. It takes place whenever a higher vapor pressure exists on the surface than in the overlying air. From moist land surfaces the amount of moisture removed per unit area per hour may exceed that removed from water surfaces because of the higher temperature of the land surface from radiant heating. Contact with such surfaces also raises the temperature of the surrounding air. With increasing temperature, the water-vapor capacity of the air increases rapidly to reinforce the effect. However, most land surfaces are only intermittently moist, and they account only for about one-third of the earth's surface. For that reason the oceans, which cover the other two-thirds of the earth's surface, are the major sources of water vapor in the earth's general circulation.

As moist air cools, its moisture-holding capacity is reduced. This may result in the condensation of water vapor, which eventually falls back to the earth's surface as precipitation in one form or another. The never-ending process of evaporation and condensation is known as the hydrological cycle. It is powered by the sun's energy.

Land surfaces affect the weather in various ways. Perhaps of most importance are the major mountain systems, most of which are so oriented that they lie across the path of prevailing winds. This lifts and cools the air and may change wind direction and speed as well.

Part of the solar energy received by land surfaces may be transported to other areas by air movement, while solar energy which warms oceans is partially transported by both air and water movement.

The atmosphere rotates with the earth and must be considered as a part of the earth system. At the same time, the atmosphere has a primary circulation between equator and poles because of the great difference in solar energy reaching these areas. From much study and research, the three-cell theory, which seems to explain the primary circulation of the earth's atmosphere, has evolved. Any such simplified or theoretical circulation model is obscured by the earth's strong secondary circulation patterns and pressure systems. But it is very helpful in gaining a general understanding of the global weather. Following are the salient features of the theory (Figure 5.1). The Northern Hemisphere is used for illustration.

1   Air is heated in equatorial regions and rises to great heights. Here it starts northward but slowly turns to the right because of the earth's rotation. By the time the air has reached latitude 30° it is moving eastward. As more air from the equatorial region arcs northward toward 30°, it piles up, forming an area of high pressure in the general vicinity of 30°.

2   Some of the air in this high-pressure area is forced down, back to the surface.

a   At the surface a portion of this air flows southward, but rotation of the earth causes it to arc to the right. This air forms the northeast trade winds. By the time this air reaches the equatorial region, it is moving almost due westward (east wind).

Figure 5.1   Three-cell circulation pattern of the earth's atmosphere.

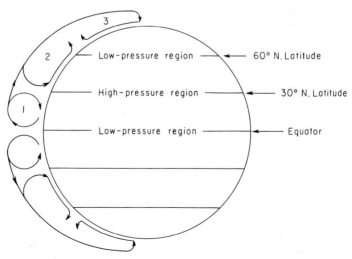

b The other portion of this descending air turns northward. The earth's rotation deflects it to the right also. This portion becomes the prevailing westerlies, a broad southwesterly flow generally between latitudes 30 and 60°.

3 The other portion of air from the high-pressure system at 30° flows on northward aloft toward the pole. It cools gradually as it moves, and at the polar region it sinks back to low levels.

4 Pressure builds up at the pole, and the cold heavy air moves southward at or near the surface. It is deflected to the right, forming a northeasterly low-level wind.

5 At about latitude 60°, the cold northeasterly flow collides with the prevailing westerlies, which are moving from the Southwest.

6 This shifting line of collision between the two flows is called the polar front.

This theory is given here because it explains the location of persisting bands of high and low pressure in the earth's atmosphere. In short, because of the ascending air, semipermanent low pressure persists near the equator and near latitude 60°. Near latitude 30° and at the polar region, semipermanent high pressure persists. The Pacific high-pressure system is one unit of this high-pressure band. Air from that system markedly influences fire weather in the western portion of the United States. The Bermuda high is another unit in this high-pressure band. At times it influences fire weather in the eastern United States (pages 131–133).

These semipermanent pressure systems are not rigidly fixed. They tend to shift northward or southward as the sun's angle changes seasonally. Also, at times the individual cells become displaced eastward or westward from their normal locations.

Local vertical motions are superimposed on the large-scale cell movement. Some of these are several hundred miles across, and some are small, of the size indicated by thunderstorm clouds. The vertical motions are migratory, although the large ones may persist over an area for a number of days. These vertical motions may affect fire weather drastically.

Atmospheric pressure is about 15 pounds per square inch at sea level, and pressure becomes progressively less with increasing height above sea level. The atmosphere may be divided into two principal parts. The lower part is called the troposphere, and the upper part the stratosphere. The boundary between troposphere and stratosphere is called the tropopause. All weather which affects the earth's surface occurs in the troposphere. The most significant feature of the troposphere is that mean temperature decreases with increase of altitude until the tropopause is reached. For some distance above the tropopause the temperature profile shows little change. The tropopause is about 60,000 feet above sea level over tropical regions and about 30,000 feet over polar regions. Temperatures at the tropopause range from about −80°C over tropical regions to about −55°C over polar areas.

The tropopause is divided into tropical, subtropical, and arctic sections. These sections may overlap. At the overlappings there is a temperature discontinuity, and these are the places where jet streams develop. The jet stream is a tubular-shaped ribbon of high-speed air, moving generally from the west and at an elevation of 20,000 to 40,000 feet. It may have a width of some 300 miles. At its core the winds average about 110 miles per hour in winter and about 50 miles per hour in summer. In extreme cases, the winds may reach 250 miles per hour. These jets frequently meander from arctic areas to the middle latitudes during the summer, indicating extreme variability of the tropopause breaks. Petterssen (1956) and Riehl, Alaka, Jordan, and Renard (1954) give detailed information on the jet stream. Schaefer (1957) suggested that the jet stream may influence the occurrence of fire-setting lightning storms. Possible relationships between the jet stream patterns and surface weather are very complex but are gradually becoming better understood through research. Some association has been identified in the Rocky Mountain region between critical fire weather and the presence of the jet stream directly overhead.

TEMPERATURE, AIR MOISTURE, AND ATMOSPHERIC STABILITY

Temperature is the degree of heat measured on a finite scale. Heat is a form of energy. From the point of view of thermodynamics it is energy in transit. Heat and temperature should not be confused. If a sample of gas is suddenly reduced to half its volume by increasing the pressure, its temperature will be markedly increased but its total heat energy will remain unchanged assuming that none is lost or gained in the compression.

All bodies radiate heat. The character of radiation varies with temperature of the radiating body. The surface of the sun has a temperature of about 6000° absolute, and radiation from it is of short wavelength. The sun's radiation has virtually no effect on air temperature because clear air is almost transparent to shortwave radiation. Energy from the sun is absorbed by the earth's surface. This energy is reradiated back into the atmosphere as longwave radiation. Part of this longwave radiation is absorbed by water vapor in the air and reradiated. Because shortwave radiation readily passes through moist air while longwave radiation is trapped, the water vapor in the air gives greenhouselike protection to the earth, helping to stabilize the earth's temperatures.

The earth's surface, however, does not absorb heat uniformly.

Consequently, the same amount of solar energy causes different temperatures on the earth's surface, depending on the nature of that surface. Bare ground or sand becomes hot under direct rays of the sun, whereas the temperature of a water surface changes relatively much less.

Forest cover has a pronounced moderating effect on both soil and air temperature due to a combination of influences. Forest canopies intercept and absorb the sun's rays, active photosynthesis converts a part of the radiant energy into plant food, and transpiration releases moisture into the air. The proportion of the sun's energy used up in photosynthesis is small. Consequently, the principal differences on a mesoscale basis between forested and bare ground areas are due to differences in the absorptive and reflective properties of the surfaces receiving radiation from the sun.

Radiation received by the earth's surface in unit time is affected by the angle of the sun's rays. This varies with latitude, season, time of day, and topography. The more directly overhead the sun is, the more rays strike the earth per unit of area. This is modified by topography. In the Northern Hemisphere, southern slopes receive more radiation than northern slopes, with the contrast increasing with latitude. As the sun approaches the horizon late in the day, the incoming energy becomes less than the outgoing radiation from the earth's surface. When the sun sets, the earth is receiving no direct radiation, but radiation from the earth continues, so that the surface of the earth continues to cool until shortly after sunrise.

These radiation relationships create a variable temperature range. When there is much water vapor in the air, nighttime outgoing radiation is largely absorbed and partially reradiated back to the earth. This keeps the temperature from falling much at the surface. Conversely, when air moisture is low, large daily temperature fluctuations occur. This effect is well illustrated by the wide average daily temperature ranges of summertime in the plateau region of the western United States as compared with sections of the Deep South, Midwest, and East, where the air normally contains much more moisture. The average daily temperature range in August is only 21°F at Chicago as compared with a range of 43°F at Elko, Nevada. In extreme cases, daily temperature ranges in excess of 60°F have been noted at high mountain-valley locations. Figure 5.2 shows summertime temperature changes in lower levels of the atmosphere during a 12-hour surface maximum-to-minimum period at Spokane, Washington. The temperature range in this instance was approximately 30°F.

The capacity of air to contain water vapor changes greatly as the temperature changes. For example, at 0°F and sea-level pressure, a kilogram of air is saturated by about 0.95 gram of water vapor, giving this

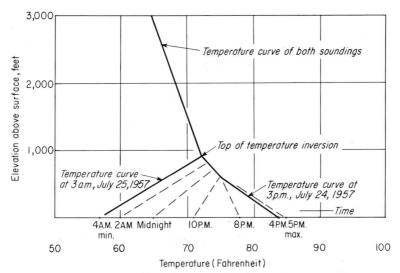

Figure 5.2 Summertime temperature changes in lower levels of the atmosphere at Spokane, Washington. Broken lines show approximate temperature profile at the times shown.

air a humidity of 100 percent. At 110°F and sea-level pressure, a kilogram of air requires almost 60 grams of water vapor for saturation, or over 60 times as much. Figure 5.3 shows a scale of temperature with water vapor required for saturation. Roughly, the vapor for saturation doubles for each 20°F temperature increase.

Relative humidity is defined as the ratio between the amount of water vapor a unit of air contains at a given temperature and the amount of water vapor the unit of air requires for saturation at that same temperature and pressure. For practical use, the effect of pressure is not great and can be disregarded. Referring to Figure 5.3, if a 1-kilogram parcel of air with a temperature of 89°F contains 15 grams of moisture, then relative humidity would be 15 grams/30 grams × 100, or 50 percent.

Figure 5.3 Grams of water vapor required to saturate one kilogram of air at different temperatures.

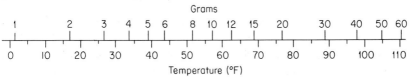

Similarly, if the temperature of the parcel dropped to 69°F, the air would be saturated and the relative humidity 100 percent.

Dew-point temperature is defined as the temperature at which condensation begins in a cooling mass of air if its water vapor remains constant. Dew-point temperature is affected but slightly by pressure change and hence is a fairly conservative quantity in identifying air masses.

If a parcel of air is lifted or lowered, its dew point will change at about the rate of 1°F per 1,000 feet. If the parcel is saturated, its moisture, expressed in grams per kilogram of dry air, is called the saturation mixing ratio. Mixing-ratio values are not affected by pressure change. Hence these values are very useful in checking moisture continuity through an air profile. Mixing ratio is thus defined as the ratio of density of water vapor to the density of dry air.

If a parcel of air is lifted or lowered, its temperature will change at the rate of 5.5°F per 1,000 feet so long as condensation does not occur. Average lapse rates in the atmosphere[1] tend to be less than this and are often quoted as 2°C or 3.5°F per 1,000 feet. Using the dew-point and temperature lapse rates, one can calculate what happens to the free-air temperature and humidity as a parcel of air is lifted over a steep mountain range. Referring to Figure 5.4, if one assumes lifting a parcel of air having a temperature of 90°F and a dew point of 62°, then the temperature and dew point would decrease as indicated and condensation would occur after about 6,000 feet of lifting. Relative humidity values are shown at each 1,000-foot interval on the right side of the figure. On a hot summer afternoon the relationships shown would be close to the actual free-air condition.

As an air parcel is forced up or down, the temperature varies with pressure change if there is no external exchange of heat. Such a process is called *adiabatic,* and the cooling rate of 5.5°F per 1,000 feet frequently occurs for convective and mechanical lifting by mountain slopes in relatively dry air masses. For example, on hot sunny afternoons, the lower few thousand feet of the atmosphere usually has this temperature structure. When cumulus clouds can be seen at the hottest time of the day in the summer, it is a safe bet that a dry adiabatic lapse rate exists between the surface and the cloud base. Close to the earth's surface, superadiabatic lapse conditions frequently precede the formation of cumulus clouds.

When a parcel of air is lifted past the condensation point, then heat is released by condensing water vapor, and this tends to increase the temperature of the parcel. Even so, as the parcel continues to rise, its

---

[1]Lapse rate is the change in temperature per 1,000 feet of elevation.

temperature continues to fall, although at a slower rate. The saturated adiabatic temperature change with elevation is known as the moist adiabatic lapse rate. (See temperature in cloud of Figure 5.4.)

Stability of the atmosphere is defined as the state in which vertical distribution of temperature is such that an air particle will resist displacement from its level. In the case of unsaturated air, the lapse rate for stability will be less than the dry adiabatic lapse rate; in the case of saturated air, the lapse rate for stability will be less than the moist adiabatic lapse rate. The dry adiabatic lapse rate represents neutral stability. This condition is shown graphically in Figure 5.5. Let the line *aa'* indicate a dry adiabatic lapse rate several thousand feet in depth. If an air parcel is pushed upward by an external force from *a*, its temperature will be the same as that shown by the line representing the environment temperature. This means that the parcel would be at neutral stability at all points along the line *aa'*. Thus it would tend to remain at the point where the lifting force was removed.

On Figure 5.5, let the line *bb'* indicate an environment which has a

Figure 5.4 Temperature and dew-point lapse rates and humidity increase in a rising column of air.

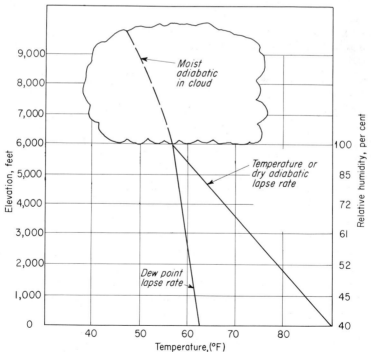

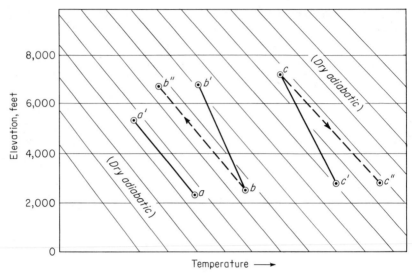

Figure 5.5 Atmospheric stability: lines *aa'*, neutral stability; *bb'* and *cc'*, stable.

lapse rate less than the dry adiabatic rate. If a parcel is forced from point *b* to the same pressure as at *b'*, it will end up at point *b''*. This parcel would then be colder and thus denser than the environment air, and as a result it would tend to sink back until it reached a point where its temperature would be the same as the environment temperature, that is, back to point *b*. Reversing the situation, let *cc'* indicate an environment which has a lapse rate less than the dry adiabatic rate. If a parcel from point *c* is moved downward to the same pressure as at *c'*, it will end up at point *c''*. In this case the parcel would be warmer and thus lighter than the environment, and consequently it will be forced up by the denser surrounding air to equilibrium at point *c*.

Though air temperature normally decreases from the surface upward, there are frequent exceptions. Wherever there is instead a temperature increase with altitude, this inverted state of temperature is known as an inversion. The layer through which this occurs is the inversion layer. Local inversions are often important factors in the fire environment. In Figure 5.6 a temperature profile is shown by the curve *abcd*. If a parcel is displaced from a to the pressure level of point *c*, it will have a temperature indicated by *a'*. This parcel would be very much colder and thus denser than the environment, and it would return quickly to its initial pressure altitude once the displacing force is removed. This would be a very stable situation. Again on Figure 5.6, let the line *ee'* indicate the environment temperature. If a parcel from *e* is displaced to the same pressure as at *e'*, it will arrive at *e''*. This parcel would be warmer at every level than the environment air, and the surrounding denser air would force it to continue to rise until it reached a point where its temperature and density was the same as the environment.

A lapse rate greater than the dry adiabatic is called a superadiabatic lapse rate and indicates atmospheric instability. These superadiabatic conditions are often found in the first few hundred feet immediately above the earth's surface due to strong surface heating with light surface winds. This represents a strong temperature and density gradient in the layers of air near the surface. These gradients usually weaken after the first few hundred feet, with temperature changes above conforming to the dry adiabatic rate. Superadiabatic lapse rates are seldom found in the free atmosphere, although it is reasonable that this condition can occur and may persist in local combinations. Byram and Nelson (1951) have found evidence of a relationship between superadiabatic lapse rates near the surface and extreme fire behavior in the Southeast. Taylor and Williams (1967) have assembled detailed evidence of similar relationships in their study of the Hellgate fire in southern Virginia.

From the foregoing discussion and examples, the following may be stated as axiomatic: The degree of air stability is directly related to the rate at which the temperature of the air changes with height. Lapse rates

Figure 5.6 Atmospheric stability and instability: inversion *abc*, stable; *ee'*, unstable.

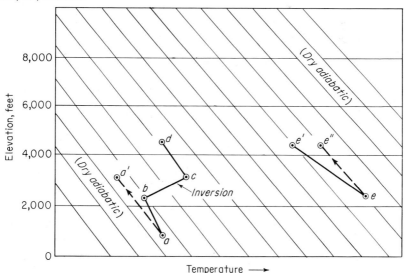

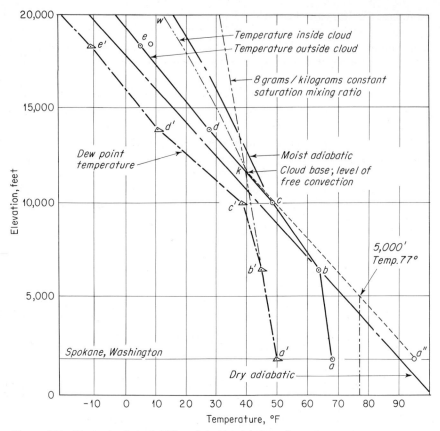

Figure 5.7 Atmospheric instability related to condensation.

greater than a dry adiabatic indicate atmospheric instability, a rate between a dry and a moist adiabatic is known as conditional instability, and lapse rates less than moist adiabatic indicate stable conditions.

In the discussion of stability so far, only those cases in which condensation was not involved have been considered. In Figure 5.7, situations involving condensation can be examined. Let curve *abcde* indicate the temperature profile a radiosonde instrument reports and let *a'b'c'd'e'* indicate its dew-point temperature curve. As surface heating warms air in the low levels, it tends to be forced aloft dry adiabatically until the temperature is denoted by *a''kde.* The average mixing ratio in the lower 5,000 feet or so is about 8 grams of water vapor per kilogram of air, as shown by *a'b'.* As the lower-level air rises and mixes, the mixing ratio would be as indicated by *a'b'k,* and at point *k,* condensation would occur. Point *k,* in this case, is the level of free convection. Above point *k,* the condensed air continues to rise, cooling at the moist adiabatic rate, as denoted by the line *kw*. The temperature inside the cloud will be as shown by *kw* and outside the cloud as shown by *kde*. The space between these two temperature curves is known as the positive area. The greater the positive area above the level of free convection, the greater will be the instability. In this case there could be a thunderstorm of marked intensity. This is an example of conditional instability. In level country, it would be necessary that the surface temperature reach about 95°F to release the conditional instability. In mountainous country, however, the thunderstorm could be activated by heating of high ground nearby, and under these circumstances the temperature where the radiosonde was released need not necessarily become as high as 95°F. For example, assume that nearby mountains have an elevation of about 5,000 feet mean sea level. At that elevation, a temperature of only about 77°F is needed to release instability. For further treatment of stability and instability see Byers (1959).

The situation illustrated in Figure 5.7 was developed on the assumption that the lifting of air was caused by surface warming. This is only one of several processes by which the necessary lifting may occur. Among the several possible mechanisms to produce this effect are orographic and frontal lifting.

Cumulus clouds will develop in many cases of air lifting but may not progress beyond the cumulus stage. These clouds may fail to develop further for two reasons. First, the air a short distance above the level of free convection may be so dry that cloud tops evaporate as fast as the bases form. Second, the temperature structure above the cumulus clouds may be sufficiently stable so that the clouds cannot grow. The second case is explained in Figure 5.8. Let *abcde* indicate temperature profile, and let *a'b'c'd'e'* indicate the dew-point curve. The mixing ratio in the lower levels is 9 grams per kilogram, and should the lower air be lifted, condensation would occur at point *k*, with a surface temperature indicated by *a''* of 73°F. Above point *k* the air would rise at the moist-adiabatic rate to point *x*, where the rising parcels would have the same temperature as the environment air. Consequently, there would be no further lifting. The inversion indicated by *cd* would effectively cap the cloud growth; clouds would occur in the area denoted by the line segment *kx*. The positive area in this case is denoted by the triangle *ckx*.

On occasion extremely low humidities occur both east and west. West of the Rockies and on their eastern slopes humidities as low as 1 percent have been recorded. Over the central and eastern portions of the United States, humidities down to 5 percent are of record, though rare. In such occurrences the surface dew point temperatures are always well

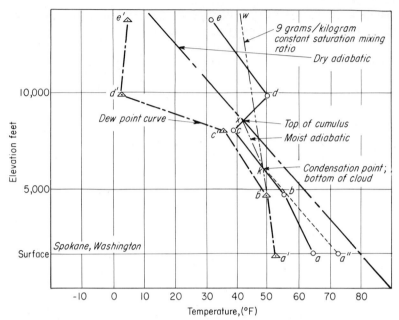

Figure 5.8 Condition of atmospheric stability. Cumulus clouds would form at point *k* but would not develop significantly beyond point *x*.

below zero. This means that condensation in this air has occurred at elevations many thousands of feet above sea level in the free atmosphere and that the air mass has lowered to the surface with very little mixing in the process. More detail is given on this important phenomena in the discussion of subsidence (pages 147–150).

AIR MASSES

Air is constantly being cooled or heated by contact with the earth. In warming, the surface air expands and is forced aloft by cooler, denser air from over nearby cooler surfaces or from more distant higher-pressure areas. This cooler air in turn is heated, thus transporting heat energy aloft. Evaporation at the earth's surface accelerates with heating, and if accompanied by convection the water vapor is carried aloft. Cool air at the surface is more dense and does not tend to rise. But moist air masses are lighter than dry air masses at the same temperature and pressure, therefore they are more buoyant. This is because water vapor is lighter than dry air and replaces a part of the dry-air volume. The molecular weight of the H_2O in water vapor is only 18 while that of the typical NO mixture at sea level is approximately 29. For that reason water vapor extends convection beyond the direct effects of heating and cooling of dry air alone.

If a large body of air remains over an area for a long period of time, it takes on the current temperature characteristic of that region. Such an air mass becomes relatively homogeneous, the air at each level having about the same temperature and moisture. These air masses may range from a few hundred miles to more than 2,000 miles across.

In general, the two major types of air mass are the warm air mass and the cold air mass. Large cold-air masses form in the polar regions and/or adjacent land areas where the surface is cold. During the long periods of darkness over cloudless polar regions, the radiating cooling process is uninterrupted. Warm air masses form principally in tropical areas and are usually rather moist. Cold air masses, on the other hand, contain little moisture. The depth of each air mass depends on the temperature of the surface at the source region and on the length of time the forming air mass remained over the source region.

When air masses leave their source regions in the Northern Hemisphere, the cold air mass moves in a general southerly direction and the warm air mass in a general northerly direction, both movements in response to pressure gradients and to major airflow patterns aloft. However, air masses moving over North America do follow certain general paths. Figure 5.9 shows the most frequent paths followed. The movement of cold air masses is more affected by obstructing mountain ranges than is that of warm air masses. Stable cold air may be deflected, slowed, or even

Figure 5.9 Typical paths of air masses entering the United States.

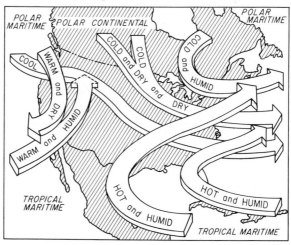

stopped in its movement by intercepting high mountains. Warm, moist air masses normally drop copious precipitation when they move over mountain ranges because of the cooling caused by lifting.

When a cold air mass begins moving southward, various modifying actions start to work on it. Some of these are listed below.

1   The cold denser air in motion invariably runs under any warmer air in its path. In doing so, it frequently lifts the warm air sufficiently to cause precipitation, which falls through the cold air. Some of the heat released by condensation is carried into the cold air by the precipitation. This happens principally in the leading edge of the cold air. Also, there will be some mixing with the warmer air at the face of contact between the two air masses.

2   As the cold air moves southward, it usually moves over progressively warmer ground surfaces which warm it.

3   The cold air mass usually comes under the influence of progressively longer periods of sunshine. This speeds up modification. Speed of movement also affects the rate at which air masses are modified. An air mass moving rapidly from a cold source region will arrive much colder than a similar one moving slowly.

Cold air masses which move southward over land surfaces are much more slowly modified than those which move over the oceans. As a consequence they may retain their identifying characteristics and intensity longer and penetrate to much lower latitudes. In the winter these cold-air surges occasionally move all the way overland to the Gulf of Mexico.

When a cold air mass moves from Siberia, or the ice-covered polar region, southward over the Pacific Ocean to the United States coast, it becomes much modified during the long overwater trajectory, picking up a considerable amount of moisture and heat energy. It reaches the west coast of North America as a rather unstable body of air with much different characteristics than it had at the source region.

As warm air masses move northward, they too modify. If the warm, moist air moves over a cold surface, the lowest levels of air may be cooled to the condensation point, and under these circumstances widespread fog may form. If the warm air is lifted by any process, the condensation temperature is usually reached and precipitation occurs, thus removing some of the moisture.

Air masses discussed so far are formed by contact with the earth surface. An air mass can also be formed by descent of air from great heights in a subsiding motion. This may represent an overturning of the strata by movement across mountainous topography, the stimulation of vertical downward movement by steep pressure gradients, or a combination of factors. Since such air was extremely cold at the source elevation, it cannot contain much water vapor. As it descends, it is heated by compression. This creates a marked temperature inversion at the air-mass base. Because of this it is not readily modified from below; that is, convection columns do not readily penetrate it. Consequently, on infrequent occasions, this air may reach relatively low levels with little modification. Subsiding air masses occasionally reach low levels over the southwestern United States. Their development has special importance to fire weather, as described in the section on large-scale subsidence.

As an air mass moves, it causes weather which is contingent on its temperature and moisture structure and in accordance with thermodynamic changes brought about by orographic lifting or other lifting processes. The relationship between temperature structure of the air mass and temperature of the surface over which it moves may determine resulting weather. For example, showers are likely to occur when a cool, moist air mass moves over warm land (Berry, Bollay, and Beers, 1945).

PRESSURE SYSTEMS AND WEATHER FRONTS

The weight of the atmosphere creates pressure of approximately 15 pounds per square inch at sea level. This is equivalent to 29.92 inches of mercury or close to 32 feet of water. Pressure decreases with elevation, but it varies also with time. There is a small diurnal fluctuation in the nature of a tidal effect, but of principal importance to meteorologists is the dynamic variation in pressure associated with the movement of air masses. Each large air mass can be identified as a pressure system.

High-pressure systems are characterized by anticyclonic or clockwise circulation and are usually referred to simply as *highs.* The temperature structure within highs varies considerably depending on their origin and formation. In the Northern Hemisphere, Canadian, Arctic, and Siberian highs are usually cold, while Pacific and Bermuda highs are usually warm.

One can easily locate anticyclones if one has access to pressure readings from many places for the same time. To do this, the readings first must be adjusted to a common altitude for comparability and entered on a map at appropriate locations. Then lines may be drawn connecting places having the same pressure. Such lines are called isobars. If a series of such lines are drawn—evenly spaced pressurewise—then the pressure systems will become evident. Anticyclones are domes of high pressure, the pressure becoming progressively higher as one moves toward the center (Figure 5.10).

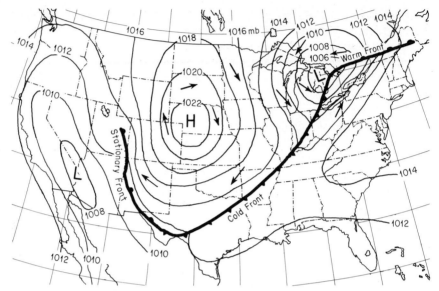

Figure 5.10 Illustration of high- and low-pressure systems.

Low-pressure systems are characterized by cyclonic or counter-clockwise circulation and are usually referred to as *lows*. Lows are valleys of low pressure and can be located in the manner indicated above. There are three distinct types, the frontal low, the heat low, and the semipermanent low. Examples of semipermanent lows in the Northern Hemisphere are the Aleutian low and the Icelandic low. These two lows and the Pacific and Bermuda highs are caused by the earth's primary circulation, as previously explained.

When a large dome of air settles over an area, creating a high, it takes on a clockwise movement imparted by rotation of the earth. Contrariwise, a low takes on a counterclockwise rotation. Air flowing spirally away from a high-pressure system tends to descend as it moves. Since such air is being heated by compression as it loses altitude, it normally has a low relative humidity. As a result, a high-pressure system usually brings fair weather. The reverse is true of the low. Air is converging as it flows spirally inward toward lowest pressure, and it rises. This air has been exposed to convective mixing at the surface and has usually picked up a considerable amount of water vapor. It cools as it rises, frequently reaching the condensation point. For this reason, a low usually brings unsettled weather. These statements regarding weather associated with pressure systems are only general. See Figure 5.10 for an example of high-and low-pressure systems. It shows a migratory high centered over Nebraska, a frontal low centered over Lake Huron, and a heat low over the Far West of the United States.

Warm and cold highs and heat and frontal lows have a direct bearing on fire weather in the United States and Canada. For this reason, the characteristics of each of these systems are listed.

Warm High-pressure System

1 The system tends to be very deep and is formed by descending air.

2 Air in the system is warm—level for level—because it has heated by compression as it has descended.

3 Air is always extremely dry at moderate and high levels, because it has descended from higher levels which are initially very cold and hold little moisture.

4 Vigorous frontal activity does not occur in connection with these systems because of their relatively warm, homogenous air.

5 The systems are occasionally almost stationary for days, although they may migrate slowly.

6 These systems are similar in structure to the semipermanent highs, such as the Pacific and Bermuda highs.

Cold High-pressure System

1 The cold dense air in this system is rarely deeper than 15,000 feet, and at times it may be very shallow. Shallow cold air may warm rapidly, and in such cases the system may take on the characteristics of a warm high.

2 Air at low levels is cold, while (a) aloft the system may be more like a warm high, or (b) sometimes at higher levels low pressure and associated cold air is present. Such cold lows may control the movement of the cold high.

3 The system is migratory, frequently moving rapidly after leaving the source.

4 Very vigorous frontal activity usually occurs in connection with this system.

5 This system is usually born in the polar regions and is therefore much more intense in winter than in summer.

Heat Low-pressure System

1 System has moderate depth, extending up to 10,000 to 15,000 feet.

2 There are no fronts in connection with this system.

3 Principal location in the United States is over the desert South-

west and California, although the heat low may extend northward to Washington and Oregon or Idaho and Montana (see Figure 5.10).

4   Air is very hot at low levels, and the dry adiabatic lapse rate in extreme case may extend to 15,000 feet above the surface.

5   When a heat low becomes well developed, scattered dry thunderstorms readily occur.

6   The system is not truly migratory, although the axis of the low-pressure trough may shift from the West Coast to the northern Rocky Mountain region or slightly east of these mountains. The system tends to reform each time over the desert Southwest.

7   This system is principally a summer phenomenon, although weak developments may occur in late spring and in early fall.

Frontal Low-pressure System

1   Develops as a wave on the front where warm and cold air meet.

2   At times this low may become quite intense, particularly during winter months, but when this happens copious precipitation results at both the warm and cold frontal areas. Thus the intense frontal low does not usually produce dangerous fire weather.

3   These lows go through a process of development, maturity, and decay (Byers, 1944). The normal life is short, usually two or three days, although some of these lows may last a week or slightly longer.

4   When the air in the warm sector is too dry for warm-front lifting to cause precipitation, then this system can contribute to adverse fire weather by virtue of the cold-front wind shift which follows, which may also be dry.

5   These systems are migratory, usually moving eastward rather rapidly.

Movement and Interaction of Systems

Weather in the middle latitudes is caused by a procession of high- and low-pressure systems moving in an easterly direction. This procession tends to shift to the north during the summer and to the south in the winter. Speed of movement of the systems varies somewhat, but on the average is about 30 to 35 miles per hour in winter and about 20 to 25 miles per hour in summer. Bowie and Weightman (1914, 1917) made early analyses of high- and low-pressure-system tracks across the United States. More recently (1959–1960), W. H. Klein has conducted similar studies reported in U.S. Weather Bureau Research Paper no. 40, in which such tracks have been further defined.

As these systems move, interaction between cold and warm air brings alternate periods of fair and unsettled weather. As long as mean amounts and frequency of precipitation are maintained, critical fire weather does not occur. Under normal conditions, warm, moist air from the Gulf of Mexico periodically moves over the central and eastern portions of the United States. Usually this air contains adequate moisture, so that precipitation occurs when any frontal activity develops. At times, however, high-pressure systems stagnate over the central and/or eastern portions of the United States, developing critical fire weather in these areas. In the Lake states principally, and in the New England states secondarily, this may happen in the spring. Otherwise the high-pressure system stagnation is mostly in the late summer and early fall.

During the summer, the Pacific high moves northward, and in midsummer it covers virtually all the eastern portion of the Pacific Ocean from the Gulf of Alaska southward to low latitudes. In this position the Pacific high has a pronounced effect on weather throughout the western half of the United States. At intervals, dry, subsiding air from this system moves over the western states aloft. The greatest frequency of surges of dry air from the Pacific high occur over California, thus explaining the very dry summers in much of that state. At times the Pacific high will shift westward, so that it is completely offshore. When this happens, then the heat low-pressure system, or trough, of the desert Southwest usually shifts westward to California and may extend northward to the western portions of Oregon and Washington. This is the normal pattern when northern California and western Oregon and Washington receive dry thunderstorms. When the Pacific high noses inland, the heat trough shifts eastward and may extend from Arizona to Utah and on up to Montana. See preceding discussion (Critical Fire Weather Patterns) and study of this subject by Schroeder (1964), (pages 5–6).

When two air masses of different densities are adjacent to each other, they create a discontinuity called a front. The front is stationary if air in both the air masses is moving parallel to it, although in such cases the cold air is usually moving diametrically opposite to the warm air. A cold front exists when cold air is pushing under warm air. A warm front exists when warm air is pushing against cold air and overriding it.

The slope of a frontal surface will depend on the temperature and speed of both the warm and cold air. The denser cold air tends to hug the surface in both cases. Surface friction tends to hold the cold air back at low levels, and this results in steepening the frontal surface. Cold frontal surfaces usually have a slope of from 1 to 50 to 1 to 150. In the warm front, surface friction causes the cold air to assume a wedgelike shape. The slope of the warm-front surface is much less abrupt, averaging between 1 to 100 and 1 to 300.

As a cold front advances (Figure 5.11), it lifts the warm air abruptly, and precipitation occurs if the warm air contains sufficient moisture.

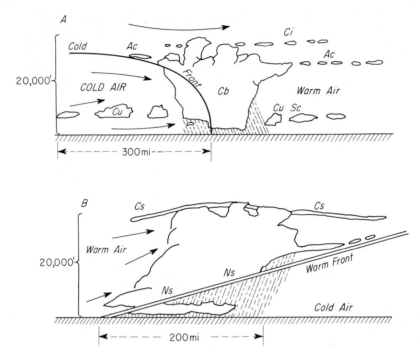

Figure 5.11 Idealized cross-section illustrating *A.* Cold-front passage. *B.* Warm-front passage. *(After Byers, 1944.)* Accompanying cloud types are *Ac*, altocumulus; *Ci*, cirrus; *Cb*, cumulonimbus; *Cu*, cumulus; *Sc*, stratocumulus; *Cs*, cirrostratus; *Ns*, nimbostratus.

Thunderstorms and/or squally weather are characteristic of cold-front passages. When no precipitation occurs, the system is called a dry cold front. Since the cold air is heavy and the air mass very stable in such a system, it moves over the ground, scouring out every drainage and ravine. It hugs the ground going downhill or uphill. Because of this characteristic of onrushing, very stable air, the dry cold front will push a fire in the direction it is moving almost without regard to topography. Most often there is a sharp wind shift at the time of a cold-frontal passage. If a fire is burning when such a front strikes it, the right flank of the fire normally becomes the head.

    The warm front normally does not present the sharp discontinuity characteristic of the cold front (Figure 5.11). Rather, the warm front is more of a zone of change. Stratified clouds and drizzle or gentle steady rains are characteristic of warm fronts, presenting no particular problem to fire control.

WIND

Air in motion, called wind, may move in both horizontal and vertical directions. Some of the vertical motions may be caused by rough terrain. All wind is caused by unequal distribution of pressure, which in turn is created by unequal distribution of temperature. Surface friction reduces the force of wind at the ground level.

Byers (1944) indicates a correlation between steepness of lapse rate in the lower atmosphere and surface wind speed. This does not mean that a steep lapse rate causes strong surface winds. It does mean that vertical mixing of the atmosphere is activated to the degree that winds aloft transmit their energy downward to create stronger surface winds. This is related to the tendency of surface wind speeds to be higher during the hottest part of the day than they are after radiation cooling has begun. Gisborne (1941) found the average highest wind speed consistently at the hottest time of the day in measurements made at five levels between the ground and 156 feet at Priest River, Idaho. His June, July, and August measurements were made on a tower in a dense timber stand.

A more stable lapse rate develops with the nighttime change in temperature structure. This allows less mixing. As nocturnal cooling at the surface progresses, inversion conditions develop. The inversion cuts off the surface layers from those above the inversion and reduces or eliminates the transfer of energy from aloft. While low-level surface winds are generally weakest at night, the reverse is noted on mountain ridges; that is, ridge winds tend to be stronger at night and weaker during the daytime.

In plains areas east of the Rocky Mountains, wind flow is more often induced by pressure gradient. Fire control men in these areas may be rather sure of wind direction and speed. Change of the pressure gradient will cause change of speed, and change in isobaric orientation will cause direction change. Such changes will usually be gradual where frontal action is not involved. Sharp direction change will occur mostly with cold-frontal passage, and wind speed usually increases sharply with these passages. Day to night change in wind speed is not as pronounced as in mountainous areas. The chief concern of the fire control man in these areas should be the expected time of arrival of the next cold front and whether or not the frontal passage will be dry.

Byers (1944) also indicates that friction slows not only the surface wind but also the higher currents as this effect is transmitted upward by eddy diffusion through successive layers of air to 1,500 to 2,000 feet or more above the surface. Not until then does wind achieve the speed one would expect from the surface pressure gradient. The layer of air thus affected may be deeper in mountainous country.

In relatively large mountain drainages, afternoon increases in wind speed may be sudden and marked when valley-floor temperature becomes high enough to break up the local valley inversion and re-create a dry adiabatic lapse rate in the lower 4,000 to 5,000 feet of air. The timing of this effect will vary from one valley to another, depending on the height of surrounding mountains and on the depth of stable air from nighttime radiational cooling. This radical wind-speed change will not occur unless there is substantial wind flow aloft, above the dry adiabatic gradient level. It is not uncommon to experience a sudden wind increase of from 15 to 20 miles per hour under favorable conditions in the summer at Missoula, Montana. This effect is most pronounced when the wind aloft coincides in direction with normal updrainage air movement.

Under these circumstances, men can be forewarned of the direction and approximate wind speed which may develop. If a fire is burning under the influence of stable air in the valley bottom, then behavior of the smoke plume will be a significant guide. If the plume rises and spreads out lazily, then the fire will probably not experience much wind change. If the plume rises to the gradient level and then streams off strongly, afternoon winds will be markedly stronger on the fire and direction will be indicated by smoke drift at the gradient level.

Fires will be easier to control at ridge tops if the daytime temperature lapse rate is steep from the surface to the elevation of nearby mountains and well above the mountains. The reason is that all slopes receiving solar energy will experience upslope winds under these conditions. Also, any air which may be lifted by flow against the mountain will not tend to return to its previous elevation on the leeward side. This increases the height to which firebrands are carried and greatly increases their airborne travel time, thus reducing probability of spot fires on the leeward side.

When very stable air is lifted over a ridge without condensation, the air will tend to return to its initial elevation. Under these conditions, the winds on the immediate lee side of the ridgetop will be extremely gusty and variable because of eddy effect but will have a downslope momentum. A fire can more easily spot over the ridge under these conditions and may be carried downslope under influence of very stable air.

Upslope surface winds are caused by solar heating. They normally commence each morning 15 to 45 minutes after the sun's rays strike the slope and cease quickly when sunshine leaves the slope. Downslope surface winds are caused by radiational cooling. Their beginning and ending dovetail with the stop and start of upslope winds. These winds are most noticeable under cloudless skies and weak pressure gradients.

The temperature difference between air heated by the mountain slope and air at the same levels over the valley creates unbalance, which establishes a circulation. The upslope wind is a portion of this circulation. The depth of these winds depends on the extent of the slope and duration of slope heating. Since the air is accumulating as it rises up the slope, the greatest depth—300 to 650 feet—exists near the top of the slope during the afternoons. Highest wind speeds are found near ridgetops and may range from 4 to 10 miles per hour. These winds are strongest on southern slopes. Defant (1951) indicates that this circulation is extremely sensitive to change in the sun's insulation. The temporary shading by a cloud will cause a quick response in decreased wind. Figure 5.12 shows the circulation of these upslope winds. They create a strong tendency for fires to stop at ridge tops. Experienced fire control men take advantage of this pattern in backfiring in mountain terrain.

Downslope winds are caused by nighttime radiational cooling, which causes development of a thin skin of air on the slope surface, more dense, level for level, than air over the valley. This density unbalance sets up a circulation which will be deepest at low portions of the slope. Inasmuch as the air in downslope movement becomes progressively more stable, these winds will not become as deep as upslope winds.

Adiabatic cooling and heating effects operate in both the upslope and downslope winds, and these tend to moderate and stabilize wind flows. Surface heating supplies sufficient energy to offset this cooling effect on the upslope wind, and radiational cooling is sufficiently strong to offset the heating effect in the downslope wind.

Figure 5.12 Schematic illustration of air circulation during daytime in a mountain valley and over a mountain range. *(American Meteorological Society, 1951. After Burger and Eckhart.)*

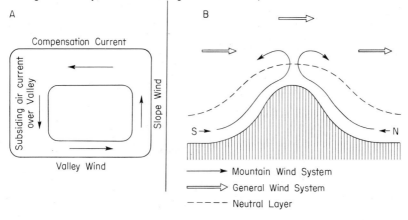

Mountain and Valley Winds

Discussion of local winds has been with respect to individual slopes only. In rugged terrain, the local upslope and downslope winds combine into an overall pattern which is called mountain and valley wind. It has become traditional in mountain country for the fire fighter to expect an up-canyon wind during the day and a down-canyon wind at night. But wind movement in mountain topography is very complex and there are many important exceptions.

Much of the time, general winds generated by existing pressure systems dominate. They obscure or may completely cancel out the convective effects generated by surface heating. But whenever general winds are light and there is a large range of temperature between daylight heating and nighttime cooling, convective winds of local origin become dominant. This is a rather common summertime situation in rugged terrain and becomes important to the forest manager wherever the critical fire season is also in the summertime. For that reason topographic wind systems warrant special study. The more detailed treatment accorded this subject in *Fire Weather,* Agriculture Handbook no. 360 (Shroeder and Buck, 1970) is particularly recommended for supplemental reading.

Wide differences in surface heating occur. They result from differing angles of exposure to the sun's rays, differing types and conditions of cover, and differing physical characteristics of the surfaces being heated. The result is a similar range in convective airflow. Nevertheless, all produce an upslope flow in the daytime and a downslope flow at night. Within this broad relationship several wind systems may be distinguished to facilitate generalizations.

Warm Air Patterns   On level ground, hot air from surface heating may surge upward like bubbles from a boiling pot. But on sloping or vertical surfaces it tends to follow the warm-air sheath upward, as in a chimney. Consequently, mountaintops and ridge crests are the focus of the principal exodus of warm air.

Valley versus Plain   The air over a valley heats up more during the daytime and cools down more at night than it does over the adjacent flatlands. Although the relationship is complex, the most important factor is believed to be the smaller volume of air over the valley (Shroeder and Buck, 1970). The resulting pressure differences cause air from the plain to flow up the valley in the daytime and down the valley at night. This is the familiar general effect cited above. Usually the narrower and deeper the valley, the faster and deeper the convective air flow. Variations occur too with differences in prevailing exposure to the sun.

The Up-valley Wind   As the warm air circulation becomes a positive up-valley wind, it tends to pull in the upslope currents along the side slopes. But since the depth of airflow may only partially fill the valley, this effect fluctuates on the upper slopes, causing frequent changes in local wind direction from up-valley to upslope. Turbulence in the valley also occurs at bends and tributary junctions.

The Down-valley Wind   As slopes cool, a reverse flow develops. It moves in a much shallower layer like drainage of water but deepens in steep valleys and canyons. As it accumulates, it builds up an inversion which may fill the lower valley. Usually the downslope drainage of cool air slows by midnight, but the general flow down the valley may persist until the morning reversal starts.

Effect on Gradient Winds   When convection is strong, it tends to lift prevailing gradient winds well above the surface. As cooling occurs, they descend and again move along the surface of exposed topography. On the other hand, gradient winds may modify, interrupt, or entirely cancel out the usual pattern of convective airflow.

Case studies in California by Schroeder and Countryman (1959–1964) develop this subject in further detail.

The Sea-breeze Front

Another familiar form of local convective air movement is the sea breeze. In coastal areas during clear weather, and particularly during the summer, a strong difference in surface heating of land and water surfaces develops. Warm air rises over the land and is replaced by the heavier cool air from over the water. This creates an onshore wind or sea breeze. At night, if land surfaces cool below the temperature of water surfaces, the reverse circulation develops with an offshore wind.

Along the Atlantic Coast, sea breezes are often a critical factor in the control of wildland fires. Williams (1968) reports on the effect of sea breezes on fire behavior in coastal areas of North Carolina. In the area studied, a definite front develops usually in midafternoon, moving inland at 2 to 5 knots per hour against prevailing winds and with a strong upward component. The wind changes in direction 45° or more during passage and veers in a counterclockwise direction most of the time. The wind is usually stronger following passage of the front. Wind speeds are usually 12 to 16 knots.

When such a front moves over a forest or brush fire, a strong convection column develops over the fire and rapid but very erratic spread of the fire front ensues.

THUNDERSTORMS AND LIGHTNING

Thunderstorms are an extremely unstable phenomenon. They will not occur unless at least the following two conditions are satisfied: First, there must be adequate air moisture to cause condensation and to support cloud growth above the level of free convection. Second, the environment-temperature lapse rate must be steeper than the moist adiabatic through a deep layer above the level of free convection.

A layer of moist air tends to become unstable whenever it is lifted sufficiently to cause condensation. Adequate lifting to cause thunderstorm activity may occur in a number of ways: (1) solar surface heating, (2) cold-front movement, (3) warm-front action, (4) orographic or lifting by flow over ascending land surfaces, (5) solar heating of high-level land masses, and (6) advection of cold air aloft. In many thunderstorm developments, several of these lifting forces are acting simultaneously. The majority of thunderstorms throughout the United States occur between noon and 6 P.M. local time, and this seems to indicate that daily solar energy is by far the most important in triggering these storms. Figure 5.13 shows the average number of thunderstorm days each year throughout the United States. Byers and Braham (1949) and Petterssen (1956) are suggested references.

Thunderstorms are important in the fire control picture in three separate ways: (1) rainfall, (2) thunderstorm-induced winds, and (3) lightning fires set.

Rainfall and higher humidity are the principal benefits from thunderstorms. Eastern and central portions of the United States receive more rain from each storm, on the average, than occurs west of the Continental Divide. Because of moist air from the Gulf of Mexico, summertime surface dew-point averages range from the middle and high 50s in the Great Lakes region and New England states to the high 60s and low 70s from Texas to Georgia and Florida. These high moisture values may be compared to average summertime dew-point readings in the 30s and 40s over the plateau region and the Rocky Mountain region west of the Continental Divide. Since the air east of the Divide contains more moisture, thunderstorms in that section can precipitate more moisture. In addition, a higher percentage of rain reaches the ground from thunderstorm clouds in these Eastern areas. This is because the cloud bases are much lower and the humidity is much higher below the clouds. Thunderstorm cloud bases will average from 2,000 to 5,000 feet above the surface east of the Divide. West of the Divide bases usually range from 8,000 to 12,000 feet, and a sizable proportion of the rain usually evaporates in falling these long distances to the surface. In extreme cases cloud bases as

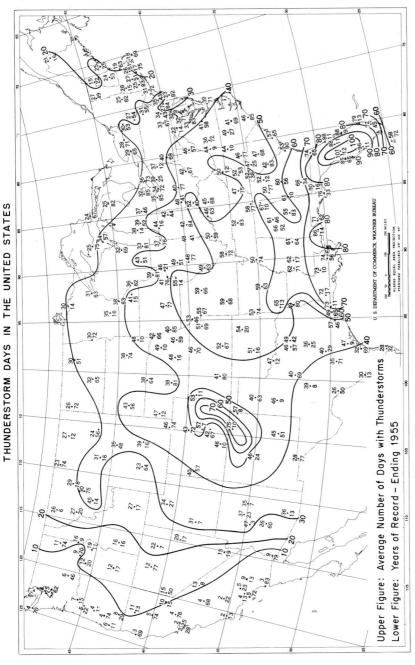

THUNDERSTORM DAYS IN THE UNITED STATES

U. S. DEPARTMENT OF COMMERCE, WEATHER BUREAU

Upper Figure: Average Number of Days with Thunderstorms
Lower Figure: Years of Record – Ending 1955

Figure 5.13 Average number of thunderstorm days annually in the United States.

high as 15,000 feet above the surface have been observed. It is because of these very high cloud bases that so-called "dry" thunderstorms frequently occur west of the Divide.

Not all the effects of thunderstorms are bad west of the Divide. Except for the western portions of Washington and Oregon, at least 90 percent of the scanty summertime rainfall comes from these storms. The low country of southern Idaho, central Washington, eastern Oregon, Nevada, and California has an average July–August rainfall of less than 1 inch. Slightly more than this occurs over the higher mountains.

The occurrence of lightning and man-caused fires throughout the Western states for the period 1940 to 1955 is given in Table 5.2. Seven states have a lightning-fire load exceeding 500 fires a year. Acreage-burned data are not available by states. During the same period, however, the National Forests in the six western regions report that lightning fires accounted for 33 percent of the total acreage burned. Lightning fires are a more serious fire fighting problem than is apparent from a review of Table 5.2 alone because of their tendency to concentrate both in time and place. Barrows (1951) reported that nearly 1,500 lightning fires occurred in Region One of the U.S. Forest Service (Montana, northern Idaho, and northeastern Washington) in the middle 10-day period of July, 1940. This created a nearly overwhelming overload for the fire organization.

As discussed in Chapter 4, ignition and persistence of fires depend

Table 5.2 Average Annual Number of Lightning Fires in the Western United States, 1940–1955*

State	Lightning fires		Total number of fires
	Number	Percent	
Arizona	1,252	84	1,486
California	936	26	3,608
Colorado	147	36	413
Idaho	1,000	69	1,458
Montana	608	71	852
Nevada	29	34	86
New Mexico	483	79	614
Oregon	969	52	1,860
South Dakota	107	62	173
Utah	82	35	236
Washington	506	28	1,807
Wyoming	98	62	157
Total	6,217	49	12,750

*Data courtesy Intermountain Forest and Range Experiment Station, U.S. Forest Service.

Figure 5.14 Ignition of partially dead ponderosa pine tree from lightning strike. Picture taken 30 seconds after strike occurred. *(U.S. Forest Service photo.)*

on the nature and condition of forest fuels. This is strongly reflected in the occurrence of lightning fires. For that reason high lightning frequency does not necessarily mean a high frequency of lightning fires. For example, the greatest frequency of thunderstorm activity in the West (Figure 5.13) is over southern Colorado and northern New Mexico, but Table 5.2 shows that Colorado does not have a bad lightning-fire problem. Again, thunderstorm frequency is relatively low over California and portions of eastern Oregon and Washington, but because of dryness of fuels in the summer, these areas have many more lightning fires than occur in other sections where the thunderstorm frequency is much greater.

Lightning storms occur in the Lake states, the Deep South, and Eastern areas, but because they are mostly wet storms accompanied by high humidity, the problem of lightning-set fires in most years is of minor importance compared with the West (Figure 9.1, Chapter 9).

Hagenguth (1951) indicates that lightning-stroke amperage ranges from about 2,000 to 130,000 amperes. That a wide range exists is borne out by fire lookouts and other observers. What if any effect amperages have in causing lightning fires is obscure.

Research on fire-setting lightning fires has been carried on near Missoula, Montana, for many years (Barrows, 1968). This research has been directed toward (1) a better understanding of lightning storms, (2) the specific characteristics of lightning strikes that cause ignition of forest fuels, and (3) the possibilities of reducing the number of such strikes through seeding of thunderstorm clouds. From evidence accumulated by Fuquay (1972), neither the voltage nor the amperage of the lightning stroke are the deciding factors. Yet the fire-setting stroke *is* distinctive. A longer current flow phase is its dominant character.

SPECIAL WEATHER CONDITIONS THAT FAVOR RAPID SPREAD OF FIRE

In the records of all forest fire-fighting agencies, only a small proportion of the fires that occurred reached a size of 10 acres or more. Most of these responded to fuel and weather conditions in a predictable manner, but always there are a few which behave in an erratic manner. These frequently account for a disproportionate part of the fire-fighting costs and damages.

One type of erratic behavior consists of a change in the usual relationship between rate of spread of the fire and slope of the terrain. There is little published mention of fires burning strongly downhill, yet fire control men agree that some of the worst fires develop when this occurs. With reference to unexplained extreme fire behavior Byram (1954) states: "Yet this . . . rapid downslope spread may happen in the middle of the afternoon when surface winds, if any, would be upslope. Fires have traveled across drainages—upslope and downslope—as though these did not exist." There are similar accounts of the behavior of fires under the influence of Santa Ana winds in southern California.

In mountainous country, very stable air usually tends to lie in the valleys with little movement, and under these conditions it favors easy fire control. But when low-level, very stable air is in motion, it tends to hug the surface. Because of this tendency it often creates special problems in the control of fires. There are three separate developments in which very stable air has been known to force fires strongly downhill. These are (1) passage of a dry cold front, (2) large-scale subsidence, and (3) thunderstorm downdrafts.

Dry Cold-front Passage

At times, as outlined in the discussion of fronts (pages 131–136), a cold air mass will move under warmer, less dense air which contains so little moisture that no condensation occurs as the warm air is lifted. The cooler air is sufficiently stable so that it scours out every ravine or drainage, moving downslope with slightly greater speed than it moves upslope. Any fire which the cold air influences will be spread almost without regard to topography. Dry, cold frontal passages occur rarely during the fire season west of the Divide. East of the Divide the occurrence is more common, with a greater frequency during periods of dry weather. This development has undoubtedly been responsible for cases of unexplained fire behavior. The role of dry cold fronts in creating critical fire weather is reviewed in detail for the United States by Schroeder and others (1964) and by Schroeder and Buck (1970).

Large-scale Subsidence

Subsidence is the settling, or lowering, of a mass of air. This motion is common to all warm high-pressure systems. Petterssen (1956) indicates the high incidence of a high-pressure pattern when subsidence is occurring. In an earlier investigation, Petterssen et al. (1944) indicate typical 6-hour vertical motions for subsiding air ranging from −4,820 feet at 30,000-foot elevation to −1,890 feet at about 10,000 feet. Subsiding air may originate at great heights, in extreme cases at or near the tropopause. At the point of origin, this air is very cold, but it has a high potential temperature.[2] Because of the extremely low initial temperature, the air contains little water vapor. As it lowers, this air is heated by compression. Since its potential temperature at point of origin is high, and since it is heated at the adiabatic rate, the result is a warm, exceedingly dry air mass when this air reaches lower levels.

It is easy to detect the base of these subsiding air masses by using an

[2]*Potential temperature* refers to the temperature an air mass would have if brought down to sea level.

adiabatic diagram. Their characteristics are a strong temperature inversion and a very sharp moisture decrease beginning at the base of the inversion. One can follow the change in movement of this air as it lowers by plotting the temperature and moisture values from successive radiosonde observations.

Subsiding air is usually much modified before it reaches the surface of the earth. When the base of this air reaches 8,000 to 10,000 feet above sea level, surface-induced convection currents begin to modify it. Modification by this convection is effective only during the daytime period. If there is considerable moisture in the lower strata of air, the overlying very dry air is so modified that there will be little noticeable effect at the earth's surface. At times, however, the subsidence mechanism persists strongly, with one surge of dry air following another. When this happens, the modifying convective columns become drier and drier and have less effect on the subsiding air. Under this condition, the convective circulation tends to bring the very dry air—modified only slightly—to the surface. See Figure 5.15 for a diagrammatic example of convection columns working on the base of a subsiding air mass.

As the subsiding air lowers, it may have horizontal motion imparted to it by the horizontal pressure gradient. If there is little pressure gradient at the surface, then horizontal motion may be unimportant. Under these

Figure 5.15   Idealized convection pattern modifying dry air at base of subsiding air mass.

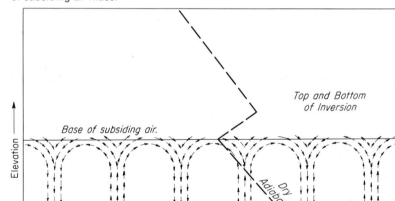

conditions the dry air will reach the surface in spots, and these spots will represent the descending portions of the convective columns.

Schroeder (1950) gives a detailed description of weather developments which bring high fire danger to the Lake states. He does not mention subsiding air, but he shows that high fire danger occurs under the influence of stagnant or slow-moving high-pressure systems. On several occasions W. R. Krum (1956) plotted appropriate soundings from the vicinity of serious fires in the Southeast and the New England states. In each case, when bad fire weather persisted for several days, he found very dry air a few thousand feet above the surface. It is believed that pure subsiding air does not reach the surface over the eastern half of the United States, but there is much evidence that modified subsiding air does reach the surface and that it causes some of the most severe fire weather situations.

Over the western portion of the United States, severe subsidence occurs more frequently than over the eastern portion. This is because of the topography, which seems to encourage stagnation of high-pressure systems over portions of the plateau region.

At times, high pressure may cover the entire western plateau region. High mountains border the plateau region on the east, west, and south and act to restrain the dense, stable air at low levels from moving away from the plateau. As a result of this damming action by the mountain, the very dry air from aloft flows over the denser air pocketed by the mountains toward low pressure on the leeward side. Since this air is drained off from the subsiding mass at moderately high levels and is heating adiabatically as it moves down the mountain slope, it arrives at low levels as a warm, extremely dry air mass. The Santa Ana winds of southern California and the Chinooks of Montana, Wyoming, and Colorado are the result of this type of development. Other examples are the Mono winds of central California, the northerly winds of the Sacramento Valley, and the east winds of Washington and Oregon. Usually the high-pressure system and the necessary leewardside low-pressure systems are located and oriented in such a manner that only one of this family of winds will be occurring at one time. However, cases have been identified by Krumm in which one huge subsiding air mass over the plateau region, with low pressure on the opposite sides of the mountains in several directions, has resulted in a Santa Ana, a Mono, an east wind, and a Chinook, all blowing simultaneously. In one such situation there was a prairie fire in Montana, a major fire in southern California, and troublesome fires in Oregon all occurring at the same time.

When this extremely dry subsiding air reaches the ground surface, there is little change in burning conditions from day to night. As a matter of fact, in southern California there is some evidence that Santa Ana winds may become worse after sunset. W. R. Krumm states that he has observed Santa Ana winds at night drive a brush fire down a steep mountain slope virtually to the sea.

At times subsiding air overlies cool, shallow marine air in portions of northwestern Oregon and western Washington. This can produce a very erratic fire weather situation. Humidity is high in this marine air mass, the top of which is marked by low stratus clouds overhead. Above these clouds, in the very dry air, fire danger is high and fires have burned vigorously on the higher mountain slopes with mild east wind conditions.

The most intense subsidence developments in the West occur in the fall and early winter, since high-pressure systems over the plateau region become stronger at that time of the year. While high pressure over the plateau region results in the most widespread situations of this nature, subsidence of high-level air also occurs in the West with other pressure-system combinations. For example, subsiding air from the Pacific high occasionally spills over the Coast Range of northern California and flows down the eastern slopes. The same thing happens at times on the east slopes of the Sierras in the Inyo-Mono section of California. In both of these areas there is a history of fires running down steep slopes under stable subsiding-air influence.

Thunderstorm Downdrafts

A downdraft occurs in the mature and dissipating stages of each thunderstorm cell. The onset of these winds is very abrupt, and the winds may be strong. Usually the winds will be of short duration—15 to 30 minutes—but in some cases may last almost an hour. Downdrafts blow radially away from the thunderstorm cloud at the surface. Strongest winds will be in the direction the thunderstorm is moving, but significant speeds may occur on the sides also. If a thunderstorm is moving directly toward a fire, the downdraft will drive the fire approximately in the direction of thunderstorm movement. If a thunderstorm approaches within 5 miles of a fire, there is danger that the fire may be affected (Figure 5.16). The air in these downdrafts is very stable and will drive the fire almost without regard to topography. Downdrafts may be troublesome in some areas east of the Continental Divide, but the moderate to heavy rains that usually accompany them may put fires out. West of the Divide, however, downdrafts are extremely dangerous. Krumm (1954) points out that these downdrafts are much stronger over the Rocky Mountain and plateau regions because of the much higher thunderstorm cloud bases. From dry thunderstorms in these regions, winds that reach between 60 and 70 miles per hour in peak gusts and that may drive fires down steep slopes have been measured. Frequently there is no rain at the surface before or after such occurrences.

The high cloud base and the deep, dry adiabatic environment from the surface to the cloud base obviously contribute to the violence of these winds. Byers and Braham (1949) indicate that the downward movement of air from the thunderstorm is initiated in the cloud by frictional drag of the falling raindrops. Krumm (1954) indicates that additional impetus occurs below the cloud, which he explains as follows:

> As the rain falls from the cloud base and evaporates into air below the cloud, it cools this air, resulting in progressively lower potential temperature at successive elevations below the cloud. It is likely that a moist adiabatic lapse rate is caused through perhaps 5000 to 6000 feet below the cloud base, after which there is little rain left for evaporation, and consequently a lesser rate of cooling occurs. Under circumstances of a progressively lower potential temperature than the environment, the cooler air would sink . . . and would probably accelerate in sinking.

The more severe of these downdrafts occur from thunderstorm clouds; however, there have been occurrences noted when there was no thunderstorm activity. If rain falls from any high-based cloud when surface temperatures are high and largely evaporates before reaching the surface, then local wind will blow radially away from the location of the rainfall.

Fire control men, in the plateau and northern Rocky Mountain regions particularly, need to be aware of these downdraft occurrences. With experience these dangerous winds can be foreseen in time to assure safety of personnel on a going fire. The beginning of rain—virga—from the cloud is the key indication to look for. As a thunderstorm moves past a fire, the direction of downdraft winds affecting the fire will change as the storm moves. If the storm moves to the north and east of the fire, the wind direction on the fire will change in a clockwise direction. Conversely, if a thunderstorm "sideswipes a fire" on the south and east, then the winds on the fire will change in a counterclockwise direction. This is illustrated in Figure 5.16. On the fire illustrated, fire fighters would be safest on the north and west sectors.

Other Special Conditions Conducive to Erratic Behavior

Instability Whenever a superadiabatic lapse rate exists near the ground or whenever active convection is occurring in the vicinity of a fire, a strong convection column quickly forms over the fire with a much

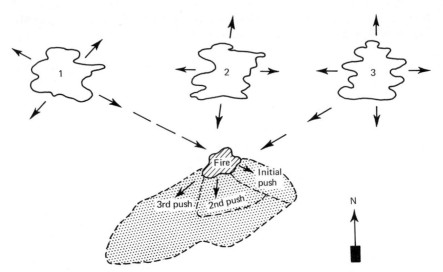

Figure 5.16 Potential effect of a passing dry thunderstorm on the spread of a fire.

increased combustion rate. Where fires occur in high-energy fuels, this condition may make fires uncontrollable for considerable periods.

Breakup of Inversions A converse situation exists when fires burn in stable air below an inversion. Usually such fires are slow-moving and easily controlled. But when the inversion is shallow, it may be overcome quickly by convection from below induced by the sun's radiation or by the fire itself. Sudden increases in the aggressiveness and rate of spread of fires are at times ascribed to the wiping out of an inversion and the release of the energy being suppressed by this barrier.

Wind Shear It is common, particularly in mountainous country, for wind direction and speed to vary at different levels above a given location. This often reflects local modification by topography and other factors already discussed, but it may be entirely the result of frontal movements. Whatever the cause, such conditions are often important to the success of fire control in their immediate area. Spot fires may be set in unanticipated quadrants, turbulence may be severe, and the convection column may be sheared off or may assume horizontal dimensions.

RELATION OF WEATHER MODIFICATION TO FOREST FIRE CONTROL

Precipitation has a profound effect on the ignition and spread of free-burning fires. For that reason, possibilities of inducing precipitation or of otherwise modifying the weather to reduce the severity of the fire problem are receiving growing attention in forest fire research as well as in meteorological research. There are two areas of principal interest. The first is the possibility of inducing increased precipitation in a specific target area to maintain favorable moisture conditions or of inducing precipitation as an emergency measure in a fire area. The second is the possibility of reducing the number or severity of fire-setting lightning strikes through cloud modification.

The potential of weather modification starts with the fact that 0°C or 32°F represent the melting point of ice but not necessarily the freezing point of water. Water vapor in the form of cloud droplets will remain in the liquid state far below the normal freezing point under certain conditions. This relationship enters into normal precipitation regimes. Two precipitation mechanisms are recognized: the ice-crystal or cold cloud and the warm cloud. The first is based on early research by Bergeron and Findeisen and has long been accepted by meteorologists. It holds that nearly all precipitation in temperate latitudes starts as ice crystals in supercooled clouds. Since vapor pressure over ice is less than that over water at below freezing temperatures, any ice crystal will grow rapidly at the expense of supercooled water droplets. If the water droplets are much more numerous than the ice crystals, the ice crystals grow large and drop out. Thus precipitation is initiated.

In the warm-cloud process, many believe that growth of water drops through collision in a saturated atmosphere is the principal mechanism that triggers, for example, tropical rains. Others believe that chance collision alone cannot account for the volume of water that precipitates and hold that salt or other hygroscopic nuclei operate in a mechanism similar to the cold-cloud ice-crystal growth.

In 1946, Dr. Vincent Schaefer brought about a new understanding of supercooled water vapor and ice-crystal relationships beginning with his studies of the causes of icing of aircraft. He demonstrated that ice crystals formed spontaneously at −39°C, but if suitable nuclei were present, they would form at temperatures much higher than this. His associate Dr. Vonnegut found that tiny crystals of silver iodide were very active as nuclei for ice crystals at temperatures up to −4°C.

These findings are the principal basis for weather modification efforts. Such activity has demonstrated that the water vapor in a supercooled cloud can be converted to ice crystals through cloud seeding. But the amount of precipitation is negligible unless moist, supercooled air continues to be fed into the system. Obviously, there must be moisture aloft before it can be precipitated. This drastically limits the chances of benefits from cloud seeding in fire emergencies. Some increase in precipitation through cloud seeding where moist air is lifted by topography ("orographic" lifting) has been demonstrated as a means of increasing the winter snow pack, but this too has very limited potential for reducing the fire problem.

The seeding of clouds to reduce their lightning-fire potential is based on several theories. One holds that heavy overseeding can produce so many tiny ice crystals that there is no supercooled water vapor left on which they can grow. This interrupts growth of the cloud and converts it to a cirrus formation, which tends to dissipate without building up its lightning potential. However, the relationships are very complex and are not yet fully understood. Continuing research in this field is needed. This will, it is hoped, yield much new insight into the lightning phenomenon and its fire-setting proclivities, even though no practical method is found for directly reducing lightning strikes through cloud seeding.

Attention is called to the paper entitled *Weather Modification and Forest Fires* (Donald M. Fuquay, 1967), which reports on the lightning-storm study often referred to as "Project Skyfire." This study has been conducted near Missoula, Montana, for many years by the Intermountain Forest Experiment Station of the U.S. Forest Service.

Chapter 6

Combustion of Forest Fuels

In Chapter 1 the general nature of the combustion process in woody fuels and its basic relationship to forestry were considered. In chapters following, the effects of fire on the forest, the physical attributes of forest fuels that determine their fire potential, and the weather relationships that vary the level of that potential were also examined.

With this background, a more specific analysis of what is known about the combustion process is in order. *What* happens when forest fuels burn and *why* they burn as they do has, for the most part, been reasonably well established, but only a few of the quantitative relationships in the process have been determined. For this reason emphasis is given in this chapter to quantitative measurement and evaluation of combustion phenomena. This discussion can serve as a foundation for the development of more accurate criteria and guidelines for fire control activities.

THE COMBUSTION PROCESS

Oxidation, Combustion, and Heat of Decomposition

Combustion is one of many types of oxidation processes. Some of these, including combustion, are chain reactions which take place rapidly at high temperatures. Other oxidation processes, such as the hardening of a coat of linseed oil in a paint film, take place very slowly at ordinary temperatures. Over a period of time, the oil film combines with oxygen in the air and hardens as it oxidizes. The process is slow, and the rate of heat release is so gradual that the temperature rise is negligible. However, there are conditions under which initially slow oxidation can terminate in a high-temperature chain-reaction combustion process. For example, a loose pile of rags or cotton waste saturated with linseed oil will undergo a temperature rise when the oil starts to oxidize because the cotton waste is a good insulator and retains much of the heat generated. The temperature rise increases the oxidation rate and vice versa, until a point is reached when the pile of cotton waste begins to smoke and ultimately bursts into flame.

The hardening of a film of linseed oil bears little resemblance to combustion. But some processes that resemble combustion are not oxidation reactions. An example is the thermal decomposition of wood—an exothermic reaction which occurs when wood substance is heated. This is usually referred to as the pyrolysis of wood. It always precedes combustion. In this reaction, wood breaks down into secondary products and releases heat. As soon as pyrolysis becomes active, flammable gases are released and ignition can take place from a pilot flame. Lacking such a source, the wood must reach a much higher temperature before spontaneous ignition can occur. If the wood specimen is well insulated, the temperature rise from pyrolysis will, in turn, increase the reaction rate and hence the rate of heat release. The accelerating rise of temperature continues until the volatile material ignites spontaneously or is distilled off and charcoal remains. It is difficult to state at what temperature the exothermic reaction becomes self-sustaining and provides the threshold to ignition. The rate of heating and the method of measurement strongly influence the values obtained. For rapid heating in an oven in which the temperature of the wood samples lags considerably behind the oven temperature, Stamm and Harris (1953) give the exothermic-reaction temperature as 523°F. However, for heating in an oven in which the temperature difference between the oven and sample is kept small by raising the temperature of the oven very slowly, the exothermic-reaction temperature may be much lower, possibly 300°F or even less. Since the exothermic reaction itself is often initiated by bacterial action and bacteria are killed at from 115°F to near the boiling point, this may well be the minimum temperature range for initiating pyrolysis under favorable natural conditions.

The heat of decomposition may result in combustion and is a common cause of fires in industrial processes. Such fires may arise when well-insulated wood-composition products are stored without sufficient cooling after receiving a final heat treatment. As mentioned in Chapter 4, the exothermic reaction is probably important in the persistence of ground fires in organic soil, although this relationship has not yet been fully established through research. The exothermic reaction does not require oxygen, so an insulated underground fuel would be a favorable environment.

Fires resulting from either the linseed-oil type of oxidation reaction ✹ or from the exothermic reaction are usually referred to as *spontaneous-combustion* fires. Such fires are a familiar problem in industrial and municipal environments but are rare in forest fire statistics.

Chemistry of Combustion

Combustion is a chemical phenomenon. A general formula illustrating its mirror-image relationship to photosynthesis has been cited in Chapter 1. A more specific formula for combustion can be illustrated by the equation for complete combustion of D-glucose sugar:

$$C_6H_{12}O_6 + 6O_2 \rightarrow 6CO_2 + 6H_2O + 1{,}211{,}000 \text{ Btu} \qquad (6.1)$$

This equation states that one molecule of the sugar, $C_6H_{12}O_6$, combines with six molecules of oxygen to give six molecules of carbon dioxide and six molecules of water plus 1,211,000 Btu of heat per pound mole of sugar burned. A pound mole is the weight of a substance in pounds equal to its molecular weight. The molecular weight of D-glucose is 180, so the heat of combustion is 1,211,000/180, or 6730 Btu per pound of sugar. A British thermal unit, or Btu, is 1/180 the quantity of heat required to raise the temperature of one pound of water from 32 to 212°F. The heat of combustion of a fuel may be defined as the quantity of heat released when a fuel has undergone complete oxidation or burning. In fire behavior work, a convenient unit of measure is Btu per pound of fuel.

Chemically, wood is a very complex substance, with cellulose and lignin the main constituents. Even the molecular weight of these basic substances is not known. However, the proportion of carbon, hydrogen, and oxygen atoms in wood can be expressed to a close approximation by the formula $C_6H_9O_4$. This formula does not represent the wood molecule, but in combustion calculations it can be treated as such. Its weight will therefore be referred to as the equivalent molecular weight.

All forest fuels contain moisture, the presence of which should be indicated in the combustion equation even though the moisture is chemically inert. The same is true of the nitrogen in the atmosphere. The equation for the complete combustion of wood with a moisture content M percent of its oven-dry weight is

$$4C_6H_9O_4 + 25O_2 + [0.322MH_2O + 94.0N_2] \rightarrow 18H_2O + 24CO_2$$
$$+ [0.322MH_2O + 94.0N_2] + 4,990,000 \text{ Btu} \qquad (6.2)$$

Moisture in the fuel and nitrogen in the air are shown as bracketed quantities because they do not take part in the combustion reaction. Throughout this text the fuel moisture content will always be expressed as a percent of the oven-dry weight of the fuel. If M is expressed in percent, it must be multiplied by a constant which is equal to 0.01 times the ratio of 4 pound moles of fuel to 1 pound mole of water. The equivalent molecular weight of wood is 145, and the molecular weight of water is 18, so the desired constant is $0.01 \times 4 \times 145/18$, or 0.322. The nitrogen symbol in Eq. (6.2) must be multiplied by a constant which is equal to 25 times the volume ratio of the quantities of nitrogen and oxygen in the atmosphere (other gases in the atmosphere being neglected). Because there is about 3.76 times as much nitrogen as oxygen by volume in the atmosphere, the desired constant is 25×3.76, or 94.0.

The heat of the combustion reaction in Eq. (6.2) is shown as 4,990,000 Btu for the 4 pound moles of fuel. This would be equivalent to $4,990,000/4 \times 145$, or 8600 Btu per pound of fuel. This figure, as well as the heats in Eqs. (6.1) and (6.2) based on the pound mole, is known as the "low" heat of combustion because it is based on the assumption that the water formed in the combustion reaction remains in the vapor or gaseous state. For low moisture contents, most of the water vapor in the combustion gases comes from the combustion reaction, but for moisture contents greater than 56 percent, the initial fuel moisture contributes the larger amount of water vapor.

The overall density of the combustion gases on the right side of Eq. (6.2) at a given temperature and pressure is affected by the initial fuel moisture. For low moisture contents, the gases are slightly heavier than air. If the fuel moisture content is greater than 23 percent, then the combustion gases are slightly lighter than air. Complete combustion is assumed in both instances.

Phases of Combustion

Although combustion of woody fuels has been termed a two-stage process in Chapter 1, it is often useful to identify three stages of combustion in a moving fire front. They overlap and all exist simultaneously. First is the preheating phase, in which fuel ahead of the flames is brought to its kindling or ignition point. Heating drives off moisture and begins the generation of flammable hydrocarbon gases. Ignition of these gases initiates the second phase and supplies more heat to rapidly complete the distillation process and the resultant flaming combustion. In the third and final phase, the residual charcoal is burned in what has previously been referred to as glowing combustion. Some carbon monoxide is formed as an intermediate product, which burns with a low blue flame to produce carbon dioxide; but for the most part the carbon burns as a solid, with oxidation taking place on the surface of the charcoal. Carbon dioxide only is produced.

The amount of heat energy released by the flaming stage compared to the glowing stage varies with fuels. Often glowing combustion associated with low flames from heavy fuels produces more British thermal units but at a slower rate. But considerable overlap enters in since only 30 to 40 percent of the heat of combustion of wood is in its carbon.

If combustion is not complete, some of the distilled hydrocarbons will remain suspended as very small droplets of liquid. These, plus residual carbonized particles which float in the air, are the familiar smoke that accompanies most fires. Some of the water vapor may also condense to give the smoke a whitish appearance.

The residual charcoal following the flaming stage varies in composition depending on the temperature at which distillation of hydrocarbons took place. If it was at the low end of the range 400° to 500°F, it will retain considerable tar coke and the carbon content may be as low as 60 percent. But at usual temperatures in a forest fire, the distillation will take place at 1500° or greater. At this level the charcoal is 96 percent carbon (Stamm and Harris, 1953, page 442).

Even though there is some overlap, the three phases of combustion can be plainly seen in a moving fire. First is the zone in which the leaves and grass curl and scorch as they are preheated by the oncoming flames. Next is the flame zone of burning gases. Following the flames is the third but less conspicuous zone of burning charcoal.

Combustion and the Energy Yield.   The energy which maintains the chain reaction of combustion is the heat of combustion[1]—a quantity which can be measured for any particular fuel. Heat transferred to unburned fuel raises its temperature to the point where the fuel, or the gases distilled from the fuel, can react with the oxygen in the atmosphere, and in so doing give off more heat. This, in turn, raises the temperature of

[1]Often referred to in engineering handbooks as heat value.

additional fuel, and thus the chainlike nature of combustion becomes established.

The heat energy released by burning forest fuels is high and does not vary widely between different types of fuels. The heat of combustion is given in Table 6.1 for a number of substances which approximate forest fuels. A little arithmetic shows that the burning of 1 pound of an average woody fuel gives off enough heat to raise the temperature of 100 pounds of water about 86°F. To raise the temperature of 100 pounds of water (about 12 gallons) from a temperature of 62°F to the boiling temperature (212°F at sea-level pressures) would require about 1.74 pounds of an average woody fuel if it burned with maximum efficiency. The combustion of about 1 pound of pitch would accomplish the same result.

The heat of combustion varies slightly for the wood of different species. It is a little higher for a coniferous species such as pine than for the hardwood species. This is a result of both the higher resinous content and higher lignin content of the conifers.

Heat Losses   The heats of combustion shown in Table 6.1 are the maximum values obtainable because they represent complete combustion conditions obtained in a bomb calorimeter. The heat evolved under forest fire conditions is not precisely known, but it is less because combustion is not complete under natural conditions. In addition, certain heat losses must be taken into account in estimating the energy budget of forest fires. For this reason it is necessary to use a smaller heat value which may be defined as the heat yield, in fire behavior work. Physically it is, to a very

Table 6.1   The Heat of Combustion of Some Woods, Woody Materials, and Pitch as Given by Carmen (1950)

Substance	Heat of combustion for oven-dry material, Btu/pound
Wood (oak)	8,316
Wood (beech)	8,591
Wood (pine)	9,153
Wood (poplar)	7,834
Pine sawdust	9,347
Spruce sawdust	8,449
Wood (shavings)	8,248
Pecan shells	8,893
Hemlock bark	8,753
Pitch	15,120
Average (excluding pitch)	8,620

close approximation, the quantity of heat per pound of fuel burned which passes through a cross section of the convection column, or smoke plume, above a fire which is burning in a neutrally stable atmosphere.[2] The only restriction on the height of the cross section above the surface of the earth is that it be in that part of the convection column which radiates a negligible amount of energy and receives a negligible amount of radiation from the fire. Probably any height greater than five times the flame height would be adequate, because most of the radiant energy from a fire originates in the combustion zone. Like the heat of combustion, the heat yield is measured in British thermal units per pound. Numerically, it is equal to the heat of combustion minus the heat losses resulting from radiation, vaporization of moisture, and incomplete combustion.

Total radiation measurements on a fire are difficult to make and nearly always have a sizable margin of error. In addition, the fraction of the energy given off as radiation may be affected by the intensity of the fire as well as by the size and shape of the burning area. Measurements of the heat radiated from wood-crib fires (Fons et al., 1960) gave an average of 17 percent of the heat of combustion based on 15 fires. To this needs to be added a part of the heat in the concrete slab under the fire plus some correction for unburned fuel. Based on this data, a working value of 20 percent may be assumed. If a heat of combustion of 8600 Btu per pound is assumed, this places total radiant energy at 1720 Btu per pound.

In estimating the heat yield, not all radiant energy can be considered lost. Some is absorbed by the smoke in the convection column directly above the fire. Also, that part of the radiation responsible for the temperature rise of preheated but unburned fuel cannot be considered lost. So the actual loss would be less than 1720 Btu per pound of fuel, possibly 1200 Btu per pound.

Because of the presence of moisture, heat is required (1) to raise the temperature of water in fuel, (2) to separate the bound water from the fuel, (3) to vaporize the water in the fuel, and (4) to heat the water vapor up to the flame temperature. However, only requirements 2 and 3 can be treated as heat losses. Also, for high-intensity fires, requirement 3 may be only a partial loss[3] but will be considered a complete loss. These heat requirements are summarized in Table 6.2, which also includes the vaporization heat requirement for the water of reaction. Complete combustion is assumed for the Table 6.2 values. Requirements 1 and 4 are not heat losses because the heat is stored in the combustion products (CO_2

[2]The reasons for basing the standard on a neutrally stable atmosphere are given in Chap. 7.

[3]For small fires, the heat required to vaporize the fuel moisture should be considered a heat loss. For large fires, it may be only a partial loss because part of this moisture sometimes condenses high in the convection column in the form of a white cloud cap.

Table 6.2   Water Heat Requirements for the Combustion of 1 Pound of Wood Fuel

Nature of heat requirement	Heat requirements in Btu with oven-dry percent moisture content of:				
	0	10	25	50	100
For initial moisture:					
1. Raising the temperature of water from 62 to 212°F	0	15	37	75	150
2. Separation of bound water from wood (heat of desorption)	0	31*	48*	50*	50*
3. Vaporization of water	0	97*	243*	486*	972*
4. Heating of superheated vapor from 212°F to a flame temperature of 1600°F	0	70	175	350	700
For water of reaction (based on 0.559 pound of water):					
5. Vaporization of water	543*	543*	543*	543*	543*
Total water heat loss (sum of requirements 2, 3, and 5)	543*	671*	834*	1,079*	1,565*

Heat requirements are expressed in Btu for moisture contents of 0, 10, 25, 50, and 100 percent. Asterisks indicate actual heat losses.

and H_2O vapor), in the residual inert nitrogen, and in the excess entrained air.

The weight of the water of reaction as computed from Eq. (6.2) is 0.559 pound per pound of wood fuel burned. The heat required to vaporize 0.559 pound of water is 543 Btu and is independent of the initial fuel moisture. Because of the constancy (for any given fuel) of the heat stored in the vapor of the water of reaction, engineers sometimes subtract this heat from the heat of combustion to obtain what is known as the "low" heat of combustion.

The heat yield for complete combustion for any given moisture content can be computed by the following procedure. Add the radiation loss, 1200 Btu per pound of fuel, to the total water heat loss (the last row of values in Table 6.2). Subtract the result from the estimated heat of combustion, 8600 Btu per pound (Table 6.1). Repeat the computation for different moisture contents, and plot the results as a function of fuel moisture. This procedure is illustrated in Fig. 6.1, which shows the heat yield as a function of fuel moisture.

Because curve A is computed for complete combustion, it represents the maximum, or limiting, value of the heat yield for forest fires. However, one of the largest heat losses may be a result of incomplete combustion. Actually, this is heat not produced rather than heat lost, but it amounts to the same thing. Most of the loss takes place in the second phase of combustion, in which the distilled gases are burned. Combustion appears to be more complete on small fires than on large fires; hence the heat yield should be greater for the small fires. Incomplete combustion on major fires is indicated by the occasional flashes which can extend upward several hundred feet in the convection column. In the intervals between flashes, part of the distilled-fuel fractions are escaping unburned.

Although the efficiency, or completeness, of combustion for forest fires is not known, the heat loss must be estimated in making energy calculations. There are several rough guidelines for doing this from the appearance of the smoke and flame, intensity of fire, and average moisture content of the fuel which burns. The combustion efficiency should be greatest for a low-intensity fire in a dry fuel, such as cured grass, which burns with bright-yellow flames and very little smoke. For a major high-intensity fire burning with dull-red flames and giving off large quantities of dark smoke, the combustion efficiency should be considerably lower. The increase in quantity of smoke with increasing fuel moisture for a fire of any size indicates decreasing combustion efficiency with increasing moisture content.

Curve *B* in Fig. 6.1 represents a tentative heat-yield estimate for

Figure 6.1   Heat yield of combustion as a function of fuel moisture content. *A.* Complete combustion. *B.* Estimate for small fires. *C.* Estimate for large fires.

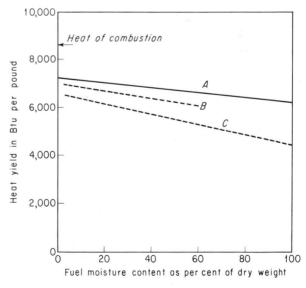

small fires (flame height 1 to 4 feet) as a function of fuel moisture content. The curve is terminated at about 60 percent because small fires will not burn at higher moisture contents in most fuels. Curve *C* is a similar estimate for high-intensity fires (flame height 50 to 200 feet). High-intensity fires can burn in fuels with much higher moisture contents than can low-intensity fires. Also, the average moisture content of the fuel which burns in a large fire is higher than for a small fire because of the larger proportion of green material, such as needles and green brush, which is consumed.

It will be observed from all three curves, *A*, *B*, and *C*, that the moisture content of fuel does not reduce heat yield sufficiently to account for the very profound effect fuel moisture has been found to have on the ignition and spread of fire.

FACTORS AFFECTING THE RATE OF ENERGY RELEASE

Figure 6.1 can be used to estimate the energy released in a forest fire if the quantity of fuel per unit area and its average moisture content are known. This energy is an important quantity, but of even more immediate significance to fire behavior is the *rate* of energy release. This rate is closely related to fuel energy but depends also on the fuel combustion rate.

Fuel Moisture

The effect of fuel moisture on the burning rate of wood fuel is so pronounced and so obvious that no measurements are needed to illustrate its overall effect. However, the mechanisms by which water affects the burning rate are not so simple. Curve *A* in Figure 6.1 shows that the presence of a relatively large amount of water in wood produces a relatively small decrease in the heat yield for optimum or complete combustion conditions.

The most important effect of fuel moisture in reducing the burning rate may be described as a smothering process in which water vapor coming out of the fuels dilutes the oxygen in the air surrounding the fuel. For the higher moisture contents, the pressure of the heated water vapor coming out of the fuel may nearly equal the atmospheric pressure. The sum of the pressures of all the gases (oxygen, nitrogen, carbon dioxide, and water vapor) surrounding the fuel must equal the atmospheric pressure. Hence if the pressure of the water vapor itself is nearly equal to the atmospheric pressure, then most of the oxygen as well as other gases will be excluded from the space immediately adjacent to the fuel. Combustion of flammable gases cannot occur under this condition. First enough water has to boil out of the fuels to permit enough buildup of oxygen to support combustion. The smothering effect of water vapor or any other inert gas is closely related to the phenomenon of flammability limits.

The flammability limits for the gases distilled from wood substance are not known but should approximate those for vapors of liquid hydrocarbon fuels. This comes in the familiar area of the functioning of a gasoline engine. The engine can operate only when its oxygen-gas mixture ignites and burns. The upper flammability limit determines how "rich" a gas-air mixture can be and still burn. The corresponding lower limit determines how "lean" the mixture can be and still burn. These limits, as given by Newman (1950), do not vary greatly for the vapors of several liquid hydrocarbon fuels. Benzene vapor, for which the upper and lower limits are, respectively, 6.75 and 1.35 percent by volume, is a representative example. This means that if there is more than 6.75 percent or less than 1.35 percent of benzene vapor by volume in an air–benzene-vapor mixture, combustion cannot take place. Newman (1950) also gives data for computing the flammability limits when the air contains an inert gas such as water vapor. If the air is replaced by a mixture of air and water vapor to form an air–water-vapor–benzene-vapor mixture, the benzene-vapor content (in percent of the total volume of the mixture) is decreased for the upper flammability limit and simultaneously raised for the lower limit. For example, if the air–water-vapor component is by volume 22 percent water vapor and 78 percent air, the upper and lower limits for benzene vapor by volume become about 5 percent and 1.6 percent of the total volume of the air–water-vapor–benzene-vapor mixture. As the water-vapor content of the air–water-vapor component of the mixture is still further increased, the two flammability limits come closer together and meet at a critical value of about 2.4 percent (that is, benzene vapor will be 2.4 percent of the total gaseous mixture by volume). The air–water-vapor component now contains about 36 percent water vapor and 64 percent air by volume. If the water-vapor content is higher than 36 percent, the benzene vapor will not burn. The flammability-limit values would probably be somewhat different for the burning of gases distilled from wood, but the basic principles would be the same.

Because the products of the combustion reaction must share a part of their heat with the inert moisture evaporated from the fuels, there is a resulting reduction in flame temperature. This could possibly have a significant effect in reducing the rate of fire spread. Flame-temperature measurements show considerable variation. The thermocouple measurements of Fons (1946) for several different kinds of fuel give a mean value of 1500°F. Vehrencamp (1955) gives 2000°F for the flame temperature but states that his value may be rather high. A compromise choice might be 1800°F for fuels with a low moisture content and 1600 or 1700°F for fuels with a high moisture content of 40 percent or more based on conventional measurement. However, recent studies of thermocouple technology indicate that actual flame temperatures are 300 to 500° higher than readings obtained by conventional techniques. Consequently the above values are conservative.

Wind

Air movement is always a major factor in combustion rate since it directly affects the rate of oxygen supply to burning fuel. Also, strong winds increase the rate of fire spread by tilting the flames forward so that unburned fuel receives energy by radiation and convection at an increased rate. These two mechanisms are especially important in causing smaller fires to build up their intensity.

The speed of the wind, both at the earth's surface and aloft, appears to have a dominant role in controlling the convection process over large fires and hence in determining the intensity that such fires will reach. The relationship of air movement to fire behavior is discussed in Chapter 7.

Heat Transfer

Heat is transferred in three primary ways, by conduction, convection, and radiation. The carrying of embers and firebrands ahead of the fire (the familiar phenomenon of spotting), although dependent on convection, is a type of ignition-point transfer and is equivalent to a fourth means of heat transfer.

As a heat-transfer mechanism, conduction is of much greater importance in solids than in liquids and gases. It is the only way heat can be transferred within opaque solids. By means of conduction, heat passes through the bottom of a teakettle or up the handle of a spoon in a cup of hot coffee.

Convection is the transfer of heat by the movement of a gas or liquid. For example, heat is transferred from a hot-air furnace into the interior of a house by convection, although the air picks up heat from the furnace by conduction.

Radiation is the type of energy one feels when sitting across the room from a stove or fireplace. It travels in straight lines with the speed of light. Radiative heating of fuels ahead of a flame front decreases rapidly with distance. For a fire that occupies a small area and can be thought of as a "point" (such as a small bonfire or a spot fire), the intensity of radiation varies inversely as the square of the distance from the fire. For example, only one-fourth as much radiation would be received at 10 feet as at 5 feet from the fire. If the fire is stretched out in one dimension, such as a long line of low-intensity backfire, the intensity of radiation does not decrease so rapidly with increasing distance from the fire. In this case the intensity varies inversely as the distance from the fire; the intensity at 10 feet would be about half as great as at 5 feet. For a fire front of two dimensions, as is approximated by the wall of flame at the front of a large fire, the intensity of radiation drops off even more slowly. This tendency for radiation to maintain its intensity in front of a large fire is an important factor in the rapid increase of the fire's energy output.

Convection, with some help from radiation, is the principal agent of heat transfer from a ground fire to the crowns of a conifer stand. Hot gases rising upward dry out the crown canopy above and raise its temperature to the kindling point. Although convection initiates crowning, both convection and radiation preheat the crown canopy ahead of the flames. The effects of both radiation and convection in preheating are considerably increased when a fire spreads upslope, because the flames and hot gases are nearer the fuels. The opposite is true for downslope spread.

Convection and radiation can transfer heat only to the surface of unburned (or burning) fuel. Radiant heat may penetrate a few thousandths of an inch into woody substances, and this penetration may be of some significance in the burning of thin fuels such as grass blades and leaves. However, radiation, like convection, for the most part transfers heat only to the surface of fuel material. Conduction consequently may be considered the only means of heat transfer inside individual pieces of fuel. For this reason conduction is one of the main factors limiting the rate of burning in heavy fuels, such as logging slash, heavy limbs, and logs in blowdown areas. Materials that are poor conductors of heat, such as punky wood, ignite more readily than do the better conductors, such as sound wood, but they burn more slowly.

Convection is perhaps the most important single heat-transfer mechanism in determining behavior of the free-burning fire. Its role in ignition and in sustained combustion is easily demonstrated with a kitchen match, by comparing the flame and its rate of travel up or down a vertically held matchstick. It is convection that gives significance to the geometry of arrangement of fuel particles in the fuel bed and of fuel components in the forest stand. It is convective heat transfer that accounts for most of the effect of topography and of wind. In very intense fires the migration of superheated gases over considerable distances, away from their origin, is a convection phenomenon that accounts for many aspects of unusual behavior of the conflagration-type fire.

The predominant role of convection in the wind-driven fire was well illustrated by small model fires in liquid fuels with a pattern of cotton tufts dispersed downwind. (Byram, Clements, et al., 1963, 1966.) When wind was applied to these stationary fires, the convection column was displaced rather than deflected and turbulent jets of flame descended to lick the surface. These darted out to ignite cotton tufts well beyond the range of preheating by radiation. Such ignition distances across surfaces free of fuel were equivalent to very wide firebreaks if converted to full scale.

Fuel Size and Arrangement

The effect of physical characteristics of forest fuels has been discussed in some detail in Chapter 4. The most relevant factors after fuel moisture content relate to size and arrangement of the fuel member.

For a given amount of fuel per unit area, the rate of burning increases with increasing surface area of the fuel provided there is an adequate oxygen supply. This is why a pile of finely split kindling burns faster than does a pile of larger pieces of wood containing the same volume of fuel.

The effect of size and arrangement of fuel on combustion can be illustrated by the following example. Consider a large pile of dry logs all about 8 inches in diameter. Although somewhat difficult to ignite, the log pile will burn with a hot fire that may last for two or three hours. The three primary heat-transfer mechanisms are all at work. Radiation and convection heat the surfaces of the logs, but only conduction can transfer heat inside the individual logs. Since conduction is the slowest of the three heat-transfer mechanisms, it limits the rate of burning. Consider now a similar pile of logs that have been split across their diameters twice, or quartered. Assume that the logs are piled in an overall volume somewhat greater than the first pile, so there will be ample ventilation. This log pile will burn considerably faster than the first one because the burning rate is less dependent on conduction. The surface area was more than doubled by the splitting, so that convection and radiation are correspondingly increased in the preheating effects. The burning surface is also increased by the same amount.

Assume that the splitting action is continued until the logs are in an excelsior state and occupy a volume thirty or forty times as great as in their original form. Convective and radiative heat transfer will be increased tremendously in the spaces throughout the whole fuel volume, and the rate of burning might be increased to a point where the fuel could be consumed in a few minutes instead of hours.

The effect of fuel arrangement can be visualized if a volume of excelsiorlike fuel, such as that just described, is compressed until it occupies a volume only four or five times that of the original volume of logs. The total surface and radiative conditions are the same as before compression, but both convective heat exchange and oxygen supply are greatly reduced. There will be a corresponding decrease in the rate of combustion.

Fuel size and fuel arrangement have their greatest effect on the lower-intensity fires and in the initial stages of the buildup of a major fire. When a fire reaches conflagration proportions, the effect on fire behavior of factors such as quantity of firebrand material available for spotting and the frequency of its ignition may be greater than the effect of fuel size and arrangement.

FUEL-WATER RELATIONSHIPS

Moisture in fuels has such a significant effect on combustion and fire behavior that it is a key variable in fire danger rating (Chapter 8). The moisture part of a fire danger rating system is equivalent to a method for keeping books on the forest fuel moisture budget. An understanding of the variations in the flammability of forest fuels requires a knowledge of the factors which control the moisture of the fuels.

The moisture content of the nonliving fuels has a wide range. It seldom goes below 2 percent but can exceed 200 percent for fuels such as punky wood and duff after a prolonged rain. The moisture content of living vegetation is less variable. For the living material which burns in a high-intensity fire, such as green leaves and needles, twig endings, and brush up to 3 inches in diameter, the moisture content usually ranges from 75 to 150 percent of its dry weight.

The main weather variables which control the moisture of nonliving fuel are rainfall, relative humidity, and temperature. Wind and sunshine are important factors in fuel drying, but they exert their influence by modifying the temperature of the fuels and the temperature and relative humidity in the thin air film adjacent to the fuels.

The only way in which fuels with a moisture content of 25 or 30 percent can gain a further appreciable increase in moisture is by rainfall. However, fuels exposed to the open sky on a clear, cloudless night gain considerable moisture in lowland locations by collecting dew. The mechanism involved is radiation cooling and is described by Byram (1943).

Woody materials can literally take moisture out of the air, although the presence of air as such has nothing to do with the hygroscopic process. The water which wood takes from the air is called bound water.

Its properties are different from those of free or ordinary water; the boiling point is higher, the freezing point lower, its density greater, and its vapor pressure lower. Energy is required to separate the bound water from wood, as indicated in Table 6.2. When wood substance is taking moisture from the air, the process is called adsorption. When wood is giving up bound water, the process is known as desorption. The amount of bound water in fuels is determined to some extent by temperature, but relative humidity is the main controlling factor. Wood that is neither gaining nor losing moisture in an environment of constant relative humidity and temperature is said to be in equilibrium with that particular humidity-temperature combination.

Temperature and relative humidity also have a pronounced effect on the rate at which bound water is lost or gained by forest fuels when equilibrium conditions do not exist. Actually, equilibrium conditions are a rare exception rather than the rule. Forest fuels are usually gaining or losing moisture as the temperature and relative humidity go through their daily cycle. Superimposed on the daily cycle are smaller random fluctuations in the two variables which cause them to change from minute to minute. Variations in temperature and relative humidity, in combination with fuel size, produce complex lag effects. In the case of the thinnest grass blades, the lag may be of an order of magnitude that can be measured in minutes. The lag time increases with size of fuel and for large logs may be of such a length that it would have to be measured in terms of months or even years (Chapter 8).

The complex field of wood-water relationships is discussed in greater detail in publications by Stamm and Harris (1953); Stamm (1946); Byram and Jemison (1943); Byram, (1963); Nelson (1968); Simard (1968); and in Chapter 8.

COMBUSTION OF FOREST FUELS

Before considering combustion as it actually occurs in the fuels of the forest, it is desirable to define specific combustion and fire behavior terms and to establish units of measurement, which thus far have been used in a general sense only.

Available fuel, the quantity of fuel that actually burns in a forest fire has been discussed in Chapter 4. It varies widely with fuel moisture conditions and with fuel thickness and geometry of arrangement. But it varies too with the duration and intensity of fire; for example, more fuel usually burns in a fire spreading with the wind than in a fire spreading against the wind.

The primary unit for the measurement of available fuel in energy calculations is pounds per square foot. But the more common unit in field measurements is tons per acre. Conversion factors for different units are given in Table 6.3 for several basic quantities used in combustion and fire behavior.

Total fuel is the quantity of fuel which would burn under the driest conditions with the highest-intensity fire. The virtue of introducing the concept of total fuel is that it sets a maximum value for the available fuel. Total fuel is measured in the same units as available fuel.

Available fuel energy is the amount of energy released when the available fuel burns. It is measured in British thermal units per square foot and is numerically equal to the product of the available fuel and the heat yield.

When dealing with convective phenomena over large fires, the available fuel energy must be replaced by what may be defined as the fuel energy available for convection (Chapter 7). With the exception of fuels

Table 6.3   Units and Conversion Factors for Some of the Basic Variables Employed in Combustion and Fire Behavior Calculations

Variable	Unit of measurement	Conversion factor per unit and alternate units
Quantity of fuel (available and total)	Pounds per square foot	21.8 (tons per acre)
	Tons per acre	0.0459 (pounds per square foot)
Fuel energy (available and total)	Btu per square foot	
Rate of spread:		
Forward rate of spread	Feet per second	0.682 (miles per hour)
	Feet per second	60.0 (feet per minute)
	Miles per hour	1.47 (feet per second)
	Feet per minute	0.0167 (feet per second)
Rate of area spread	Acres per hour	12.1 (square feet per second)
	Square feet per second	0.0826 (acres per hour)
Rate of perimeter increase	Chains per hour	1.1 (feet per minute)
	Feet per minute	0.909 (chains per hour)
Fire intensity	Btu per second per foot	
Total fire intensity	Btu per second	
Combustion rate	Btu per second per square foot	
Heat yield	Btu per pound	
Heat of combustion	Btu per pound	

which have components which require a long time to burn out, such as logs and heavy limbs, these two energies are ordinarily equal.

Total fuel energy bears the same relationship to the available fuel energy as does total fuel to available fuel.

Rate of spread is a general term used to describe the rate at which a fire increases either its area or linear dimensions. In fire behavior, one of the most useful measures is the forward rate of spread, for which the primary unit is feet per second. A related unit is miles per hour. Other units are given in Table 6.3, including units for area rate of spread.

Fire intensity is the rate of energy release, or rate of heat release, per unit time per unit length of fire front. Numerically, it is equal to the product of the available fuel energy and the forward rate of spread. It is also equal to the product of the available fuel, the heat yield, and the forward rate of spread. The primary unit is British thermal units per second per foot of fire front. Because fuel requires time to burn, the heat release will not be confined to the leading edge of the fire but will extend back through the depth of the zone in which combustion is taking place. For a fire backing slowly into the wind, this may be only a few inches deep, and the fire intensity may be as low as 5 Btu per second per foot of fire front. In a major fast-spreading fire, the depth of the burning zone might be $1/4$ mile or more and the fire intensity in the neighborhood of 30,000 Btu per second per foot of fire front.

Total fire intensity is the rate of heat release for a fire as a whole. The primary unit is British thermal units per second. Total fire intensity is not as useful a concept as fire intensity, but it affords an effective means of comparing the total rate of energy output of a fire with that of other sources such as a thunderstorm or a house furnace.

The *combustion rate* is the rate of heat release per unit of burning area per unit of time. It might also be termed the unit area burning rate in forest fuels. The primary measurement is British thermal units per second per square foot of ground area. This is an important basic variable related primarily to fuel size, fuel arrangement, and fuel moisture. Factors such as size of burning area and wind speed may have a relatively small influence on the combustion rate, but this has not yet been determined. The combustion rate should not be confused with fire intensity, which is a different type of variable.

Fire Intensity and Associated Fire Characteristics

Fire intensity expressed in British thermal units per second per foot of fire front has more meaning if it can be associated with specific characteristics, such as what the fire looks like, what it sounds like, and how fast it travels. This can be accomplished by starting at the bottom of the fire-intensity scale and working up to the higher-intensity fires.

Fire intensity can be written as the simple equation

$$I = Hwr \qquad\qquad (6.3)$$

where I = fire intensity in British thermal units per second per foot of fire front

  H = heat yield in British thermal units per pound of fuel

  w = weight of available fuel in pounds per square foot

  r = rate of spread in feet per second

Equation (6.3) can also be written as $I = Er$, where E is the available fuel energy which is equal to the product Hw.

For a homogeneous idealized fuel which has a constant combustion rate R, the fire intensity may also be written as

$$I = Rd$$

where d = depth of burning strip of fuel.[4]

Figure 6.2 shows the rate of spread in feet per second plotted as a function of wind speed in miles per hour. The data[5] in this figure were obtained on small test fires on the Francis Marion National Forest in South Carolina. The light fuels were fairly uniform mixtures of grass and pine needles in rather open longleaf and loblolly stands and weighed approximately 0.1 pound per square foot, or about 2 tons per acre. Wind speeds are shown as negative for fires burning against the wind. This method of representation results in a complete wind-speed scale ranging from negative wind speeds through zero (calm conditions) up into the positive, or headfire, winds. The rate-of-spread curve is shown as a broken line in the headfire region of the diagram because the scarcity of points makes its position uncertain there. It will be noticed that backing fires spread faster into the stronger winds than they did into the lighter winds. This relationship has not been confirmed by test fires in the laboratory except in nonflaming fuels (Murphy et al., 1966), though it has been observed at times in field-test fires. There are two clues to this observed effect. One is that highly porous fuel arrangements which are

---

[4]Some refer to the distance the flaming zone extends back from the leading edge as the *width*. To avoid confusion, the term *depth* is used in this chapter.

[5]Rate of spread as such was not the main purpose of the experimental fires on which the data for Fig. 6.2 were obtained, and no attempt was made to isolate the effects of fuel moisture. Some of the scatter for individual observations is a result of fuel moisture variation. Most of the observed points are for fires backing into the wind rather than burning with the wind because the test fires were part of a prescribed burning study.

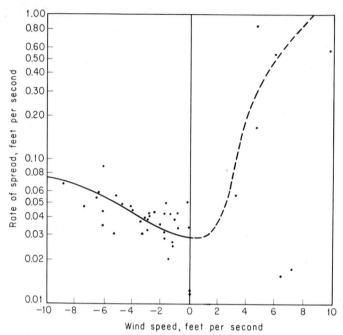

Figure 6.2 Rate of spread (mostly for backing fires) in light grass-needle fuels for different wind speeds measured at approximately 3 feet above the ground.

penetrated in part by the wind increase their burning rate with the increased ventilation induced by stronger winds. The second is a probable eddy effect in the airflow.

Estimates of fire intensity can be readily made from the rates of spread shown in Figure 6.2. For example, consider a fire spreading 0.04 foot per second. Combustion efficiency on these low-intensity fires at the lower fuel moisture contents should be high, so the heat yield might be as much as 6500 Btu per pound of fuel (dry-weight basis). If the available fuel is 0.1 pound of fuel per square foot, Eq. (6.3) shows that the intensity of this fire would be $0.04 \times 6500 \times 0.1$, or 26 Btu per second per foot of fire front. Very few fires burning in forest fuels would have an intensity as low as 2 or 3 Btu per second per foot of fire front. Most prescribed fires burning against the wind travel at a rate of 0.03 to 0.06 foot per second. If the available fuel is 0.10 to 0.15 pound of fuel per square foot (roughly 2 to 3 tons per acre) their intensities in this case would range from about 19 to 58 Btu per second per foot. The burning zone would be less than a foot deep, and the flames about 12 to 20 inches high. The flame length would be somewhat longer, possibly $2^{1}/_{2}$ feet, because the flames would be tilted over by the wind. By moving briskly one could step over the fire without getting burned.

Going up the scale of fire intensity into the headfire region of Figure 6.2, a fire spreading 0.25 foot per second would have an intensity of about 160 Btu per second per foot of fire front if the available fuel is 0.1 pound per square foot and the heat yield is 6500 Btu per pound. This intensity is probably near the maximum for headfires or flanking fire[6] that could be used in prescribed burning work. Ordinarily, backing fires are used in prescribed burning, but in the older stands flanking fires are used as well as headfires, which are not permitted to run for long distances. A fire with an intensity of 160 Btu per second per foot would have flames 4 or 5 feet in length.

On that sector of their perimeter which burns with the wind, a majority of wildfires probably have intensities in the range from 100 to 1000 Btu per second per foot of fire front. For an available fuel of 0.1 pound per square foot and a heat yield of 6500 Btu per pound, a fire would have to spread at a rate of 1.54 feet per second to develop an intensity of 1000 Btu per second per foot. This is nearly twice the intensity of the fastest-spreading experimental fire represented in Figure 6.2. Ordinarily, a fire with this intensity would be burning in heavier fuel but not spreading so fast. For example, if the available fuel was 0.3 pound of fuel per square foot (a little over 6 tons per acre), the corresponding rate of spread to give an intensity of 1000 Btu per second per foot would be about 0.51 foot per second. This would be considered a fairly hot fire. The flames would average about 9 feet in length, and considerable radiant heat could be felt 30 or 40 feet from the blaze. The roar of the flames would be accompanied by occasional explosive and whistling sounds. Foliage and small twigs on much of the green understory brush would be consumed and thus become a part of the fuel. There would be occasional flashes into the crowns in conifer stands, especially where there was draping of dead fuels over brush and the lower part of the crown canopy was less than 20 feet of the ground.

An approximate relation between the flame length h in feet and the fire intensity I is given by the equation

$$h = 0.45 I^{0.46} \tag{6.4}$$

which on comparison with Eq. (6.3) can be written as

$$h = 0.45(Hwr)^{0.46} \tag{6.5}$$

[6]A flank fire represents the spread roughly at right angles to the direction of forward spread.

This is well supported by a study of scaling laws (Byram, 1966). Equation (6.5) is represented by the diagram in Figure 6.3 in which the flame length, h, is plotted as a function of the rate of spread, r, for different values of the available fuel, w. The heat yield, H, was given a constant value of 6000 Btu per pound of fuel. A diagram of this sort could serve as a rough guide for estimating the width of firebreak needed to stop a fire of any expected intensity provided that severe spotting has not started. For example, assume that the width of a firebreak needs to be 1.5 times the flame length. Then this width can be estimated from estimates of the available fuel and the expected rate of spread.

Equations (6.4) and (6.5) will give too low a flame for high-intensity crown fires because much of the fuel is a considerable distance above the ground. However, this can be corrected for by adding half of the mean canopy height to h. For example, if Eq. (6.5) gave an estimated value of h of 40 feet and the mean canopy height is 60 feet, then the corrected estimate is 70 feet.

Equations (6.4) and (6.5) are better approximations for low-intensity than for high-intensity fires. They are based on the assumption that the leading edge of the fire is a long straight line and that the fire intensity is constant. However, the leading edge of a high-intensity fire tends to curve

Figure 6.3 Approximate relationship between flame length, available fuel, and rate of spread.

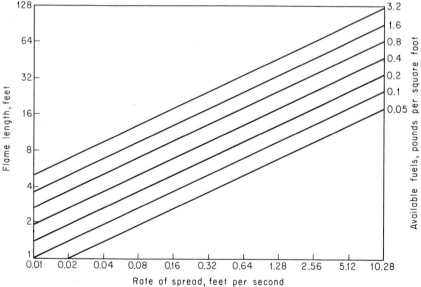

and form a prong-shaped head (or heads if the fire is large enough). Also, a high-intensity fire has a tendency to pulsate or burn in surges, which can produce a rather wide fluctuation in flame length. In addition, the sudden ignition of unburned gases in the convection column can result in flame flashes which can momentarily extend several hundred feet into the convection column aloft.

Levels of Fire Intensity

The preceding discussion might indicate that the nature of the fire-intensity scale is such that as wind speed increases, as fuel moisture decreases, and as the general fuel flammability increases, the expected fire intensity would increase in a smooth curve from the lower to the higher intensities. It is more realistic to visualize fire intensity in terms of stair steps or a discontinuous-type scale, because of the tendency for intensity to increase rather abruptly from one level to another of considerably higher intensity because of fuel arrangement or more specifically fuel stratification. For example, consider a low-intensity fire burning in a rather dense pine stand 50 feet in height which also has an understory of dense brush. Below the dense brush is a surface layer of heterogeneous dead fuel consisting of pine needles and cones, leaves, some grass, and limbs and twigs of various sizes. A low-intensity fire can burn in this surface fuel and not consume the brush. As the intensity increases in the lowest level, a point is reached when the leaves and smaller twigs on the brush start to burn. The intensity and rate of spread may now increase rapidly until a considerable part of the brush foliage is burning. The next abrupt increase comes when the pine crowns start to burn, in which case the fire is said to be crowning. Actually, these changes do not necessarily come all at once but are accompanied or preceded by sporadic bursts of intensity and flashes of burning into the fuel of the next higher level. There are times when lulls and gusts in the wind as well as variations in fuel and density of stand can cause a fire to alternate from one level to another. This is greatly facilitated by the presence of "ladders" of draped needles and moss which may be present below the crown canopy, as discussed more fully in Chapter 4. Also, height of canopy base and canopy compactness have a pronounced effect. The rather open short crowns in stands of southern pine require a considerably higher fire intensity to sustain a crown fire than do the compact, deeper crowns in spruce and fir stands in the Northern and Western states.

Since fire intensity levels fluctuate a great deal even in a uniform fuel, it is not appropriate to regard them as plateaus of constant fire intensity. It is more realistic to think in terms of zones or regions in which available fuel is approximately constant. Although the concept of available fuel is essential in energy calculations, its wide fluctuations make it an elusive and difficult quantity to measure or to estimate. More fuel becomes available as the fire passes from one intensity level to the next. The magnitude of the increase in available fuel differs considerably between different fuel and stand types. Possibly from 1 to 5 tons per acre are added when the foliage and smaller twigs in the understory brush burn. Depending on the conifer species and density of stocking, an additional 5 to 20 tons per acre may be added when the crown canopy burns.

THE MECHANISMS OF FIRE PROPAGATION

The sight of a fire eating its way through the dry weeds of a vacant city lot or through the fuels of the forest is so familiar that the process seems very simple. Actually, the phenomenon of fire spread is highly complex. Some of the dominant mechanisms for major fires are of a meteorological nature and will be considered in Chapter 7. For low-intensity, slow-spreading fires, the simpler combustion mechanisms dominate. Even the combustion processes in fire spread are not the same for fires of all intensities. This can be illustrated by starting with some of the simpler examples and progressing to higher-intensity fires.

Flow of Fuel and Heat and Transport of Ignition Points

Probably the simplest type of fire spread for solid fuels is the flame traveling slowly but at a fairly constant speed down the stem of a vertically held kitchen match. If the match is moved upward at a speed equal to the rate of downward motion of the flame, the latter will appear to remain stationary. Fuel is moving upward through the stationary base of the combustion zone. Simultaneously heat is flowing into the fuel in the opposite direction at the base of the combustion zone. The heat flow distills volatile fractions from the match, which combine with oxygen in the combustion zone to maintain the rate of heat output. That the whole process is in a rather delicate equilibrium can be illustrated in several different ways. Any agent which results in cooling in the combustion zone, especially near its base, will cause the match flame to go out. Anything which tends to separate the flame from its fuel supply, such as a sudden puff of air, will have the same result.

    Although radiation may make a minor contribution, conduction is the main heat-transfer mechanism controlling the rate of heat flow in the match stem. The situation is somewhat different for a low-intensity fire spreading in a layer of dry pine needles in calm air. Again the flame can be visualized as stationary if the fuel is assumed to be on a horizontal tray moving toward the flame at the same rate that the flame moves relative to the pine needles. Fuel is thus flowing through the front of the combustion zone, and heat is flowing in the opposite direction to the unburned fuel. In this case, the dominating heat-transfer mechanism appears to be radiation.

A still different situation exists when a fire is spreading under the influence of a light wind in a fuel of some depth, such as an area of dry grass. The basic process of the flow of fuel into the fire and flow of heat from fire to fuel is the same as in the previous two examples, but convection is now a more important heat-transfer factor. Some of the hot gases are carried into direct contact with unburned fuel when the flames are tilted over by the wind. Also, radiative heat transfer is increased accordingly.

Qualitatively, the flame propagation in the three preceding examples can be described by a combustion model which is the same in each case even though there is considerable difference in the relative significance of the three heat-transfer mechanisms. The basic process is a flow of fuel into the combustion zone and a flow of heat in the reverse direction into the unburned fuel. For this type of combustion model, Fons (1946) has made a theoretical analysis to obtain equations for the rate of fire spread in specially prepared fuel beds.

Proceeding to fires of higher intensity, it is found that the heat-transfer mechanisms are accompanied by an entirely different process which begins to dominate the fire propagation as the intensity increases. This mechanism is not a true heat-flow process. It can best be described as a transport of discrete ignition points ahead of the main flame front, although all three heat-transfer mechanisms are still involved. In fire spread by the extension or transport of ignition points, the combustion state is established in cold, unburned fuel with an extremely small transfer of heat; thus the simple combustion model based on a continuous flow of heat and fuel is no longer valid.

The transport of ignition points can be brought about in three ways. First, radiation from an extensive flame front may be intense enough to ignite isolated patches of light or flashy fuels. Second, turbulent motions on the leeward side of a flame front may bring hot gases momentarily into contact with flashy fuels and establish new ignition points. An example is that type of flame front which tends to break or roll like waves on a beach. The third source of ignition points is the transport of burning embers, or spotting, which appears to be the dominating fire-propagating mechanism for the highest-intensity fires.

Ignition Probability

One of the most important combustion factors involved in fire propagation by transport of ignition points is ignition probability. Since falling embers are the most important source of ignition points on the worst fires, ignition probability will be discussed from the standpoint of spotting; but most of the discussion applies also to the other sources of ignition points.

Like available fuel, the ignition probability is a widely variable quantity and as yet has not been determined experimentally. It increases rapidly with decreasing fuel moisture, hence with decreasing relative humidity. It is known that the ignition probability for most firebrands is essentially zero when fuel moisture is 25 to 30 percent. From this point it builds rapidly to the 5 percent moisture content level and is at maximum below 5 percent. As might be expected, it varies considerably with the firebrand. It is also known that ignition probability, like the combustion rate, is greatest for oven-dry material. In addition, both appear to be considerably affected in the lower fuel moisture content range by a change of only a few percent in fuel moisture.

The importance of the relation between fuel moisture and ignition probability in the behavior of large fires can be illustrated by a hypothetical example. Suppose that from the convection column over a large fire, 10,000 embers per square mile per minute are dropping in front of the fire. Assume that the surface fuel moisture content is such that only 0.1 percent of these firebrands catch and produce spot fires, thus giving only 10 spot fires per square mile. If, however, the surface fuel moisture is low enough for 5 percent of the embers to catch, then there would be 500 spot fires per square mile. As they burn together, these spot fires would greatly increase the rate of spread and intensity of the main fire; this in turn would increase the rate of production of new firebrands. Thus relative humidity (working through fuel moisture) has a twofold effect on rate of spread in certain types of extreme fire behavior. First is the effect on fuel combustion rate and rate of spread of the ordinary flame front. This effect would be present on small and large fires alike. Second is the effect in accelerating rate of spread and fire intensity by increasing the number of ignitions from falling embers ahead of the flame front. This latter effect would be present only on fires where spot fires were ignited in sufficient number or built up fast enough ahead of the flame front to exert a definite effect on fire behavior. The actual number of ignitions will depend not only on fuel moisture but also on the nature of the surface fuels in which firebrands fall and the fraction of the ground area covered by the fuels.

Fuel characteristics that make plentiful and efficient firebrands have not been completely identified. The material would have to be light enough to be carried aloft in updrafts yet capable of burning for several minutes while being carried forward by the upper winds. Decayed punky material, charcoal, bark, clumps of dry duff, and dry moss are efficient firebrands (Chapter 4). Leaves and grass tend to be inefficient firebrands except over very short distances. On the basis of their capacity to cause ignition, firebrands can be put in two definite classes: (1) flaming and (2) glowing. Although flaming firebrands have a far higher ignition probability than the glowing type, ignition by the latter is much more common outside the heated zone. The type of firebrand material determines whether or not it will be flaming or glowing, but a more important factor may be duration of flight. Flaming firebrands are normally very short-lived so have a much shorter range and are most uncommon in long-distance spotting.

Ignition Temperature

In the discussion of forest fuels in Chapter 4, distinction between fuels based on how they burn was made. The first fuel ignited may be either the flash-type fuel easily and quickly ignited by a match flame or the smoldering-type fuel which ignites much more slowly yet is capable of being ignited under some conditions by a single spark. This same distinction is important in firebrands. Dry, undecayed grass, leaves, and needles are almost impossible to ignite directly by a lighted cigarette or glowing piece of charcoal, yet they are easily ignited by a match flame. But a match flame is normally too short-lived to establish glowing combustion in punky fuels or in charcoal.

Temperature of the firebrand is a critical factor. The flame temperature of a match is 2300° or higher.[7] The effective temperature of glowing material is much lower. It quickly forms a film of ash which excludes oxygen and slows up the combustion rate. So the surface temperature of such a firebrand is likely to be 1200°F or below. But exposure to this lower temperature persists much longer.

The ignition temperature of solid fuels is not a constant and is not a specific point except for carefully defined sets of conditions. If glowing and smoldering are the ignition criteria, then the ignition temperature may be somewhere in the temperature range from 400 to 700°F. If the appearance of flame is taken as a criterion, then the ignition temperature is higher. From measurements on the internal temperatures of rapidly heated wood cylinders, Fons (1950) estimates their surface temperature to be about 650°F when they ignite. He found that cylinders placed in a heated atmosphere would glow but would not flame until the temperature

---

[7]In many former publications flame temperatures are given as 1600 to 1800°F since this is the thermocouple reading. Studies show that actual temperatures are 300 to 500° higher.

of the surrounding atmosphere was between 800 and 900°F. This temperature probably corresponds to the ignition temperature of the gases
distilled from the wood cylinders and is in good agreement with the
ignition temperatures of the vapors of the liquid hydrocarbon fuels, most
of which range from 700 to 1100°F.

Combustion Relationships in Fire Behavior

Most of the above characteristics of combustion of forest fuels are
common to all free-burning fires. Typically 80 to 90 percent of such fires
remain small and of low intensity. The small fire that remains small or at
low intensity is entirely controlled by its environment. It increases in its
rate of energy production with time up to a certain level, then it maintains
that level until fuels or burning conditions change. But when fuels and
burning conditions combine to produce a very high rate of energy release,
the fire interacts with its environment and may modify it drastically. In
the language of experienced fire fighters, at a certain threshold "it began
writing its own ticket." It then takes on unusual behavior which is beyond
direct control by conventional fire fighting methods and may become one
of the few conflagration fires that account for 90 percent or more of the
damage suffered each year. The behavior of such fires is critical to the fire
control man because of their great damage potential. The mechanisms of
such behavior are considered more fully in Chapter 7 and in Chapter 16.

Forest Fire Behavior

The term *fire behavior* is a general descriptive term to designate what a fire does. It is an apt term for wild-land fires in several respects. The ignition, buildup, propagation, and decline of any large fire in forest fuels represents a complex chain-reaction process. The variation often seems infinite, and fire fighters of long experience often state that no two fires are ever alike. They are, of course, speaking of the total fire fighting job including both the fire and its physical environment. Such a belief is well sustained by research. The large number of variables (some eleven to twenty) that affect the fire suppression job make the mathematical odds almost overwhelming against any two fire suppression jobs being exactly the same. Even the behavior of small free-burning fires alone, in supposedly uniform fuels, shows erratic variation—to the frequent discomfiture of the field research man. For such reasons a going fire tends to take on a personality of its own and its dynamics easily equate with the behavior of a living thing in the mind of the fire fighter. However, most variations can be accounted for, and by slow stages the ability to predict behavior is being progressively improved.

The critical challenge to the fire control man is to achieve as complete an understanding as possible of what a fire is doing and what behavior may be expected in the period ahead. The completeness of this understanding sets natural limits to the degree of success attainable in fire control. No natural phenomenon has ever been completely controlled until it first was completely understood. This principle applies to progress in the prevention and control of wild-land fires.

NATURAL HISTORY OF A FIRE

The natural history of a fire implies a time sequence. For each combination of fuel and environment, both fire intensity and rate of spread increase with time until they reach a plateau, as described in the preceding chapter. This may require minutes or hours. Unfortunately, from the point of view of the fire control man, the more critical the burning conditions and the more abundant the potential fuel, the longer will the buildup continue and the higher will be the level of intensity reached. There are several reasons for this. As the rate of heat energy release increases, the area over which new ignitions occur keeps increasing. At the same time the convection set up by the fire keeps increasing in strength. This increases the rate of oxygen supply and also increases the distance at which spotting will occur. In heavy volumes of mixed fuels a fire may keep on increasing its rate of forward spread over several hours. In grass fuels the maximum rate may be reached in 20 minutes or less. When the maximum is reached, it will be maintained at that rate until burning conditions change, the fire gets into different fuels, or the fire is interrupted by barriers. Often the corresponding fire-fighting job increases in size and difficulty in a ratio roughly corresponding to the square of the time elapsed from ignition. Thus successful control of fires becomes highly time-dependent, as will be discussed in subsequent chapters.

Aside from this overall relationship of time to fire behavior, the many additional variables that determine the behavior of a fire may be grouped into the three general categories of fuels, weather, and topography. All three have been discussed, though topography has been considered only in relation to air moisture and air movement. Its more direct effects on fire behavior can best be examined as they modify the effects of factors in the other two categories.

Typically, one part of a fire spreads more rapidly than the rest. Usually this is due to wind or slope or their joint effects. This creates a pennantlike or fanlike pattern with the fastest-spreading portion at the apex or farthest point from the origin. This pattern is repeated so frequently that it is accepted as conventional behavior and the parts of the fire's perimeter are separately designated as follows (Figure 7.1): *(a)* the head or head fire, that part of the perimeter enlarging itself most rapidly; *(b)* the flanks or side fire moving at right angles or obliquely to the direction taken by the head fire; and *(c)* the rear or base of the fire or the tail fire, spreading in the opposite direction to the head fire. Always the rate of spread is at a diminishing rate from head to flank to rear. But the ratio varies widely depending on wind or slope and available fuels. Associated with these differences in rate of spread are strong differences in fire intensity. These relationships are recognized and utilized in the prescribed use of fire. The backing fire or flank fire is often artificially created to produce the kind of burn needed for specific land-management purposes. This is discussed further in Chapter 18.

As was discussed in Chapter 6, combustion of forest fuels, except for ground fuels and punky wood, is normally a two-stage affair. There is first a flaming stage, then a glowing stage. In the more flashy fuels—grass, needle litter, dead leaves, twigs, etc.—nearly all the heat energy is released quickly in the flaming stage. Living fuels also release virtually all

Figure 7.1 Typical pattern of fire spread.

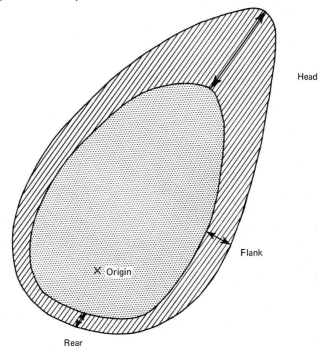

their energy in flaming combustion. In the thick or compacted fuels, a high percentage of the heat is released more slowly in glowing combustion. These differences in rate are fundamental factors in determining fire behavior.

The pattern for Figure 7.1 represents a rather rapidly moving fire with an active flame front. The faster it is moving, the deeper will be the flame front at the head of the fire and the greater the ratio between the rate of spread at the head and the rear, assuming that fuels are relatively uniform. Flash fuels may act as a fuse to more dangerous fuels; otherwise rate of spread is not critical to the fire control man unless it also represents a high burning rate and high fire intensity. If the fire in Figure 7.1 is burning in standing dry grass, there will be practically no glowing combustion and the dynamic part of the fire will soon become a doughnut pattern, then a shallow fire front in an open crescent. Though not so apparent in heavy mixed fuels because the pattern is then operating on a much larger scale, the same thing happens to the pattern of all spreading fires. When the head, flanks, and rear become far enough separated that radiation and convection begin to operate separately in each sector, the fire begins to lose its identity as a single dynamic unit. As it does so, a part of the burn begins to cool.

Always the period of maximum heat output of the flaming fuels in any one spot is sustained for only a few minutes. Because of this, a number of small fires burning together build up a much higher level of heat energy than will develop from a single fire front moving through the same area. This principle is utilized to raise heat levels in controlled burning when flammability of fuels is low. It also helps to clarify the violent behavior induced by a large number of spot fires burning together and is believed to be the triggering action in the fire storm. This phenomenon will be discussed later.

If the fire represented by Figure 7.1 is burning in heavy mixed fuels, flaming combustion will take place over a much deeper front around the entire perimeter and glowing combustion of fuels in the interior may persist for some hours. The fire control problem is usually closely identified with the moving fire front. The rate at which it engulfs new fuels, and the time required for flaming combustion to be complete[1] determine the fire intensity and the amount of area producing high levels of heat energy at one time. These relationships too are highly significant to fire behavior.

---

[1]Fons defined the period of flaming as *residence time.*

Variations in the Burn Pattern

The pattern of initial spread, as well as the principal direction of spread, is determined mostly by the speed and direction of the surface wind and by topography. Both wind and topography have a marked influence on heat transfer by radiation and convection. Local variations in fuel and cover type also affect the pattern, but their effect is usually less than that of wind and topography. They are important, however, in the rate of buildup of intensity.

In the absence of wind and in flat terrain, a fire will spread at about the same rate in all directions, so that the initial spread pattern is an approximately circular area with the point of ignition in the center, as shown in Figure 7.2A. If there is a wind which maintains a constant direction, the burned area will assume the shape of an elongated ellipse, with the long axis parallel to the direction of the wind, as shown in Figure 7.2B. The ratio of the two diameters of the elliptical area will depend on the surface wind speed. Often the direction of the wind is not constant but may vary through an angle of 30 or 40°. In this case, the initial pattern of spread will assume a fan-shaped area, as indicated by Figure 7.2C. An extreme but infrequent example of a variable wind is a situation in which there is no definite prevailing wind direction. This condition can occasionally exist on sunny days when the atmosphere is turbulent and gusty winds can come from almost any direction. The initial spread pattern will resemble that of Figure 7.2A but will be larger and have a more irregular perimeter.

In mountainous terrain, both wind and topographic factors control the pattern of initial spread and direction of travel. In the period just following ignition, wind may be the dominant factor, but as the fire intensity builds up, topography is more likely to dominate, especially on the steeper slopes. A fire starting on a slope will have an initial spread pattern similar to that of Figure 7.2B, with the long axis pointed upslope. The pattern may be modified somewhat if a general slope or drainage has a number of spur ridges. This tendency can create a pattern of spread dangerous to men in the area. The pattern is illustrated in Figure 7.2D. The fire is burning slowly in flat or gently sloping terrain near the base of two spur ridges. After spreading from the indicated ignition point or origin, it may start to run up the sides of both ridges simultaneously and to form two heads. Since the two heads may spread along the ridge slopes faster than a man can travel upslope, the U-shaped area between the heads may become a trap. The rapid upslope spread can occur very suddenly, and the fire can travel 5 miles per hour or more on steep slopes.

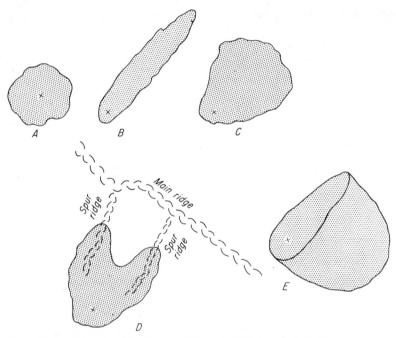

Figure 7.2 Characteristic shapes of fires in initial spread. *A.* No wind and flat terrain. *B.* Effect of wind and/or slope. *C.* Variable wind. *D.* Initial fire spread pattern when fire advances up two spur ridges simultaneously. *E.* Pattern when a change in wind changes one flank to head fire.

Mountainous terrain creates many variations in the fire pattern in addition to those shown. Under some circumstances, a fire traveling up a steep slope to a ridge top will set spot fires far down on the opposite slope, which in turn may quickly burn a swath back up to the ridge top. On very steep slopes, burning pine cones, logs, or other rolling material may create the same effect on a smaller scale. Such behavior creates a very ragged fire front. When spot fires have been set far ahead, a very irregular fire pattern is also created. These topographic variations are often critical to the fire fighter.

A critical pattern which occurs frequently on larger fires, but which can and does occur on fires of all sizes, is represented by Figure 7.2*E*. It is a modification of Figure 7.2*B,* in which a fire makes an initial run with a brisk prevailing wind. Then the wind changes almost to right angles of its former direction, turning a whole flank of the fire into a headfire. This often happens with the passing of a cold front. It can result too from the downdraft from a passing thunderstorm or from the circulation induced by a sea-breeze front as described in Chapter 5.

The Convection Column

The buoyancy of heated air enters into every weather phenomenon discussed in Chapter 5. The convective forces it represents are also critical in all flaming combustion in forest fuels as discussed in Chapter 6. So it is logical to expect that variations in convective forces enter strongly into fire behavior.

The convection caused by a fire is usually well defined by the rising smoke column. Its size and rate of growth and dynamics are in direct relation to the heat energy being produced by the fire.

A low-energy fire, or a fire that is smoldering or dying out, may produce a smoke plume rather than an active convection column. A smoke plume results from convection just as the smoke plume from a chimney does. But it is inert and its only significance to fire behavior is the evidence that some combustion has taken place. Smoke plumes from smoldering fires are often quite prominent in early morning but tend to dissipiate as the sun's rays create convective circulation. Often convective forces not induced by combustion cause smoke plumes to rise several hundred feet, so that they superficially resemble an active convection column. It is important to distinguish between them. When there is considerable wind, the smoke plume may dissipate almost as formed so that an occasional puff of smoke only is visible; or it may become a light-colored wedge of smoke reaching the ground and drifting downwind. When the wind is light, the smoke plume may extend upward a considerable height, particularly in early morning as cited above. The most distinctive features of a smoke plume are (1) lack of pronounced vertical or "inside out" motion, (2) relatively light color, (3) relatively high transparency.

A high-energy fire produces an active convection column with a strong vertical component and a characteristic inside-out rolling motion. When strong winds are present, the convection column is tilted or displaced, often retaining its identity with the convection column almost horizontal downwind. Under some atmospheric conditions, however, such as created by a high-speed flow of dense, stable air downslope, convection may remain largely disseminated without well-developed convection columns.

Since heated air tends to follow the warm-air sheath upslope close to the ground, as discussed in the section on mountain and valley winds (Chapter 5), convection from a going fire in steep topography often hugs the slope and emerges as a recognizable convection column only at the ridge top.

The convection column seems to create an air curtain around itself. For that reason, when it is well developed, the wind tends to flow around it as if it were a solid obstruction.

Studies of the mechanism of the convection column usually account for only a part of the energy through warm-air buoyancy. Conversion of some of the heat energy into mechanical energy, or feed-in of energy from the wind field, apparently enters in also.

In general, conditions which favor free convection stimulate the burning rate of the fire; conditions which resist convection hold it down. Wind may be regarded as substituting for free convection. The analogy is close to that of opening or closing the dampers on a wood stove.

The development and behavior of the convection column is a good criterion of atmospheric conditions as well as of fire behavior. When an inversion exists, the convection column will extend only to the altitude at which its temperature equals the air temperature, with the smoke spreading out horizontally at that point. The strength and direction of winds aloft in the absence of an inversion are revealed by the degree and direction of tilt of the convection column or by its being sheared off. As will be discussed later, massive convection columns extending to high altitudes characterize most conflagration fires. These reflect a particular atmospheric condition.

Low-intensity versus High-intensity Fires

Most wild-land fires that appear in the statistics of protection agencies are relatively low in intensity. They are the fires that are controlled by direct attack with conventional methods of fire fighting. They mostly behave as expected and remain within the fire suppression capabilities of the local protection force long enough to be controlled. Generally such fires fall below a heat output of 1,000 Btu per second per foot of fire front. As in the formula approach to rate of spread and resistance to control discussed in Chapter 4, such fires can be treated as "thin" or two-dimensional. Their convective activity is light and is often disseminated but, of most importance, the edge of the fire can be worked.

In contrast to these fires, a small number quickly outgrow the stage where direct attack can succeed and soon become "too hot to handle." Intense radiation and surges of superheated gases prevent the close approach of men and machines to the head of the fire. The attack force then finds it necessary to resort to indirect methods of control. They are faced with a problem in three dimensions where the magnitude of the problem is more nearly represented by the amount of heat energy being released than it is by the number of chains of fire perimeter or of projected fire line. Such fires can reach an intensity of hundreds of thousands of British thermal units per second. Such levels of intensity are possible even on a quarter-acre fire. So the rate of energy output of two fires of equal perimeter can range all the way from that of smoldering spots to that of a small tornado.

The need of a clearer concept of the three-dimensional nature of a high-intensity fire was first given emphasis in the board of fire review on the McVey fire in the Black Hills of South Dakota in 1940.

Fires can be considered as two-dimensional or three-dimensional only in a relative sense, because even a low-intensity fire has a shallow convection region over its flames. Also, there are conditions under which a high-intensity fire may form a convection column only intermittently.

The height that smoke rises above a fire is not always an indicator of the height of the convection zone above a fire. Smoke from a small fire may reach a height of 1,000 feet or more, but active convection may reach only a small fraction of this height. Such a fire forms a smoke plume rather than a dynamic convection column.

It is natural to think of a high-intensity fire as a large-scale model of a low-intensity fire. Both tend to build up to the combustion rate dictated by fuel and environment, and the same basic combustion processes and heat-transfer mechanisms are operating. But there is an important difference. The high-intensity fire produces enough energy to interact with and to modify its environment, so that it becomes a phenomenon in atmospheric physics and meteorology as well as in combustion. As such, it too can perhaps be modeled, but only in relation to atmospheric forces with which it is interacting at the time. As a physical phenomenon, a fully developed conflagration has more in common with a thunderstorm than with a low-intensity fire in surface fuels.

Fire Behavior and How it Relates to Fire Environment

What is known about the behavior of the free-burning fire in natural fuels has been learned through a variety of methods. One prolific source has been the analysis of past experience through statistical analysis of fire reports. A second, which has been responsible for most quantitative information on rate of spread, has been the study and measurement of small experimental fires in the field and in the laboratory. Third is an energy analysis of the fire system discussed in the next section. The fourth, which may be termed the case study method, consists of careful documentation of all environmental factors at the time of a fire and an examination of their probable relationship to the behavior observed. The first will be discussed further in Chapter 14. Since the characteristics of the low-energy small fire differ from those of the more dangerous high-energy fire and since fire statistics fail to describe these distinctive aspects, the case study has special value in developing information on the interaction between high-intensity fires and their environment. Though case studies seldom provide enough quantitative data for statistical significance, they do provide means of establishing the life history of a fire and the chronology of events. They also develop quantitative evidence of the qualitative relationships between fire behavior and environmental factors. In Chapter 16 case studies of several large fires are reviewed.

To give a case study its maximum usefulness, each environmental factor needs first to be analyzed. The following are pertinent.

Relation to Time of Day More fires occur from late morning to midafternoon than at other times of day. This is the time of day that fine fuels are most flammable and thermal turbulence near the ground is at a maximum on a warm, sunny day. Most of the time, higher humidities, decreased wind, and more stable, cool air return shortly after sundown. This drastically reduces rate of spread and intensity of the fire. A high proportion of fires that escape control by the first attack force are successfully controlled at this time. But under special conditions described in Chapter 5, high wind speeds and low humidities may prevail during the night, resulting at times in peak fire intensity. Nighttime conditions of this kind are dangerous to fire fighters and are often responsible for the escape of fires believed to be under control. The ability to recognize and to forecast these reversals of the usual diurnal regime is often critical.

Available Fuel The available fuel, as discussed in Chapters 4 and 6, is always a critical factor. For a given rate of spread, the fire intensity is directly proportional (at constant heat yield) to the quantity of fuel that burns. However, there are times when the effect of an increase in the available fuel on fire intensity appears to be considerably greater than one would expect from the actual increase. This phenomenon appears to be associated with the energy-conversion rate in the convection column discussed later. It could occur when a fire needs only a small amount of additional fuel to supply the energy needed to form a convection column, or chimney, and thus acquire vertical structure.

Fuel size and arrangement are important fire behavior factors, especially in low-intensity fires or in the early part of the buildup of high-intensity fires. Extreme fire behavior is most likely to occur in heavy, mixed surface fuels such as logging slash, or in natural cover where the fuel is well distributed vertically to a considerable depth, such as in dense conifer stands where the fuel extends, with some degree of stratification, from the soil to the top of the crown canopy. Intense fires also build up in stands of evergreen brush and can readily cross over water in swamps if the brush or dry swamp vegetation is dense enough.

There are five basic fuel factors needed to describe fuel in terms of its capability for supplying energy and supplying it fast enough to meet the energy requirements of a high-intensity fire. In a simplified form for moving fire these are: (1) combustion period, (2) critical burnout time, (3) available fuel energy, (4) fuel energy available for convection, and (5) quantity and quality of firebrand material available for spotting. A sixth factor, the total fuel energy, need not be included because it merely places an upper limit on the available fuel energy and the fuel energy available for convection.

The combustion period is the time required for a fuel to burn up completely and depends primarily on fuel size, fuel arrangement, and fuel moisture. It probably depends to some extent on fire intensity, but the nature of the relationship is not yet known. The combustion period may range from a few seconds for thin grass blades to several hours or longer for logs and heavy limbs.

Critical burnout time is the maximum length of time that a fuel can burn and still be able to feed its energy into the base of the forward-traveling convection column; its magnitude depends primarily on fire intensity. This is synonomous with residence time as used by Fons.

The fuel energy available for convection is that part of the available fuel energy which is fed into the base of the convection column. For fuels with a combustion period equal to or less than the critical burnout time, all the fuel energy is available for convection. If the combustion period is longer than the critical burnout time, then the fuel energy available for convection is less than the available fuel energy.

Available fuel energy was defined in Chapter 6, as were firebrand characteristics.

The operation of the basic fuel factors can be illustrated by an example. Consider a high-intensity fire spreading in an area of plentiful heterogeneous fuel, a considerable part of which is in the form of flammable logs and heavy slash and the rest a mixture of smaller material such as twigs, pine needles, and grass. Although the relationship between fire intensity and the critical burnout time remains to be determined, it will be assumed, for the sake of illustration, that the latter is 10 minutes. Those fuel components with a combustion period less than 10 minutes will have a fuel energy available for convection equal to their available fuel energy. However, since logs and heavy limbs may require several hours to burn out, their energy available for convection may be comparatively low; they could still be burning after the fire had moved several miles, so should have only a negligible effect on the behavior of the fire front.

If the forward rate of spread of this particular fire was 1.8 miles per hour, the flame front would have advanced 0.3 mile in 10 minutes, or in a time equal to the critical burnout time. A slower-moving fire with a critical burnout time of 20 minutes and a forward spread of 10 chains ($^1/_8$ mi) per hour would advance 3.3 chains.

Fuel Moisture and Drought   There is a close relationship between the occurrence of large fires and prolonged drought (Chapter 1). Drought affects fire behavior in several ways. Progressive drying of the deeper fuel layers as well as the heavier fuels, such as dead limbs and logs, makes more available fuel and increases the combustion rate. Excessive drought causes premature curing of vegetation and dieback in tree and shrub crowns. It has a similar effect on all green vegetation. In swamp and bog areas it lowers water tables, eliminating natural barriers and exposing organic soils to fire. This greatly increases the difficulty of holding fire lines. This problem is most severe in areas with organic soils, but it exists wherever dead, dry, buried roots or pockets of organic material can result in breached fire lines.

Drought reduces all punky fuels to a very low moisture content. This increases the probability of ignition from falling embers, so that spot fires become more prevalent and more persistent. This, in turn, increases the likelihood of pseudo front formation and fire storm effects.

The disastrous Maine fires of 1947 followed a severe summer drought. All the six to nine fires that merged in the final conflagration had already been worked on several times by conventional methods for that locality and were believed to be fully under control. But due to the drought, deep-burning, smoldering fuels required intensive mop-up. Local fire fighters were not accustomed to such requirements and had not been trained in how to do it.

Relation to Temperature   Heating of fine fuels by the sun's radiation can significantly reduce the heat energy required for ignition. But this effect is obscured because heating also rapidly reduces the moisture content of such fuel. After ignition has occurred, initial temperature of the fuel has only a minor effect. Yet hot weather is usually associated with high fire danger. Outbreaks of forest fires, with increase both in size and number, tend to occur in periods when the prevailing temperatures are above normal. This relationship is most pronounced in the Western states, but it is also important in the East and South. However, in the states east of the Mississippi River, some of the largest and most intense fires have burned when the temperature was low and falling. Such fires, which may be described as cold-front fires, made their major run during the passage of a dry cold front (Chapter 5). The low temperatures were accompanied by low relative humidities (25 to 40 percent) and strong surface winds.

Probably either high temperature or low temperature as such has much less significance than other conditions associated with it. High temperatures in the Western states during the summer are often accompanied by turbulence, by low relative humidities, and by upslope convective winds. The combination of low humidity and high temperature means rapid loss of moisture from the dead fuels. It also means a high transpiration rate for living vegetation, which can lower its moisture content if the available soil moisture is nearing depletion.

Relation to the Wind Field   Studies of the relation of wind speed to rate of spread of small fires show a rapid acceleration in rate of spread with increasing wind speed. Show, from his early studies, often described the relationship as approximately proportional to the square of the wind speed. This approximation has long served as a guidepost. McArthur (personal communication) found this relationship generally valid for grass fires in Australia. His data, as did Show's, apparently included considerable acceleration from spotting. The relationship changes with moisture content of the fuel. Consequently, a family of curves is required to describe the rate of fire spread in each fuel. The most typical relationship found by American investigators for fires in forest litter, excluding spotting effects, is that of an increase in rate of forward spread in direct proportion to the wind speed, up to 5 to 6 miles per hour, at this point it increases at a rate approximating the $1^{1}/_{2}$ power rather than the square of the wind speed. This holds true for the first 20 to 30 minutes following ignition at wind velocities below 30 miles per hour. At very high wind speeds, lateral spread of a fire is inhibited and in light fuels the fire may be blown out.

In forest cover, the wind speed near the ground is greatly reduced. A 30-mile wind may be translated into a 5 to 6 mile wind within a dense, closed timber stand. In southern pine stands, Cooper (1965) found that the typical reduction was close to 50 percent. Even above the treetops the inertial effect of contact with irregularities of the earth's surface and cover reduce the speed of prevailing winds. Consequently, wind speeds usually increase with height above the surface. This tends to create a stratified condition.

A very critical wind field phenomenon is the passage of a cold front

(Chapter 5). The four largest fires of the Southeast in 1955 and 1956 made their major runs during the passage of a cold front. These are characterized by strong surface winds with considerable turbulence, low humidities, and low temperatures that last from 6 to 10 hours. Prior to the arrival of the cold front, warm dry winds from the southwest prevailed. These had produced an elongated fire oriented in a general southwest-northeast direction. The shift of the wind to the northwest after the passage of the dry cold front caused the right flank of the prefrontal fire to become the front or leading edge of a new, fast-moving fire (Figure 7.2E). This wind field pattern is often repeated.

   Relation to Topography   Like the influence of wind, the influence of topography on the rate of spread of fire is so marked that it has always been considered an important fire behavior factor. A fire spreading up a steep slope resembles a fire spreading before a strong wind. As a first approximation, the effects of slope and wind on small fires can be equated, but the analogy cannot be carried too far. If spotting and whirlwinds do not occur, the rate of buildup of fire spread in heavy fuel, in level country, and under the influence of a brisk wind is slowed down when the fire's intensity becomes high enough to produce a strong indraft opposite the direction of fire spread. This self-regulating process does not occur when a fire builds up intensity in spreading upslope. Nevertheless, topography as such has undoubtedly been given more credit than it deserves in influencing the behavior of major fires. Many major fires, such as those which burned in the Lake states many years ago or in the Southeast since 1954, have burned in flat or slightly rolling country where topography had little effect on the overall behavior of the fires.

   Ordinarily a fire will spread upslope, but high-intensity erratic fires have spread not only upslope but downslope as well. Such fires have been known to travel across drainages (upslope and downslope) as though they did not exist (Chapter 5).

   Relation to Atmospheric Instability   Case studies used in the early work on the possible causes of extreme fire behavior, such as those carried out by Byram (1954) and others, indicated that an unstable atmosphere with its accompanying thermal turbulence was associated with severe fires. However, additional case studies showed that severe fires were also occurring at night when the air was stable. In addition, not all fires build up to a high intensity during the afternoon hours when instability is greatest. If applied to either a stable or unstable atmosphere, analysis of energy relationships shows that the normal changes in the stability of the atmosphere should have a negligible effect on the energy budget of large fires, although this does not rule out the possibility of stability affecting fire behavior in other ways. Scesa and Sauer (1954) came to a similar conclusion in their analytical work on free convection.

Even though atmospheric instability may not have an important direct effect on the behavior of large fires, stability conditions can influence fire behavior in several different ways. First is the direct effect on the energy of small fires; low-intensity fires burning in relatively quiet air can capture a considerable part of their total energy from an unstable atmosphere. This phenomenon could contribute to the rate of buildup on small fires burning upslope. Turbulent air and gusty variable winds can cause small fires to build up more rapidly and to behave erratically.

The most significant effects of atmospheric-stability conditions on fire behavior appear to be indirect in that they operate through the wind profile. Another potentially significant indirect effect, not yet fully understood, is the possibility of a slightly stable atmosphere contributing to the violence of convective phenomena on high-intensity fires. This may be an important mechanism in the sudden and unexpected buildup of intensity on some of the blowups which occur at night.

Total Environment   The above list of environmental factors may be further extended. But to do so would increase the overlap and duplication of the more basic underlying relationships. These are the nature and quantity of available fuels, the geometry of their arrangement on both a micro and mesoscale, their moisture content, and the rate at which oxygen is supplied to the combustion process. Various combinations of these factors impart different behavior characteristics. Some of the more important characteristics from the point of view of the fire fighter are considered separately in the following section.

One very important factor is the state of the atmosphere and the degree to which it dominates or is modified by the dynamics of the thermal energy produced by the fire. This potential has been explored in the chapter on fire weather. It is pertinent to note that nearly all fire behavior phenomena that are unique to high-energy fires have an important atmospheric component. These phenomena are considered in the following section.

Distinctive Behavior Phenomena of High-energy Fires

Large high-energy fires which must be visualized on an area basis are often referred to as mass fires. They may be either stationary or moving but are of conflagration proportions. This is the type of fire created by incendiary bombing and by atomic explosions. Mass fires may occur in either forest or urban environments when initiated by such agents. In peacetime, they are limited chiefly to forest environments, and most of the phenomena such fires display in urban environments are duplicated at times in high-energy forest fires. For this reason the experience and technical knowledge of forest fire control and forest fire research men are often drawn on to improve the understanding of their behavior (Countryman, 1964; Countryman and Chandler, 1966).

Phenomena of special practical and scientific interest that are characteristic of the development of such fires are discussed in the following sections. These will continue to challenge the scientist, the planner, and the practitioner in the years ahead.

The Phenomenon of Blowup The term "blowup" has long been used by fire control men. More recently it has become accepted as a useful term by research men as well. To fire control men it usually means any sudden increase in fire intensity or rate of spread sufficient to upset existing plans for the control of a fire. It implies a rapid and often sudden increase in fire intensity from a relatively low to a much higher level. In this sense it often represents the transition from a low-intensity to a high-intensity fire and from a two-dimensional to a three-dimensional fire control undertaking.

The transition from a low-energy to a high-energy state operates as a cycle of reinforcement. Low fuel moisture means high combustion rates and thus short combustion periods. A decrease in fuel moisture also means an increase in available fuel, and hence in available fuel energy. Both these processes promote an increase in fire intensity. Growing fire intensity, in turn, lengthens the critical burnout time, and this means an increase in the fuel energy available for convection. In this way a cycle of reinforcement is established which favors the growth of fire intensity. As the intensity grows, both the available fuel energy and the fuel energy available for convection increases still further (as, for example, when crowning begins). The atmospheric factors become increasingly more significant as the fuel energy available for convection continues to increase. Eventually, the point is reached when convective energy exceeds energy of the wind field in the lower levels. Convection can now begin on a large scale. The fire can then build its convection column, or chimney, very quickly, and the most rapid part of the blowup is under way. It is at this stage that spotting and ignition probability may become dominant fire behavior factors. Whirlwinds and strong updrafts can produce ember showers over large areas of unburned fuel. Turbulent rolls on the leading edge of the flame front may bring flame sheets in direct contact with fresh fuel.

The transition from a low-energy fire to a high-energy fire is seldom a gradual process. Typically at some point there is a sudden surge in the burning rate and a blowup is under way. Usually the apparent cause is a pickup in wind speed or the start of crowning or of rapid growth of numerous spot fires. But it is seldom that a blowup can be properly ascribed to a single factor.

A fire sometimes appears to increase its intensity rather suddenly when it has reached some definite size. Although many fires may increase their rate of energy output when they have reached a size of 40 to 60 acres, any simple relation between size and sudden growth of intensity is more apparent than real. Fires burning in heavy dry fuel on a steep slope may be in the process of blowing up before they have reached a size of 5 acres. Other fires may attain a final size in excess of 1,000 acres without ever blowing up. The tendency of a fire to blow up, or to build a dynamic convection column, is more closely related to rate of energy output than to size of fire.

Spotting   Spotting is perhaps the most troublesome characteristic of all of high-intensity fires. Long-distance spotting depends on the presence of favorable firebrand-producing and firebrand-igniting fuels, as discussed in Chapter 4. Short-distance spotting can occur, though at varying frequency in all fuel types. In long-distance spotting, burning embers may be carried several miles from the main fire to ignite new fires. In fire records for the United States, spot fires set 7 miles ahead of the main fire have been authenticated. A. G. McArthur cites a case in West Australia where a spot fire was set 18 miles from the main fire and states that spotting several miles ahead in eucalyptus stands is common. Although the spot fires occurring at long distances are spectacular and effective in spreading fire over large areas, the spot fires nearer the main flame front have a much greater effect on fire behavior.

Showers of burning embers within $1/4$ or $1/2$ mile of the main fire front occasionally produce disastrous firestorm effects by igniting large areas almost simultaneously. The numerous spot fires that result quickly merge to create a pseudo flame front with greatly increased burning rate, higher intensity, and increased turbulence. Such a front may closely resemble the ordinary flame front but with higher flames, higher intensity, and higher rate of spread. The operation of firestorm effects to create pseudo flame fronts is likely an important factor in the rate of spread of most fires which travel 3 miles per hour or faster.

Spotting is closely related to strong convection and updrafts which carry the burning embers aloft, possibly to heights of 5,000 feet above the surface, where they are carried forward by the upper winds. Often the direction of the upper winds is different from the direction of the surface winds, so long-distance spotting may not necessarily be in the direction of spread of the surface fire.

Any fire burning in a strong wind is likely to be accompanied by some spotting, even though the fire may not have any significant vertical structure or pronounced convective activity. This condition can be especially troublesome to fire fighters when fire burns in the tops of dead snags. Strong winds can blow the resulting embers horizontally several hundred feet. However, this type of spotting is not as crippling to fire control efforts as the convective type of spotting, which can scatter more embers over much greater distances. As yet there are no fire control methods which can cope effectively with a high-intensity fire when spotting takes place on a large scale.

Fire Whirlwinds Fire whirlwinds are one of the most striking features of fire behavior. From the standpoint of fire fighting operations and personnel safety, their importance is comparable to other extreme fire behavior characteristics such as long-distance spotting and ember showers, with which they are closely associated. Actually, fire whirlwinds are one of the most important direct causes of spotting.

These whirlwinds, or fire devils as they are sometimes called, come in a wide assortment of sizes and intensities. They range from little twisters less than 2 feet in diameter at the ground to tornadolike whirls several hundred feet across which in both size and intensity are comparable to small tornadoes. Although size and intensity of rotary motion are related in a general way, there exists no simple relationship between them. Some of the smaller whirls can have a surprisingly high speed of rotary motion and updraft, as demonstrated by their ability to lift debris from the ground.

There are probably two types of fire whirlwinds. The first and more frequent type is analogous to the dust devil in that it apparently forms at or near the surface over a heated area. It appears to grow upward as it increases in intensity. The second type appears to be similar to the tornado both in structure and method of formation. It seems to be closely associated with very strong convective activity. Whirlwinds of this type appear to originate high in the convection column (possibly 1,000 feet or more above the fire) on its downwind side and burrow downward until they reach the surface. These whirlwinds may appear to form at the surface because they are ordinarily invisible until they contact the surface. The vortex then rapidly fills with debris or flame, depending on whether the point of contact is outside or inside the fire area.

Since both fire whirlwinds and spotting are closely associated with strong convective activity, they are most likely to occur when a fire burns into heavy fuel, when two fires burn together (such as the joining of a headfire and a backfire), or whenever an extensive area becomes ignited all at once.

Fire whirlwinds occur under varying topographic conditions ranging from rough mountainous topography to flat coastal-plains land. They can exist in either stable or unstable air. Surface wind speeds can range from near calm to perhaps 30 miles per hour.

Graham (1957) lists 28 examples of stationary slash-disposal fires in Oregon and Washington on which intense fire whirlwinds developed, some of which reached tornado proportions. An interesting feature of these whirlwinds was their tendency to form near ridgetops on the leeward side. It may be that the lee slopes merely furnish a sheltered zone of reduced wind speed which enables the whirlwinds to keep their bases anchored in the parent heat source. Unlike the ordinary convection column, a large whirlwind can readily separate itself from the burning area. The tendency of fire whirlwinds to break away from the parent heat source, spreading new fire as they go, is one of their most troublesome characteristics. Their movement can be a real threat to both fire control operations and crew safety.

Some of the best examples of whirlwinds associated with a convection column are given in the description and excellent photographs by Hissong (1926) in the report of the large fire on an oil-tank farm at San Luis Obispo, California, in 1925. These whirlwinds had true tornado characteristics. The photographs show long, funnellike structures suspended from far up in the convection column. Of those that reached the ground, some contacted the surface a considerable distance from the base of the fire and were observed from as much as 3 miles from the fire. Small buildings were destroyed by the whirlwinds. In his study of the Chicago fire on the night of October 8–9, 1871, Musham (1941) states that fire whirlwinds were probably the major factor in the destruction of the city. These whirlwinds, too, must have reached near-tornado proportion because they lifted burning planks and dropped them on buildings far ahead of the main body of fire.

The fire whirlwind has been successfully modeled in the laboratory (Byram, 1962, 1970). Based on models developed at the U.S. Forest Service's Southern Forest Fire Laboratory, very high velocities of spiraling hot gases are easily generated. A rotation rate of 23,000 to 24,000 revolutions per minute, a horizontal component of 20 to 25 miles per hour, and an updraft velocity in the center of the whirl of 40 to 50 miles per hour were developed by the model used. Of equal significance was a threefold increase in the burning rate.

Apparently the rotational flow in a vortex is quite an efficient method of converting heat energy into mechanical energy. It helps to explain the lifting capacity often demonstrated by fire whirlwinds and helps too to explain many aspects of erratic fire behavior, including sudden upsurges in the burning rate.

The Firestorm Another phenomenon which can give insight into the behavior of high-intensity fires is the mechanism of the so-called firestorm. It is a stationary fire as compared to the moving fire front, but its burning rate, and hence also its energy production, are at the peak over a sufficient area to create violent indrafts from all directions.

The classic example of such a fire from which this descriptive title evolved was the burning of Hamburg, Germany, in late July, 1943, during World War II. It was the result of hundreds of incendiary fires set simultaneously by bombing raids which rapidly burned together in a spectacular holocaust (Bond, 1962). Indrafts were said to be so violent that they caused automobiles to be tumbled end-over-end down Hamburg streets toward the center of convection.

The most significant feature of the firestorm is the merging of many separate fires. Small fires begin to interact and to stimulate each other at a certain critical spacing dictated by the rate of energy release and by convective forces. This can be illustrated by birthday candles. If placed closely enough together, the individual flames suddenly merge to create a single hot flame at a greatly accelerated burning rate. The merging of spot fires in advance of a fire front creates a pseudo flame front as described in the preceding chapter. This greatly increases turbulence and stimulates burning rate. Though the burning area, the convective force, and the velocity of indrafts may be below the level of a fully developed fire storm, the mechanism is the same. This principle is utilized in the prescribed use of fire (Fenner, Arnold, and Buck, 1955) and is discussed further in Chapter 18.

Vertical Structure of the Convection Column Over major fires and over fires to which one would be most likely to apply the term *blowup* (because of the sudden and often unexpected buildup of turbulent energy), there is a well-developed convection column which may extend high into the atmosphere. The shape of a convection column is determined by the winds aloft. If there is a low-level wind with a fairly deep zone of decreasing wind speed, the convection column will tend to curve upward slightly throughout the zone. If the speed of the winds above this zone is low, then the convection column will tower to a great height and form a white water-vapor cap. If, above the zone of low wind speed, there is a rapid increase in wind speed, the convection column will fracture, lose its updraft velocity, and tend to drift horizontally. The direction in which spot fires are likely to occur can be anticipated by noticing the direction in which the upper part of the column tends to lean and also the direction of smoke drift aloft if the column fractures. Spotting can occur on a large scale with either the towering or fractured type of column, but it seems to be worse with the latter type. Figure 7.3 illustrates the two types of convection columns.

Updraft velocities in the hot central core of the convection column are not known, but they may exceed 70 or 80 miles per hour on high-intensity fires. However, a fire often burns in surges, in which case huge bubbles of hot gases can be seen to travel rapidly upward in the column. These surges are accompanied by an outward and downward roll in the column's outer periphery. These rolls may be present far up into the convection column which, over a large fire, appears to be continuously turning itself inside out.

Large fires exhibiting extreme fire behavior have convection columns with white water-vapor caps reaching a height of 25,000 feet or more. Such columns reach their most massive development in the firestorm. Since about 70 percent of the total mass of the atmosphere is below this level, these fires have literally pierced the atmosphere. They are truly three-dimensional phenomena and have storm characteristics like other disturbances in the atmosphere.

Character of Wildfire Flame   On large fires the tendency to pulsate or burn in surges, along with certain characteristics of high-intensity flame fronts, causes a much greater variation in flame height than occurs on small fires. The problem of estimating flame heights on major fires is complicated by the flame flashes, which may extend 400 to 600 feet into the convection column. Such flashes may result in overestimates of the average flame heights, which usually range from 50 to 150 feet on high-intensity fires (Chapter 6).

There are considerable differences in flame movement and motion on large fires. Flame spirals with both horizontal and vertical axes develop. Occasionally, the flame front resembles huge waves rolling on the beach. At other times, the flames and gases may travel rapidly upward, accompanied by strong indrafts toward the burning front. There are not many closeup observations on record of the appearance of the flame fronts of major fires because experienced fire fighters seldom document their observations or remain very long in the dangerous

Figure 7.3 Examples of convection columns over large fires. *(U.S. Forest Service photos.) A.* Towering convection column. *B.* Fractured convection column.

locations favorable for such observations. For a similar reason, it is even more difficult to get direct and detailed observations of pseudo flame fronts in firestorm areas.

Formation of Heads Unlike a fire backing into the wind, head fires of all intensities do not maintain a burning front in the form of a long straight line or gently rounded curve. Instead, the fire tends to form a narrow, rounded head or at times a sharp prong where the intensity is greatest. If fuel and topography create differences in the rate of spread, several separate heads are likely to form as the fire gets larger. Although variations in fuel and topography are the primary influence, heads appear to form even in uniform fuels and in flat country. On major fires, the distance between high-intensity heads, each with its own convection column, may be a mile or more. A conflagration covering 50,000 acres may have five or six high-intensity heads. High-intensity fires of 5,000 acres or less in flat country are likely to have only one high-intensity head with occasional smaller ones.

The Use of Models to Advance Understanding of Fire Behavior

Discussion of what is known and of what is being learned about fire behavior is not complete without some reference to fire models. They are perhaps the most important single device in the process of converting the unknown to the known, thus taking the mystery out of fire behavior. They are important too in clarifying the known. Their role in research is well explored in the reference cited.[2]

A model is always an idealized set of conditions for the fire itself or its environment. Its purpose is to simplify or to make more manageable the measurement and integration of the effect of all fire behavior factors. It is an essential device in fire research because of the many variables operating in the natural environment. But the fire model is also important to activities of the fire control organization, particularly fire control strategy and tactics, fire control planning, and training of men in wildfire behavior and control.

In research, wherever many factors enter into a phenomenon under study, it is very difficult to evaluate the separate effect of each. This is true particularly of fire behavior in the natural environment. So the usual approach is to exclude or to hold constant all environmental factors except the factor of immediate interest, then to vary it by a known amount and measure the effect on fire behavior. This requires rather rigid

[2]*The Use of Models in Fire Research*, NAS–NRC Committee on Fire Research, 1959.

controls, and since this is difficult to accomplish on a full scale, a variety of small-scale fire models are employed.

Fire models are of wide-ranging character, depending on their purpose. They may be categorized as follows:

Physical models:
    Small fires outdoors
    Small, controlled laboratory models using gas, liquid and solid fuels.
    Large outdoor physical models
Graphic models
Mathematical or conceptual fire models

Physical Models Most small field test fires are fire models of a sort. Usually the fuel and its arrangement are controlled and weather conditions are carefully selected. Though at full scale for ignition and early spread, the fire is kept small and measurement and study of fire behavior are limited to these phases only. Consequently, the data obtained will represent the early stages only of a fire's life history. Nevertheless, such data can be very valuable if such limitations are taken into account and are the source of most information on rate of spread of the fires in natural fuels.

In the laboratory a meaningful model becomes essential, though it may bear little superficial resemblance to a wild fire. Simple models are legion. An ignited kitchen match can serve as an effective demonstration model of the relative role of radiation and convection in the burning rate by the simple expedient of comparing rate of spread along the matchstick in the vertical position when the flaming end is above, when it is below, and when it is at various angles. Various small laboratory bench fires using gaseous, liquid, and solid fuels serve as useful models of other relationships. One study involved a small pan fire in a liquid fuel. When the fire was exposed to moderate-speed wind, it was demonstrated that direct transport of superheated gases can cause ignition of kindling fuels at distances well beyond the range of possible ignition by radiation (Chapter 6). The model designed to test the mechanism of the fire whirlwind, which has been described in a preceding section, is an excellent example of isolating a particular relationship of interest through a physical model.

Simple laboratory models of such relationships are often an essential first step toward their more complete measurement and understanding. But an integration of several relationships is usually necessary to describe the free-burning fire in a fuel complex. For that reason models of increasing complexity and sophistication are a natural trend in forest fire research.

At the Forest Service's Northern Forest Fire Laboratory at Missoula, Montana, field test fires in model arrangements of logging slash were carried out to test the effect of amount, arrangement, and condition of fuels. In the laboratory, carefully calibrated model fires in trays of ponderosa pine needles are designed to represent a cross-section of a fire front in matt type fuels. Studies have been conducted of heat transfer and fire spread using such models (Anderson, 1969; Rothermel, 1969).

One fire model, designed by W. L. Fons at the Forest Service's Southern Forest Fire Laboratory at Macon, Georgia, consisted of a specially constructed wood crib on a moving platform. It was ignited at one end and the fire was permitted to travel to the other. As the flame moved through the crib, the platform was moved at the same rate, permitting a fixed set of instruments to record essential measurements. This was designed to represent a section of the moving front of a large fire in well-ventilated fuels, extending from the leading edge back into or through the flaming zone. Design of this model and data obtained are described in a series of reports referenced in the bibliography. The reference cited (Byram et al., 1966) is the last report of the series.

At the Riverside, California, Forest Fire Laboratory, outside models of mass fire arrangements to represent the typical fuel loading of a city were constructed in the desert. These represent full-scale fire intensity but a model-scale conflagration-type fire. Such models necessarily become complex. They are designed to define the conditions favoring fire storms and other special phenomena exhibited by high-intensity mass fires (Countryman, 1969).

Graphic Models A graphic model is a visual device. It is designed to clarify a relationship and to promote easy visualization of the consequences of change in its primary factors. The model on which the Hornby fuel classification was based (Chapter 4) is a good example. Such devices have been used as the basis for planning fire control systems and are of frequent use in fire control training, fire prevention, and fire danger rating. They are discussed in subsequent chapters. Operations research, which is being applied increasingly to fire control problems, nearly always starts with a graphic model. In forest fire activities, most of the graphic models used require no computation and provide a concise substitute for detailed description. However, in operations research the model itself is likely to be computer-oriented or mathematically based.

Mathematical or Conceptual Fire Models   A   more   sophisticated type of model is the mathematical or conceptual model as applied by the fire physicist. Such an approach is necessary to the development and application of the natural physical laws that enter in.

In the first edition of this text, Mr. George Byram developed in some detail the abstract fire system model with which he was working in 1953. It provides a unifying concept and a base from which to examine the relationship between a fire and the total wind field. As such it is described briefly as a conceptual model in the following section. For more detailed study, the first edition should be consulted.

Limitations in Fire Models   All fire models simulate reality but fall short of it in varying degrees. In meeting the objective of simplifying relationships, minor factors are neglected and the model is usually based on a single set of idealized conditions. If fire-modeling laws are observed, this will permit approximations close enough for many purposes, but it is easy to forget that they are approximations only. Consequently, there is a strong tendency to apply models beyond their field of usefulness. To avoid this, the assumptions on which they are based and the range of conditions under which the model is valid need to be carefully defined and frequently rechecked.

A Conceptual Fire Model and Its Potential Application   This   fire system model as developed by Byram has four essential parts: (1) the earth's gravitational field, (2) a compressible fluid (that is, the earth's atmosphere), (3) a boundary surface beneath the compressible fluid (that is, the earth's surface), and (4) a heat source at or near the boundary surface. The fire then becomes only one of the four component parts of this model.

Fire behavior is determined by the interactions between the four component parts of the fire model. Some of these are very complex, especially for high-intensity fires. Others are more simple, such as an interaction involving only the boundary surface and the gravitational field. In level country, the direction of the gravitational field is perpendicular to the earth's surface and fire behavior is quite different than it is where the angle is much less or much greater than 90° up or down a mountain slope.

The most involved interactions are between the heat source and the atmosphere. Though not yet fully understood, they concern the energy relationships between the fire, the winds aloft, and the vertical temperature gradient of the atmosphere. To explore these relationships, two energy-criterion equations were developed. One of these represents the energy flow in the wind field, P_w, which is directly proportional to the cube of the wind speed. The second, P_f, is the computed rate at which thermal energy is converted into kinetic energy in the convection column over a fire.[3] The ratio between these two values is significant. Theoretically, when P_w is greater than P_f, the fire is completely dominated by the wind field.

Figure 7.4 illustrates the application of these criteria to an actual fire. P_f is a horizontal line because it was computed for a neutrally stable atmosphere. The level of P_f in this case far exceeds the value of P_w up to about 7,500 feet elevation. This would indicate that the energy of this particular fire should dominate the wind field at the time. This was confirmed by a case study. The evidence from other case studies indicated that blowup fires were likely to develop when P_f is greater than P_w for 1,000 to 4,000 feet above the fire. However, P_f is always less than P_w on the start. The transition when it equals, then exceeds, the inertial forces of the wind field may correspond to the sudden surge in burning rate (or blowup) often experienced in the development of high-energy fires.

Although strong convection over a fire is favored by low wind speeds both at the surface and aloft, the energy criterion shows that the rate of heat output or fire intensity is equally important. It also indicates that vertical structure is not determined by the actual magnitudes of the wind speed and intensity of the fire so much as by the relative values of P_w and P_f, that is, by the dimensionless ratio P_f/P_w. This ratio between

[3]

$$P_w = \frac{\rho(v - r)^3}{2g}$$ (7.1)

$$P_f = \frac{I}{c_p(T_o + 459)}$$ (7.2)

Equation (7.1) applies to the wind field, and Eq. (7.2) applies to the heat source. In Eq. (7.1), P_w is the rate of flow of kinetic energy in the wind field at some height, z, above the fire, g is the acceleration of gravity, ρ is the air density at height z, v is the wind speed at height z, r is the forward rate of spread of the fire, and $(v - r)$ represents the wind speed relative to the fire front, not a fixed point on the ground. In Eq. (7.2), P_f is the rate at which thermal energy is converted to kinetic energy in the convection column at any height, z, above the fire, I is the fire intensity, c_p is the specific heat of air at constant pressure, and T_o is the free-air temperature at the elevation of the fire.

The quantities in Eqs. (7.1) and (7.2) and the units in which they are measured are shown in the following tabulation:

Quantity	Units
P_w and P_f	Foot pounds per second per square foot
g	Feet per second per second
v and r	Feet per second
I	Btu per foot per second
c_p	Btu per pound per degree Fahrenheit
T_o	Free-air temperature, °F
ρ	Pounds per cubic foot

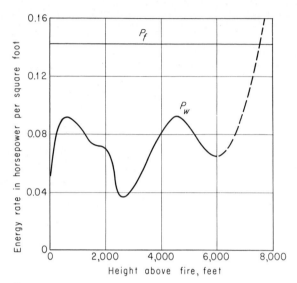

Figure 7.4 Application of energy-criterion equations. P_w represents the rate of flow of kinetic energy in the wind field above the Wood River Valley fire. P_f represents the energy-conversion rate in the convection column as a function of height above the fire.

buoyant forces and inertial forces, chiefly the wind field, has significance to the behavior of all fires.

Other Mathematical Models As stated in the discussion of the convection column, it tends to form an air curtain around itself. This causes the wind to flow around it much as if it were a solid object. Since this relationship is not taken into account in the preceding formulas, some physicists prefer a different mathematical approach in which total output of energy rather than energy per foot of fire front is used to express the equivalent of P_f and in which P_w is expressed as pressure exerted by wind on a barrier around which it can flow. The formula for wind pressure, or in this case F, then becomes:

$$F = \frac{C_d\, A\rho U^2}{2g} \tag{7.3}$$

where F = force in pounds on a cross section of the smoke column
C_d = drag coefficient (may vary from 1 to 1,000)
A = projected area of drag body in square feet
ρ = fluid density in pounds per cubic feet (free air)
U = fluid speed in feet per second
g = gravity in feet per second squared

Most basic research in forest fire behavior is concerned with mathematical models. These take the form of mathematical descriptions or equations by which the prediction of fire spread, fire intensity, or other aspects of fire behavior can be approximated. Though this process is complex and moves forward slowly, it gives much promise of steadily improving the ability to understand and to anticipate fire behavior in all natural environments. This is well illustrated by the previously cited work of Anderson and Rothermel (1968, 1969), at the U.S. Forest Service's Northern Forest Fire Laboratory, in developing equations for fire spread and intensity with varying fuel properties. These properties include moisture content, mineral content, loading, depth of fuel, and size-class distribution.

The Wind Profile

A vertical profile of the winds aloft usually shows considerable stratification in wind movement. Both wind speed and direction are likely to differ at different elevations above the surface. Though many variations occur, wind speed ordinarily increases with height up to several thousand feet above the surface. Byram (1954) found considerable evidence that when the opposite condition exists, blowup fires are more likely to occur. This was described as a situation where increase of wind speed above the surface was limited to the first 1,500 feet or less. Above this was a deep zone of decreasing wind velocity. This type of profile is illustrated by Figure 7.5. The A curve was based on 10 A.M. soundings. At that time the wind speed maximum was at the surface. Curve B represents a similar sounding six hours later. Arrows indicate the wind direction at different levels. Low-level jet winds such as illustrated by curve B are identified by Byram as the danger signals of blowup conditions, though they are not yet well understood. Those in the daytime are often associated with thermal turbulence or passage of a dry cold front, while nocturnal jets are ascribed by meteorologists to inertia oscillations in the earth's atmosphere that occur every 24 hours.

The use of wind profiles to sample the wind field aloft and to detect significant changes has many limitations. The most important is the difficulty of obtaining accurate data. The ascent of a pilot balloon needs to be observed and traced from two positions by theodolites placed at a measured distance from each other on a base line to ensure against error in wind speed and direction. Observations made by meteorologists in the course of daily weather forecasting are too infrequent and too far apart to be of much assistance in quantitative appraisal of fire behavior. Even very accurate measurements cannot be regarded as fixed. Most of the time the

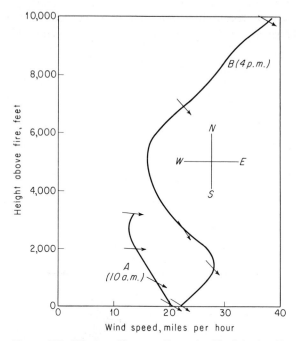

Figure 7.5 Wind profiles over Roanoke, Virginia, for 10 A.M. and 4 P.M., October 23, 1953. The Fort Lewis fire, about 10 miles to the southwest, reached its peak intensity and made its major run during this period.

wind field is in a state of flux, particularly when gusty or turbulent airflow prevails. So the measurements can produce only a sample or an approximation of the state of upper winds.

These limitations have been a severe handicap in the practical use of wind profiles in local forecasting. They have also been a handicap in efforts to carefully reconstruct the wind field in case studies after a high-intensity fire has occurred.

Nevertheless, what is happening in the atmosphere for a good many thousand feet up, as expressed by the wind profile, is obviously much more significant to fire behavior than the horizontal wind speed only at some spot near the ground. It is hoped that simpler, faster, and more accurate methods of obtaining wind profiles will develop. As this occurs, they will become a much more reliable gauge of the local wind field and hence of the dynamic environment with which high-intensity fires interact.

Fire Behavior Warning Signals and Their Interpretation

As stated at the beginning of this chapter, the degree to which fire behavior is understood places a ceiling on the efficiency attainable in all fire control activities. This is direct and crucial in fire fighting but applies as well to all fire planning and action programs.

In fire fighting there is a special premium on anticipating the behavior of a fire as far as possible in advance. This need is met in part by forecasts of fire weather and by operation of a system of fire danger ratings (as discussed in Chapter 8, which follows). Recognition of the warning signs of a potential blowup, or of conditions that favor the transition of a two-dimensional fire to a high-intensity three-dimensional fire, is particularly important (Figure 7.6). All sources of information need to be drawn on. To the experienced fire control man, firsthand observations are essential. A review of the more important conditions that are likely to generate a runaway fire is in order at this point.

Fuels For a given rate of spread and heat yield, fire intensity will be directly proportional to the weight of available fuel. Heavy volumes of fine fuel mean a hot, fast-moving fire. In mixed fuels, the availability of kindling fuels and vertical arrangements conducive to crowning become critical. Fuels alone can generate a high-intensity fire under moderate or even low fire-danger conditions. So the experienced fire man looks first at the fuels in which the fire is burning or into which it may spread.

Fuel Dryness For the several reasons previously discussed, fuel moisture content is the next most critical factor. It determines the ease of ignition, the amount of available fuel, and the burning rate for each class of fuel. Whenever relative humidities are as low as 20 percent or less, the moisture content of flash fuels and the outer surface of other fuels will also be low and ignition probability from falling embers will be high. Under prolonged drought conditions, ground fuels and heavy fuels will also be dry, greatly increasing the available fuel and fire intensity. Fires then crown more readily, and ground fuels burn more persistently. In a fire danger rating system these conditions will be expressed as a high spread index and a high intensity or drought index.

Topography Steep slopes greatly speed up the burning rate and the rate of spread of a small fire. When the head of a fire or a spot from it becomes established on a steep slope, a fast run to the top can be expected. The local mountain and valley winds generated by convection

Figure 7.6 Transition of a two-dimension to a three-dimension fire through crowning. *(U.S. Forest Service photo.)*

in sunny weather (Chapter 5) have a strong influence on the behavior of any fire in such terrain, and it can be expected to respond to the diurnal shifts in up-canyon and down-canyon air flow. Except under drought conditions, moisture content of fuels on steep north and east exposures will be significantly higher than on south and west exposures. This results in a slower rate of spread of a fire front on such slopes. Turbulence of airflow through ridge saddles and at forks in canyons with corresponding erratic fire behavior are also to be expected. Though an inversion may fill canyons after sundown with dense moist air, ridgetops may be exposed to brisk, low-humidity winds through lowering of the strata of gradient winds.

The Wind Field As outlined in Chapter 5, several of the more dangerous atmospheric conditions conducive to rapid fire spread can be forecast. For the most part they can be identified on the ground also by observation and by sample measurements of wind speed and direction and relative humidity. Observation of the behavior of the smoke column is very helpful. Probably the most critical is the arrival of a dry cold front. Next, particularly in the West, is the onset of foehn-type winds or subsidence of upper air, with its extremely low humidities, to the surface. Thunderstorm downdrafts are ordinarily of significance only in the West under conditions as described. Under conditions of strong local convection on a hot day, gusty and variable winds are likely to generate a fast burning rate but with rapid and unpredictable fluctuations in direction and rate of spread. The presence of dust devils and of bumpy flying also indicates thermal turbulence from unstable air which may extend several thousand feet above the terrain. This too spells trouble for the fire fighter.

Similarly, a combination of a strong, low-level wind aloft—even though surface winds are very light—with decreasing wind speeds in the upper strata has often been associated with conflagration fires. This combination is apparently favorable to the feed-down of energy to the surface. When such a condition exists, rapid growth of small fires and blowup of low-intensity larger fires is to be expected.

Early Spotting A fire should be regarded as capable of developing extreme behavior if in its very early stages it has a tendency to spot for any considerable distance, say 600 feet or more. Such spotting indicates the presence of susceptible fuels and of updrafts or whirlwinds capable of lifting up embers large enough to burn half a minute or longer before reaching the ground. A pattern of spot fires along the same straight line or curve accentuates this warning.

Dynamics of the Convection Column After a convection column has formed, the blowup may have already occurred or at least be well under way, so the characteristics of the column may be more significant from the standpoint of safety than of fire control tactics.

Motion or pronounced movement of the convection-column gases is a more immediate indicator of high fire intensity than is convection-column shape. Color changes as well as motion are indicative of the onset of high-intensity burning. An increased burning rate means a drop in combustion efficiency, which, in turn, results in much darker smoke with a dense, solid appearance.

Because of extraneous smoke and lack of perspective, shape and motion characteristics of the convection column can be observed better at a distance of several miles than at close range, although the direction of lean and the smoke drift aloft can sometimes be observed from nearby.

Chapter 8

Fire Danger Rating

The preceding discussions of fuels, weather, and fire behavior have
presented the reasons for the wide fluctuations in the fire potential that
may occur in time and by place. As both time and place change,
simultaneous changes in the fire potential or fire danger are likely to
occur. So it is not surprising that unaided personal evaluation of the fire
potential for a specific area at a specific time has been found to be difficult
and unreliable. Fire control officers may be asked the question: How
serious is the danger of fires starting, spreading, and doing damage today?
But it has been common for even the most experienced among them to
reach widely different conclusions. The purpose of fire danger rating is to
supply an objective basis and uniform guidelines for such evaluations.
This requires conversion of as much as possible of the empirical and
subjective approach to a measured and numerical basis. A first step in this
is to provide for separate evaluation of the variations of the fire potential
with time.

First it is important to be clear on what is meant by *fire danger*
and *fire danger rating.* Fire danger is the "resultant of both constant

217

and variable fire danger factors, which affect the inception, spread, and difficulty of control of fires and the damage they cause." Fire danger rating is "a fire control management system that integrates the effects of selected fire danger factors into one or more qualitative or numerical indices of current protection needs" (U.S. Forest Service, 1966).

As indicated, fire danger is a comprehensive term. Constant and variable factors include everything that influences whether a fire will start, spread, and do damage. All three potentials must be present. If all fire risk could be positively excluded from an area (including lightning), no fire danger would exist there. Under conditions when fires cannot spread—for example, when there is a snow cover or most fuels are wet—there is no fire danger. Finally, if fires can start and spread but do no damage, fire danger is also absent. Though such a situation was often believed to exist among early settlers and much more recently among graziers, it is rare in practice except for small areas.

HOW FIRE DANGER RATING BEGAN

A brief review of the early development of fire danger rating will provide for a better understanding of current practices in this field.

The history of this development is a lively and fascinating story, with a sequel in each forest region. Though the purpose was the development of an objective basis for decisions, a rather high degree of empiricism was always involved. So the story is built around persons and personalities in both fire control and in fire research. Only the highlights can be related here. It developed as a means of bolstering the judgment of the forest administrator in determining where and when short-season fire protection men were needed in a protected area. It was a natural concomitant to the establishment of large-scale areawide protection of the National Forests, which was organized shortly after the formation of the Forest Service in the Department of Agriculture in 1905 but was reorganized and strengthened after the great Idaho fires of 1910 and at subsequent intervals. Early leaders in the Service became increasingly conscious of the importance and variability of fire danger.

Coert Dubois, writing in 1914, had a clear concept of the elements affecting fire danger, of the need for some means of rating it, and of the fact that fire danger basically could be expressed in rate of spread. He had the concept but not the means of measuring and integrating the elements of fire danger. Shank (1935) was one of the first to develop a systematic method of evaluating fire danger. His method was based on cumulative measurement of relative humidity, with current danger indicated by total deviation from a norm or base assumed to indicate "normal" fire danger for the season. The method identified general burning periods but was not sensitive to significant day-by-day changes. Being entirely cumulative, it tended to underestimate current burning conditions when they were on the increase and to overestimate them when on the decrease.

Systematic attack on the problem of fire danger rating dates from the advent of organized research in fire weather in about 1925, mostly represented in the person of H. T. Gisborne. He published a study on the subject in 1928, and in 1933 he devised a "fire danger meter," an ingenious cardboard slide-rule device correlating five variables and expressing their combined effect in seven fire danger classes (Brown and Folweiler, 1953). The variables taken into account were:

1 Moisture content of fuels, represented by the weight of a standard-sized fuel stick exposed in a specified manner
2 Relative humidity of the air
3 Calendar date within the fire season (a measure of condition of vegetation and solar radiation)
4 Activity of fire-starting agencies (essentially lightning)
5 Visibility distance

The seven fire danger classes were defined in terms of both fire behavior and fire control organization as follows:

Class 1 Brush burning and other fires do not spread enough to require any trenching. No special protection organization needed.

Class 2 No spread under dense timber on north slopes. On open areas and on south slopes fires spread during the heat of the day. No special protection organization needed.

Class 3 Fires spread slowly and hold overnight on north slopes and under dense timber and make short runs in open and through slash. Running crown fires are very rare, however, except with fresh and strong winds. Requires skeleton fire control organization.

Class 4 Fires crown in single trees and groups but do not make long runs in full timber on north slopes. Occasional crown runs on south slopes and flats with moderate fresh winds. Requires full regular control organization.

Class 5 Occasional runs in full timber on north slopes but seldom crossing topographic divides. Fast spread certain on south slopes, cutover areas, and heavily fueled old burns. Requires first "overload" fire control organization with extra personnel added.

Class 6 Big runs common on all exposures within a single drainage but only occasionally crossing pronounced topographic barriers. Full fire emergency provisions and organization.

Class 7 Explosive conditions with fire spreading at rates up to 1,500 or 2,000 acres per hour including densely timbered north slopes during afternoon and evening. Topographic and other usual barriers such as rivers and large cultivated fields ineffectual during peak of day. Requires complete mobilization of all available forces.

In developing this first meter, Gisborne defined organization steps first and matched them with his appraisal of the corresponding fire behavior conditions, starting from no spread to the most explosive conditions known to occur. He then prepared his meter, calibrating it so that any combination of the variables selected could be resolved into one of the seven classes.

Measured by later standards, the meter had several imperfections. It included a mixture of flammability and organization factors almost impossible to correlate directly on a single numerical scale. Only the first three variables, fuel moisture, relative humidity, and calendar date affected flammability. One of the most important, wind, was omitted (but was soon added). The system was specifically tailored to fit the control organization, fire season, and fire behavior of a particular forest subregion—western Montana and northern Idaho. The classes were too few and unequal in size, and they were not very sensitive to changes in flammability. Like Henry Shank, he was concerned chiefly with developing guidelines for scheduling the placement of lookouts and other short-term personnel who made up the summer fire organization. For that purpose, it was more important to identify the beginning and end of the fire season than day-to-day changes in burning conditions. Also, the classes were interpretable only in terms of a particular kind of fire control organization in the area—that maintained by the U.S. Forest Service. There was grave doubt as to the applicability of such a scheme to other areas and organizations.

But the meter was based on sound principles; it filled a need, had vitality, and properly marks a milepost in the scientific development of fire control. Other agencies and National Forest Regions were urged to adopt the Gisborne meter. This elicited lively controversy and stimulated penetrating thinking and research on the part of fire control organizations in all forest regions of the country.

The result was a wide variety of new fire danger rating systems. This had both advantages and disadvantages. The advantages were a concerted attack on the problem and a broadening of the subject until it had grown far beyond Gisborne's original concept. Most of all, it resulted in the adoption everywhere of a systematic guide to the judgment of the forest fire control manager. Lack of perfection in all rating schemes also served to spur on each new inventor to produce something better. The disadvantages were the development of some nine to eleven rival systems of fire danger rating in the United States for National Forest protection areas. These eventually became an obstacle to the correlation of fire plans and policies within the U.S. Forest Service and posed a quandary to cooperating protection agencies. This has led to their replacement by a single national system.

A careful review of all factors affecting fire danger will clarify the available alternatives in developing a fire danger rating system.

ELEMENTS OF TOTAL FIRE DANGER

Since many factors affect total fire danger in one way or another, meaningful categories are needed by which they can be differentiated. This is done by grouping them into two broad classes, the constant or fixed factors and the variable factors. Constant factors can be dealt with through planning a year or more in advance, whereas variable factors combine to cause rapid but dynamic fluctuations in the potential fire fighting job. For efficient functioning, the fire organization needs to be aware of these fluctuations and of their magnitude. This is the objective of fire danger rating. *Fire danger rating is concerned only with that part of total fire danger that may vary throughout the day and from one day to the next.*

There is necessarily some overlap in the identification of fire danger factors as constant or variable in nature. Many have both fixed and variable aspects and may need to be considered in both categories, thus requiring some arbitrary distinctions. So-called "normal" or "seasonal" fire risk is considered a constant factor in terms of the average number of fires to expect. But fire-setting lightning storms and high concentrations of visitors, as during hunting and fishing seasons, are variable factors of fire risk. Forest fuels, even the special fuels created by logging operations, are treated as constant factors, but the vegetative stage of grass and annual vegetation is everywhere recognized as an important variable in fire danger. Similarly, the moisture content of fuels, which is regarded as a variable factor, may strongly control the fuels available to burn at a given time and may become a fixed factor in this respect. High moisture content in the heavier fuels may be just as effective in reducing the fire potential as their physical removal would be.

Constant Elements of Fire Danger

Climate   Climate, as distinguished from weather, is treated as a constant or fixed factor. It is a primary determinant of vegetative cover type and so of the quantity and nature of the natural fuels present. It also determines relative frequency and duration of critical fire weather. Consequently, and though far from a fixed quantity, it is the commonly used base on which fire plans are built.

Values at Stake   The values that may be adversely affected by fire are obviously an important factor in total fire danger. They are the justification for fire control expenditure and have a direct bearing on the intensity of protection. From this point of view, values threatened by fire comprise a fixed factor of chief concern in overall policy and current planning. However, the amount of damage done by a particular fire is closely related to its intensity, which in turn is closely related to burning conditions. This makes actual damage a dependent variable even though potential damage is fixed. But because it reflects location and does not directly affect fire behavior, it is not included among the variable factors used in fire danger rating.

Topography   The topography of an area is a truly fixed factor, but it is highly important in creating significant variations in fire danger from place to place. The effect of slope, as discussed in Chapter 7, is similar to the effect of wind. The steeper the slope, the faster the rate of spread, other things remaining unchanged. Under strong solar radiation, wind is generated on slopes, and nighttime inversions occur. These affect fire danger (Chapter 5). The relative elevation of an area and its aspect—that is, north, south, east, or west—also cause much variation in fire danger because of associated differences in local climate (Hayes 1941, 1944, 1949). Fuels on a south-facing slope may be dry enough to burn furiously, while similar fuels on an adjoining north slope will not carry fire. Variations of this kind need to be taken account of in applying fire danger ratings.

Solar Radiation   The radiant energy received from the sun on the earth's surface varies appreciably during the season with changing length of day. It also varies some from year to year because of atmospheric and solar changes, but it is relatively fixed and predictable at a given time and place. Its effect during the season is well reflected by meteorological measurements. It is properly treated as a fixed factor, but differences should be recognized in comparing seasonal fire danger between areas of widely different latitude.

Variable Elements of Fire Danger

Many of the variable factors overlap. Humidity, temperature, and precipitation are variable factors. But the chief significance of each is in the effect it has on fuel moisture.

An examination of the relationships of the common variable factors that influence or enter into fire danger rating follows.

Fuel Moisture Moisture content is of central importance since it directly controls the current combustibility of fuels. The capacity of fuels to vary in moisture content depends on their character. Dead fuels may be grouped as follows:

1 Fine fuels—grass, leaves, needles, tree moss, and loose surface litter. These fuels can absorb or lose moisture very rapidly, and their flammability can accordingly vary from none to high in a few hours. These are the kindling fuels.
2 Medium fuels—sticks, branch wood, medium-deep duff. These change moisture more slowly and cumulatively. Where they constitute the key fire-carrying fuels of an area, their moisture content is critical in suppression.
3 Coarse and heavily compacted fuels—logs, deep duff, and peaty material. These fuels change moisture content slowly and cumulatively over long periods; in large logs the change may span several years. Under drought conditions they may enter more and more into the first wave of heat energy produced by the fire. When very dry, they greatly increase the task of mop-up for the fire fighter, and when they burn completely they are likely to cause damage to the site, particularly in organic soil areas.

Wind Air movement is of major importance both as to speed and direction. The wind can change markedly in both direction and intensity from hour to hour. It is regarded as a primary variable since at low speeds, up to 5 to 6 miles per hour, it stimulates the rate of spread of a fire in direct proportion to its speed. For a considerable range above low speeds, the rate of spread corresponds to the 1.5 power of the wind speed. Wind also increases the rate of drying whenever fuel moisture is above the equilibrium point with air moisture.

Air Temperature Air temperature and relative humidity are closely associated (Chapter 5). Rising temperature rapidly reduces the relative humidity of the air and speeds up the drying rate of fuels. Air temperature or, more correctly, the ambient temperature affects the susceptibility of plant tissue to damage (Chapter 3), and temperature of the fuel as influenced by direct radiation and air temperature directly affects the energy required for ignition. Severe fire situations are frequently associated with high air temperatures. Temperature is both a daily and a seasonal variable and also has a cumulative effect on current fire danger through its effect on fuel moisture. This is analogous to the way that temperature summations give an index to the stage reached by a plant in its growth cycle.

Barometric Pressure   The pressure of the air mass at a particular time and place is mostly significant as an index of air-mass movement and hence of weather change, especially wind speed and direction. It is used daily by the fire weather forecaster. At high elevations, where low barometric readings are normal, less oxygen is available for free combustion. This has some effect on fire behavior but is so seldom a critical factor that it has not been used in fire danger measurement.

Upper Air Conditions   Upper air conditions (Chapters 5 and 7) are highly variable and are known to have influence on fire behavior, but so far they have not been incorporated into danger ratings.

Precipitation   The amount of precipitation and its duration are primary variables affecting fuel moisture and consequently fire behavior. Rain has an immediate effect on a going fire as well as on fire danger. It quickly wets kindling fuels and can check spread of a fire in both medium and fine fuels almost immediately. If it persists, it can reduce current fire danger to zero. As an element of fire danger, precipitation is also of longer term significance through its cumulative effect on fuel moisture. These effects can be expressed as

1   Current. May be expressed as days since last rain of a specified amount.
2   Seasonal. Cumulative seasonal precipitation gives a general index of moisture content in the coarser fuels. When compared to the normal for a given period, it becomes a useful indicator of the trend toward either drought or flood conditions.
3   Yearly or cyclic. A sequence of unusually dry or wet years has a powerful influence on fire danger. This comes about through their cumulative effect on the moisture content of logs, deep duff, and organic soils, increased growth of grass and annual vegetation in wet years, and increased dieback and needle fall in dry years.

Though primarily of concern as a short-term variable, precipitation is also a controlling factor in climates. It can be predicted in terms of normal seasonal or annual rainfall and treated as a fixed factor in some phases of planning.

Groundwater Level   In some areas, the height of the water table gives a direct index of the cumulative effect of surpluses or deficiencies in total precipitation and hence is related to the moisture content of the coarser fuels. A low water table has the further effect of exposing muck and other organic fuels to drying out. In some Southeastern areas, whether swamps are wet or dry is a major factor in gauging fire danger. When wet they serve as fire barriers, when dry as fire accelerators.

Relative Humidity and Dew Point The amount of moisture in the air compared to its capacity at any given temperature measures its drying power and hence is correlated with fuel moisture. Drying power of the air changes markedly from day to day and hour by hour. As a current variable it is most significant in controlling flammability of fine fuels. Cumulatively, it is used to show the trend of moisture content of medium to coarse fuels.

Condition of Vegetation The seasonal cycle has a pronounced effect on the availability of kindling fuels. Whether grass, weeds, ferns, brush, or other foliage fuels are green, curing, or dry has a tremendous effect on both the quantity and flammability of such fuels. In hardwood types, whether the leaves are green on the trees or dead on the ground can spell the difference between very little and high fuel hazard. Seasonal variations may vary the calendar date of a vegetative stage by two weeks or more from the average. In addition, severe drought or killing frosts may change the vegetative condition abnormally and suddenly. These characteristics of seasonal changes make the vegetative stage an important variable factor.

Fire Risk or Ignition Sources The activity of man and lightning in starting fires is a major component of total fire danger, having both fixed and variable aspects. While subject to change in trend through fire prevention action, man-caused fires are reasonably predictable by statistical examination of past experience. Lightning is seasonal in nature, but storms can be predicted fairly well on a short-range basis. How many fires they may start is less predictable. A common practice is to regard normal fire risk for an area as more or less fixed but unpredictable as to specific time and place.

Visibility One truly variable factor that is no longer included in systems of rating fire danger is atmospheric visibility. This is an important factor in the efficient detection of fires, and it assumes importance to fire organizations whenever poor visibility and high fire danger coincide. Since it has no effect on fire behavior, it is measured and its effect on the fire organization is dealt with independently of the other elements of variable fire danger.

Variable Elements Used in Fire Danger Rating

Several of the preceding variables are indirect in their effect or else they overlap. Some are significant only in relation to one class of fuel, some are difficult to measure, and some do not affect fire behavior. This has led to the selection of different elements for use in fire danger ratings in different forest regions and to considerable diversity in the relative weights given each. Nevertheless, the differences in field practice are more apparent than real. There are only three important variables; fuel moisture, vegetative stage (or availability of flash fuels), and wind speed. However, many difficulties arise in obtaining meaningful measurements. Correct sampling of fuel moisture in a forest fuel complex is particularly difficult. Relative humidity, fuel moisture in calibrated sticks, and days since last rain have all been used and each has validity in representing certain fuels. Vegetative stage is important in all fuel types, but the relative importance of annual vegetation in determining the degree of fire danger varies greatly by cover type. A further complicating factor is that no satisfactory quantitative method of measuring vegetative stage has evolved. Wind speed can be accurately measured, but free wind speed is reduced from 50 to 80 percent in a forest stand. This requires interpretation when the rate of development of a fire in a closed stand of timber is sought. However, the free wind speed in the open represents the potential to which the fire will eventually respond and is now accepted generally as the standard in determining fire danger ratings.

However arrived at, all rating systems make use of the moisture content of fine fuels and wind speed. They may use these to produce a burning index or a spread index for grass, but none of the systems in the United States stop there. They take account of cumulative drying effects in the intermediate and heavier fuels to produce a more meaningful index of the potential burning rate of forest fuels. This is done either by cumulating daily drying factors since the last rain or by measuring the moisture content of a calibrated fuel moisture stick. Most danger ratings of the 1940 to 1960 period were essentially a locally modified burning index.

BASIC PROBLEMS OF FIRE DANGER RATING

The danger rating systems that developed following the introduction of Gisborne's bold innovation had a common general purpose but differed in the variables utilized, in the relative weights given each, in the times and places measurements were taken, in the specific purposes served, and in the manner in which ratings were expressed. These deviations often represented valid difference in fuels, climate, and needs.

In developing a fire danger rating system, the first problem is to formulate objectives defining what the danger rating system should be designed to do. Once that is determined, decisions can be made on the following six basic problems of developing an operating system. Each justifies separate review, since the best answer can vary with differing fire environments. The differences in operating systems reflect differences in how one or more of these problems were resolved.

What to Measure

As already discussed, only the factors subject to daily variation at a given location are relevant. Of these, factors such as visibility affect performance of the fire organization rather than behavior of the fire, so they should not be integrated with behavior factors.

Of the variables affecting current danger, fuel moisture and wind stand out. Moisture content directly controls fuel flammability (Chapter 6). Although wind does not strongly affect ignition, it speeds fuel drying (which does increase ease of ignition) and it directly affects the rate of combustion and hence fire spread. Any danger rating scheme must include some measures of fuel moisture and wind. Air temperature and solar radiation affect fuel temperature, which in turn has a direct but not major effect on ignition and an important effect on the drying rate of fuel. High air temperatures also affect local winds (Chapter 5). The other current variables except visibility are significant mainly as they affect fuel moisture content and amount of available fuel. This is the primary significance of vegetative stage or condition.

To sample the correlated effect of precipitation, temperature, humidity, and wind, calibrated fuel moisture indicator sticks or slats were long used as a part of the measurement. With these sticks, each calibrated to weigh 100 grams oven-dry, the percentage of moisture content at any time is easily measured. Though research has demonstrated that equal accuracy in the low moisture range can be attained by the use of weather measurements, fuel moisture sticks have continued in use for some purposes.

Questions of economy may strongly influence decision on what to measure. Some elements are easier and cheaper to measure than others. There are strong reasons of economy and convenience to utilize data normally gathered at weather stations. Relative humidity, dew point, or air temperature sometimes are used because they are more readily available than more direct measures of fuel moisture such as indicator sticks and are also more sensitive to moisture changes in fine fuels.

In summary, what to measure entails the job of selecting the most significant yet economically measurable elements affecting current fire danger.

When to Measure

Since current fire danger varies from day to day and hour to hour, when to measure it is an important consideration. The main questions are the following:

Season or Period   From a fire control standpoint, there is no reason for taking measurements during periods when fire danger is not important. The winter is an obvious example over most of the United States. The problem is to know during what periods fire danger may be significant. The usual answer to this problem is to rely on past experience, as accredited by analysis of fire statistics, but to maintain a few danger-measurement stations out of normal season long enough to detect abnormal off-season periods of critical fire danger. This is a valuable practice. It often provides timely confirmation that critical fire danger can and does occur outside of the fire season. Danger measurements are sometimes discontinued at certain stations for short periods of low danger within the normal fire season. But key stations are continued.

From a cumulative and statistical standpoint, there are strong reasons for continuous daily measurements throughout the fire season. Most meters include cumulative features that virtually require it. Continuous measurements are necessary for comparing seasons in total. For these reasons, at least the key stations are usually operated continuously during the season.

Time of Day   There is considerable diurnal change in fire danger. The normal pattern is to be lowest at night, rising during the morning, usually reaching a peak shortly after midday. The question is at what time or times during the day it should be measured. The aim is often to rate danger at an average afternoon level for the day rather than at the highest for the day. A reading taken fairly early in the day, that can be used to give an indication of what the peak for the day may be, is often desirable. A practical consideration is the time of day observers are available to take measurements and the cost of taking and handling them. At a guard station, for example, noon is a more convenient time from a work standpoint than midafternoon. It is also important to schedule measurements so that they can be transmitted to a central dispatching point in time for most effective use. In practice, fire danger-rating measurements are taken on some fixed daily schedule one or more times per day with additional measurements taken as current danger may dictate. Correlations have been worked out between time of measurements, so that ratings taken at one time can be converted to their equivalent at another with a fair degree of accuracy.

Where to Measure

Since fire control is applied to very large and often heterogeneous forest areas in terms of microclimate, topography, and timber cover, difficult questions arise as to where danger measurements should be taken. Basically, the problem is to determine at how many points measurements should be made to give an adequate sample, and specifically where individual points should be located. There are several things to consider.

Fire Occurrence Logically, fire danger ratings should represent areas in which fires are most likely to occur. In the northern Rocky Mountains, for example, over 65 percent of all fires originate between the middle and top of the slope and only 7 percent on level areas (Barrows, 1951). Danger ratings made mostly on level areas (essentially valley bottoms) do not represent conditions on the middle or upper slopes, where most of the fires occur. An offsetting factor, however, is the fact that in this region the most dangerous fires occur at the lower elevations.

Fuel Types and Topography If at all feasible, direct measurements in the more dangerous fuel types are sought even though they may comprise a small portion of the total area. Usually too, in mountainous country, low-level and high-level fire danger stations are established to enable better interpolation of ratings. Studies by Hayes (1941, 1944) and others have shown that altitude and aspect have a strong influence on fire danger ratings. Valley-bottom and slope relationships in the northern Rocky Mountains, based on these studies, are summarized by Barrows (1951):

> **At Lower Elevations** On the north slopes burning index is lower during all periods of the day and night than at valley-bottom stations. On south slopes burning index is slightly higher during all periods except the evening transition period when it is about the same as the valley bottom.

> **On the Mid-Slope Areas (Thermal Belt)** On north slopes burning index is about the same as the valley bottom during the day and evening

transition period, and is higher at night. On south slopes burning index is higher at all times than in the valley bottom or at any other elevation.

At Upper Elevations   On north slopes burning index is about the same during the morning transition period as at the valley bottom, is lower during the day and evening transition period, and is higher at night. On south slopes burning index is higher than at the valley bottom at night and during the morning transition period, and is lower during the day and evening transition period. In general, there is less difference between north and south slopes at upper elevations than at midslope or at lower elevation.

This conforms to the general relationships discussed in Chapter 5, though the so-called thermal belt above the nighttime inversion is a highly variable relationship. Whether it exists and whether it would be a significant factor in fire spread needs to be determined for each mountain-valley regime.

Values at Stake   The location of high values in a protected area may need to be taken into account. Often such values are concentrated in small areas and priority may be given to locating fire danger stations either in such areas or in contiguous areas from which the threat of fire is most likely to come.

Cost Limitations   As always, cost is an immediate and often controlling consideration. The establishment, operation, and maintenance of danger stations are expensive, especially if they must be located at places other than where people normally are, as lookouts (provided the towerman lives at the site), guard stations, equipment headquarters, and the like.

Though expensive, fire weather systems that use automatic telemetering are coming into increasing use. They are designed to measure and record fire weather and to transmit the data at specified times or on command to a central receiving office. With such a system, fire control officers, in sampling fire danger, need no longer depend exclusively on reports from locations where fire control personnel are stationed.

How to Measure

Some of the most difficult technical problems of danger rating have centered on developing means of measuring variables known to be significant. Fuel moisture is an excellent example. Research has confirmed its critical relationship to ignition and spread of fire in all classes of fuels. How to obtain a representative measurement for a fuel complex or of even a single class of fuel has required painstaking research. Moisture content can be measured directly by use of sample duff beds or by representative fuel indicator sticks of different sizes and shapes that are exposed in various ways. It can be measured indirectly, both currently and cumulatively, by relative humidity or days since last rain of specified amount. Similarly, a great deal of research has been devoted to devising cheap and efficient means and techniques of measuring precipitation and wind. Standard Weather Bureau instruments are excellent but too expensive for general forest use, so cheaper yet sufficiently accurate rain gauges and anemometers have been developed.

The establishment and maintenance of danger measurement stations, entails solution of questions regarding specific location of stations, standards for the mounting and exposure of instruments, and procedures to ensure accuracy and consistency in the taking and reporting of data. As a case in point, should stations be situated in the open or placed in forest stands more nearly representative of actual forest conditions? Much thought and research have been given to this question. It has been resolved in favor of open stations where observations can be standardized and made more consistent.

How to Integrate Measurements

Since a danger rating is a composite figure, the different elements included in it must be weighted and integrated. This entails some of the most fundamental problems of danger rating. For example, what is the relationship between specific measures of wind and fuel moisture and rate of spread? Is their effect on rate of spread also directly related to ignitibility of fuels, and hence indicative of fire occurrence, risk remaining constant? What is the effect of days since the last rain of specified amount, or of the average moisture content of $^1/_2$-inch round sample fuel sticks for the last 5 days on fuel flammability? What is the specific effect of current or cumulative levels of relative humidity?

The unique feature of danger rating is not so much the measurement of individual factors as the determination of their joint effects on ignition and spread. The problem is complex. In part, the solutions that have been achieved are based on controlled measurements and fairly close mathematical correlations. In part, however, they rest on empirical observation and experience. Various combinations are tried based on available measured data. If the resultant rating does not jibe with what is observed on the ground during actual fires, it is adjusted so that it does. Fire danger ratings as developed, though usually numerical in expression, should not be thought of as accurate mathematical correlations of completely measurable phenomena. Wind speed, temperature, humidity, and the weight of a calibrated fuel moisture stick can be precisely determined at a specific time and place, but the determination of their joint effect is at a much lower order of accuracy. If the measurements are not fully representative of the local protection area to which they are applied, this further reduces accuracy of the ratings.

How to Apply Danger Ratings

A final and crucial problem is how to apply danger ratings, once developed, in the practice of fire control. A simple burning index based on a single class of fuel can be so designed that it will predict the rate of spread of fire in that fuel quite successfully. Because of this, there was a strong early tendency to develop a separate rating scheme for each important fuel type. This trend was modified, however, by the need to have a unified scheme for a whole state or a National Forest region. When modified to cover a range of fuels to serve this purpose, the rating scheme then becomes less and less a direct measure of fire behavior but instead a set of key numbers from which interpretations can be made. The eight to eleven rating schemes that were developed in the 1935 to 1945 period ranged from a one-fuel burning index to very complex sets of index numbers. Beginning in 1958, work in the United States toward unifying all existing rating schemes into a complete national system was initiated. Though there is doubt that a national system for general use can be as simple and as accurate as a single fuel system, the advantages are so great that progress toward achieving such an objective will no doubt continue.

STRUCTURE OF FIRE DANGER RATING SYSTEMS

In Figure 8.1, the basic structure adopted for the national system in the United States is shown. It represents a consensus among fire danger experts and gives recognition to the fact that no single index is adequate for all purposes. Four aspects or phases are recognized: risk, ignition, spread, and fuel energy.

Risk represents the relative activity of fire starting agents, both natural and human. But risk is significant only in relation to fuels. To make an estimate of the probability of fires starting, the risk must be combined with the probability of ignition. More specifically, the fuel susceptible to ignition by the kind of firebrand to which it is being exposed (Chapter 4) is the critical second term in the computation. For example, fires caused by cigarette butts in a recreation area tend to become more and more prevalent and persistent as the moisture content of punky wood

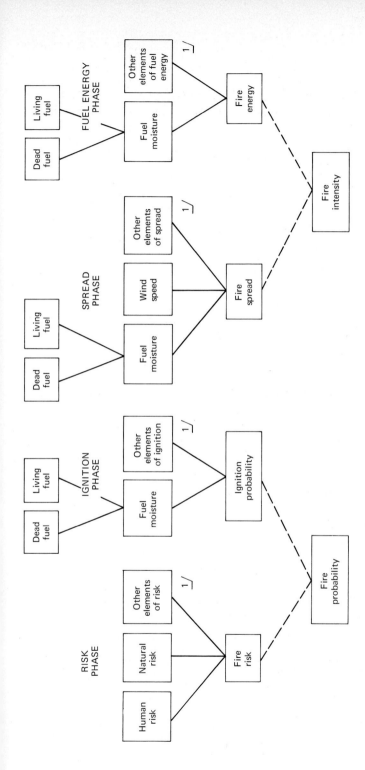

1/ Significant weather or fuel elements to be identified and evaluated by continuing research.

Figure 8.1 Basic structure of national fire danger rating system. *(U.S. Forest Service.)*

and duff recedes. When both fire risk and the ignition probability of a specific fuel can be related numerically, a meaningful index of fire probability can be developed. This can tell the fire control manager how many fires to expect.

Ease of ignition or relative flammability of fuel is significant in other respects as well. A fire spreads by a series of ignitions. Consequently, ignition probability is closely related to the burning rate of the fuel. But neither ease of ignition nor burning rate alone determine rate of spread of a fire; wind speed, other characteristics of the fuel type, and the topography also enter in. When these are taken into account to predict rate of spread, the result is a burning index or fire spread index. Usually, fuel type and topography are considered separately in such determinations. When made specific in this way, a spread index becomes very useful in estimating the potential size of the job of controlling a small fire. But it may not correlate well with the damage done nor with the behavior of the fire if it is not controlled in its early stages. Damage is more closely related to the rate of energy release and the level of heat energy developed. These primarily reflect the volume, arrangement, and flammability of available fuels. When such elements are also taken into account, an index of fire intensity can be computed which is related more directly to severity of damage from wild fires and to large-fire behavior.

If reliable indicators of each of these components were available to the forest manager, they would be valuable to him in several ways. Good data on the relative risk of fires starting from each source of ignition and kind of use would permit much better apportionment of the prevention effort and much better efficiency in that activity. Such data, coupled with the relative probability of ignition, would yield an estimate of the number of fires to expect per 1,000 acres or other unit. Reliable estimates of this kind would enable the manager to sharpen the daily management of the detection and communication systems and the dispatching service. A reliable index of fire spread when related to fuel type and topography provides an estimate of the probable size of a fire at given intervals after ignition. This is valuable to the dispatcher[1] in deciding the fire fighting force needed to control the fire. If this is coupled with the index of fire probability, then both the number and size of fires to expect per day or per week can be estimated and the potential of the current fire fighting job is given dimension. This permits alert management of all fire fighting resources. If, in addition to the rate of spread of a fire, reliable data on the

---

[1]A dispatcher is a person who receives reports of discovery and status of fires, confirms their location, takes action promptly to provide the men and equipment likely to be needed for control in first attack, and sends them to the proper place. For additional needs he acts on orders from the fire boss. (U.S. Forest Service, 1966.)

rate and quantity of heat energy it will release can be estimated, then the damage it will do can be more closely estimated and the full difficulty of controlling it can be better appraised. Consequently, the average energy release per fire times the number of fires, which gives a number expressing the energy release per day, becomes significant as a measure of the severity of the fire load per day. When summed up for the season, it gives a significant measure of the severity of the fire season.

Each of the questions answered by these indicators or indexes enters into decision making in all forest fire control organizations. When only a single index is available, it tends to be used for all purposes, although no single correlation can do so accurately. Consequently, a complete system needs to be on a multi-index basis. The first step in developing a national system was the devising of a single fire spread index. Components of this spread index are illustrated by Figure 8.2, taken from the U.S. Forest Service handbook on this subject.

Across the top of this graph are the four weather measurements plus the estimated herbaceous stage for the area of interest. Dry-bulb temperature is repeated to avoid confusion in the graph. Starting with herbaceous stage and the dry-bulb and wet-bulb temperature relationships (which may be utilized in any one of three forms: relative humidity, depression of the wet bulb, or dew point), the moisture content of the fine fuels can be determined from prepared tables. This, when correlated with wind speed, can be used to identify the relative rate of spread of fire in fine fuels (grass, leaf litter, pine-needle litter). But in a forest stand, the fine fuels are usually only one component of the fuel complex. Branch wood and other slower-drying components of the litter also must be taken into account. This is done by recording how long they have been exposed to drying influences and the rate of drying each day, gauged by temperature and relative humidity of the air and expressed in the form of a "buildup" index. This, when associated with the fine fuel moisture, is used to identify a more representative or adjusted fuel moisture content. When correlated with wind speed, this yields a fire spread index representative of a timber cover. These are the general relationships on which most fire danger rating is based.

In developing the national system, five classes of fuels are taken into account. Three of these are dead fuels, two are living fuels. The dead fuels are classified according to their time lag in drying. Time lag is the time required for a fuel to lose approximately 63 percent of the difference between its initial moisture content and its equilibrium moisture content. A range of 200 hours for the three time-lag classes was adopted. The three time-lag classes are the 1-hour, the 10-hour, and the 100-hour classes. Their respective ranges are 0 to 2 hours, 2 to 20 hours, and 20 to 200 hours.

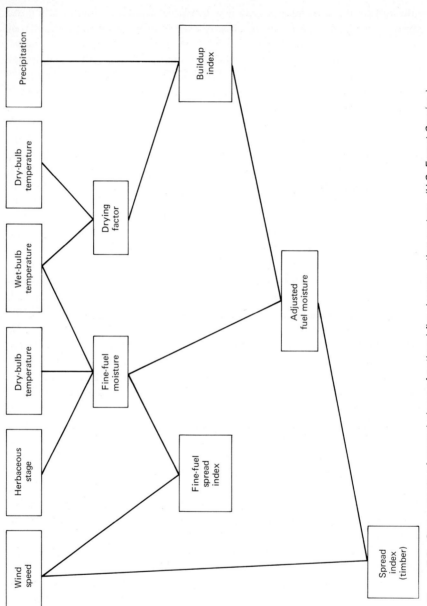

Figure 8.2 Components of spread phase of national fire danger rating system. *(U.S. Forest Service.)*

Their significance is illustrated by data for the fine fuels in the 1-hour class. They will lose approximately two-thirds of the moisture they hold above equilibrium at 80°F and 20 percent relative humidity in the first hour and on up to 99 percent at the end of five hours. This means they can dry out almost completely during a dry, warm day.

The other classes are similarly related under a given set of drying conditions. Beyond the 200-hour range, drought from cumulative or prolonged drying over several months or years is also significant though more difficult to identify mathematically. It often increases available fuels by causing dieback in living fuels and deep drying in organic soils, logs, and stumps. It is usually complicated by transpiration and water table effects. Since drought often sets the stage for conflagration fires, a separate drought index has also been given attention (Keetch and Byram, 1969).

Two classes of living fuels are identified. They are (1) grass and other herbaceous plants, and (2) twigs less than 1/4-inch in diameter and the foliage of woody plants. This is believed to include the range of living material that can be dessicated and burned by a moving flame front.

Additional steps toward establishing a more complete national system in the United States were taken by a special research unit which was set up in 1968 (Deeming, Lancaster, Fosberg, Furman, Shroeder, 1972). This system is designed to be flexible by making use of fuel models to represent a range of naturally occurring fuel situations. Nine such models were set up in 1972. This permits a more direct evaluation of local fire danger by the device of "plugging in" the appropriate fuel model.

SIGNIFICANT VARIATIONS IN DEVELOPMENT OF FIRE DANGER RATING SYSTEMS BY AGENCIES

As outlined in preceding discussions, danger ratings in the United States were at first closely tailored to a single fuel type (Gisborne, 1928). Later they were adapted to represent fuels and weather of a forest region. These were in the regional pattern adopted by the U.S. Forest Service in administering the National Forests. The result was nine distinct rating schemes within the U.S. Forest Service during most of the period 1938 to 1963.

In Canada, beginning with the Wright Tables (1933–1946), fire danger rating also developed early. It assumed a more national status from its beginnings at Petawawa Forest Experiment Station in Ontario through the progressive development of forest fire danger tables for each major fuel type in each Canadian province (Beall, 1939–1947; Villaneuve, 1948; Williams, 1963). As in the United States, continued study has been given to devising a truly national fire index. Its objective is to consistently identify the kind of fire behavior to expect from each combination of variable fire danger factors. The resulting *Forest Fire Weather Index* or *FWI* was issued in published form in 1970. As described by C. E. Van Wagner (1970), it is a measure of fire intensity, that is, energy output rate per unit length of fire front in the standard fuel type. The standard fuel type is rather heavily weighted by fuels in lodgepole pine and jack pine forest types. In a similar manner to the national system under development in the United States fuels are classified according to their drying rate or time lag. In the Canadian system, three distinctions are recognized: (1) $2/3$ day, fine fuels typical of pine litter; (2) 12 days, the duff layer; (3) 52 days, slow-drying fuels which continue to lose moisture in long term drought. For administrative use, index ratings are grouped into conventional fire danger classes.

In Australia, several fire danger rating systems were tried out prior to 1950 (Cromer, 1946). But such ratings did not come into regular use until 1963, when A. G. McArthur devised a comprehensive system based on fire behavior studies (Luke, 1961; McArthur, 1963, 1966). The Australian fire danger ratings have been designed especially to serve as a guide to safe practices in prescribed burning.

Danger Rating Scale

Initially, danger ratings were identified only by descriptive classes. The first Gisborne meter had seven such classes. When used as a guide to administrative action, the boundaries between certain classes grew in importance, since action was geared to the crossing of class boundaries. It was found too that classes were unequal and that more discrimination within classes was needed. This led to the development of a numerical scale by which to identify the progression from low to high fire danger and by which classes could be defined. A 100-point scale was adopted for this purpose. The original concept was that zero would be at the point where a set fire would soon die out, and the top or 100-point level of the scale would constitute the most flammable condition that could occur naturally, with the range between equally divided. Under this concept, the midpoint would be expected to mark the threshold of high and extreme fire danger. In practice, the 100-point scale did not conform to this concept. Most ratings were made proportional to rate of forward spread of small fires or to the rate of perimeter increase. Both follow a geometric progression, with increase in flammability and with time. When such a progression is fitted to an arithmetic 100-point scale, the points of the scale do not assume equal importance to the fire control man. This is evident by referring to Figure 8.3. This is an illustration of the type 8-100-O fire danger meter used for many years in the southeastern United States. Class 1 includes index number 1 only, Class 5 includes all the scale above 50. Though nearly all burning-index ratings were fitted to a 100-point scale (some of the 8 to 100 series to a 200-point scale), each differed in how it was done and danger classes were not identical.

The spread index of the national fire danger rating scheme in-

Figure 8.3 Forest fire danger meter, type 8-100-O, developed by the Southeastern Forest Experiment Station, U.S. Forest Service. *(U.S. Forest Service photo.)*

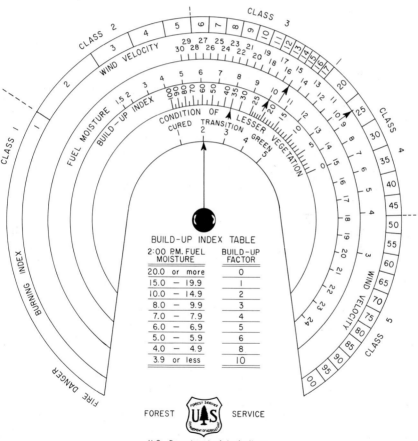

troduces uniformity in the scale. The completed system also provides for five classes of fire danger with a color code for each. But it permits flexibility in the identification of these fire danger classes for local administrative use.

Form of Presentation

The combined effect of the variable factors on fire behavior must obviously be arrived at by a series of correlations. The most direct and unequivocal manner of applying such correlations is by means of tables and curves derived from experimental data and computations. These permit graphic determination of the rating for a given set of measurements. However, beginning with the first Gisborne system, a slide-rule type of gadget or so-called meter has been a prominent feature of most rating schemes. Both horizontal and circular slide-rule patterns have been employed, usually of pocket size. These permit faster determinations and have the advantage of reducing the errors that arise in the more complex manipulation of tables and graphs. However, in spite of much ingenuity in taking account of all variables in a slide-rule device, there is usually some loss of accuracy due to rounding off, telescoping scales, etc. Probably the most important factor favoring the use of slide-rule types of danger meters has been in their public relations value. They attract attention, their manipulation arouses curiosity, and their design imparts an air of scientific precision. Attention-getting qualities of this kind are often not given much weight by the scientist, but they are of great importance in training nontechnical personnel and in educating the public.

A further step in recognizing the public relations potential of fire danger rating was in the development of the fire danger board. It was first developed as a substitute for the fire danger meter in the Northwest region of the United States for Washington and Oregon. The principle was adopted and further developed in the central Rocky Mountain region for Colorado, Wyoming, and South Dakota, and later for Arizona and New Mexico, where heavy dependence was placed on local resident cooperators both to detect and control forest fires. The fire danger board was a medium-size display panel for use under shelter at key locations where it would be observed by forest users and fire cooperators on foot. The state of each factor used in the rating, as well as the rated fire danger, were represented by a color code and clearly posted by use of slides and pointers. This substituted for a danger meter and made the rated fire danger a more graphic and more understandable situation.

From these beginnings have developed the large roadside fire danger display boards illustrated by Figure 8.8, page 255, and the color code described later.

Elements Measured   The variables actually measured and used in fire danger rating have already been discussed. By 1940, vegetative stage, fuel moisture in a calibrated stick, relative humidity, and wind speed had become the standard components of fire danger rating. But variations in arriving at the significant fuel moisture measurement persisted. Throughout most of the West, $1/2$-inch round ponderosa pine fuel moisture sticks served in place of the basswood slats used in most of the East. In the 1958 revision of the California system, three different correlations to produce separate ratings for grass, brush, or timber were used, related to the fuel of principal interest. The grass-burning index reflected an adjustment for percent of curing, the brush-burning index took into account the seasonal changes in moisture content of brush crowns, and large-log moisture studies were drawn on to identify the cumulative drying or buildup in timber fuels. Such distinctions have contributed to the development of the national system.

The dry bulb temperature was given additional weight in one of the older systems (Brown, 1939) because of the close association between very high temperatures and conflagration fires in the high plains and foothills of South Dakota and Wyoming. No doubt this represented strong convective activity.

So far no measurement representing the wind field above a fire, other than horizontal wind speed, has been devised for use in fire danger rating. Further investigation of wind profiles has promise in this respect.

Cumulative Features

The system developed in the Lake states was the first to utilize weather measurements and days since last rain to substitute for fuel stick moisture determinations. The success of this method has led to further refinement, such as the buildup index of the national system and the drought index initiated in the southeastern United States in 1955.

SPECIFIC COMPARISON OF FORMER REGIONAL SYSTEMS

The form these variations took in practice is well illustrated by comparing two regional systems representative of the East and of the West in the United States. Such a comparison can further clarify the various issues in developing a danger-rating system. The two systems selected for this purpose are the 8-100-O fire danger meter used in the Southeast and the model 8 burning index meter used in the Intermountain and the Rocky Mountain states of the Northwest. Both served large forest areas for the decade prior to 1964 and had evolved over a much longer period. They were developed independently and differ in several important respects, though they also have much in common. The model 8 meter is the successor to Gisborne's original danger-rating system.

The meters themselves differed. That for the 8-100-O is a circular slide rule (Figure 8.3) developed in 1954 by the Southeastern Forest Experiment Station. That for the model 8 burning index meter is of the envelope and movable slide type (Figures 8.4*A* and *B*) first developed by the Intermountain Forest and Range Experiment Station in 1955. Both meters

Figure 8.4   Burning Index Meter.

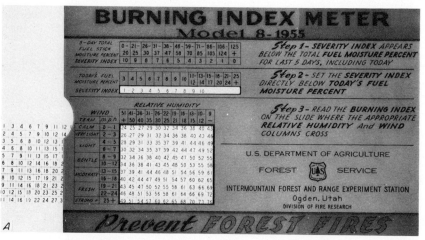

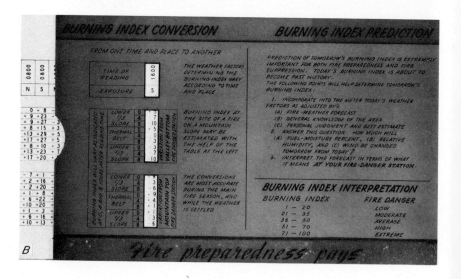

Figure 8.5 Typical open fire danger measuring station. *(U.S. Forest Service photo.)*

have a 100-point burning-index scale, though the meaning of *burning index* is not identical. The model 8-100-O is linear in relation to average occurrence of fires per day. The model 8 burning index is a nonlinear numerical description of the ease with which a fire will start and spread.

The fire danger stations at which fire weather data were measured were to similar specification and similar data were taken. Wind speed was measured in the open at 20 feet above ground level with similar corrections for obstructions. Both systems used fuel moisture indicator sticks, though of different specifications. The 8-100-O used a set of three weathered flat basswood slats (venetian-blind stock) calibrated to fall in the range of 95 to 105 grams dry weight. The model 8 used a set of four $1/2$-inch pine dowels calibrated to weigh exactly 100 grams oven dry weight. Both systems used the same especially designed fuel moisture scale for weighing the indicator sticks where the percent moisture could be read directly, even though the dry weight of the stick varied from 100 grams. Both systems required similar exposure of the sticks in the open under a screen shade on a wire support over a prepared bed of litter. In the East, 4 inches of hardwood leaves were used, while a $1/2$-inch bed of pine needles was used in the West. Shading was by 14- to 16-mesh wire screen. Up to six layers of screen wire were used in the full-shade period in the East, but only two were used in the West.

The integration of fuel moisture measurements into the burning index was similar but not identical in the two systems. For the 8-100-O system, fast-drying fuels were represented by a visual determination of the vegetative stage plus the moisture content of the basswood slats. Slower-drying fuels were represented by a buildup index derived from cumulated 2 P.M. slat-moisture readings reduced by precipitation. In the model 8 system, fast-drying fuels were represented by relative humidity and $1/2$-inch moisture stick measurements; slower-drying fuels were represented by a severity index based on cumulative five-day measurements of $1/2$-inch stick moisture. The different drying regimes in each case were weighted and combined with wind speed to produce a number on a 100-point scale. In the 8-100-O system, the first three fire danger classes occupied only the 0 to 20 section of the scale; in the model 8 system they occupied 0 to 50 on the scale. But the two remaining classes, high and extreme, had similar significance to fire control officers.

The measurements required to operate these two systems were as follows:

Model 8	**Model 8-100-O**
Dry-bulb temperature	Condition of lesser vegetation (visual)
Wet-bulb temperature	Precipitation
$1/2$-inch stick moisture	Basswood-slat moisture
Wind speed	Wind speed

FIRE DANGER CLASSES AND COLOR CODES

As brought out in the discussion of the development of fire danger rating, each system, beginning with that of Gisborne, used descriptive classes of fire danger regardless of whether they were also identified in relation to a numerical 100-point scale. This pattern has been continued with the fire spread index. Five classes of fire danger are identified with its ratings. These are low, moderate, high, very high, and extreme. Each fire danger class represents the net effect of several factors which can be combined to identify a broad but fairly distinctive level of potential fire load to a fire fighting agency. Though imperfectly identified with firespread index ratings, the general progression as described in U.S. Forest Service handbooks is about as follows:

Low Fuels require an intense heat source to ignite, such as lightning. Fire spreads by flame in flash fuels only and persists overnight only as a smoldering or creeping fire in ground fuels. Spotting does not occur. Mop-up procedures only are needed to control fires.

Moderate   Fine dead fuels ignite from most firebrands but most of the time fail to kindle heavier fuels. Fires in open, cured grassland may spread rapidly with the wind, but woods fires spread at slow to moderate rates. Fire intensity is low except where fine dead fuels are concentrated. Short-distance spotting may occur but is not a serious problem. Control of fires is relatively easy at all stages.

High   All fine dead fuels ignite readily and all sources of risk have a fire-starting potential. Fires spread rapidly in most fuels and short-distance spotting is common. High-intensity burning occurs on slopes and in fuel concentrations. Crown fires may occur. Tendency in mixed fuels is for fire intensity to keep on building for several hours. Control is difficult if it is not completed in the early stages of buildup.

Very High   Fires start easily from all causes, spread rapidly, and increase quickly in intensity. Spot fires are a constant threat. Long-distance spotting and fire whirlwinds may occur. Direct attack on the head of a fire is feasible for only the first few minutes after ignition occurs.

Extreme   All fires start quickly, spread furiously, and burn intensely. Small fires reach the blowup stage more quickly than in the "very high" category. A high percentage develop violent behavior and become runaway fires which defy conventional methods of control. Spotting, crowning, and high-elevation convection columns are common characteristics. Direct attack is rarely possible and may be dangerous except immediately following ignition.

Color Codes   As discussed earlier in this chapter, colors were used early in the development of fire danger boards. Later, in the Denver region, they were used both for this purpose and as a part of the code for action plans devised to fit fire danger. This feature has been incorporated into the national system of fire danger rating being developed by the U.S. Forest Service. The color code is as follows:

Low	green
Moderate	blue
High	yellow
Very high	orange
Extreme	red

ESTABLISHMENT AND OPERATION OF FIRE DANGER STATIONS

Fire danger stations provide the essential information on which fire danger rating is based. They reflect the decisions made in respect to the questions of what to measure and where to measure it. In their operation, they also reflect the decisions on how and when to obtain the measurements. To serve their purpose properly, each should sample an important area and each should operate according to strict standards of consistency and accuracy, otherwise the potential value of the system may be seriously impaired. Specific standards for the establishment and operation of fire danger stations have been drawn up by each fire control agency. These are incorporated in administrative handbooks, copies of which may usually be obtained on request. The most important specific requirements may be related to the following categories.

Site Location

The area the site is intended to represent must be determined in advance, as this influences the selection of the site. Originally, timbered sites were often used, but there are so many erratic variations in natural shielding from sun and wind by timber cover from one spot to the next that open locations have become the standard. Elevation, topographic relation, and exposure to wind and sun are important factors. Accessibility is also an important factor, since an observer must be available. A poor site is often accepted because it is close to a forest employee. Automatic telemetering stations have the virtue of freeing the selection of the site from requirements in this respect. Though costly, they are being installed in key locations where access by fire control personnel or cooperators is difficult or time-consuming (Figure 8.6).

Installation

Usually an enclosure is necessary to protect the fire weather equipment from disturbance by animals or other agents. Instruments of proved adequacy for the purpose must be mounted according to specifications and kept in repair.

Equipment

Usually a standard shelter in which equipment such as the psychrometer, maximum-minimum thermometer, and similar equipment are housed is a prominent feature. This provides uniformity in the degree of shade and shelter under which air temperature is measured. Psychrometers in use may consist of the hand-operated sling psychrometer, the hand-fan psychrometer, the electric-fan psychrometer, or the separately mounted mortarboard psychrometer. Special significance has so long been associated with relative humidity, particularly in western regions of the United States, that most fire agencies prefer to continue to determine

Figure 8.6 Automatic telemetering fire danger station which automatically measures and transmits, either on demand or on a programmed schedule, the fire weather data needed to rate fire danger at this site.

dry-bulb and wet-bulb temperatures and to refer them to the proper psychrometric table for the elevation of the site in order to obtain a current measurement of relative humidity. However, in computing the spread index as described, the difference between the wet-bulb and the dry-bulb readings, which is known as the wet-bulb depression, can be used instead. Anemometers to measure wind speed are a universal feature, but they too vary a great deal. Many are standard Weather Bureau equipment, but many forest installations utilize lighter and less expensive equipment. They may be equipped with a buzzer, a flasher, a counter-timer, or a dial recorder. The wind speed is determined by referring the counted number of buzzes or flashes in a specific time interval to a conversion table or, in later dial models, by reading it directly. Wind direction is nearly always determined, though it does not enter into the ratings. It is indicated by a wind vane to the nearest 45°, or it may be transmitted or recorded to the nearest degree by a direct or remote dial converter.

A maximum-minimum thermometer may also be utilized, since it provides a useful supplement to the dry-bulb–wet-bulb record for later analysis.

A rain gauge is essential equipment, since the amount of precipitation is one of the primary factors in determining relative dryness of fuels. It may be of several types, including the self-recording. Mostly measurement of precipitation is accomplished by catching a sample in a vertical-sided can of known cross section and measuring the depth with a graduated stick.

At certain stations a hygrothermograph may be maintained in order to obtain a continuous record for research or other use. The chart may be of only the 24-hour capacity or may operate unchanged for seven days.

Since the moisture content of fuel moisture sticks does not enter into the U.S. Forest Service's national fire spread index, they are no longer required at fire danger stations. This eliminates the exacting requirements for proper mounting, shading, and weighing of the sticks and for integration of their moisture content into ratings. This simplifies the operation and maintenance of fire danger stations. It also enables all weather stations to become forest fire danger stations without introducing new measurements. The determination of vegetative stage and the computation of a buildup index are the only additions required.

The phasing out of fuel moisture sticks is not universal. They have had the special advantage of automatically correlating all factors affecting the moisture content of a stick without any computation. Because of this they have found supplementary uses, particularly in helping to identify conditions favorable to success in prescribed burning. So long as calibrated sticks are obtainable at a reasonable cost, there will be some continuing use of this kind.

Maintenance

A high standard of maintenance is essential. This includes the enclosure, the control of weeds and grass on the site, the installation and mounting of each instrument, and the maintenance of all instruments (Figure 8.5).

Operation

A written set of instructions on the exact procedure to use in taking each daily measurement is an important feature, since observers are seldom technically trained and substitutes may be used. Frequent checking is necessary to ensure that all standards are met.

Recording

Requirements include use of the proper form, neat and legible entries in pencil, prompt recording after observation, missed data explained, and all data properly recorded. A daily record sheet for computing fire spread ratings is illustrated by Figure 8.7.

Computations

Although computations are never complex, they seem always to be a common source of error on the part of observers who take time out from nonrelated jobs. The most common sources of error are in determining relative humidity, in computing the buildup index, and in computing the proper spread index. The use of a fire spread index meter to substitute for tables reduces the number of errors. But the primary remedy is through training of observers and systematic follow-up inspection to maintain a high degree of quality control. Self-inspection outlines are very helpful to observers in this process.

USES OF DANGER RATINGS

Fire danger ratings expressed as index numbers have the advantage that they can be treated statistically in various ways, even though the number itself is more empirical than quantitative in meaning. The ways in which danger ratings can be used have expanded over the years.

The established uses of danger ratings, as drawn from actual practice by state and federal agencies, may be listed in the following eight categories. Four of these are usually identified with prevention activities. They are listed in approximate order of importance.

1 Manning and specific action guides
2 Calculation of initial attack strength
3 Estimating fire occurrence load in high-risk areas
4 Informing the public of impending fire danger
5 Issuance and cancellation of burning permits
6 Activation or lifting of woods closures
7 Planning and conducting prescribed burns
8 Appraising fire damage

Manning and Specific Action Guides

This was the first objective of fire danger rating and is still the most important single use. As such, dependence on the ratings varies widely.

WB FORM 612-17 (REV. 1-65) — U.S. DEPARTMENT OF COMMERCE, WEATHER BUREAU

10 - DAY FIRE DANGER AND FIRE WEATHER RECORD

AGENCY: **U.S.F.S.**

STATION ELEVATION: **3400** Ft.

PSYCHROMETRIC TABLE USED: **27** In.

DAY OF THE MONTH	STATE OF WEA-THER	HERB. STAGE	DRY BULB	WET BULB	WET BULB DE-PRES-SION	DEW POINT	REL. HUM.	FINE FUEL MOIS-TURE	BUILDUP YESTER-DAY OR CORRECTED	DRY-ING FAC-TOR	BUILDUP INDEX TODAY	DIR.	SPE-ED	ADJUST-ED FUEL MOISTURE
1	2	3	4	5	6	7	8	9	10	11	12	13	14	15
2¹	3	2	42	40		38	85	S	64	0	64	5	14	S
2²	2	2	66	48		29	24	10 0	64	3	67	5	11	13 0
2³	0	2	68	47		21	17	9 5	67	4	71	5	5	12 0
2⁴	3	2	57	52		48	73	19 0	71	1	72	6	8	20 0
2⁵	1	2	71	51		31	23	9 0	72	4	76	5	10	10 0
2⁶	3	2	73	55		41	31	10 0	76	3	79	4	6	12 0
2⁷	3	2	77	55		36	23	9 0	79	4	83	3	20	10 0
2⁸	6	2	53	53		53	100	30 1	23	0	23	3	2	30 0
2⁹	2	2	64	51		40	41	13 0	23	2	25	6	3	18 0
3⁰	1	2	71	55		43	36	11 0	25	3	28	5	12	16 0
31	1	2	75	56		41	30	10 0	28	3	31	2	2	15 0
SUMS	✕✕	✕✕							✕ ✕			✕✕		
MEANS	✕✕	✕✕							✕ ✕					

FINE FUEL MOISTURE (cols 4-9); *BUILDUP INDEX* (cols 10-12); *WIND* (cols 13-14); *SPREAD* (col 15)

DAILY (24-HOUR) DATA *(Recorded at Basic Observation Time)*

DAY OF THE MONTH	MAX-IMUM (TEMP)	MINI-MUM (TEMP)	MAX-IMUM (HUM)	MINI-MUM (HUM)	KIND	TIME BEGAN	TIME ENDED	AMOUNT	TIME BEGAN (T-STORM)	TIME ENDED (T-STORM)	AVG. CLOUD COVER		
33	34	35	36	37	38	39	40	41	42	43	44	45	46	47
2¹	46	40	98	64	7	08	09	0 05			3		
2²	14	35	96	24	0						2		
2³	70	34	88	17	6	DN	DN	0 03			0		
2⁴	73	34	86	42	6	13	14	0 02			3		
2⁵	73	44	85	23	0						1		
2⁶	75	34	90	31	8	15	16	0 04			3		
2⁷	80	45	93	22	0				14	15	3		
2⁸	77	50	100	84	6	DN	CONT'D	0 86			3		
2⁹	66	48	96	38	6	DN	11	0 02			2		
3⁰	73	44	100	30	0						1		
31	76	43	100	30	8	10	10	T			1		
SUMS					✕✕	✕✕	✕✕		✕✕	✕✕			
MEANS					✕✕	✕✕	✕✕		✕✕	✕✕			

WB FORM 612-17 (REV. 1-65)

OBSERVER'S SIGNATURE: *John Doe*

UNIT			STATION NAME						STATION NUMBER				
SAMPLE N.F.			SAMPLE, UTAH						4-20309				

BASIC OBSERVATION TIME (Local standard time)			PERIOD OF RECORD (Month, dates and year)										
1500 MST			FROM May 21, 1965					TO May 31, 1965				

INDEX
SPREAD INDEX

TIMBER	FINE FUEL															
16	17	18	19	20	21	22	23	24	25	26	27	28	29	30	31	32
0	0															
28	37															
19	23															
11	11															
33	36															
21	25															
56	60															
1	1															
9	14															
22	34															
10	16															

REMARKS

48	49	50	
			SNOW ON THE FUELS.
			RAIN DURING THE NIGHT AND CLEARED OFF.
			SHOWER 1515 TO 1545, AFTER BASIC OBS. TIME, WAS MEASURED AT 1500 ON 26TH.
			THUNDER AND LIGHTNING TO SW.
			RAIN ON TO 1600
			AND ON TO 1100
			RAIN A FEW MINUTES AT 1000

CHECKED BY: J. B. Doaks

USCOMM-WB-DC

Figure 8.7 Sample 10-day record at a fire danger station. *(From U.S. Forest Service handbook on fire danger rating.)*

Organizations with fixed levels of men and equipment tend to use them only as a general guide. Other fire organizations with ample reserves employ the ratings as detailed guides to daily adjustments in manpower and equipment to conform to predetermined standards of preparedness for selected levels of fire danger. As the dependence on measured fire danger increases, the importance of anticipating fire danger conditions for at least a day ahead also increases. This places a high premium on fire weather forecasts. In fact, where strong reliance is placed on fire danger ratings by practitioners, the accent is usually on tomorrow's weather.

Specific response to changes in fire danger does not depend on the existence of large reserves of manpower and fire fighting equipment. In the central Rocky Mountain region, a system of step-up plans provided a daily set of preparedness actions to be observed which enabled a fire organization, based chiefly on volunteer resident cooperators, to maintain for many years an excellent standard of protection at minimum cost.

The success of most forest fire organizations in preventing unacceptable fire losses depends on effectively meeting the challenge on a relatively small number of occasions each year. To identify these occasions and to forewarn of their development is the function of fire danger rating and of fire weather forecasting. Together they can greatly facilitate meeting the triple requirements of effective action at the right place at the right time.

In forest regions of the western United States, with a relatively short fire season, fire danger ratings still serve well to identify the beginning and the end of the fire season as well as to indicate unusual deviations from the average. So they enter into the scheduling of men to fire control positions. In the South they are depended on to define the intermittent periods when fire lookouts are needed.

Calculation of Initial Attack Strength

The use of fire danger ratings to guide the manning of fire control positions and the availability of fire control equipment is in anticipation of fires that may occur. The second phase in which fire danger ratings are a valuable guide is in decisions on the strength of attack to be made after a fire is reported. The number of men and amount of equipment available are always limited. Where burning conditions are critical, travel is slow and more than one fire is likely, it becomes very important to have a good basis for deciding whether a particular fire will require 2, 10, or 50 men to control it. By taking account of the expected rate of spread of fire at the site under current burning conditions and the probable rate of fireline construction, the probable strength of attack required to control a fire at various time intervals after it starts can be computed. Such computations can guide decisions on how many men or how much equipment to send to the fire on the start. Such guides are projected as a part of the national system for the United States.

Estimating Fire Occurrence Load in High-risk Areas

In a heavily used forest area in which exposure to live cigarette butts, for example, is nearly constant, the number of fires they start will closely reflect changes in the flammability of fuels. For that reason the number of fires will also show very good correlation with the ratings of a valid ignition index for that area. If records of fire occurrence and of fire danger measurements are maintained for the area, they provide a good opportunity to analyze fire risk. The number of fires per day at each danger class will reflect the class of fuel as well as its moisture content; but if both risk and fuel are constant, the number of fires should be directly proportional to changes in the ignition index. If so, significant rates of future occurrence can be computed.

Some computations for the purpose of identifying occurrence rates have been based on number of fires per unit of burning index. Such computations have been useful in showing trends but, since the burning index was not designed to reflect ignition only, rates were not proportional to its scale, so a rate per unit of index had very limited validity.

Table 8.1 illustrates the type of analysis that can be made when fires are identified with a burning index class (Crosby, 1954). This is based on burning index ratings obtained from the former Lake states meter. Spread index ratings of the national system can be used for similar determinations.

The data represent a five-year period for a forest protection area. As

Table 8.1   Number of Fires Related to Daily Burning Index Classes

Burning index class	Average burning index	Days per season	Fires per season	Fires per day	Fires per unit of burning index
Safe	1	34	0	0	0
Very low	2	32	0.6	0.02	0.010
Low	4	39	1.2	0.03	0.007
Moderate	8	46	3.7	0.08	0.010
High	16	34	9.9	0.29	0.018
Very high	32	24	18.7	0.78	0.024
Extreme	64	5	11.8	2.36	0.037
Total		214	45.9		

shown in the last two columns, not only the number of fires per day but the number of fires per unit of burning index increases with daily burning index. The latter shows that the burning index is not properly reflecting ignition index. Even so, occurrence factors determined by this approach give a good estimate of the number of fires that can be expected on a day identified with a particular burning index.

Regressions can also be determined relating burning indexes to number of fires, area burned, or other significant factors. Close correlations often cannot be expected but are indicative and useful.

One use of fire occurrence factors is in measuring the effect of prevention activities. Suppose that after an intensive prevention campaign was initiated, the number of fires dropped sharply. Was this the result of the campaign? Not necessarily; the campaign may have had no effect. The season may have been much wetter than average, and an even smaller number of fires might have been expected with no extra prevention effort. Similarly, if there had been more fires, the extra prevention effort still may have been effective, since, if the year had been extra dry, many more fires might have been expected. Without some norm or base for estimating fire occurrence, as is provided by fire occurrence factors developed for a specific area, valid conclusions about prevention efforts are impossible, especially over any short period.

Computed correlations between burning index or spread index and fire occurrence can be used to appraise changes in fire risk and the need for different or more intensive prevention effort. If occurrence records are built up over a number of years and related to burning index ratings, a pattern is established. Any deviation not explainable by danger ratings points to the need for immediate investigation.

Fire occurrence may be thought of as the net result of the exposure of fuels to fire weather and fire risks over a given period of time. By careful analysis, the role of each in the resultant occurrence of fires can be appraised.

Informing the Public of Impending Fire Danger

Current fire danger expressed in descriptive fire danger classes is a highly effective way of making the public more fire-conscious. Large display boards along roadsides or at key locations in public places serve in this way. They take many forms. Some take the form of a thermometer or barometer, some a dial or computer. They supplement other displays, such as the smaller fire danger board already described, and sharpen interest in current reports of fire danger in newspapers and via radio and television. They are highly regarded and widely used for such purposes.

One of them is shown in Figure 8.8. To maintain their effectiveness, it is essential that they be kept current. The public quickly loses respect for a rating which persists in giving a verdict of high fire danger, for example, throughout a period of heavy rains.

Issuance and Cancellation of Burning Permits

Use of fire for debris burning, slash disposal, camp or warming fires, and for various land management purposes is controlled by various federal, state, and local laws and regulations. Many states have specific permit laws. National Forests, National Parks, and state park and recreation areas all have strict control of fire either through state law, federal regulation or local ordinance. Fire danger ratings give a valuable and consistent basis for determining times and places where such restrictions should be applied or lifted and are widely so used.

In Table 8.2, debris-burning fires for the period 1942 to 1947 for 14 Eastern states are arranged by fire danger class at the time of their occurrence. According to analyses made in 1949, 85 percent of the debris fires that escaped control and 91 percent of the area they burned were on

Figure 8.8 Public roadside fire danger display board indicating current burning conditions. Superior National Forest, Minnesota. *(U.S. Forest Service photo.)*

Table 8.2 Number of Debris-burning Fires, Total Area Burned, and Average Size of Fire, by Fire Danger Classes in 14 Eastern States, 1942–1947*

Fire danger class	Number of fires	Area burned, acres	Average size of fire, acres
1	222	1,437	6.5
2	1,206	11,439	9.5
3	4,670	67,347	14.4
4	3,575	66,180	18.5
5	7	138	19.7
All classes	9,680	146,541	15.1

* Jemison, Lindenmuth, and Keetch (1949). Based on Type 5-W meter.

Class 3, 4, and 5 days. Similarly, in one protection area in the southern Appalachians, 76 percent of the fires that escaped from debris burners over a 6-year period were on Class 4 and 5 days. These data well illustrate the practical value of danger ratings as a guide to policy and practice in issuing or canceling burning permits.

Activation and Lifting of Woods Closures

Fire danger ratings, especially when associated with protracted drying of intermediate and heavy fuels, serve as a defensible basis for closing certain forest areas to the public. Cumulative ratings, such as the buildup index of the national system, are preferred for this purpose. The spread index or any index that changes materially with changes in wind speed, is not a good closure index. Woods closures are usually by proclamation, and cannot be activated or lifted with changes in wind speed. Such closures may be partial, such as to campfires or to hunting, or they may be made complete for specific high-hazard areas. Current fire danger conditions defined in terms of relative humidity or fuel moisture only are used in the Northwest to determine when logging operations should be shut down and special precautions taken in other respects.

Planning and Conducting Prescribed Burns

In carrying out prescribed use of fire, it is seldom sufficient to confine the fire only to predetermined limits of area. Usually the fire intensity and consequently the fire's behavior must also be kept within predetermined limits to accomplish the intended purpose. This calls for special diagnosis of the fuel and weather conditions favorable to such controls and for use of fire danger rating techniques to anticipate behavior of the prescribed fire.

In the Douglas-fir region, clear cutting by patches results in areas of very heavy logging slash surrounded by green timber. To accomplish successful disposal of the slash, burning conditions are sought when the heavy fuels will be dry enough to support a clean-burning fire but kindling fuels in the green timber will be damp enough to keep down the risk of firebrands from the burning slash spotting into the adjacent forest. Paired fuel moisture sticks in the open and in the timber have been used very successfully in identifying such conditions. In Australia, complete guides for diagnosis and selection of burning conditions favorable for carrying out extensive burning operations in eucalyptus forests have been developed (McArthur, 1962). These are based on the familiar concepts and techniques of fire danger measurement.

Appraising Fire Damage

Fire damage in a forest stand is closely related to fire intensity. Ordinarily, the hotter the fire the greater the damage. This relationship is utilized in statewide fire records throughout the Southeast. Correlations between fire damage and fire danger class have been developed (Lindenmuth, Keetch, and Nelson, 1951, and later unpublished studies by Bruce) which enable reasonably satisfactory estimates of statewide fire damage each year. As might be expected, the estimate of damage for a single fire by this method alone may be considerably in error.

On federally owned lands, appraisals on the ground are ordinarily made of the larger burns. But particularly in young pine stands, it is often very difficult to estimate the amount of defoliation and the percentage of kill that will result until the following growing season. Here too, the burning conditions at the time, with particular reference to temperatures and fire intensity, enable much more reliable estimates immediately after control of the fire.

DANGER RATING IN PERSPECTIVE

It is common human experience that not more than three factors can be kept in mind at one time. Consequently, the use of objective devices to simplify the mental process of bringing together all factors affecting variable fire danger is sound. A further strongly supporting factor is the advantage of substituting an objective method for the opinions of individuals in justifying fire expenditures. These are borne out by the continuing extension and acceptance of fire danger rating systems until they have become a nearly universal feature of fire control on wild lands.

Over a 40-year period, fire danger rating systems have gone through much evolution. Gradually, what to measure, how, when, and where have become well defined and standardized. How to integrate measured factors is also in the process of standardization. No doubt the process will continue. As indexes for fire risk, ignition probability, and fuel energy are developed for the national system in the United States, application of ratings can be expected to become more flexible and the findings more accurate.

Certain weaknesses in the original concepts and in conventional features have, however, proved difficult to correct and will continue to slow down progress.

Perhaps the most important has been the high degree of complexity introduced into danger rating. This grew out of the fact that the first danger rating schemes were overambitious. They undertook to tell the forest manager what to do about the fire situation before they had firmly established their ability to measure its potential. This was closely linked to the fact that quantitative data were lacking by which to define relationships. There was a tendency toward pseudoscientific theorizing to fill the gap. As a result, the more empirical the rating, the more complex was the approach to it. As relationships have become more clearly defined, danger rating has become more forthright and simpler. But this has taken many years. The popularity of the burning index, which was the simplest of the concepts developed, bears out the virtue of the old adage to keep it simple.

Certain specific features of the rating scheme have also been troublesome. Perhaps the most troublesome has been the numerical scale. Units of burning index scales are of unequal value for the several purposes used. Although often done, the adding, averaging, and dividing of numerical values from these scales and relating the derived values to various aspects of fire business was not valid mathematically. This can be corrected in the future by using specific scales properly weighted for the purpose.

Next in importance is the weight given to wind in fire danger ratings. Wind greatly stimulates forward spread of small fires following ignition. But when a proportional adjustment is made in a spread index, wind tends to dominate the scale. This results in deceptively low spread ratings when there is little or no wind. Yet, as developed in Chapter 1, many conflagrations occur under conditions of very light prevailing winds. More research is needed on atmospheric relationships. Perhaps ways can be found to supplement horizontal wind speed to give a more accurate picture of the fire potential.

Closely related is the question of atmospheric variables as a valid part of fire danger rating. Though it has long been recognized that atmospheric conditions aloft were important, direct measurements are not used in danger ratings. As fire weather forecasting advances, this could be an important next step toward more accurate measurement and prediction of the fire potential.

The value of fire danger rating in imparting to the public an intelligent awareness of the threat from wildfires is unmeasured but very high. Its potential in this respect has often been underrated but ranks close to its importance as an operating tool by fire control agencies.

Part Two

Control of Forest Fires

Fire as a dynamic phenomenon, its relation to weather, its interactions with the forest environment, and its relevance to the quality of man's environment as well is presented in Part One.

In Part Two, this basic information becomes the background to action programs and is used in presenting principles and methods employed in successful protection of wild land from fire and the structure of planned fire control systems by which they may be consistently applied over large areas.

There are three lines of defense on which an effective system of protection of wild lands from fire must be based. The first consists of measures to prevent fires from starting. The second consists of timely provisions to control the fires that do start while they are still small. The third consists of measures to minimize the size and destructiveness of fires that start and become aggressive in spite of these provisions. They provide the general sequence of the presentation.

Methods and techniques for doing different parts of the fire control job are given in Chapters 9 to 13. Systematic planning of fire control systems to ensure consistent accomplishment of each fire control job and effective integration of effort to meet objectives are described in Chapter 14. Special problems of operating fire control systems are identified in Chapter 15, and problems in control of large fires with case histories in Chapter 16.

Chapter 9

Prevention of
Man-caused Fires

A fire prevented does not have to be suppressed and does no damage. If all fires are prevented, the whole objective of fire control activities is accomplished too. Consequently, all fire control organizations, forest, rural or urban, give primary emphasis in carrying out their jobs to preventing as many fires as possible. It is the first line of defense.

Fires occur when flammable fuels are exposed to firebrands. Fire prevention can be accomplished either by removing the source of the firebrand or by removing the fuel it may ignite. The alternative chosen is influenced by the values threatened by fire. The need for controlling or eliminating fire risk[1] increases as fuel hazards and values increase. So it becomes a truism to the fire control planner that high fire risk must not be permitted in any area which has both high fuel hazards and high destructible values. To bring this about it is often more feasible to reduce fuel

---

[1] *Fire risk and fire hazard* as used in forest fire literature are defined as follows. *Fire risk:* (1) the chance of fire starting as determined by the presence and activity of causative agents, (2) a causative agent. *Fire hazard:* a fuel complex defined by kind, arrangement, volume, condition, and location that forms a special threat of ignition or of suppression difficulty.

hazards than positively to reduce or eliminate the sources of risk. The control of fuels is discussed in the next chapter. The general principles and the highlights of the effort to control the many sources of fire risk are presented in this chapter.

Lightning is a serious source of risk throughout Western mountain areas of the United States, where it usually accounts for 30 to 64 percent of the forest fires reported, even though only 9 percent of the nation's total. Research has been devoted to reducing the number or severity of fire-setting lightning storms (Chapter 5). This may in time lead to effective means of reducing this threat. But most of the work in fire prevention will continue to be devoted to the many sources of man-caused fires, which comprise the other 91 percent of the total.

Effective control of each source of risk requires knowledge of how it operates locally and of when and where it is most likely to start fires. To develop such knowledge, analysis of past fire experience in each protection area is needed. This depends on records of how, why, when, and where fires have started in the past. Such information can be obtained from individual fire reports if they are accurately prepared. Usually this requires that all data be recorded by the officer who was personally in charge of the operation immediately after each fire is controlled.

The individual fire report is important since it is the primary source of all fire statistics. Each report represents fire fighting experience under a given set of circumstances. National statistics represent the firsthand experience of thousands of men each year. Local fire statistics may be brought to bear to reveal fire fighting experience over a period of years. Analysis of a ten-year record can often serve to diagnose both the successes and failures of men who have fought fire in a particular protection unit. But accuracy and reliability of such diagnoses depend on the accuracy and adequacy of the individual fire reports on which they are based.

The data most frequently used for guidance of prevention programs are the specific causes of fires that occurred, the time and place of occurrence, and the class of people responsible. Conducting a fire prevention program without reliable information of this kind is like operating a ship without a rudder; it uses up energy but does not get anywhere. (See Figure 14.1, Chapter 14.)

MAJOR CAUSES OF FOREST FIRES IN THE UNITED STATES

Eight major cause categories of forest fires have long been used in fire statistics. These are Campfires, Debris Burning, Incendiary, Lightning, Lumbering, Railroad, Smoker, Miscellaneous. Though of long standing, this classification includes a mixture of activities and agencies inconsistent for many purposes. Frequent proposals for revising it have been made, but the disadvantage of breaking the continuity of the statistical record kept such changes to a minimum for over fifty years. However, in 1964, the U.S. Forest Service and its cooperators adopted some rather far-reaching changes in the fire cause classification. At that time railroad fires, which had shrunk in importance on the National Forests, were included in a broader category by that agency termed *Equipment.* This includes all fires due to use of machines. However, several state agencies retained a separate record of railroad fires. The term *Forest Utilization* was substituted for *Lumbering* and was broadened. *Campfires* and *Debris Burning* were discontinued as general causes, and *Recreation* and *Land Occupancy* were substituted. The eight general causes then became Equipment, Forest Utilization, Incendiary, Land Occupancy, Lightning, Recreation, Smoking, and Miscellaneous.

The redefinition of these eight general causes is given in a supplement to the 1956 edition of the *Glossary of Terms Used in Fire Control* issued by the U.S. Forest Service in 1966 for interim use. These definitions follow:

    1   Equipment. A fire resulting from use of equipment.

    2   Forest Utilization. A fire resulting directly from timber harvesting, harvesting other forest products, and forest and range management except use of equipment, smoking, and recreation as related to the above activities.

    3   Incendiary. A fire willfully set by anyone to burn vegetation or property not owned or controlled by him and without consent of the owner or his agent.

    4   Land Occupancy. A fire started as result of land occupancy for agricultural purposes, industrial establishment, construction, maintenance, and use of rights of way and residences except use of equipment and smoking.

    5   Lightning. A fire caused directly or indirectly by lightning.

    6   Recreation. A fire resulting from recreation use except smoking.

    7   Smoking. A fire caused by smokers, matches, or by burning tobacco in any form.

    8   Miscellaneous. A fire of known cause that cannot be properly classified under any of the other seven standard causes.

A potential ninth category, *Unknown,* has been recognized in some earlier classifications. However, it is not a very useful identification and was often overused. It was abandoned for that reason. It is again omitted in the 1966 revision and the reporter is required to assign every fire to the most likely cause based on information available.

With conscientious reporting practices, it is reasonable to require the reporter to decide on the most likely cause, since he is in the best position to analyze the evidence. But when reporting is done by someone other than the "man who was there," the statistics for cause of fires may become distorted by a tendency to throw too many fires for which the cause is uncertain into one or two catch-all categories.

The distribution of fires by major causes throughout the United States is shown in Figure 9.1 for the 50-year period 1917 to 1966.[2] This is for areas under protection only for each of five state groupings into which the United States was divided for this purpose and for the United States as a whole. Records for shorter periods show considerable change through the years. The number of fires, size of fires, and area burned have reduced. Some shifts have occurred too in the proportion of fires ascribed to certain general causes, particularly on publicly owned lands. On the National Forests and Parks, fires ascribed to railroads and to campfires have reduced in both numbers and proportion of the total. There have been changes too in some regions in the proportion of fires ascribed to smoking, though much of this change reflects changes in reporting practice. Nevertheless, when all reported fires for protected federal, state, and private lands of the United States are added together by regions or for the United States as a whole, the pattern of general causes remains remarkably stable. The causes of wildfires in 1968, for example, are very similar in distribution to the 50-year average shown in Figure 9.1. This reflects environment, which changes slowly on a regional or national scale. Consequently, the 50-year record shows the more significant differences in the nature of the fire prevention problem in the various forest regions. The cause categories in Figure 9.1 are in accordance with the former cause classification except that equipment fires have been deleted from the miscellaneous category and added to railroad fires to initiate the new Equipment (machine-use) category.

Differences between regions are well illustrated by the proportion of fires of incendiary origin. At 39 percent in the Southern group of 13 states including Virginia, Kentucky, and Tennessee, it is the largest cause of all. In the North Central group, which includes Missouri and southern Illinois, it is still very important, with 16 percent of total fires. In the Eastern group of 12 states it becomes a minor cause at 10 percent and in the Pacific Coast states including Alaska and Hawaii at 9 percent. In the Rocky Mountain states, it fades to 2 percent and is unheard of in most of the wild-land country of these 12 states.

[2] Taken from the 50-year insert in the 1966 *Forest Fire Statistics*, prepared by the Division of Cooperative Forest Fire Control, U.S. Forest Service.

It will be noticed that the number of lightning fires follows an opposite trend. In the Rocky Mountain group, they account for 61 percent of the fires. Here the lightning fire problem sets the pattern for fire control systems. Still important locally, lightning accounts for 31 percent of the fires in the Pacific group. In the North Central and Southern groups, it fades to a minor cause at 2 percent; and in the Eastern group, where it becomes the unexpected or surprise fire in most areas, it accounts for only 1 percent of the fires.

Debris-burning fires are of varied origin. A debris-burning fire is any fire spreading from a fire set to burn rubbish or garbage or for the purpose of land clearing, range, stubble, or meadow burning. Those used as a land-management practice tend to be associated with incendiary fires, since many of the latter are used for the same purpose on the lands of absentee owners. In the North Central group, fires so classed dominate the fire control problem at 28 percent of the total. If incendiary fires are added, deliberate burning accounts for 44 percent of the total. Debris-burning fires are the third-highest cause of fires in the Eastern group, at 21 percent of the total. Incendiary fires are not so closely related here, but they add another 10 percent, due to set fires, for a total of 31 percent. Close to this proportion is the Southern group, with 19 percent of its fires classed as debris-burning and a total of 58 percent due to deliberate burning. This cause becomes secondary at 9 percent in the Pacific group and a minor cause at 4 percent in the Rocky Mountain group.

Smokers' fires are a prominent cause in all regions. The most prevalent in the Eastern group at 26 percent, they are also important in the North Central group at 21 percent, in the Pacific group at 20 percent, in the Southern group at 17 percent, and, as the second-highest cause, even in the Rocky Mountain group at 10 percent of the total.

Machine use and campfires account for quite consistent though secondary proportions of the fires in all regions.

Miscellaneous causes rank second in the Eastern group at 23 percent of total fires. In descending order, they account for 17 percent in the North Central group, 14 percent in the Pacific group, 12 percent in the Southern group, and 7 percent in the Rocky Mountain group. The proportion of fires in this category is important. When it becomes large enough to compare with other major causes, it is obvious that the classification needs revision. If the specific causes can be identified, this may be brought about by separating out the most common cause or causes to form new categories or by revision of the classification system as a whole. *Miscellaneous* otherwise has little significance as a category. Widely varying sources of risk, fuels, and circumstances enter into these fires, so few generalizations can be made that will be useful in an action

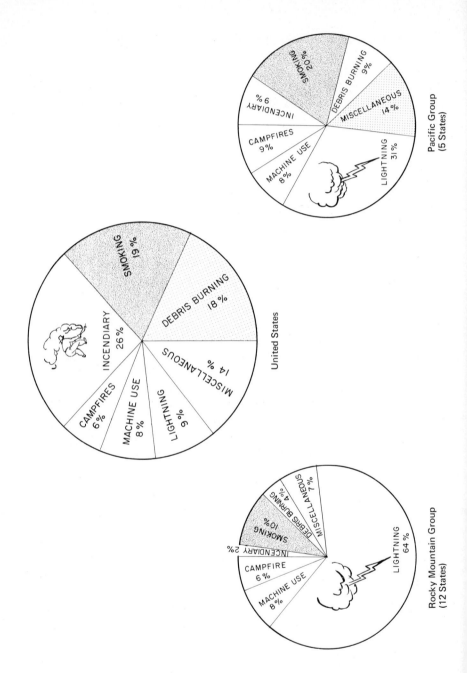

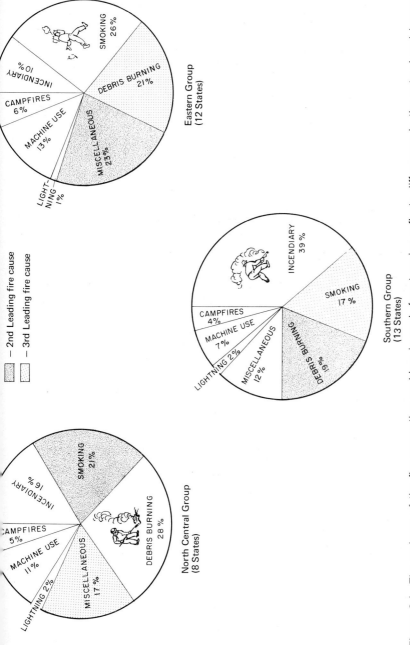

Figure 9.1 The makeup of the fire prevention problem in each forest region reflects differences in the natural and human environment as revealed by this 50-year record.

plan. However, it is perhaps significant that miscellaneous fires of often unusual specific causes seem to increase both in frequency and in proportion on wild lands tributary to large urban population centers.

The number of fires and acres burned on protected federal, state, and private lands for the same period (1917–1966) is shown in Figure 9.2. This graph needs to be interpreted in the light of a great increase in the acres protected. The 150 million acres protected in 1917 increased nearly nine times to 1,125 million acres in 1966. Consequently, *number of fires* and *acreages burned* apply to a constantly changing and expanding area. Nevertheless, the graph does have interest and significance. Though the number of reported fires more than doubled, from about 40,000 per year to over 100,000, this was far below the 1:9 ratio of area increase. Of even greater importance, the acres burned, which had been close to 20 million per year prior to 1917, were fluctuating between 2 to 3 million per year at the end of 1966. Although this level of loss of forest resources is not now considered acceptable, it does indicate marked success of the cooperative program between federal, state, and private agencies to reduce fire losses.

As illustrated by this graph, the number of reported fires is an incomplete measure of the fire problem and of fire losses. Figures for the acreage burned, when coupled with the number of fires, are much more

Figure 9.2   Fifty-year record of number of fires and area burned on a continually augmented "protected area" for the United States.

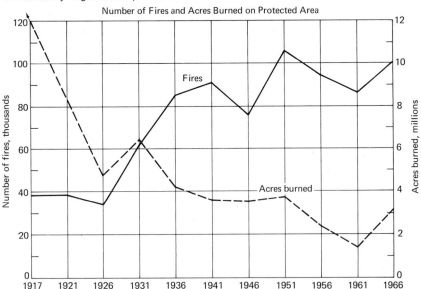

significant as long as the same area or similar fuel types are compared. The figure for burned area alone can be just as incomplete as number of fires alone unless it is classified by cover type, severity of burn, and values at stake. For such reasons, statistics on total area burned and total number of fires for the whole United States have little meaning without further information and analysis.

Fire statistics, such as fire occurrence by major causes and the acreage burned by states or regions, are useful in depicting the nature and magnitude of the fire problem and in furnishing some clues as to why fires occur in that area. But much more local information is needed before a plan of action to prevent fires in a specific protection unit can be effective.

Specific Causes of Forest Fires

The first step in obtaining more specific information about man-caused fires is to determine, if possible, the cause behind the cause and to learn more about the class of people responsible. Much of this information can also be obtained from carefully prepared fire reports. In addition to the general cause classification, fires are further classified in three ways. The first is the general land-use category of the activity that caused the fire, second is the specific cause under each general cause, and third is the class of people responsible. Though these more specific breakdowns vary from time to time and differ between agencies, the following illustrate these three classifications as applied by the U.S. Forest Service in instructions for the preparation of fire reports.

The land-use categories chosen are Lightning, Agriculture, Forest and Range Management, Harvesting Other Products, Highway Activities, Hunting and Fishing, Incendiary, Industry, Power and Reclamation, Railroad, Recreation, Residential, Timber Harvesting, Other.

Specific causes under both the land-use categories and the general causes break down the cause classes to further identify the source of the fire. For example, Forest Utilization, which is the second of the general causes, includes the land-use categories of Timber Harvesting, Harvesting Other Forest Products, and Forest and Range Management. For each of these the following specific causes are provided for in the fire report: Blasting, Burning Building, Burning on Right-of-way, Cooking Fire, Hot Ashes, House or Stove Flue Sparks, Prescribed Burning, Safety Strip Burning, Slash Disposal, Warming Fire, Other.

The persons responsible may be listed under one or more of the following eight categories: Owner, Permittee, Contractor, Public Employee, Local Permanent Resident, Seasonal, Transient, Other.

For example, suppose that members of a logging crew working for a timber sale contractor fail to extinguish a warming fire they set on a cold morning. It spreads later in the day in their absence, causing some damage and requiring action by local forest fire-fighting forces. This fire then becomes a statistical fire; that is, it will be included in the number-of-fires and area-burned record for the local area and it will be classed as follows: General cause class—Forest Utilization, land-use category—Timber Harvesting, specific cause—Warming Fire, class of people responsible—Contractor.

Keeping track of the relative frequency of each specific cause helps to define the problem and specifying the class of people responsible helps to define the audience toward which the fire prevention message needs to be directed.

When it is clear which activities and which group of people are responsible for most of the fires on the local unit, the forest manager still needs to ask himself more about the human part of the fire prevention equation. Just how and why did these people cause a wildfire to start?

Human Behavior and Fires

It is often extremely difficult to get at the real reasons why people start fires (Folkman, 1965; Shea, 1940). The apparent or stated reason may not be the real one, which may be deeply rooted in anthropological, cultural, and psychological patterns and habits. Unless these things are understood, effective progress cannot be made in making people not only forest fire conscious but positive in their actions to prevent them. Man-caused fires are commonly ascribed to carelessness, and this is true in the general sense of the word. But there are different shades of what is commonly called carelessness, such as heedlessness, indifference, and thoughtlessness as well as more or less culpable negligence.

Smoker and camper fires are almost entirely due to carelessness in one form or another, since there is no positive motive to set a forest fire. Why do they happen? One reason may be basic indifference. As has been brought out, the American people have come through a pioneer era during which forest fires and forests in general were regarded with considerable indifference and lack of understanding. Wild lands are commonly looked on as undeveloped and unimproved areas. In such areas, the restraints to be observed in one's own house, and even on city streets, no longer seem to apply and are abandoned without substituting any new ones. Smoking habits on city streets may thus become a menace in the woods.

The transformation of this underlying basis of general public indifference into a positive recognition of the value of the natural and a positive desire to protect it has been a central theme in fire prevention efforts for well over two generations. It has been highly successful among urban forest users but much less so among nonurban local residents.

Some people are more heedless than indifferent. People dislike being told to do things and instinctively rebel. Some will not believe there is danger; they think *they* are different and know better than forester advisers about safe practices. Ignorance and heedlessness are closely related. Others are neither indifferent nor heedless but thoughtless or negligent. Habits can be extremely strong and hard to break. Many a forester has, to his eventual chagrin, unthinkingly committed the same acts that he preaches against in fire prevention. By such acts he may create antagonism among local people—antagonism that could lead to incendiary fires. The urban habit of flipping a match or cigarette is extremely difficult to break. Much prevention effort is directed at habit breaking. Novelty ashtrays in cars, "fag bags" to hold cigarettes and matches, admonition on prevention posters to "break your match," and similar attempts are examples of habit breakers. Some people, and this applies heavily to debris burners, are not indifferent or necessarily heedless or thoughtless but rather lazy or negligent or inadequately informed on safe burning practices and the consequences of unsafe practices. Significant errors can be made in prevention work by concentrating effort on the overcoming of indifference, for example, when the need is to help break habits and give positive and practical help on what to do and how to do it easily.

Motives behind incendiarism are often extremely complex and subtle, and unless they are understood in a particular situation, preventive action may be futile.

A classification of incendiary fire motives used by the Florida Forest Service and specifically applicable to a Southern situation illustrates this:

1 Fires set for direct personal economic gain to
   a Burn property of others to protect owned property
   b Improve grazing, control of stock, or hunting
   c Facilitate logging or naval stores operations
   d Clear for collecting fish bait, firewood, or other materials
   e Receive pay—hired to burn
2 Fires set for indirect economic gain to
   a Make landowner come to terms on use of land
   b Obtain employment
   c Kill timber to make its sale necessary
   d Control pest and diseases, ticks, chiggers, snakes, etc.
   e Force sale of property at reduced price
3 Fires set to attain a goal or personal satisfaction
   a Spite against large ownership

    b   Personal grudges and neighborhood quarrels
    c   To make public forest employees work or to cause their removal
    d   Because they feel the woods need burning (habit)
    e   Obeying an impulse, malicious mischief, drunk and disorderly conduct
4 Fires set to conceal a crime
    a   Whiskey-still camouflage and decoy smokes
    b   To destroy evidence of timber or cattle theft, illegal hunting, or other trespass
    c   To delay pursuit or obliterate trail
5 Fires set by mentally afflicted and immature
    a   Pyromaniacs—the true "firebug"
    b   Incompetent persons
    c   Children

Other classifications have been devised, but this is sufficient to illustrate the wide range and complexity of motives involved. Every one of the items listed has been the reason for incendiary fires. The relative importance of motives naturally varies by areas. Some are peculiar to the South, but many are not. Economic reasons and personal frustration of some sort account for most of them. The latter are behind many of the items listed in groups 3 to 5.

The incendiarist group continues to be of critical importance. As wild lands become better stocked, more valuable, and more extensive, incendiary fires become more disastrous and the spite fire becomes an increasingly potent weapon.

Debris-burning fires include fires intended as land management measures. Many are chiefly a matter of tradition and habit regardless of the benefits claimed by the burner. The burning of dead leaves and grass is looked on very much as a matter of spring housecleaning. At other times, with some merit, burning is done as a matter of self-defense against fires on neighbors' property. In general, the wildfire from debris burning represents a desire to use fire and often a rather undiscriminating belief in its benefits. This leads to unwillingness or inability to exercise the precautions necessary to confine it safely to the burner's land.

It does no good merely to say that people are mistaken in their use of fire. Motives must be recognized, and positive action must be taken to substitute more constructive attitudes and actions for those that play a part in causing forest fires. A cultural and psychological reorientation may be necessary. It must also be recognized that people often will not admit their real motives and, in fact, may not be aware of them. In probing for motives one must be prepared to dig deeply in some situations and to appreciate that the solution of the problem lies in the social sciences and not in technical forestry.

Fire is fascinating to children. One important and growing cause of fires is described as "children with matches." Fires of such origin, though often included in the miscellaneous category, occur in the statistics of every wild-land fire control agency. They have shown a tendency to increase around growing suburban areas and have resisted conventional methods of prevention. In central California, studies in 1967 showed no significant reduction of such fires in 20 Years. According to research carried out by Folkman (1965) and Siegelman and Folkman (1971) for the U.S. Forest Service, also in California, 75 percent of the children causing wild-land fires were under ten years of age (commonly five to seven), and most of them were boys.

This illustrates the importance of identifying the class of people responsible. Even the Smokey Bear appeal had not previously been directed to children this young. The majority of children who start fires by playing with matches or other igniters need only to be properly taught and properly motivated to avoid such behavior. However, because of the almost irresistible attraction of a spreading fire to many disturbed children, the problem assumes psychiatric and psychological aspects which will continue to be highly troublesome to wild-land managers in suburban and summer-home fringe areas.

PRINCIPLES AND METHODS USED IN PREVENTING FIRES

Every man-caused wildfire in a protected unit may well be regarded as evidence of something wrong. Always it is the result of a critical combination of circumstances that may be prevented from developing. These circumstances may be codified to permit logical diagnosis and prescription in the manner employed by a physician.

For example:

A smoker fire = a smoker + smoking materials + matches (or lighter) + careless smoking habits

If any one of the four elements producing the smoker fire is eliminated, there is no fire. So there are four alternative ways to prevent such a fire: (1) The smoker may be banned bodily from areas susceptible to ignition from smoking (complete closure) or he may be induced to refrain from smoking in specified areas (closed to smoking) or from discarding burning materials in hazardous fuels (no smoking while walking). (2) If some smoking combinations are found not to be hazardous or smoking can be limited to spots clear of fuels, smoking might be limited but not entirely banned (cigarettes only, smoke here, etc.). (3) It may be feasible to make the igniting agent more fire safe by such measures as banning kitchen matches or restricting use to lighters or treated matchsticks (regulation of smoking). (4) Finally, the smoker might be taught and motivated to apply all necessary precautions to avoid setting a fire. Obviously, the alternatives under 1 are the most direct and positive for a specified time and place but cannot be extended over large areas and are usually temporary in nature in forest areas. The fourth alternative would take time but would have more permanence.

This type of analysis can be applied to all fires where the critical combinations that cause fires are known. The incendiary fire may be thought of as follows:

$$\text{An incendiary fire} = \text{a man} + \text{a motive for burning} + \text{incendiary devices}$$

Obviously, the chief alternatives are either to remove the man from the area or to eliminate or suppress his motive for burning.

In all situations some control of the movement or behavior of people is required. Direct control through laws and law enforcement is an important part of the fire prevention activity but represents only one end of the spectrum. The kinds of measures that may be applied and the appropriate place for each may be considerably clarified if they are examined in the general order of increasing control of the individual in the forest environment.

When viewed in this way, three broad categories of measures become apparent. These may be identified as follows:

Education of the public
Regulation of public use
Enforcement of fire laws

Most fires caused by wild-land users, particularly the urban visitor, are the result of ignorance of fire in the forest environment. This, in turn, underlies much of his negligence or carelessness in handling fire. His ignorance cannot be completely overcome, but if he can be strongly motivated to prevent fires and is taught to observe a few simple precautions, he will not cause a wildfire. Intensive public use, which creates the necessity of dealing with people en masse, also brings with it increasing dependence on regulating the use rather than educating the individual.

Finally, there is always a small hard core of people who can be motivated only by fear of punishment. This makes fire laws and law enforcement an essential part of fire prevention.

The following discussion provides further analyses of prevention principles and methods that will give better understanding of the fire prevention tools available.

Motivation

Underlying each of these classes of measures is the question of motivation. Each kind of measure is aimed at stimulating a particular set of human motives to induce the individual to do something or to avoid doing something. The approach might be described as ranging "from the carrot to the stick," though this oversimplifies the relationship.

There is a diversity of human motives. They are often very complex and sometimes unconscious. Murray (1964) lists 20 that are classed as social motives, all of which have some relevance to fire prevention. It will be helpful here to identify the makeup of the common social motives that are important in the prevention of man-caused fires.

Motives have two factors in common, a need and a goal. Behavior that arises from a need and leads to a goal is referred to as motivation. Motivation is often conditioned by factors other than a need and a goal. It then becomes complex, and both need and goal may become obscured to varying degrees. A further generalization is that everything one does is either to gain a pleasure of some kind or to avoid something unpleasant. Motives may be classed as positive or negative on this basis. They are conditioned by the environment and often weaken or strengthen with time. Hence a powerful appeal of 20 years ago may now be weak. Always emotions play a strong part. To break a bad habit or to initiate a new kind of behavior, only motives having a strong emotional base are likely to be effective.

Maintenance of self-esteem and the many facets of self-interest provide effective motives for fire prevention. The personal loss to you, from fires in a familiar recreation area which killed wildlife and marred scenery you have enjoyed, has an impact. Even the unfavorable effects on the local economy are recognizable and have an emotional effect.

Identification of fire prevention and protection of the environment with high ideals of good stewardship, good citizenship, etc., also inspires strong sentiments. When strong sentiments in favor of preventing wildfires become prevalent, they in turn create pressure for conformity, which also operates as a strong motive. This greatly reinforces public regulation measures and provides a favorable background, as well, for law enforcement to become an effective tool in preventing fires.

Law enforcement and public regulation of the nonconformist operate through fear of the consequences of violations. When the unfavorable consequences to the violator are both social and legal, they become doubly effective. Fear is a powerful motivating force. Fear of what others will think is a strong determinant of people's behavior. But sole dependence on fear of the law generates hostility where cooperation might otherwise be gained.

Salesmanship

Although emotional factors are powerful, effective motivation in practice depends also on certain psychological principles which have been well authenticated through experience in national advertising. The more important are attention, recognition, repetition, continuity, and timeliness.

Attracting attention is almost compulsive in competitive advertising. Eye catchers, shockers, and gimmicks of all kinds are employed to gain attention. The device used to attract attention may have nothing to do with the intended message. Bathing beauties may be used to help sell wire rope, for example. The reason for attention getters is that the individual can absorb only one thing at a time, but many things compete for his attention. The subjects or messages that do not attract his attention make no impression.

After attention has been gained, the next objective is to establish a means of quick identification and future recognition. This may be done by using a catchy symbol or slogan with which the product or service can be associated. Specific messages ride on and gain effectiveness from being associated with a widely known recognition symbol. The value of an established trademark is an early tradition in industry. This principle has proved equally effective in fire prevention. Smokey Bear and the recurrent tag line "Only you can prevent forest fires" or simply "Prevent forest fires" and eventually a picture of Smokey Bear only carried the message. The establishment of a unifying symbol for fire prevention which rapidly gained mass recognition is regarded as a historic achievement.

To accomplish the recognition sought, the next essential principle is repetition. Only by repetition is a message remembered and sharpened, and the impression it makes deepened. But repeition may become tiresome. The use of a recognition symbol or trademark makes it possible to repeat the message without repetitious verbosity. This has, of course, been an important factor in the Smokey Bear example.

Continuity is another important principle in the establishment of a trademark or recognition symbol. If the effort is not sustained, the audience soon forgets and the message fades. Continuity not only maintains the message, once it has gained a measure of acceptance, but it enhances its prestige as well. Witness the prestige of trademarks maintained through several generations. This too is of significance to fire prevention.

Appropriateness of time and place are further essential principles. In advertising, they are the final step in making sales. They are the "here and now" of the goal. They can assure that motivated action will be directed toward the desired target. Without the element of right time and right place, even though all the preceding principles have been observed, the effort may be wasted. This is, of course, critical in fire prevention and has been emphasized by Davis (1952) as follow-up at the point of use (or sale). If the public is importuned by signs to use special precautions because of extreme fire hazard but there is snow on the ground or there have been soaking rains in the area, the fire prevention message loses not only prestige but respect as well.

Education of the Public

People are the primary problem in preventing fires. If everyone who uses or travels through wild-land areas were fully conscious of the destructiveness of wildfires, well informed on how to avoid causing one to occur, and sufficiently motivated to act accordingly, only a tiny fraction of the annual crop of fires would occur. Consequently, education of the public is a primary effort. It is the positive, hopeful approach to fire prevention. Its objective is to create an informed awareness or fire consciousness in all forest users. Its potential is that of saving many millions of dollars every year. Its greatest handicap is the difficulty of reaching all the classes of people responsible for fires and of communicating the "how" as well as the "why" through conventional media.

Conventional media include the following:

Books, magazine articles, news releases
Radio messages
Television programs
Motion pictures
Signs, posters, exhibits
Handouts
Slide talks and speeches
Personal contacts

Each of these means of communication is effective when skill is used in choosing the right time, place, and persons. But all are needed, since no one medium will reach all classes of people and individuals vary widely in their response to public appeals, instructions, and restrictions. A favorable response depends first of all on gaining full acceptance of the intended objective. But it depends too on the manner and circumstances of presentation. Each medium has certain advantages and certain limitations in these respects.

Books, magazine articles, and news releases are often very influential, especially if they challenge public acceptance of an undesirable situation and do so dramatically or with logic and wit. Most conservationists will long remember the impact of Rachel Carson's *Silent Spring* on the use of insecticides. Controversial magazine articles and news reports of fire damage often have similar impact. But much less dramatic factual material provides the essential base for most fire prevention programs.

Radio messages and programs have the advantage of being voice communication requiring little or no effort on the part of the listener. Radio communication reaches many who read little or who live in remote rural and backcountry areas where television is not available. Car and portable radios maintain communication and can transmit fire prevention messages to travelers.

Television has the special advantage of communicating by both sight and sound and usually color as well, so it is adaptable to a variety of applications ranging from brief commercial-type messages to full-length dramatic productions.

Motion pictures with sound share television's special advantages as a communications medium. Assuming that projection facilities are available, motion pictures have another advantage—the capability of almost infinite repetition and of flexible scheduling at any time and place desired. In the past, the fire prevention moving picture at schools and churches in backcountry communities was the badge of an active fire prevention program. Better roads and expanded radio and television coverage now place public-service moving pictures under severe competition with other forms of entertainment. When this is offset by the excellence of the public-service production, it continues to enjoy its special advantages. In addition, it is then in demand for inclusion in the programs of commercial movie theaters as well.

Signs, posters, and exhibits have their special value as codified reminders of a message or slogan already familiar to the viewer. As such, they have their highest value when so placed that their effect is to emphasize the "here and now" significance of the message. This critical element of placement can make them effective too in identifying restricted areas and in giving warning of prohibited acts. Exhibits, however, serve primarily as a medium of information. They take many forms and are designed for viewing by large numbers of people, as at conventions. They undertake to give a more complete story than is possible with signs and posters.

So-called handouts serve best when they highlight in brief, simple fashion the important points of a more detailed or complex presentation in such a way that they enable the listener to pass it on easily and correctly to a third party. They serve many other purposes as well, often representing a specific place and occasion in the manner of a tourist souvenir.

Slide talks and speeches have the same advantages as sound moving pictures or television by virtue of communicating through both the eyes and ears. Usually the presentation and the attention-getting level are of a lower order, though this depends on the speaker. The special advantage is that the presentation establishes personal contact with the audience, and since it is not fixed in advance, as in a moving-picture sequence, the slides can be selected and the presentation can be designed to fit the local audience and the local problem. A speaker without slides should take every possible advantage of visual aids to sharpen communication with his audience.

Individual personal contact permits a degree of meeting of minds that is not attainable through any other means of communication. This is its special advantage. It can be highly selective and often becomes the critical factor in making the local prevention plan effective and in filling the gaps left by other media. Its role will be discussed further in the development of the current plan of fire prevention for a protection unit.

Communication to the people through these media is a prerequisite to the successful regulation of public use and to fire law enforcement.

Regulation of Public Use

The regulation of use of wild land is very important in preventing man-caused fires. It is closely related to educating the public on one hand and to law enforcement on the other. Primarily, full public compliance depends on prior appeals and publicity to clarify the reasons for restrictions and to generate a favorable attitude toward their acceptance. On the other hand, though much of the authority to regulate use of public land is inherent in the purpose to which it is dedicated, all regulation of use requires a legal basis and must be enforceable through some specific authority. This may be federal, state, or local. On federal land this is usually under federal regulations, though state laws or local ordinances may also apply. Where the action of residents on their own lands is concerned, authority for restrictions is always state or local.

The most common form of regulation is by application of closures of various kinds. As already discussed, closures vary in degree. Areas of hazardous fuels may be closed to all access by use of locked gates or barriers on access roads. Larger areas may be closed for periods of high or extreme fire danger by posting of signs and patrol by fire prevention guards. Where access is by private road, it can be closed as a simple exercise of the right of ownership. Where access is by a road built by either state or federal funds, further authority is needed. Where fire emergency is the only reason, closures have to be limited to fire danger periods.

In National Parks and on some National Forests, "work roads" may be generally closed to recreationists though not to local residents, permittees, or contractors who have a recognized current need of access.

The more common form of closure is that of limited closure. Though this is the more often used, it is also the more difficult to bring about. The most prevalent are restrictions on smoking. Smoking may be prohibited in forest areas except at specified locations, such as campground and headquarters areas. At times such prohibitions have been applied as well to the occupants of automobiles traversing public roads in such areas. Such prohibitions are never observed very well if the effect is that of prohibiting the habitual smoker from smoking. Consequently, the conventional places where smoking is permitted often need to be supplemented on a planned basis to accomodate the smoker. Usually too, it has been found best to permit smoking in an automobile as long as the ashtray is used for both the match and the cigarette butt. To assure this, many states have special laws prohibiting the throwing of burning materials from vehicles. This is discussed under law enforcement.

A second common form of limited closure is the prohibition of campfires in wild-land areas. Even this form of closure is difficult to enforce except for limited areas or periods. Yet campfires and warming fires have been such a perennial source of troublesome wildfires that it is very important in most areas to prevent the irresponsible building of such fires. This is the initial reason for creating campgrounds with prepared fireplaces or camp stoves. Prior to full development of such facilities, provisions for campfire permits have often been used successfully. Usually the prerequisite has been a shovel, ax, and water bucket as minimum equipment in the applicant's camp outfit. This would be supplemented by instructions, given by a fire prevention officer, on how to select a safe site and on other precautions to take, reinforced by a handout.

A third important form of closure is that against planned use of fire for any of a variety of purposes when not confined by a properly designed incinerator. Such fires are usually referred to as controlled burning or debris-burning fires. On federal lands such fires are usually carefully limited by special clauses in contracts with users and construction contractors. The more serious threat is often from wildfires that escape from such activities on state and private lands. State laws must be depended on for limiting such fires. Most states have legislation on this subject. Some prohibit debris-burning fires during certain fixed periods corresponding to the fire season, with provision for extension by proclamation by the governor (Figure 9.3). Others have provision for burning permits to be issued if certain requirements are met. The issuing officers may be volunteer fire wardens or regular state and federal forest officers under a cooperative arrangement. Restriction of burning for air pollution control is increasing in most states.

Planned burning of hazardous fuels as a land treatment measure over a considerable area are usually the special responsibility of the state forester. Fire danger ratings and fire weather forecasts are critical information in handling the issuance of such permits. In California, control through issuance of such permits becomes crucial, since controlled burning of chaparral cover cannot proceed when fire danger is low (Chapter 4).

A fourth form of closure is that of bringing to a halt any activity on wild lands that carries a positive risk of fire. Under state laws in Washington and Oregon, logging operations are closed down when the relative humidity of the air drops below a certain level. Usually this is only for portions of the 24-hour period, though it may extend for several days.

In most states the hunting season may be postponed or interrupted by closing the entire state or portions of it during periods of very high fire danger. This is brought about usually through a proclamation issued by the governor. The National Forests may be closed to hunting by the regional forester for the same reason. This may be in cooperation with the state or independently. The fire-setting capabilities of such activities as blasting, target practice, setting off of fireworks, and military maneuvers greatly increase as fire danger increases. It is common to prohibit or closely regulate such activities also on public lands.

Though some of these measures are based on state law, most operate as rules and regulations under the general authority of the forest agency responsible for administration of the land. All have a legal basis and are related to law enforcement to the extent that they control activities of the individual. But regulation of use can be distinguished from the law enforcement activity by the fact that its measures are aimed primarily at reducing fire risk in a specific area, they depend mostly on education of the public for their acceptance, and they are directed to the user only.

Figure 9.3 Debris-burning fire not properly confined. A common cause of wildfires in summer residence areas.

Law Enforcement

Law enforcement is always a necessary tool in fire prevention. There is a small minority of people who are heedless, careless, or indifferent or who actively resist any regulation of their use of fire to serve what they believe are their personal interests. A few are active incendiarists. Though this group is small, it is always capable of nullifying the gains made through programs of public education and regulation of fire risks. Fire laws and law enforcement remain the only means of preventing the fire-setting activities of these people.

In the United States, most states have legislation on setting and leaving fires, on the abatement of fire hazards, and on incendiarism. These provide the essential background of legal penalties to the acts of omission and commission that lead to damaging wildfires. But legal deterrence becomes effective only through active enforcement. Here the variation is great. The degree to which fire laws are enforced varies within and between states and with one fire law compared to another. There are many reasons for this, but perhaps the most common reason for inadequate enforcement in forest fire agencies is that forest officers engaged chiefly in the other forms of public education are most reluctant to exercise police powers. Yet, just as in the enforcement of traffic laws, if the laws are enforced and convictions for their violation are well publicized, a positive reduction in the incidence of fires from negligence is commonly experienced. Where law enforcement has been weak and man-caused fires abundant, the use of specially trained law enforcement officers is frequently the best way to accomplish this. This practice has already gained acceptance through necessity in coping with difficult problems of incendiarism and fire trespass. However, some laws provide legal deterrence without special provisions for enforcement.

Perhaps the most universal and most effective legal deterrent to deliberately set fires or to careless or negligent use of fire is the civil liability of the fire starter for any damage his fire may do to the property of others. This liability exists even where other fire laws are lacking. Among landowners and permanent local residents, this liability is a strong restraining influence which may be reinforced by state law or local ordinance.

Among timberland owners, contractors, and commercial interests of all kinds, this liability is the basis for lawsuits to recover fire damages. Where the federal government, the state, or any public agency is the owner of the land and the resources damaged by a fire, it has the same right as the individual to recover damages from the person or agency responsible.

Fire trespass and litigation under it are legal subjects around which much has been written. To work effectively with lawyers in this field, special training is needed and special law enforcement officers are often employed, as cited above.

Civil liability is not effective against the incendiarist for several reasons. The incendiarist seldom has financial assets; he often becomes highly skilled at setting delayed-ignition fires, so he is difficult to identify; and evidence of how the fire started is usually consumed by the fire. When an incendiarist is caught in the act, the damage is likely to be small. So criminal rather than civil action is the primary deterrent except in the rare case where the incendiarist was acting as the hired agent of a property owner. For similar reasons civil liability for fire damage is not very influential among residents who do not own property or among transients.

All states have laws designed to prevent uncontrolled fires in grass, brush, and timber cover. These laws vary in detail and in coverage. Some apply only to the portion of the state in organized forest districts, but all follow a similar pattern. Most provide for (1) regulation of debris burning of all kinds, usually through a system of permits obtainable from fire wardens; (2) installation of spark arresters and other mechanical devices for preventing fires from glowing carbon from power saws, tractors, locomotives, donkey engines, etc.; (3) most prohibit throwing burning materials, such as cigarette stubs, from vehicles; (4) some go further than 1 and require disposal of logging slash and other fire hazards; (5) all have penalties for incendiary fires, and for acts of negligence in the use of fire, such as leaving campfires unextinguished. Most states too have special enabling acts which permit the cooperation of a political unit of the state, such as a county, with state authorities for the purpose of controlling all fires within that unit. All states have a state forester or equivalent official who usually heads up administration of state forest lands and all forest fire control activities on state and private lands. He also represents the state in cooperative fire control programs with the federal government.

State forest fire laws stipulate a range of penalties for violations. The more serious violations, such as incendiarism, are punished as felonies; the less serious, such as failure to obtain a permit to burn debris, are punished as misdemeanors.

Since state laws apply on federal as well as on state and private lands within the state, they are commonly used by the U.S. Forest Service in carrying out fire prevention programs on the National Forests and to varying degrees by other federal land management agencies. However, federal regulations also apply to federal lands and can be enforced through federal courts. Federal forest fire regulations on the National Forests cover most sources of man-caused risk and are referred to as fire trespass regulations. A complete set of such regulations also applies to National Parks. Most violators of fire regulations in the National Parks appear before special magistrates who are assigned for this purpose. Whether prosecution of an offense on National Forest land is conducted under state law or before a federal judge will vary depending on several factors. The more important are adequacy of the state law covering the offense, the delays likely, and factors of local convenience and cooperation in carrying out the action.

Though fire law enforcement is an essential part of any fire prevention program, it needs to be carried out with discretion and with a background of full understanding of the local situation. This applies particularly to incendiary fires. In some localities in the South, incendiary fires are regarded by most local residents with indifference or approval in the belief they do more good than harm, and a high proportion of fires so classed are not set with criminal intent. In such localities, the legitimate place of prescribed burning needs first to be recognized. Where appropriate, it should then be utilized to satisfy legitimate needs. This provides an opportunity to publicize the critical distinction between the carefully controlled burn and the destructive wildfire. After a course of action of this kind, a vigorous law enforcement program is likely to win the full support of responsible local residents and to be highly successful. Without local action and participation of this kind, legal prosecution of violations is likely to be looked on as persecution by outside interests. Negative local attitudes arising in this way often strongly influence judges and juries.

To summarize, the forest manager's concern with forest fire law and its enforcement is primarily that of how much fire prevention it can accomplish. He is justified in allocating priorities in the total fire control effort accordingly. Though fire law enforcement is an essential part of fire prevention, it is not a panacea. Basically it serves best as an educational tool to be used wisely and firmly. To be effective, enforcement must be preceded and accompanied by prevention education, much of it by individual contact in each community. Many instances can be cited in which enforcement was the key factor in reducing woods fires. But such reductions are always transitory unless the effort has been backed by on-the-ground prevention education. In the final analysis successful enforcement depends on both local and general public support.

NATIONAL FOREST FIRE PREVENTION PROGRAMS

From the vantage point of the foregoing discussions, fire prevention action programs can be examined with perspective. Two existing national programs will be reviewed first: the National Cooperative Forest Fire Prevention Program, often referred to as the Smokey Bear Program; and the Keep Green Program sponsored by American Forests Institute. The critical problem of developing effective local programs will then be examined.

The National Cooperative Forest Fire Prevention Campaign

The U.S. Forest Service, other federal agencies concerned with wild-land management, and state forestry organizations have long recognized the importance of active fire prevention work. The Forest Service has pressed fire prevention programs since its organization in 1905 and has exerted national leadership. State organizations have in turn taken the lead in their respective areas. Close cooperative relationships have existed for many years between the Federal Forest Service and state forestry agencies in forestry work on state and private lands. The basic pattern began with the Weeks law of 1911, which has been greatly broadened and strengthened by the Clarke-McNary act of 1924 and subsequent legislation. Under this legislation federal funds are available to support state programs of fire control and tree planting on state and private lands. Over the years, prevention materials and programs of all sorts have been developed and applied. Almost everything has been tried, from the old warning and scare posters of the 1920s and earlier to the more recent and more subtle appeals to personal motives and citizen responsibility generally.

The prestige and effectiveness of forest fire prevention among the American people has increased markedly in this period. This is chargeable mostly to the Cooperative Forest Fire Prevention (C.F.F.P.) campaign which was organized in 1942, soon after entry of the United States into World War II. The circumstances at the time are described by Clint Davis (1951):

> The danger of uncontrolled forest fires hampering an all-out rearmament program was well recognized. Lumber—billions of feet of it—was needed for cantonment construction, crating, aircraft carrier decks and numerous other defense needs. Huge amounts of pulpwood were needed for paper, cardboard, explosives and chemicals.
>
> Demands on range lands were heavy for the production of meat, leather, and wool to feed and clothe our troops. Important watersheds had to be protected from fire to prevent any interruption of water flow for domestic use and hydroelectric power so essential in keeping the wheels of industry humming around the clock.
>
> Forest fires were also recognized as a threat to defense and security measures within the nation's boundaries. Columns of smoke would nullify the effectiveness of air raid detection systems. Smoke screens might well protect submarines and other means of enemy harassment. Forest fires had already proved a problem in the vicinity of airfields and artillery training grounds. Smoke interference often made it necessary to shut down essential training programs for pilots and gunners for periods of days. In other areas troop training was hampered because it was necessary to use GI's to combat and control fires encroaching upon military installations. Another threat, that of the enemy firing our forest, was always prevalent.

Prevention of man-caused fires was an obvious answer to the problem; it was something that the American people could do by not doing something—starting fires—and required a minimum of manpower or equipment.

At the same time, the advertising industry made available to the war effort on a public-service basis the massive power of professional advertising in promoting voluntary, individual action to meet national problems. The War Advertising Council was organized in January, 1942. A liaison with fire prevention was logical and early effected by the U.S. Forest Service. A wartime forest fire prevention campaign was organized and was so successful that it continued during the war along with war bond and scrap metal drives and blood donor and other programs. This marked the first time that the full strength and skill of top national advertising talent in simplification, dramatization, repetition, and in artwork were put behind fire prevention work.

At the end of the war period the challenge of the human problem of preventing forest fires and the popularity of the program so impressed the Advertising Council that instead of going on to other public-service programs they continued to sponsor the forest fire prevention program. As a public service contribution, some of the country's leading advertising agencies donate their services in creating advertising materials for Council campaigns. A large number of industrial and business corporations cooperate. American business, large and small, including advertising medium owners, contribute all the time and space needed to display the advertising for the Council's public-service campaigns.

Utilizing this continued service, fire prevention work was organized on a permanent basis as the C.F.F.P. campaign. It is sponsored by the U.S. Forest Service, the fire control agencies of the U.S. Department of the Interior, and the state forestry agencies working through the National Association of State Foresters. Many other organizations have also taken an important part in the program. Specific Council assistance is assigned to the advertising agency of Foote, Cone, and Belding of Los Angeles, who annually contribute professional services worth thousands of dollars. Materials for a special Southern state program (started in 1958) are contributed by Liller, Neal, Battle, and Lindsey of Atlanta, Georgia. The impact and contribution of professional advertising talent in applying basic merchandising principles were early felt.

One of the first recommendations by the advertising experts was the development and constant use of an identifying slogan or tag line for all materials. After much study the slogan, "Remember, Only You Can Prevent Forest Fires," was adopted. The experts pointed out that this slogan contained several important elements. It puts forest fire prevention on a personal basis, and it intrigues the interest of each individual to analyze how he or she can do something about forest fire. [Davis, 1951]

A second contribution was establishment of a dramatic recognition symbol. After a number of tries, a bear, christened Smokey, was first presented in 1945 as an effective fire hero and mouthpiece for prevention messages. Five years later, a bear cub, rescued from a forest fire in New Mexico, was made the living prototype of Smokey in a master stroke of publicity genius. The bear was flown to Washington and photographed with the President, high officials of the administration, and various other well-known people. It became a prominent member of the Washington Zoo. Smokey, wearing blue jeans, hat, and a purposeful look, became a permanent standard bearer and symbol of prevention and has been worked into the basic structure of the campaign to the extent that it is popularly known as the Smokey Bear campaign.

The C.F.F.P. campaign has had a tremendous impact on the public. On a recognition basis, Smokey Bear rates with leading national trademarks. Advertising contributed by publishers and many business and other organizations has blanketed the country. Radio and television programs carry it. Millions of posters, placards, bookmarks, blotters, comic books, songs, and other items for use in all sorts of media and places are distributed annually.

Under provisions of a special act of Congress in 1952, Smokey Bear was "copyrighted" for fire prevention, and educational uses of the symbol on belts, books, games, and other merchandise are approved by the chief of the Forest Service.

Each year a new campaign is planned, usually featuring some particular theme. Samples of magazine and newspaper advertisements, radio scripts and recorded messages, car and bus cards, and television scripts and films are sent to mass media cooperators without charge. Samples of other items distributed by states and federal field units are shown in Figure 9.4. Materials range from those designed for mass appeals to specific how-to-do-it and other educational items for local use. While the program is aimed primarily at general use, considerable and ingenious thought is given to making it effective in local situations. Some of the material, that for use in advertisements specifically, is designed so that sponsors' and users' names can be inserted locally. The special program for the Southern states is an effort to more closely localize appeals and action to distinctive Southern problems, particularly the problem of wildfire from incendiarism and debris burning, which had shown little response to prevention programs of the past. Special materials and posters for this purpose are contributed by advertising firms of the South as described above.

In 1968, Haug Associates, Inc., of Los Angeles, California, undertook a national survey of the public's image of Smokey the Bear and of

You have so many reasons to
PROTECT YOUR FORESTS

Remember–
only **YOU** can prevent woods fires!

Only you can prevent forest fires.

Only you can prevent forest fires

Figure 9.4 Forest fire prevention material prepared for the Cooperative Forest Fire Prevention Program. *(U.S. Forest Service photo.)*

Remember– **Only you can**
PREVENT FOREST FIRES !

the public's attitudes toward the Smokey Bear symbol. The study was conducted in three regions, the East, South, and California. Within each region, six areas, consisting of three medium and three smaller cities, were selected for sampling, which was done through 1,800 interviews. Half the interviews were divided equally between adult men and women. The other half were equally divided between two groups, children aged 6 to 12 and teen-agers aged 13 to 18.

The highlights of this survey showed that Smokey was well known and well liked by all age groups. The name was correctly associated with the symbol by 98 percent of the children, 95 percent of the teen-agers, and 89 percent of the adults. All understood Smokey's function and believed that human irresponsibility was the major cause of forest fires. Among younger children, Smokey was their favorite symbol over four other top symbols created by national advertising. Some teen-agers felt Smokey was for younger children, and his image was slightly more favorable among adults than teen-agers. As might be expected, the primary source of awareness of Smokey was through television, but signs and posters ran a close second. Comics were prominent among teen-agers, and books, magazines, and newspapers figured importantly among adults. Almost 90 percent of the adults who recognized the Smokey symbol felt that he was doing a good job. This is said to be a remarkable showing compared to any similar creation. In effect then, after more than 25 years' operation of the Smokey Bear program, its success when measured by criteria such as those described has remained remarkably high.

Keep Green Programs

Forest industry naturally has a tremendous stake in protection against fire. Private forest owners, faced with an imperative need for protection, have for many years banded together in protective associations, their organized effort antedating development of general statewide protection. The longest and strongest development of the protective associations is in the West. Prevention work has always been done by these organizations, strengthened by general assistance from industry and other private forestry associations. This work led to development of a national prevention program known as the Keep Green movement. It is a popular-front program complementary to the Cooperative Forest Fire Prevention campaigns sponsored by the federal and state protection agencies and begun at about the same time.

The immediate genesis of the movement is best described in the words of W. B. Greeley, probably its major proponent (1949):

One evening in 1941 Governor Martin of Washington called a meeting of forest-minded people at Olympia. Real problems confronted us. How could we make the state of Washington safe for tree farms which were appearing here and there on the lands of owners who had determined not to cut out but to stay in business? We had been burning over 150,000 acres of forest land yearly.

Early in the evening, someone referred to Washington's pride in being the "Evergreen State" and said that it was the job of all of us to keep it that way. The chairman turned the meeting into a rapid fire of questions to almost everyone in the room: What can the lumbermen do to keep Washington green? What can the sportsmen do to keep Washington green? What can the teachers do to keep Washington green? And so on, covering most of the groups of people in the state. On the rousing mandate of this meeting, Keep Washington Green was organized soon after. It set itself the task of breaking down public indifference and negligence toward man-caused fires, by the use of every educational means we could command. The first leader engaged to wake up the people of Washington to their common responsibility was Stewart Holbrook.

Oregon began a similar program a few months later, in 1941. Minnesota adopted a Keep Green program in 1944. Out of these grew the national Keep America Green campaign.

It is an educational program designed to acquaint people with the value of trees and the economic and social contribution that forests make. To a high degree its success depends on localizing the program to the state, county, and community level. This is accomplished by enlisting active sponsorship of local newspapers and radio stations and active participation by schools and by such groups as civic organizations, labor unions, women's clubs, youth groups, and veterans' organizations.

American Forest Institute, formerly American Forest Products Industries, Inc., representing the major forest industries of the nation, has been national coordinator of Keep America Green since 1944. Since that time, state Keep Green programs have been started in most of the major wood-producing states.

The American Forest Institute, Inc., supplies television station-break slides, spot radio announcements, leaflets, stuffers, and many other items for general distribution in much the same way as does the C.F.F.P. campaign.

The usual first step in organization is the creation of a statewide central committee headed by a leading citizen and made up of representatives of government, professions, civic groups, and industrial groups interested in forest fire prevention. Initiative and sponsorship may come from any one of such groups including the forest industry, state forestry departments, timber protective associations, Federation of Women's Clubs, or Junior Chambers of Commerce. The purpose of the central committee is to produce a plan of action, supply campaign materials, and stimulate and coordinate the effort.

In well-developed campaigns, local Keep Green committees are organized. These may be county or community committees or committees within the framework of existing organizations such as service clubs. From there on, work may take on a wide variety of forms, including talks and movies to all sorts of groups, poster campaigns, school education work, slogan and essay contests, pageants, Boy and Girl Scout activities, and Green Guard youth organizations, depending on local interest and needs.

Keep Oregon Green, one of the first and strongest of the state programs, is illustrative both of state organization and work done. The work is directed by the Keep Oregon Green Association, with a board of trustees representing the major industrial and other forestry groups of the state. Action is directed by an executive committee appointed by the governor. It employs an executive secretary with an office in Salem. There are a statewide Newspaper Committee and Radio Committee and a series of county committees also appointed by the governor. The Association is mostly financed by private contributions. Only about a fifth of the annual budget comes from state governmental sources. Individual memberships in the Association, on as wide a basis as possible, are strongly encouraged.

A variety of programs has been undertaken. The Oregon Green Guard of young people from 6 to 18 years of age has been an important medium. The program is carried out through both conventional and unconventional media including newspapers, radio and television, posters, placards, auto tags and stickers, stamps, pamphlets and leaflets, and various novelties. A sample of some of them is shown in Figure 9.5.

The Keep Green campaigns have depended on considerable local financing and a strong local initiative for their excellence. These are strong assets; but since they depend on a few individuals, they are often transient in nature. As a consequence, the campaigns have varied widely in effectiveness among the states.

Coordination with the Smokey Bear Program has been in effect at state and national levels almost from the start. Keep Green committees have often been the media for distributing certain C.F.F.P. materials, though they have always supplemented them with more localized appeals identified with the Keep Green campaign. In recent years such committees have been placing more dependence on use of the Smokey Bear

Figure 9.5 Oregon Keep Green publicity material.

materials and American Forest Institute has been giving lower priority to the Keep Green campaign in their overall program.

Local Action Programs

The preceding sections have given information on the two national fire prevention programs and on how they operate. These programs are aimed at reaching large segments of the public and emphasize the use of mass media. Although they reach down to many specific groups, an understanding of how particular prevention problems are met and solved cannot be gained by a general description of prevention programs. Much of the most effective prevention work is done at the local level. Particular fire-causing groups often offer special problems.

To show how prevention principles, approaches, and media are used in meeting particular problems, two case examples are presented. Both are actual situations and illustrate specific approaches that have been found successful. They are selected as samples of the major cause groups and of the educational and law enforcement measures that have been applied.

FIRE PREVENTION THROUGH COMMUNITY EDUCATION

The following describes a cooperative project between the Tennessee Department of Conservation, Division of Forestry, and the Tennessee Valley Authority, Division of Forestry Relations.[3]

Situation   The problem area was the Beech River watershed, including 193,000 acres of gently rolling land, 40 percent forested, in west Tennessee. Nonforest area was cultivated, pastured, or abandoned because of severe erosion. Eighty percent of the woodland area was included in farms, mostly small tracts, averaging 41 acres. Nine out of every ten forested acres supported hardwoods.

Most of the area had been under state-organized protection for only two years prior to the prevention project. Substantial portions of the area had been burned over for years by residents seeking to improve pasture, kill snakes and boll weevils, or clear land. Local residents estimate the annual burn to have been from 10 to 25 percent. The general attitude of residents was that forests were of low value. "Shotgun" prevention programs had made only slight progress with prevention education.

Cause Analysis   Available fire records for the watershed were analyzed and fires located on maps by cause. The chief cause appeared to be carelessness in allowing escape of fires designed to clean up agricultural wastes and misguided

---

[3] Report furnished by courtesy of these two organizations.

attempts to improve woodland pasture. This was the reason for 65 percent of all fires; hunters started 11 percent, and there were other miscellaneous causes. Average number of fires per season varied with rainfall: With rainfall 10 inches below normal, there were 70 fires; with normal rainfall, 44 fires; with 10 inches above-normal rainfall, 18 fires.

Action Planning   An intensive campaign of rural meetings, fire prevention movies, news and radio releases, and posters and exhibits was planned. Each fire was to be vigorously investigated in the field, and neighbors and witnesses were to be questioned to emphasize the seriousness of the situation. Major effort was to be concentrated in a personal contact campaign planned for the entire area to enlist cooperation of all family heads. A recent forest school graduate was to be engaged for the specific purpose of conducting the program.

Action Taken   All fire control personnel—fire control assistants, lookouts, and fireguards—were trained in fire prevention techniques, and fire prevention was included in their work assignments. This broadened the effective force. Causes of fires were vigorously searched by the project forester, who was not required to perform any suppression duties. No punitive action was taken when guilty parties were apprehended, as the Division felt public opinion was not far enough advanced to sustain such action. Friendly warnings were issued, however, and the whole fire picture discussed with offenders. The project forester personally contacted over two thousand family heads in an attempt to interest them in forestry. He classified, in terms of the fire problem, each person interviewed as a definite risk, a possible risk, indifferent, or strongly in favor of fire control. He made an effort to enlist interest according to the abilities of the persons questioned. He marked growing stands for thinning, improvement, and harvest cuts, pointing out forest values and results of fire prevention at every opportunity. The fire control organization held two general fire prevention meetings, issued 85 news releases, broadcast 4 radio programs and 52 spot announcements, and distributed 10,000 pieces of literature and 1,000 posters to supplement the personal contact campaign.

Results   Fire incidence was reduced by 50 percent during the two-year period. In comparing fire seasons for 1950 to 1951 (before the prevention program) with 1952 to 1954 (during and after the program), some interesting observations can be made on the basis of numbers of fires occurring in generally comparable fire weather. For seasons with rainfall 10 inches below normal, there were 30 fires after the campaign compared with 70 before. With normal rainfall, there were 18 instead of an average of 44; with 10 inches above normal rainfall, there averaged 6 instead of 18 fires. The number of fires continued to decrease after 1954. Former hot spots were eliminated.

Creation of an interest in forestry meant not only a reduction in fires and elimination of a negative attitude but a positive interest in growing trees. During the two-year period of the project, 450 landowners planted about 800,000 trees a

year for erosion control. The year after the intensive campaign, private landowners in the area planted 1,550,000 trees.

REDUCING INCENDIARISM THROUGH DIRECT PERSONAL CONTACT[4]

The Broad River area of North Carolina includes about 125,000 acres in
parts of four counties. The area is 90 percent forested, mountainous,
relatively inaccessible, and thinly populated.

The Situation   Prior to 1943, the fire history was bad, with a high incidence of fire occurrence, much of it incendiary. Local citizens were indifferent,
and fires of 1,000 to 2,000 acres not uncommon. No local help was available for
suppression, and there were no satisfactory district wardens available in or
adjacent to the area. Local people were engaged mostly in farming or forest work.
Hunting was the major form of recreation. About two-thirds of the fires started in
the part of Buncombe County lying within the area.

The Buncombe County ranger was slightly acquainted with a local young
married man who spent much time hunting. This man was above average in
intelligence and more or less the leader of his group of associates. This group had
long been suspected of setting fires, but insufficient evidence had prevented any
convictions.

The Solution   It was planned that the Buncombe County ranger would try
to promote friendship with this particular young man by arranging some hunting
trips with him and his group. The county ranger had good dogs and hunted quite a
lot himself. This plan was put into operation for three reasons:

1   To see if friendship could be developed and thereby secure local help for
fire fighting.
2   To see if information could be gained as to party or parties setting the
fires and to the motive
3   To see if friendship and interest could be aroused in this man to the point
of eventually appointing him a district fire warden

During the fall of 1942 and winter of 1943 several hunts were arranged with
this group. The county ranger was careful not to discuss forest fires, and only
when a burned area was entered while hunting did he suggest that they move to an
unburned area where hunting would be better. The fall of 1942 was wet, and no
fires occurred in this area. In the early spring of 1943 the county ranger went in to
this area on a fire. He took help with him as was usual but stopped by the home of
this local friend to see if he would help. The man was not at home, but the county
ranger left word that he was going on to a fire, specifying the place, and was

---

[4] Information given by B. H. Corpening, District Forester, North Carolina Division of Forestry.

pleasantly surprised a couple of hours later when this person with several of the local men showed up at the fire and volunteered their help.

Results   This was the beginning of the end of wildfires in the area. Since 1945 no fires of incendiary nature have occurred in this section. Fires of any kind are rare. This local person was made a district warden in 1944 and continued in that capacity until 1949, when he moved to an adjacent county, continuing to hold his warden appointment. A friend of about the same age was appointed warden in his place, continued the good work, and is now the most dependable warden in Buncombe County. The area into which the district warden moved was known as a hot spot of the county. His wife's people lived there. Almost immediately forest fire occurrence dropped in this area too. Since 1951 the area has no longer been considered a problem section, and the warden is rated as one of the best in the county, seldom has any fires in his community, and assists the county ranger in other parts of the county when called on.

Diagnosis and Prescription

The approaches in the two preceding examples differ. Chief dependence in the first case is on mass media and group contacts and in the second on individual personal contact. Nevertheless, both illustrate the successful outcome of (1) a careful analysis of the problem, (2) a diagnosis, and (3) the application of a prescription especially drawn to fit the local situation.

This is also a highly effective approach in developing integrated fire prevention plans and programs for each forest protection unit. How this may be accomplished is developed further in Chapter 14, illustrated by problems on the ground typical of the sort with which the local forest manager must cope.

Hazard Reduction

Fire prevention concerns control of both fire risks and fire hazards. Chapter 9 is devoted to methods of controlling the many sources of man-caused fire risk. This chapter moves on to the less publicized aspect of preventing fires through control of the quantity, arrangement, continuity, ignitability, or burning rate of forest fuels. Though such measures are potentially costly, the principles and techniques come entirely within the scope of the forester's land-management activities on the ground. So, unlike programs of educating the public and of enforcing fire laws, the assistance of outside experts is not required. Instead, it is a part of the exercise of responsible ownership. How well it is accomplished is a good gauge of the quality of the owner's management. In fact, ideally, the control of fuel hazards is so well built into forest land management that it ceases to be identified as a separate fire control measure.

PURPOSES AND PRINCIPLES OF HAZARD REDUCTION

The benefits of hazard reduction extend much further than fire prevention. Potentially, control of fuels means control of the size and difficulty of the entire fire-fighting job. Several principles are involved.

First, the direct prevention of fires through hazard reduction means removal of fuels exposed to sources of high risk. This is well illustrated by the cleared and burned railroad right-of-way. It is also illustrated by the developed campground from which all dead fuels have been removed.

Next comes an extension beyond the concept of mere prevention of ignitions to that of preventing or limiting spread following ignition or of preventing the rapid buildup of heat energy. In terms of fire prevention, the objective becomes prevention of large or uncontrollable fires rather than simply a reduction in the total number of fires.

With this broadened significance in mind, hazard reduction may be classified according to its intended purpose, as follows:

1 Removal of all ignitable fuel in limited areas of special risk. The cleared and burned railway right-of-way is an example, as already mentioned. It is illustrated also by the zone kept clear of fuels around sawmill burners, city dumps, etc. It is represented on a more extensive scale where forest or grass areas are burned over under control to avoid subsequent ignition from known sources of risk. The common purpose is the automatic prevention of ignitions by removal of fuels.

2 Removal of all fuel in a strip close to or around the source of risk in order to confine any fire that may be ignited to a small isolated area. This kind of measure frequently substitutes for complete removal in cases cited under 1 above. Cleanup of fuels or exposure of soil in a strip along roadsides to create firebreaks to confine roadside fires is a familiar example. The purpose is both prevention of ignitions and containment.

3 Removal of fuel in a strip where the purpose is to exclude fire from a high-value or high-hazard area. Firebreaks around a forest plantation are a typical example (Figure 10.1).

4 Removal of fuels to reinforce natural breaks and to create new ones by which an area can be broken up into blocks to facilitate control of wildfires. This is a familiar pattern in California brushlands (Figure 10.2). In Southern plantations, a skeleton system of access roads and firebreaks combined usually serves this purpose.

5 Use of prescribed burning, when coarse and intermediate fuels are moist, to safely remove flash fuels from considerable areas. Similar use on smaller areas to strongly reduce fuel hazards. The purpose is to reduce the energy output and the rate of spread of wildfires so they will be much easier to control and will do less damage. Such burning is practiced extensively in Australia and is familiar throughout the southern pine region. It is also used to a limited degree in ponderosa pine in the western United States.

6 Breaking the vertical continuity of fuels and the horizontal continuity of tree crowns in coniferous stands by cultural measures such as pruning and thinning and the removal of undergrowth. Although the value of hazard reduction of this kind is commonly recognized, it is not

Figure 10.1 Four-year-old slash pine plantation protected by a 9-foot plowed break which reinforces road at right. *(U.S. Forest Service photo.)*

commonly practiced because of costs. However, many examples of such work by the Civilian Conservation Corps of the 1930s could be cited. Its particular purpose is to reduce the threat of crown fires. In South Australia, where pine plantations border on towns, a system of thinning, pruning, and complete slash disposal has been practiced as a means of creating "crown fire free" areas. This affords improved protection to both the town and the plantation (Douglas, 1967).

7   Removal of dead snags or trees that would throw spot fires if ignited. This is a familiar requirement in timber sale areas on the National Forests but is most fully recognized and practiced in the Western regions of the United States. The purpose is assurance to the fire fighter that his efforts will not be frustrated by a succession of spot fires from embers flying overhead (Figure 10.3).

The application of hazard-reduction measures to serve these purposes requires decisions based on careful evaluation and planning. As pointed out in the previous chapter, high risk and high fuel hazards cannot be allowed to persist where high values are at stake because of the near certainty of disastrous fire losses. It is often more feasible to treat the fuel than to reduce the risk to a safe point. But what form of fuel reduction to apply and to what portions of the area must then be determined. High hazards should always enter into priority decisions. Precise determination by computations is not to be expected, but by taking all relevant factors into account, good judgment in such decisions can be consistently applied.

Critical fuel hazards created by logging may call for a variety of

Figure 10.2 Fuelbreak systems in California. *A.* In coniferous forest. *B.* In chaparral cover of southern California.

Figure 10.3 Wide, snag-free corridors in the Tillamook burn, Oregon, created to alleviate problem of snag-to-snag propagation of fire by flying embers. *(Courtesy American Forestry Association.)*

remedial measures depending on the size of the area; the exposure, continuity, and probable duration of the hazardous fuels; and on the kind and location of risk to which they are exposed. As discussed in Chapter 4, small areas of logging slash up to several acres in extent may not be a serious threat if widely separated and surrounded by low-hazard fuels. But the situation changes abruptly if the contiguous green fuels cure to become flash fuels. Even then, if fire risk is very low in the area and the flash fuel period is short, such fuels may be tolerated. The fire hazard will be less serious on north and east exposures in mountainous terrain (in the Northern Hemisphere) and wherever the ground is shaded by foliage of living trees. Hazardous fuel accumulations placed upslope from each other or along the axis of winds which prevail during periods of high fire danger are to be avoided. They may permit fire to jump quickly from one to the next through ignition by flying firebrands in spite of intervening barriers to continuous spread on the ground.

In most of the southern pine region of the United States, because of close utilization, there is very little heavy material in the logging slash. Also, activity by insects and fungi is at a high level because of the prevalence of higher humidities and temperatures. Consequently, logging slash decays rapidly and normally ceases to be a hazard after three years. This contrasts with coniferous types in much of the western United States, where logging slash may remain a high hazard for 20 years or more. Here, material not in direct contact with the ground seems to be in a microclimate which is either too dry or too cold most of the year to permit much decay activity. This strongly affects the need for hazard reduction.

The importance of these considerations varies with the degree to which hazardous fuels are exposed to fire risk, as discussed in the preceding chapter. One general principle is that fire hazards that will generate fires beyond the fire control capability of available fire-fighting forces must not be permitted to develop or persist. In practice, this means that under all except extreme fire danger conditions, fuel hazards should be maintained at a level that will permit the local first attack force to control any fire that starts before it causes unacceptable damage or requires emergency assistance from outside to bring about its control.

FIREBREAKS

Of the seven different methods of applying hazard reduction in the foregoing, only the use of controlled fire under 5 and the removal of snags under 7 are commonly applied in depth. All other forms of hazard reduction are restricted to limited areas. These usually take the form of clearing flammable material from a strip of specified width and location. This may be carried to the point of complete exposure of mineral soil and cultivation of the soil, or it may be limited to removal of flash fuels only. In either case, the strips on which fuel has been removed or reduced are referred to as firebreaks.

A firebreak is a natural or constructed barrier utilized to stop or check fires that may occur or to provide a control line from which to work. It is distinguished from the fire line by being constructed in anticipation of future fires. It often consists of two parts: (1) a lane or strip cleared of brush and other understory fuels, and (2) a narrower strip, within this lane, which is cleared down to mineral soil. Many firebreaks consist of a plowed furrow or two only. The total width of the break may vary from a minimum of this kind (3 to 4 feet) up to 100 feet or more, depending on cost and need. A forest road or a maintained right-of-way such as a power or telephone line often serves as a firebreak. Firebreaks for each of the first four purposes listed are quite similar in construction even though there is considerable difference in their intended function. However, they do vary in width, in degree of removal of living and dead fuels, and in their placement.

Where the purpose is removal of fuel from high-risk areas, much of the hazard reduction may not be identified as firebreak construction. This may be true in the cleanup around campgrounds and often along public roads.

Where the purpose is to isolate a source of fire risk, the firebreak often becomes a supplemental provision to the removal of fuels. For example, a sawmill in or near a forest area, particularly if it operates a refuse burner, is a potential source of wildfire. Most state laws require removal of flammable material for a specified distance around such an installation plus an exterior firebreak dug to mineral soil.

Where the purpose is to keep fires out of a high-hazard or high-value area, the firebreak must provide effective defense against a wildfire that has developed momentum in outside fuels. This may demand a wider firebreak than it is feasible to build and maintain. This is because convective heat transfer greatly increases the distance from the flame front over which ignitions will occur, even in the absence of spotting (Byram et al., 1963; Anderson, 1969). The minimum width is that required to prevent ignition by direct radiation, the maximum is not yet well defined but should be greater than the potential horizontal length of flame to be expected at the head of a fire (Chapter 6, Figure 6.4, page 176). When fire danger is high and fire is burning in heavy mixed fuels, particularly on slopes or with a brisk wind, this width can become prohibitive for a constructed firebreak. But the effective width can be increased at least 50 percent by reducing the angle between the axis of direction of spread and that of the firebreak. This is illustrated by Figure 10.4.

Where firebreaks are intended to keep fire out of a specific area, an experienced fire control officer can predict, with considerable confidence, the most likely direction from which a threatening fire will come. Accord-

Figure 10.4   Effect of angle of approach of a fire on effective width of a firebreak. Note intercepts at *a, b, c,* and *d.*

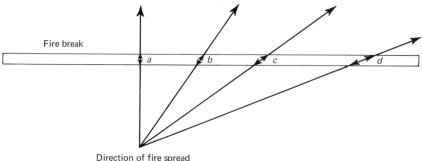

ingly, firebreaks can often be planned to reduce the likelihood of a fire heading across the firebreak at right angles where the effective width of the break is the least.

A second method of increasing the effective width of a firebreak is to backfire from it. Use of a firebreak as a base for backfiring in advance of an approaching wildfire often becomes its most important function in fire emergencies. Time is always critical in carrying out fire control tactics. So the existence of a prepared line in a strategic location can make the difference between a fire controlled at small size and a fire that becomes a disastrous conflagration.

Where the purpose of firebreaks is to break up a protected area into firebreak blocks, they are usually referred to as fuel breaks. They may have little relation to sources of risk. But to be skillfully designed, their pattern must take fire behavior into account in relation to local fuels and topography. Normally, fuel breaks will buy the most protection if they reinforce the places where a spreading fire will naturally slow down. The ridgetop location is a familiar example (Figure 10.2).

All barriers, artificial or natural, need to be taken into account in planning fire control strategy. In addition to firebreaks constructed as such, there are often artificial barriers such as roads; railroads; power, gas, oil, and telephone line rights-of-way; and breaks created by various forms of occupancy in forest areas. In almost any forest area intensively developed for timber production, a network of roads is established that constitutes a partial firebreak system as well. In fact, firebreaks are constructed and used to break up a forest area into small control units only where sufficient roads and other suitable barriers are lacking. Streams, water bodies, swamps, interspersed agricultural lands, cover types of naturally low flammability, and topography all may constitute important natural barriers to the spread of fire in particular situations. Dispersion of timber cutting to avoid creation of large, continuous slash areas is an important aspect of natural barriers. Staggered clear cuttings, as extensively applied in the Douglas-fir type of the Northwest, intersperse cutover areas with blocks of green timber of less flammability.

A closely integrated purpose of firebreaks is to furnish access to men and to fire fighting equipment. Nearly always, firebreaks serve this function to some degree, ranging from an incidental value up to the primary justification. Firebreaks are often combined with roads regardless of the purpose for which the road was constructed. On federal and state forests in the Lake states, for example, a gridiron system of combined roads and firebreaks was constructed over large areas by the Civilian Conservation Corps in the 1930s at $1/4$- to $1/2$-mile intervals. After 30 years, only the firebreaks accompanied by roads or serving as roads retained firebreak value because they were easier to maintain. At the same time, 50-foot firebreaks between plantations were so reduced in width by the growth of planted trees that they no longer imposed a barrier to crown fires. In California, the most ambitious firebreak project of the 1930s became known as the Ponderosa Way. When finished, it was 650 miles long. Its purpose was to provide better defense against grass fires from high-risk lands in the Sacramento Valley, fires which each year invaded the ponderosa pine timber slopes above. Though it was expected to be an automatic barrier to some fires, its chief use was to enable fire fighters to backfire against rapidly advancing fires from the grasslands. Wherever feasible, it was constructed under the forest canopy in order to reduce maintenance. All heavy dead fuels were removed on a strip of 50 to 200 feet and a road served as the center line wherever topography permitted.

Evaluation of this firebreak 20 years later showed that it had not been feasible to give such a big project much maintenance. It demonstrated too that continuity was unimportant, and that many sections had little or no advantage. But it demonstrated also that shaded breaks, traversed by roads, in areas where good silvicultural practice in the form of thinning, pruning, and removal of competing understory vegetation had been practiced, plus removal of all heavy fuels, can create a long-lasting reduction in fire hazard and a semipermanent or built-in firebreak system.

This precedent has contributed to the progressive development of firebreak and fuel-break systems in both northern and southern California (Green and Schimke, 1971; White and Green, 1967). Recent fuel-break projects have been aimed at breaking up the continuity of high-hazard fuels by strategically placed broad bands of low-hazard cover. Intensive treatment within these broad fuel breaks brings about a long-lasting reduction in fire hazard by replacement of brush and understory vegetation with grass and low-growing shrubs of low flammability (Figure 10.2A and B). In Figure 10.2B, the elimination of chaparral brush from a broad fuel break is illustrated. The term *firebreak* is, then, limited to the jeep trail of bare soil in its center. Figure 10.2A illustrates the much narrower fuel break used to reenforce the effect of topography in limiting the spread of fire in the mixed conifer type of northern California.

As already implied, firebreaks and fuel breaks have universal value to the fire fighter as "fortified" locations at which to take a stand and from which to backfire against an oncoming fire. For such a purpose they need to be strategically placed and to have only enough width or be clean enough to make it easy to control the backfires set. The backfire rapidly creates a barrier wider than any firebreak that could be constructed.

In southern California and in parts of northern California as well, brush fields (or chaparral) become so dense that foot travel through the brush becomes almost impossible. Similarly, steep terrain and dense cover combine to greatly restrict access by vehicles of all kinds. Fire, however, travels rapidly in the brush whenever burning conditions permit it to spread. These factors place a high premium on the access value of firebreaks for movement of men on foot and for movement of mechanized equipment. This makes firebreaks an essential provision as well for the safety of fire fighters. Consequently, a system of firebreaks and fuel breaks has become a continuing feature of the planned fire control system in such areas.

Construction and Maintenance of Firebreaks

Methods of constructing and maintaining firebreaks may be classified as mechanical, chemical, vegetative, and burning. They may be employed singly or in combination.

Mechanical Most firebreaks are constructed by mechanical means employing common land clearing equipment, usually power-operated. Where topography and cover permit, fire plows are most commonly used. The simplest break is a few plowed furrows, often separated and currently burned out in between. Disks and road graders are also used. Where forest cover is not completely removed and larger trees are left to create shaded firebreaks, some clearing and burning by hand may be necessary to reduce forest fuels. In brushier and rougher areas and where the timber is not too large (mostly 12 inches in diameter or smaller), caterpillar tractors with special blades are more commonly used. Costs are naturally highly variable and no averages can be given, since cost may vary from $10 to $12 a mile to several thousand dollars depending on the width and character of the break desired and the character of the terrain. A heavy disk, single or double, or a fire plow is the most commonly used maintenance equipment in the East. Such disks are usually tractor drawn, but they have also been mounted under or behind trucks. The drag harrow and other cultivator equipment is also used.

Maintenance is a major item in the firebreak investment. Over a 10-year period, it usually costs more than the initial construction. Breaks do not stay clear but usually revegetate quickly with trees and other vegetation. Leaf or needle fall often renders them ineffective as a direct barrier in less than a season.

Erosion is often a major problem, particularly in mountainous terrain and with mechanically constructed and maintained breaks. A firebreak that soon becomes an impassable and destructive gully cannot be tolerated. In areas of unstable soils, firebreaks cut to mineral soil are often impractical because of erosion.

Chemical   Herbicides for both herbaceous and woody plants are extensively used in right-of-way maintenance by railroads, highway departments, power companies, and on firebreaks as well. Chemicals employed to keep firebreaks free of flammable vegetation are of two general types: (1) the inorganic poisons which kill all vegetation and sterilize the soil for at least a period and (2) the toxic organic compounds, usually of hormone derivation, which are more selective in their lethal effects and more temporary since they oxidize without leaving any poisonous residue in the soil. The most effective of the former is sodium arsenite. But it is attractive and highly lethal to game animals and to livestock. It is very soluble so tends to leach out of soil and is not entirely satisfactory as a soil sterilant in most locations. The second type of herbicide which has rapidly dominated the field is represented by the biological chemicals known as 2-4-D and as 2-4-5-T.

Fire retardant chemicals which retain their effectiveness when dry, such as diammonium and monammonium phosphate, have value in creating temporary firebreaks, particularly in grass and other fine fuels when sprayed on and then allowed to dry. Leaching by rain limits the period of effectiveness. However, new work in this field gives promise of much increased application of chemicals to create a nonflammable strip as a substitute for complete elimination of plant materials.

Vegetative   Lush ground vegetation is an excellent firebreak cover so long as it remains green. The maintenance of a green firebreak during the fire season offers much future promise. In the Southeastern states this has been achieved successfully by developing grazed firebreaks. These are cultivated, heavily fertilized, and seeded to low-growing forage mixtures in much the same way improved pastures are developed. Stock graze them heavily and produce an effect like a golf green. Besides producing a very good firebreak in this way, considerable value in forage is realized and maintenance is much simplified

In California, the development of green belts through irrigation is still on an experimental scale but also offers much promise.

In the Landus region of France, the extensive planting of maritime pine (*Pinus pinaster*) with few breaks in its continuity was blamed for the disastrous fires of 1949 that caused much damage and loss of life. The French plan for keeping such fires more controllable depends primarily on a master plan of green firebreaks consisting of intermingled cultivated land, grazed pastureland, and planted strips of poplar and other hardwoods but with practically no visible investment in firebreaks and firebreak maintenance as a specific objective.

Burning   The burning of protective strips is a practice of long standing. Farmers, railroads, highway departments, and others frequently burn out roadsides and rights-of-way to remove fuel accumulations and to encourage growth of green vegetation. Burning may be done between control lines created by plowed furrows, but it is often carried on during safe periods with no prepared lines. Various burning torches and other devices used in backfiring are pressed into service. Mechanized outfits have been devised which have strong capabilities for both ignition and extinguishment. These are used in combination to burn out strips of standing green or dead grass or other light fuel under good control. Prescribed burning of larger areas is separately discussed in Chapter 18.

Effectiveness of Firebreaks

Wide differences of opinion exist on the effectiveness of firebreaks. There are instances where they have been effective and others where they have not. In the United States, the major development of firebreaks was during the period of the Civilian Conservation Corps (CCC) between 1932 and about 1938. Thousands of miles of firebreaks were constructed, mostly in the Lake states, the South, and California. Most of them have not been maintained as such. Many have been converted into roads. The great development of forest road transport systems since the CCC days has reduced the earlier need for firebreaks by increasing accessibility.

Firebreaks for containment purposes are generally effective and continue to be widely used. Such breaks are usually close to the fire source, and an effective barrier often can be constructed and maintained at reasonable expense. In most situations, they only need to stop small fires near their point of origin that have not had opportunity to develop strong fronts.

Firebreaks to protect a particular area or piece of property from outside wildfires or to break up a large wild-land area into control units are seldom effective as direct and unaided barriers. If a fire starts near a break and spreads toward it, the break may greatly slow its development and will provide a ready-made control line on one side of its perimeter. Similarly, a more aggressive fire approaching a break at an oblique angle may not cross it. This may considerably limit its spread. But in most other circumstances, particularly where spot fires are being set, firebreaks may have little effect in reducing the spread of a fire and so may be of little assistance in the fire-fighting job. But as already discussed, where heavy brush cover makes access difficult, and where it generates hot, fast-moving fires, firebreaks assume a very important role as routes of safe access and as lines of defense where fire fighters can backfire against an approaching wildfire. This function of access and safety of men greatly exceeds the conventional function of firebreaks in much of California.

As always, the capabilities of the local forest fire control organization are important. A strong, fast-moving, and well-equipped organization finds limited use for preconstructed breaks except in areas of extreme fuel hazard or under conditions of high or extreme fire danger. Roads, cleared rights-of-way, streams, and various other natural and artificial breaks are pressed into service as firebreaks and function successfully as backfire lines whenever strategically located in relation to a going fire. In a managed forest area, these low-cost or no-cost breaks often occur at sufficient intervals to fill such needs.

The problem in constructing firebreaks is that of evaluating probabilities (Davis, 1965; Murphy et al., 1967). A firebreak at the right location at the right time may be invaluable. But if the probabilities are such that the chance for a firebreak to function as intended will come only once per 50 years or more, then the investment in constructing it may be of low priority.

AREA FUEL REDUCTION

The purpose of area treatment is to reduce fuel hazards over an area to facilitate control generally. The relation to firebreaks is analogous to the military distinction, considering an area as a whole, between defense based on fixed lines and defense in depth.

Area treatments may achieve several objectives either singly or in combination. They are designed to reduce

1 Rate of spread
2 Fire intensity and hence damage and difficulty of control
3 Likelihood of fires starting by reducing ignitability of fuels
4 Difficulty of access to men and equipment
5 Difficulty of constructing effective control lines

Area treatments can be classified in three general groups: (1) disposal of slash following timber cutting; (2) fuel reduction following wildfire, blowdown, hurricanes, insect epidemics, or other forest catastrophes; and (3) prescribed broadcast burning in green timber areas to effect general reduction in fuel volume and hence hazard. All these groups commonly involve prescribed use of fire. Methods and techniques of using fire are given in Chapters 17 and 18. The purpose here is to present and orient the problem as a part of hazard-reduction work.

Slash Disposal[1]

Fire hazard on an area increases greatly following timber cutting primarily because a large volume of the finer and potentially flammable fuels from the tree crowns lose most of their moisture and are concentrated on the ground surface. The increased hazard is controlled by the following conditions:

1   The quantity of slash created. This is affected by the volume cut by species, the method of logging, and the care exercised during logging. Much slash results from road construction and damage to residual trees in addition to slash from harvested trees.

2   The distribution of slash, that is, whether slash is patchy or more or less continuous. This is a function of the character of the timber stand and method of logging. With tractor skidding, for example, much of the slash is windrowed along skid trails.

3   The flammability of slash. There are substantial differences between deciduous and coniferous species as well as within these groups. There are substantial differences too due to arrangement of the slash. If slash is lopped or flattened to place it in close contact with the ground, moisture contents remain higher and kindling fuels are less effective.

4   The duration of hazard. This is controlled by the volume of the slash created and by the rate of disintegration. Tree species and environments differ markedly in this respect.

5   Microclimatic changes resulting from more open stand conditions following cutting. These include higher surface temperatures and increased air movement near the ground, which accelerate both drying of fuels and rate of spread should a fire start. Marked changes in surface vegetation also follow logging. Together, such changes may exert a larger total effect on hazard than the slash itself.

6   The size of the area cut. In general, the larger the area, the greater the total hazard.

7   The frequency and pattern of logging roads or skid trails that may serve as firebreaks and that improve accessibility. Roads may, however, increase risk since they permit more hunters, berry pickers, fishermen, and others to enter the area.

The total increase in hazard after cutting is highly variable. In selective hardwood cuttings or in partial conifer pulpwood thinnings, the

---

[1] Slash is defined by the U.S. Forest Service (1956) as "Debris left after logging, pruning, thinning, or brush cutting. It includes logs, chunks, bark, branches, stumps, and broken understory trees or brush."

increase may not be serious. In heavy cutting of western conifers, the increase is great; an area may be changed from one of low hazard, both in terms of rate of spread and resistance to control, to extreme on both counts as a direct result of logging. Furthermore, the hazard is of long duration, since slash accumulations may remain dangerous for from 10 to 40 years.

Because of the volume and duration of the hazard and the large areas involved, slash disposal is most critically a problem in western conifers, mainly the Douglas-fir, western white pine, ponderosa pine, and mixed pine and fir types. Accumulations of undisposed or partially disposed slash over large areas are a matter of deep concern. Fire history has abundantly demonstrated the high hazard of cutover areas and of slash in particular. As emphasized in Chapter 1, many of the worst fires of the past have either originated in slashings or achieved major momentum in such fuels.

Data presented by Barrows (1951), based on study of 9,994 fires burning in the western-zone national forests of western Montana and northern Idaho between 1931 and 1939, illustrate the comparative susceptibility to wildfire of cutover, previously burned, and green forests. The comparison in terms of area burned per million acres protected is as follows:

Type of forests	Acres
Cutover forests	22,400
Burned-over forests	16,500
Green forests	2,000

As shown, the ratio of cutover to green forests in rate of area burned is over 10:1, with previously burned areas a close second. For the same period and general area, a measure of the relationship between fires on cutover lands with slash treated or not is given by Lyman (1947) in Table 10.1. As shown, the ratio of area burned in untreated and treated slash areas is nearly 7:1. The average area of untreated slash protected during the period was about 8,000 acres, and consequently nearly half of it burned during the nine-year period. A much larger area of treated slash was protected.

The data assembled by Barrows and Lyman illustrate the high hazard on cutover areas in general and of untreated slash in particular. Similar data can be cited for other forest areas throughout the western United States. The situation is worse than the statistical data alone indicate, since slash areas often trigger large fires in adjacent uncut stands.

Slash disposal is basically a managerial problem. The work is

Table 10.1. Effect of Slash Treatment on Number of Fires and Areas Burned in the Western White Pine Type, 1931-1939

Cutover lands with slash	Total fires occurring	Fires 300 acres or larger, percent	Total area burned, acres
Treated*	58	1.7	554
Untreated	24	21.0	3,526

* Includes slash which was piled but not burned.

expensive, and not all slash can or need be disposed of. The question is fundamentally how much slash disposal, when, and where. As in the case of firebreaks, the cost of disposal must be weighed against the total hazard offered by an area, considering both slash and other fuel hazards, the exposure to risk, and the capabilities of the fire control organization. Something short of complete disposal must often be accepted as a practical matter. In many Western areas, slash created by logging or other cutting in overmature or partially dead stands may be only a part of the total fuel hazard present. In such situations, slash disposal measures confined entirely to the new material cut may be of little benefit. A plan based on the total fuel complex, taking full account of topography, natural firebreaks, and sources of risk, will be much more effective.

There are two general methods of slash disposal that require use of fire: (1) pile (or bunch) and burn and (2) broadcast burn. They may be applied singly or sometimes in combination in treating an area. Lop and scatter and chipping of slash are also employed but do not require fire (Lindenmuth and Gill, 1959).

Pile and Burn   The essential feature of pile-and-burn methods is that logging slash and other debris are assembled in separate piles and burned. Substantial hazard reduction results from piling alone in some situations. The most frequent practice is to prepile and then burn during some safe period, usually late fall or early winter. A less common method during periods of low fire danger is known as swamper burning or progressive burning. A fire is started in some spot clear of living trees and slash is piled on it to burn just as it is trimmed from newly felled trees. Or, after logging is complete, a somewhat similar method may be employed by starting a fire and gathering all nearby slash to burn progressively as it is handled.

The basic advantage of prepiling is that the work can be done at any time working conditions permit, with burning done fairly quickly during a safe period. A disadvantage is that safe burning periods, when the piled slash is still dry enough to burn but fire will not spread away from the piles, are often of limited duration. Field experience demonstrates that there is often a temptation to burn when fuels are too dry or too little time is allowed to elapse in igniting adjacent piles, with the result that fires spread and damage living trees. At times burning is undertaken when the slash is too wet. Then only the fine fuels will be removed and only a temporary effect is accomplished. If burning is delayed to wait for a safe time, dangerous slash may be accumulated for several years. Even with the best of burning conditions, tree damage is common because of poor burning technique, inadequate space for piles, or poor location or construction of piles. Various methods, including roofing slash piles with waterproof paper (Ash, 1951; Fahnestock, 1954), have been devised to overcome some of these difficulties.

A major problem with pile-and-burn methods is the cost. In the past, most of it was done by hand labor, which has become increasingly expensive. For lack of any consistent and easily applied direct measure (Chapter 4), slash volume is commonly reckoned in terms of volume of timber cut. Disposal costs are naturally variable but may range from $1 to perhaps $5 per thousand board feet of timber cut. With cuts ranging up to 30,000 or more feet per acre, the costs of piling and burning slash obviously may exceed $150 per acre. With very heavy cuts, the cost is prohibitive. Burning may then become impractical as well because of the lack of space in which to put piles. Figure 10.5A shows an area in which slash was piled by hand and gives an idea of the size of the job (Figure 10.5).

Because of the cost of handwork, less expensive mechanical means of bunching slash have been developed and extensively applied. The equipment used usually consists of a crawler tractor equipped with a special blade or a bulldozer blade with special teeth attached (Figure 10.5B). This equipment can be used successfully on slopes of less than 35 percent and where down timber is not heavy. Mechanical piling or bunching has been successfully applied in most western conifer types where terrain, slash, and cover conditions permit. For example, bulldozer piling is extensively employed in making clearcuttings in lodgepole pine and Englemann spruce stands. Here, as in ponderosa pine, the bulldozer action scarifies the ground, exposing mineral soil needed for natural regeneration. The method also permits knocking over snags and unwanted live trees and bunching them along with large limbs and other heavy debris on the ground. Silvicultural and hazard-reduction objectives are combined. An effective cleanup of the site after logging is accomplished at much less total cost than hand labor and frequently in situations where the job physically could not be accomplished without use of power

Figure 10.5 *A.* Logging slash piled for burning. Seed-tree cutting, western white pine type, Idaho. *(U.S. Forest Service photo.) B.* Piling slash and associated forest debris with bulldozer equipped with special teeth. *(From R. W. Steele, Montana State University.)*

equipment. Tractor piling results in fewer and larger piles than hand methods. Although the piles are jumbled and somewhat mixed with dirt, they will burn satisfactorily in the fall if bunched compactly. Separate piles burn much better than slash windrows.

Broadcast Burning   Slash disposal by allowing fire to spread more or less completely over the ground has been practiced in several forms over many years. In the early days of American logging, it was common practice to fire slash areas indiscriminately. A major reason was low cost. Slashings were simply touched off and fire was allowed to run wild over the area. Slash was more or less destroyed, and so was timber remaining on the cutting area and often nearby as well.

A restricted form of broadcast burning, referred to as spot burning, is applied to some extent, principally in ponderosa pine. Much of the slash left after logging is more or less bunched in spots and windrows. This is due both to selection cutting by groups and to tractor logging. During periods when fire will not spread over surface fuels generally, these concentrations can be burned. Sometimes additional bunching is done by pulling tops, etc., into piles. With ideal weather conditions and skillful personnel, the bulk of the slash hazard can be reduced in many situations without undue damage to the residual stand. Fire may cover 30 to 50 percent of the total area, burning hard in some places where slash is concentrated and lightly in nearby natural surface fuels. Spot burning is treacherous, however, and can be done only during periods of limited duration. There is ever-present danger of excessive damage to residual trees or of the slash fires developing into disastrous wildfires. The time and place to do this kind of work must be selected with much care in close relation to fire weather and fire danger.

The most extensive application of broadcast burning as a means of slash disposal is in clear-cutting of old-growth conifers, mostly in the Douglas-fir and western white pine types. In most such areas, slash disposal by piling methods following clear-cutting is both impractical and prohibitive in cost. Also, the ground needs to be cleared to obtain satisfactory reproduction of desired species. Here, all merchantable material is removed, the balance of the stand felled, and the accumulation of fuels burned broadcast. Methods and techniques for doing this work are given in Chapter 18.

Hazard Reduction Following Forest Catastrophes

Forest disasters of wildfire, hurricane, and insect and disease epidemics often create dangerous fuel volumes of dead timber over extensive areas, constituting an intolerable hazard.

It is a common saying that one wildfire breeds another in coniferous forests. Spread of the Michigan fire of 1881 was accelerated by dead timber in the 1871 burns (Chapter 1). A whole cycle of fires was generated by the Great Idaho fire of 1910. Much of the area burned by the Tillamook fire of 1933 disastrously burned again in 1939, 1945, and 1951 (Figure 10.3). Instances of fire-killed timber resulting from the residue of one wildfire helping to trigger a second and sometimes a third fire can be cited almost endlessly. Considerable work has been done in areas of fire-killed timber to reduce the hazard to tolerable proportions.

The situation in western Montana and northern Idaho, centering around the western white pine type, furnishes a good illustration of the general problem. The area has been visited by severe fires in the past, in 1910, 1919, 1924, 1929, and 1934 to name some of the bad years of more or less recent times. A single fire in green timber usually kills most of the stand, leaving a jungle of dead materials of high fuel volume and hazard for many years that threatens not only the burned-over area but surrounding green timber as well (Figure 10.6). As has been emphasized, fire history has shown the acreage burned in fire-killed areas to be much

Figure 10.6   Result of a hard single burn in heavy timber, Idaho, soon after the fire. The fuel hazard on such areas increases for 10 to 15 years and may continue high for over 20 years as the dead timber gradually decays, is blown down, and breaks up. *(U.S. Forest Service photo.)*

higher than in green timber, the fundamental reason being the more hazardous fuels present. The question is what to do about it. The following factors bear on the situation:

1 The duration and intensity of the fuel hazard. Fuel hazard in burned-over areas last much longer than in green-timber slash areas. As brought out by Lyman (1945), the hazard reduces little for 20 years and may persist in substantial degree for 40 years or more. Decay will eventually reduce the fuels, but it is a slow process, with many years of high fuel hazard intervening.

2 The proportion of standing to down fuels. Snags are by far the worst hazard from the standpoint of rate of spread and difficulty of control. A fire starting in a snag area is frequently uncontrollable. Fuels on the ground are much less hazardous, and their danger is further mitigated when shaded by tree reproduction and other vegetation.

3 The size of fire-killed areas and their distribution with respect to surrounding green timber.

4 The presence or absence of natural regeneration. Most areas covered by a single burn naturally regenerate abundantly, presenting the dilemma of good natural reproduction whose existence is threatened by the fire hazard of a maze of snags. Good natural regeneration can seldom be expected following a second fire.

5 The amount of fire-killed timber that can be salvaged and removed from the area.

6 The presence of natural fire barriers, topographic or otherwise, and general accessibility.

7 The risk of fires starting. Other things being equal, the more areas are frequented by man or lightning, the greater the total danger.

8 The relation to disease or insect control. In the western white pine type, blister rust is a major problem, and in control areas all stand treatments must be considered in relation to their effect on control of *Ribes*, alternate host to the disease.

9 Topographic features, altitude, aspect, and exposure to prevailing winds that can be expected to influence the ignition and behavior of fires in the area.

10 The strength and general effectiveness of the fire control organization and the probable effect of hazard-reduction work on total fire control and costs.

11 The cost of hazard-reduction treatment.

12 The site quality of fire-killed areas and the general intensity and objectives of forest management being practiced. Watershed, recreation, and other forest values must be considered along with timber production.

As indicated by the range of considerations listed above, what to do in a specific situation is a matter for administrative analysis and decision.

Two general courses of action are possible: fell the snags or burn broadcast. Felling snags only is much cheaper than burning and greatly reduces the hazard by slowing rate of spread. Where adequate restocking by natural reproduction has taken place, it will soon shade the felled snags and often reduce the hazard to tolerable level. Figure 10.7A and B shows the difference in fuel hazard between standing and felled snags when good natural reproduction is present. Although control is difficult because of the logs on the ground, rate of spread is fairly low. Also, once on the ground and shaded by reproduction, the dead trees decay more rapidly than when standing. During the days of the Civilian Conservation Corps, literally millions of snags were felled on thousands of acres of burned-over lands. This work has been continued since, though on a lesser scale, chiefly as a regular part of timber-cutting operations. The development and widespread use of the power saw have greatly facilitated snag felling.

Broadcast burning in fire-killed areas in the western white pine type was done to some extent in the 1930s and continued into the 1940s. Application since has been limited due principally to the cost of the work, reluctance to sacrifice good natural reproduction, ability to make quicker attack on fires by road and by air, lessening of fuel hazard on old burns due to natural decay and previous fuel-reduction work, and the fact that snag felling alone is a reasonably adequate treatment in many situations. The worst fuel areas of the region have been broken up and fire hazard has been much reduced. This has been done with the hope that extensive new burns will not develop.

The general story of fuel reduction on burned-over areas in the northern Rocky Mountains, as very briefly sketched here, is illustrative of the general nature of the problem and of approaches followed in seeking a solution. Similar work has been done in other western areas, particularly in the Tillamook burn in Oregon and in problem areas in Washington, and California in particular. Specific problems and methods vary with the environment.

Hazard reduction following natural blowdowns and insect and disease epidemics applies the same principles and procedures followed in slash disposal and fuel reduction work in burned-over areas. Fuels along roads or other areas of high risk are reduced by piling and sometimes by spot-burning methods. Some broadcast burning is done. In blowdowns, opening the area to access by roads or by firebreaks usually demands high priority. In insect- and disease-killed timber, removal of as much of the standing dead timber as possible through salvage usually gets high priority, followed by felling of remaining snags. No generalizations can be made on how much or what kind of work should be done. Each situation must be carefully appraised.

Figure 10.7 Showing removal of snags. *(U.S. Forest Service photo.)* A. Hazardous 20-year-old snags over good natural reproduction in the western white pine type, Idaho. B. Same general area immediately after felling snags. Although there is much dead fuel on the ground, the reproduction has closed over it and the fire hazard is greatly reduced. *(U.S. Forest Service photo.)*

Broadcast Burning of Natural Fuels

Broadcast burning of forest and range lands, so-called light burning, has been and is being done for a number of purposes and is a practice of long standing in certain areas. The purposes intended usually fall in the following categories:

1   To reduce fuel hazard, and hence as a prevention measure.
2   To improve pasture conditions by removing leaf litter and other dead vegetation and by killing competing trees and "brush." (Historically, this is the major reason for widespread use of fire on both forest and range lands.)
3   To improve hunting and increase game populations.
4   To reduce harmful insect and animal populations, chiggers, snakes, and so forth (usually ineffective).
5   To improve general visibility and accessibility for the user and particularly for the hunter by eliminating reproduction and understory brush.

The usual aim is to encourage a relatively light fire to spread broadcast over an area. This is practiced to some extent in ponderosa pine; to an increasing extent in woodland, brush, and range-land areas of the western United States; and quite commonly in the pine types of the lower South, where woods fires have long been common. The benefits from much of this burning are controversial, though in most cases a degree of hazard reduction is brought about. This may consist only of removing the flash fuels which will be replaced in one year, or it may eliminate fuels that have accumulated over a period of years. Methods and techniques of using fire as a tool in wild-land management are given in Chapters 17 and 18.

RELATION OF HAZARD REDUCTION TO FOREST ENVIRONMENT

In Chapter 3, effects of fire on soil and microclimate were presented. When such effects involve large areas or result from burning of heavy volumes of fuels, they cause drastic changes in the local environment. These changes consist of changes in exposure to sun and wind, in the acidity of the soil, in plant species, and in the appearance of the area. Each of the former has already been considered; changes in the appearance of the area have not.

The immediate effect of fire on the appearance of a burned-over area is always unfavorable. It scorches green vegetation and blackens tree stems, and it usually kills small trees. Such effects disappear with time.

The visible evidence of a mild burn in grass and litter may vanish in a few weeks with the onset of new spring growth; that from the burning of heavy volumes of slash from clear-cutting of timber or from a wildfire which killed mature trees may require several seasons to disappear, since it takes that long for new green vegetation to become reestablished and several decades for a new tree cover to develop.

Nonetheless the longer-term effect of fire is quite often a more attractive appearance. It eliminates dead material, clears out heavy undergrowth, and creates forest openings. This is exemplified by the open, grassy nature of the virgin ponderosa pine stands of much of western United States, which has frequently been visited by fire. Shorter-term effects of fire may be controlled to operate this way. Where logging or natural causes result in heavy volumes of dead fuel, the use of fire to clean up the debris is often the quickest and most effective way to restore an attractive appearance to the area. Consequently, hazard reduction is rarely the sole benefit of such work.

Large segments of the American public strongly oppose the cutting of timber in all forest areas in which they are interested. The reasons for such opposition naturally vary in detail, but the primary reason is obviously related to the appearance of a cutover area which has been logged according to traditional practices of the past. Typically, such an area presents a scene of desolation. Many standing trees are broken or severely damaged, skid roads and logging roads have done much violence to the forest floor and terrain, and the ground is heavily littered with broken tree trunks and branches in grotesque disorder. This is a common result of concentrating on getting out the merchantable timber cheaply and failing to apply hazard-reduction measures. In eastern hardwoods this kind of logging still prevails, since it is done by small operators—usually by a contractor instead of the owner. In old-growth timber stands of the West, heavy logging equipment is used. Though this equipment is more skillfully employed, much breakage occurs and there is usually much added cull material due to defect in old trees. As a consequence the volume of logging slash is often so great that all the ground between skid trails is covered to a depth of several feet. Natural decay proceeds so slowly that hazard-reduction measures are the first step in rehabilitating such areas.

In western forest areas, necessity has already induced considerable progress. Patch cuttings followed by broadcast burns in the Douglas-fir region have previously been described. Following a clean burn, they reproduce promptly and soon lose their blackened appearance. They have won more acceptance by the public than less drastic partial cutting or thinning operations that leave damaged trees and considerable debris from logging much in evidence. However, extensive burning of slash fuels during safe periods often results in heavy drift smoke. This interferes at times with aerial operations and may greatly aggravate the effects of local air pollution. Preliminary study gives promise of minimizing this problem through careful selection and forecasting of the atmospheric conditions when wood smoke from such sources will be rapidly dissipated. This is an added function of the fire weather forecaster (Murphy et al., 1970).

It is inevitable that logging of overmature timber stands will continue to produce large volumes of waste debris to be disposed of in some way. But as cutting moves into young, managed stands, the problem should be much alleviated.

State and federal park officials have found that even in parks the removal of a tree is normally accepted without protest if done in such a way that aesthetic considerations are not ignored. This usually means complete removal of all resulting debris. Foresters also find that even on roadsides, partial cutting, thinning, and pruning may be accepted with approval if a good cleanup of all slash is carried out and a pleasing appearance is created. This places a premium on "good housekeeping" in all cutting operations.

It is now appropriate to reexamine former concepts of how much the forest manager can afford to spend for reduction of fuel hazards following cutting. A good cleanup of slash fuels carries values far beyond the direct advantage to fire fighting. It enhances all recreational values and is favorable to game and forage. It strongly influences public attitudes and may determine whether or not any commercial forest management will be permitted on many publicly owned forests in the future. If skillfully done, salvage cutting can be carried on successfully even in high-value recreation areas. As stated at the beginning of this chapter, maintenance of a favorable forest environment through control of fuel hazards depends primarily on the landowner. The degree to which he assumes this responsibility reflects the quality of his stewardship.

Chapter 11

Forest Fire Detection

In spite of the best of fire prevention provisions, some wildfires occur and must be controlled. But before anything can be done toward controlling a fire, its existence must be known. Consequently, its detection is the vital first step in action taken to control a fire. Four steps preceding actual attack on a fire are usually recognized. These are defined as elapsed time intervals and are stated as follows:

Discovery—time from origin of a fire until it is first seen by someone who reports it

Report—time from first discovery to receipt of report by someone responsible for taking action

Getaway—time taken from receipt of report to departure of fire control forces

Travel—time from departure of fire control forces to arrival of first man or men at the fire

Each of these four steps can be executed with more speed and precision if adequate facilities are available and good planning is carried out. This requires the development and proper functioning of systems of fire detection, communication, and transportation. Since fire detection is a primary function and a fire function only, it will be considered separately in this chapter.

Factors Affecting Visibility and Detection

Smoke is normally the telltale evidence on which detection depends. Consequently, the visibility of smoke under various circumstances controls the success of most detection. Typically, green fuel or moist fuel becomes involved in even a small fire in forest cover. This contributes moisture and particulates to produce a dense white smoke. This kind of smoke against a dark forest background or against the horizon is easily detected at considerable distances and provides the rationale on which most detection is based.

Since the obvious objective in forest fire detection is to discover fires when they are small, the visibility of a relatively small smoke over distances of 10 miles or more becomes important. To enable the setting of standards against which detection may be measured, a standard-size smoke has been defined at various times (Byram and Jemison, 1948; McArdle, 1936). Usually it is defined as the smoke normally emitted from a fire of $^1/_8$ acre or a defined smaller area of burning forest litter. For study and planning purposes, simulated smokes are often used. The smoke candle developed for this purpose gives smoke of the same color as that of a fire in forest fuels at a standard rate. Smoke pots in which fuel mixtures are burned have also been devised at various times. Artificial smokes, such as the smoke candle, which lack convective heat may deviate considerably in shape from a natural smoke column and often fail to rise above treetops. Nevertheless, they are more convenient and safe to use so are often employed for administrative tests.

External Factors   The maximum distance at which a given object such as a standard smoke can be seen is termed the *visual range*, and, when referring specifically to the smoke column, as *visibility distance*. The size of the smoke column is only one of three external factors which determine the ability of the eye to detect a fire at a distance. The other two factors are the transparency of the atmosphere and the degree of contrast between the smoke and the background against which it appears to the eye.

The importance of the transparency of the atmosphere is obvious when visibility is seriously reduced by fog, smog, or drift smoke. But lesser degrees of impairment that may appear only as distant haze are also important though much more difficult to evaluate. A special hazemeter was at one time developed to measure the dependable range of distance at which a standard smoke column could be detected under haze conditions at a given time (Byram, 1935). Though no longer available, it permitted better evaluation of the effect of light haze or drift smoke.

The contrast between a smoke and its background is also an important determinant. A luminous gray-white smoke against a dark green forest background can be seen for long distances. When the background is a logged-over area, cured grass, or weeds of much lighter color, the same smoke will be visible for a much shorter distance or not at all. Haze tends to reduce the contrast between smoke and all backgrounds below the horizon. It produces maximum obscurity and maximum reduction in this respect toward the sun. Fortunately, when the background to the smoke is the horizon instead of forest cover, the same physical effects that illuminate the haze illuminate the smoke much more strongly, so that a new and strong contrast between the smoke and a sky background is set up. For such reasons, when looking toward the sun, a small smoke on the horizon can be detected for a long distance while one below the horizon may be missed entirely.

Personal Factors Affecting Distant Detection Since detection of smokes depends on the eye, personal factors also enter into it. Individuals differ in their ability to discern distant small objects, but this resolving power cannot be accurately measured by standard eye tests. A simple and more appropriate eye test was developed by Byram (Byram and Jemison, 1948). It consists of testing how far an observer can see a black spot $1/16$ inch in diameter against a white background. Such tests are useful in the selection of lookout observers.

The observer's search techniques are important. Skill does not depend on long-continued peering for smokes but rather on a fast, running glance from near to far to detect any slight abnormality in the panorama. Training helps to develop search techniques, but skill depends on experience.

The personality of the observer also enters in. Unpublished tests of some eighty lookouts refuted the preconceived belief that the highly introverted individual who liked to be alone was likely to be the most successful lookout observer. Instead, restless, more extroverted individuals rated best in performance.

Systematic Methods of Detection

Organized detection of fires is ordinarily accomplished by means of one or more of the following conventional methods and facilities:

1 By lookouts planned and designed for the purpose
2 By aerial patrol over planned routes under specified circumstances and frequencies
3 By ground patrol, also over planned routes at specified times
4 By prearrangement with local residents and cooperators

Unorganized detection also occurs. It consists of action taken to
report fires by any individual who happens to see the fire and recognizes
that action to control it is needed. For statistical purposes, forest fire
agencies do not consider a fire to have been "discovered" until the person
who sees it either takes effective action to control it or reports it to
someone who takes such action.

The objectives of organized detection are twofold. These are (1)
Discovery and report of every wildfire in time to control it at small size
with available forces. To accomplish this during daylight hours, the
planning objective is usually set at 15 minutes. (2) Location of the fire
with sufficient accuracy to enable attack forces to start for the fire
immediately and go to it by the most direct route. Usually this means no
error in location greater than $1/4$ mile even when the location is 10 to 15
miles from the observer. When two lookouts can see the same fire, the
intersection of their azimuth readings greatly increases the accuracy of
the location. Each of the four systems of organized detection are capable
of meeting both of these objectives under favorable circumstances, but all
fail at times. Each calls for different structures and facilities. Typically,
more than one method is employed in large protection units. All methods
depend primarily on the ability of the human eye to identify a small smoke
column, often at considerable distances.

FOREST FIRE LOOKOUTS

Structures for fire lookouts are the most distinctive and most specialized
of fire control facilities. They have long been a universal symbol of
organized protection. Nearly all protection agencies use lookouts, though
they vary in the degree to which they depend on them. In 1952, 36 of the
43 states which were maintaining organized forest fire protection were
operating forest fire lookouts. These comprised 2,455 steel towers with
cabs, 584 wood and stone structures, and 94 tree cabs. About 2,000
lookouts were in use on National Forests and National Parks at the same
time. So, in the United States, over 5,000 lookouts were in active use in
1953. By 1968, the number used by federal agencies had shrunk to about
1,200 and the number used by states to about 2,300. This represented an
overall reduction of 30 percent, and this trend continues. No doubt the

number will reduce further, through at a slower rate (Zimmerman, 1969).

Lookout structures have evolved over a considerable period. Since their purpose is so highly specialized, the distinctive design and operating requirements considered essential to their successful functioning are described.

Elevation   The observatory must be sufficiently elevated to provide an unobstructed view from it over the treetops and any other local obstructions.

In flat country, this usually requires high towers which can clear the mature forest canopy. If the location is in a young stand, its height at maturity would be the proper criterion. Where the site is on a hill or ridge, clearing away of nearby obstructing trees may greatly reduce the height of tower necessary and may be preferable.

In mountainous terrain, the most important factor is usually the shape of the high point selected as the lookout site. A flattened top may require considerable tower elevation in order to gain a sufficient view down its slopes. If angles and distances are measured so that the profile of the top can be defined, it is not difficult to determine the exact height from which the desired view can be had with the minimum tower elevation (Show Kotok, et al., 1937).

In all cases, the elevation required determines the necessary height of tower. It is a waste of money and effort to place a higher tower on a lookout site than is needed to clear local obstructions. The gain in angle of vision from the highest tower that can be built for points 5 miles or more distant is too slight to be worthwhile. This can easily be verified by checking mathematically the effect of various tower heights on the slope of lines of sight into distant topography.

Varying requirements for tower height have greatly influenced the standards accepted for lookout structures. In most of the eastern United States, lookout sites are commonly on flat ground or on low hills or ridges where the timber cover is the chief obstruction. Such settings call for relatively high towers of 60 to 120 feet. To build such a tower at reasonable cost, the cab or observatory is reduced in size to provide only for observation. Where needed, living quarters are provided separately on the ground. Commonly the floor of the cab, which rests on a steel tower (Figure 11.1), measures 7 by 7 feet.

Where low tower elevations up to about 60 feet suffice, it is more common to provide an observatory and living quarters combined. This usually involves a 14- by 14-foot floor plan and a heavier but lower tower or base. Lookout structures of this type are most common in the Western regions of the United States (Figures 11.2 and 11.3).

Figure 11.1 Typical steel lookout tower used in the eastern United States. *(U.S. Forest Service photo.)*

Figure 11.2 Standard lookout on masonry substructure where only low tower is required. *(U.S. Forest Service photo.)*

Unobstructed View Unobstructed view from inside the lookout observatory or cab requires windows from which the entire panorama can be seen with minimum obstruction. From the fire finder or alidade[1] in the center of the cab or observatory, the view must be so little obstructed horizontally that a reading on any smoke in the panorama can be obtained by horizontal adjustment of the alidade. This means that the corner posts, the stovepipe if a wood stove is used, and the framing between windows must not create any obstruction of more than 4 to 6 inches. This not only assures that an azimuth reading can be taken on any smoke that may show up but also enables the observer to see all the territory from any position near the center of the observatory by simply moving his head slightly to change the angle of his view (Figure 11.4). Large-pane windows are also preferred. The vertical angle of vision must also be unobstructed within

---

[1]An alidade is a straightedge equipped with sights. It is the essential part of a fire finder, a device for locating fires.

Figure 11.3 Lookout observatory on treated wood tower. *(U.S. Forest Service photo.)*

certain limits. The windows must come low enough that a line of sight from the fire finder to country below will not be cut off by the window ledge. The upward angle seldom needs special attention, since it is rare for an observatory to be far below nearby topography.

Permanence of Structure The high construction cost and rapid deterioration of most wooden lookout towers and observatories at lookout sites have always been serious problems. Materials and construction standards that will ensure an adequate service life for the structure and that will hold annual maintenance to a minimum are accordingly essential features. Steel towers and pressure-treated wood towers meet this requirement. At times the cost of a pressure-treated wood tower exceeds that of a steel tower of equal dimensions. The lower maintenance cost of steel towers, their longer life, and their salvage value in case relocation is desired are regarded by many as justification for a higher initial cost.

Lookout structures of limited height in recreational areas and lookout substructures are often built of masonry. In these instances costs are higher but permanence is assured (Figure 11.6).

Protection of the Observer   The ability to protect the observer from direct sunlight, wind, and storms is a rather obvious requirement for a lookout structure. The provisions for such protection must be stricter in a combination dwelling-observatory than in an observation cab alone.

Protection from the sun's glare is a common problem. Internal measures to accomplish this consist of rigid standards for keeping windows clean; the use of interior paint that has low reflective characteristics in colors restful to the eye, such as pale green; and the observer's

Figure 11.4   Lookout observer reporting fire to dispatcher. Note fire finder and interior arrangements with no obstructions above window ledges. *(U.S. Forest Service photo.)*

use of special glare-reducing goggles which do not reduce the visibility of smoke yet protect the eyes from strain.

Exterior provisions consist of shutters hinged above the windows and supported in a near-horizontal position to shade the windows. In lieu of this, long overhang eaves are at times substituted. Windows set at an angle from the vertical to avoid reflections and tinted glass to reduce glare have also been tried but have not been generally adopted because of high cost for the small advantage gained.

Protection of the structure and of the observer against lightning is essential for all lookout structures. This protection consists of a complete protective net of copper wire or cable. In brief, it consists of a lightning rod or its equivalent on the roof with conductors carried down each corner of the observatory and—in wooden towers—down each tower leg. The four down conductors are tied together at the roof line, at the floor level, and underground at the tower base where they are fully grounded. All large metal objects in the observatory are grounded to these conductors. This is necessary for wooden observatories and towers. The legs of steel towers can be grounded and the down conductors dispensed with. Requirements are further simplified where the roof and cab are also of metal. However, complete lightning protection must always be a standard requirement. Model specifications have been made available to protection agencies in the United States through scientists of the General Electric Company.

Though not an essential feature, a catwalk around the outside of the observatory is a regular feature of most 14- by 14-foot observatories. It aids in close observation, makes the observatory less confining, and makes it easy to clean the windows from the outside (Figure 11.3).

Housekeeping Arrangements   The 7- by 7-foot cab is an observatory only and is occupied only during specified hours. A dwelling unit may be required with it. The 14- by 14-foot observatory is designed to serve both as an observatory and living quarters. This sets up rather exacting specifications. Nothing can be permitted to obstruct the view, yet a bed, cooking equipment, and storage space for personal effects and food must be provided. A bank of cabinets under the windows, a screened food cooler in the floor, a trapdoor in the ceiling to permit some attic storage, etc., are common provisions to meet such needs. Where little or no tower elevation is required, a substructure rather than a tower is sometimes provided. It may be developed as a garage or storeroom. Such an arrangement makes it easier to meet all requirements (Figure 11.2).

Specialized Equipment   The first essential is provision for taking accurate azimuth readings on distant smokes. This may be accomplished with a map board and alidade. But more commonly a specially made fire finder is installed. Several states have developed special low-cost fire finders of plastic and aluminum which they manufacture or procure by contract. The Osborne fire finder is the most common instrument available commercially. It can be accurately adjusted and has cross hairs permitting vertical as well as horizontal readings on the location of a fire. It can be adjusted, too, to miss corner posts when they would otherwise obstruct the line of sight on a smoke. Most other fire finders in use also have such adjustments, but only the Osborne is equipped to take vertical angles. The vertical-angle reading from an Osborne fire finder becomes useful only if a carefully oriented panoramic photo of the visible terrain is used.

Panoramic photographs themselves are very useful as a working tool and are quite commonly employed in Western regions of the United States. Each photograph carries a horizontal reference line corresponding to the elevation of the lookout station from which it is taken, and it usually covers one-third of the panorama. Accurate azimuth and vertical-angle graduations are assured by use of a special photo-transit camera and appear along the base and margins of the pictures. These pictures then serve as a reference picture map. They can quickly acquaint a new observer with the identity of the terrain as it appears from the lookout. This is facilitated by accurately labeling the names of streams, ridges, peaks, lakes, and the various local installations on the pictures and by preparing profile maps or sketches to identify the ridges and drainages partially hidden by intervening topography. Besides this value in more quickly acquainting the lookout observer with his territory, the vertical angle is often useful in describing the location of a small smoke. The dispatcher or fire officer to whom the lookout observer is reporting can, in effect, look over his shoulder by using a duplicate picture containing the location. This was originally intended as the primary function of the photographs. In actual practice, except during the training period, vertical-angle locations are not much used. But the graduated photographs are such valuable references that their use has far exceeded utilization of vertical-angle identification.

The next essential equipment on which the observer's value depends is his radio equipment or telephone. Often both are operated. This is common where the lookout point serves as a communication hub to other lookouts or as a relay point for messages (Figure 11.5). These are discussed in the section on forest communications (Chapter 14).

Binoculars are another working tool that is regarded as standard equipment. Their primary value is to check on or verify suspected smokes. In an early and still valid study of the function of binoculars for lookout service and the most desirable specifications for the purpose,

Figure 11.5 Lookout observor reporting fire weather observations by radio. *(U.S. Forest Service photo.)*

Curry (1933) listed the following service values. Binoculars are especially useful for (1) periodic examination of areas of known high risk, (2) distinguishing fires which may produce only intermittent puffs of smoke, (3) more accurate azimuth readings, (4) improving the lookout observer's estimate of the size of the fire and its rate of spread.

Several factors operate which are so far unmeasured by available equipment. Studies have shown that the distance at which a small smoke can be seen varies with its vertical-angle relation to the sun and observer as well as with the transparency of the atmosphere at the time (Buck and Fons, 1935). These variations are important in planning the spacing of lookouts and in determining the relative dependability of detection service in each quadrant of the panorama from daylight to darkness.

The variation in atmospheric transparency is often erratic and troublesome in this respect. Fog, drift smoke, dust, and in some areas industrial and city smog may make a lookout partially or wholly valueless at certain hours or for several days under certain weather conditions. When visibility is dangerously reduced in such ways, other means of detection have to be substituted. Over most of southern California, fire lookouts have been abandoned for this reason.

McArdle (1936) and Brown (1939) decided that for most practical purposes a lookout observer can give detection service to an area of approximately equal radius in all directions and that the pattern of coverage can, on the average, be assumed as circular without serious error even though this may not be true at a particular hour of the day. This somewhat oversimplifies a series of complex relationships with which the lookout observer must contend.

Classes and Combined Functions of Lookout Observers and Stations

Three classes of lookout points are commonly recognized: primary, secondary, and emergency.

Primary   The primary lookout point normally covers such extensive or important territory not served by other means of detection that occupancy is planned for the entire fire season. For the same reason, no interruption in service can be permitted for any reason except the temporary lack of fire danger in the territory served or visibility so reduced that the lookout cannot function.

Secondary   The secondary lookout has less important or less extensive coverage that is not duplicated by primary lookouts or other means of detection. It may vary widely in importance. As distinguished from the primary lookout, occupancy for the full season is not regarded as essential. Therefore a shorter continuous season or intermittent occupancy is usual.

Emergency   A third category, the emergency lookout, is also utilized in some areas. Such a lookout is manned only intermittently when conditions of high to extreme fire danger exist, on occasions of unusually high risk or reduced visibility, or when a check on the existence or location of a reported or suspected fire in its visible area is needed. This type of lookout is typical of warden or cooperator detection and of prevention patrol points.

Other Functions   In addition, and often irrespective of classification, both the lookout observer and the lookout station frequently perform more than one function. The lookout observer may double as a fire prevention guard or, if his station is a convenient hub of communication, he may serve as a lookout dispatcher. He may also have important duties as a fire danger station observer, fire weather reporter, and as a switching and relay operator for radio and telephone communications. He may serve part-time as a maintenance man on fire roads, trails, structures, and equipment.

He may also serve as a lookout fireman. The lookout fireman combination may involve any one of the three categories of lookouts. A lookout fireman is a lookout observer who also fights fires in nearby territory. Usually he functions in this way only for territory where he can make first attack on a fire more quickly than the nearest available fireman or crew. This combination of duties becomes of increasing importance as access by road decreases and travel time to get to fires becomes a critical factor in successful control.

Where attack on nearby fires becomes an important function at a primary lookout station, continuous detection service may be provided by assigning a second man or fireman at the station, by employing a married couple (with the wife taking over the detection duties whenever the lookout is called to a fire), or by making arrangements for quickly moving in a substitute lookout observer.

Lookout fireman stations are commonly secondary lookouts, where justification for full-season employment of the lookout fireman depends on the combined function. At one time this combined position was used very commonly in the northwestern portions of the United States when access by road was poor but risk of lightning fire was high. As access by road increased and wherever smoke jumpers came to be used for first attack, much abandonment of such positions took place. The substitution of aerial detection for ground methods has also replaced many secondary lookouts, so that lookout fireman positions are no longer common in the United States.

The combined lookout fireman function usually places a greater premium on housekeeping facilities at the station and may require additional storage or sleeping provisions. Road access to the lookout to permit the lookout fireman to make prompt use of all existing roads by car is also desirable. Otherwise, there is little difference in the design requirements of such a station. The only difference in working equipment is the addition of a standard unit of fire fighting tools and reliable vehicular transportation.

Potentially the most important combined function for many lookouts is that of serving as an information center and fire prevention contact to users and visitors of all kinds. Many lookouts are placed on points from which a magnificent panorama greets the eye. When accessible, they may be visited by large numbers of travelers and recreationists. This imposes a responsibility on the lookout observer that may become a very important part of his job. Often a second man is needed. On some heavily frequented points, fire prevention contacts and informational services become so important that the position is maintained for this joint function where detection service alone would not justify it. This is frequent in

Figure 11.6 Modified lookout structure at scenic point where public contact requires special provisions. *(U.S. Forest Service photo.)*

State and National Parks and is recognized to lesser degrees in National Forest practice.

Such combinations are at times given recognition by the special architectural design of the lookout structure, which is planned to serve visitors and to satisfy aesthetic requirements of the location and surroundings. The lookout observatory retains its usual function unmodified, but sleeping quarters for the lookout may be separate from it (Figure 11.6).

A fire danger station is often maintained at a fire lookout station because the lookout is continually available and can report readings regularly. Such duties can be incidental to detection duties. Many lookout stations, however, are not representative locations for the taking of fire danger data.

PLANNED FIRE LOOKOUT SYSTEMS

Some of the essential principles of planning to set up an optimum system of fire lookouts or to improve an existing system will be outlined. (Techniques are detailed by Brown, 1935; Show et al., 1937; and Hornby, 1936).

Mapping   To deal with detection coverage in systematic planning, it must be reduced to a measurable quantity. This is accomplished by mapping the areas for which an existing or prospective lookout point can give dependable service. Such areas are termed *visible* or *seen* areas. The first term is preferred. The usual definition is the pattern of area that can be seen directly (either the ground surface or treetops) from a given location at a specified elevation above ground. Visible areas are mapped in three ways: (1) by use of profiles on a topographic map, (2) by sketching from a panoramic photograph taken at the site, and (3) by field sketching at the site. Techniques developed for such mapping during the 1930s are described in the references cited above.

Accurate mapping of areas in which fires can be discovered from a given point enable the planner to show visible area graphically on a map and to transfer it to tracings which can be superimposed on other maps of the area in any desired combination. Such maps and tracings are referred to as detection coverage. Mapping of visible area also permits its conversion to acres which can be classified by risk zone or fuel type and treated mathematically in making desired comparisons or evaluations.

Detection Radius   A normal radius of dependable detection service needs to be established in order to fix the outer limits to the coverage credited to a lookout. Radii of 8, 11, 15, and 20 miles have been used at times. In most of the western United States, a radius of 15 miles is accepted as the standard, since visibility is normally good during the fire season and smoke from a small fire can usually be seen to this distance. In the South and Southeast, where visibility is poorer, a 6- to 8-mile radius is most often used. A circular pattern is assumed for planning purposes.

Risk Zones   In planning detection, because the purpose is to detect the maximum number of fires rather than to simply cover area, frequency of fire occurrence needs to be taken into account in rating the importance of lookout coverage. Both man-caused and lightning fires vary widely in their frequency of occurrence in one area compared to another. But lightning fires are more erratic and predictions of their frequency are less dependable unless based on a long period and zoned on the basis of ignitable material as well as lightning strikes. In many areas, zoning of lightning risk is not worthwhile. Man-caused fires tend to be concentrated more sharply in local areas. When the points of origin of all fires for a period of years are plotted on a map, zones of similar occurrence can be delineated separately for lightning and man-caused fires. Special techniques have been developed to compute appropriate risk ratings for each risk zone (Show et al., 1937). Usually this is done by giving weight to an occurrence area closely in proportion to the rate of occurrence. Differences between fuel types can also be recognized in this way.

Lookout Selection   After potential coverage of prospective lookouts has been converted to a basis where each pattern of visible area can be shown on a transparency and its acreage computed and weighted for variations in hazard or risk, an objective means of building the most efficient detection system needs to be applied.

In the system developed in California (Brown, 1935), this consisted of starting with the highest-rated point. Its coverage was superimposed on the unit map. Then the remaining points were made to compete for the rest of the area not yet covered. The point that could add the most to the coverage of number 1 was accepted as number 2. This was continued down to the point where net coverage that could be added by a new lookout fell below a predetermined minimum. At this point the lookout system was regarded as complete. In the process, a priority system was set up for both construction of lookouts and their seasonal occupancy. If only two lookouts could be financed, numbers 1 and 2 were the best, and so on down the list. Usually this resulted in classing some of the lookouts as primary and some as secondary.

Where detection points were also to be used as the location from which firemen would make first attack on fires, the system of selection became more complex and was arrived at graphically by trial and error to obtain a maximum of both detection coverage and smokechaser coverage (Hornby, 1936). However, the principles remain the same, and the tendency for each new lookout or lookout fireman station to add less to the total than had the one just preceding made fire control planners quite conscious of the operation of the law of diminishing returns.[2]

Coverage Standards In mountainous country, it is impossible to get even close to 100 percent coverage of all the area by any system of ground lookout points that can be devised. The character of the topography is an important factor. In country of short steep slopes and deeply cut drainage with few or no high points dominating the rest, it requires more lookout points to get a desired percent of coverage. In long-slope topography with broad valleys and a few high points, the problem is simpler. This factor influenced the adoption of combined lookout-smokechaser coverage in the system devised by Hornby (1936). Because of this factor the coverage standards set for planning need to have considerable elasticity.

Coverage of 75 to 80 percent of the protection unit by one or more lookouts of which approximately 60 percent is covered by two or more lookouts was commonly sought. This may require 30 or more lookout points per million acres of protected area. In California the percent of coverage was usually expressed as coverage of weighted fire risk rather than of gross area. Usually direct coverage of 70 percent or more of the fire risk within a specified detection radius produces an effective detection system if the terrain consists of flat, rolling, or long-slope mountain topography, since most areas not directly visible to a lookout point are not very far below the line of sight of more than one lookout or else are directly visible to a lookout beyond the detection radius. But where deep canyons and sharply cut topography prevail, it is inevitable that some dangerous areas will remain invisible to all lookouts. Detection planning helps to define such areas.

AERIAL DETECTION

Aerial detection is in several respects a different service than that provided by fixed detectors. It provides more uniform, more flexible, but less continuous coverage. A lookout provides more limited, more fixed, but also more continuous coverage. Consequently each is superior in certain situations and each can supplement the other in a large protection unit.

---

[2] This law or principle states that as any factor in production (in this case number of lookouts) is increased, the output per unit factor will eventually decrease.

The more important advantages of aerial detection are the facts that

1   A single observer can cover more area in less time and often at smaller unit cost than by any other method.

2   Coverage is completely flexible. There need be no blind spots and the "when" and "where" to search for fires can be varied at will.

3   The location of the fire and the best route to it can usually be determined more accurately because of the ability of the plane to circle the fire at close range.

4   Conditions surrounding the fire, such as fuels, terrain, and natural barriers that may affect its behavior or the difficulty of controlling it, can usually be observed and reported more accurately and in more detail for the same reason.

5   Aircraft used in detection patrol are available to scout large fires and to perform other emergency fire services of various kinds.

The more important disadvantages are:

1   Observations are intermittent. If a smoke plume from a small fire becomes visible a few minutes after the patrol plane has passed over, it may not be discovered until the plane again flies the same route one to four hours later or perhaps the next morning.

2   Adverse flying conditions may limit flying at critical times. Thunderstorms and high winds are hazardous to small planes. Poor visibility due to drift smoke sometimes interferes with landing and takeoff.

3   The location of small intermittent smokes is more difficult to identify in featureless terrain than when intersecting azimuth readings from two lookouts are obtainable. The azimuth reading from a single lookout is also superior at times.

4   Highly qualified pilots and observers are needed, particularly for mountainous terrain, but are often scarce.

5   Special backcountry landing fields and aircraft servicing facilities may be needed.

How much time can safely be allowed for discovery is a decisive factor in determining the place of aerial detection. In California, the need to detect fires within 15 minutes of their start in fast-burning fuel types set the standard for discovery time in that region. This was based on daytime occurrence of man-caused fires which usually start during the hot part of the day in flash fuels. Similar standards apply, for similar reasons, in the South and elsewhere in the United States. It is not feasible to meet such standards with aerial patrol.

Throughout the northwestern United States lightning-caused fires predominate. They are normally on a much slower time schedule. They are typically set in late afternoon or evening when fire danger conditions are moderate, and they burn for some time, usually overnight, as smoldering fires in a snag or in the forest duff. Most of the time they can be detected and reported by a patrol plane before they gain headway. This is the type of fire on which successful aerial detection is based in Alaska, in the Lake states, and over much of Canada. However, the threat from flash fuels and dangerous man-caused fire risks is never entirely absent and may be aggravated by drought. This may require special provisions. If fuels and fire risks can be reasonably well identified by time and place, this may be accomplished by instituting more intensive aerial patrol.

Most protection agencies use airplanes for emergency and supplemental detection even through regular patrols are not maintained. Privately owned planes under contract are usually employed. However, the U.S. Forest Service maintains a small fleet of planes for both uses, and many of the state services maintain one or more of their own planes for such purposes. A notable example is the Texas Forest Service, which has operated a small fleet of planes for many years for regular and emergency service.

Requirements for ground facilities are greatly modified by use of aerial detection. Where full dependence is placed on aerial patrol, no lookout structures are required. This, in turn, simplifies the communication system. Increased dependence on aerial patrol in northern Idaho and western Montana has resulted in the abandonment of large numbers of lookouts and many miles of telephone lines and trails. The reduced investment in fire facilities and the reduced cost of annual maintenance are advantages of the aerial patrol system. However, requirements for emergency landing fields may create sizeable offsets.

Happily, where lakes or other water surfaces are numerous and well distributed, as in the Superior-Quetico boundary waters and in canoe and wilderness areas of the United States and Canada, they can serve as ready-made landing fields for float planes and hydroplanes which then become the standard aircraft for detection patrol (Figure 11.7).

In rugged country, suitable sites for landing fields are rare and may require high development costs to bring them to reasonable standards of safety. High elevations require more clearance and longer runways. The specifications are interrelated with the type of plane to be landed and its requirements. In 1952, there were 48 landing fields and 64 airstrips on the National Forests. This number has not increased materially, though such facilities have been supplemented a great deal by helicopter landing spots.

Forest patrol planes for mountain areas must have good stability as well as ability to climb steeply and to land at low speed on short runways, often with crosswinds. The ideal patrol plane for fire detection has not yet

Figure 11.7 Seaplane on fire detection patrol. Superior-Quetico boundary waters canoe and wilderness area, Minnesota. *(U.S. Forest Service photo.)*

been produced. Existing planes which best meet the above requirements do not give the observer an unrestricted view of the terrain below. Usually, he must observe from one side only, and struts and wing surfaces interfere to varying degrees with observation. High-wing types have advantages in this respect. Some twin-motor planes have a much better safety margin, but costs favor single-engine types. Jet planes are normally unsuitable. Flight elevations are varied to get desired coverage and depend chiefly on topography. They vary from 2,000 to 5,000 feet above the average ground elevation. This is because observations at oblique angles are likely to give better visibility to smokes against dark backgrounds and to make small smoke columns a better target than when viewed vertically, or nearly so, from above.

So far, not much specialized equipment is required to enable aerial patrol to function except for the plane itself, its radio equipment in the wavelengths needed for full functioning, and the usual facilities at its hangar, its landing field, and at strategic emergency landing fields. The aerial observer is the key figure in the performance attained. His important functional equipment consists of accurate maps and aerial pictures on which to determine the correct location of any fires seen and his radio equipment designed for immediate report back to his base.

The map needs to be prepared in strip or pleated form for convenience in handling. A special key or grid system for locating fires on the map and reporting them accurately is highly desirable. A report form or checklist to ensure proper records and reporting is also needed.

The observer needs much experience and training to function effectively. Attempts to have a single individual serve as both pilot and observer have not been successful; experience has demonstrated that a passenger observer is best. But the pilot *can* assist, particularly on his side where much of the view is cut off from the observer. Techniques of observing, the proper positioning and routing of the plane, and use of profiles to determine the best flight elevation are described in detail in current air operations handbooks used by the U.S. Forest Service and by several state and provincial agencies. Though such handbooks are not available to the public, they are normally freely accessible to the student or technician.

The function of detection and first attack can sometimes be combined when smoke jumpers are used. This is often accomplished in the northwestern United States, where heavier planes are used for emergency patrol after lightning fires. Two to four parachute firemen are carried in the plane. They can parachute directly to any fires discovered and begin control action without delay.

When aerial patrol is combined with a skeleton system of fixed lookouts, there are several advantages. The lookout points serve admirably as radio contact points with the patrol planes. They serve too to ensure against "sleeper" fires missed by the patrol. So airplane hours can be saved when either or both risks and/or fire danger are low.

PLANNED AERIAL SYSTEMS

The use of aircraft to detect fires is nearly universal among forest fire fighting agencies in the United States and Canada, but the degree of dependence varies from occasional emergency use to total dependence. The determination of the degree to which aerial detection should be employed always enters into the development of a detection system. This requires analysis of the advantages and disadvantages of aerial detection in the area of interest.

Technical data on which planned aerial detection should be based consists of information on the optimum elevation and direction of flight in relation to topography and different positions of the sun and the effect of shadows and variable backgrounds on the visibility of small smokes from the air. Whereever such information is available, specifications for aerial patrol routes can be more accurately defined.

The first step in planning, as with fixed lookouts, is to analyze recent history of occurrence and to identify the high-risk areas. The location and extent of high-hazard fuels, like recent logging slash, are also identified. These data provide the basis for setting priorities in aerial detection coverage.

In flat country it is usual to start with a grid pattern of parallel routes about 10 miles apart, then modify it to give more intensive coverage to high-priority areas, particularly those in which high risks, high-hazard fuels, and high values are all present. Flight routes may be so planned that every flight will cover such areas twice. Considerable ingenuity is sometimes required to devise an optimum pattern. Consequently, even in flat country the regular flight pattern may deviate a great deal from that of a parallel grid.

In mountainous areas flight routes are designed in relation to topography. Drainages and subdrainages then become the unit. Topographic shadows obscure or blot out the view of stream bottoms in rugged topography whenever the sun approaches the horizon. Smoke plumes in such location do not show up until they come above the shadow angle. Within these limits the best detection is toward the sun. Flight routes are designed accordingly. Flight elevation above the terrain is usually maintained at 1,500 to 5,000 feet. Ordinarily, the lower the flight elevation, the sharper the detection of small smokes. This is because they are larger targets at oblique angles and are likely to have more contrast with their backgrounds. But in rugged topography there are large blind areas when the aircraft flies low over the terrain. This must be taken into account in designing aerial routes. A series of aerial photos taken at different elevations or profiles made from topographic maps may be used to establish the optimum flight elevation.

This type of planning is needed to establish what is usually referred to as the regular aerial detection patrol. It becomes the conventional patrol under nonemergency conditions. But to realize the full potential of the flexibility that aerial detection affords, provision must also be made for special and emergency patrols. These may be of several kinds in relation to changing fire danger and fire risks and to areas of high-hazard fuels.

As fire danger increases, the importance of speed of attack on fires also increases. This places a premium on quick detection and short elapsed time from ignition of a fire to attack on it. For that reason additional patrols are usually instituted as fire danger increases even though there is no coresponding change in risk. This may be done by increasing the number of regular patrols or by instituting special patrols which concentrate on problem areas. If carried to the point of giving continuing intensive coverage to large areas, costs soon exceed those of a lookout system.

The second contingency calling for special patrols arises from threats from increased risk. The most prevalent in this category is the fire-setting lightning storm. In protection units where at least a skeleton system of lookouts is operated, the probable location of strikes from such a storm and its route of travel can be quite closely identified and the specifications for a special lightning-fire patrol can be tightly drawn. Where no fire lookouts are being operated, the lightning-fire patrol becomes more generalized. Typically, fire-setting lightning storms occur during midafternoon and early evening hours. When fire danger is high, a special effort is made to detect lightning-set fires and to get men on them before darkness. This is the purpose of many special lightning-fire patrols. Unfortunately such patrols are not always possible, since flying conditions are often adverse.

Special early morning patrols to pick up any undiscovered lightning fires are nearly always employed following lightning-storm activity. Fires which have smoldered overnight usually produce a smoke plume that is easily seen at sunrise but that dissipates as soon as atmospheric convection becomes active, to be replaced by an occasional puff of smoke visible only a short distance away. By midafternoon, when an easily seen smoke column develops from a much larger and hotter fire, the chance for control at small size may be lost. To take advantage of the improved opportunity to detect fires in the early morning interval, the use of additional aircraft is worthwhile, particularly where coverage of large forest areas is involved.

Sole dependence on a system of aerial detection has been most successful in the following circumstances:

1 Where the principal risk of fires is from lightning and rate of spread of fire is low.

2 When extensive rather than intensive protection from fire is being practiced, as in much of Alaska and in some wilderness areas.

3 In northern lake country where patrolling float planes may perform several functions. They may be equipped with water tanks quickly filled by a scoop on take off so they can pick up water from a nearby lake and drop it on a fire to hold it in check until it can be reached by ground fire fighters.

4 Where the protected area is scattered and sufficient natural barriers exist to reduce the risk of runaway fires.

More commonly aerial detection is integrated with other methods or is used as an emergency service. The air-ground systems developed in the northwestern United States have already been mentioned. These are most successful when each form of detection is used where it pays off best. Primary lookouts are used to cover most areas of man-caused risks and fast-burning fuels. Blind areas and critical fuels in such areas are covered by ground patrols during critical periods. Aerial patrols give more extensive coverage. They may supplement the lookouts by giving intensive coverage in blind areas and when haze or smog seriously reduces visibility of smokes from lookouts but not from aircraft. Special patrols may be scheduled following lightning storms or during hunting season. When fire danger is low, aerial detection may be used alone, since it can give rather uniform detection service when speed of attack on a fire is not critical. In some areas where the lightning-fire season ends early but man-caused fire risks continue to be a problem, a few primary lookouts supplemented by ground patrol of high-risk areas may be used instead.

In protection units where fast-burning fuels and abundant sources of man-caused fire risks exist, aerial detection may be used only on an emergency basis or where lookouts are not on duty in early or late season. In areas of this type aerial detection may often be dispensed with entirely.

OTHER MEANS OF DETECTION

Though fire lookouts, the oldest means of detection, are giving way in many areas to aerial observers, other means of detection are also important and may dominate under certain circumstances.

Detection by Ground Patrol

When equipped with a car and field radio and in close touch with a fire dispatcher, ground patrol can function effectively as an organized means of detection.

The primary advantage of the method is its flexibility. The patrol route can be varied and observation can be concentrated on dangerous areas at times of high fire danger or of high exposure to risk. Further advantages are that the function combines well with fire prevention activities and with first attack on small fires. Rarely is a patrolman restricted to detection duties alone. Often he arrives on the scene before a camp or warming fire in a dangerous place has escaped control, and he can therefore prevent its becoming a wildfire. Similarly, cigarette fires may be found and extinguished before they have become more than a smoldering spot. Such work is highly valuable in reducing both costs and losses.

The disadvantage is that it is not possible to provide enough continuity of detection by such means to make them fully dependable. The patrolman may be at the wrong place at the time a fire starts. Usually ground patrol is of most value where it is operated as a supplement to regular lookouts. If the patrolman does not carry a means of communication with him, he is handicapped in all functions. He must operate independently in taking action on fires and much delay may occur in reporting them. Prevention activities are less impaired, but they lose flexibility.

Usually detection patrol is used within the more dangerous risk areas, expecially those not well covered by fixed lookouts. Examples are extensive but heavily used recreational areas, active logging operations, and slash areas exposed to public risk. Such patrol may be by horseback or on foot as well as by a patrol car. Unless a field radio is carried, such patrol is limited in its value for detection. However, a somewhat different form of foot or horse patrol is sometimes used that has potentially high detection value but little value to prevention or first attack. This is patrol of ridgetops or other high country which permits distant coverage of more area than is obtainable from any one lookout site. In the past, such patrol was used to a limited extent but without mobile communication. Therefore the patrolman was out of touch too much of the time and often had difficulty locating a fire accurately without the aid of azimuth readings. Provision for fire finders at strategic points plus a mobile radio now offers possibilities for more effective ridgetop detection patrol.

Detection by Cooperators

As a partial or complete substitute for fixed lookouts and ground patrol, systems of organized detection by resident cooperators have proved highly successful in some regions. The facilities needed consist of local means of communication and simple alidades with or without maps at strategic observation points near the residence or place of work of willing cooperators. Some kind of alidade is important to assist a cooperator in locating a distant smoke. It should be designed for mounting out of doors. Investment in facilities is at a minimum and detection service is at minimum cost. In the central Rocky Mountain region, chief dependence for detection of fires was placed on resident cooperators for many years. After making a careful survey of areas visible from each cooperator's home or place of business, such detection can function well as part of a planned detection and fire dispatching system. Such systems are particularly successful where most fires are accidental or of lightning origin in accessible country, and where public sentiment against wildfire is strong. It is difficult, by such a system, to develop coverage that is comparable to what a well-planned system of lookouts can provide, but it is an excellent supplement to incomplete lookout coverage and a marked advantage over no organized detection.

Besides cooperative detection service that has been planned and organized to some degree, chance discovery and volunteer reporting of fires by forest workers, forest users, and forest travelers often accounts for a significant proportion of the fires. This is particularly true in heavily frequented areas where most fires are man-caused. Much of the time, discovery is by someone at the scene, before a sufficient smoke column forms to be seen by the nearest lookout or by a patrol plane. Although such discoveries may appear to be too uncertain to influence planning, they do reduce the need for fire lookouts in many areas. The probability of such discovery increases with the number of visitors, though not at a uniform rate.

Detection by Nonvisual Means

Conventional detection of fires as discussed so far depends primarily on visual detection of smoke from the fire during daylight hours. This has both advantages and disadvantages. The advantages are that smoke normally rises. Typically too it is a dense white smoke against a dark background or against the horizon and is highly visible when viewed from an oblique angle close to 90° from the vertical. Because of this, smoke from fires in locations shielded from an observer by timber cover or equivalent topography can usually be detected as well as fires in areas where the ground surface is visible. Aerial detection greatly reduces the shielding, but with varying degrees of loss to the intercept size of target and in background contrast.

Disadvantages also arise from dependence on smoke and its visibility. Smoldering fires produce little or no smoke. Often a lightning-set fire of a quarter acre or more burning in forest duff produces a visible puff of smoke above the treetops only at intervals. Very dry fuels produce hot flames but little smoke. Under some conditions of air drainage or subsidence, smoke follows the airflow instead of natural convective channels. This results in delay in detection and in errors in locating the fire. Finally, as has already been mentioned, haze, drift smoke, smog, and fog may greatly reduce the visibility of smoke or completely block out the view from a fixed lookout.

Detection by Infrared Sensing Equipment Heat-sensing devices have been developed which can identify a source of heat. These operate in the infrared part of the spectrum to which the eye is not sensitive. At night such devices have been shown to be capable of detecting a few square feet of flames or glowing coals as much as 11 miles distant provided they are in the direct line of sight. On a sunny day this capability is, however, greatly reduced. Shielding by timber cover or topography that intercepts the line of sight to the heat source prevents detection by this means. Consequently such devices are inferior to the human eye for detecting fires from a fixed fire lookout.

But when infrared equipment is airborne, a new set of capabilities is provided. Studies by Hirsh and others (1966, 1969), show that shielding by timber cover can be minimized if the scan angle with the terrain is less than 60 percent from the vertical. This specification makes it necessary to fly at 15,000 feet in order to cover fully a 5-mile strip on each side of the aircraft. Within such a strip, infrared sensing equipment can identify very small sources of thermal energy down to 1 square foot, in darkness as well as daylight and through haze or smoke by use of a continuous automatic scanning device. The infrared emissions at the source are picked up by an electronic signal. This is amplified and converted to a visual thermal view of the terrain. It may be photographed for study of the imagery on the ground.

Location of heat sources is determined both by orienting infrared photographs to aerial maps and by use of doppler radar to identify location by coordinates.

This kind of operation has already proved its value in scouting wildfires and has so far been used chiefly for such service. Potentially it is a very valuable tool in detecting small fires which do not produce enough smoke to be readily detected by visual means or that are burning at night. A smaller instrument designed for manual operation has been in use for some time in Australia. In the United States a portable infrared scanning device that can be mounted on the wing of an aerial patrol or smoke-jumper plane for low-level operation gives promise too of greatly extending the potential of this kind of detection service. The detection of smoldering, lightning-set fires by infrared sensing devices is coming into increasing use throughout the western United States. Many believe that detection systems of the future will be based on such equipment.

Detection by Television Equipment It is possible to substitute a rotating televison camera for the lookout observer and to project the panorama as seen from the lookout on a screen at the dispatching headquarters. If observations are transmitted in this way from several lookout points so that their observers can be dispensed with, the savings in costs significantly offset the presently higher investment and maintenance cost of the electronic equipment.

Tests have confirmed that reasonably good detection can be attained by means of the television camera. The camera apparently distinguishes contrasts as well as the eye but is inferior in detecting movement and in depth perception. The net result is that it is a fair substitute for the eye but definitely is not superior. High costs have so far limited use of this method to tests and demonstrations. If, in the future, the costs of such a television system can be drastically reduced, there is a potential in many areas for developing systematic detection by this means.

INTEGRATED DETECTION SYSTEMS

In most areas, existing methods of detecting fires are the result of past planning and development activities with varying degrees of later modification. Awareness of formal planning of the past easily leads to unquestioned acceptance of the existing system as the best obtainable. But both fuels and risk are subject to critical change. Hazardous fuels following logging, wildfire, or insect or disease epidemics may quickly develop and may quickly or gradually disappear. New access roads and new uses may change the pattern and intensity of fire risk, and the ratio between costs of alternative methods of detection keeps changing. An annual check should be made of the performance of the existing detection system and, at not less than ten-year intervals, a systematic analysis of the cumulative record should be made to determine what improvements may be needed.

In northern Idaho and parts of the Douglas-fir region in the United States, combined systems of primary fire lookouts supplemented by aerial detection have evolved since 1940. The lookouts serve as communication hubs and as insurance against "sleeper" fires not visible at the time of a scheduled aerial patrol. Carefully planned systems of this nature which combine primary lookouts with both aerial and ground patrol have demonstrated the soundness of drawing on all available means of solving the detection problem on the ground.

How does one recognize the improvements needed or, conversely, the weaknesses in the existing detection system? A positive answer requires analysis of the fire record. Statistics for a ten-year period are usually required for the purpose, but shorter periods will serve if data are properly interpreted. Some of the questions such data can answer are

1 Who has been making first discovery of the fires that have occurred? How many discoveries were by lookouts, by aerial patrol, by planned cooperators, by the traveling public, or by others? This can determine whether the planned system is functioning as intended. If, for example, lookouts got credit for discovering only 30 percent of the fires in their visible area but most of the remainder were discovered by someone nearby before the smoke could become visible to the lookout, the insurance value and backup function of existing lookout coverage may still provide a good return.

2   Have there been dangerous delays in detection? This can be answered by analyzing the elapsed time between origin and discovery of each fire of the record. Delays when fire danger was low should be discounted if the likelihood of damaging fires was also low. Delays under more active burning conditions should be carefully checked to determine whether they are likely to be repeated. Similarly, the record of fires discovered by chance should be reviewed to determine the probable outcome if the chance discovery had not occurred.

3   How can dangerous delays in discovery be corrected? If delays in discovery tend to concentrate in a particular area, this may localize the problem. If they are traceable to a particular activity or can be identified with a particular time of day, days of the week, or to a particular seasonal period, the problem becomes easier to resolve. Perhaps it can be solved by ground or aerial patrols during certain periods, by use of a secondary or emergency lookout, or by imposing a local closure to public use during high fire danger periods. Possibly a survey by infrared sensing equipment after lightning storms can improve the record if the delays have been in discovery of lightning-set fires.

4   Are present costs of detection reasonable, and how do alternative methods compare? Though a complete answer to this question may be difficult to give, it is important to the administrator. Situations have existed, for example, where a fire lookout was being maintained to give coverage to a locality where several fires from debris burning could be expected each year. But local residents and topography were so placed that a fire-prevention patrolman located in the area could make prompt discovery and, through prior contact with the burners, could probably prevent such burning when conditons were dangerous. Consequently more could be accomplished by not maintaining the lookout and at less cost. At the other extreme, in one situation a fire lookout with extensive coverage of low-risk but high-value area was discontinued because of the very few first discoveries made from the lookout. But shortly after this economy measure, a fire started in this area and gained so much headway before it was discovered that it became a conflagration with costs and damages exceeding the computed cost of maintaining the lookout for approximately one hundred years. For such reasons decisions to reduce standards of detection should not be made lightly.

As pointed out at the beginning of this chapter, both state and federal forest fire agencies in the United States have continued to reduce the number of lookouts they maintain since a high point in the early 1950s. Most of these reductions have been preceded by analyses such as described followed by planning of an integrated detection system. Others have resulted simply from attrition due to increased cost of operating lookouts, to overtime pay requirements, high cost of maintenance, and high frequency of vandalism of lookout structures during off seasons. There are serious problems in maintaining fire detection service from lookouts, but these should not be permitted automatically to reduce desired standards of detection. To ensure this, a redefinition of the minimum standards needed for detection of fires in the forest planning unit should be drawn up prior to making new analyses.

Such standards will vary with fire danger and may be influenced as well by the strength and capabilities of the fire control organization. The purpose is to ensure that every fire that occurs will be discovered soon enough that it can be controlled by the local fire fighting force without serious damage. Because requirements to accomplish this will vary with fire danger and with fuels, considerable flexibility needs to be introduced in planning and in operating the system. Supplemental aerial detection of fires is well adapted to provide this since it can be intensified when fire danger is high and its coverage can be concentrated as needed on high-risk areas. Ground patrol has similar flexibility but more limited scope.

In developing an integrated detection system, costs to fire control funds tend to become the measuring stick. Unfortunately, when savings in such costs are used as the sole guide, offsetting disadvantages from changes in the fire detection system may be overlooked. The abandonment of lookouts which provide important but unevaluated public contact and fire prevention service is a case in point.

Two general principles should be observed when significant modification of the fire detection system is undertaken. First, the assumptions on which the previous planning was based and the conclusions reached at the time must be understood. This enables changes to be made more intelligently. Second, the accuracy of supporting data for revisions must at least equal that on which the original planning was based. Better yet, since it usually undertakes a higher degree of discrimination than the original plan, replanning should aim for a higher accuracy than was previously attained. Recognition of such requirements often discourages replanning of existing systems. But wherever or whenever records of performance demonstrate the need for changes, the time and effort required for redesigning the system are a wise and economical investment.

Chapter 12

Forest Fire Suppression

Fire suppression is always a challenge. Whenever fire danger is present, a wildfire grows in intensity and in rate of spread with time. The difficulty of controlling it grows simultaneously. At worst, a fire is capable of defeating every method of control yet devised; even at best, it may yield only to certain fire-fighting techniques. Its behavior varies with fuels, weather, topography, and other factors of the local environment. Consequently, no two fire suppression jobs are exactly alike, and how to control a particular fire cannot be detailed in advance. Nevertheless all fire fighting is based on certain underlying principles and is carried out through a few basic methods developed through experience. These are the subject of this chapter. They form the bases for systematic forest fire control.

As stated in the introduction to Part Two (page 261), fire suppression enters into both the second and third lines of defense and may be thought of as coming in two categories, namely (1) fires controlled at small size or damage by local fire suppression forces and (2) fires which cannot be controlled at an acceptable size or damage by the local organization and which require emergency assistance from outside the protection unit. The second category introduces special problems in organization and logistics, which justify separate attention. These are identified in this chapter but considered further in Chapter 16.

SUPPRESSION PRINCIPLES AND METHODS

The general principle underlying forest fire fighting is closely akin to the operation of the combustion formula (Chapter 1). For more graphic use in training fire fighters, the three essential components of combustion can be restated as *fuel, oxygen,* and *kindling temperature.* Combustion can proceed only when all three are brought together. But each in the presence of the other two has an affinity for joining them in a three-way process that can be visualized as a closed fire triangle. Each then forms one side of the triangle. Viewed in this way, the fire triangle can serve as a useful fire training model. To extinguish fire, the process must be reversed and at least one of the components must be separated from the other two.

The analogy can be carried further. If the ignition and combustion of each class of fuel in a fuel complex is thought of as a separate triangle, then the chain reaction of progressive ignition of all available fuel present, with the accompanying buildup of burning rate and intensity, then becomes a series of interlinked triangles (Figure 12.1). When linked together, the separate triangles then become more powerful and complex. Often it may be more urgent to break the linkage between triangles than to treat them separately. For example, if measures can be taken to reduce a crown fire to a surface fire or to prevent a surface fire from building into a crown fire, this breaks the linkage or weakens it and a principle in fire fighting is well illustrated. But further extension of such analogies needs to be treated with caution as, carried too far, they can confuse rather than clarify.

Basically, the aim of all fire fighting is to remove one essential component of the combustion triangle. This is done by (1) removing the fuels, (2) reducing the temperature of burning fuels, or (3) excluding oxygen.

Removal of fuels is the most common method used in conventional forest fire fighting. Usually this is done by creating a barrier strip or fire line free of fuels around a fire. To be effective, the fire line must create a gap between burning and unburned fuels wide enough to prevent the ignition of unburned fuels from either radiated or convected heat. In heavy mixed fuels of low moisture content, this may be difficult to accomplish. In addition, there is always a threat of spot fires being set by flying embers. A fire line by itself is seldom adequate to stop the fire. Even

Figure 12.1 The fire triangle graphically represents the three essential components of combustion. Linked triangles can then represent the progressive ignition of each class of fuel present.

so, it does provide a definite line of demarcation from which to work, and when reinforced by firing out the unburned fuel inside the line, it becomes an effective method of confining a fire.

The fire line width required to check the spread of a fire depends on fuels, terrain, and burning conditions and varies from a narrow, hand-raked or scraped path a foot or less wide up to bulldozed firebreaks of 20 to 50 feet. The difficulty of the job of creating a fire line also varies within wide limits with differences in fuel types, terrain, and topography. This is an important consideration when calculating the manpower and equipment needed to control a given fire. The development of fuel classifications for resistance to control was an attempt to improve estimates in this respect (Chapter 4). How the fire line is utilized will be discussed further under methods of attack.

The second most important means of breaking up the combustion process or fire triangle in forest fire fighting is that of reducing burning fuels below the kindling temperature. In industrial fire fighting, water and chemicals are the mainstay. In forest fire fighting, water has been less prominent because of the lack of readily available supplies of water. Water is heavy to transport and usually difficult to deliver at the scene of a forest fire.

For these reasons mineral soil is important in forest fire fighting. It is a partial substitute for water and can be employed effectively to exclude oxygen, knock down flame, and to cool down burning embers. It has less cooling power than water and does not materially increase the moisture in the burning fuel, so it is inferior to water in these respects. But even where water is available, skillful use of mineral soil is important in nearly all mop-up operations and will no doubt continue to be a part of the techniques of direct action on most forest fires.

Water is most effective in quenching flames when flaming combustion predominates. It is applied in various ways. The most common method of application is spraying by means of fire hoses and nozzles, though drenching from the air as discussed later in this chapter has become an acceptable method also. The purpose is to wet as much of the surface of the burning fuel as possible and to cool burning material below the kindling point. Water is also used in solid streams to churn up deep-burning fuels and to produce deep wetting. Burning material is also puddled and mixed with wet soil. With backpack pumps, many detailed techniques have been developed to extinguish fire in various materials with a minimum of water.

Wetting agents can increase the efficiency of water and make it go further by reducing its surface tension. Such supplements have found increasing acceptance among protection agencies. The advantage varies with fuels and with methods of applying water. These are discussed further in Chapter 13.

When natural supplies of water are not available at the site, water is commonly brought to a fire by means of tank trucks and at times by aircraft as cited above. Use of tankers is discussed in Chapter 13. The effectiveness of tank trucks depends, of course, on the degree of access to the fire area. Access may be augmented by the use of hose lays. Techniques of organizing the use of water by such means on a fire were very clearly developed for training purposes in a booklet entitled *Water vs. Fire* (Neuns, 1950). A review of this booklet is recommended.

In country not generally accessible by road, specially designed portable power pumps become very important. They are light enough to be taken in by backpack and set up at any nearby source of water, and hose lines are laid to carry water to the fire itself. To supplement power equipment of this kind, backpack fire pumps are utilized in most fuel types to permit application by the organized fire crew independent of other equipment.

The third important means of breaking up the fire triangle is through the exclusion of oxygen. Both water and mineral soil owe much of their extinguishing value to their smothering effect. Water and steam do this by diluting or displacing free oxygen; soil and other inert materials by excluding oxygen. One of the oldest methods of fighting fire in short grass and other fine flash fuels is by beating out the flames. Lack of oxygen for even a second or two is sufficient to extinguish the flames so long as the process is exclusively that of flaming combustion. If glowing combustion is present to any degree, unburned gases soon reignite. Smothering is used a great deal in mop-up operations on small fires through techniques of mixing or burying small live firebrands in mineral soil. But since some oxygen is always present in the natural environment of forest fuels, effective exclusion of oxygen requires careful techniques. The burying of larger burning materials in mineral soil is not generally regarded as good practice for this reason except as a temporary measure. Partial exclusion of oxygen reinforced by cooling or other effects is much more common in practice.

The concept of the fire triangle is, of course, based on the physical means of extinguishing fire. It can be argued that it is negated by the use of chemicals. But the effect of fire retardant chemicals can be interpreted in similar terms. They are believed to affect both the oxygen supply and the fuel. Presumably they restrict oxygen access by coating or sealing the burning surface, and they convert the fuel they impregnate from a flaming fuel to a smoldering fuel.

Accepted techniques to use in fighting small fires are well described for training purposes by many of the states and by each of the National Forest regions in so-called fireman's handbooks and in handbooks for fire wardens. These are useful reference but will not be detailed here.

Methods of fire fighting are classified in two ways. The first is based on the relation of the fire control line to the edge of the fire; the second is based on how the fire-fighting crew is organized. In the first category, several conventional systems have been recognized at various times, but all may be categorized as *direct* or *indirect*. Similarly, several methods of organizing a crew of men to build fire line have become recognized, though all may be identified with two or three degrees of independence of action of the individual fire crew member.

Control-line Methods

The Direct Method   In the direct method the fire line is built at the edge of the fire, or the edge and the interior of the fire are worked on directly (Figure 12.2*A*). No backfiring or burning out is done. It is the usual method of attack on small fires and is frequently used on slow-moving larger fires. The direct method, where applicable, has the advantage of keeping the fire to minimum area and damage and of quickly checking the production of heat and the rate of spread. On large fires it also has the advantage of more safety to the fire fighter, since he is working directly on the fire edge and can usually retreat safely into a cool area behind the fire front if a blowup occurs.

On small fires particularly, the term *hot spotting* is often associated with direct attack. This means giving first attention to cooling down the head and any hot spots which threaten to ignite new fuels. The purpose is to slow down or to stop the spread and to reduce the output of heat energy to make the fire more manageable. Mineral soil and water spray are commonly used, and beating out the flames in grass and other flash-type fuels is often employed. Such action takes priority over building fire control line, which may be entirely dispensed with. Action of this kind, by which the whole burning area is treated systematically, is at times referred to as the area method.

Where fire control line is built at the fire edge, there is often considerable difficulty in making sure that no live embers are left outside the fire control line. Some training manuals recognize the "2-foot method," which means the fire control line is constructed entirely in unburned fuels approximately 2 feet from the fire edge.

Usually the direct method results in quick and positive control of the small fire, but it cannot be employed where heat and smoke are too intense for men to work directly at the fire edge. Commonly this is true at the head of a spreading fire, even though the rest of the perimeter can be worked directly. If fire line is being built, it usually has the disadvantage, too, of requiring more work per unit of fire perimeter, because the actual edge of the fire is normally irregular with many indentations. A further disadvantage with a rapidly moving fire is that fire line which closely follows the perimeter is often poorly located amd may be very difficult to hold. Spotting, superheated gases, and direct radiation from hot, burning fuel close to the line may set too many fires across the line.

In California brush types and in most grass types which support hot, fast-moving fires, a special form of direct attack called cold trailing is often employed. The fires characteristic of such types are almost entirely flaming combustion. As a consequence, when the fire stops spreading for any reason, such as the usual night change in burning conditions, change

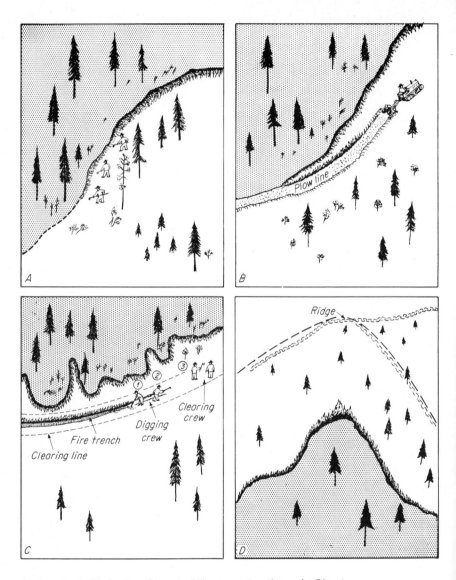

Figure 12.2 Methods of control-line construction. *A.* Direct method. *B.* Parallel method. *C.* Indirect method used with irregular fire edge to shorten control line and make it easier to hold. *D.* Indirect method employed to take advantage of a better control-line position and to anticipate fire spread.

in wind velocity or direction, change in slope such as occurs at a ridgetop, or lack of continuity in fuels, the fire cools rapidly and the edge tends to die out, leaving only scattered nuclei of smoldering fuels. When this occurs over any significant part of a fire's perimeter, it offers an opportunity for men to work directly on the fire edge and to mop up the separate spots. Complete control of the fire can then be brought about with very little construction of continuous fire control line and often too with minimum effort and minimum danger to fire fighters. Lacking such action, a fire that appears dead can often build up, with rising fire danger from smoldering spots, to conflagration proportions in a few hours.

Cold-trailing techniques often provide a valuable strategic measure to the fire boss on large fires when there is suddenly a second chance to make direct attack effective. The principal fault of the method is that it is slow, requires skillful work with hand tools by experienced men, and requires following all the irregularities of the fire's perimeter. In earlier brush fire history in California, cold trailing was the primary method of controlling large fires.

Indirect Methods Indirect methods always involve reinforcement of the fire line by burning out or backfiring. The so-called parallel method is a compromise method between direct and indirect. In the parallel method, the most advantageous location for the fire line is selected close to the perimeter but at some little distance back from the fire edge (Figure 12.2*B* and *C*). The fire line cuts across indentations and avoids locations that would be difficult to hold. As construction of the line proceeds, any unburned fuels between the fire line and the edge of the fire are immediately burned out. Other indirect methods depend on more extensive backfiring (Figure 12.2*D*).

At this point the relation of backfiring to the location of the fire line and to the organization of fire crew needs to be considered. In these relationships there is a significant distinction between two primary techniques of backfiring. This is recognized by the use of the terms *clean burning* or *burning out* to designate one form of backfiring. Clean burning or burning out means burning a narrow strip of fuels between the fire line and the fire edge just as line construction proceeds. This requires no special technique except that no more fire should be set at one time than can be handled by the working crew. In backfiring, especially on very large or fast-moving fires, the fire line around the head of the fire may be located at a considerable distance from the fire edge. This may require burning out of areas as large or even larger than the burning area itself. In such cases all fire lines must be completed before backfiring starts and skillful techniques must be employed in getting a complete burn under circumstances where calculated risks must be taken. Techniques are discussed later. Burning out can be practiced by a qualified crew foreman. Backfiring requires more experience and should be undertaken only by men fully trained in fire behavior and fire weather and experienced in the techniques that can be safely employed in the locality.

Crew Organization Methods

The second category of fire fighting methods is based on how the fire crew is organized to do the job. Three distinctions are usually recognized. These may be termed (1) the "man-passing-man" or squad method, (2) the "progressive" methods, and (3) the station or "individual assignment" method.

The Man-passing-man Method The man-passing-man method, sometimes called the squad method, was commonly used in the western United States for a long time without any distinctive name. A descriptive name was adopted when it became necessary to distinguish it from other methods.

In most forest cover there are two main operations to perform in building a fire line: (1) swamping out or clearing away all flammable brush and down material on a strip 6 to 10 feet wide on a selected location, similar to clearing for a forest trail, and (2) digging, raking, or scraping away litter, rotten wood, and duff down to mineral soil to create the equivalent of a footpath 16 to 24 inches wide near the center of the strip that will serve as a safe barrier against creeping fire. With heavy litter and deep duff and particularly on steep slopes, the second operation may move very slowly.

The two main operations require different tools, so the fire crew is usually operated in two sections with the swampers ahead. In each section the men are kept well spread out and each man completes the work to be done on a piece of line. When he reaches the point where the man ahead of him started and has joined the front end of his piece of line to the piece ahead, he moves on up ahead of the front man in his section and starts on another piece of line. This causes the men to rotate in each section and the only men who do not change position are a lead man or line locator who selects the location for the fire line and the foreman, who may bring up the rear, inspecting the work done. Unless a second crew is coming in behind the line-building crew, the foreman keeps dropping off members of his crew at intervals to guard and strengthen the constructed line. This causes the crew to become smaller as it proceeds. This is necessary where the line is built close to the edge of the fire and the fire burns up to it in a short time, as in the direct or 2-foot method where no burning out or backfiring is done.

One variation of this technique has been systematized as the "rotary crew method." It is well exemplified by the system worked out at one time in the Nebraska Sand Hills for direct attack in fighting severe grass fires by hand methods. The grass cover is similar to the sage grass prevalent in the Southern and Central states. It is tall and dense and supports a hot flame. The soil is nearly pure sand and easy to dig with a shovel. The lead man fills his shovel with sand, jumps in close to the flames, and throws the sand by a special motion to knock down and cool a maximum but small sector of the hot flank or head. He then quickly moves out of the zone of intense heat and, while he prepares to repeat, the next man moves into the lead behind him and he becomes the last man in line. When this method is well organized, so that men do not get in each other's way and each takes his turn facing the intense heat, the crew moves smoothly in a rotary fashion in either a clockwise or counterclockwise direction depending on whether the control action is proceeding to the left or right. The method works best with a crew of ten men or less. Adaptations to a variety of conditions, degrees of heat, and tools are possible.

The advantages of the man-passing-man method lie chiefly in its flexibility. Men can be pulled off the crew for special assignments without disrupting forward progress. There is a degree of competitive stimulus, too, in moving up to the head of the line when the work behind is caught up. A high degree of teamwork and esprit de corps can be developed in a rotary crew.

The disadvantages are (1) a higher rate of accidents through men passing tools in motion and men bunching up too closely, (2) loss of time in difficult terrain as men move around each other, (3) a tendency for the squads to become separated so that, on a fast-spreading fire, it may not be feasible to complete the fire line swamped out by the clearing crew or to hold the rather long stretch of incomplete fire line behind them. Such situations also induce danger to the fire fighters since the foreman is less closely in touch and a spot fire or a quick run by the fire may split his crew.

Progressive Methods The primary difference between the squad method and so-called *progressive methods* is that the crew moves ahead as a single unit and each man retains his position in the line as in a military formation. The first of these methods to become accepted has been known as the "one-lick method." In its idealized form, the one-lick method is based on the idea that if it takes one man ten strokes with a hand tool to produce an acceptable piece of fire line 6 feet long, then it can be done by ten men each taking only one stroke each 6 feet as they pass by. By repeating strokes (licks) at some such predetermined interval—for example, every two steps—the whole crew can move forward quite rapidly by a system of two steps and a lick, two steps and a lick, and so forth, leaving a completed fire line behind them. Such a system has its limitations. It is more regimented and somewhat less flexible than other methods and requires skilled foremanship. To work smoothly and efficiently, it also calls for considerable practice. But in difficult terrain and cover where the fire line is the only easy route of travel, it is by far the fastest method of building fire line with hand tools. There are also fewer injuries since men do not get in each other's way. The crew is not so widely scattered, as no one can lag behind, and it is under better control of the foreman in difficult and dangerous locations. It has proved particularly successful with teen-aged youths. The fast pace set in initial attack cannot be maintained for long periods. This requires alert coaching by the foreman.

The method is based on the crew that does nothing but construct line. A burning out and holding crew must follow them or there must be enough time to complete the line before such work is begun, so that the crew can reorganize for this purpose.

There are many modifications of the one-lick method. That is why there is some confusion in distinctions and why it was necessary to adopt the general term *progressive methods* to cover all systems where each member keeps his place in a forward moving crew. It is, of course, not essential that only one lick of work be done at each pause. Longer pauses and more swings with the hand tool can be introduced for the smaller crew or where the job is more complex. Some have experimented with a progressive method where men are spaced rather wide apart, each with a section of line to do. The first man to complete his section to the piece of finished line ahead shouts "up" to the man ahead and takes over where his neighbor was working. Each man ahead then moves up a notch. You might call this the move-up or step-up method or "bumping from the rear." There is a system too where the foreman keeps calling the signals. Such systems closely approach the older systems until the only essential difference is that all crew men keep in a predetermined formation in progressive methods comparable to the man-passing-man methods.

The Individual Assignment Method   The third method, known as the individual assignment method, is used mostly in mop-up, in the final stages of a fire control operation, or on a fire that is spreading slowly. Each man or team is assigned a definite beat for which he or the team is responsible. Men are consequently distributed at intervals all the way around a more or less static fire perimeter. This has the advantage of a clear definition of responsibility and of the job to be done for each fire fighter. When the men assigned in this way are experienced fire fighters who need little supervision, they respond by effective independent action and rapid production of fire control line. The method has the advantage that all parts of the fire's perimeter are immediately subject to control measures, and responsible men have room to operate without interference. The disadvantages are that the system is relatively inflexible. If the fire should increase in its rate of spread or intensity before the control line is completed or if an unexpected threat such as spot fires should develop, it is difficult to shift men to meet such emergencies. It usually has the disadvantage too of some inequities in patrol-beat assignments. This may result in slow completion of the fire control line even though initial progress is rapid.

Mechanized Control-line Methods   The direct and indirect methods, discussed above, of establishing control of a fire are based on organized crews of men with hand tools often supplemented by water spray. Such crews control a high proportion (70 to 90 percent) of the fires reported each year, including most fires of $1/4$ acre or less, but they account for only a fraction of the total fire control line constructed. Most of it, if measured in miles, is constructed by various kinds of mechanized equipment. This is particularly true in the accessible and nonmountainous terrain characteristic of the eastern and southern United States. The kinds of equipment employed are discussed in Chapter 13, following. The effect of such equipment on the method of attack has relevance here.

Application of water, whether by hand pump or power pump, is nearly always a direct attack measure. It is the primary dependence for fast control of the small fire and for mop-up of the larger fire wherever water can be made available. However, it also often serves a valuable function in indirect attack. It is often used to wet down fuels outside the fire line, particularly where spotting is likely; to slow down the head of a fire as it approaches the control line; and to hold down the intensity of a backfire to make it more manageable. Techniques have also been developed involving the use of water pressure at the hose nozzle as a substitute for a scraped or dug fire control line in light fuels.

A plowed or scraped fire line produced by mechanized equipment usually requires indirect attack. Such equipment substitutes for the line construction crew. A line locator is normally required ahead and a backfiring crew may follow closely. This may enable rapid construction and burning out by the parallel method. Where bogs, rocky terrain, or dense cover limit the access of available mechanized equipment, the method of attack tends to become more and more indirect with greatly increased dependence on use of backfiring.

The need for fast action strongly influences the role played by mechanized equipment. Normally light, highly mobile equipment or a few men with hand tools can get to the fire first. This is referred to as first attack. Heavier line-building equipment is usually much slower. When it is brought in, this is referred to as reinforcement action. It may follow first attack more or less automatically or it may be held on standby awaiting call at the discretion of the fire boss at the fire.

Backfiring

Burning out or backfiring unburned fuels inside a control line determines the success of all indirect methods of controlling a fire. Success in backfiring under the burning conditions that usually prevail during the spread of a blowup fire requires both a high level of knowledge of fire behavior and prior experience in carrying out such operations. Experience in carrying out prescribed burning projects is excellent training for backfiring in fire suppression. The techniques of carrying out prescribed burning are discussed in Chapter 19. The special requirements for success in stopping the spread of a wildfire by backfiring are exacting and always require emergency planning. Often the condition of the atmosphere and the nature of local wind patterns are critical factors.

Under some conditions, backfiring should not be undertaken. This is particularly true when the release of additional heat energy is likely to create fire whirls or turbulence that will stimulate the burning rate and aggressiveness of the main fire. Ill-advised and inept backfiring by property owners in a frantic attempt to protect property in the path of a conflagration has often led to a firestorm type of disaster with much greater property loss and area burned than would otherwise have occurred. Backfiring even by experienced men has at times had similar effect. With the wrong wind pattern, backfiring sets spot fires that may endanger fire fighters and cause loss of control line. Always it represents some sacrifice of area. Nevertheless, backfiring is usually the only available technique by which a rapidly moving fire front can be checked or stopped during the main run of fire. When there is a reasonable chance to bring this about, it should be undertaken even when spotting is likely to occur rather than waiting for the main fire front to hit the line.

The purpose of clean burning or of backfiring is to create an effective firebreak between a wildfire and unburned fuels. Always the lowest-intensity fire that will accomplish the purpose is sought. But the backfire cannot always be held to low intensity, and at times a high-intensity backfire is deliberately induced. The potential of the high-energy backfire extends much beyond that of simply creating a firebreak and must also be appraised. It has the potential to either lessen or increase the dynamics of the main fire and so to modify its behavior. A surface backfire sucked in by the indraft ahead of a crown fire can bring the fire out of the crowns. It can so strongly reinforce the indraft that the convection column is raised, the rate of forward spread slowed down, and flying embers are carried so high that the danger of spot fires is reduced. Unfortunately, such effects can seldom be created with certainty. Some calculated risks are always necessary. This makes the safety of the men an especially urgent consideration. Not only must escape routes be arranged for those taking part in the backfiring operation, but all other crews and units on the fire must know of the plan and be in the clear. Four examples of backfiring are shown in Figure 12.3 to illustrate situations where it enters into fire control strategy.

Part *A* shows the most common situation, a backfire set to stop the rather narrow head of a fire spreading rapidly but not under exceptionally adverse burning conditions. Level or near-level terrain is assumed. A control line is constructed at a distance far enough in advance of the wildfire to give time to establish the line and for the backfire to spread far enough away from it to create a burned-over strip of sufficient width to stop the wildfire head. The control line may be an existing road, trail, or other barrier, or it may be constructed by hand labor, by plows, or by merely wetting down a strip and digging little if any line. Backfires are set along or near the inside edge of the line and allowed to back toward the wildfire, which normally would be spreading with the wind. The backfire would have to be set along a front wide enough that the wildfire will not flank (go around) it. The control line similarly must extend far enough beyond the backfire on either end so that it will not be flanked by the backfire. The distances between control line when backfired and the wild-fire, and the length of line backfired, are naturally relative to the situation. These distances may range from a hundred yards to a mile or more. The objective of the whole maneuver is to burn out a strip wide enough to stop the wildfire and to induce it and the backfire to come together at a sufficient distance from the control line that spot fires can be caught and the line held.

Throughout the maneuvers, it is imperative that sufficient men and equipment be available to hold the backfire and vigilantly patrol for spot fires. It must be remembered that the backfire is initially set into the wind and that smoke and sparks will be blowing over the line. Later, the backfire may be drawn into the main fire, but this is not likely to be true to start with. Spot fires from both the main fire and backfire must be

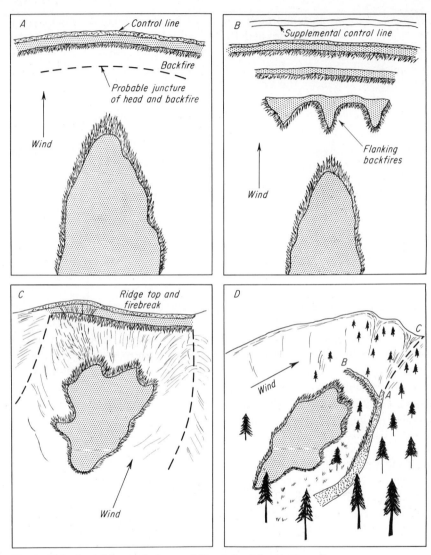

Figure 12.3 Backfiring techniques. *A.* Single backfire to stop a fire head. *B.* Multiple backfires to stop a fire head under particularly adverse conditions. *C.* Backfiring to contain a fire within a small drainage. *D.* Emergency backfiring to save a completed portion of planned control line.

expected. If the spot fires and the backfire are not held, then obviously the net result of the maneuver is only to speed the spread of the main fire. However, if there is no chance of stopping the head fire without backfiring, then it should be undertaken without hesitation provided safety of personnel is assured and flanking maneuvers do not give better promise of control with less total damage and cost.

Figure 12.3*B* is basically similar to part *A* but introduces the principle of multiple backfires to meet adverse conditions where (1) there is not time to widen a single backfire to hold or else (2) several bands of fire are needed to materially slow down or to reduce the momentum of the approaching head fire. Level ground is assumed in this illustration. Three strips of fire are set in succession. Flank lines are set on the inner line as shown. The purpose is to develop quick counter energy in the backfire by utilizing simultaneous ignition techniques, yet at the same time to keep fire whirls and other violent effects of the merging of two fire fronts away from the prepared fire control line. Supplemental lines may be established behind the main control line for added protection against the backfires.

Many variations are possible in the use of multiple backfires. In plow country, it is common practice to plow several parallel lines in front of a hot and rapidly moving head fire. One or two intervening strips are usually burned out, with extra lines often plowed that are not burned out. The idea is to slow the fire, if not stop it on the first line or so, and to have the other control lines available if needed. Applied on slopes, multiple backfires are employed to extend a burned-out strip down the slope. The backfires are set in sequence, working from the top of the ridge down in the same way that strip firing is practiced in prescribed burning on slopes (Chapter 18).

Figure 12.3*C* illustrates use of backfiring to hold an irregularly spreading fire within a small drainage. An existing firebreak along the ridgetop is assumed, as well as brushy, flammable fuels. A backfire is started inside the firebreak as indicated and allowed to work down the slope. Vigilant patrol is necessary to hold the ridgetop line against spot fires and "heads" originating either from the backfire or approaching wildfire. Depending on rate of spread and general burning conditions, control lines will be located down lateral ridges as indicated and mostly burned out after the main spread is stopped at the ridgetop. Firing both the main and lateral ridges at the same time might well result in too much area getting hot at once, which might cause an excessive number of spot fires or the generation of fire whirls.

Figure 12.3*D* illustrates the problem of a fire spreading laterally on a slope. There has not been time to complete and burn out a control line to point *C* as planned. The need is to save the line built (to point *A*) and to check the spread of the wildfire to gain time. To accomplish this, an emergency line, *AB*, is constructed and backfired across the slope in the face of the advancing fire to check its spread. Backfiring is carried to the completed line and on down it, as shown in the figure. This is an emergency measure but much preferable to doing nothing and permitting the completed line to be outflanked by the fire.

Strategy and Tactics in Fire Fighting

From previous discussion of fuels and of fire behavior it is obvious that each unwanted fire in forest fuels will present the fire fighter with a distinctive set of problems in carrying out his task. This gives forest fire fighting a special character compared to other operations of comparable cost. Blueprints or detailed specifications prepared in advance such as are used for all forms of construction cannot be relied on. Instead, the fire fighter at the scene of the fire must first size up the job to be done in bringing the fire under control and make decisions on how to do it, where to take action, and in what order to bring about quick control of the fire at minimum cost and damage. This demands the exercise of good judgment. Good judgment in turn depends on knowledge of fire behavior, on methods of fire suppression, and on specific information on fuels, weather, and topography in the vicinity of the fire. As the fire control job increases in size, information on probable extension of the burn with time, availability of additional manpower and equipment, and the elapsed time required to employ them in the control operation become critical. Knowledge too of how to organize and direct men and machines to accomplish the required work in a given time schedule becomes a vital requirement on large fires.

The terms *strategy* and *tactics* have often been used to describe this process of utilizing available forces and techniques to control a fire. These terms have much the same meaning as in military operations but have some overlap in relation to forest fire fighting. *Strategy* refers particularly to the planning and direction of large-scale operations where a variety of equipment, methods, and techniques are combined to gain advantage in controlling a large fire. It is sometimes referred to as generalship. *Tactics* normally refers to the choice of methods in building fire line and to the placement and movement of the fire fighters used. The preceding discussion of fire-fighting methods is primarily concerned with tactics—though use of indirect methods nearly always requires decisions on overall strategy as well, as is illustrated in Chapter 16.

The use of skilled tactics and the development of sound strategy in fire control operations depend heavily on experience, training, and careful advance planning, as will be further developed in Chapters 14 and 15. Study of fire behavior and of the principles of fire suppression can qualify men for fire suppression responsibilities after a much shorter period of experience than would be possible if they depended on learning by trial and error. Similarly, guidelines on how to evaluate the situation and on how to forecast probabilities can sharpen the judgment of the inexperienced. These considerations are the basis on which tactics and the overall strategy employed in controlling a fire can reach a professional level.

Tactics on the Small Fire   Control of a fire is simple in concept. On a small fire the execution may also be simple. It becomes complex only as the organized action to control it increases in complexity. Suppose you happen onto a small fire in pine litter intermingled with patches of old logging debris, a fire which has spread in an elongated oval to about 50 feet in length. It is just beginning to build up in its rate of spread and to form an active head. In a car nearby you have a shovel, Pulaski tool, and a fire rake but no nearby help. The obvious course of action is first to look over the fire to determine whether you can control its spread by your own efforts and where the threat of rapid spread is greatest. If you can handle it, the second step is to take quick suppression action.

You would choose direct attack. The shovel would probably be used first to cool down the head and the hot spots by applying dirt along the perimeter (hot spotting). Then the rake or shovel would be employed to put a fire line around the head, then on the fire edge at each hot spot, then on the rest of the perimeter. If these tactics are successful, then hot material along the edge is raked in and scattered. If it does not burn out quickly, systematic work is started to mop up all fire inside by scattering, by mixing with dirt, by scraping off hot coals from stumps and logs where fire has not yet become deeply established, and by moving burning material farther away from any dead snag or brush pile or punky log just outside the fire line. The most threatening part of the fire would get first attention, then the next most threatening, until the fire was completely controlled and finally extinguished. The whole action might take less than two hours, and one man might accomplish it with ease.

But if the head of the fire was about to run into a fire barrier, it might not need first attention. If one flank of the fire was about to ignite a pile of slash, that might be the most dangerous point. If fire was just starting to go up a tall, dead snag or was beginning to ignite branches of a bushy tree inside the fire, first attention to stop these might be most urgent. In each case a simple judgment would first have to be made.

How to attack the fire might be dictated in part by the tools available. If a backpack pump was available it would be used to cool down the head and the hot spots, instead of throwing dirt, and it could reduce the time needed to mop up the fire. If no tools were available, an improvised beater might serve to reduce the heat of the fire, and burning material might be kicked away from dangerous fuels. An improvised fire line might be made with the feet. But for best efficiency several hand tools would be needed by one man in such a situation. Choice of tools and equipment will be discussed in Chapter 18. Too often the tools supplied assume a conventional method of attack without any substitute for the conditions under which they become ineffective.

Fitting the Tactics to the Fire   Whether to attack a fire at the head or at the flanks is often debated. Control action on the small fire just described illustrates a principle applicable to all fires. The most dangerous part of the perimeter is attacked first if possible. Usually that is the head of the fire, but many exceptions occur. The advantage of controlling the head first is that the spread is checked decisively as soon as the head of the fire is stopped and the fire can be controlled more quickly at less area and damage. In flash fuels where the rate of spread is fast, work on the flanks may have little effect because the head fire can outdistance the rate of control on the flanks. In hot, slower-burning fuels, attack on the flanks starting close to the rear has best chance of success under many circumstances. On larger fires in the western United States it is considered best practice to control the head first if feasible. But when fire danger is high and bulldozers or heavy tanker equipment are not available, this is often not feasible. So it is rather common practice to start work on the flanks of a fire and to pinch it in at the head from both sides, rather than to start at the head. The reasons are (1) danger of being outflanked, (2) danger to men, (3) usual necessity of employing indirect attack methods at the head, and (4) anticipated changes in fire behavior or in strength of fire-fighting forces.

Wherever the rate of line construction is slow and a fire line is started at the head of the fire, there is a problem of close timing. Even if the center of the head is held, line must be extended both ways fast enough to catch the advancing flanks or new heads will form at both ends of the constructed line and all of it will be lost by being outflanked. On a rapidly spreading fire, on steep slopes, or where crowning is likely to occur, such a position becomes dangerous to the fire fighters. If they become outflanked, their lives are threatened. Another factor is that wherever the head of the fire is too hot for men to make direct attack on it, line must be built well in advance and fired out. To do that successfully the line must be extended around the flanks sufficiently to prevent its being outflanked either by the backfire or by the advancing front. On many fires, control of the flanks by extending control line up from the rear is the best way to provide safe anchor points for both ends of the backfire line. Flank attack also becomes good strategy when there is good reason to expect, within the time schedule of planned operations, favorable change in burning conditions that will reduce danger to men at the head or that will permit working close to the fire in direct attack. Anticipated changes in wind direction may also dictate such action. Similarly, the first attack forces may be inadequate to make any progress in attack at the head of the fire. If so, their energies will be much better employed in building safe control line on the flanks until enough reinforcements arrive to make an all-out attack at the head.

Skillful tactics come within the following guidelines. On small fires, direct attack on the head of the fire is always good advice unless some other part of the perimeter is clearly more threatening. On larger fires, the head should be controlled first if feasible and if not dangerous to men. Such action is feasible most of the time in light, flashy fuels but only occasionally in heavy, hot fuels.

An important principle in training fire suppression personnel in skilled use of tactics is to develop an aggressive attitude but to keep options open. Control the head on any small fire first if feasible. If not, drop back promptly to control work on the flanks. If the head can be expected to slow down in a time or distance acceptable in control plans, start with the flanks and do not waste energy on the head at its peak of heat production. The important thing is to avoid a defeatist attitude while also exercising good judgment so as not to waste energy or endanger men needlessly.

FIGHTING FIRE FROM THE AIR

Across roadless terrain and particularly through dense brush cover, fires often move upslope and leap barriers by spotting with an ease and speed that cannot be matched by men with ground equipment. This relative inflexibility of fire-fighting forces when confronting an aggressive fire has long been the fire boss's most frustrating problem. It is aggravated by the need to move heavy equipment and by the difficulty of keeping continuously informed of a large fire's movement and behavior. The problem of getting men and equipment to the right place at the right time is referred to as a problem in logistics, which closely parallels similar problems encountered by military field forces. The problem of getting continuous information on a fire's behavior is usually referred to as the problem of intelligence or of scouting. This too parallels military situations. Aircraft offer potential solutions to both problems, which have attracted fire control men since 1919 (Clepper, 1960). In that year the first military planes were used on fire detection patrols. Further development of aerial detection has been discussed (Chapter 11). Use of aircraft for scouting going fires was a parallel development. Finding ways to attack a fire from the air developed more slowly.

Smoke Jumpers and Cargo

The development of a system of transporting fire fighters and cargoes of fire equipment or supplies by plane and of delivering them by parachute to remote or backcountry fires was the first step. In this, aircraft and parachutes substitute for foot travel and for transport by backpack or horse pack. Control of the fire itself is, however, by conventional methods—chiefly with hand tools. This grew out of the experiments for using aircraft for bombing fires with water or chemicals which were initiated in 1935 (*History of Smokejumping*, U.S. Forest Service, 1969). It was soon apparent, with the aircraft and supporting equipment then available, that such methods were impractical.

Cargo dropping of equipment and supplies developed rapidly in the 1936 to 1938 period, and the first parachute jumps in forest terrain were carried out successfully in 1939. Starting in 1940, the use of parachute fire fighters to control small backcountry fires was initiated on a trial basis. The system was perfected and grew through the years until over 400 smoke jumpers were used and some 5,785 jumps were made in 1968 (U.S. Forest Service, 1969; Figure 12.4). The significance of smoke jumping to the structure of fire control systems is discussed in Chapter 14. More about the equipment required is given in Chapter 13, following.

Evolution in Use of Water and Chemicals[1]

After the water bombing trials of 1935 to 1936, primary attention was given to other uses of aircraft until 1947, when a joint project was undertaken by the U.S. Forest Service and the U.S. Air Force. Exploratory work was continued in the early 1950s in both Canada and the United States.

Early work in the United States concentrated on dropping water in containers of various sorts that either splashed on impact or were exploded near the ground by means of proximity fuses. Some dropping of uncontained water was attempted, but the elevation was too high and too little water reached the ground. Reasonable accuracy was achieved with water containers dropped from planes gliding at low levels, but this could not be duplicated from high levels with planes of the B-25 and B-29 class. The technical possibilities of missile dropping were, however, estab-

---

[1] Chemicals for Forest Fire Fighting, N.F.P.A. Forest Committee, National Fire Protection Assn., Boston, 1967.

Figure 12.4   Two smoke jumpers parachuting to vicinity of a fire in
Glacier National Park, Montana. Parachutes are in opening stage.
Parachutes used by men who jumped earlier are visible in trees
below. *(U.S. Forest Service photo.)*

lished. Parallel work was continued in Canada, where a technique of
dropping a salvo of up to eight $3^{1}/_{2}$-gallon water bags made of paper was
developed. An eight-bag pattern could drench an area of conifer needles
or other light fuels 10 feet wide and 90 feet long (Mackey, 1954). The
method was used successfully on small fires in nonpopulated areas as a
delaying tactic.

In the United States, missile dropping was considered too dangerous to employ in populated areas or as close support to fire fighters on the ground. Also, the technique was of limited practicality in many situations. Guided by the experience of agricultural flyers accustomed to low-level flying in applying insecticides, a technique of bulk free fall of water or chemicals from small planes was developed and tried out in California. Success was limited because of lack of accuracy in placing the liquid on the target from safe flying elevations above the rugged topography that prevailed.

In 1955, as a result of a cooperative series of tests in a project known as Operation Firestop, the potential value of chemicals to increase the effectiveness of water and the advantage of a slurry[2] in improving accuracy and effectiveness of aerial application were demonstrated. Out of this, techniques rapidly developed for dropping thickened chemical mixtures on fuels in advance of moving fire fronts. Sodium calcium borate, a by-product chemical from the manufacture of borax, was utilized and became the standard for a time. Borate was later replaced by other more effective and less toxic slurries in a continuing evolution of methods for direct aerial attack on fires in Western regions of the United States (Figure 12.5). In the Lake states region and in most of Canada where aircraft, particularly float planes, are a primary means of transportation, a water scoop, by which a tank in the plane could be filled automatically in the process of takeoff from a water surface, became a key factor in this evolution. Where water surfaces abound in flat country, a plane can drop a load of water on a fire from a low level, return to a nearby lake, refill its tank, and return with a second load in a short time. This technique has proved so effective that neither thickeners nor retardants in the water have been considered essential, though the use of wetting agents and of quickly dissolving retardants is employed in special situations.

In the southeastern United States, the use of a mixture of the fire retardants diammonium and monammonium phosphate in the form of liquid pyrophosphates won preference. These fertilizer solutions diluted without thickeners have proved to be effective flame inhibitors when applied to prevailing fuels in this region. They have the advantage of local availability at relatively low cost and require no mixing equipment.

Tactical and Strategic Considerations in Aerial Attack

The use of chemical fire retardants in forest fire fighting (Chapter 13) has brought with it a new technology and some new concepts. First of all, fire retardant solutions, regardless of their composition, are not superior

---

[2] A slurry is a watery mixture or suspension of insoluble matter such as clay.

Figure 12.5 Tanker plane dropping 700 gallons of slurry in advance of a fire in young stand of ponderosa pine. *(U.S. Forest Service photo.)*

extinguishers. If applied directly to a hot fire, their extinguishing effect is only that of their contained water; but if applied to the unburned fuel ahead of the fire, they have a high potential for interfering with its progress. The treated fuels may ignite and burn, but without flame. The resulting glowing combustion proceeds slowly. This reduces the intensity of radiation and drastically reduces the zone in which new ignitions occur. Thus the fire slows down and loses intensity in a manner that is the reverse of the reinforcement action of a growing fire described in Chapter 6. The chemical retardants lose very little of this effect as the solution in which they are applied dries out. They are designated as long-term retardants for this reason. But all thickened solutions and slurries retain considerable retardant effect by forming an inert coating on fuel surfaces; also, they dry out slowly. Consequently, all retardant solutions are very well adapted to use in indirect attack on fires. They can be used well in advance of a fire front to create temporary or preliminary fire control lines or to reinforce constructed fire lines. They also have uses in fire prevention and have many uses in the safe conduct of prescribed burning.

A second basic point is that attack on fires from the air either by dropping water or chemicals is not a complete suppression method except under very special circumstances. These are circumstances under which flaming combustion prevails and the fire could be extinguished on the ground by a water spray alone. It is further limited by the requirement that the fire be small enough or of low enough intensity that water or chemicals which can be carried by available tanker planes or ferried in by helicopter can have a decisive effect in stopping the head of the fire. In grass and other light fuel, complete extinguishment of small fires by aerial attack through either water or retardants may well become established. But aerial attack in mixed fuels can only be effective to the degree that it operates as close aerial support to ground operations. Because of the dramatic nature of aerial attack, this is often lost sight of.

The most effective application of aerial attack is on small, aggressive fires which exceed the capacity of ground forces to control by direct attack. Aerial attack has the potential of checking or of reducing the energy output of such fires sufficiently for ground forces to gain quick control. This kind of service can prevent a small fire from becoming a costly disaster. Timely support is difficult to achieve but is so important that a small-capacity plane (50 to 200 gallons) arriving during the critical buildup of such a fire may be far more effective than a 2,000-gallon tanker an hour later.

The second important service of aerial attack is that of giving ground forces more time to get to a fire in roadless areas. This is the special contribution of the water drops by float planes in the lake country. They wet down the area in which a fire is burning and are usually successful in checking its spread and preventing crowning until ground forces can get to it to complete control.

The third use is in aerial support of ground operations in the control of a large fire. Though a runaway fire has already passed the point where aerial attack could keep it small, an aircraft still has a potential for facilitating control in several respects. This potential can be realized only by close coordination and complete control by the fire boss. Under such conditions, fire retardants can be dropped to slow fire spread and to establish preliminary fire control line, reinforce fire control line already built, knock down or hold down spot fires, or increase the safety of a backfiring operation. Such tactical use requires rather high-capacity aerial tankers (1,000 gallon or more) and a lead plane to help guide the big tanker and to improve accuracy of placing its load. An air-attack boss may be placed in charge of such operations by the fire boss.

Helicopters

Aircraft gain their advantage by not being earthbound. Yet both propeller and jet airplanes are relatively inflexible in their operation. They move forward only, must move at a rate above stalling speed, can climb only at a limited angle, and can turn only in arcs. The helicopter can hover, climb, or descend almost vertically and can move in any direction almost at will. For these reasons helicopters offer a much higher potential for effective attack on fires from the air. The offsetting factors are a much more limited payload and higher cost per ton mile. These disadvantages can be overcome when a helicopter is used to give shuttle service from nearby sources of supply of water and chemicals, as it can place them with more precision and less waste. The technology of fire fighting by helicopter is still developing, but special accessories to facilitate laying of hose and application of water and chemicals are already operational.

Helijumper crews are special fire crews equipped and trained for

Figure 12.6 Helicopter hovering over pond while 450-gallon water bucket fills for attack on a nearby fire. *(U.S. Forest Service photo.)*

transport to fires by helicopter. They are equipped with protective clothing to permit them to drop into the brush from a hovering position when no landing spot is available. The special advantage of this kind of transport is that of placing fire fighters at almost any location desired in rugged topography quickly and without fatigue.

PRINCIPLES OF FIRE SUPPRESSION ORGANIZATION

Fire fighting is always in the nature of an emergency operation. It calls for fast, aggressive, and efficient action. To achieve such action, good organization of fire-fighting forces is essential. Uncertainty, slowness, conflicts in authority, and lack of teamwork are more disastrous to the success of forest fire fighting than to other forest work, but they can largely be overcome through good organization. Without good organization of fire-fighting forces, the chance to control a fire at small size or later to prevent its becoming a conflagration may be lost.

The principles of good organization are not complex, yet they are often neglected or violated in the stress of fire fighting. Analysis of the history of disastrous fires nearly always reveals that one or more faults in organization of the fire-fighting forces caused higher costs and greater losses than would otherwise have been experienced. Too often a fire reaches large size because of faulty organization of forces in its early stages, rather than from lack of know-how in the control effort

Organization by Size of Force Engaged

It is common to think of formal organization of fire-fighting forces as a requirement associated only with large fires. This is because small fires are so often controlled by small fire crews that have already been well organized and trained. Although organization of the forces on small fires may be informal, the need to observe the principles of good organization begins as soon as two or more men are engaged in the emergency task.

In all cases the man in charge of the fire is the fire boss. But his responsibility for organizing the fire-fighting force varies within wide limits depending on the number of men and the diversity of equipment and facilities employed for the job. For simplicity, the progression is described in terms of men using hand tools and situations in which the number of men is a good indicator of organization requirements.

The One- or Two-man Fire   On the small one-man fire described in the preceding section, there was no problem of organization. Know-how and willingness to meet the challenge through his own efforts are the critical factors to success. The fire fighter is his own fire boss in such situations. He must decide what to do and in what order to do it, then take action. He cannot delegate any part of the task to others. As soon as two men are engaged, a degree of organization becomes necessary. Usually one man needs to take the lead in planning and scheduling the joint efforts of the participants to create effective teamwork. In any case the two men need to coordinate their efforts.

The Squad-leader Fire   This is the type of fire where control operations are carried out by a small crew unit, usually ten men or less. This is typical of the many fires suppressed by a small tank-truck crew, plow crew, warden crew, or hastily enlisted pickup or work crew from some nearby source. The leader acts as fire boss. He has the responsibility of sizing up the behavior of the fire, of deciding the plan of action, and of carrying it through. He delegates most of the physical accomplishment to the members of his squad but must take the lead. He takes an active part in the fire fighting but also assumes responsibility for the men in his charge. He sees to it that needed work is done by the squad acting as a team, and he does what is necessary to provide for food, water, and safety of the men. He supervises the men directly and shows them how to do unfamiliar jobs acceptably.

The most common faults of the inexperienced squad or unit crew leader acting as fire boss of a small fire are the tendency to become so intent on doing the physical job himself that he fails to get production from the group as a unit and is not alert to a threat or task that is not immediately in sight, or, at the other extreme, to be a poor leader by being too inactive. If the leader in this situation does not participate in the physical task, he fails to set the pace, to properly demonstrate how to do things correctly, and to assume active physical leadership of his team in the attack. The effective leader not only sizes up the job and decides on a plan of action but also assumes physical leadership in carrying it through.

The Crew-sized Fire   Where a fire is of a size or aggressiveness to require more than one squad of men, approximately 18 to 30, the man in charge assumes the responsibility of a foreman. This means he can no longer supervise the work of each man directly. This must be done by organizing the men into squads, with a crew leader or straw boss in charge of each. In addition, if it is desirable to split the crew to work simultaneously—for example, on both flanks of the fire—he may need to designate a temporary crew foreman to lead one group. If he does so, he delegates at least part of this responsibility to him. He delegates direct supervision to the straw bosses and confines his supervison to seeing to it that they function properly.

On this size fire the foreman must usually do some special scouting to get a good estimate of the fire's behavior, and the necessity for planning is more exacting. Supplies and equipment for the crew are now also likely to require some special attention. The foreman may need more men or he may need to plan for a relief crew if more than one work shift is going to be required. So he must devote more time and attention to these things.

As fire boss, he still has the responsibility for estimating the work requirements for controlling the fire, of deciding the plan of action, and of carrying it through. But each is now somewhat more difficult. To do them well, he delegates not only the physical tasks but the immediate supervision of the workers undertaking them.

The Multiple-crew Stage Fire   When a fire has reached a size or aggressiveness that requires a force of more than one crew, additional crew foremen are needed and additional crews need to be organized. When several crews, each under a foreman, are engaged, the fire boss must further delegate supervision. He delegates supervision of the men to the foremen. They in turn delegate a portion of it, as well as the physical tasks to be accomplished, to the straw bosses. Squad leaders, also referred to as straw bosses, each report to the foreman. The foremen report to the fire boss.

The Sector-stage Fire   When a fire requires a large number of men or equipment units, there are soon too many foremen to report directly to the fire boss. At this stage the perimeter of the fire needs to be divided into convenient sectors with a sector boss assigned to each. The fire boss then delegates supervision of control operations on each sector to the sector boss, and foremen then report to their respective sector boss. The sector bosses in turn report to the fire boss, who now devotes his full time to other pressing aspects of his task relating to overall plans and strategy in controlling the fire.

The Division-stage Fire   On a very large or complex fire, the number of sectors may build up to ten or more. A fire boss normally cannot efficiently supervise and coordinate work between more than three or more sectors. The number depends on the behavior of the fire and on topography, accessibility, and ease of communication. Beyond this number, the organization problem is best solved by dividing the responsibility geographically into two or more divisions for each of which the fire suppression job can be carried on more or less autonomously.

Organization of the fire into two or more divisions is also a convenient device when two or more independent protection organizations are directly engaged in fighting it. In such cases, separate divisions may be set up when the number of men and the amount of equipment alone would not require such action. On a fire organized by divisions, the division boss position is created, and each sector boss for the sectors making up a division report to him rather than directly to the fire boss. An overall fire boss continues to carry final responsibility for plans and decisions. In cases where a fire is burning on both sides of a river or has developed two widely separated active fronts, the control work on the divisions may require little correlation. In such cases suppression work may be organized, as for two separate fires. In intermediate cases and where divisions are set up on the basis of the responsibility assumed by different agencies, the fire boss's responsibility for planning and for strategy decisions may also be delegated to the division bosses with the exception of responsibility for coordinating work between divisions. In these cases the coordinating officer is no longer a fully functioning fire boss.

Combining Men and Machines   The preceding is based on organizing men with hand tools. In Figure 12.7 a chart has been drawn up which illustrates how mechanized equipment modifies the pattern. It will be noted that the two tankers and the two tractors are each given to a supervising officer of the same status as the crew boss of foreman. It will be noticed too that the backfiring crew has only three men and the air attack boss has no men under him, yet both report directly to the fire boss on the same basis as the crew boss. The importance and difficulty of the responsibility assumed, rather than the number of men supervised, determines the place of the supervising officer in the chain of command. This relationship and the additional organization of forces by functions is illustrated by this chart. More on the organization by functions is presented in the next section.

Summary of General Principles that Apply

The preceding description of the progression in building a fire organization to fit the fire suppression job as it develops emphasizes the necessity of maintaining a clear-cut chain of command. It is short and direct on a small fire and becomes longer as the organization requirements become more complex. It parallels military practice in the relationships of the private soldier to officers in command positions. It is based on certain principles. The two most important are unity of command and span of control.

To achieve *unity of command* each person must know to whom he reports and who reports to him. He should not be expected to report to

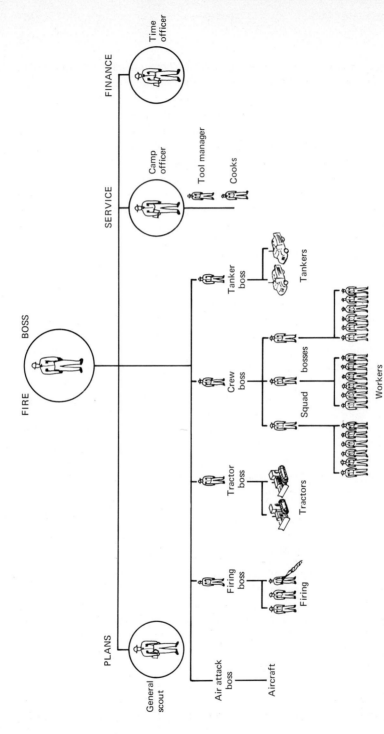

Figure 12.7 Organization of a multiple-crew fire. (From Fireman's Handbook, *U.S. Forest Service.*)

more than one superior. He must have clearly defined responsibility. He must have the specific authority needed to enable him to discharge that responsibility. If each of these things is observed, the first major requirement of good organization has been met.

A second important principle is to avoid exceeding the *span of control.* There is a practical limit to the number of men or organization units one person can direct successfully. A squad leader, a foreman, a sector boss, a division boss, and always the fire boss must not have more men, machines, or special units working under his immediate direction than he can properly supervise. Exceeding the span of control is a common failure. When a fire escapes control and reaches threatening proportions, the fire boss too often tries to carry on with a constantly augmented force of men and machines without taking time to reorganize properly. Reasonable limits to the span of control for the above positions based on much experience by the U.S. Forest Service are about as follows: (1) For the straw boss or squad leader, not over ten men if the men are working in close formation and particularly if inexperienced or not over five or six men if on specialist jobs or if widely scattered; (2) for the crew boss or foreman, not more than four straw bosses or squad leaders; (3) for the sector boss, not more than three foreman units, though the number may go to four before reorganizing; (4) for the division boss, not more than three sector bosses; (5) for the fire boss, rarely more than two fully active divisions.

Time and distance also enter into these relationships. A crew foreman can readily supervise three squads of men through their leaders or straw bosses if they are working close together. If distributed over a mile of line up a steep mountainside, he may be unable to give adequate supervision unless he has continuous radio communication with them. Authority to make decisions must be close to the work on the ground. It needs to be delegated to accomplish this. This is the purpose of sectors and divisions on a fire. If the officer in charge of a sector or division cannot be reached quickly because of distance or lack of communication when emergency decisions are required, authority to make such decisions must be further delegated or some reorganization effected to ensure against critical delay. A closely related principle is that of avoiding conflict between the various supporting functions in a large fire organization. This calls for use of specialists as well as delegation of responsibility by the fire boss. This is discussed in the section which follows.

Organization by Functions

In the progression discussed, only the supervision and management of forces directly engaged in controlling the fire were considered. In order to get men and equipment to the fire and to maintain them on the job, transportation, supplies, and various services must also be carefully organized and properly scheduled. A further important function is intelligence or making sure that the fire boss can keep constantly informed on what is happening on all parts of the fire. This function becomes highly important as the fire increases beyond the point where the fire boss can personally observe the behavior of the whole fire and the progress of the control work.

Through studies of the organization requirements of fire suppression, five broad groupings of the essential functions have been recognized. These are termed (1) the command function, (2) the line function, (3) the plans function, (4) the service function, and (5) the finance function.

On small fires, all are performed by the fire boss with help from the dispatcher at the nearby headquarters from which action is initiated. If the fire is controlled by the initial attack force, the organization already functioning by virtue of presuppression plans is sufficient. But if regular forces are insufficient and additional men and equipment must be mobilized, special attention to each function will be needed at the scene of the fire.

Figure 12.8 *A.* Line boss communicating through air-net radio to scout in helicopter. *B.* Sector boss obtaining information by radio from line boss on a dangerous spot fire. This will be the basis for instructions to crew foreman, who is standing by. *(U.S. Forest Service photos.)*

The Command Function The command function, as previously described, must remain clear-cut. There must be only one fire boss and the line of authority must be clear, as outlined under unity of command. It is not regarded as good practice to provide an alternate to the fire boss. The responsibility should be his until he is relieved. However, he may be given assistants as necessary to keep his duties within manageable proportions.

The Line Function The line function, involving organization of work on the fire line, has been described because it is inseparable from the delegation of authority necessary for the functioning of straw bosses, crew bosses, sector bosses, and division bosses under a fire boss. However, a special line boss is often assigned to assist the fire boss on large fires, particularly in rugged terrain where it is not feasible for the fire boss to participate directly in coordinating the construction of fire control line (Figure 12.8*A*). It is the line boss's job to supervise the execution of the suppression plan adopted by the fire boss. He acts as coordinator between divisions and, where no divisions have been established, may act as coordinator between sectors in place of a division boss. This position is highly valued by some fire bosses but should be used with caution. The authority delegated by the fire boss is not as clear-cut as in other functions. Consequently, an active and capable man acting as line boss has a tendency to supplant the fire boss as the real director of control line operations. This is not always undesirable if it is understood and accepted in advance, but it does tend to violate unity of command.

The Plans Function   The plans function is a continuing responsibility of the fire boss. His responsibility for making plans cannot be delegated, but the task of gathering the necessary information for current planning can be delegated in varying degrees. This can be done effectively by employing scouts equipped with radios to report fire behavior and the progress of the control effort.

The fire boss may need specialized service, such as an overnight infrared photo map of the fire area, an observer to scout the fire from the air, an air-service coordinating officer, or an aerial photo interpreter. As such services increase it may become desirable to assign a maps and records officer to assemble all information in usable form and to calculate the fire line and the manpower required to meet a desired time schedule. Special arrangements for supplemental scouting of every actively spreading fire are nearly always needed. Other specialized provisions for planning and intelligence are needed only on large or complex fires.

The Service Function   The service function is essential on all fires and becomes increasingly complex when heavy, mechanized equipment is used in quantity. For fires controlled by initial attack forces or otherwise controlled within a single work shift, this function is provided by the supporting organization largely through the dispatcher. As soon as more than one shift is involved and whenever outside equipment has to be utilized and fire fighters have to be recruited for the job, the service function has to be organized at the fire.

This function consists of keeping time correctly for men and equipment hired, of establishing and operating a fire camp to provide meals and beds close to the work, of providing for communication on the fire and to outside headquarters, of maintaining and reconditioning hand tools and small equipment being used, and of servicing the mechanized equipment assigned to the fire. To manage this variety of functions, the fire boss needs help at an early stage. As soon as it is apparent that one or more fire camps need to be established, camp bosses are also essential (Figure 12.9). To the camp boss is delegated the responsibility of ordering and receiving equipment and supplies, of organizing the camp, and of supervising kitchen and cooking arrangements for his unit. Unless such duties are so delegated, the fire boss is soon so burdened with the details of such services that his efforts are diverted from the main task of controlling the fire. To simplify these arrangements, a special team of men is at times trained for regular assignment to fires to organize these functions. Where fire-fighting crews need to be fed only a few meals, lunches or hot meals may be brought in from outside sources in preference to establishing messing arrangements. Other variations occur.

The Finance Function   Avoidance of financial tangles under the stress of the emergency created by a runaway fire becomes more and more difficult with increasing involvement of outside men and equipment. Here too the fire boss soon needs help. A timekeeper may be needed as

Figure 12.9 Base camp for fire fighters in process of being organized for full service function. Relieved crews arriving for supper and to be checked in by the timekeeper. *(U.S. Forest Service photo.)*

soon as outside labor is brought in. When a camp boss is designated, he may supervise timekeeping for both men and equipment along with his other duties so long as all are operating from his camp. But usually by the time a fire reaches the sector stage a special finance section headed by a qualified finance officer is needed. It is the duty of the finance officer to make sure that all time slips, purchase vouchers, and so forth are correct and properly drawn and that the terms of cooperative agreements made before the fire are properly observed. He assumes responsibility for handling claims for personal injury and damage to property, and his section provides the fiscal advice needed by the fire boss in his campaign to bring about final control of the fire without exorbitant expenditure. The finance officer arranges for paying off personnel when required and may be an authorized paymaster.

The officers assigned to supervisory and other special functions are often referred to as *the fire overhead.* Too much overhead is almost as great a handicap to good organization as too little. Information and instructions go through too many hands and become garbled. Overhead with too little to do get in the way and hold up the work. If anxious to contribute fully to the fire control job beyond the light duties assigned, they tend to exceed their assigned authority and to encroach on the fire bosses' responsibility. This causes confusion and may affect the morale of all the fire-fighting force.

The organization requirements have been discussed as they develop on the ground. The addition of overhead should follow closely. In other words, the organization on any fire should be built from the ground up, not from the top down.

Demobilization and Mop-up

Typically the progressive stages in successful control of a fire are in the following sequence. First, the rate of spread of the fire and its heat production are slowed down, usually by work on the head and threatening hot spots. On large fires, this may be true only on the flanks. Then a control line (including existing barriers or breaks) is completed around the perimeter. The fire is then said to be corralled, in Western terminology. Then the lines are burned out by clean burning or backfiring or the fire burns up to them and is held from crossing into new fuels. At this point the fire is considered to be controlled. But control of a fire means only that its spread is confined and that existing forces should be able to prevent any further breakover into new fuels under existing conditions. The further work necessary to make the fire entirely safe or to completely extinguish all fire is referred to as mop-up.

On small fires, mop-up continues until the fire is entirely out. On large fires, such work may be concentrated on the zone near the perimeter and mop-up may be regarded as complete considerably in advance of the time the last deep-burning fuels well inside have finally burned out.

In most forest types, ground fires in deep duff, roots, half-buried rotten wood, and mucky soil will persist after the faster-burning fuels have been consumed. This smoldering fire may look safe to the uninitiated but continues to be a threat until it is completely extinguished or burns out. The process of preventing the burned area from starting any new fire that can escape into unburned areas requires persistent and painstaking work. In dense coniferous types, it may require 50 to 80 percent of the total suppression expenditure. The average for all forest types is approximately 50 percent.

To carry out mop-up work effectively, the fire-fighting forces need to be reorganized and the force can usually be drastically reduced. Because the fight to control the fire has been won, there is a natural human tendency to relax and to accept less aggressive and systematic methods in completing mop-up than was expected in the control operations.

From the point of view of the cost of fire fighting, much research is needed to develop faster and more efficient methods of completing this part of the job safely. Closer supervision of men is needed and much smaller crews become more efficient. Experienced straw bosses and foremen are important to a thorough job. It is often good practice to bring in fresh crews to carry on this work because of the natural let-down felt by fire fighters who helped to bring the fire under control.

Conventional techniques consist of feeling for smoldering fire with the hands, digging it out, mixing it with mineral soil, puddling it with water, soaking and stirring by means of backpack or power pumps, and work with hand tools (Figure 12.10A and B). On the start, patrol beats around the fire's perimeter are often set up with men singly or in pairs given responsibility for guarding against any flareups or undiscovered spot fires on a specified piece of the line. As long as burning conditions remain highly dangerous, this is worthwhile. But it is usually more efficient to organize all mop-up men into small crews to work systematically to remove all threats close to the control line and then at increasing depth inside the burn.

On a severe hot burn, there is so little unburned fuel remaining that little mop-up work is required after control of the fire's perimeter is established. On burns in heavy virgin stands of green timber or heavy undergrowth where crowning did not occur, a large amount of unburned fuel commonly remains inside the burn after the fire has gone through. It tends to dry out and to become more flammable after the fire. In such

Figure 12.10 Mop-up work in progress. *A.* Early stage of mop-up
to cool down burning material near fire edge. *B.* Last stages of
mop-up, feeling with hands to locate and extinguish remaining
spots of smoldering fire. *(U.S. Forest Service photos.)*

cases reburns often occur, and slow, tedious work on mop-up is the
necessary price that has to be paid to make sure that the suppression
expenditure for control is not lost.

Chapter 13

Fire Control Equipment
and Supplies

In Chapter 12 emphasis was placed on principles and methods of fire fighting. All methods depend for their effectiveness on the performance of men with equipment. Both are indispensible. Some kind of equipment is always necessary even if no more than a wet burlap sack, a pine branch, or a bucket. From such a premise it is easy for an equipment specialist to make a convincing showing that equipment alone determines the success of the fire-fighting job. A fire training expert can make an equally convincing case in support of the thesis that good training and organization are the primary elements, with equipment incidental. Both specialists are partially correct. Mechanized equipment can replace men in doing physical work but always requires intelligent direction and some degree of know-how to perform an assigned task. Hand tools always demand manual skill for efficient operation. Throughout this chapter, performance attributed to any equipment assumes the operator is trained for his part of the job and is meeting the requirements for successful operation of that particular equipment.

GENERAL REQUIREMENTS

The fire triangle described in Chapter 12 gives special significance to the physical jobs for which fire tools are employed. For combustion to proceed, fuel, oxygen, and a temperature above the kindling point must combine and be maintained. It is the fire fighter's job to break up this combination, which he does by the aid of tools. He removes fuel to separate it from sources of heat, and so to limit or localize the burning process, or he works at limiting the available oxygen or at reducing the temperature of the burning fuels below the kindling point. All fire-fighting tools might be classified according to which of these three functions they facilitate most. The most efficient serve more than one function. Digging, cutting, and scraping tools employed in building fire line are devoted almost entirely to removing fuels from exposure to kindling temperatures. Flappers and beaters of various kinds depend chiefly for their effect on the temporary exclusion of oxygen, though they function also to some extent in dissipating heat. Tools used for applying dirt or sand to a fire function in the same way, but with a more pronounced dual effect in lowering temperatures of the burning fuel. Equipment used to apply water carries out a truly dual function in excluding oxygen and in rapidly lowering the temperature of the burning fuel. Backfiring equipment performs the function of eliminating fuels from the path of the main fire, just as cutting and digging tools do, but it adds to the heat energy being released. All mechanized equipment performs one or more of these functions. The only difference is in the method of performance and in the replacement of manpower by motor power.

BASIC CONSIDERATIONS IN CHOOSING FOREST FIRE EQUIPMENT

All fire equipment, whether powered or hand operated, is subject to the same basic criteria of suitability for the job. Since the fire-fighting job varies, there is considerable variation in the relative importance of each criterion in a particular environment. So there is a valid basis for variation in the equipment chosen. Each of the following criteria is important in all fire equipment and illustrates the unity of equipment problems in forest fire control.

Effectiveness

This is the capability of the equipment to accomplish a desired task to an acceptable standard. The emphasis is on the quality of the result. Mechanized earth-moving equipment, for example, is rated as ineffective if it cannot produce acceptable fire control line.

Efficiency or Productivity

This is often the deciding factor. Whether hand- or motor-driven, an item of equipment should permit or produce a maximum amount of effective work of a given kind with a minimum energy requirement. In hand tools this is strongly influenced by the experience and training of the individual worker. The emphasis is on quantity and on rate of production to a standard of effectiveness set by the preceding factor. Production per unit of energy expended is important and may become decisive in choosing mechanized equipment.

Versatility

Closely related to productivity, but often in conflict with it, is the need for versatility. A machine or hand tool may be very effective or very productive and efficient but sharply limited in the number of tasks it can perform. A choice or compromise often has to be made between productivity and versatility, since it is frequently not possible to combine both to a satisfactory degree in the same item. The wider the range of use of a specific piece of equipment, the better. The number of different items that can be stocked and brought to a fire in the first attack is often severely limited, yet these tools must do a widely variable job. Firemen trained and equipped to control small fires in backcountry, often referred to as smokechasers, must be prepared to carry their equipment on foot. This limits their hand tools to one or two general-purpose tools. A choice of more than one size or kind of plow or tanker can seldom be available for use on a particular fire or even on different fires in the same protection unit. In some situations, much of the mechanized equipment is too costly to hold for fire suppression use only. But varying degrees of dual use can ensure its availability. This too places a premium on versatility.

Portability

It is necessary to transport equipment speedily to fires, which frequently occur in areas of difficult access. It is also necessary to transport equipment without exhausting the fire fighters before they reach the fire. A major part of equipment development work has been devoted to solving transportation problems by paring down weight, by unit packaging, and by devising better means of transport. This applies to smoke-chaser packs as well as to truck-carried tractor-plow units and fire pumps. Aircraft have made their greatest contribution in helping to solve the problem of speedy transport. By parachute delivery, equipment, food, and men can be placed on a backcountry fire hours or even days ahead of surface transport. But parachute delivery is only one-way transportation. Often the return of equipment to the nearest base remains a difficult problem, and parachute delivery by its nature imposes some rather stringent limitations on weight and bulk. If properly packaged, a power saw or portable power pump can be readily delivered to the scene of a fire by parachute, but not a bulldozer, a tank truck, or a conventional fire-line plow. Helicopters can solve the problems of return transportation of parachute cargo, but they do not relieve limitations on bulk and weight. It is axiomatic that the heavier the piece of equipment, the slower and more expensive it is to move and the more limitations are imposed by existing roads, bridges, and airplane capacities. Yet heavy equipment is frequently very effective on a large fire.

Durability

Fire equipment must be rugged and not prone to break down when most needed. This applies especially to power equipment, where the whole strategy and plan of control may depend on a very few pieces of equipment and sometimes only one. A long useful life is also important.

Simplicity

A tool or machine should be easy to understand, simple to operate, and have the fewest possible parts. Most fire fighting is done under emergency conditions by men with limited equipment experience—at least on fires, and the fire rather than the equipment should be the focus of attention. As a generality, the more specialized the piece of equipment, the more skill and training it takes to operate it to full advantage. This certainly applies to complex machinery, and the availability of skilled operators may be a major limiting factor. Specialized fire equipment is not necessarily complex, but the fact that it is different from common tools, to which most men are accustomed, adds a negative factor of adjustment to its use.

Maintenance and Replaceability

Equipment must be serviced and kept in repair under rough field conditions. Such work is frequently done at night, almost always under pressure, and sometimes by inexperienced men. Minimum maintenance requirements are essential. These need to be easily understood and performed. This requires not only that regular servicing should be simple but that key parts and assemblies can be readily detached and replaced. Since much fire equipment is specialized and not stocked by conventional sources of supply, assurance of the availability of parts and maintenance service often requires advance planning.

Standardization

It is highly desirable to use the same items as widely as possible. This is important both within and between protection organizations. On project fires, large masses of equipment belonging to several fire control organizations are often assembled. The more standardized it is, the more readily it can be pooled, traded, and effectively used and the less time-consuming are the servicing and maintenance problems. Standardization of transportation methods and packaging is likewise important. Critical accessories like plow attachments, trailer hitches, and hose couplings should be standardized among cooperating agencies and can cause no end of difficulty when they are not. Each organization tends to have its own ideas as to desirable equipment and specifications. This is also true of local units within large fire control organizations. Variations to meet differences in local needs are desirable and make for progress, but they should not be carried to the point where they seriously limit interchange of equipment in emergencies.

Economy

Questions of economy are of major importance in every aspect of equipment development and use. The kind, quantity, and application of equipment must constantly be balanced against relative and total cost as well as effectiveness. Equipment frequently offers a means of making fire control dollars go farther; at other times it may become an extravagence and a burden. No control organization can operate on the basis that cost is no consideration, nor can it afford to be without efficient equipment. In the long run, equipment must pay off in savings in suppression costs and in reduced damages.

The above criteria for selection of fire equipment should constantly be kept in mind. They apply to all fire equipment and provide the guidelines for acquisition and development of the equipment needed in each situation.

HAND TOOLS IN FOREST FIRE FIGHTING

Trained men with hand tools have been the traditional forest fire-fighting force since organized forest fire control began. With the passage of time and at an accelerated pace since 1930, mechanized equipment has replaced manpower in building fire line, in applying water, and in supplying fast transportation. This could easily lead to the assumption that men with hand tools are now outdated in forest fire control. This is far from true. Though plows and bulldozers build most of the fire line around the perimeter of accessible large fires and aerial transportation aids strongly in delivering men and equipment to backcountry fires, men with hand tools, including smoke jumpers, still make the initial attack on most fires and are responsible for keeping a high percentage of small fires small. Every fire starts as a small fire and can be controlled directly by one or a few men with hand tools if they can attack it before it becomes too hot to be controlled by such means. The many small fires controlled more or less routinely in this way may properly be regarded as evidence of the successful functioning of the presuppression organization.

A great variety of hand tools, particularly digging and cutting tools, have been pressed into service in fire control operations. However, only a few have found a place as standard fire equipment among North American forest fire agencies. Some are standard commercial items developed for nonfire purposes; some are adaptations of commercial items, and some have been developed specifically for fire control use. Those used most commonly are illustrated in Figure 13.1*A* and *B*. A brief description of each tool and of its use follows, referenced to its number in the figure.

Ax (1, 2, 3)   There are many types, sizes, and weights of axes, which are the prime hand-operated cutting tool of the forest. The double-bitted $3^{1}/_{2}$-pound swamping ax (1) is the most common and is standard equipment throughout the western United States. Single-bitted axes, or poleaxes (3), are common in the East. They are used for the same general purposes but can also be used to drive wedges, etc. Lighter axes, like the $2^{1}/_{2}$-pound double-bitted ax (2) or poleaxes of about the same weight, are widely used around camp, for scouting, and for marking fire line location. The ax is a universal item yet is essentially a one-purpose tool. All it will do is cut.

Pulaski Tool (4)   The Pulaski successfully combines a cutting with a digging tool which makes it highly versatile. It weighs approximately 5 pounds with a $3^{1}/_{2}$-pound head and is specifically designed for fire use. It was first developed by Ranger Pulaski who won fame in the 1910 fires in northern Idaho. He used it first as a dual-purpose tool carried in a scabbard on his saddle horse. Later it found similar use in cars and pickups to provide the driver with means of controlling a small fire without first returning to his base to obtain fire tools or help. However, it did not come into common interregional use until it became a well-balanced, high quality tool in the hands of a manufacturer. It is often carried by foremen, scouts, and line locators on going fires and by some members of crews involved in one of the progressive methods of constructing fire line (Figure 13.1*C*).

Shovel (5, 6)   If an experienced Western fire fighter had to select just one piece of equipment, he would probably choose a shovel.

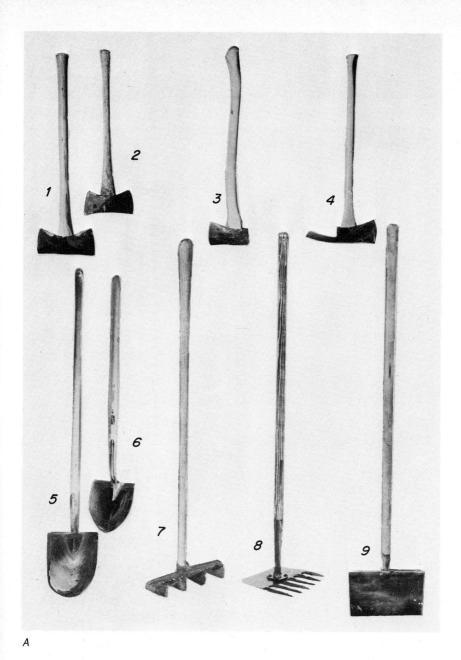

A

Figure 13.1 *A and B.* Common hand tools used in firefighting. *(Photos from U.S. Forest Service, Georgia Forestry Commission, Western Fire Equipment Co., Michigan Conservation Dept.) C.* Closeup view of Pulaski tool digging fire line. *(U.S. Forest Service photo.) D.* Closeup view of shovel in use to cool down a spot fire. *(U.S. Forest Service photo.)*

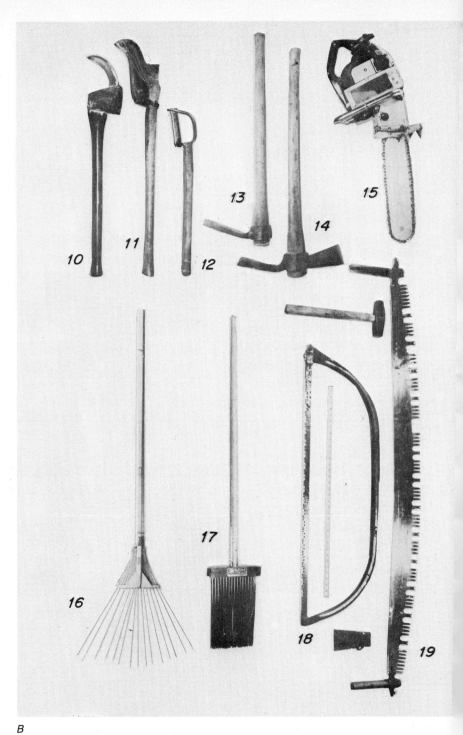

C

D

Edge-sharpened near the point, well-balanced, and strongly made, a shovel is a most versatile, simple, and durable tool, almost universally used. It can be used to dig, scrape, throw dirt, and cut to some extent. When scraping and cutting become important uses, the sharpened edge may be carried well up on one or both sides. It is usually not, however, used as a primary line-construction tool but more commonly as a supplement to other digging and cutting tools. It is much used and is particularly effective in throwing dirt to check a running fire or in digging out or burying burning material. There are many kinds and sizes of shovels, but the round-point, long-handled type is the most common. Item 6 (the successor to the so-called lady shovel) is specifically designed for fire use and is the lightest yet most effective shovel for all-around use (Figure 13.1*D*).

Council Rake, or Rich Tool (7)   Essentially, this tool consists of four heavy mowing-machine sickle-bar blades riveted to a 1-inch piece of angle iron which is attached to a handle. This tool is highly efficient for trenching work in light brush, duff, and small roots and can be used for cutting, digging, or raking. It is the most widely used hand tool for fire suppression in Eastern and Southern states. The Rich tool is the original of the type and somewhat heavier than the Council tool. Both are commonly called fire rakes.

Various types of common rakes, usually of the heavier or asphalt type, have been used in the past in needle and leaf types. Items 7 and 8 will do anything a common rake can do without clogging and are more efficient.

McLeod or Cortic Tool (8)   This is a combination heavy-duty rake and hoe for cutting matted litter and duff and clearing loose surface materials. It needs to be supplemented in rocky soils or brushy cover. The tool is specifically designed for fire work. It has long been a standard tool in California but has found increasing use throughout the ponderosa pine types. In Australia it has proved highly useful in creating fire line in pine plantations.

Swatter, or Flap (9)   This tool consists of a piece of heavy belting about 15 inches long and 12 inches wide mounted with a long handle. It is effective and widely used in beating out (smothering) fires in grass and similar light fuels.

Brush Cutter (10, Little Giant Tool; 11, Brush Hook; 12, Sandveg Tool)   There are various types of brush cutters, of which three are illustrated. They are strictly single-purpose cutting tools designed to cut smaller stems than can be efficiently handled with an ax. Power-driven brush cutters have been designed for fire use, but they are not yet commonly used in fire suppression.

Grub Hoe (13) and Mattock (14)   There are many variations of these ancient tools. They are effective in fire-line digging and about the last word in durability, simplicity, and economy. The grub hoe is a straight digging tool. With a wider, shorter, and lighter blade, it is called a hazel hoe. The mattock has a narrow but thick cutting blade on the back good for roots, and its weight (5 to 7 pounds) makes it effective (but fatiguing to use) in heavy duff and rooty ground.

Broom Rake (16, 17)   These items have been developed to provide a light but effective tool for use in light litter, leaf, and needle fuels. The broom rake (16), which can be readily adjusted for width and stiffness of the teeth, is particularly effective.

Saws (15, 18, 19)   The woodsman's crosscut log saw (19), of which there are many types and sizes for felling and bucking, has been traditionally used for the single purpose of cutting the larger tree stems. Hammer and wedge are employed to relieve pinching or binding in the cut. Special light, flexible saws have also been developed and used in the West for smokechasing on foot. The Swedish bucksaw (18), widely used in the northern forests of the Lake states and eastern Canada, has become familiar in all regions of the United States. It is rapid and effective for stems up to about 12 inches. The power chain saw (15), of which there are numerous makes, sizes, and types, has revolutionized felling and bucking in the woods and has replaced all hand saws on large operations. Very lightweight models have also entered the category of hand tools by being integrated into the line-building technique of organized crews. They offer tremendous advantage in speed and stamina in line-construction or mop-up work where much timber must be felled or bucked. Nevertheless, considerable dependence must still be placed on hand saws.

Backfiring Equipment   A variety of equipment is used for backfiring, much of which is done as a part of control-line building. Some common types are shown in Figure 13.2. Part *A* shows types fired by gas or fuel oil. The propane torch (1) carried on the back burns liquid gas, produces a very hot flame, and can be lighted with a match with no preheating. It is widely used. A disadvantage is that it must be filled from heavy-pressure cylinder tanks which are difficult to transport and use in the field. Several types of back-carried gasoline or gasoline-kerosene torches operating on the principle of the common plumber's blowtorch

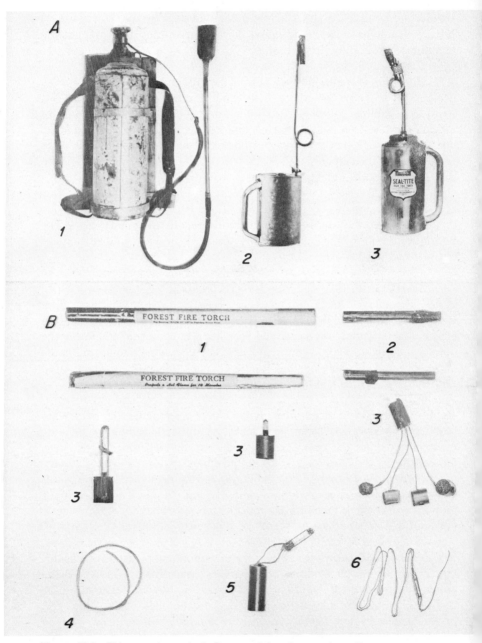

Figure 13.2 Firing equipment. *A.* Gas or oil-burning torches. *B.* Fusees and grenades. *(Photos from U.S. Forest Service, Western Fire Equipment Co., R. L. Fenner.)*

have been used in the past. They must be preheated before use but are easier to supply with fuel than the liquid-gas torches. Backpack flame-throwers have been employed to some extent in forest fire fighting, but safety hazards have limited their use.

There are a number of wick or drip torches (2, 3) in general use. Their essential features are a fuel-oil supply tank and a tube with a wick or drip nozzle in the end that can be lighted. They lack the heat of the gas torches but are safe, economical, and easy to use and will readily ignite litter fuels if they are dry enough to carry fire. They are generally used throughout the South.

Part *B* of Figure 13.2 shows backfiring equipment fired by solid fuels of the fireworks variety. Item 1 is an adaptation of the familiar railroad and highway fusee. It burns for 10 minutes and has a metal ferrule, so that the torch can be stuck on the end of a pole to give a long handle. Item 2 is a pocket-sized fusee, burns 3 minutes, and is specially designed to give heat rather than light, as do the common fusees.

There is at times need for ignition equipment to start fires at some distance from a control line, in inaccessible locations, or simultaneously over an area in strips or other patterns. Ignition grenades (3) are designed to be thrown or cast with a slingshot. The item on the left has a 15-second fuse ignited by jerking off the tip cover. It burns about a minute, emitting flames 2000°F plus. The center item is similar but with a shorter fuse. The grenades in the right-hand group are separately ignited by jerking out of the binder holding the tips together. Fuses (4) are used rapidly to carry fire from one ignition grenade to another. The fuse does not ignite fuels along the way, however. Item 5 is an electric ignition grenade. When wire-connected, a series of them can be set off simultaneously by a blasting machine. Firing as a group is necessary in area ignition in which the objective is to fire a strip or other area simultaneously. Item 6 is an electric ignition cap of the type inserted in item 5. It can be used simultaneously to fire fused ignition grenades.

Backpack Pumps   The simplest and most portable and maneuverable pumping outfit—for its size—is the common backpack pump widely used by practically all fire control organizations. It consists of a 4- to 5-gallon tank or collapsible sack carried on the back, a short length of hose, a sliding-action hand-operated pump, and a nozzle adjustable to a straight stream or spray (Figure 13.3). It is commonly carried on pickups and trucks with hand tools or power-pumping equipment. Operated by a skilled man, it is the most efficient, flexible, and economical of all pumping equipment per gallon of water used. Since the quantity of water carried is obviously limited and must often be carried considerable distances, there

A

B

Figure 13.3 Collapsible and tank-type backpack pumps. *(U.S. Forest Service photo.)*

is a premium on making it go as far as possible. Wetting agents, which will be discussed later, have proved useful in this respect. Backpack pumps are most useful in extinguishing flames in light fuels, in cooling down hot spots, in extinguishing spot fires, and in mop-up operations. They seldom enter into the operation of building a fire line, but are excellent for direct attack on small fires.

Influence of Fuel Types on Choice of Hand Tools

As discussed in Chapter 4, the wild lands of North America have a diversity of cover types, fuel types, and terrain. This has led to a similar diversity of preferred fire-fighting equipment in the various forest regions. Tradition and prejudice have played a part in these preferences, yet they are for the most part soundly based on the differences in the physical task of creating a fire line.

In the Douglas-fir forests of the Northwest, for example, the creation of a fire line usually involves heavy swamping of down material and reproduction and the removal of a deep layer of compacted duff. Often it must be accompanied by extensive felling of dead snags 3 to 5 feet in diameter. This places a heavy premium on such woodsman's tools as heavy power saws, two-man crosscut saws, and sharp axes. Digging tools such as hazel hoes, mattocks, and Pulaski tools rather than raking or scraping tools also get preference. Shovels are used to complete the fire line but play a secondary role until a preliminary fire line has been constructed.

In the lodgepole pine type of the Rocky Mountains, stems are smaller and duff is thinner, so swamping is lighter except in stagnated reproduction. But terrain is usually more rocky. The very light power saws become effective here. One-man saws, including the Swedish bucksaw, also give good efficiency per man hour with the smaller sizes of down material, so these are still used. The Pulaski tool is preferred as a hand tool over the hazel hoe, and the shovel finds increased use as a scraping tool in creating the fire line.

In the ponderosa pine type, a heavy needle litter is the most common medium in which the fire spreads, with only a thin layer of decayed material next to mineral soil. The most common job in creating a fire line is removal of this litter. It is done most efficiently by scraping tools rather than by heavier digging tools. The McLeod or Cortic tool finds increasing favor for this task. Shovels also play an important role, as in lodgepole, with mattocks and hazel hoes of lower efficiency. The presence of snags, heavy slash, or dense reproduction gives varying but less prominence to the use of axes and saws.

In the chaparral types of the Pacific Coast, the major job is usually that of swamping a wide break through dense thickets of small but tough and unyielding stems of shrub species to create a backfire line. The hand tools used traditionally for this work were brush hooks and short-handled brush cutters of the machete type to supplement the ax. The construction of fire line for indirect attack by hand tools in chaparral, a fuel type where fire moves rapidly, is both slow and arduous, so it was never very effective. This led to very early development and use of power equipment in the form of fire tank trucks and bulldozers and more recently to aerial attack with chemicals. It led, too, to dependence on prepared or natural firebreaks and use of backfiring techniques. For the fire line itself, the McLeod tool and the shovel have preference.

In broadleaf types of the Central states and Appalachians, the most prevalent fuel consists of hardwood leaves. Since they are a light fuel not attached to the ground and the associated ground cover usually consists of light brush, briars, and other stems, much more readily cut than in the semiarid types of the West, much lighter tools give best efficiency. The Council tool or the Rich tool are the most distinctive and most universally useful in building fire line. Long-handled fire rakes have largely been replaced by the broom rake. It is fast and effective where leaf litter only has to be cleared. Backpack-carried, engine-powered blowers are also coming into use for this purpose.

In the southern pine types the most common surface fuels are a fine grass and a heavy needle cast. This material over coarse sand decays slowly, causing a rapid accumulation of a flammable cover commonly referred to as "rough." After a few years' accumulation, it will support a hot, fast-moving fire. The hand tools used in hardwood types become less efficient, and tools such as the McLeod tool used in the ponderosa pine type of the West have not found favor. Chief dependence is placed on plowing breaks in advance of the fire and burning out for indirect attack and on the use of heavy swatters with shovels and Council rakes as supplemental tools in direct attack.

Grass types are involved in forest fires nationwide, as described in Chapter 4. They vary a great deal in the problem they present, depending on the density and accumulation of dead grass and the fuels with which they are associated. Direct attack by hand tools is usually by beaters or by backpack pumps. As described in Chapter 12, a successful method of direct attack on grass fires in the Nebraska Sand Hills by use of the rotary crew method to throw sand was developed in the 1930s. However, fire moves rapidly through dry grass and always places men on foot with hand tools at a disadvantage. Consequently, though fire intensity and duration are much below that of heavier fuels, mechanized equipment is usually substituted. Fast-moving plows or fire tank trucks are often used and heavy reliance is placed on backfiring from plow lines or natural or artificial breaks.

Relation of Crew Organization to Choice of Hand Tools

In the individual assignment method, the fire perimeter is divided among the men available and each man or team of two men is assigned a specific portion or patrol beat for which he or the team is solely responsible. This immediately places a premium on use of versatile or general-purpose tools, though individual freedom of action and a static area do permit the use of any specialized reserve tools that can be assigned to the beat. Usually specialized work such as snag felling and heavy swamping has been done or is not needed, and a preliminary fire control line may have been constructed. Such things usually simplify the problem of properly equipping the men. However, it is inherent in the method that self-sufficiency of one or two men requires more tools per man for efficient performance than other methods. Typically, in a Western region, a shovel, a Pulaski tool, and a backpack pump would be the minimum needed on each beat.

The man-passing-man fire crew organization is quite flexible, so minor disproportions between cutting, digging, and scraping tools on the job at hand are not so apparent. Nevertheless, they do slow up progress if not corrected. A good foreman sees to it that there are enough men with general-purpose tools that they can function in more than one capacity as needed. He may personally carry along an extra tool to be put into action as needed.

Smooth functioning of the progressive methods of building fire-line demands careful selection of tools. If conditions are quite uniform along the course of the projected fire line, proper selection on the start of cutting, digging, and scraping tools, in the correct proportion of each, will suffice. However, it is usual to encounter considerable variation in the kind of work to be done as the crew proceeds. Adjustments are made mostly by shifting men from cutting, digging, or scraping to the tasks that are slowing up progress. For example, men with Pulaski tools may be shifted from cutting to digging or vice versa. Usually the foreman also has one or two extra tools which he exchanges with crew members when reinforcement in some part of the task is needed. For example, if the fire line is being poorly completed, the addition of a shovel at the expense of a hazel hoe or a Pulaski tool may correct the situation. Similarly, a sharp ax to reinforce the cutting tools ahead at the expense of a digging or scraping tool may speed up progress, which may have been slowed by a heavier job of swamping out. Naturally the fewer adjustments needed, the more efficient the operation. Though there is somewhat less premium on general-purpose tools than in the station or squad method of crew organization, a quota of such tools provides the essential flexibility.

Devices to Ensure Effective Use of Fire Equipment

From the beginning of organized fire control, various devices and policies have been used to ensure that the right kinds and quantities of fire-fighting tools in good condition for fire-fighting use would be available where and when needed.

Perhaps the first of these is the rather common practice among most fire-fighting organizations of marking fire-fighting tools to distinguish them from equipment maintained for other purposes. This practice of distinctive marking carries with it the message "for fire-fighting use only." This helps to enforce rules against use of such equipment for other purposes which might result in loss and in poor state of usability when emergency fire needs arise. Such marking consists typically of a red paint band of specified width, applied around the handle of an ax next to the head, for example, and on specified parts of each other item of equipment. Such paint markings are usually distinctive for each cooperating fire agency and serve as a means of sorting out equipment where tools from more than one organization are used on a single fire.

A second device of equal prevalence and importance is the segregation of fire tools. Segregation provides more specifically against misuse or misplacement of fire tools and is reinforced by the practice of distinctive markings. But segregation usually goes much further in its purpose. Usually a standard list of the number and kinds of tools most commonly needed by different-sized crews is adopted. These sets of tools for different-sized crew units are set aside and plainly identified. When this is done, all equipment for a ten-man crew, for example, can be loaded out quickly without danger of important omissions or excesses (Figure 13.4). Such segregation by fire crew units is often carried further by assembling tools in boxes, so that the box is moved as a unit. It can then accompany a forest work crew or be placed in a strategic location to outfit volunteer crews. The advantages of such assembled tool units for emergency fire use are obvious and need little emphasis. Certain disadvantages must also be recognized and certain precautions need to be observed. Standard tool outfits must be based on average needs and, in country of varied conditions and cover, cannot provide properly for all needs. So they often need to be supplemented. The inexperienced person is likely to accept such outfits as complete and may allow the ready-made assembly to stifle his own initiative in selecting the best tools for the job at hand. The practice of including special and extra tools as a part of the outfit, to allow more selection on the job, helps in this respect but cannot be carried very far or the tool assembly becomes too heavy and cumbersome to be consistent with its purpose.

The next step in making sure that sharp and well-maintained tools of the right kind and quantities will be quickly available for fire use where and when needed is the strategic placement and distribution of fire equipment stocks in relation to transportation and manpower. Much thought and planning have gone into the question of how much fire

Figure 13.4 Western hand-tool and equipment packaging. *(U.S. Forest Service photos.) A.* Smokechaser pack. Individual packs like this are often used to equip crews up to about ten men. Packs are numbered in sequences; for example, a five-man crew is outfitted by taking packs 1 to 5. *B.* Twenty-five-man outfit complete with beds and mess equipment. Can be dropped by parachute or hauled by truck. With equipment packaged like this, large crews can be outfitted in a few minutes.

equipment ought to be maintained at various strategic points in a protection unit, and whether most of the equipment ought to be held at a central point or widely dispersed at many points throughout the unit. No categorical answer can serve, since the best arrangement varies with the source of manpower, kind and location of transportation, the ability to get equipment quickly from outside, etc. Where local resident cooperators are depended on to take first action on fires, a rather special situation exists, and the warden fire tool box (or fire cache) becomes a distinctive and essential feature (Figure 13.5). Where the warden assembles and leads the fire crew, the tool assembly at his residence is in the right location for best service. In all fire fighting there are usually two needs to be taken account of in distributing fire equipment. The first is equipment to provide for first attack on all fires, and the second is equipment to provide properly for reinforcement or follow-up crews for the large fire. The former calls for considerable dissemination of fire tools for small crews; the latter permits more centralization of stocks for large crews that must usually be brought from longer distances.

In general, a few guidelines can be drawn.

1   Fire crews should, if possible, start out fully equipped.
2   Tools need to be at or close to the source of manpower for all first attack action.
3   Failing either of these, tools must be available en route or on

Figure 13.5   Warden fire-tool box, containing fire tools for small local crew, being inspected by ranger and fire warden. *(U.S. Forest Service photo.)*

transportation that is capable of delivering them at the fire ahead of the crew.

4 Excessive dissemination of tools reduces the ability to mobilize them for a single major fire.

5 Too much centralization of equipment induces delays in getting on the job and divides responsibility.

These guides developed in relation to hand tools are also significant and applicable in relation to mechanized equipment.

Skill in Use of Tools

Men with tools are the essential combination, as stated at the beginning of this discussion of fire equipment. Since work with hand tools is properly a vocational activity, it is easy for the forester to neglect the importance of good hand tools and of skill in using them. Each hand tool requires a particular kind of coordination and each can produce at least twice as much per unit of energy expended if skill is developed in using it. Sports of various kinds supply close analogies. The golfer recognizes that selection of the proper driver and the skill he has developed in using it determines his success. Much of the success of controlling fires at small size has a similar dependence.

The present-day substitution of motor power for manpower in building a fire line by the mile further masks the importance of this subject. In most forest regions in the United States and Canada, use of hand tools to build fire line is progressively being limited to areas inaccessible to mechanized equipment and to the occasions generally when such equipment would arrive too late to make an effective first attack. But most of the time the very first chance to control a fire at small size is when it is only a few yards in diameter. At this point skillful use of hand tools in direct attack may quickly eliminate the need of building fire line or of using mechanized equipment.

In mountainous terrain and primitive areas inaccessible to mechanized equipment, the cost of placing smoke jumpers or other firemen on a small fire is high. Their services pay off only if they employ skilled hand methods. The training of men in fighting fire with hand tools is discussed further in Chapter 15.

Camp and Mess Equipment

Camp and mess equipment is closely associated with hand tools. In Eastern and Southern regions of the United States, camp and mess equipment is rarely used on fires. However, special provisions must often be made to feed fire fighters a few meals at or near the scene of the fire.

Usually this is done by arrangement with local food establishments for sack lunches or hot meals either individually or in bulk. The Georgia Forestry Commission meets this need by moving in a fully equipped trailer kitchen supplemented by one or more trailers equipped as dining cars. Such equipment is held in readiness for use of large fires. Several other state organizations in the United States have similar provisions.

In backcountry and wherever slow-burning ground fuels may require mop-up of several days' duration, special camp and mess equipment becomes important. The increasing emphasis on such equipment becomes noticeable as one moves northward, moves up in elevation, or goes from well-populated, accessible country into the backcountry.

Throughout most of the western United States, fire control tradition has called for continuous operations on a two-shift basis until each fire was completely controlled. This normally means establishing a fire camp and providing food and beds for fire fighters near the scene of the fire until mop-up of the fire is complete. This has made camp and mess equipment an integral part of the fire equipment stocks maintained. Early requirements for moving in camp and mess equipment by packhorse have influenced its design. For the most part it is designed to be of light weight and minimum bulk (with nested cooking pots, stove used as container, etc.). Delivery of such equipment by parachute has similar requirements. Gradually the heavy pots and pans of an earlier period have been replaced by aluminum and other light materials.

In fire equipment stocks, camp and mess equipment is often assembled into convenient units, such as a 10-man outfit or a 25-man unit. Usually such equipment is integrated with the work tools needed by the same number of men, though the mess equipment may be held separately (Figure 13.4).

With delivery by parachute, return of the equipment is often difficult due to inaccessibility of the location or present-day lack of pack animals. Return of equipment often is by helicopter, but costs are high. This has placed a premium on converting as much of the equipment as possible to inexpensive disposable items—paper cups and plates; plastic knives, forks, and spoons; and paper beds instead of wool blankets.

This trend has been accentuated in many areas by the increasing practice of bringing in prepared food either freshly cooked or frozen instead of providing for complete messing facilities in the fire camp. On the average, in all regions of the United States, more use of mechanized equipment in building the fire line and in completing mop-up has reduced the number of men engaged and has shortened the time during which a fire camp is needed. These too are significant factors in the trend.

POWER EQUIPMENT IN FOREST FIRE FIGHTING

The history of forest fire fighting has also been a history of the development of all kinds of equipment to facilitate the job. The evolution of specialized hand tools has already been discussed. The gasoline-powered portable pump was the first power equipment to become identified with forest fire fighting, though miscellaneous mechanized equipment was often pressed into service. The farm plow pulled by horses, then special plows of various kinds pulled by tractors and other vehicles also became an early feature of the mechanization of fire fighting. The bulldozer started a little later but paralleled this development by making it possible to mechanize fire-line building in mountainous terrain and through heavy brush and timber cover. The power pump on wheels in a wide range of vehicles and pump-tank capacities has increasingly held sway as the symbol of forest fire fighting since the 1930s. Each of these will be discussed, as well as the use of aircraft, which has added a third dimension to the attack on fires.

Before continuing, however, it may be helpful to consider the special advantages offered by power-driven equipment and some of the reasons all forest fire agencies have devoted much time and talent to the development and adaptation of such equipment.

More Power   The ability to concentrate more power is perhaps the first in importance. A small tractor with a specially designed plow can replace a 30- to 50-man crew in creating fire line and is, of course, much easier to manage. A power pump greatly increases the radius of action and the striking power of water.

More Speed   The potential ability to speed up all phases of the fire control operation through motorized equipment is a key factor. Though more speed is at times difficult to realize, it is always the promise. Power and speed often conflict. The big tractor and the city-style tank truck may have a powerful striking force but are slow-moving.

More Endurance   Fire fighting usually demands hard work and fast action under emergency conditions. This soon causes fatigue even among men well conditioned to such work. Typically, on a runaway fire, men respond well in meeting emergencies until they tire, then they tend to feel defeated if a repetition of strenuous effort is required. Where and when machines can take over to press on without pause, the chance to stop the fire is greatly improved.

Better Availability   Typically, forest fire agencies have limited forces of men, and most fires in wild-land areas are remote from other sources of labor. Even where advance planning and training have been carried out, there is likely to be considerable delay in making outside sources of labor effective on a fire. But equipment held on a standby basis can be activated quickly by a few men. Often this better availability is decisive in heading off a runaway fire.

Lower Cost   The high cost of labor often makes it cheaper to do work with machines than by manpower. This is true particularly where labor must be held on a standby basis in order to be available for fire fighting.

More Effective Use of Men   As previously discussed, performance by machines depends on man. Often, skilled operators are required. When employed by the forest fire agency, instead of being mere laborers they become an asset in making equipment function more fully in first attack on fires. Wherever motor power can substitute for manpower, better use of the other capabilities of employees becomes feasible.

Overall Aspects   Disadvantages of power equipment will be considered specifically in relation to each type of equipment. However, it is well at this point to consider some of the overall disadvantages of a high degree of mechanization of fire control on wild lands. First of all, mechanization has been devoted mostly to building the fire line. Though this is a prerequisite to the conventional method of controlling a fire by indirect attack, it tends to become an end in itself which diverts attention from the fire and from the fact that moving dirt and clearing away cover may or may not have an effect on the fire, depending on its behavior and on the other measures taken to control it. Most mechanization takes the form of directly substituting machine work for handwork. This tends to give it a narrow function. A more productive approach is that of fully exploiting the things machines can do that men cannot do in fire fighting. This process has not yet been fully exploited. For that reason, even though compromises must always be made in developing fire equipment to meet the various criteria discussed, a substantial increase in both the effectiveness and efficiency of existing mechanized equipment for forest fire fighting still remains to be achieved.

Major Types of Power Equipment Used

Most power-driven equipment has been adapted and developed for fire suppression use from prototypes used in agriculture or industry. A few are used without special adaptation, and one, the rotary trencher, is an original fire control development. Some equipment pumps water, some clears firebreaks, some digs trench, and some does more than one job. Following is an introduction to the general types which will serve as a guide to their more detailed consideration.

Plows (Disk or Moldboard)   Originally agricultural equipment, plows have been adapted and highly specialized for fire suppression. A plow is primarily a trench digger, but the exposed mineral soil of the furrow plus the overcast soil removed from it creates a firebreak up to 5 feet in width in sandy soil. When its power source is an armored tractor or truck, considerable removal of brush cover may also be accomplished.

Bulldozer   Bulldozers are widely employed in construction work and used without special adaptation in fire suppression. The most versatile of all power equipment used to create fire line, the bulldozer is an effective line clearer, trench digger, and road builder.

Rotary Trencher   An original tool in fire suppression. The essential element of the rotary trencher is a rotating flail that both constructs a fire trench and throws dirt.

Pumper   Pumping units function both as first-attack and as line-building equipment. Their primary function is that of direct attack on small fires or of reinforcement of the attack on large fires. However, when a strip is watered down (or blanketed with some chemical) so that it will not ignite, it functions as a temporary fuel break just as effectively as if it were cleared and trenched.

Combined Units   Power units are combined with each other and with hand tools in various ways. A plow is often either mounted on or towed behind a truck that also may be equipped with a pumping unit and hand tools, plus armor on front to smash through brush and small trees. The total unit can constitute a versatile, fast-moving, and complete piece of fire suppression equipment. Tanks and pump are sometimes mounted on a crawler-tractor plow unit, permitting the operator to quiet hot spots and control spot fires very effectively as an adjunct to line plowing. Truck tankers are always equipped with hand tools. A pickup truck, carrying a tank and pump or at least backpack pumps and hand tools, is the backbone of first attack for many organizations. To some extent, tractors drawing plows are also equipped with a bulldozer blade to aid in clearing line. Considerations of equipment productivity, versatility, cost, etc. apply with particular force to combined use. A combined unit is usually less efficient at a particular job than a specialized tool, less mobile, and more expensive. Its advantage is that a wider range of jobs can be done by one unit.

Plows and Other Line-building Equipment

The plow is an efficient trench digger. One of the most ancient tools, the plow has been adapted and improved into a specialized and highly effective fire suppression tool. The development of fire plows is a long and fascinating story of equipment engineering trial and error. All plows in current use are specially designed for fire work and bear only a general resemblance to their agricultural ancestors.

Fire plows were first developed and put into general use in level, sandy soils and fairly lightly stocked forest stands. As plows and their power source were improved and their capabilities better appreciated, their use was extended into areas of rougher terrain, rockier soils, and heavier ground cover. Plows are widely used in the South and in the Lake states, where they form the backbone of fire suppression equipment. Plows are used to some extent in the Southwest, but only in limited areas elsewhere in the West. Their use is restricted because of difficult accessibility, steep terrain, rocky soils, and heavy timber stands. In such areas bulldozers are preferred. There are, however, considerable areas in the West in which plows can and are being used.

Kinds of Plows A large number of sizes and kinds of fire plows have been developed in different regions, each designed to meet particular problems and conditions. Each plow has its advocates, advantages, and limitations. The following general classification will help to classify them by general types and introduce some terminology.

Weight A primary consideration in a plow is its weight. This controls both the kind of job a plow can do and the power necessary to pull it. Table 13.1 gives a general weight and power classification. Fire

Table 13.1 Weight and Power Classification of Fire-line Plows

Weight class	Approximate weight, lb		Drawbar horsepower required to pull
	Tractor-mounted plows	Self-contained sulky plows on trailing wheels	
Light	250–600	500–600	18–25
Medium	700–1,000	1,000–2,000	20–40
Heavy	. . . .	2,000+	40+

plows must be extremely rugged to withstand conditions of use that have little parallel in agriculture.

Means of Moving Dirt All fire-line plows (except the reversible hillside plow in extremely limited use) are middlebusters, that is, the units are bilateral and throw dirt equally to right and left. The primary cutting instrument is a middlebuster or double-bottomed plow point, usually preceded by a rolling disk coulter or fixed knife (fin) to cut through sod and debris to help open the trench. The furrow is widened and dirt is thrown each way over the ground on the sides (the berm) by either disks or moldboards. These are often assisted by supplemental wings mounted on either side to make the total width of exposed mineral soil wider and to firm the overcast so that it will not fall back into the trench behind the plow, as may occur in soddy ground. As to means of dirt moving, plows are usually classified as disk, moldboard, or middlebuster types. The last applies to plows with relatively small moldboards with limited side throw of dirt which primarily dig a trench.

Attachment Plows are of two types. Self-contained (or sulky) plows are those mounted on trailing wheels as a separate unit. Such plows are pulled by the prime mover with the controls largely independent of the prime mover. Dependent plows are without wheels and are attached to the power source (tractor or truck) and completely controlled from it.

Plow Penetration Penetration of the plow point into the ground is accomplished either by the weight of the unit itself (with supplemental weights sometimes added), by changing the angle of the point in relation to the axis of the prime mover, or by direct down pressure hydraulically applied. Self-contained sulky plows with trailing wheels get plow penetration by the weight of the unit plus adjustment of the plow-point angle. Dependent plows mounted on truck or tractor usually have a hydraulic down-pressure mechanism and also plow-point angle adjustment to keep the plow in the ground.

Means of Transport Tractors with plow units are slow-moving and highly dependent on truck power to get to fires quickly. Some sulky plows are designed as trailer units and can be towed on roads at normal road speeds. This can increase flexibility. As designed, the light tractor-plow units are hauled on $1^1/_2$- or 2-ton flatbed trucks, medium units on 2- to $2^1/_2$-ton trucks, and the heavy units on truck-tractor combinations. A variety of folding ramps and tilting truck beds have been devised to facilitate loading and unloading such units (Figure 13.6).

Most fire plows were initially designed and constructed by state and

Figure 13.6 Hydraulically controlled tractor-drawn fire line plow unit loaded on tilt-bed truck. Note armoring on tractor to protect operator and bulldozer blade to knock over trees and clear ground for the plow. *(Courtesy Mississippi Forestry Commission.)*

federal control organizations to meet their particular needs and ideas. A few have gone into commercial production, but many still in active use continue to be assembled in shops operated by using agencies. This is because progress toward standardization has been slow and the market has been too specialized and limited to attract commercial manufacturers. Primary development of plows has been in the Southern and Lake states, where they are widely used. Figures 13.6 to 13.10 illustrate common types of plows, their attachment, and their transportation and give some idea of the kind of fire line they produce.

Plow Performance   Plow performance in building fire line depends on such factors as operator skill, machine capability, power, terrain, and ground cover. Comprehensive studies of plow performance made in the South by the U.S. Forest Service in 1955 are drawn on for most of the following generalizations.

The power and speed of the prime mover sets the ceiling in rate of line production, modified to some degree by the strength of the plow and

Figure 13.7 Fire-line sulky plow (Ranger Super Pal sulky plow). Note arrangement of rolling coulter, middlebuster point, double disks, and side wings to widen trench. Rubber-tired wheels permit towing on roads by pickup or truck. *(U.S. Forest Service photo.)*

Figure 13.8 Truck-drawn fire-line plow. Michigan hydraulically controlled plow pulled by truck with four-wheel drive that is also carrying slip-on tanker. *(Courtesy Michigan Department of Conservation.)*

Figure 13.9 Truck-tanker-plow unit plowing fire line. Operator can direct a stream of water on the fire as he plows. *(U.S. Forest Service photo.)*

the degree of side throw of dirt permissible in constructing a clean line. For most tractors, this is between 2 and 3 miles per hour, and $2\frac{1}{2}$ miles per hour (or about 200 chains) is regarded as the maximum rate at which a plow can make good line.

The following mechanical and physical factors affect rate of fire-line production:

1 Slope. Upslopes, downslopes, and sideslopes slow down production at a progressively faster rate until the limits of the piece of equipment are reached. Production downslope increases somewhat with gentle slopes and then decreases sharply with steeper slopes. Most power equipment loses efficiency rapidly on slopes over 30 to 35 percent, and 45 percent is about a practical maximum.

2   Stand size and density. A plow unit is not designed as a land-clearing tool. It must either ride down trees and plow through them or go around. It can ride down small trees up to about 4 inches in diameter even if these are numerous. Above this it must dodge them or be seriously slowed down.

3   Brush cover. Provided the unit has the weight and power to smash through, the effect of brush is mainly to obscure the view of stumps and other obstacles and to require frequent stops to clear out trash clogging the plow. In general, the heavier the brush, the slower the rate of production with any kind of equipment.

4   Soil. All plows naturally work best in sandy soils. The harder and heavier the soil, the more power is required and the slower is production within the limit of the equipment. Only the Talladega plow is specially designed to work in rocky, gravelly soils with light tractors. With skill, combination middlebuster point and disk combinations will also do good work in rocky soils, but they require more power.

5   Down timber and stumps. Plows are almost universally pulled

Figure 13.10   Fire plow, in action on a fire, operating with a small fire crew. This is a Mathis plow in South Carolina. *(U.S. Forest Service photo.)*

behind a power source that is designed to smash down and ride over brush and small trees but not to clear the ground. Down timber and larger stumps that cannot be dodged are consequently major deterrents to plow use; they may stop a plow completely. Where a plow unit is used in such cover, it must be preceded by land-clearing equipment, normally a bulldozer. A bulldozer blade or pushing bar is sometimes mounted on the tractor-plow (Figure 13.6) to solve this problem in a single unit.

The above factors, very briefly described, operate largely in setting limits. A given piece of equipment is designed for certain conditions and operates successfully within its range. The heavier units naturally have the wider range of successful operation since they can perform where a lighter plow cannot. But they are also expensive where their weight and power are not needed, and they are slower and more expensive to transport to fires.

In addition to the capability of the equipment itself, the skill and experience of the operator must be considered. If a man thoroughly knows a piece of equipment and has confidence in it, he gets much more out of it than from another with which he is unfamiliar. Operator skill contributes much more than can be measured in faster rate of line construction. It means courage based on knowledge when difficult conditions are encountered. It means avoidance of hangups, breakdowns, and other causes of delay when the machine is urgently needed. It means better control line. A skilled line locator working with the machine operator is a strong asset. In difficult situations he can sometimes double plow performance.

The wide range of conditions under which plows operate has more effect on the rate of fire-line production than the type and weight of plow. However, as a general guide for plows in general operation, 200 chains per hour is fast, 140 medium, and 90 or less is slow.

General Considerations in Use of Plows   The preceding discussion has introduced the principal types of plow units and their characteristics. When employed in fire control work, several special criteria and considerations enter in that affect efficiency of plow operation and that may serve to more clearly define the role of this equipment. These are listed in outline form.

1   Quality of plow line constructed. Little supporting manpower can be counted on to improve the fire line. Consequently, a plow should be capable of producing 90 percent or better clean line free of organic material (Figure 13.10).

2   Drawbar pull. A plow should be designed to require minimum

power to operate. A hard-pulling plow requires a larger and more expensive tractor, costs more per unit of line produced, slows down the rate of progress, and reduces the margin of reserve power needed for fast plowing in emergencies.

3 Simplicity of design. The item should have the fewest possible parts, mechanisms must be easily adjusted and maintained, and controls and adjustments must be easily understood by the operator.

4 Plow attachment. It should be possible easily and quickly to attach a plow to a regular tractor drawbar. It is often necessary to swap tractors and plows without regard to makes and to use industrial or farm tractors, especially in an emergency. Sulky plows have an advantage in this respect; most can be attached immediately to anything that can pull them.

5 Plow penetration. The plow must penetrate ground readily and construct satisfactory plow line, preferably by its own weight. Such plows tend to be lighter-pulling. If down pressure is used, it must be positive and flexible. Penetration is largely controlled by plow design.

6 Plow depth adjustment. Adjustment of plowing depth must be easy, rapid, and simple and done in only one place on the plow. Efficient plow operation requires frequent depth adjustment. The shallower the better, as long as a satisfactory fire line is produced. Dynamometer tests on a light plow showed that 200 to 400 additional pounds of pull are required for each additional inch in depth below 3 inches.

7 Horizontal plow flexibility. A plow should be free to swing 90° right or left of the main axis of the tractor, with a positive stop to avoid hitting the tractor treads. This is essential in backing, making sharp turns, and in reducing plow side bind.

8 Vertical plow flexibility. The plow must be able to follow inequalities in the surface readily, without either emerging from or burying itself in the ground, and to ride up over obstacles without undue shock or strain to plow or prime mover.

9 Plow raising. A simple and securely locking mechanism is necessary to hold the plow above ground in a traveling position. On tractor-mounted plows, the plow should rise to a vertical position easily and be held rigidly by a positive lock.

10 Plow backing. During plowing operations it should be possible to execute backups easily without raising the plow to a carrying position or digging it into the ground. Backups are frequent. Sulky plows tend to lack maneuverability in backing.

11 Separation of plow from prime mover. It should be possible completely to uncouple the plow from the tractor in a matter of seconds without use of special or uncommon tools. Units do get stuck on stumps, become mired, and so forth, and must be uncoupled when time is of the essence.

12 Interchangeability and ease of part replacement. This is extremely important. Insofar as possible, all critical parts should be interchangeable on a given plow and quickly replaceable using common tools. Repairs have to be made under time pressure and usually under difficult working conditions.

Bulldozers   A bulldozer is a versatile and widely used power tool in the forest. A general knowledge of bulldozer-equipped tractors is assumed; the aim here is to indicate their uses in fire suppression. The basic advantage of the bulldozer is that it is a highly maneuverable and complete tool. It is unsurpassed for control-line clearing and trench digging in heavy going. On slopes where it can be operated (up to about 60 percent), nothing can equal a heavy bulldozer in rapidly smashing through brush almost impenetrable to hand crews, removing down logs and stumps, knocking down trees and snags, and clearing a strip to mineral soil. A bulldozer operated by a skilled man is an inspiration to behold. The machine can also build or improve roads, construct aircraft landing fields, clear safety strips, and prepare campsites.

Another major advantage of the bulldozer, and especially in the western United States where it was first developed, is that it is widely used in forest work. It is consequently generally available, along with a supply of skilled operators. It is also one of the few tools that does not have to be adapted for fire suppression use. Building fire line is not basically different from many forest jobs for which a bulldozer is commonly used.

In some areas of the West, southern California, and the Northwest Coast especially, the bulldozer is often used as a first-attack tool. It can clear fire line, dig trench, and assist in the mop-up of deep-burning fuels. More frequently, however, bulldozers are used as a reinforcement tool following first attack by hand-tool crews or tankers. When so used they are effective in completing the control line, widening backfiring strips, clearing the way for a plow unit, pushing over snags, etc. Being very versatile, their operation can be coordinated effectively with other equipment. Few large fires in the West are fought without using some bulldozers.

The bulldozer does have limitations. It is basically designed to push dirt and other materials and does not have the speed or efficiency of a well-designed plow in constructing fire line in situations where plows can be used. The larger bulldozers, which are most effective in fire-line work, are also heavy, offering the same transport problems as do the heavier tractor-plow units. While somewhat more maneuverable on steep slopes than a plow unit, production falls off rapidly on adverse slopes over about 45 percent. They are also stopped, or nearly so, by wet ground or rock outcrops.

In fire-line construction, bulldozers often work in pairs. One bulldozer leads, smashing through and partially clearing the line. The second machine completes the job. The two machines supplement and protect each other. If one gets stuck or hung up, the other can free it. Also, if one machine breaks down, the other can clear a strip around it to protect it from the fire. The operative bulldozer can then continue to build line.

A typical Western fire-line organization for two bulldozers is about as follows, in order of progression:

1   Line locator (with radio) who determines the general location of the line with respect to the fire
2   Line spotter immediately preceding the bulldozers who determines the specific line location
3   Head bulldozer with operator
4   Second bulldozer with operator
5   Backfiring crew with torches to burn out between line and fire
6   Mop-up and holding crew

The entire unit would be under the direction of a foreman.

Light Mechanized Equipment

There has long been a gap in the mechanization of the job of creating fire line. In most locations where the plow or bulldozer cannot go or cannot get soon enough, fire line must be cleared by hand methods. This has been usual in backcountry, but the problem is common too in rugged terrain where rock or steep slopes prevent operation of heavy equipment. It becomes critical as well in bogs and other areas where the ground is too soft to operate heavy equipment.

The development of special "swamp buggies" and of amphibious equipment to facilitate fire-fighting operations in swampy country is a special field which continues to challenge the equipment developer. It will not be detailed here.

The development of light, mechanized fire-line equipment that would greatly increase the output of a few men and that could be delivered to roadless locations by parachute and placed in service on a fire as readily as a power saw has long been sought. It has been a special objective of men interested in forest fire equipment particularly in the northwestern United States. Models have been developed of several types of fire-line trenchers, beaters, flails, and sand casters of the garden tractor class. All have shown promise of considerable usefulness yet have failed to win a place as standard equipment in fire control practice.

One type, known originally as the Bosworth trencher and later as the rotary trencher or the one-man flail trencher, has gone through much evolution and appears to have the best prospect of continuing use. It is based on a different principle in clearing fire line. Instead of digging or scraping by a pushed blade or plow point, it clears a shallow trench to mineral soil with a rapidly revolving flail driven by a gasoline motor and turning at right angles to the direction of travel. This is potentially a more efficient method of moving loose material.

The original light, hand-propelled model developed in the 1930s was replaced by a heavier, self-propelled model in 1957 (in Field Trials.) This model, in turn, was superseded by returning to a light, hand-propelled model which was first tried out in 1961 and successively modified. Resulting manufacturer's specifications were issued in 1966 (Equipment Development Report No. 5100-14, 1966). This model has a total weight of 56 pounds. It is adapted to parachute delivery and can be carried to a fire by packboard. In forest litter, one man can make fire line faster with it than three men using hand tools. Two-man and four-man crews built around the operation of one man with this trencher have been found efficient. A six-man team built around the operation of two trenchers was found to be most efficient in deep duff and heavy ground cover. Use of this machine by smoke-jumper teams is increasing.

Water-using Equipment

The profound effect of fuel moisture on ignition and spread of wild-land fires and on the fire intensity they develop has been discussed in relation to fuels, fire behavior, and fire danger rating. It follows that a soaking rain is the best fire-fighting agent of all, and the local application of water has a powerful and immediate quenching effect on flaming combustion. Consequently, water has a high potential in the extinguishment of fires. How much of this potential is realized in fire fighting depends on the equipment used to apply it and on the techniques of use.

The backpack pump has already been described in the category of hand tools. Its use illustrates the general character of the role of water in current practice. Unlike digging, cutting, and scraping tools, its effect is not through the removal or rearrangement of fuel but through cooling and smothering. Consequently, pumps of all kind are not commonly thought of as tools for constructing fire line, though they may function in this way temporarily by wetting down barrier strips of fuel in the path of a spreading fire. They are most valuable in direct attack on small or low-intensity fires where total extinguishment can be realized, second in the support of both direct and indirect attack where fire line is being built, and third in the mop-up of all fires. The degree to which water and water-using equipment is used for these purposes still varies a great deal among states and forest regions in the United States and Canada. Some use of water is universal, but fuels, accessibility, and organizational factors strongly influence conventional practice.

The most important limitations in using water arise from the fact that it is heavy to transport, that fuels such as punky wood, duff, or sawdust when very dry are difficult to wet, and that water itself is much less effective in extinguishing glowing combustion than flaming combustion. Much of this is due to the physical qualities of the fuels supporting glowing combustion. They are poor conductors of both moisture and heat. They contain enough oxygen to enable combustion to persist even when cut off from outside air and they are likely to support exothermic reactions (Chapter 6). Each of these factors enters into local variations in the dependence placed on use of water for fire fighting.

Water in Direct Attack   Water is very effective in extinguishing flame. This is the reason backpack pumps are efficient in controlling fires spreading in light fuels. However, in patrolling high-risk areas for fires, more striking power with water is needed than can be supplied by a single backpack pump. This need has been met by a wide range of inexpensive power pumps mounted on a vehicle, usually a pickup-type truck. The water tank may range from a 50-gallon to a 200-gallon tank. At 8 pounds to the gallon, a pickup is easily overloaded and slowed down by larger water tanks.

Such an outfit is excellent for attack on small fires. If the fire has not yet become established in heavy or coarse fuels, extinguishment of flaming materials may leave little or no mop-up to do and the patrolman can leave the area as safe in a short time. On small, smoldering fires, supplemental work to dig out and expose burning fuels will be needed to facilitate complete wetting. Complete extinguishment then requires more care and is slower. Techniques are those of mop-up rather than of building fire line.

Water in Support of Fire Control Line   This is also a well-established use of water in both direct and indirect methods of attack, though the full potential of providing water at the right time and place is difficult to realize. A coordinate and often very critical use of water in support of indirect attack is in backfiring.

Larger-capacity tank trucks than the outfit described for a fire patrolman are preferred for support of the fire control line on larger fires. This support is generally in the form of (1) cooling down hot spots in advance of the fire crew to enable men to work closer; (2) treating spots inside the line that threaten to ignite aerial fuels or fuels outside; (3) wetting down of fuels outside that are exposed to radiation or sparks; (4) extinguishing spot fires as they occur; and (5) extinguishing the fire edge where such action can reduce the amount of fire line to be worked with hand tools.

On wild lands where few roads exist, the portable power pump with hose packed in by man pack or by horses was the first power equipment used and has continued as standard forest fire-fighting equipment in roadless areas throughout the western United States and Canada. Since the pump and hose cannot be put into place as quickly as a pump on wheels, it cannot function as quickly in direct attack on small fires. But it provides strong reinforcement action and functions well in the supporting activities on larger fires described above.

Portable pumps depend on sources of water. But hose-laying techniques permit more or less indefinite extension of the end of the hose uphill or in horizontal distance through establishing relays. These consist of sumps or collapsible tanks at the point where water pressure becomes too weak. These then serve as the water source for a second pump. Once a pump is established at a water source, it functions in support of the fire line in the same way that a tank truck does. The difference is that a tank truck with live hose reel (that is, a reel so designed that water can be pumped through the hose while still on the reel) has a much better chance to function in direct attack on a fire. But the water supply of the tank truck is definitely limited and may become exhausted at a critical time. Because of this there is always a strong incentive to increase the water-carrying capacity of tank trucks. Where this means less versatility and reduced ability to make direct attack on small fires with water, the advantage of the larger capacity is quickly offset. The portable pump placed on a natural source of water usually has an unlimited supply. There is a highly developed technology in the use of portable pumps and in the operation of hose lays. The booklet *Water versus Fire* presents some of these in graphic fashion (Neuns, 1950). Figure 13.11 shows a hose-laying sequence where water is used to create the preliminary fire control line. It is evident that the water-carrying capacity of a tank truck to support this operation must be large and must be supplemented by other tankers in relays.

Water-use techniques need to vary with the type of fuel and cover. Where the fire is confined to grass, weeds, and surface litter, surface wetting is sufficient to completely quench the fire and no other work is necessary. Where the fire is in high-energy fuels such as dry logging slash, it is seldom feasible to extinguish much of the deep fire edge directly. But skillful use of water can slow down spread and cool down the fire enough

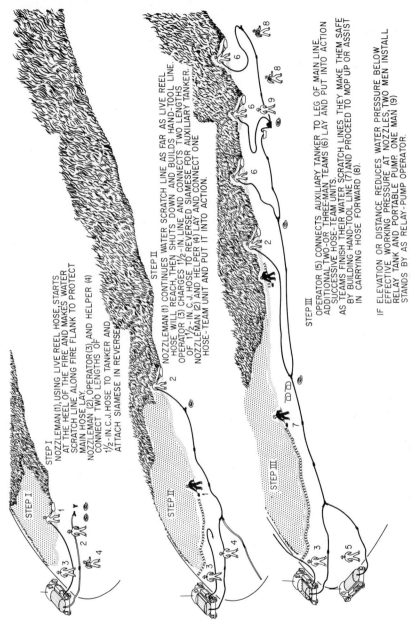

STEP I
NOZZLEMAN (1), USING LIVE REEL HOSE, STARTS AT THE HEEL OF THE FIRE AND MAKES WATER SCRATCH LINE ALONG FIRE FLANK TO PROTECT MAIN HOSE LAY.
NOZZLEMAN (2), OPERATOR (3), AND HELPER (4) CONNECT TWO LENGTHS OF 1½-IN. C.J. HOSE TO TANKER AND ATTACH SIAMESE IN REVERSE.

STEP II
NOZZLEMAN (1) CONTINUES WATER SCRATCH LINE AS FAR AS LIVE REEL HOSE WILL REACH, THEN SHUTS DOWN AND BUILDS HAND-TOOL LINE.
OPERATOR (3) CHARGES 1½-IN. LINE AND CONNECTS TWO LENGTHS OF 1½-IN. C.J. HOSE TO REVERSED SIAMESE FOR AUXILIARY TANKER.
NOZZLEMAN (2) AND HELPER (4) LAY AND CONNECT ONE HOSE-TEAM UNIT AND PUT IT INTO ACTION.

STEP III
OPERATOR (5) CONNECTS AUXILIARY TANKER TO LEG OF MAIN LINE. ADDITIONAL TWO- OR THREE-MAN TEAMS (6) LAY AND PUT INTO ACTION SUCCESSIVE HOSE-TEAM UNITS.
AS TEAMS FINISH THEIR WATER SCRATCH LINES THEY MAKE THEM SAFE BY BUILDING HAND-TOOL LINE (7) AND PROCEED TO MOP UP OR ASSIST IN CARRYING HOSE FORWARD (8).

IF ELEVATION OR DISTANCE REDUCES WATER PRESSURE BELOW EFFECTIVE WORKING PRESSURE AT NOZZLES, TWO MEN INSTALL RELAY TANK AND PORTABLE PUMP. ONE MAN (9) STANDS BY AS RELAY-PUMP OPERATOR.

Figure 13.11 Progressive sequences in a complex hose lay. *(Courtesy U.S. Forest Service.)*

to permit men to work close to it. The dependence is usually on confining the fire and letting it burn out clean. In mixed forest fuels with heavy litter and duff and lower fire intensity, the most profitable use of water is in support of clean burning or backfiring. It is then used to wet down outside the line, to cool down backfire heads that get too hot, and to extinguish spot fires. If used very much inside the fire line, it is likely to prolong the suppression job by slowing down the burning out process.

Water in Mop-up   The use of water can completely extinguish small fires rather than merely control their spread, and it has a similar potential for the final extinguishment of large fires. As in small fires, the task is simple where combustion is limited to light fuels. Surface wetting to knock down flame and extinguish sparks is sufficient. But deep duff, punky wood, and organic soil may all be present in mixed forest fuels. When fire is well established in such fuels it is very difficult to extinguish.

In early use of portable pumps in forest country, repeated failures were experienced in the effort to extinguish all fires by surface wetting. Both authors recall instances of approximately a 1-acre spot fire on which water was pumped for approximately six hours on each of three succeeding days, after which it was declared fully extinguished. After a lapse of three days of continuing high fire danger, the whole area was again alight, so that the net effect of the wetting was only to prolong the task of mop-up. Two factors were operating: first, fuels supporting glowing combustion were abundant; second, water applied to the ground surface in a forest environment drains off through natural channels and leaves many dry pockets below the surface. Combustion persists in these pockets and spreads by gradually drying out the adjacent fuel again. To overcome this problem, skilled techniques have been developed for the use of water to extinguish smoldering fire. One very effective technique with a portable power pump placed on an abundant source of water is the employment of a high-pressure, solid stream of water through the hose nozzle to penetrate the surface and to churn up and puddle the organic fuels below the surface. Another technique depends on use of hand tools to uncover sources of fire, to puddle burning fuels, and to otherwise extend the effect of a more limited source of water from a tank truck. The use of wetting agents to facilitate such techniques is discussed in the subsequent section on use of chemicals.

Types of Power Pumps Used   In the discussion so far, the general role of backpack hand pumps, of portable power pumps off the road, and of pumps mounted on tank trucks has been described. Requirements for the first two are reasonably uniform, but that of the tank truck varies widely. Though detailed equipment specifications are beyond the scope of this chapter, consideration of a few of the specific characteristics which are important in the choice of available power-pumping equipment will be helpful.

Both two- and four-cycle engines are used. The two-cycle engine set the standard for early off-the-road portable pumps, since such engines, lubricated through oil in the gasoline, are the most powerful for their weight. However, four-cycle engines, like those in automobiles, are considered more reliable and require less exacting maintenance. They are commonly used on the larger tank trucks. Since World War II, increased use of aluminum and other light metals has progressively reduced the minimum weight of the four-cycle engine, until it now competes with the two-cycle engine for most uses.

Pumps used are of two general classes, the positive-displacement pump and the centrifugal.

There are several kinds of positive-displacement pumps. The three of some importance in forest fire control are the gear pump, the rotary pump, and the piston pump. In this category the gear pump has been most used. All have in common close spacing between the gears, rotors, impellers, or pistons and the housing which encloses them. For this reason they cannot be used with water containing fine sand or other abrasives, which quickly cut out the pump. A second characteristic is that a fixed quantity of water is forced through the pump with each revolution. For this reason a pressure-relief bypass valve is needed in the hose line on the discharge side of the pump. Otherwise, if the water is shut off at the end of the hose, the hose bursts or the engine stalls. The special overall characteristic which has given such pumps prominence in forest fire control in the past is their ability to develop relatively high pressure at low power output. Two-cycle positive-displacement portable pumps commonly deliver about 20 U.S. gallons per minute and operate at 100 to 250 pounds of pressure per square inch at the nozzle. Heavier piston pumps may develop as much as 700 to 800 pounds of pressure.

Centrifugal pumps have a rotating vane or impeller which spins the water and forces it out through centrifugal force. The spacing between impeller and housing is not as close as in the positive displacement pump, so the centrifugal pump is much less sensitive to abrasives. In other words, it can pump muddy water with little or no damage. For similar reasons, centrifugal pumps do not require a pressure-relief bypass valve. In general, centrifugal pumps move a larger volume of water at lower pressures, but they are heavier in weight. However, it would be misleading to say that centrifugal pumps are always low-pressure pumps or that they are always heavy. Pressure can be built up by stages to equal that of positive-displacement pumps, though as pressure is built up the volume of water delivered reduces rapidly. Portable four-stage centrifugal pumps weighing only 40 to 55 pounds are now in use which deliver 70 gallons per minute at 50 pounds pressure, 44 gallons at 200 pounds pressure, and 25 gallons at 250 pounds pressure. Such pumps now dominate the field.

Essential accessories used on most power pumps are a pressure gauge, a pressure-relief valve for all positive-displacement pumps, and shutoff valves for the suction and discharge openings (except on portable pumps). A Siamese (double) coupling with shutoff valve is often mounted just ahead of the pump discharge opening. Its purpose is to avoid the back pressure of a head of water in the hose line when the pump engine is restarted after an interruption in the operation.

Tank-truck units are normally equipped also with a suction intake hose so that the tank can be filled from a water source by the unit's own pump. When so equipped, they can also pump directly into hose lines from a fixed water source.

Ejectors   With a perfect pump, atmospheric pressure would permit water to be lifted by suction 33.9 feet at sea level. Because pumps are not 100 percent efficient and become less so with use, from 20 to 22 feet is regarded as a working maximum at elevations of less than about a mile. This means that the water source cannot be more than this distance below the pump when filling tanks or pumping direct. There are often situations where the available water source is at a greater distance, as from bridges, canyon roads along streams, and so forth.

An ejector, also termed eductor, can be used in meeting such situations. It is a simple device, which in one form has long been used by housewives to empty laundry tubs without floor-level drains, and operates on the same general principle that causes a bystander's hat to follow a speeding bus. Water is carried in an extra line from the pump down to the water intake, where the ejector is mounted. Pressure through this line to the ejector draws additional water through the intake and delivers a greater amount, but at lower pressure, through a second line back to the pump. An ejector may be used to lift water 80 feet or more vertically and, on level or slightly sloping situations, for distances up to 200 feet. They are also commonly used within suction distance limits to speed tank refilling.

Tank Truck Units and Supporting Equipment   When a power pump is mounted on a vehicle it becomes part of a more complex mobile unit. All the pumps and engines described have been included in such units at various times and places. No one standard combination has been accepted by all forest fire agencies. Yet there has been a trend toward standardization through the development of so-called slip-on units.

The Slip-on Unit   The slip-on unit has evolved in response to two very practical limitations in the development, operation, and depreciation of tank truck units for wild-land fire fighting. These are cost and obsolescence.

The cost factor is always important. In many areas the fire season is of short duration, 3 to 4 months, or the occasions when a tank truck can be used to advantage are intermittent and occur only a few times per year. It then becomes quite costly to tie up a truck on a year-round basis for the limited fire service needed.

The factor of obsolescence is equally important. Even though there is no lack of justification for holding a truck for exclusive fire use, such use seldom accumulates much mileage in travel. At the end of ten years with only a few thousand miles on its speedometer, it may still be in excellent condition, but it has become obsolescent. It is now impossible to replace parts when needed, and since it is now an unfamiliar model, it becomes more difficult as well to give it proper maintenance. The slip-on unit is designed to solve both problems.

An assembled slip-on pumper unit is not permanently attached to the carrying vehicle. The equipment consists of a water tank with baffle plates to prevent water from surging in transit, a live hose reel, and often an additional folded or rolled hose supply, pump, and engine, all assembled as a unit. Although the engine is usually integral to the unit, a power takeoff from the vehicle engine is sometimes used. The unit can be carried on any flatbed truck or pickup of sufficient body width, length, and weight capacity. Besides the advantage of the slip-on unit in permitting other uses of the carrier when not needed for fire service, it can be removed from the carrier and placed at a fixed water source for continuous operation, releasing the carrier.

Slip-ons are made in various sizes and equipment combinations, from 50-gallon units carried on a pickup or jeep to 1,500-gallon capacities requiring a heavy truck. Hand tool outfits for five or more men are usual components of the lighter units. All have their uses, proponents, and critics. Anything over about 200 gallons capacity is considered a large unit.

Figure 13.12 shows one of the slip-on tanker units designed by the U.S. Forest Service for possible use in all National Forest regions. This particular model is assembled as a 75-, 125-, or a 200-gallon capacity unit, with only minor changes in specifications. It is top-mounted (pump and engine on top of the tank) and adapted to use with any one of several

Figure 13.12 Slip-on tanker unit in use in West Virginia. *(U.S. Forest Service photo.)*

4-cycle engine-driven pumpers. A distinctive feature over previous models is the plastic (fiber glass reinforced) tank which is noncorrosive and considerably lighter in weight than previous metal tanks. With the pumper mounted, the unit can deliver water from the tank to a fire, from a natural source of water to the tank, or from a water source direct to the fire. The pump and engine unit can be removed and placed at the water source to function as a portable pumper.

Integral Pumper-Tankers   Integral units have the tank and pumping equipment built into the vehicle so that no part can be easily removed for separate use. They are built to fight fire only. Practically all city fire department pumpers are of this type.

As would be expected, integral units are of all sizes and kinds. Some are modifications or adaptations of city or armed-forces units. Others are made up from component parts and specially mounted on standard commercial trucks (Figure 13.13). Power to drive the pump is usually transmitted from the vehicle motor, but separate motors are also used. Two types of pumps are used in some cases, a piston type for high pressures and a gear or a centrifugal type for high-volume delivery. A live reel is almost always carried, plus additional folded or rolled hose for distances beyond the reach of the live reel. Two to four hose lines can often be served at the same time within limitations of pressure and quantity of water delivery that can be sustained.

Tank trailers pulled by trucks and sometimes by tractors are also used to supplement water supply to pumping units. They are used to sustain pumpers in action on a fire. Canvas or other fabric slip-on tanks are used, which can be placed on anything that will carry them. In an emergency, almost anything that can carry water has been pressed into service, including commercial tank trucks and even concrete mixers.

Tanker trucks, whether slip-on or integral units, almost always carry a complement of hand tools and backpack pumps and usually have space for a small crew. As such, they are a complete fire-fighting unit accenting use of water. In many areas they are used as a first-attack unit. With a well-developed utilization road system, a tanker truck can be brought within a quarter of a mile of almost any spot, and usually much closer. Tankers, where available, are used, at least as support units, on nearly all large fires.

Tanker-Truck--Tractor-Plow Combinations Pumping units are often combined with power line-building equipment. In Michigan, for example, a basic fire-fighting unit is a truck with four-wheel drive, armored to smash through brush and equipped with a hydraulically controlled dependent fire plow, a slip-on tanker unit, some hand tools, and radio. Such a

Figure 13.13 Tanker truck with pump, carrying 300 gallons of water and fire crew with hand tools, used to make first attack on fires in northern California. *(U.S. Forest Service photo.)*

unit can deal effectively with a wide range of fire situations. There are a number of such vehicle–water-plow combinations (Figures 13.8 and 13.9). Tanks and pumps are also mounted on a tractor-plow unit. Here, water is used strictly as a supplement to cool down hot spots, permitting line building in more advantageous locations. It is also useful to catch spot fires and strengthen line. The hose is operated by a tractor driver.

Hoses Of the many kinds of hoses made, only a few are commonly used in forest fire fighting.

Hard rubber (noncollapsible) hose of $3/4$- or 1-inch inside diameter is usually used on live reels in length up to about 250 feet. Water can be pumped through it while it is wound on the reel. Collapsible hose can also be used on a live reel but must be stretched out, filled, the nozzle closed, and the hose rewound. Rubber hose is expensive and fairly heavy in larger diameters. It is always used with high-pressure fog units. Live reels are sometimes power-operated for quick rewinding.

Fabric-jacketed (often cotton) rubber- or synthetic-lined hose is commonly used in 1- and $1^{1}/_2$-inch diameter, with forestry specifications calling for burst pressure tests up to 600 pounds per square inch. Working pressures of around 350 pounds per square inch are expected. This hose can be used on live reels, folded, or rolled for rapid extension and coupling for longer distances.

Unlined linen hose has long been used in roadless areas, with synthetic fiber hose substituting for it in part. Whether to purchase and stock this class of hose or to give preference to the cotton-jacketed rubber-lined hose is often debated. The comparative advantages and disadvantages of rubber-lined and linen hose which enter into hose selection are as follows:

Cotton-jacketed rubber-lined	**Unlined linen**
Advantages	Advantages
Less friction and no water loss through seepage.	Light weight, small bulk, and lower cost.
Thorough cleaning not so essential	More resistant to hot embers because seepage through fibers keeps hose wet.
Will withstand more abrasion and rough handling under pressure.	Unlimited shelf life if properly stored.
Disadvantages	Disadvantages
Greater weight and bulk.	Larger friction loss.
Costs more.	Leakage until thoroughly saturated.
Limited shelf life, the rubber lining deteriorates in time even when not in use. Should	Must be thoroughly cleaned and dried after use or it will

have water run through it at least once a year. More subject to damage from hot embers.

mildew and deteriorate even though most linen is treated for mildew resistance by manufacturers.

Nozzles The whole purpose of pumpers, tankers, and hose lays is to bring water to the fire. The nozzle and the skill of the operator at the point of application determine the success or failure of the whole undertaking. Water can be highly effective or largely wasted, depending on how it is used.

By varying nozzle type, rate of delivery, and pressure, a wide variety of water patterns can be obtained, ranging from a hard, solid stream that can cut like a digging tool, through sprays of increasing fineness, to a fog. The diameter of the water column at a given distance from the nozzle can also be controlled; both wide- and narrow-angle spray patterns are used. It is essential that the operator be able quickly to adjust the pattern of water delivery to the need. A solid, cutting stream may be best in knocking down a hot fire in heavy fuels; for penetrating deep, smoldering duff; or for dealing with fire high in a burning snag. A fine spray or fog may be best in other situations, as in leaf and grass fuel types.

There are many kinds of nozzles, and no one type or kind will serve all purposes. They should be selected to best fit the pressure, the rate of delivery available, and the kind of job to be done. For example, there is no point in using a nozzle designed for 30 gallons per minute delivery when 20 is all that can be furnished or in using two hose lines when desired pressure can be maintained in only one. Similarly, high-pressure nozzles are ineffective without sufficient pressure.

High-pressure fog nozzles have been very effective inside structures and are popular among urban fire fighters. They have proved ineffective on wildfires outdoors. The fog cannot be fully directed, but the high pressure creates a pattern of air entrainment around the target area which tends to stimulate the burning rate around its margins.

Most nozzles used are combination types adjustable to deliver a straight stream or varying fineness of spray. Such a combination nozzle is illustrated in Figure 13.14. Additional versatility is gained by use of interchangeable tips at a fraction of the cost of the complete nozzle. For low-volume spray or stream delivery in hard to get at places, an applicator, essentially consisting of a 4-foot rigid tube with a delivery tip screwed on the end of a nozzle, is efficient.

An essential feature of any nozzle is a quick-acting shutoff valve. In knocking down a fire or extinguishing the burning perimeter, water is

Figure 13.14 Stream and fog combination nozzle. *(U.S. Forest Service photo.)*

most efficiently used in short bursts. It takes skill and experience to use just enough water to do the job and then shut off the nozzle immediately. Such practices save water. This is critical when a limited-capacity tank truck and a long haul to the water source both impose limitations. The know-how of a good nozzle man in meeting different fire situations cannot be imparted in a textbook. Much of this type of information is given in manuals issued by fire control organizations.

Gravity Water Systems In mountainous country, a natural water source may be above the point of desired use on a fire, and gravity can sometimes be used in lieu of a power pumper. Gravity pressure develops at the rate of 43.3 pounds for each 100 feet of vertical drop. At least a 50-foot drop is necessary to develop useful pressure. A gravity intake, or sock, is used, consisting of a cone-shaped piece of canvas about 10 inches in diameter at the large end, which is held open by a metal ring. The other end tapers down to a threaded male coupling to which the hose is attached. A gravity water system provides an ideal facility for mop-up of fire in smoldering fuels.

Water Sources Much can be done in advance of wildfire to augment natural water sources in an area. Some organizations give water development much emphasis. Such work consists of locating available sources on maps, constructing access routes to natural water, digging water holes, developing springs, establishing storage basins or tanks at strategic locations, and digging wells. Michigan (Stewart, 1934) developed a technique of rapid washing-in of temporary wells in a few minutes where soils are suitable and the water table is not lower than about 20 feet. Advance planning of water sources is profitable in all areas where dependence is placed on use of water in first attack. Existing and proposed sources of water and programs for their systematic development become important features of fire plans in such areas.

CHEMICALS IN FOREST FIRE FIGHTING

Use of chemicals is an important factor in the choice and maintenance of pumping equipment and is a prerequisite to direct attack on fires from the air.

Combustion itself is a chemical reaction. Consequently, it is logical to seek chemical means of inhibiting, retarding, or stopping it. Unfortunately this has proved difficult. In part this has been due to an incomplete understanding of the combustion process, in part to the nature of combustion itself. Robbing a large fire of energy on the same scale that such energy is being produced remains an impossibility. But chemical means of inhibiting combustion or of slowing down or extinguishing a small fire or a small portion of a large fire have continued to make progress since 1955. This process will continue. Although chemical means of breaking the combustion chain reaction has future promise, as illustrated by basic research by Friedman and Levy (1957) with the haloginated hydrocarbons, the most obvious effects of chemicals used are physical in nature.

It is known that salts of most alkali metals have an inhibiting effect on the combustion reaction. One of the most familiar is sodium bi-carbonate. When heated it undergoes the reaction

$$NaHCO_3 = CO_2 + NaOH$$

The CO_2 has a blanketing effect and both the salt particles and the gas exert a cooling effect. These appear to be sufficient to account for the practical value of sodium and potassium bicarbonate as extinguishers of flaming materials indoors, but the value of these effects is considerably decreased on outdoor fires. However, the research cited above indicated that the inhibiting effect actually realized was chemical in nature. This may later prove true of certain other retardant effects that appear to be chiefly physical in nature.

In the 1930s, a considerable list of chemical agents which have fire retardant properties was established through a special research project conducted by the U.S. Forest Service's Forest Products Laboratory (Truax, 1939). Three of these which appeared most promising in these preliminary tests, namely monammonium and diammonium phosphate and ammonium sulfate, became the subject of much further research and development by the U.S. Forest Experiment Stations following exploratory tests in 1955. These tests were carried out by cooperating fire agencies in a project which was known as Operation Firestop. A by-product chemical, a mixture described as sodium calcium borate, was also the subject of much research during this period, since it was the first slurry mixture dropped on fires from aircraft. Prompt application of what was learned through this research activity, accompanied by intensive equipment development, resulted in revolutionary developments in ten years. The use of chemicals for attack on fires by aircraft became firmly established and the expanding use of chemicals in more conventional fire control ground operations was well launched (N.F.P.A. Forest Committee, 1967).

Prior to this intensive development, some experimental work had been done with wetting agents (Fons, 1950), but findings had been much slower in affecting fire control practice.

The chemicals that have found a place in forest fire control may be classified for convenience into the following categories and subcategories:

> Water-modifying agents
>> Wetting agents
>> Viscous agents
>> Foams

Water-carrying slurries
Flame-inhibiting chemicals

They will be discussed more specifically in this order.

Wetting Agents

By a wetting agent is meant a chemical that reduces the surface tension of water, causing it to spread or penetrate more readily over surfaces and through porous materials. Pure water has a surface tension of 73 dynes per centimeter. For fire-fighting use, addition of a wetting agent to a concentration that will reduce the surface tension to 30 to 35 dynes per centimeter is considered desirable. Wetting agents give an advantage wherever complete wetting is a problem.

Fons (1950) made laboratory and field tests of 14 wetting agents. On the average, he found that wet water from these agents spread two to eight times as far on a smooth surface and penetrated eight times as far into uncharred wood as plain water. He found that it penetrated charcoal and charred wood five times as much as plain water.

In terms of advantages in fire suppression, the potential in heavy litter and duff fuels was a possible savings of 23 percent in the water required and 13 percent in the time required for complete mop-up of a small fire. Wet water showed superiority in knocking down flame quickly and in reducing the incidence of rekindling following mop-up operations. Dead fuels remained wet 50 percent longer when sprayed with wet water; and once they had been treated and dried out again, they could be sprayed with plain water with the same result as the original treatment.

But wet water is not superior in all situations. Because it forms a thinner film on aerial fuels and the surface of undecayed litter, it has less heat absorbing capacity per unit of surface of such fuels. So such surfaces dry out more quickly. Also it does not increase the cooling and smothering potential of water. Consequently, on a hot fire where all the water applied is being quickly evaporated, wet water gives no advantage. The primary advantage comes from more rapid wetting of ground fuels and less waste of water by runoff from fuel surfaces.

Consequently, wet water gives the greatest advantage in extinguishing fire in the fuels which support glowing combustion. Since this is a time-consuming task in the mop-up of fires in mixed fuels, it offers the greatest return when employed in this activity. Low rates (3 to 6 gallons per minute) and special techniques of application are needed for maximum effectiveness.

Most wetting agents foam in solution. Some foaming of wet water seems to be a desirable property in mop-up activities. The films formed between the particles by the foam hold the water until it can penetrate. However, excessive foaming is undesirable and to be avoided in selecting a wetting agent. Though wetting agents vary in their attributed qualities, their spreading and penetrating capabilities do not differ widely. For that reason a number of wetting agents appear to be about equally useful in forest fire control. Most are corrosive to some degree to iron or galvanized iron tanks. For that reason the use of a rust inhibitor is desirable when wet water is to be left in a tank.

Viscous Agents

Just as the reduction of the surface tension of water gives certain special advantages, agents that significantly increase surface tension of water also have special advantages in some applications. These include thickening agents of various kinds which increase the ability of a fluid to resist flow. Relative resistance to flow is known as viscosity. It is measured in several ways and, though increased viscosity and increased surface tension are associated, they are separate parameters. For use in rating fire control chemicals, viscosity only is identified and measured.

Several viscosity agents by which water may be thickened are available. With any of these, viscosity up to a firm gel can be created. For application by pumps from fire trucks, a viscosity similar to that of a thin syrup is preferred. This is rated at 150 centipoises (units of viscosity), with that of plain water rated at 1.002 at 20°C.

The particular advantage of thickened water is that it sticks to surfaces and clings to fuels in a layer several times the thickness of the film formed by plain water. Because of this, it can absorb much more heat. This gives it special value for (1) pretreating fuels outside the fire line to prevent ignition in backfiring operations and (2) in the direct and parallel methods of building fire line.

On test fires it has shown advantages for direct attack on high-intensity fires and shows particular promise in protecting structures against exterior ignition. In addition to its holding more water in contact with a surface, it tends to seal the surface. This adds a smothering as well as a blanketing effect. It has shown value in mop-up in this way in extinguishing fire in logs and heavy material.

However, it does not penetrate a fuel bed and does not wet fuels below the surface. So it can serve to best advantage as a supplement rather than as a substitute for wet water. In use it has the disadvantage of causing very slippery footing. It is likely to lose viscosity in storage due to contamination by trace amounts of chemicals or by bacterial action. But since it is easy to mix as needed, this problem is easily solved for ground tankers. It is, however, more complex for aerial tankers. Increased viscosity in hose lines causes considerable friction loss. At the nozzle, it produces a more solid hose stream and causes water spray to disperse less in the air. This is of advantage when the stream is being directed at a specific target such as a tall burning snag. In spite of the several positive advantages described, viscous water has been slow in gaining a place in ground operations in forest fire fighting.

Foams

Stable foams are highly effective in extinguishing fires in flammable liquids. These foams are stronger and more stable than those typical of the wetting agents in use. Their smothering action is the primary factor and they have been highly developed for this purpose. Several types of foam are used, with expansion rates from 8.5 to 18 gallons per gallon of water.

For various reasons they have also been of interest to forest fire fighters. The potential value of stable foam that can persist for two hours or more is that of acting as an insulating agent against firebrands and against radiation. Among the uses visualized are a blanket of foam on the roof of a building threatened by a forest fire, over susceptible fuels such as logs and snags, along the outside of a backfire line or the fire control line, or perhaps in depth to completely fill the interior of a threatened structure. A wide strip of foam has often been tried out as a substitute for a fire control line. Like viscous water, it does not wet fuels below the surface and has little or no smothering effect on glowing combustion. For that reason it has been common experience in deep litter fuels for the fire to continue to spread under the foam and soon to cross any barrier created by this means. Consequently, the potential is in a special-purpose category with some possible advantages over viscous water.

One handicap to use of foam where it could be effective is the need for special mixing devices and nozzles, though it is possible to feed the foaming agent into a water hose line by means of a proportioner. Another handicap is the effect of wind. Even a moderate wind tends to carry foam away and to dissipate it. If and when a forest fire tanker unit can be adapted to the application of foam at will without loss of other capabilities, foam will no doubt find increased employment on wild-land fires.

Water-carrying Slurries

Early in the effort to find means of applying water to fires from aircraft, it was found that water dissipated so rapidly falling through the air that something was needed to bring it down with little loss in a definite pattern and in a predictable trajectory. Fine clays mixed into the water to the consistency of a thin batter served this objective very well and have continued in use for air tanker operations. The clay most commonly used was a special high-swelling sodium type of bentonite clay mixed with water at the rate of 0.75 pound per gallon of water. For aerial delivery, a dye is added to make the slurry more visible on the ground.

In earlier practice, sodium-calcium-borate, which produces a slurry similar to bentonite, was widely used. It was assumed to have flame-inhibiting properties. However, later research demonstrated that such properties, if present, were of a very low order. It was discontinued in favor of bentonite for short-term fire-retardant effects and by other clays and viscous agents carrying more active retardants for longer-term retardant effects. The latter have gained dominance.

Clays of the bentonite type have several advantages besides helping to deliver water in a predictable pattern and intensity. Such clays hold a high percentage of water and remain wet for one to two hours under summer drying conditions. The clay coats fuels with an inert layer of mud which retains some insulating value and gives considerable resistance to ignition after the water evaporates. It forms a very stable slurry, is inexpensive, is readily available, and is noncorrosive and nontoxic.

It has the disadvantage of being abrasive and erosive to pumping and handling equipment and requires special equipment and facilities for availability in fire fighting.

Flame-inhibiting Chemicals

Of the many chemicals that have some fire retardant properties, ammonium phosphates and ammonium sulfate have been found most effective for forest fire control. The phosphates, which consist of monammonium and diammonium phosphate, are approximately 1.5 times as effective as ammonium sulfate and are much superior to most other chemicals tested. This is because they act as retardants to both flaming combustion and glowing combustion. Ammonium sulfate is effective against flaming combustion only.

The precise manner in which these chemicals interfere with combustion has not been fully established. It is believed that they react with the products of combustion to form incombustible products and that they interfere with access of oxygen by creating a glazed layer over the fuel. This effect is independent of moisture. Fuels that are treated with water solutions of these chemicals and then allowed to dry retain their fire retardant character. For that reason these chemicals are referred to as long-term inhibitors or retardants—as compared to water or inert slurries, which are shorter-term in their effects.

Monammonium phosphate, often referred to as MAP, and diammonium phosphate, similarly referred to as DAP, are used in both ground and aerial application. DAP is more soluble and has a neutral pH, while MAP is somewhat acidic. DAP is usually preferred for these reasons, though it is necessary to apply more DAP than MAP for a given phosphate level. Both vary a great deal in solubility with temperature of the water. In the range of 32°F to 212°F, MAP ranges from 18.5 to 63.0 percent and DAP from 30.5 to 52.0 percent.

Both are obtainable in crystalline or powder form and in several grades for use as fertilizer. The concentration of these chemicals in solution is described either in terms of percent of solution by weight or percent of P_2O_5 equivalent. By weight, solutions of 10 to 15 percent are commonly used. This corresponds to a P_2O_5 equivalent percent of approximately 8.

For use in ground tankers and backpack pumps, water solutions of this order can be used effectively. A viscous solution with DAP applied experimentally along the outside of a backfire line was found highly effective in preventing ignition of fuels outside of controlled burn areas and areas being backfired out. It is similarly effective in strengthening the fire control line through areas of high-energy fuels.

For use in aerial tankers in the southeastern United States, DAP-MAP mixtures available as liquid fertilizers are quite commonly used without thickening agents; elsewhere, solutions of DAP and MAP are usually thickened with viscous agents such as CMC (carboxymethylcellulose) or with a clay carrying agent. Attapulgite clay is often used in commercial fire retardants. Also included in slurry to be stored for emergency use by aerial tankers are additives to inhibit corrosion (usually sodium dichromate), at times an additive to prevent spoilage of the thickener, and a dye to give visibility to areas treated from the air. Several manufacturers now produce retardant slurry mixtures in powder form ready to mix. Because of convenience and developing price competition in this field, it has become common to purchase slurry formulations which have been produced commercially. Several such formulations are now available.

Although, as previously stated, ammonium sulfate is a less effective retardant than ammonium phosphates in a ratio of 2 to 3, it has certain advantages that retain a place for it in forest fire fighting. These are easy solubility and low cost. It has over twice the solubility of DAP, so it is not sensitive to temperature or to impurities in the water and is easily mixed. It can be thickened with industrial gums or clays in the same manner as phosphates. One manufactured fire retardant product consists of a 15 percent by weight ammonium sulfate solution thickened by attapulgite clay, with pigment and a corrosion inhibitor added.

AIRCRAFT AND ACCESSORY EQUIPMENT

The use of aircraft to overcome the problem of transport of men and equipment to a fire in roadless country began with the dropping of specially packaged equipment and supplies from fixed-wing aircraft by free fall. Then it progressed to delivery by burlap and other disposable parachutes and finally to delivery by conventional nylon and other parachutes designed for use by military personnel but declared excess for such use.

Though limited dropping of supplies and equipment by parachute is possible from all propeller planes, only a few aircraft are well designed for such use. The old Ford trimotor of World War II fame was for a long time the preferred aircraft for parachute operations. It could slow down to 80 miles per hour or less without stalling, could climb steeply out of mountain canyons, and could land and take off from short, bumpy runways even when carrying a load of freight. For such reasons it was the first "flying platform" for launching parachuted fire fighters.

A series of military and nonmilitary types of airplane have since been utilized for both smoke jumping and cargo dropping. However, to be well-adapted to this use, all must have a low stalling speed, good climbing ability, and short runway requirements for takeoff and landing. Canadian aircraft designed for backcountry use meet such requirements exceptionally well.

This is well exemplified by the so-called Otter and Beaver, which are widely used in fire control operations. The twin-engine Canadair excels for heavy-duty attack on fires with water. It can pick up 12,000 pounds (1,500 gallons) of water from a lake surface in 15 seconds at 70 miles per hour in two 750 gallon tanks and can drop the water at two locations or in two sorties. This makes it possible to employ this technique of water bombing effectively on much larger and more intense fires.

Several types of propeller aircraft manufactured in the United States have been widely used in fire control activities, but most are not replaceable because of obsolescence caused by competition with jet planes in commercial use.

Jet aircraft are too fast-moving for nearly all uses in forest fire control. This leaves some questions of future availability of properly designed fixed-wing aircraft for forest fire activities. Helicopters and, possibly, unconventional types of aircraft will no doubt meet such a deficit.

As discussed in Chapter 12, the helicopter is exceptionally well adapted to fire control uses. It permits close inspection of the perimeter of a fire from the air and can place water or chemicals on a fire with more precision than a fixed-wing aircraft. Similarly, it can be used to place incendiaries in carrying out a difficult backfiring operation.

Helicopters with a capacity of 500 to 700 gallons of retardant or water can safely drop it from an elevation of only 50 to 100 feet above the ground when traveling at 25 to 50 knots.

Racks for laying fire hose by helicopter and dispensers for accurately placing water or a fire retardant on a desired target are in regular use. A rapidly developing technology of helicopter use in a variety of fire control missions is to be expected.

Aerial Tankers

Most aircraft used in the United States for dropping water or chemicals on fires operate under contract with forest fire agencies and are not a part of the permanent fire equipment. In California, 21 air-tanker bases are operated. In 1968, the State Division of Forestry in that state and the U.S. Forest Service had 29 tankers under contract at these bases. Smaller planes (50- to 200-gallon tanks) utilized for this purpose are usually agricultural spray planes modified for the purpose. Larger tankers (200 to 2,500 gallons) are ordinarily converted military planes on which tanks have been mounted. Such planes are equipped with a large gate, controlled by the pilot, which can empty the tank in a few seconds. In the larger planes the tanker capacity may be separated into several compartments which can be emptied separately. This gives greater flexibility to the operation.

To operate effectively, the tanker plane must have good payload capacity, good maneuverability, and the ability to climb steeply. When the liquid or slurry is released, it cascades down, forming an elongated oval of the solution on ground fuels. In timber stands some is intercepted by the tree crowns. This is undesirable where crown fires are not likely. A higher proportion of the less viscous liquids and slurries penetrates the crown canopy to coat surface fuels.

Equipment for Mixing, Pumping, and Storing Retardants

A specialized technology involving specialized equipment, has developed around aerial tanker operation. This equipment includes devices for mixing chemical solutions and slurries, pumps for handling abrasive and corrosive materials of this kind, and distribution and storage systems for the mixed slurry. Since air tankers can operate effectively over a radius of up to 200 miles, such facilities can be highly centralized. Where air-tanker use is frequent, as in California, permanent chemical mixing plants have been developed. Large tank capacities, up to 40,000 gallons for storage of slurry, and facilities for storage of dry chemicals and for mixing, pumping, and loading are in proportion. A continuous-flow injector mixer has been developed. Such facilities are the responsibility of trained specialists and will not be detailed here. At temporary sites, canvas tanks and pumps lined with plastic often hold the reserve supply for helicopters or small tankers, and a portable mixer on a trailer serves to mix the retardant at a sufficient rate. Descriptions of such facilities and requirements for their successful operation are contained in the second edition of the N.F.P.A. publication entitled *Chemicals for Forest Fire Fighting* (1967).

Parachutes

The smoke jumper's parachute is naturally a critical item. The most distinctive feature is that it can be steered within limits to a selected landing spot. This feature depends on two slots which create air jets when the parachute is inflated in its descent. Guidelines which can change the direction and velocity of these jets give the smoke jumper considerable option in determining his landing spot. The parachutes are made of nylon, with a 32-foot canopy which affords slow descent. The gradual evolution of smoke-jumper parachutes since 1940 is an interesting story in itself.

Parachutes for dropping supplies, sometimes referred to as freight parachutes, have also gone through considerable evolution. In early practice in the United States, techniques of packaging were developed by which many items could be dropped by free fall. This was followed by development of the burlap parachute, which did not need to be returned to the base. Such practices were made obsolete by the availability of ample supplies of surplus military parachutes originally manufactured for personnel use. This has resulted in improved reliability in delivering supplies by parachute as well.

Protective Equipment

Protective clothing and equipment for smoke jumpers has been subject to considerable change with time. But most change has been in the material used. The equipment still consists of the same essentials. An emergency 28-foot parachute in a chest pack with a quickly attachable harness is always carried. The remainder of the outfit consists of a two-piece padded suit, a football-type helmet with a wire mesh face mask, a nylon let-down rope, and heavy logger boots. These have each proved their value in practice and together have built a very impressive safety record during the entire history of this operation.

A similar type of suit and face mask has been found effective in protecting helicopter crews who must jump into the brush while the helicopter hovers at brush-top height.

FIRE EQUIPMENT DEVELOPMENT

Most of the progress in devising better forest fire equipment has come about through a teamwork effort generally referred to as fire equipment development. Always it involves new ideas or concepts and must be supported by varying degrees of applied research. Often it involves development of a new system of doing things. The most frequent participants have been foresters who became specialists in forest fire control or were trained in forest fire research, mechanical engineers specializing in forest fire equipment, and technicians of many categories.

The tradition in the U.S. Forest Service for seeking progress in forest fire control by this means is closely identified with David P. Godwin, who was in charge of this activity for many years. He coordinated the development of equipment and techniques for delivering supplies and equipment to the scene of a forest fire during the 1935 to 1940 period and arranged the first trials of parachuting fire fighters in 1939 at Winthrop, Washington (Clepper, 1969). An organized system of forest fire control through primary dependence on aircraft and smoke jumpers was successfully developed by 1947. It has continued active operation in much of the backcountry of the western United States and Alaska since that time. Its success has depended on an intensive and continuing program of equipment development.

Equipment development activity has been widely disseminated among forest fire agencies and is everywhere a crucial part of the history of progress in forest fire control. The story is different for each forest region. Usually it reflects local personalities and distinctive problems of the local environment. Whether or not the effort is fully productive depends on two things: first, the amount of research devoted to fire equipment needs, and second, the availability of funds and facilities to carry through planned projects. Among state agencies, the research and development work carried on for many years for the state of Michigan by Gilbert Stewart at Roscommon, Michigan, gave that state a leadership role in fire equipment development in the eastern United States for several decades.

Nevertheless, many contributions have been made through the inventiveness and ingenuity of individuals working with very limited facilities. Many fire control men are equipment-minded and most have ideas for improving the fire equipment used in their area. Such ideas need to be encouraged, yet efforts to carry through on a new equipment idea are likely to be ineffective when time and supporting facilities, funds, and engineering know-how are limited.

History to date indicates that the best progress toward a creative contribution to forest fire equipment is to encourage the man with the idea to carry its application only far enough to demonstrate its soundness, or to build a model. At that point the development and testing necessary for the next step should be planned as a special project. The author of the idea may participate as a team member in this equipment development project, but it needs to be placed in the hands of competent manufacturers or engineers for further technical development. By such a process the period of development may be much shortened and fewer good ideas will be lost or discredited.

The publication known as *Fire Control Notes* was initiated by David P. Godwin. Its original purpose was to disseminate new equipment ideas between agencies and forest regions and to serve as a clearinghouse to reduce duplication of effort. Though its subject matter has broadened considerably with time, it has continued its emphasis on new equipment ideas and development.

Chapter 14

Designing Fire Control Systems

The purpose of this chapter is to give an understanding of the design and structure of existing fire control systems and of the principles and guidelines that may be applied to revise such systems when readjustment is needed.

All systematic fire control depends on advance planning. Consequently, every level of the fire organization participates to some degree in this activity and some distinctions are needed.

First of all, the area serving as the planning unit is a basic consideration. The planning unit is the smallest unit for which a separate plan is developed. In state and private organizations in the United States, this may be national through an association of state foresters, regional through interstate compacts, state through the state office, or the unit may be the county within the state or a geographic subunit such as a protection district. Federal organizations have parallels in the geographic scope of fire control systems.

The function to be served is the second distinction. The operating system in an area may be regarded as serving all three lines of defense in systematic fire control. These are:

1   To prevent as many fires as possible from starting
2   To control the fires that do start while they are still small
3   To minimize the size and destructiveness of the fires that start
and become large in spite of these provisions

A separate plan or approach designed to attain each of these objectives is
made for each planning unit, then all are integrated either through a more
or less formal master plan or informally through current operating plans
and instructions.

The degree of success in 1 determines the size of the problem in the
succeeding phases, and a high degree of success in 2 reduces the requirements for 3. Study of the record on any protection unit will show the
relative success being attained under 1, 2, and 3. Though there are no
precise standards by which to measure success, comparison between
areas having similar problems is usually sufficient to identify the areas in
which improvement through redesign of the system is most needed.

Necessity for Planning

There are several needs that require advance planning of the fire organization and its facilities. The following are the most common:

1   The problem of maintaining readiness to attack a fire at any time
and place within the protected unit
2   Need for flexibility to enable the organization to gear its response to wide fluctuations in the size of the fire fighting job from day to
day
3   Need of prompt action for success
4   Need to solve problems of poor access and slow travel in parts of
the protected area
5   Need to serve large areas with minimum forces
6   Need for utilizing inexperienced men with a minimum of direct
supervision
7   Need for cooperative arrangements
8   Need to coordinate plans and systems

Although wildfires may start almost anywhere in a protected unit
and may spread anytime fire danger exists, the probability that they will
start and spread at a particular time varies widely. Fire danger ratings, fire
weather forecasts, and analysis of fire risks enable the fire manager to
greatly reduce the uncertainties and to operate his organization more
efficiently.

Success in control usually demands quick action, but wild-land
protection units are large and many fires occur at a considerable distance

from the nearest attack unit. Such handicaps to speedy action are often aggravated by poor access of critical areas and slow travel. Such problems can be met by planned alternatives such as improving and extending the road system, increasing the number and speed of travel of the units used in first attack, moving them closer to fire risk areas, and other measures to improve the effectiveness of equipment and the efficiency of men.

A further important reason for planning is that the control action may often be taken by inexperienced men. In many wild-land management units, fire control is only a part of the overall activity. Fire control specialists and special fire-fighting units are always limited in number and coverage. In localities where the fire problem is critical, they may be assigned in adequate numbers to carry out most fire control activities. Where it is less critical, fire control work may become the part-time responsibility of a large number of individuals whose main job is something else. In either case, fire emergencies from time to time may make heavy demands on the talents and facilities of the organization. Careful planning minimizes the disrupting effect of this process and enables amateurs to become effective.

In practical terms, two kinds of planning are involved. The first is concerned with designing systems, the second with operating them. The purpose of the first is the strategic placement of facilities to make effective control of fires possible. The purpose of the second is to ensure the realization of the full potential of facilities to make the control of fires effective. The first concerns equipment and facilities of all kinds, the second concerns systematic selection, training, and management of personnel. Planning of equipment and facilities is relatively long-term in nature. A well-designed fire detection system, for example, may operate successfully for ten years without change. But planned action by personnel must always be subject to short-term modification. Training to ensure the performance essential to planned action is discussed in Chapter 15.

As used in this text, the term *fire control system* may designate any function of the fire control organization for which separate objectives are set and a separate plan is drawn up. Examples are unit plans for fire prevention, detection, communication, transportation, dispatching, or first attack. The term refers as well to the operating plan into which these separate plans must be integrated.

Objectives to Be Met

Fire control systems must be designed to advance fire control objectives. The overall objective of all fire control activities is to produce human benefits at a favorable cost, but exact appraisal of accomplishment by such criteria is not feasible. Instead, the fire control manager and the planner of fire control systems work toward more specific but intermediate goals such as some quota of number of fires or acres burned or a particular set of standards of performance.

Maximizing accomplishment at minimum cost for each separate goal will not necessarily achieve the ultimate objective. For example, the cheapest way to prevent fires might be to completely exclude all use and development in the area, but the cheapest way to get quick detection might be through having plenty of cooperators in the area, or it might be through extending aerial patrol that was already covering an adjoining area. The cheapest way to get quick, dependable action on a fire in the area might be through crews employed for other work projects in the unit. Superimposed on each other, these separate plans might easily conflict and could be costly. Each must be integrated with the other. Then their combined accomplishment must be tested to make sure that together they produce maximum protection at a cost in keeping with the losses to be prevented. This is the essence of integrated planning.

Concepts in Systematic Planning

The orderly development of fire control systems in the United States engaged the attention of early research men and wild-land administrators beginning with Coert Dubois (1914). This paralleled the growth of systems of fire danger rating described in Chapter 8 and was a part of the same effort to develop and apply objective guides to the building of fire control systems. In fire danger rating, these took the form of measures to gauge the variations in the size of the fire-fighting job with time as discussed in Chapter 8; in fire prevention, they developed in the pattern of statistical diagnosis and prescription as described in Chapter 9. In presuppression planning, these took the form of minimizing the time required to attack a fire following its inception or its discovery.

Time requirements became an overriding guide. This had always been so in urban and industrial fire-fighting systems. It is equally important to the success of forest fire fighting, even though poorer access and longer distances normally make it necessary to accept slower attack. The relation between speed of attack and success in controlling fires at small size in California was well explored through studies by Show and Kotok (1929). From these they developed time standards for attack on fires in California fuel types which were termed hour-control standards (Show and Kotok, 1930). Such standards became the pattern for criteria of adequacy of existing and proposed fire control systems in the western United States during the succeeding two decades. Since the time required to attack a fire includes discovery, report, getaway, and travel, it is a composite item. To bring it to a minimum, the time required for each step must have separate attention. The elapsed-time record, which is still an important part of individual fire reports used by most fire agencies, was devised to permit ready comparison between actual performance and accepted standards for speed of action at each step in the time sequence.

A second important concept was "coverage." Detection coverage is the area within which a small fire can be detected by an observer at a lookout or other vantage point. It is independent of time for a fixed location but becomes time-dependent when the observer is in an aircraft. A time-dependent form of coverage originally known as fireman or smokechaser coverage represents area in which a fire can be reached within a given time limit, starting from a designated point. This will be discussed in relation to transportation planning.

Formal planning of fire control systems using criteria of time standards and of coverage received much attention on the National Forests prior to 1945. Up-to-date improvement and redesign as conditions change is of continuing interest to all fire agencies. To make it productive, the methods and criteria underlying the system to be revised should first be understood. The principles described for each of the following planning systems are intended to assist in this respect.

FIRE PREVENTION ACTION PLANS

In Chapter 9, national, regional, and local public education programs were considered. Though carefully planned, they do not constitute a complete plan of fire prevention, since management of fuels (Chapter 10) as well as risks must be considered, and regulation of use becomes an important tool. The complete fire prevention action plan is best illustrated where it becomes the responsibility of a unit manager on the ground. The unit considered in the following pages is approximately that of an important ranger district on a National Forest.

The fire prevention plan for a local protection unit may be obscured or may actually be nonexistent despite an impressive collection of supporting data having some bearing on the local prevention of fires. An important distinction needs emphasis. A fire prevention plan consists only of a proposed program of action. A collection of data is not a plan and has little significance except as it relates to planning.

The fire prevention plan itself will usually consist of a schedule of projected measures to be carried out. Since most are on an areawide basis, current map records are usually a part of the plan. Identified risk zones may each be singled out for special action. Fuel types which support high-intensity fires may also be identified and closed to recreational use or isolated by firebreaks. A sign and poster map may be needed to provide a complete basis for selection and posting of appropriate signs to best serve the local problem.

Planned patrol of crucial areas during critical periods of fire danger, including assignment of personnel, routes of travel, and time of day, are essential elements. However, they are usually integrated into the presuppression plan and are often not separately identified as a part of the fire prevention plan.

The fire prevention plan for a local unit will vary with the type of fire control organization. State organizations and private protective associations are often protecting lands of other owners. This may limit areawide planning to short-term arrangements. It may also result in concentrating public education programs in the state forester's office and omitting specific provisions for reducing fire hazards except for those covered by local legislation. On federal lands and on state-owned lands, the more complete control of activities on the land permits the inclusion of the regulation of use and the treatment of fuels. This broader scope is illustrated in the problem cases given in the following section.

Fitting Plans to Local Problems

Public education programs are designed to instill an attitude of acceptance and support of fire laws and regulations and to teach people how to take the more elementary precautions necessary to prevent fires from their own activities. The accomplishment of these things is a prerequisite to successful fire prevention. It sets the stage. But unless skillfully supplemented by a local action program, they may fall far short of bringing about significant reduction in fire losses.

The relationship is akin to using a shotgun or a target rifle when shooting at a distant target. Each local problem often requires separate attention as a specific target. The busy forest manager may accept the idea that the fire prevention job is already being done by the specialists, so his responsibility is limited. This is far from true. At best, specialists even including law enforcement officers can relieve him of only a part of the job and responsibility. His responsibility demands such control of fuels and sources of risk in his protection unit that fire costs and losses will be at a minimum. This requires skill in the selection and application of prevention measures to fit the local problem.

How can he go about this in an orderly manner? The case examples cited in Chapter 9 are suggestive of how the public education phase of the job may be extended and adapted to local use. But beyond that, the local forest administrator needs a plan definitely tied to the fire prevention problems on the ground throughout his forest unit.

Such a plan may vary a great deal in detail and emphasis depending on the makeup of the fire problem. But experience has demonstrated the following general approach to be highly effective. Basically it consists of analysis, diagnosis, and prescription. A final step of coordination and integration is also needed when diagnosis and prescription must be applied piecemeal.

The Fire Risk Map   From the individual fire reports for the protection unit, the location of fires that occurred the preceding year or for a period of years can be posted on a map. This is sometimes called a fire business map. Figure 14.1 is a diagrammatic representation of such a map, on which the starting points of fires for the preceding five years have been posted. Man-caused fires are shown by a spot, lightning fires by a cross. When several years' record has been assembled in this way, patterns of occurrence become evident. If activities and access have not changed significantly, a ten-year record brings them out even more clearly. On western forests, a 20-year record of lightning fires often shows a surprisingly definite pattern of occurrence. For the area shown in Figure 14.1, most of the fires fall in fairly definite concentration areas around which a zone boundary can be drawn.[1] When this is done, the map may be referred to as a risk zone map. Counting the fires on the map, it will be seen that an average of about 11 fires per year have been occurring. As is typical, about 80 percent fall in identified risk zones with about 20 percent scattered in other areas. Lightning fires occur erratically but average only about one per year, so these are not an important factor in this unit.

Areas of Special Risk   Six special risk areas are defined by the zone boundaries drawn. These are numbered consecutively, 1 to 6, on the map. The next step is to diagnose the reasons for the high frequency of fires in each of these particular locations as is done below. Then after considering all available means of reducing the frequency, the combination most likely to be productive in this particular locality can be identified.

Area 1   This is the location of the dump for the small town of Jackson, an unincorporated town with no local ordinances concerning burning at the dump. The local grocer dumps cartons and waste paper which he usually ignites as he leaves; others dump flammable trash.

---

[1] A general rule in drawing such a boundary is that, except as modified by fuels or barriers on the ground, it be half the distance outside of the average spacing of fire locations inside.

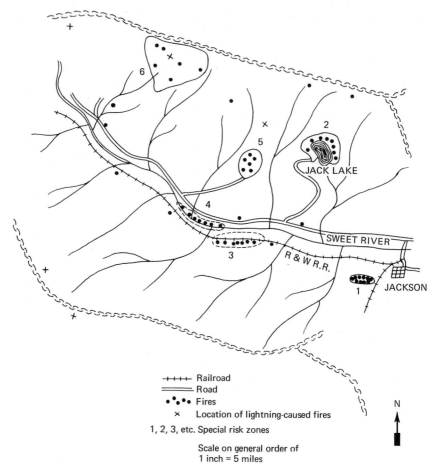

Figure 14.1   Fire risk map (Jackson District).

Children sometimes amuse themselves playing with fire in the dump.
Three times in one year fires escaped from the dump on dry, windy days.
One jumped the railroad track to the east and burned two outbuildings at
the edge of the town. Another burned grass and brush to the intersection
of the two railroad tracks to the northeast and set two spot fires across the
river near the road.

REMEDIAL ACTION   The important need is to induce some
reliable person to accept responsibility for regulating the burning. A
volunteer fire department is located at a small town 5 miles away. They

may be persuaded to visit the dump once a week with their fire truck and do the burning. If so, signs should be posted accordingly. Instructions and specifications for operating a town dump without danger of fire are available through the National Fire Protection Association. This information should be utilized. If the dump is operated by the county, the sheriff or other official may make county equipment available to maintain a wide firebreak and perhaps a metal fence around the dump.

The forest protection agency may find it effective to enter into a cooperative agreement by which the local officer extends assistance or supervision. If there is a forest fire warden in the community, perhaps he can become effective if given specific authority.

Area 2—Jack Lake   This is a frequently used though undeveloped fishing and picnic area. Eight fires have required attention in this area in the last five years. Careful review of the individual fire reports leave in some doubt the specific cause of four of them, which were classed as smoker fires. The other four resulted from abandoned camp and picnic fires. Although all fires were small, they were a threat to a very desirable recreation area on the lake and to a heavy timber stand above the lake. Users of the area might be classed as local residents, though picnic parties usually come from a farming town some 40 miles distant.

REMEDIAL ACTION   The development of a camp and picnic ground with fireplaces should greatly reduce the fire risk. Timely posting of "no smoking" signs should be a useful supplement. Supervision of use and contact with visitors should also be inaugurated in this area as soon as possible.

Area 3   A 1-mile stretch of the railroad seems to have one to four fires every year. Investigation following each fire indicated that red hot fragments from brakeshoes, burning fusees, or hot carbon from sanding the flues of the diesel locomotive were the most likely causes. Three additional fires along the track also occurred outside this area.

REMEDIAL ACTION   A joint study with a representative of the railroad is indicated. Failing that, frequent checks and patrol of this area by a well-instructed forest fire prevention guard should clarify the specific cause. If heavy use of brakes along this 1-mile stretch is inevitable in the regular operation of freight trains, then a special double width of cleared and burned right-of-way for this distance may be effective. If the fires are from fusees dropped by brakemen as they slow the train approaching Jackson, instruction on how to place the fusees to avoid fire can help. If it turns out that the locomotive engineer habitually sands his flues at this point, this can be done at a less hazardous location.

Area 4   Just beyond Area 3 but across the river, there is another stretch of about a mile between the road and river in which one or more fires have been occurring every year. The fire reports indicate that most of these are due to picnic or warming fires. The river at this point has several deep pools used as swimming holes by teen-agers from Jackson.

REMEDIAL ACTION   Endeavor to get Boy Scouts or other youth groups to organize swimming activities and to undertake some responsibility for the area. Develop and post spots for picnic and cooking fires until funds permit more complete development. Arrange patrol of the area during fire danger periods.

Area 5   Area 5 is a timber-cutting area in which logging operations are in progress and are expected to continue for 2 years. Six fires occurred there in the three years since the logging operation started. Two of the fires were clearly from power saws and one was from a tractor exhaust. The other three were classed as smoker fires but may have been of similar origin. All but one of the fires were found and controlled by the logging contractor. One fire was discovered during a holiday weekend when all men were out of the area. It spread in the logging slash and was controlled only with great effort, after doing considerable damage to logs and logging equipment.

REMEDIAL ACTION   Logs are being hauled on the access road. It should be closed to all other travel as both a safety and fire measure. Armed with test information on the various ways the operation of power saws can start fires, a project should be organized through the logging contractor to make sure that all necessary precautions are being observed. Smoking regulations should be drawn up and posted, and spark arresters should be installed on all tractor mufflers. When logging is complete, the area should remain closed to recreationists until the hazardous fuels have been disposed of or their flammability has been greatly reduced.

Area 6   Although this is a larger area with a lower concentration of fires, it comprises a definite risk area high on the ridge above Sweet River. It is an old burn of about twenty years ago with considerable open brush and grass cover. Five fires classed as man-caused plus one lightning fire have occurred here in the last five years. Information from the fire reports shows that all the man-caused fires have occurred in the fall hunting season and were apparently due to warming fires set by hunters.

REMEDIAL ACTION At the end of the spur road below, where hunters leave their cars, post special signs appealing to hunters and develop one or more fireplaces for warming fires. Up on the ridge, at one or more natural gathering points for hunters, develop simple but safe campfire areas. During the hunting season, work out a cooperative hunter patrol with the game warden to check on all camp or warming fires.

Completing the Action Plan

The brief diagnosis and prescription for each special fire risk area are suggestive only. If the exact circumstances of how and why each fire started can be learned, the kinds of remedial action that may prove helpful keep increasing. The forest manager can modify both fuels and risk, so his fire prevention plan is a challenge to his resourcefulness. Reduction of hazardous fuels is covered in Chapter 10. Though most of such projects are handled separately, they are also a definite part of the local fire prevention program.

What would be desirable to do always exceeds what can be done with available personnel and facilities, so action priorities must be established.

The most dangerous threat is probably fires from risk zone 1 unless all burning in the dump can be stopped when fire danger is high. Though prevailing winds are from the west, dry winds from the northeast or southeast are experienced at times when a cold front passes through. Such a combination could cause a fire near Jackson to sweep upriver and to become a local disaster. Risk zone 5 is almost equally dangerous because of the high-energy slash fuels and steep brushy slopes north of the area. Area 2 at Jack Lake would be next in priority because of high recreation values. Lack of hazardous fuels near the lake reduces the threat somewhat. Areas 3 and 4 would rate next. Existing fire barriers, ease of access, and abundance of lush vegetation along the river reduce the threat most of the year. But a fire gaining headway on either side of the river under conditions of high fire danger would quickly sweep to the top of the river divide. Area 6 is lowest in priority since the fire season usually ends before the hunting season starts.

With these things in mind, the town dump becomes the first project to get attention, and fire prevention measures in the timber cutting area come next.

In both cases, and also in each of the other four high-risk areas, much depends on personal contact. Even if funds do not permit current construction of campgrounds, if the town dump cannot be redeveloped for some time, and if new work on burning railroad right-of-way cannot be done until next year, progress can still be made. The forest manager himself, through personal contact, will need to work on the problem of the town dump, the railroad, and the timber cutting. He may be in position to exercise authority on the timber-cutting operation but must depend primarily on enlisting cooperation in reducing the fire threat from the dump and the railroad. The national fire prevention programs should make this kind of cooperation easier, but it becomes effective only through personal contact. In the neighborhood, favorable personal contact with a few of the "opinion makers," who are not necessarily the leaders, is often sufficient to win remarkable compliance with reasonable precautions against fire.

To extend the advantages of personal contact, it is desirable to provide for a fire prevention patrol of recreation areas and of other areas where construction or other activities carry a fire risk. Until there can be reasonable assurance that fire risks are being controlled, the fire control officer should give high priority to a prevention patrol with radio communication during the periods of a critical fire danger. The scheduling of patrols and of any closures planned should be in close relation to changes in fire danger. These relationships are considered further in Chapter 15.

In conclusion, action plans to fit local fire prevention problems take up where state and national programs leave off. They must start with an analysis of past fire experience in the unit by which high-risk areas can be defined and must take into account the where, when, why, and who of individual fires in each risk area for clues to remedial action. First action prescriptions and then their priorities must be established. Finally, a plan of action utilizing available personnel and facilities is devised to accomplish as much of the high-priority fire prevention work as is possible. In such a program, personal contact and cooperation of others in fire prevention can go far to overcome lack of personnel and facilities.

DESIGN OF FUNCTIONAL SYSTEMS

In Chapter 11, techniques for planning systems of fire lookouts, for planning detection by aerial patrol, and for developing combined systems of detection were described. These well illustrate the development of a functional system designed to meet a single objective, in this case to ensure reliable and speedy detection of fires.

Planned functional systems of communication and of transportation have also had special attention in the past in an effort to reduce report time and travel time following detection. But unlike the detection system, both the communication system and the transportation system are multipurpose in character and are essential to all land-management activities. Consequently their design is usually supplemented rather than formulated by fire control requirements. Nevertheless, both are basic factors in the success or lack of success of forest fire control.

Fire Communication Systems

Means of communication are particularly critical to the functioning of the fire control organization because speed and reliability in putting through fire messages are necessary. Typically too, a small number of fire control personnel must serve a large protected area. This places a further premium on good point-to-point communication.

The wild-land communication system may be visualized as the nervous system of the fire organization, enabling quick awareness of external stimuli at some central point and quick response. It provides the essential link that enables a widely disseminated group of men to work together as key members of an organization. It is the means by which dispersed supervision, cooperation, and coordination of activities can take place on a person-to-person basis. It is the prerequisite to successful functioning of all systems of detection.

The performance specifications and structure of the system were necessarily the function of the wild-land manager and planner when the communication system depended chiefly on a ground-line telephone system assisted by some commercial metallic lines in generally un-developed areas. As metallic lines owned by the fire agency replace this system, which has in turn been progressively replaced by radio communi-cation, technical engineering requirements became more dominant. This has resulted in increasing dependence on the engineer and technician for installation and maintenance. However, effective service for fire control activities is best assured where operation of the system and specifications for its performance remain the prerogative of the forest manager. The planning and revision of communication systems should properly be the joint effort of qualified engineers and forest administrators.

Though the communication system on a forest area must serve all activities and is not solely a fire control problem, requirements for speed and reliability are normally much more exacting for fire purposes and must usually set the pattern.

Some of the principles and requirements in need of special emphasis in planning are discussed below.

Speed and Reliability   The time it takes to transmit a fire message is a controlling factor in setting the standard of communication for the fire control organization. Emergency fire messages must go through promptly. In a well-designed plan of communication, this requires:

1   Direct communication between the fire detector and the man responsible for initial action on a fire
2   Definite plans for fire dispatching
3   Provisions for 24-hour service
4   High-order maintenance to ensure minimum chance of failure of communication during the critical fire season
5   Alternate means of getting through in case of unavoidable failure during emergencies
6   Clear channels requiring elimination of overloading and of competition between users likely to either delay communication or to reduce its effectiveness
7   Elimination of static interference
8   Good outlets to commercial communication channels

Supervisory Relationships   The communication system should be so designed that every man or station that must function as a part of the fire organization can also be reached by the communication system and each man can report directly to his immediate supervisor. This often means that the shortest distance to a communication outlet will not serve properly.

Relation to Plan of Organization   The pattern of communication needs to conform also to the desired overall pattern of organization. This may be illustrated by comparing a highly centralized fire organization to a highly decentralized organization on a National Forest where the principal channels of communication are by telephone. In the former organization, a central dispatcher receives all reports of fires and initiates all action. Such a system requires direct communication between the dispatching center and every lookout, crew, or individual throughout the forest who may enter into planned first attack on fires. It also requires direct and dependable contact to outside sources of manpower and supplies through mainline commercial facilities. In a highly decentralized system, where all dispatching is normally done from the ranger's headquarters and where only emergency communication direct to the supervisor's headquarters is needed, the ranger headquarters becomes the communication hub.

With a centralized system, the communication net for the whole forest centers about the supervisor's headquarters and is distinguished by main trunk lines radiating out to all the protection units. With a decentralized system, there is a series of small nets, each centered at the respective ranger headquarters. Diagrammatically, the comparison is that of a big wheel in the first instance and of a cluster of small wheels in the second. If a change in the form of organization is desired, changes in the communication system may be essential. Each form of communication network has its special advantages and each is the best solution in certain situations. The choice is often influenced by the geography of the area involved.

Kinds of Communication Facilities Used   The most commonly used facilities are fire agency and commercial telephone systems and high- and very-high-frequency radio systems, chiefly FM (frequency modulation). The grounded telephone system of earlier days and the AM (amplitude modulation) radio have become obsolete for planning purposes. The grounded telephone line was the simplest telephone line to build and maintain. For several decades it was the symbol of organized fire control in the backcountry of the western United States. But high noise levels from static and the labor required for its maintenance became a major handicap in backcountry. These factors led to its abandonment in favor of radio.

Where it has not been made inoperative by power transmission lines, the metallic circuit telephone is still highly regarded as reliable communication for main trunk lines. But the skilled labor requirements for maintaining a main trunk line including phantom circuits and transpositions, even where power-line interference is not troublesome, are burdensome to forest fire-fighting agencies. Consequently, ownership of such lines even by federal agencies has dropped markedly since World War II, and commercial lines have become the chief dependence in this category.

The high- and very-high-frequency radio systems have special characteristics that affect their service value in fire communication. Communication by means of high- or so-called medium-frequency field radios has the advantage of being less limited by intervening rough topography. This advantage is offset to a considerable degree in AM equipment by interference from atmospheric static. To an even greater degree than with the grounded telephone line, this handicap is worst when lightning storms are active and in late afternoon during hot, dry weather over rugged terrain. This difficulty is greatly reduced be substituting FM equipment. It can also be met in part by increasing the power output of both transmitting and receiving sets. But this solution is severely limited by the interference caused by the communication of distant organizations operating on the same wavelength.

Communication with very-high-frequency (VHF) or ultra-high-frequency (UHF) equipment is limited somewhat by mountain topography, since transmission conforms closely to line-of-sight paths. This is overcome by placing automatic relays on ridgetops or other strategic topographic locations that can extend this kind of coverage to mobile equipment in the valleys. With the aid of such provisions, even where many locations remain at which messages cannot be sent or received, UHF has become the standard means of local and emergency fire communication (Figure 14.2).

Need of Flexibility   In planning fire control systems, communication must be designed not only to serve the organization in its regular functioning but must also be capable of the expansion and flexibility required to provide emergency communication for temporary periods on large project fires wherever they may occur. Radio-equipped motor vehicles and portable field radio equipment are admirably adapted to providing the needed flexibility, but additional wavelengths must be available to avoid interference when control operations on such a fire are in progress. Usually provision for emergency radio communication is made by reserving certain UHF frequencies for the purpose. Often these are in pairs, with reception on one wavelength and transmission on a second.

Relationships to Commercial Facilities   Most forest fire agencies own and operate communication facilities mainly for reasons of necessity. Commercial facilities normally do not extend into wild-land areas, and even where they are accessible they are seldom adapted to giving direct backcountry service. Consequently, most forest and radio networks do not duplicate other communication. Typically, they give backcountry points and stations their only contact with the outside world, which means a headquarters town or city, which in turn brings varying degrees of association with commercial facilities. Association with power feeder lines creates problems in telephone communication, as already discussed. These may be met by leasing commercial circuits to serve as the last leg of the backcountry telephone circuit or by complete abandonment and substitution of a VHF or UHF radio network. To avoid local interference to VHF radio reception, voice transmission is often brought in by wire from a strategically placed relay point outside of or overlooking the headquarters city, and operation is by remote control.

Figure 14.2 Forest warden, Virginia Division of Forestry, in contact with his headquarters by radio from the scene of a fire. *(U.S. Forest Service photo.)*

Dial telephone circuits have caused many problems in extending commercial telephone service to forest installations. But in the more populated areas, even a fire lookout may now be on a dial circuit. In California, the brush fire organization in Los Angeles County is served very efficiently by a teletype system.

Commercial telephone facilities and services can be expected to further replace forest telephone networks and to more closely supplement forest fire radio networks. Shortwave radio networks, on the other hand, are likely to continue as the more or less exclusive domain of forest fire agencies within their assigned wavelengths. Forest fire agencies have gradually been getting out of the telephone business, but operation of shortwave radio networks promises to continue as an important part of their activity.

Surface Transportation Systems

Forest transportation involves both means and facilities for moving men and equipment from place to place. It serves all activities and becomes important to fire control as it affects the time required to make effective attack on a fire. Transportation in the context of time, and methods of improving it to speed up action on fires, is always of special concern to the fire control planner.

In building an improved system, the planner has two general approaches by which he can cut down the travel time to fires:

1   Through strategic placement of first-attack units to reduce travel distance or by increasing their rate of travel through use of a faster vehicle
2   Through improvement of access and of speed of travel by improvement of the transportation system on the ground

Both are involved in integrated planning. But since the kind of transportation system also determines the kind of fire control system possible, the second approach will be given chief attention here.

In intensively managed areas, roads and other means of access constructed for other purposes provide most of the access needed in fire control activities. In more extensively managed and roadless areas susceptible to fire damage, fire control requirements dominate the need for access. This general principle is well illustrated by the evolution of fire control systems in the United States.

For the first two decades after National Forests were created in the western United States, huge roadless areas had to be protected from fire. Fire fighters had to be moved on foot and equipment by man pack or by pack mule. Trails to facilitate such movement became critical to fire control systems and comprised most of the fire transportation system. Even "way"[2] trails were highly regarded.

As use and development created a skeleton system of roads, critical needs for fire control shifted to the supplemental roads needed to enable fast attack to be more uniform in the protected area. Where ground transportation systems remained primitive, this placed a high premium on air transportation. Fast transport by air represents use of the first approach and is discussed later. Where waterways remain the chief travel routes, fast motorboats to substitute for slower-moving water craft closely parallel this trend.

Travel Time   The time required to get to a fire after it is reported is often the most critical limitation in preventing large fires from developing. Early emphasis on this relationship (Show and Kotok, 1929) led to the

---

[2] A way trail is an ungraded and largely unimproved foot trail but well enough marked to follow.

development of criteria for determining coverage within certain time limits. These were hour-control standards developed locally for each forest cover type. Though much of the data and techniques may now be regarded as obsolete, the principle of improving the efficiency of fire control through faster action retains full validity. The model for coverage of area by a fireman or a fire crew is described for this reason.

Coverage   The method used for defining the coverage attainable within any desired time limit from any location at which one or more fire fighters (smokechaser, fire guard, fire crew) might be stationed was devised in the early 1930s (T. W. Norcross, 1931). The locations for which such computations were carried out were termed time centers and became a primary focus in transportation planning. The approach to hour-control coverage is illustrated in Figure 14.3. If a forest fireman can travel across country at 2 miles per hour, the outer limits of the area he can reach in a half hour is roughly a circle with a 1-mile radius. If he can travel on a trail at the rate of 4 miles per hour and has a trail in one direction only, his coverage assumes the shape shown in *A*. If he has access by trail in three directions, his coverage becomes spider shaped but still limited, as in *B*. But if he has even a narrow road on which he can travel safely in an auto at 20 miles per hour, he can reach a point on the road 10 miles distant in a half hour. Within that time he can also reach a strip on both sides of the road on foot at shorter distances. This strip decreases from a 1-mile width across country at the starting point and a 2-mile reach on trails down to the vanishing point at 10 miles, where time for any foot travel in this time interval would run out. The standard of the trail, the topography, and the use of saddle horses create variations in the rate of travel, but these are of minor moment compared to the presence or absence of roads. It follows too that the rated speed on a road, which might range from 10 to 50 miles per hour, becomes of considerable importance. Roads were classified accordingly on the basis of the average safe speed a loaded tank truck or other first-attack vehicle could maintain.

This model (Figure 14.3) for measuring accessibility has attracted the attention of operations research workers and has the potential for guiding computer solutions under a given set of restraints.

Road Patterns   Application of the Norcross system of coverage produced a road pattern in flat country of isosceles triangles which theoretically gave maximum coverage at minimum road investment. Unpublished computations carried out in 1935 demonstrated that no fixed or idealized system would apply, as long as (1) the ratio between cost of road construction and cost of maintaining firemen and (2) the ratio

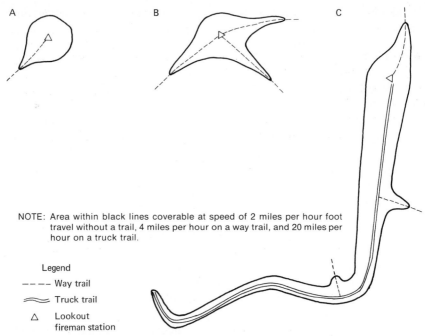

NOTE: Area within black lines coverable at speed of 2 miles per hour foot
      travel without a trail, 4 miles per hour on a way trail, and 20 miles per
      hour on a truck trail.

Legend

– – – – Way trail

〰〰 Truck trail

△   Lookout
     fireman station

Figure 14.3 Relative working range (or coverage) of a smokechaser on foot and by road. *A*, with one way trail only; *B*, with
three way trails only; *C*, range when smokechaser is equipped with
auto and roads are available over which to operate it.

between road speed and speed of foot travel did not remain fixed.
However, the same studies did show that a fireman station becomes
increasingly effective as the number of radiating roads from it increases.
Most road systems, regardless of the purpose for which they were built,
create natural time center locations from which rapid access to a
maximum area of country is possible. Skillful use can be made of such
locations to speed up attack on fires in local areas.

Cost Relationships   In theory the proper guides to application of
travel time coverage are costs. In Figure 14.3, it is evident that the fireman
with an automobile in *C* covers approximately three times the area
covered by either of the firemen on foot in *A* and *B*, even though he has
only a single road for auto travel. By a well-designed system of radiating
roads, this ratio can be increased up to ten times that of the area covered
by foot travel only. Consequently, roads can greatly reduce the number of
firemen required. Where simple rut roads or ways can be built very

cheaply, the cost of many miles of such roads can be offset by the reduced number and cost of men required for coverage. On the other hand, when the cost of men on foot is low, more time centers but fewer miles of road result. This was the original basis for developing a fire road system. The principle retains validity for undeveloped areas, though its application in most of the United States is now obscured by the high-standard, high-cost, multiple-purpose roads which prevail in most critical areas.

Coverage Without Foot Travel The model for coverage on foot grew out of the concept of first attack by one or two men with hand tools operating from a fixed location as the standard. This is typical of control of lightning fires in green timber areas of the northwestern United States and parts of Canada. Wherever this is not the accepted standard of first attack, the coverage concept needs to be modified. This is the case, for example, where first attack is mechanized and depends on getting a tank truck, a plow unit, or other equipment to the fire. In some areas, four-wheel-drive equipment is depended on for first attack and is designed to travel across country. In others, tractors and plows are moved to the roadside nearest the fire. In southern California, travel on foot through dense chaparral cover is limited to prepared ways and firebreaks. Each situation requires a different approach to the problem of reducing travel time. The approach used in southern California was that of planned coverage of the roadside only since human risk was confined to it and risk of lightning fires could be largely disregarded (Brown, 1937).

Wherever fires spread rapidly, as in the southern pine region, and chief reliance is placed on heavy equipment such as tractor plow outfits, assurance that such a unit can be delivered to the scene of a wildfire within certain time limits requires careful determination of travel time and of strategic locations at which such units should be stationed during critical fire danger periods. This is an important principle wherever heavy or slow-moving equipment is to be used in the initial attack on fires.

All-purpose Roads All roads and trails have values aside from fire control and their construction is a part of the normal development cost of wild-land properties. Consequently, fire control requirements are only a part of the answer to the need for transportation planning. On National Forests, "all purpose" road planning criteria have replaced coverage within time limits as the principal planning tools. For that reason criteria such as road speeds and travel time in making first attack on a fire are no longer the primary guides in planning road systems on the National Forests. This easily leads to the impression that such criteria are obsolete. On privately owned forest areas under management and on well-developed multiple-use forest properties, this may be true. All-purpose roads commonly exceed the minimum standards needed by fire control forces for access and speed of travel. But even on such properties, logging, thinning, and other cultural practices which greatly increase fire hazards are often carried out without regard to first establishing the faster access necessary to maintain fully adequate insurance against fire.

Moreover, extensive tracts of wild land, especially in the United States, are reserved as wilderness or primitive areas, as National Parks, or are otherwise dedicated to a single use such as watershed, wildlife, or recreation. All such areas pose special problems to systematic fire control. Always the primary problem is that of getting fire-fighting forces to wildfires quickly enough to avoid unacceptable losses. This is sometimes expressed as "force enough fast enough." Solution of this problem is one objective of transportation planning. Since all roads are banned in wild and primitive areas and limited in other areas dedicated to a single use, other transportation facilities must be substituted to varying degrees. Aerial transportation is considered briefly in the section following. Waterways can also substitute for roads. To develop an integrated plan of transportation to properly serve fire control needs, all available forms of transportation must usually be drawn on. This broader concept should be the starting point.

Early Planning in Summary   The road networks produced to permit coverage within time limits based on the model described contributed much to the development of road systems in backcountry throughout the western United States, and many miles of these networks built in the 1930s by the Civilian Conservation Corps are still in use. The advantages were a systematic approach to accessibility and emphasis on the principle that if time is saved in attack on a fire, money is saved. Disadvantages were too great a premium on cheap roads and illogical road patterns in mountain terrain.

In developing a multiple-purpose forest road system, the best current procedure appears to be to first apply nonfire criteria to define the main routes and tributaries needed by prospective use and development of the area and then to apply tests of coverage within time limits to ensure addition of the further access roads necessary to enable prompt attack.

Aerial Transportation

The use of aircraft for detection and for direct attack on fires with water and retardants has been outlined in preceding chapters. These uses take advantage of the position of the aircraft above the terrain. Basically, however, the contribution of aircraft is transportation. Aerial transportation of men and equipment to backcountry airfields and aerial delivery of men and supplies in backcountry by parachute have greatly relieved the requirements of road systems wherever employed. This is the main reason for using smoke jumpers for first attack on fires. One or several men can be placed on a backcountry fire by parachute from a central point 50 miles away in the same time that a backcountry fireman can get to it from 2 to 3 miles away on foot. By utilizing this principle, whole systems of widely disseminated firemen and lookout firemen in backcountry were replaced by smoke jumpers at a central point. The advantages were better availability for attack and more flexibility in regulating strength of attack, as well as some savings in cost.

The smoke-jumper system also has definite limitations. These arise primarily from the high cost of complete facilities at the central base and from the limitation of smoke-jumper services to fire fighting only in the backcountry they serve. Both are cost factors. To hold unit costs at or below those of other systems of protection, an area of several million acres of roadless country in which smoke jumpers can operate effectively must be available. However, with a strong base operating, satellite bases at lower unit costs can serve smaller problem areas of approximately $1/2$ to 1 million acres in extent. In addition to providing first attack in the roadless area, they usually provide supplemental and emergency service throughout an extensive tributary zone. This has helped to solve the problem of costs.

Helicopters have the potential to replace fixed-wing aircraft and parachutes in aerial attack systems. They are being used increasingly to return smoke jumpers and their equipment to base after completing a fire-fighting mission. They are slower and have less payload. Their slowness in reaching a destination 50 to 100 miles away could result in serious delay in making first attack, but this delay is minor at 10 miles. The unit cost of moving men and equipment by helicopter is high but can be expected to decrease in time, at least in relation to that of fixed-wing aircraft. As this occurs, the handicap of slowness may also be overcome by decentralizing the operation to reduce the distances to be traveled. Consequently, though the special advantages of the helicopter will no doubt bring it into increasing use in forest fire control, it cannot be expected to replace fixed-wing aircraft and parachutes directly in an existing smoke-jumper system. Rather, a carefully planned alternative system of first attack by helicopter will need to be developed.

ELEMENTS OF THE INITIAL ATTACK SYSTEM

Almost equally important to speed of attack on fires is the strength of attack. In fact, speed of attack means nothing until coupled with an output of measures capable of stopping the spread of a fire and of slowing and stopping the combustion process on small fires. One or two highly trained men with hand tools can supply such measures in sufficient strength to control most fires a quarter acre or less in size. But in some fuels and under some burning conditions the thermal energy being released from even a fire of this size is sufficient to overwhelm any direct attack that can be mounted by hand methods. Mechanized equipment is highly productive wherever it can be used to strengthen the hand of the small first-attack unit in such situations. The small, fast-moving tank truck and some plow units, as described in Chapter 13, have these special virtues.

Because of the rate at which the production of heat energy grows in a wildfire, it is seldom good practice to sacrifice speed for strength of attack. Consequently, heavy equipment functions best in reinforcement action rather than first attack. This places a premium on the performance of the small group of men usually referred to as the initial attack force.

Men as Planning Units

All the systems discussed are designed to make men more effective, but the end result always depends on men's performance. If it is well above average, it may offset many handicaps imposed by inadequate planning and facilities. But if it is far below the standards on which the system is based, the system will fail. It is the purpose of the fire control manager to recruit and train men to meet specific standards of performance, but the planner must always assume some level of performance in advance.

The level of performance most often assumed for men is that of well-qualified individuals under reasonably efficient management and good supervision. Allowance for the normal quota of errors can be made. But it must be assumed, for example, that the lookout observer is fully qualified and will be at his post watching for smokes during specified hours, that the communication system will not be out of order through any neglect of maintenance, that the fireman or fire crew will be at their posts ready to go, that the fire truck will not fail to operate as intended, that they will not take the wrong road, and so forth.

In addition to quality of performance, quantity of performance per man per unit of time (such as chains of fire line per man-hour) is also an essential planning unit. It is expressed in man-hours, man-days, or man-months. When the period of time is fixed, it is expressed simply as number of men. When planning the number of men to send to a fire in the first attack, both fire danger and fuel type affect the manpower needed. So a fire may be rated as a one-man, a two-man, a five-man, or a twenty-man fire. Fuel-type ratings assist in making such estimates.

The use of men as planning units is well illustrated by early studies in which the control of a fire was visualized as a problem in plane geometry (Hornby, 1936). If a surface fire is making a forward spread of 5 chains per hour, it is increasing its perimeter at approximately 16 chains per hour. To control the fire, fire line must usually be built and held around the whole perimeter or the perimeter itself must be worked. Obviously a crew that can build and hold line at a rate faster than 16 chains per hour can control it. But what is essential? Any fire making definite forward spread is well checked as soon as the head and forward flanks are controlled. For planning purposes, enough manpower to control the fastest-spreading half of the fire is considered enough to ensure safe control. But the perimeter keeps on increasing while the work is going on. Computations on this basis show that at 16 chains per hour, 80 percent of the original perimeter or 12.8 chains would be the critical job. On some fires, nearly double the original perimenter would have to be worked. The importance of travel time is illustrated by similar computations. For high fire danger and fuels rated at medium resistance to control, the average number of men required grows from 1 to 50 in $2^1/_2$ hours.

The output per man in a fire crew engaged in fighting a fire by hand tools tends to decrease as the number of men increases above certain limits. Unpublished statistical analyses show, however, that the work accomplished by a team of two men is more than twice that of one man. At this high point the output per man is maintained up to five men, then decreases slightly per man to the point where ten men are working as a unit. Beyond this number it drops off rapidly to as low as 40 percent of this level of output per man for a fifty-man crew. This trend is well borne out by experience. It needs to be taken into account by the planner of fire control systems and by the fire boss on large fires.

Similar trends in the output per man soon show up with time. Fire fighting is strenuous work. Typically, the rate at which fire line can be constructed by hand labor drops off rapidly after a few hours. Fatigue alone may cut the output per man at the end of 12 hours to one-fourth the initial rate. It becomes a much less dominant factor when men are operating mechanized equipment instead of using hand tools (Chapter 13).

Because of loss of output per man as the number of men in a unit increases and as the hours of operation increase, the strong tendency to mass large numbers of men to fight a runaway fire and to hold them on the fire line for long hours is usually an exercise in false security. This has significance in the case studies of large fires in Chapter 16.

The Fire Crew

The first problem in planning is that of getting at least one man to the scene of a fire within the time limits adopted for that location. Early planning was based on the theory that any fire could be controlled by one man if he could get to it soon enough. But provision for reinforcement action is always needed. Commonly, additional men are sent in as first reinforcements to make up a small fire crew. Second reinforcements often follow while the fire is still small. If the fire escapes control by first attack and local reinforcement action, an emergency buildup of manpower and equipment from outside the area begins.

In practice, one-man attack is not very successful except on lightning-set fires in green timber, under moderate to low fire danger, or on roads when reinforced by a tank truck. If the fire spreads into heavy mixed fuels, a strong, organized crew or mechanized equipment is needed. Studies and experience in California demonstrate convincingly that attack on a fire in brush fuels needs always to be strong as well as fast. This is supported by similar experience in other fast-burning fuels. But the cost of increasing one-man attack units to some higher number has prevented orderly transition from one-man attack to small-crew attack where needed except in southern California, where cooperative arrangements have made financing feasible. Instead, other work crews and cooperator crews are integrated into the system wherever possible. As special funds for preventing conflagration fires on federal lands have become available, they have largely been devoted to financing large, specially trained reinforcement crews, "hot shot crews," "red hots," and so forth rather than to the financing of increased first-attack strength.

The small, specially trained crew of three to ten men with or without mechanized equipment is a highly effective fire fighting unit. This has been demonstrated in practice by federal, state, and private agencies and is a natural choice of fire control managers. But it is imperfectly utilized. The most important reason is cost. In many protection areas there is too little fire-fighting activity to justify a full-time standby crew for even a short peak-season period. Instead, good planning provides substitute measures. The financing of special fire training and of work-crew or cooperator-crew standby time during high fire danger is helpful. Financing of a nucleus unit or a tank-truck or plow operator who are kept on standby during the fire season is also common. Dependence is then placed on diverting a few men from other work to make an effective first-attack unit. Similar provisions for bulldozers and bulldozer operators often provide for first reinforcements. As pointed out in the discussion of mechanized equipment, a plow unit with its operator substitutes for the physical labor of perhaps twenty men. Therefore a plow with driver is a strong first-attack unit which is more readily available and easier to maintain on standby that its equivalent manpower.

One solution to the problem of maintaining trained crews of fire fighters has been through cooperative arrangements between fire control agencies and correctional institutions. This is illustrated in California, where a joint Conservation Camp Program between the State Division of Forestry and state correctional authorities has been carried on since 1945 (Clar, 1969).

Volunteer cooperator crews of local residents long served as a substitute for regularly financed first-attack units in the Rocky Mountain and Intermountain Regions of the United States and are still important in many areas. Such forces make up the primary fire control system on privately controlled lands in Australia.

The Fire Dispatching System

A system for sending men and equipment to fires as needed is called a fire dispatching system. It can function only through an adequate communication system. How highly developed it needs to be depends on the severity of the fire problem and the form of organization in effect. Where the local manpower and equipment are adequate to take care of all except rare emergencies, the local unit can operate largely as a self-sufficient fire-fighting group. Dispatching then consists only of internal communication and of activating local arrangements with cooperators. No dispatcher is employed. Such activities are assumed as a part of the job of managing the forest property. This is typical of many intensively managed forest properties where the threat of a conflagration-type fire is slight.

In units where there is little or no reserve manpower and equipment but where fuels and fire danger create frequent emergencies, more dependence must be placed on outside assistance. This calls for increasing activity by a central dispatcher who coordinates the movement of men and equipment between local units.

As the potential threat increases, the scope of geographic coverage in the dispatching also increases. This is illustrated in California by the successive levels of dispatching that become involved on the National Forests as a growing fire-fighting emergency increases the requirement for specified classes of men, equipment, and supplies that must come from increasingly wider areas. Organizationally, these levels are ranger district, supervisor's office, regional interforest zone, regional office, and western United States interregional coordinator. In the Northeast, the principle is illustrated among state organizations by the arrangement among the Northeastern Interstate Compact states and the province of Quebec by which member forest fire fighting forces can be pooled to meet major fire emergencies.

The Planned Fire Season

The "normal fire season" is an important part of all wild-land fire plans. Some of the earliest efforts to plan fire control systems were concerned with establishing a "normal" fire season and the proper rate of buildup and of reduction in manpower in order to match the strength of the fire organization to the potential size of the job (Chapter 8). This is still an important purpose of fire danger ratings. But intermittent employment of men in step with short-term changes in fire danger is usually undesirable or impractical. Such adjustments can best be applied to the management of equipment and men that are already available.

The most common planned system provides for the availability of sufficient men, equipment, and facilities for the average or more commonly the "average worst" year. By *average worst* is meant the average if easy years are omitted, or it may mean the average of the three or four more difficult years of the last decade.

Based on this average fire season, positions are financed on a time schedule by calendar dates. But whether or not a lookout or a prevention patrol needs to be on duty on those dates is usually decided by current fire danger ratings. Danger ratings continue to be used during the season even through no new employment of men is contemplated. Danger ratings give the alert when conditions are dangerous and provide the basis for administrative decisions on standby status and overtime duty.

So-called "stepup plans" geared to fire danger ratings combine presuppression arrangements and dispatching action. Presuppression arrangements depend on the persistence of certain weather conditions. They determine the resources that will be quickly available to the dispatcher. Action to be taken after a fire is reported depends on several other factors separately identified for decision.

OPERATING PLANS

The different kinds of planning and the differing organization levels at which it takes place often lead to confusion. Most commonly, what is meant by the fire plan is the current operating plan for fire activities. Since it provides a good focal point for all matters concerning fire control facilities, equipment, and manpower, a description of its makeup at different administrative levels will illustrate the distinctions to be made.

At the lowest administrative levels, an operating plan is a direct action plan consisting essentially of a statement of the men and equipment available and action to be taken in case of fire. As the size of the unit and the scope of the job increase, the plan becomes more complex.

Supporting policy and procedures and provisions for backup to direct action become an increasingly large part of the data.

The preceding section on fire prevention action plans was based on an administrative unit equivalent to a state fire district or a ranger district on a National Forest. At this level it serves as the planning unit for current action plans only. Planning for systems of detection, communication, transportation, and first attack is usually carried out at a higher administrative level. Nevertheless, the conversion of policy directives and planning decisions into action designed to solve the distinctive problems on a particular local unit often demand administrative planning of a high order.

The prevention action plan is intended to illustrate this. However, it would be only a part of the operating plan. Other important components would consist of manning schedules showing the assignments of available personnel and the positions to be occupied during the fire season. The specific changes in manning and standby to correspond with changes in fire danger are an important feature. Guides to dispatching and instructions to the dispatcher as assigned may be posted. The labor supply and equipment available for first attack will be posted in chart form and its location may be shown on a map of the unit as well. A list of specialists, such as tractor or plow operators, truck or transport operators, aircraft pilots, etc., along with a listing of cooperative agreements covering use or rental of locally owned emergency equipment is also important. This represents the local reserves that can be drawn on.

Beyond this the further resources needed if a disaster fire develops will come from outside and will normally be the primary responsibility of higher authority.

Supplemental reference material may consist of such data as danger ratings posted to date on a chart; maps showing land ownership and the protection boundary; maps with printed azimuth circles at the location of each lookout and a string or other device for plotting lookout readings; and maps showing roads, the communication net, and the distribution of equipment stocks. Maps showing the location and extent of high-hazard fuels and the cause and location of recent fires are also important.

At the next administrative level, the larger unit such as a National Forest serves as the planning unit for the kind of plans that may be described as design or placement plans. These would include the detection system, the communication network, the planned road and firebreak system, and the planned location of fire crews and other first-attack units. Reference maps for the larger unit may also cover the same information as that posted at each district headquarters.

This will ordinarily be the center for receiving fire weather forecasts and for transmitting fire danger measurements. Action to implement changes in manning schedules will ordinarily be limited to interdistrict assignments only.

BUILDING A COOPERATIVE SYSTEM

Fire fighting is always a cooperative undertaking. A spreading fire threatens everything in its path impartially and is no respecter of political or property boundaries. This fact, plus the sudden and dramatic challenge that fire usually poses, has always inspired a higher degree of cooperation among property owners in developing a common defense than most other forms of community action. This is well exemplified by the bucket brigades of the days preceding the power pump and the volunteer fire departments that continue to operate effectively in smaller communities in most developed countries.

The first organized forest fire control developed as a cooperative venture, first in defense of improved property then in defense of forest resources as well. Timber protective associations grew out of cooperation between timberland owners. Fire control on the National Forests and other federal lands initially depended heavily on community cooperation as well.

Although the forms of cooperation and the participants change with time and circumstance, success of the whole enterprise of protecting wild lands from fire must continue to depend on cooperation between individuals and between private, state, and federal agencies of all kinds. The ideals and spirit behind successful cooperative defense against fire have enabled poorly equipped amateur fire fighters to win many battles. When such a spirit is lacking, well-equipped and well-financed forces often fail.

Cooperative relationships enter into each phase of building a fire organization, and their successful development can greatly reduce costs. The fire prevention program is based largely on inducing cooperation of the individual, and it succeeds to the degree that individuals respond. Cooperation in detecting and reporting fires both by planned cooperators and by the traveling public prevents many runaway fires and in some areas replaces fire lookouts. Cooperation also enters into organized detection. Many fire lookouts give coverage to areas in two or more protection units and customarily report fires to the agency responsible even through no sharing of costs of the lookout have been arranged. Cooperative detection and reporting of fires seen from private and commercial aircraft and at times by neighboring aerial observers gives valuable supplemental coverage in some areas.

In all communication systems, a fire emergency message is given priority without question. Cooperators and wardens are often given a telephone or radio outlet to make their cooperation effective, and assignment of radio wavelengths among fire agencies is the result of interagency cooperation.

In initial attack, it is usual practice among cooperators that whoever can get to the fire first also makes the first attack. Similarly, in fire emergencies it is common for a cooperating agency to make equipment and men available to the agency in trouble even though fire danger is high in its own area. The pooling of resources to meet an emergency situation is the usual objective of interagency and interstate compacts.

Forest fire fighting and structural fire fighting have operated independently and have tended to remain as separate specialties in the United States, although volunteer fire organizations in suburban and rural areas often deal with grass and brush fires. Urban and forest fire fighting in most areas appear to have little in common. However, in some areas on the West Coast and particularly in Los Angeles County, California, the problems with which both types of organizations must cope tend to merge. In most outdoor recreation areas and in summer residence colonies, structural fire problems are created far from city fire fighting facilities and are often aggravated by danger of exterior ignition from

Figure 14.4 Forest fire sweeping across site of a mountain summer home. *(U.S. Forest Service photo.)*

grass or brush fires. In such areas the best solution is to first form an association of property owners which acquires the specialized fire equipment it may need and can then develop cooperative arrangements with local forest fire-fighting forces to ensure coordination of effort. As populations increase, these problems will multiply. Consequently, the development of close working arrangements or mergers between forest fire-fighting agencies and structural fire fighters is an essential need in building the fire organization (Figure 14.4).

In Australia, these functions are merged. Volunteer fire organizations known as bush fire brigades assume full responsibility for the protection of all private land and property outside the larger cities, and they cooperate as well in fighting fire on government-owned lands.

In summary, it may be said that systematic fire control may be initiated by cooperation alone even in the absence of financing, and it is made stronger at every level by building in more cooperation.

Chapter 15

Operating the Fire Control Organization

The purpose of this chapter is to give emphasis to the problems that characterize the operation of a fire control organization and to measures employed for meeting them. The principles and practices of administration apply to fire control as to any other organized activity; no new ones are added by the requirements of successful fire control. Yet these requirements do demand distinctive emphasis on certain aspects of administration and management. This is well illustrated by the frequent failure of nonfire organizations to respond effectively to a fire emergency even though they are effective in similar work they are doing. Special requirements relate to the need for advance preparation for emergencies of uncertain time and place and quick response when they occur. They add up to exacting requirements for correct action at the right time and place, which in turn have certain implications to all aspects of administration and management.

FIRE CONTROL ADMINISTRATION

The essential characteristics of a good fire organization are clear lines of authority, quick response when action is needed, and interunit flexibility that can rapidly increase fire fighting striking force when emergencies occur. Not all of this can be assured through internal planning (Chapter 14). Small units, such as a private protective association or a county unit organized on a self-sufficient basis, are likely to be efficient and economical in suppressing small fires and in meeting normal fire-load situations. But they lack the resources to cope with periodic overload conditions which unfortunately lead to the major fire losses.

Several factors in addition to size enter into the effectiveness of the diverse federal, state, and private forest fire agencies operating in the United States. One important factor is the difference in responsibility assumed by the agency. Federal agencies normally have full responsibility for management of the land they protect.[1] States have similar responsibility for state-owned areas but must operate also to give public service protection to privately owned lands. In most states this activity dominates. The difference this makes in fire prevention activities has been discussed in Chapter 14. It affects other fire control activities as well. When an agency is protecting land owned by others, it is in the capacity of a contractor. To keep costs within reasonable limits, the owner must usually provide some degree of self help. On large, commercially owned tracts of timberland, this may be carried to the point where state fire crews operate for the most part to provide emergency or reenforcement backup only to local work crews and equipment.

The uses to which the land is dedicated are also important. In the United States the U.S. Forest Service has the largest area under protection dedicated to multiple use, but several other federal agencies protect important areas dedicated to special uses such as the National Parks, Indian reservations, military reservations, and federal wild-land areas reserved for a variety of other special purposes.

Fire control activities are integrated to varying degrees with other land-management activities wherever the protection agency also has responsibility for managing the land. Where a small central core of fire professionals are employed, integration of other activities with fire control strengthens the organization. But where such individuals are lacking, the fire activity is weakened. This is well illustrated on the National Forests, where the ranger district serves as both the administrative unit and the basic unit in organizing forest fire control. This normally assumes that the district will function as a relatively self-sufficient unit in prevention and presuppression, with outside assistance only in the suppression of large fires. The corresponding delegation of responsibility

---

[1] Under cooperative agreements considerable privately owned land is also protected under contract. However, this is incidental.

works well as long as fire activities, as measured by conventional criteria, constitute a substantial part of the district workload. Regularly allotted fire funds are then likely to be sufficient to finance several subprofessional staff men. This provides a skeleton fire organization which strengthens the planning and supervision of fire activities and makes it relatively easy to maintain standards. But when fire activities make up only a minor part of the average workload, such funds may be entirely lacking. It is then assumed that fire work can be absorbed below a certain level as an incidental part of the overall job. In such situations fire planning and expertise in other phases of fire control must depend on outside sources, yet responsibility and authority for all local fire activities are still retained by the local unit manager. He finds it difficult to maintain standards, and a locally weak fire organization often results.

Wherever fire control work is closely integrated with other activities, there is a strong tendency to regard it as a temporary specialty with expertise readily acquired by experience. On this basis men who are highly successful in fire work are promoted into nonfire positions and inexperienced men are assigned to responsible fire positions to gain experience. At times this places the organization concerned in the position of fighting fire with amateurs at the professional level, compared to many of the stronger state organizations in which fire men devote their whole professional career to fire control activities.

In nearly all fire control organizations on public land, the administrative district is the key field unit. A professional-level man is normally in charge of the district; fire control is usually one of several activities being carried on, usually through subprofessional assistants, and it is seldom the principal activity. Size of the district varies from areas of about 75 square miles up to several hundred square miles in Canada and some Western national forest ranger districts in the United States.

Among state fire organizations, the county which is the most important local political unit usually becomes an important field unit as well. A county is generally too small to be an effective administrative unit, so it is common for several to be grouped into a district. County spirit and participation in fire control are highly desirable, but not to the point where local autonomy interferes with free intercounty movement of manpower and equipment. In the fire districts made up of counties, a professional-level man is in charge and fire activities are generally the sole or dominant responsibility.

Organization and administrative levels above the district vary with the organization. There is sometimes a regional or other major administrative subdivision within the state or province, as in Michigan. Above the ranger district in the U.S. Forest Service, there are three administrative levels: the National Forest, the National Forest Region, and the Office of the Chief in Washington, D.C. In private organizations, the district or other operating unit usually reports directly to top authority for coordination of its activities.

Financing needs to be in accord with the form of organization and should provide both strength and flexibility to meet unusually heavy suppression expenditures. Suppression costs of more or less normal seasons can be anticipated and budgeted with fair accuracy. But there is no way to budget in advance for the cost of the critical fire fighting emergencies that occur only occasionally, often at intervals of 5, 10, or even 50 years. This problem is met in several ways. One method is to build up a reserve fund in easy years. Another is provision for deficit financing for unusual suppression costs. This means that a control organization is given authorization to incur suppression costs in excess of its normal budget, constituting, in effect, a blank check for unusual fire costs. Sometimes, as in some private protective associations, there is power of extra assessment to cover unusual costs. Another partial solution to the problem is simply intraunit flexibility through bigness. If an organization is large enough, a bad fire situation in one area can be alleviated by drawing men, money, and equipment from other, less critical areas without serious strain on the total budget. A very large organization like the U.S. Forest Service seldom encounters unusually severe fire control needs in any one year in more than two or three of its nine regions in the continental United States. Even in a large state, control conditions in a given year are seldom extreme statewide.

Insufficient ability to finance overload situations can be fatal to effective control. There have been instances where action on fires had to be suspended or limited for lack of money, but such situations have become rare. Lack of financial strength is a chronic and serious weakness of small, autonomous control units.

Recruitment

Personnel recruitment problems are difficult in fire control. Despite the magnitude of the job, relatively few professional-level men are recruited directly into fire work, and the core of full-time professionals is small. Much of fire control is integrated with other forest work, and top fire men are often transferred to nonfire positions. A prime reason is that fire suppression work is intermittent and seasonal, making it difficult to establish full-time professional workloads and career ladders at competitive pay levels. This problem is even more acute at the subprofessional level. The backbone of most state, private, and federal organizations is made up of local, experienced men who are the county rangers, foremen of all kinds, machine operators, and so forth. They are indispensable but increasingly difficult to hold, especially on a seasonal basis. Competent temporary labor for fire suppression is also difficult to obtain. General scarcity of manpower, together with its rising cost, is a prime reason behind the mechanization of fire suppression, as pointed out in Chapter 13. In some areas, even enough temporary manpower to back up machines is hard to find. Constant effort is consequently necessary to recruit and keep needed manpower. More attractive professional and subprofessional positions and career ladders in fire control need to be developed.

Fire control cannot, however, be fully professionalized. The tendency for the work to concentrate in a few months of the year and for emergency overloads to develop suddenly makes part-time assistance of many kinds necessary. Traditionally, this was done by employing temporary men for the fire season only and by giving fire work first priority during that period in the work programs of designated personnel. As it has become more difficult to hold experienced men, planned year-long employment has increased, either by converting key fire season jobs to a year-long basis or by pooling funds to ensure year-long employment on various projects.

Local residents, timber operators, graziers, summer-home owners, summer-camp operators, and others who have an economic interest in protection from fire can help to solve the problem. Planned detection by cooperators has been discussed in Chapter 14. First attack by local wardens and cooperators continues to be a valuable contribution as well in many areas. Availability of local work crews for fire fighting may at times substitute for services of a standby crew. Quick discovery and reporting of fires by the first person in the vicinity to see it commonly cuts elapsed time below that of discovery by a lookout, and prompt amateur action to hold a fire in check until it can be mopped up by trained fire forces often prevents a costly fire emergency.

TRAINING

No forestry enterprise requires as great and unremitting emphasis on training as does fire control. For reasons discussed in Chapter 1, the professional forester who finds himself in charge of a wild-land protection unit is commonly in need of professional-level training in one or more of the following: forest fire behavior, fire weather, fire danger rating, fire foremanship, fire suppression organization or fire generalship, and in techniques of training his employees for each of the various specialized positions in the fire organization. In support of agency programs, he may also need special training in such subjects as techniques of fire planning and public education.

Professional Training

Training at the professional level in a federal agency may be initiated by the bureau but it is ordinarily carried out by the regional organization. Among states, it is usually carried out at the state level but is often a subject of joint interest of regional groups of states. As an example, members of the Northeastern Forest Fire Protection Commission[2] have carried on a continuing program of training in large fire organization.

A variety of methods are employed to extend professional-level training in forest fire subjects. An obvious one is that of assigning men to universities for the advanced training desired. This is productive for fire research men who need advanced training in supplemental and nonfire subjects, but most universities are not prepared to meet the many needs of fire control agencies. Consequently, most training, even though at a professional level, is conducted as an agency or interagency activity.

Special agency training schools are often conducted by states and state compact groups and by the U.S. Forest Service, the National Park Service, and the Bureau of Land Management in the United States. These may include specialized training in new activities but often serve as an agency-oriented refresher course in fire control as well as other subjects for new professional employees.

Special programs such as the redesigning of fire control systems are at times the subject of special regional interagency schools when initiated.

A further step in this area has been the development of training in decision-making on large fires or in so-called fire generalship. This has been marked by the development of a special facility called the fire control simulator. This is a device by which a spreading fire and its smoke can be projected on a forest background to simulate actual fire behavior under realistic operating conditions. By means of the simulator, exercises are developed to give trainees experience in making decisions under the stress of real-life fire emergencies. These decisions concern sizing up the fire, ordering and assigning resources, planning attack strategy, adjusting plans and strategy as the situation changes, looking out for the safety of their men, directing and coordinating simultaneous operations, and, at the end of the exercise, participating in group evaluation of the decisions made. Only men with considerable background and experience can profit fully from this kind of exercise, and much depends on the skill of the

---

[2] Since September, 1969, this has included the province of Quebec.

instructor. However, simulators have also been adapted to training men in the use of correct tactics in controlling the small fire, usually referred to as training in first attack.

The simulator was first developed in 1962 by the Division of Fire Control of the U.S. Forest Service working with the International Electric Corporation of Paramus, New Jersey. It has evolved since that time into a popular working tool among all fire control agencies. It has stimulated interest both in training and in problem solving and has helped to raise standards.

But decision making is only one aspect of the leadership skills required to control high-energy fires. An equally important but less prestigious need is that of good foremanship. This is the ability to lead men and to coordinate their efforts to attain efficient accomplishment. This is the ability that most often makes key subprofessional men indispensable to their agencies. For the same reason, it is sometimes regarded as of a subprofessional nature compared to the planning and decision making implied by generalship. Yet the latter is unproductive without good foremanship.

The professional fire control manager and trainer needs to practice good foremanship and needs to train men in how to practice it. Unfortunately he is in poor position to do so unless he has had an opportunity to acquire such skills. During the 1930s, most professional foresters in the United States had a period of apprenticeship as technical foremen, which gave them advantages in this respect. Young foresters have had less opportunity to receive this kind of training since that time. It is worth emphasizing that the success of the fire boss at each level of organization discussed in Chapter 12 depends on good foremanship. Often he must supply it himself.

Subprofessional and Vocational Training

Subprofessional training may include phases of the training already listed, but it is predominantly training in forest fire-fighting methods. This is the subject of many agency handbooks and manuals and is aimed particularly at training men of short-term employment in methods of first attack on small fires. A further logical division is the general category of vocational training, where skill in carrying out a particular task such as operating mechanized equipment or building fire line is the primary goal. Both subprofessional and vocational training are needed to qualify men for most positions in the fire organization, so distinctions have significance here only as they relate to the choice of method.

Some of the more common positions for which men must be

qualified by training are fire lookout, lookout fireman, prevention patrolman, fire crew foreman, fire crew member, fire warden, resident cooperator, tank-truck operator and crew, nozzleman, tractor operator and plow crew, dispatcher, and operators of all kinds of mechanized fire equipment including portable pumpers, bulldozers, power saws, trenchers, backfiring equipment, and so forth. Both specialized and general training are required. Most of these men need to be trained in skillful use of hand tools in fire fighting, and most of them need to know how to operate field radios and telephone equipment. All need training in safe practices and orientation in just how they fit into the protection organization, what the standards of performance expected and the hours of duty are, what to do in emergencies, what forms and records they must prepare, and other matters affecting their pay and welfare.

The amount of turnover in the protection forces from year to year naturally affects the size of the training job. But it is always a more important task in fire control activities than in other forestry undertakings. In planning and carrying out such a program, every method of training and every training aid that has evolved in other fields of work has a place, but the period in which to carry out formal training is always limited and must usually be closely planned and scheduled in advance.

Group training fits such specifications best and is the standard. But many kinds of special training may be required for only one or two men who have special duties on a single protection unit. Good practice will usually dictate pooling of the training needs between protection units to bring together a sufficient group of each kind of specialist such as lookout observer, tank-truck operator, tractor operator, pump operator, dispatcher, and so forth to justify a special training program designed to meet the requirement of their particular job.

On National Forests and National Parks, special training is often accomplished by organizing "guard training schools," which include the seasonal forces from all ranger districts, plus regional schools for highly specialized and interunit supervisory positions. Most state fire organizations apply the same principle by organizing training by districts or state subregions. Protection agencies often cooperate in interagency schools as well.

At such training schools general training and orientation is usually given the group as a whole, then it is broken into organized groups to facilitate the various types of specialized training needed. Men in the group who are already experienced in the job for which they are employed should be included but given special attention to make sure that they too will benefit fully. Enlisting their help in training "green" men, or grouping them to permit more advanced training for their jobs, or offering them special training to permit them to qualify for additional jobs are all effective measures.

In general, the four-step method of training is the best adapted to the purpose. Essentially it consists of the following: 1. explain, 2. demonstrate, 3. let student try it, 4. check student's performance. Lecturing alone is usually found to be least effective. The group conference method can be effective if properly used. It accomplishes most where men of considerable experience are included and where the purpose to be served is to develop the students' judgment and to make safety of personnel and other good practices a habitual part of their thinking. All these methods are used in the highly developed program of training smoke jumpers.

Charts, models, demonstrations, training films, and individual practice and testing are familiar and valuable aids in all group training. Organized training in groups of this kind should never be regarded as complete in itself. If well done, it can greatly speed up the attainment of acceptable performance, but it needs to be followed up by training and drill on the job, by written job instructions, and by thorough inspection, testing, and supervision.

Every foreman, crew leader, dispatcher, and warden who has supervisory duties needs to be enlisted in the task of planned training of men on the job. Much of it can be drill in proper techniques, but it can take many forms, such as competitive performance tests, self-inspection checklists, group evaluation of crew performance, and so forth.

Written instructions are quite commonly used and are valuable particularly where men must work alone or must assume responsibility for action in the absence of their supervisor. Positions such as lookout observer, local warden, crew foreman, isolated fireman, and local dispatcher come in this category. Written instructions need to be addressed to the incumbent personally and to cover the special arrangements and circumstances that pertain to his particular job. Such instructions serve as a notice and reminder list to the incumbent of the performance standards expected. In this way they supplement the group and job training that has preceded. They are valuable too as a means of making clear any special duties or any variation from general instructions that may be distinctive to that particular position.

Training in fire suppression is far more effective if brought to a climax by practice on an active fire. Well-planned group training usually provides for this. A practice fire may be difficult and costly to arrange but is very important in units where few fires occur and large fires occur only at long intervals.

Prescribed burning projects are for this reason a valuable training ground for fire control personnel. Though such projects are usually carried out under conditions of low or moderate fire danger, they give firsthand familiarity with fire behavior and particularly with the effects of variations in technique, timing, and sequence of ignitions. This well justifies a policy of assigning full responsibility for executing such projects to the fire control organization, a practice which is quite common.

The closer the trainer can come to typical field conditions for his tests and demonstrations, the easier it is to translate training objectives into field performance. The same principle applies in the operation of equipment of all kinds. For that reason, training on the job becomes important.

Safety

Safety is closely akin to training and needs attention in every training program. General safety standards for woods work apply fully but need special emphasis because of frequent use of unskilled men in strange environments, under pressure of an emergency.

Safety hazards are in two general categories: (1) those inherent to the operation of equipment of all kinds in fire control activities, (2) those created by the fire itself. The former are much more prevalent and account for most injuries. But wildfire is always potentially dangerous. The principal tools needed to control it safely are an understanding of fire behavior, an alert anticipation of what to expect of a fire at a particular time and place, and efficient means of communicating such information to fire bosses.

Safety hazards from equipment of all kinds arise chiefly from inept use or operation of such equipment. Consequently, developing skill in use of equipment is the first and most important step in reducing safety hazards. Closely related is training in such matters as how to handle and how to carry hand tools and portable equipment to avoid injury to the carrier or to others. This type of safety needs to be made a part of the responsibility of each worker.

Safety hazards from the fire itself are usually the responsibility of the fire boss. They are closely related to its behavior. On level ground in mixed forest fuels, a very fast-spreading fire front seldom moves forward faster than 3 miles per hour. Though this rate of spread makes the fire difficult to control, men on foot can move out of its path with very little difficulty. But going uphill, a fire speeds up while men on foot slow down. Consequently, men on a steep slope above a high-energy fire are in a potentially dangerous position. This type of situation leads to a general safety rule. *Don't attempt to outrun a fire up a steep slope.* Either be in a position to sidestep to the flanks or avoid placing men in such situations entirely.

Some grass and brush fires do move faster even on level ground than a man on foot. Such fires have a shallow flame depth, as brought out in Chapter 7. Where there are variations in the fuel, even minor breaks cause discontinuity in the flame front. By taking advantage of such discontinuities, it is possible to escape into the cooling burn behind the flame front. This is the best practice for those who may be caught in the path of brush and grass fires. Starting a backfire and moving into its widening circle, to avoid being hit by the flame front is also a successful technique, which evolved on the Western plains of the United States when prairie fires were prevalent.

As discussed under strategy and tactics in Chapter 7, safety hazards from the fire itself are related to the method of attack as well as to its behavior. Men are in a hazardous position at the head of an aggressive fire if they are unable to build and hold fire line there and the flanks are still spreading freely. Similarly, men attempting to bring a fire line downhill to contain a fire coming up from below are also in jeopardy.

But perhaps the most dangerous behavior of all is that caused by many spot fires set well ahead of the main fire which then suddenly merge in a violent firestormlike manner. This too dictates great caution in placing men in advance of the head of a fire when spotting is prevalent. Because it is easier to see what a fire is doing at close quarters and to identify the safest lines of retreat, fire fighters are usually safer in the direct or parallel methods of attack than when they are placed at some distance ahead of a fire in indirect attack (Chapter 12). Any high-intensity fire can be dangerous, but fire fighting requires a bold, aggressive spirit for success. It cannot be a completely safe undertaking. The proper balance requires that safety hazards be brought down to the minimum but that necessary chances be accepted.

In some organizations, notably the U.S. Forest Service, a special safety officer is made a part of the organization on large fires. It is his job to ensure that practices conform to safety standards. This includes participation in carrying out strategy and tactics in such a way that unnecessary safety hazards are avoided. It is also his job to facilitate first aid and transportation of accident victims and proper reporting of accidents.

SUPERVISION

Supervision is often thought of as the spark plug by which plans are activated and teamwork is achieved. This kind of functioning does characterize good supervision. But its more important though less obvious task is that of developing personnel through training on the job. The success of this function determines the quality of performance, since it must constantly be engaged in narrowing the gap between the standards set and the standards realized in practice.

Errors in fire fighting are often costly. If the chance to control a small fire is lost, the chance to avoid disastrous costs and damages may also be lost. Consequently, all fire control agencies give much emphasis to codifying accepted standards and procedures. This facilitates supervision. The general progression, then, for subprofessional personnel becomes that of organized training followed by training on the job, usually supported by written standards and procedures and tested by inspection which compares performance to standards and identifies shortcomings for corrective action.

Inspection

Inspection in fire control activities may take several forms. To be constructive, the standards of performance sought must be clearly understood and feasible to attain, and the approach needs to be that of a challenge to the individual for personal improvement of habits and skills. When it is of this character, self-inspection, checklists, and written instructions become highly effective.

But like performance of all tasks, inspection in practice is not always constructive. It can deteriorate into a form of fault finding for not meeting standards that have not been clearly defined or that cannot realistically be attained. This is one of the first evidences of poor supervision.

Besides its function in controlling the quality of personal performance, inspection is highly important to the proper maintenance of fire control equipment and facilities. Periodic inspection of fire equipment is an essential function. Even when stored in good condition, safety hazards such as loose ax handles or deterioration of equipment through corrosion, mildew, insects, or rodents are common problems in stocks of hand tools. Corrosion, weak batteries, and deteriorated spark plugs are common problems of mechanized equipment in storage.

Inspection ensures that equipment is in good condition, that it is properly placed, and that it is ready to go whenever needed in an emergency. Functioning in this way, it is an insurance policy against avoidable error or delay in meeting a fire emergency. Codified instructions and standards and the effort to meet them tend to dominate the local supervision of fire activities. So it is easy to assume that this comprises supervision in forest fire control. But supervisory functions that may more properly be termed management are also essential. They become increasingly critical as they become associated with the allotment of funds by centralized authority in the fire control organization.

MANAGEMENT IN FIRE CONTROL ACTIVITIES

It is the forest manager's job to buy the maximum protection from fire with the funds available to him. To accomplish this he must solve a series of problems. Perhaps the most critical is that of being prepared to fight fire whenever the need arises. Plans are never automatic, even when fully supported by funds. They become effective only through the manager, and only through him can they gain the flexibility necessary for efficient day-to-day operations. He must find ways, for example, to substitute for the services or coverage of any of his fire control personnel whenever, for any reason, they cannot function as intended. He must often also make decisions on when to use his personnel on an overtime basis.

Typical management problems which call for frequent attention and follow-up are:

1 *Maintaining a state of readiness to fight fire*   Fire weather forecasts and fire danger ratings are valuable in keeping the manager informed of the existing and prospective fire potential. But he may find it difficult to adjust his organization accordingly. Use of cooperators; keeping his key men in touch by radio or other means; holding equipment operators, equipment, and men on standby; arranging for emergency dispatching service; providing for backup forces when regular forces are called to a fire; and coordinating actions with cooperating agencies are all examples of the types of action open to the manager as fire danger becomes critical.

2 *Desirable degree of professionalization*   One extreme is almost complete specialization and functionalization, as in a city fire department. The other is a high degree of integration of fire control with other forest work. Both extremes and all degrees of integration are to be found in North America, and opinion differs on desirable trends. Detection and suppression functions can be rather highly specialized but prevention and hazard reduction cannot be, since they depend on actions of many people and organizations outside of fire control. A high degree of integration of fire control with other forest work makes it difficult to use specialized equipment and sophisticated methods, but it does make more manpower available for fire control. The desirable balance between specialization and integration must be determined by organizations and based on field experience in forest resource management.

3 *Maintaining good communication*   As brought out in Chapter 14, the functioning of the fire organization is closely dependent on its communication system. In much the same way that the aerial observer gives flexibility to fire detection, mobile radio equipment gives flexibility to forest communication. This is of critical importance in the management of fire activities, since communication needs do not remain fixed either in time or place. The recurring pattern of need is set by the fire season. But superimposed on it is the suddenly expanded emergency need created by the simultaneous occurrence of several fires or by a single runaway fire. Because radio equipment could be easily transported and quickly placed in emergency service at the scene of a going fire, such uses were the initial impetus for developing and adapting radio communication for use in wild-land areas. But always the available radio channels are at a premium. Consequently, the channels used are often in danger of the kind of congestion and interference experienced on the old party line of telephone tradition.

One of the important management measures used to minimize time required for messages is the use of code in verbal transmission. This starts with the international call signs in the 10-code used by police, fire departments, and other two-way mobile radio operators. The "10-4" reply to a message, meaning "OK" or "acknowledged" is commonly familiar. A supplementary four code has been adopted by the U.S. Forest Service in which "4-11" is an emergency fire call. Beyond such codes, all routine reports to be transmitted by radio can be converted to code form to shorten the time required for their transmission. Often this results in greater accuracy of transmission as well.

4 *Balance between use of power equipment and hand tools*   For reasons given in Chapter 13, the use of power equipment in suppression has increased tremendously. Power equipment has become an economic necessity in most of the United States. In many situations it can do a job that would be impossible to accomplish by manpower and hand tools alone. Nonetheless, it is also true that high reliance on power equipment can be excessively expensive and can divert attention from the fact that, in many situations, trained and fast-moving small crews of men can suppress most fires more cheaply than can machines. If power equipment is provided, the decision that then must be made is whether it would be cheaper to send it to most fires for insurance or practice even though a substantial proportion of them could be successfully suppressed by manpower. The optimum combination of power equipment and hand labor also must be determined.

5 *How to make specialized equipment efficient as well as effective* This problem is closely related to decisions on the balance between use of hand tools and power equipment, but it persists after such decisions have been made. It has several aspects.

Lack of accessibility of the protection unit to specialized equipment may limit the potential of such equipment. Tractor-plow units, bulldozers, or heavy tank trucks cannot operate in or across swampy ground. Tank trucks can seldom operate off of a road, and bulldozers and tractor-plow units must go on their own power to a fire from the nearest road. These limitations are important but can often be minimized by the manager. During high fire danger periods, good management may dictate movement of such equipment to strategic locations which enable quick access to critical areas with the operator on radio communication. This may enable such equipment to participate in first attack on fires or to provide quick reinforcement, thus increasing its value.

Contact by radio or other means of communication with the operator of slow-moving equipment is highly important. The dispatcher can start such equipment toward a fire without delay and complete or correct the instructions on how to reach it while en route. In case of false alarm, the equipment can be headed off promptly.

Versatility in use, as discussed in Chapter 13, is an important problem to the forest manager. The slip-on tanker unit is a good example of a solution to the problem of tying up truck units when not needed for fire. Sulky plows that are easily moved on roads and easily detached from mobile units also provide a solution to the manager. The manager is also faced with the problem of making outside equipment from other projects or agencies more efficient when pressed into use on a fire. Problems of obsolescence, which were discussed in relation to fire trucks in Chapter 13, extend to all specialized equipment. They can be met in part by substituting rental for purchase of expensive equipment, such as airplanes, helicopters, or even bulldozers.

Finally, problems of maintenance need to be the constant concern of the manager. Good maintenance of fire equipment bears much the same relation to its proper functioning that good training and supervision do to the quality of performance of personnel. Most of the nontechnical men in year-long positions in fire organizations have earned their place through high-quality performance and know-how in maintenance of all kinds of forest fire equipment. With some merit, many inspectors judge the level of performance to be expected of a fire agency by the quality of maintenance of its equipment and facilities.

6 *Hazard reduction in relation to suppression strength*   To what degree can a strong suppression organization be capitalized upon to reduce the need for slash disposal or prescribed burning in depth? The question can also be reversed to ask how much hazard reduction work is necessary to make effective suppression at reasonable cost possible. The local manager is likely to ask this question in terms of how much hazard reduction work must be done to keep the fire-fighting job within the capabilities of his own organization. Strong differences of opinion center on this point.

7 *Skill without practice*   A successful control organization does not see much wildfire. An effective fire prevention program keeps down the number of fires that have to be controlled, and a highly effective presuppression organization may routinely extinguish nearly all of them before they gain headway. Successes of this kind limit the fire experience gained by local personnel. This may extend to protection units as large as

a National Park or a National Forest. The manager must deal with this problem. Conventional training needs to be supplemented by provisions such as the detailing of trainees to outside fires.

8 *Support without headlines* How can continued public support for fire control be maintained when losses are held to a low level? A successful organization does not make headlines, and its very success can engender public complacency and a feeling that fire control expenditures are out of line with needs. A large fire, which nobody wants, is always news, and a series of them is a powerful lever for getting increased support for fire control. The problem is basically one of public relations. Means must be found to dramatize personnel, improved procedures and equipment, and instances of successful prevention and suppression to take the place of black headlines when large fires occur. Perhaps a recurrent tag line like "And so another potential conflagration was stamped out" should be developed and emphasized, as "Only you can prevent forest fires" has been so successfully exploited in prevention.

9 *Cost* Modern fire control is expensive. There is constant need for close cost control and good financial management. Research, prevention, hazard reduction, detection, and suppression costs must be scrutinized and balanced. Beyond these financial management problems are larger economic questions of justification of costs in relation to losses and damageable values at stake, as discussed in Chapter 19. It is possible to spend too little as well as too much; in the past, sights were often set too low.

10 *Maintaining simplicity in spite of increasing technical complexity* To the student and practitioner alike, the development and operation of a modern, fully equipped fire control organization can seem very complex. It necessarily is in many respects. Yet by the nature of its job, a control organization needs to remain simple in basic organization and operation to maintain the high degree of manageability it must have. How to make procedural guides, handbooks, and other necessary operational material contribute toward greater flexibility and resourcefulness in meeting the shocks and stresses of control practice, rather than stultifying it, is a difficult problem of fire control management.

One comforting thought is that organization and management of fire control on wild lands is not so complex if it is considered a step or a job at a time. A large pulp and paper mill seems exceedingly complex to a visiting forester. One wonders how such a unit could ever be contrived. The answer is that no one person did or could; an operating mill represents years of cumulative knowledge and the experience of many men. In a less apparent way, a control organization can be just as complex, and the answer is the same. It was built a step at a time, and problems are also largely met one at a time.

Chapter 16

Control of Large Fires

Large, uncontrolled fires are a universal problem among forest fire-fighting agencies. In many respects, such fires are a problem distinct from the day-to-day operation of the control organization, and though the point at which they become a dire emergency naturally depends on the strength of the organization, the nature of the threat does not vary. It is distinctive and common to all fire agencies.

Certain distinctive aspects in the organization of suppression forces for the big fire are identified in Chapter 12. But the problem extends much further than the organization of forces to deal with the fire itself. It often places the whole organization under strain and may impose a severe test of the adequacy of the regular organization and of its personnel, equipment, and plans. Errors or failures in performance in making first attack on a fire are a frequent reason for fires becoming large. At times this is followed by similar failures at later stages, when there was a chance to control the fire at less damage or cost than was finally incurred. Avoiding such failures and overcoming the effects of any errors made become a part of the emergency job of controlling the large fire. The organization engaged in the contest has much in common with an athletic team engaging its strongest rival. After the contest is over the simile persists. Diagnosis of each weakness in performance and remedial action to ensure better performance next time are as important to the manager of fire control activities as to an athletic coach.

SIZE RELATIONSHIPS

The size of a fire is usually expressed as the present number of acres in a going fire and more commonly as the size of the burn when the fire is controlled. Size alone may have little significance, but in protected areas most fires that become large do so in spite of efforts to control them, so they are mostly wildfires with high energy output and high intensity. It is this type of large fire which is the chief subject of this chapter.

Statistically, large fires are a small portion of the total number but account for most of the burned area and damage. In 1971, only 1.6 percent of the fires on United States protected areas burned 300 acres or more, but they accounted for 73 percent of the damage. This is a typical pattern. In a statistical study of 22,485 fires occurring on the National Forests of Montana, northern Idaho, and eastern Washington during the period 1931 to 1945, Barrows (1951) reported that less than 1 percent of the fires accounted for 98 percent of the area burned. In a southern California study of 3,035 fires on four National Forests. Show (1941) found that 3 percent of the fires covered 90 percent of the total area burned from 1922 to 1939. A limited spot study in Georgia of 45 of the larger fires occurring between July 1, 1954, and July 1, 1956, showed that only 0.2 percent of the total number during the period accounted for 56 percent of the total area burned, even though small fires in southern pine commonly reach several acres in size. Similar statistics can be quoted for nearly any period for sizable areas of protected wild land, such as a million-acre unit.

FIRE AGENCY RELATIONSHIPS

Large fires are the most unwanted and discouraging development in organized fire control. Often they demonstrate failure of the third line of defense (page 261) and always failure to some degree of the protection organization in accomplishing its mission. The bigger the fire, the more severe the loss, the higher the cost, and the less accomplishment for the money spent. Years of successful protection may be largely nullified by a single large wildfire. In such situations the responsible agency may find itself in the position of winning most of the small battles but of losing the big ones. Several factors are conducive to such a development.

The more effective the control organization, the less frequent fires become. As they become less frequent, fewer men develop fire-fighting skills through experience on the job. Unless this is offset by a vigorous program of training, it greatly increases the threat of big fires. As fires become less frequent, the fire agency also finds it more and more difficult to maintain an aggressive program of fire prevention and a readiness to make fast attack on a fire whenever fire danger is present. Another important factor is the strong tendency for both private and public support and financing of the forest fire fighting organization to diminish as fire damage decreases. This finds expression in the reduction of funds in the name of economy and in reduced cooperation in preventing, reporting, and controlling fires. The reduced cooperation is elusive and ordinarily consists simply of conversion of active cooperation to passive cooperation, but the result is nevertheless strongly negative. Following a disastrous fire, funds and action programs can be restored much more easily, but often at the cost of locking the door too late.

Large fire is a relative term, since the significance of a large fire as a problem depends on the resources required for its control rather than on the size of the area it has enveloped. The point at which a fire becomes a special problem varies somewhat too with the strength of the fire organization. In the practice of the U.S. Forest Service, a Class E fire of 300 acres or more is regarded statistically as a large fire, though a 300-acre grass fire might easily be controlled by a single plow crew and would not be classed as a problem fire.

Fires which require men, equipment, and organization beyond that available and within the control of the local fire organization become the large fires of this discussion. In administrative practice they become known as project fires, campaign fires, overload situations, or sometimes conflagration fires.

THE LARGE-FIRE ORGANIZATION

Large fires generally pose a twin problem of both fire-fighting resources and organization, though usually the problem of effective organization is the more critical. It is no small feat to build up, in a few hours, a large, complex organization that can function efficiently. It requires competent men fitted skillfully into a new and expanding organization and a high degree of teamwork among individuals who have probably never before worked together in the same relationship. Various devices are used to facilitate this process. On a National Forest where the ranger district is the local unit, the ranger may relinquish his position as fire boss to be available for action on other fires or because a better qualified fire boss is available, and current fire plans may provide in advance for quickly moving in resources from other districts. Where central dispatching is employed, the dispatcher has been in the action from the start, so no transition is required if and when the fire requires men and equipment from outside the district. Another means of facilitating the organization of large fires is through special advance training of officers to fill the key staff positions that are usually needed. This may extend to training men to serve as overhead teams or to developing small groups of specialists who can provide special services, such as communication, scouting, timekeeping, and aerial services, with minimum supervision.

The five functions around which the large fire organization is usually built have been discussed in Chapter 12. These are (1) the command function, (2) the line function, (3) the plans function, (4) the service function, and (5) the finance function. On many fires, not all of these functions are carried out by separate staff men, and the order in which staff men are added may vary as well. Yet each of the five functions must be served in some way. Consequently a clearly defined model organization for large fires provides useful guidelines. The progression described (page 389–394) conforms closely to practices of the U.S. Forest Service and most Western states (*Fireman's Handbook,* 1966) but needs to vary as the difficulty and importance of the different functions vary. Several factors are important.

Accessibility is particularly important. In backcountry without road access, dependence must be placed on hand tools and light equipment that can be delivered by parachute, mule pack, or motorboat. A fire camp is necessary from the start, and since travel is primarily on foot, sectors and divisions are much shorter. To avoid wasting too much time in foot travel en route to or from the fire line, side camps are usually necessary. Supply service and communication are crucial, and the sector boss and the division boss, when assigned, must be more self-sufficient. Usually it takes too much time and effort for a line boss to participate directly in line construction to make such a position worthwhile. A camp boss is needed from the start, and an assistant at each side camp. Specialists may be needed to facilitate aerial support. Where it is confined to delivery of equipment and supplies by parachute or otherwise, the camp boss may organize this activity. Where water or chemicals are being applied to the fire, an air-attack boss may be assigned. If a small helicopter is available to the fire boss, this can simplify the organization since he can do his own scouting and can usually see the fire's entire perimeter at will. If radio communication to all sectors of the fire is good, the fire boss can coordinate progress in building the fire line also.

In accessible terrain where all parts of the perimeter of a large fire can be reached, plows or tank trucks are likely to be depended on primarily and a much smaller number of men is likely to be used. Because of easy road access, fire fighters are brought to the fire by truck or bus and the fire boss's headquarters may be at some distance from it. Close liaison is easy to maintain with the men and equipment assigned. Sectors can be much longer and divisions may not be used.

In addition to accessibility, the degree to which the activity is mechanized strongly affects the big fire organization. As illustrated in Chapter 12, Figure 12.3, a tractor-plow unit, a bulldozer, or a large-capacity tank truck with one or two men assisting the operator takes the place of a foreman and organized crew with hand tools. This permits organization of line building, backfiring, and mop-up on several miles of fire line with a minimum number of men, probably less than thirty. Each operator acts as the boss of his operation, and the fire boss can coordinate the effort without much difficulty. Organized in this way, the fire boss often finds it feasible to send in relief operators and crews for the second shift, thus permitting the men in the first attack to return to their own headquarters for the night.

The nature of the fuel in which the fire is spreading is also decisive. In mixed forest fuels with deep duff and much punky wood, smoldering combustion will persist and will require protracted mop-up. This may require the establishment of a nearby fire camp. Longer duration affects the services needed as well. A camp mess, a tool sharpening and repair unit, and so forth are then usual.

In grass and brush types that support hot, fast-moving fires, there is little mop-up to do when the fire is stopped. Accordingly, even for a very large fire, most of the personnel may operate from their own regular headquarters with camp and mess facilities limited to a temporary communication center for the fire boss to which lunches are brought.

Variations in the messing arrangements are a natural corollary to the differing situations discussed above. As discussed briefly in Chapter 13, frozen foods and hot meals delivered to the scene of the fire have become increasingly common in forest fire fighting. This is due to several factors: (1) shortening the time to completion of control and mop-up, (2) improved aerial service, (3) high cost of emergency messing arrangements in fire camps, (4) scarcity of experienced camp cooks, and (5) ready availability of frozen meals and prepared foods.

ANALYSIS OF ACTION ON LARGE FIRES

Because successful control of a fire so often depends on correct action and close timing, it is profitable to review the outcome of what was done at all stages of the fire that became large. Often even a supposedly minor act of omission or commission proves to be the chief contributing cause of failure to control a fire at small cost and damage. So there are many parallels to the ancient proverb which was given new life in 1758 by *Poor Richard's Almanac*[1]: "For want of a nail the shoe was lost; for want of a shoe the horse was lost; . . . ." A review of action on large fires also serves many other purposes. Often it can serve to confirm the values and weaknesses of all kinds of equipment, the capabilities of personnel, and the validity of the methods and tactics used in fighting fire. Perhaps of most importance is the training value of such reviews to all participants, particularly to inexperienced personnel.

Beginning in California in the early 1920s, boards of fire review were conducted in the California Region of the U.S. Forest Service for most of the large fires that occurred. These were organized by the top fire men in both administrative and research positions. Their purpose was to determine why the fire reached large size and what could be done to avoid a repetition of the errors made. At first, personnel failures and what to do about them were a prominent feature, but it was soon realized that the training value of such reviews to the participants and the value to the agency in identifying improvements needed in training and in current policies, practices, and methods were much more important.

The success of these reviews in advancing fire control practice led to their adoption by the U.S. Forest Service for use in all National Forest regions in the late 1930s. Similar practices have subsequently been adopted by most forest protection organizations.

Though the earlier reviews were conducted on a quite formal basis, most of the objectives of such reviews can be realized through an informal approach at all levels of the fire organization. The important requirements are that the reveiw be conducted by experienced men capable of unbiased appraisal, that it be held while all circumstances and events are still fresh in the minds of participants, and that it be confined to using the fire as an object lesson on how action can be improved next time.

Some kind of review of most problem fires is usually held by the responsible fire agency. Reports and summaries from such reviews are rarely published. One exception is the state report on the Badoura fire in Minnesota (Lawson, 1959). Generally, the supporting data become very voluminous but can often be made available for reference to the student. Abstracts of several reviews of this kind by the U.S. Forest Service appear in certain issues of *Fire Control Notes* (Headley, 1939, 1940; Brown, 1937, 1940).

---

[1] John Bartlett, *Familiar Quotations*, 14th ed., Little, Brown and Company, Boston, 1968.

Standards of Accomplishment

Analyses of action on large fires cannot be very productive unless definite standards of performance have been developed against which the individual case can be compared.

Usually this starts with the overall fire control policies of the fire agency. These are supplemented by instructions and performance standards at various administrative levels. Success is usually measured by (1) the time required to complete the fire suppression job, (2) the damage done, and (3) the costs incurred.

Standards of elapsed time have already been discussed. For larger fires these are within an overall framework of agency policy. The long-held fire suppression policy of the U.S. Forest Service (Chapter 19) provides that action will be aimed at overnight control of all fires; failing that, overnight of the second day, etc.

Fire danger ratings and fire weather forecasts provide a basis for standards of readiness and for dispatching. Dispatching guides are often set up based on these and other factors. The dispatcher must exercise resourcefulness in apportioning available fire-fighting resources, and some margin of error must be accepted. But he is subject to criticism if available information is disregarded or existing instructions are violated.

In suppression action itself, failure to recognize the potential of a fire, failure to ask for reinforcements when needed, failure to use proper strategy and tactics, and failure to organize and use available men and equipment effectively are common deficiencies. Such deficiencies can each be identified by an experienced fire boss but are seldom apparant from the record alone. Standards of quality of suppression action cannot be as firmly applied as standards of equipment performance, for example, since they often depend on the exercise of judgment. However, this is the province of field manuals and written instructions which often undertake to set such standards in some detail.

Case Histories of Large Fires

A common deficiency of most analyses of large fires is that the details and sequence of what men did in their efforts to bring the fire under control overshadow what the fire did. This is a natural outcome. Usually all participants are so fully engaged in other emergency duties that no one is available to make objective and continuing firsthand observations of the fire itself. So the fire's overall behavior, and particularly the time and sequence of significant changes in its behavior, are uncertain and are likely to be poorly reconstructed from circumstantial evidence. This seriously limits the validity of conclusions drawn as to the adequacy or inadequacy of the efforts made to control it.

The case study can usually correct this difficulty. Ideally, it is planned in advance and carried out by a trained research team who moves in as soon as it is apparent that a blowup fire is in progress. By means of observations and measurements, such a team develops a detailed time history of the fire. Usually this is in the form of a detailed log of events and a carefully drawn map showing the spread of the fire at various time intervals. In addition to such information, detailed weather measurements are sought and evidence of the occurrence of blowup fire phenomena such as described in Chapter 7 is assembled. How far such a team can go in establishing such things as the rate of energy release, the force and extent of meteorological interactions, and the magnitude of such phenomena as convective forces, fire whirlwinds, spotting, and crowning depends on several factors. Perhaps the most critical is timing. If the team can arrive soon enough to observe, to photograph, and to instrument various aspects of the fire behavior just as they develop, the case study can be carried much further. However, this depends also on the technical competence of the men engaged and on adequate meteorological, photographic, and other equipment for the purpose (Countryman and Chandler, 1963).

Case studies of blowup fires are important as a source of new knowledge in addition to their value in appraising a particular problem in fire fighting. This is because many of the phenomena they exhibit are absent in small or low-intensity fires. But these studies must usually be carried out under a good many handicaps. Rarely can they be planned in advance, since large fires and particularly blowup fires are not anticipated very far in advance and may not occur for long periods. Consequently, most case studies are made after the fire has made its run. Comprehensive studies of disaster fires in Australia have developed an excellent record of the behavior of the large fires in the Australian environment and have made definite contributions to this subject. (Wittingham, 1964; Douglas, 1965; McArthur, 1958, 1967.) Use of carefully instrumented large-scale test fires to study mass fire phenomena has progressively increased the significance of technical case studies since 1960, as illustrated by the report of the Loop fire disaster in California (Pyles et al., 1966) and the study of the Sundance fire of northern Idaho (Anderson, 1968).

As better understanding and prediction of large-fire behavior develops, analysis of action on large fires and the more comprehensive case studies as well will become more meaningful and consequently more valuable in training men and in planning fire suppression strategy.

HOW FIRE-FIGHTING SYSTEMS OPERATE

In training men, it is difficult to provide an experience to parallel that of being a participant in the fight to control aggressive fires. Some of the essential ingredients are the challenge imposed by the fire itself, the need to visualize its behavior in relation to time and place, the necessity to make decisions under pressure, the necessity of closely coordinated teamwork, and always a job to do that will never be exactly duplicated.

This difficulty led to the development of the fire control simulators described briefly in the preceding chapter. Simulators are particularly valuable in training men in decision making.

The progression in fighting a large, fast-moving fire is that of flexible response to the fire's behavior. Typically, the fire boss must act on incomplete information, then he must adjust and adapt further action as new information is received or as changes occur. Experienced men foresee the probable need for such adjustments in advance and plan accordingly.

A vivid picturization and word description of going operations on conflagration fires in 1967 is contained in the article entitled "Forest Fire, the Devil's Picnic" in the *National Geographic* of July, 1968. This is an excellent supplement to the narrative accounts that follow.

How fire-fighting systems operate in practice is illustrated by the following four accounts. These can help to integrate the application of principles and relationships set forth in preceding chapters. These describe suppression action in different forest regions and were written by men with firsthand experience with the fire control practices of their organizations in the forest regions in which they operate. These accounts have much in common, though they describe action by federal, state, and provincial organizations under a diversity of forest types and topography. All but one of these accounts are written in the first person for each key role and permit the reader to experience vicariously the responsibility of the fire boss, the dispatcher, and various other key positions in the forest fire control organization. Along with this feeling of responsibility, the sense of triumph over potentially overwhelming natural forces that comes from careful planning, effective execution, and close teamwork also comes through to the reader. The first two cases describe critical fire situations created by drought and more fires than the local force could handle. The last two describe campaigns to control single, fast-moving fires. Typically, in fighting a runaway fire there is a period of seeming confusion and uncertainty. This is reflected in part in the narratives. But all the cases described are intended to picture the application of best practices under adverse conditions. These contrast to the board-of-review type of report which points out weaknesses or errors in policy, planning, or execution that can be corrected by available means.

Following each account is a brief paragraph pointing out distinctive aspects of the situation or incident described. These are placed last, with the suggestion that the student first read the account in the capacity of a role player and that he then review it to clarify the particular aspects to which the notes call attention.

Case 1

Bitterroot National Forest, Montana

The Bitterroot National Forest in Montana is one of 16 National Forests located in Montana, northern Idaho, and northeast Washington which are administered as the Northern Region of the U.S. Forest Service with headquarters at Missoula, Montana. The region is characterized by winters of heavy snowfall but dry summers, heavy mixed fuels, deep duff, and numerous dry lightning fires. Because the fire problem has long been recognized as difficult, each National Forest has a well-developed fire organization with special fire personnel at each ranger headquarters. Because the regional headquarters is a dispatching center and is nearby, the forest supervisor's office is relieved of responsibility for special services and in part as well for dispatching of outside manpower and equipment.

"Hit 'Em Hard While They're Small"[2]

Tom Smith and Mark Boesch
Bitterroot National Forest, U.S. Forest Service

It was 0730 on the morning of August 10. The Darby District of the Bitterroot National Forest was ready to begin another busy summer day. Dispatcher Boesch turned to the brush crew forman, about to leave for the Lick Creek timber-sale area with his four-man crew.

"Clarence, we'd better have hourly checks beginning at 0930. I'll have the weather forecast from the Supervisor's office by then, and we'll have an idea of what's in store for us. If I don't miss my guess, you fellows will be on fires before the day is over."

"Okedoke," Clarence Lindquist replied. A few minutes later he and his

[2] Updated by W. R. Moore, Regional Division of Fire Control at Missoula, Montana, January, 1971, after consultation with original authors and fire staff men of Bitterroot National Forest.

crew pulled away from the ranger station in the carryall after making sure it was fully gassed and ready for a lot more miles than the ten or so that would take them to their brush-piling job.

District Ranger Foskette came into the office about that time.

"What's the picture for today, Mark?" he asked his dispatcher.

"The brush crew's on the way to Lick Creek, Red. The East Side trail crew will be working Trail 159 on the way to Coyote Meadows. They should be checking in soon. We should be hearing from the Tin Cup trail crew any minute, too. I have a hunch we're going to be busy today. Here's the weather picture, based on yesterday's readings."

The dispatcher handed the ranger the sheet that had on it not only the weather readings he had taken at the weather station the evening before, but also the estimated readings for this day. Ranger Foskette studied them carefully.

The dispatcher had predicted for this day of August 10 that moisture content of the $1/_2$-inch fuel sticks would be 5; there would be a severity index of 8; humidity of 15 per cent; a wind average of 10 miles per hour during the afternoon, making a burning index of 65. Lightning was also predicted.

"Wow!" Foskette exclaimed. "We better pray for rain with that storm."

"Heck of it is, these August storms don't give us much rain," Boesch said. "When they do, it's generally spotty. Right now we've got dry spots on the district. Rock Creek is one. Hasn't rained up there since July 20, and only a trace then."

"Lucky thing we haven't had any hot storms the past two weeks the way this weather's been building up," Foskette said. "But we're bound to catch it sooner or later."

"This could be the day," Boesch said. "We'll know about it when we get the forecast from Hamilton" (Supervisor's office).

"Well, I've got to check some of the range today," the ranger said. "This dry weather isn't doing the grass any good either. I'll take the mobile unit. Call you first from Smitty's, up Rye Creek."

"Right, Red. I'll let you know what develops."

Bad as this weather was, Red Foskette couldn't just let everything else drop and sit tight there at headquarters, waiting for something to happen. That's what he had his dispatcher on the job for. Boesch had been dispatching for ten years. If he wasn't capable of taking action on a fire bust now, he never would be. And he had good men to aid him. There was the headquarters guard, a man with wide experience who could fill in behind the dispatcher at headquarters, or who could go out and take over a fire. There was also a station fireman, a skilled smokechaser who had seen a lot of fire action. And there was the packer-truck driver, who could either take a string of mules up the trail to a fire, or could drive a truck load of fire fighters and/or equipment to the end of a road. The Darby District Ranger was a resource manager of 391,000 acres of forest land. He was as concerned with fire as anyone else, but he had other things to look after, too, such as grazing, timber sales, road, trail, and other improvement work. He had skilled, key men to help him in these various duties. The assistant ranger did a lot of the timber work, helping to supervise the cutting by private operators of some ten million board feet each year. Today the assistant and his helper would be working at head-quarters on scale books. But the alternate ranger was up Tin Cup Creek, inspecting the trail reconstruction job that was going on there.

When the two-man East Side trail crew checked into headquarters by radio relay via the Deer Mountain lookout, Boesch gave them the same orders he had given the brush crew foreman. The same was true when the Tin Cup crew checked in.

Following the radio business, Boesch gave orders to his headquarters men to make sure all the station vehicles had been gassed up the night before and now were ready to go. He told them to check all the equipment. Then he mentally checked what they had available. This included 2 pickup trucks, a Dodge powerwagon, and a 1-ton stockrack truck. There were 25 smokechaser packs made up, two 10-man loose tool outfits, 1 Pacific Pump with 1,200 feet of hose, 4 handi-talkie radios, 1 jeep pumper unit, and two 25-man standard fire-fighting outfits, the latter sufficient to fully equip 50 men on a fire. Finally, there were 2 chain saws. Soon the dispatcher heard the men warming up both chain saws out in the shop, making sure they were ready for use on a fire. Then they were testing the handi-talkies, calling the lookouts to make sure these vital radios were functioning properly.

It was now 0815. Boesch opened the front door of the office. Beginning to get a little warm.

"Going to be a hot day," he said to his clerk, who was busy typing a timber-sale contract.

Boesch went back to the fire desk and opened his Dispatcher Binder. He turned to the section where the cooperators were listed. These people—farmers, ranchers, dude packers, townsmen, and logging and mill crews—had all been contacted early in June. All were listed there in the Binder, along with their experience, capabilities, and the kind of equipment they had to offer. The latter included trucks, jeeps, mules and horses, school buses, chain saws, and even bulldozers. Boesch was personally acquainted with most of these cooperators and could talk to them on a first-name basis. Now he began calling them, seeing who would be available for fire duty that day.

Some of the ranchers in the valley had hay down. Even so, most of them agreed to come to his aid if Boesch needed them badly enough. Most of them were grazing permittees. They had a big stake in this business of stopping fires.

Jack Lykins, a commercial packer on the district, had a full string available, shod and ready to go, with his own truck to haul them wherever they might be needed.

The sawmills had their crews working, and they would spare what men they could in an emergency. They, too, had a stake in this business, since they could not long remain in business without Bitterroot Forest timber.

The two restaurants in the town of Darby were alerted to be prepared to make double lunches for fire fighters. They knew what to put in these lunches—four big sandwiches, fruit, several candy bars, cookies or pastry—enough to do a man all day if necessary.

As Boesch called the various cooperators, individuals and crews, he made notes on his ready pad on who and what was available and even how to contact them. That was not only for his own use, but for someone else who might have to fill in for him here at the desk when the going got heavy.

By the time Boesch was through working on the list of fire cooperators, it was 0900, and the forest dispatcher, Tom Smith from the supervisor's office at Hamilton, was calling all five of the Bitterroot districts on the radio.

"Here's the weather forecast," Smith said. "And it's a bad one. Increasing cumulus clouds today, followed by moderate, scattered lightning storms with little or no rain over the Nez Perce, Bitterroot, Beaverhead, and Deer Lodge forests. Humidity will range from 15 to 25 percent over southern areas. Maximum temperature at 3,000 feet 90 to 95 degrees. Winds will be light to gentle, but moderate and gusty in vicinity of lightning storms." Smith then suggested that each district review its manpower situation and arrange to have necessary men available for immediate action.

Boesch gave his 10-4 radio code, indicating he had received the forecast, then after the other districts had done the same, he got back on the radio again with Smith.

"Tom, in view of that forecast, maybe you'd better alert that boomer crew of yours and have them available. Looks like we'll be needing them."

"Will do," Smith replied. He was proud of his crew of young cooperators he had organized to chase smoke and fight fire. Their ages ran from eighteen to the early twenties—about a dozen young huskies who had been trained through previous smokechasing and fire-fighting jobs to do a good job of hitting the trails with fire packs, all of them being in fine physical condition.

"I'll alert Fred Fite, the regional dispatcher" (Region One Headquarters at Missoula), Smith told Boesch. "We'll probably be needing smokejumpers too."

After this radio business with Smith, Boesch called the two Darby lookouts to give them the weather forecast—Deer Mountain, in the Sapphire Range on the east side of the Bitterroot Valley, and Ward Mountain over on the west side in the high, rugged Bitterroot Range. The two lookouts wrote the forecast in their logs. Then Boesch got a weather check from them.

"Scattered cumulus in the southwest," Deer Mountain said.

"Yeah, looks like we're going to get that storm all right," Ward Mountain agreed.

The forest dispatcher called Darby. "The patrol plane will take off from the Hamilton airport at 1000," Smith said. "They'll be flying Flight B, down Darby's west side, through the West Fork District, over into Idaho for a look at the Magruder and Salmon River country, back over into the Sula District, over Darby's east side, then both sides of the Stevensville District. Pass the word to the other districts."

As Boesch gave this information to the districts that lay south of him, he also checked with them on the manpower they had available that day. They were accustomed to swapping forces back and forth in the kind of bust that was now shaping up.

It was now 0930.

The crews began checking in via radio. Boesch gave each one the weather forecast and told them to be sure and check in again at 1030.

At 1000 Deer Mountain called. "Those clouds are really building up," he said. "That storm is on the way."

Calling Ward Mountain, Boesch got much the same report. Then he called Smith. "Tom, how are you doing with recruiting your boomer crew?"

"Have six of them standing by here. Can probably get four or five more within an hour or so."

"Better send what you have here for stand-by," Boesch told Smith.

"Will do," Smith agreed. "One of them has a car. They'll ride up in that. And Mark, I checked with Fite. He has plenty of jumpers available. In addition there are seven 25-man suppression crews available throughout Missoula. Don't hesitate to call for help. I've notified Vern Hamre, who is at Stevensville, of what's shaping up."

"10-4," Boesch said. Hamre was the Bitterroot fire control staff officer.

It is 17 miles from Hamilton to Darby. Those six men would be at the district headquarters within thirty minutes.

Boesch was looking out the front door toward the southwest, seeing the angry-looking cumulonimbus himself now, when the boomer crew pulled into the station. About the same time the brush crew was calling from Lick Creek. Boesch stepped over to the radio.

"Bring your crew in, Clarence," Boesch told foreman Lindquist. "We'll be getting lightning soon."

He got the verification of that when he heard one of the West Fork District lookouts calling his headquarters, reporting lightning on the southern edge of that district.

"Not much rain with it, either," he heard the lookout say grimly. "But it looks like Darby will get the worst of this one."

From then on the radio stayed busy, with Boesch glued to the fire desk. Ranger Foskette called from the Smith ranch, was apprised of the situation, and said he would start back for headquarters at once. The East Side trail crew checked in, and Boesch told them to stay in contact with Deer Mountain for possible fire duty. The Tin Cup crew called and was told to check in again at 1100, and every half hour after that. The patrol plane checked in from over on the West Side, one of their routine 15-minute checks, this being a safety factor. The observer gave Boesch their location, then called Smith. Boesch heard the observer tell the forest dispatcher that they would not be able to make their scheduled patrol because of the menacing storm. Smith ordered the observer to keep a watch on the route of the storm and to continue checking in regularly with the district dispatchers.

It was 1100.

Deer Mountain called to report that the storm had entered into Darby District and was putting down lightning at the head of Trapper Creek on the West side of the Valley.

Boesch now had available at his headquarters station the six-man boomer crew of Smith's, the five-man brush crew, the assistant ranger and his helper, the headquarters guard, the station fireman, and the packer-truckdriver. The storm was now moving along the west side of the district, lightning plastering the head of Trapper Creek, then moving north to hit sections of Chaffin, Tin Cup, and Rock Creek. But as it neared the deep drainage of Lost Horse Creek, it veered eastward, crossing the wide Bitterroot Valley where it set a barn on fire, killed two cows in a field, started plastering the forest again in Sleeping Child Creek, and then moved northeast across the Shalkaho Drainage, and finally passing out of the district over the head of Gird Creek. All the while the forest patrol plane flew near the storm, watching the areas of hot lightning concentration.

Even before the storm passed out of the district, about half an hour after it first arrived, Deer Mountain was calling in the first fire location.

The fire was at the head of Tin Cup Creek, one of the worst areas on the district. Dispatcher Boesch was glad now of having that crew in Tin Cup. Almost immediately he was able to contact them by radio. He gave Alternate Henderson the fire location, and they agreed that four of the seven trail men had better get started for it. They were all set to go, having fire packs in their camp. With a 3-mile hike ahead of them, they should be able to hit the fire within two hours.

Boesch contacted the patrol plane and asked him to swing over the Tin Cup fire. He would be there in about five minutes, and after a good look at it would be able to give the dispatcher a better idea of its potentialities. Boesch might have all of that Tin Cup crew on this fire before it was over with. But he couldn't sacrifice too much of his manpower on the first fire.

It was 1130.

Ward Mountain now called in. He had a fire over near Bald Top Mountain on the East side of the Valley in the Sleeping Child Drainage.

"Looks bad," he said. "Spreading fast."

He reported the smoke as being white, with a heavy volume. Having the location of it plotted on his board, Boesch saw that it was burning in an open area near Bald Top. Lots of grass in there and down lodgepole. Likely that was the cause of its fast spread.

"This is one for you, Clarence," Boesch said to the brush crew foreman. He didn't send all of Lindquist's crew with him. Those brush men were all skilled fire fighters and could act as straw bosses on project fires. He let Lindquist take one of those with him, then gave him three of Smith's boomer crew—good men, but a little less experienced than the regular crew men.

"I'm going to put in an order for smokejumpers on that one, too," Boesch told Lindquist. "Be sure and take a radio with you."

The headquarters guard would get them outfitted with what they needed. Boesch stayed at the fire desk. He now called the forest dispatcher. He had quickly made out a smokejumper request form, and he gave Smith the necessary information for relay on to the regional office. That fire was already close to a half acre, so he ordered eight jumpers, a half DC-3 load.

"Wind's kicking up," Smith told him. "They might not be able to jump."

"I know," Boesch said, "but I've got a five-man ground crew on the way."

Smith agreed that was a good idea—the old insurance business. Then he told Boesch he had four more of his boomer crew who would soon be ready to start for

Darby. He would keep recruiting. West Fork now had two fires going, even though they'd had less lightning than Darby.

Then the Sula District Dispatcher was calling. He'd pulled his brush crew in—wanted to know if Darby wanted the five men.

"Send them right away," Boesch said, "and thanks, Terry."

The patrol plane was calling Darby now. He hadn't made it to that Tin Cup fire yet. Instead, the observer had spotted another fire just above Lake Como in the Rock Creek Drainage. This one, too, looked bad. Boesch knew that country well. He knew it was steep as a cow's face there. The fire was burning about halfway up the slope. If it reached the top it would have bad fuels and would spread all over the country. Wasn't doing much yet, for the fuels were light where it had started. Just one snag burning. But the wind was throwing sparks from that snag. And when it fell, the burning tree would likely roll down to the creek bottom where there were more bad fuels.

Boesch called Smith. He asked if the rest of that boomer crew had got started for Darby.

"No," Smith said, "but they're ready to leave now. Got five of them with their own transportation."

This was good news. He asked Smith to tell the men not to come to Darby, but instead to wait at the Lake Como road for the crew he was sending from Darby. They would go to the fire up Rock Creek.

Ward Mountain called then. He could see the Rock Creek fire throwing up smoke now—couldn't see it before because of a high ridge that shut him off. That one was beginning to spot, Boesch knew. Then he had Ward Mountain give him a report on the Bald Top fire.

"Doesn't seem to be spreading so fast now," was the word.

Boesch told him to watch for that jumper plane. Probably, he thought, the fire had made its initial run through the grass. But there was a lot of down lodgepole in the area. It would need a chain saw. He made a note of that.

Rock Creek was one for the assistant ranger, Bernie Swift. Boesch gave him two of Smith's boomer crew, one of whom was of straw-boss caliber. Then Swift left, taking a handi-talkie, extra loose tools—enough to give each man a Pulaski and shovel—and smokechaser rations.

"I'll get the rest of the stuff you'll need in to you, Bernie," Boesch said as the assistant went out the door, "one way or another."

The forest dispatcher was calling on the radio.

"Mark, what about the helicopter at Missoula? Possibly you can use it to stop the head of that Rock Creek fire."

"Fine, Tom," Boesch said happily. "We can sure use it. Have the pilot set down here at Darby."

"Will do," Smith said.

The headquarters guard went out to the wide area back of the ranger station to mark a set-down spot for the 'copter. This was not the first time the 'copter had been called for this kind of duty.

Now the patrol plane was calling. There were two fires up Tin Cup. One of them, the one Deer Mountain had seen, was on a ridgetop. It wasn't as much of a threat as one lower down, about a mile away. It was beginning to spread in bad fuels.

"Swing down the canyon over the trail camp," Boesch ordered the observer. "Henderson will get on the radio. Give him that dope, and ask him to take the rest of his crew up there."

"10-4," came the acknowledgment. Then the observer added, "I tossed out some of Tom's pink toilet paper to mark those fires."

"Good dope," Boesch said, and smiled. But humorous or not, he knew the value of this. This scheme, which Smith had originated, worked wonderfully in helping ground men find a fire. The pink color of the toilet paper could be seen a long distance as it unraveled itself earthward. And it marked an area well as it spread out over the trees and rocks.

Having a minute, Boesch called both restaurants in town and asked them to start making double lunches.

Now Medicine Point, one of the Sula District lookouts, was calling Darby. He had just picked up a fire in Chaffin Creek. Just one snag burning. Boesch plotted its location quickly on his board—about a mile from the end of the road. Two good smokechasers could get there within an hour. He sent one man from Smith's boomer crew, plus one of the brush crew men. He decided not to send a radio with them. They could use the streamers in their smokechaser packs for signaling the plane if they needed anything. Ordinarily they would take a radio, but this one looked fairly easy, and Boesch wanted to hold a radio or two in reserve for higher priority.

Ranger Foskette came in just as Deer Mountain was reporting another fire. This one was in the head of Sleeping Child, near Coyote Meadows. This was high lodgepole country. The fire wasn't doing much, but it could. Plotting its location, Boesch saw it was not much more than a mile from the East Side Trail crew's location. He gave them orders through Deer Mountain to proceed to the fire. They had smokechaser packs with them, plus their radio. In about half an hour he would know the story on that one.

Ranger Foskette was busy reading the log the office clerk had been keeping as Boesch was busy working the fires. Darby now had six fires going, but also had men on the way to all of them.

"That Rock Creek fire worries me," the ranger said. "Maybe I'd better head up there."

"The 'copter will be here shortly, Red," Boesch told his ranger. "Why don't you use it to scout?"

"Good idea," Foskette said. "I'll go over, grab a quick lunch, then be all set."

The headquarters guard was busy. He had detailed several of the men standing by for fire duty to begin making up more smokechaser packs. Boesch could now hear the patrol plane talking to Alternate Henderson, giving him the word about the two Tin Cup fires. He heard Henderson 10-4 on taking the rest of the men up there, then get promptly off the air. Boesch got on the radio and asked the plane to swing over for another look at Rock Creek.

Now Ward Mountain was on the air, calling in another fire, this one up

Skalkaho. It was close to the Tenderfoot logging road. A bad area—logging slash in there, and open yellow pine country, the fire burning on a south slope. It was beginning to spread.

This was one for Bill Helm, the headquarters guard—a man with lots of fire experience. Before dispatching him, Boesch checked with Smith to see if he'd be able to recruit any more men.

"I've got two here," Smith said. "But I've also got Stevensville's five-man brush crew coming. Figured you would need them. They should be here at Hamilton in about ten minutes."

"That's fine, Tom. Send those seven men out to the Skalkaho road turnoff. Bill Helm will meet them there with the necessary tools."

Stevensville was the district north of Hamilton. Smith, as forest dispatcher, was doing his job of coordinating the Bitterroot Forest forces, helping to cope with this threat on the Darby District.

Boesch sent two of the experienced Sula men with Helm, along with a ten-man loose-tool outfit, and had them stop at one of the restaurants to pick up ten double lunches. They could eat part of those lunches on the way to the fire. Helm also grabbed a chain saw, one of his favorite weapons.

It was 1230. Darby now had seven fires going.

Ward Mountain called. The jumper plane was over the Bald Top fire. Rock Creek was kicking up more smoke. Boesch called one of the sawmills. He spoke to the foreman, who promised to have a ten-man crew ready for instant use when needed. Another sawmill promised the same. Both crews would have their own overhead.

Now the patrol plane called. He couldn't get on the air earlier because of the traffic. He had scouted the Rock Creek fire carefully. The snag had fallen and rolled nearly a quarter of a mile downhill, setting spot fires along the way.

"You've got about six different fires burning there now," the observer reported. "Some are still spots. But two of them are spreading out. That country's mighty steep. No chance for jumpers."

The observer should know. He was an ex-smokejumper.

Now Smith was calling from Hamilton. He'd talked to the DC-3 that was circling Bald Top. Too much wind up there at the present time. They couldn't risk letting the men drop to that one.

There were eight good fire fighters in that plane. Boesch wanted to get them into action.

"Ask them to swing over Tin Cup," he said to Smith. "Maybe they can jump on the lower fire. We'll have trouble there if it starts to crown."

"Will do," Smith said.

Then Boesch called the patrol plane.

"Go over and have a look at Bald Top," he said. "Find where that ground crew is, and see if they'll be able to handle it."

"10-4."

It was 1245.

Would there be any more fires showing up? Boesch thought so. That's why he had held smokechasers in reserve. And he still had cooperators to call on—individuals he had alerted earlier. Ranger Foskette was back from dinner. He got a refresher from the log, then went out to where the helicopter was setting down, taking a radio with him.

Boesch was on the phone again, calling one of the dude packers, Jack Lykins, and ordering him to load his mules and take them to Lake Como to where the trail took off for Rock Creek. He made several other calls. These to other cooperators—men who owned boats with outboard motors. He asked them to get their boats and motors to Lake Como right away. In 15 minutes they could make a trip from one end of the lake to the other, saving Lykins 5 miles of packing. Then he had the packer-truckdriver take several men to help him load one of the twenty-five-man outfits onto the truck. He would haul it to Lake Como, and the stuff would be loaded onto the boats, then taken up to where Lykins could start packing. Bernie Swift and his men had been able to take a short cut around the rugged side of the lake. But there was no short cut for the mule string. They would have to use the good trail around the far side of the lake. But once at the head of the lake, they would only have to pack that twenty-five-man outfit a mile or so to where it was needed.

The patrol plane called then to say that the ground crew was about fifteen minutes away from the Bald Top fire, and it looked like they could handle it okay. It was just about $1/2$ acre in size.

Boesch told the plane to go look at the fire near Coyote Meadows, then swing over for a look at Skalkaho.

But just then the trail crew called from Coyote Meadows, saying they had just got there and could handle the fire okay.

That was one of them, anyway, Boesch thought. He called Medicine Point to see how Chaffin Creek was doing. Still that one snag smoking. Those two smokechasers should just about be there, Boesch thought. When there was time, he would have the patrol plane swing over for a look at it.

The patrol plane was calling again. Another fire, this one in Little Sleeping Child Creek. It wasn't more than a mile from the Patterson Ranch. Al Patterson was a per diem guard and had a tool cache. Quickly Boesch called him and gave him the necessary information on the fire.

"You can grab your tools and get started for that one, Pat," Boesch told the per diem guard. "I'll call the Lovely boys and have them come up to give you a hand."

The Lovely brothers had a ranch about a mile below Patterson's. They'd been alerted earlier that morning and were standing by. Now they loaded two saddle horses onto their stock truck and in a few minutes were on the way. That fire would be manned by three capable cooperators in less than an hour. They were trained men who could put the fire out and return home without further instructions.

Ranger Foskette was now calling on the radio. It was only 20 minutes since he had walked out of the office, but already the helicopter had set him down on a large flat rock above those Rock Creek fires.

"Going to need about ten men up here, Mark," Foskette told his dispatcher. "I've sent the 'copter back to start ferrying them in. With luck we can handle this situation. I've just talked with Bernie below me. He's been trying to get out to you, but he must be boxed in. He's putting his men on the fires below. This is goat country. Worst fuel is up here on top. But I think we can keep those fires from getting up this high."

"Will it be safe working up there, Red?" Boesch asked.

"Yeah, it's okay," Foskette said. "Fuels are scattered there below us. Worst danger is for Bernie and his boys, from rolling rocks. I've warned him about them."

Now Smith was calling from Hamilton. He'd just heard from the jumper plane over Tin Cup. Wind was a lot better there. They could put all eight of those jumpers on the lower fire.

"The spotter says it looks like they can use them down there, too," Smith told Boesch. "That lower fire is a couple acres and wanting to go. The upper fire is maybe a quarter of an acre and is burning downslope. About four men can hold it."

That tricky wind, Boesch thought. It was true of a lot of those rugged west side canyons. Normally, fires burned a lot faster upslope this time of day, but in places like Tin Cup, the wind could really fool you. He gave Smith a quick go-ahead on putting the jumpers in. Good to get these huskies into action.

Now the patrol plane was calling from Skalkaho.

"This fire is spreading pretty fast," Boesch was told. "It's in that yellow pine now. Must be 3 acres anyway. Looks like you'll need some follow-up."

"Can you see anything of Helm and his crew?" Boesch asked.

"Yeah, they're on the road. They've got about a mile to go yet. Should be on the fire in 20 minutes."

Boesch cleared, then got busy. He called one of the sawmills and got their ten-man crew headed for the ranger station. They would be there in 10 minutes. Then he called another mill and got their ten-man crew headed for the station. They'd be there shortly, too. One of these he would put on Rock Creek via helicopter. The other would go as reinforcements to Skalkaho.

Skalkaho was a 'dozer chance, too. He got one from a logger, working about 5 miles away. He could walk his 'dozer up the Tenderfoot road. He got another 'dozer from another logger, then called the County road department for their transport to haul it. Both 'dozers would be on the fire in 2 to 3 hours.

The packer-truckdriver was back from Lake Como now. The other twenty-five-man outfit was loaded onto his truck, and he was soon off for Skalkaho.

Boesch still had seven good smokechasers and fire fighters left at his headquarters. Past experience had taught him that this was necessary. The day wasn't over yet. There would likely be more fires showing up. And there was lots of work for those men right here at headquarters, keeping stuff moving and running the numerous errands.

And so it went, with two more fires picked up later that afternoon, one by the patrol plane, the other by one of the lookouts. One of these fires was in remote back country. Boesch used two jumpers on that one, getting them on the fire within an hour and a half of the call, whereas it would have taken ground men 6 to 8 hours to get there. The other fire was closer in, and Boesch put four of the seven reserves on it.

By nightfall every fire on the Darby District was manned. Several were under control. Skalkaho was 5 acres, but Helm was sure he would have it under control by the ten o'clock deadline the next morning. Those two 'dozers had saved his men a lot of tough line building. Boesch had ordered an air drop of tools, grub, and beds for the Tin Cup men. Henderson had the drop site marked. Among other things, such as tools and beds, he'd had them drop a pump with 4,000 feet of hose. The pump with 500 feet of hose could be used on the lower fire, which was near the creek. The rest of the hose was used on the upper fire. Avery Hughes, one of the trail crew men, had worked out an ingenious system of gravity feed from a water source high up in goat rocks. No pump was needed. All they had to do was start that water from the pot-hole into the hose which ran down the steep hill. That gave them plenty of pressure. It was a system the Darby District had been using with great success for several years now. Henderson expected to have his Tin Cup fires controlled by the ten o'clock deadline, too.

Rock Creek was six small fires spread out over a steep slope, the largest just under an acre in size. The 'copter had got all ten of the mill crew up there to help Ranger Foskette. He and his assistant working below had the situation under control. Lindquist and his crew held the Bald Top fire to an acre. The threat of project fires was over. Ten fires from one storm were held down to six Class A and four Class B.

Darby District, thanks to good beforehand thinking and preparedness, with the dispatcher using his meter to estimate rate of spread for slope exposure and fuels, which gave him a good idea of manpower and equipment needs, plus willing and able cooperators and good teamwork on the part of forest and district headquarters, had again come through a tough situation, keeping the small ones from becoming big ones.

Notes: This case illustrates the benefits of careful advance planning and of skilled local dispatching by which available forces are apportioned and dispatched to head off a threatening disaster. Though somewhat idealized, it illustrates effective utilization of an experienced and highly qualified staff at ranger headquarters and full dependence on a local dispatcher who is thoroughly familiar with all available resources. Other assets that are skillfully utilized are frequent radio contact including recurrent radio checks with available crews, weather and fire danger forecasts, aerial detection and scouting, use of local resident cooperators, and use of smoke jumpers.

Case 2

Fire Control in Ontario

The Forest Protection Branch of The Ontario Department of Lands and Forests is responsible for forest fire control over an area of 313,080 square miles contained in the provincial fire district. The fire district includes about 75 percent of the land area in the province.

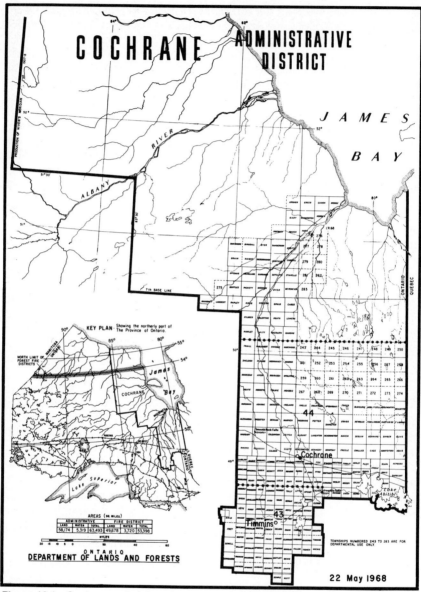

Figure 16.1   Cochrane administrative district, Province of Ontario, Canada.

This is only one of the Departments of Lands and Forests' areas of responsibility. The total department function is the management of the renewable natural resources in Ontario. This is accomplished through the administration of public lands, timber management, fish and wildlife management, parks, and research. Personnel, accounting, law, and operating activities support these other activities as well as the forest protection activity.

The cabinet minister responsible for lands and forests is assisted by a deputy minister and eleven branch chiefs. Each branch chief is responsible for the total work program of his branch. There is a branch for each activity listed above.

The province is divided into three regions for administrative purposes. A regional director is in charge of each region. These areas are further broken down into districts and the districts into divisions. There are 21 forest districts in the province, each containing from two to four chief ranger divisions. The chief ranger in each division is responsible, under the direction of the district foresters, for the accomplishment of the field work required for the above branches.

The Cochrane Fire District is 53,398 square miles in area. A further 10,155 square miles is administered for purposes other than fire. The district is located in the Northeastern Region of Ontario. The district's northern boundary is formed by Hudson Bay and James Bay, as illustrated by the accompanying map (Figure 16.1).

Commercial stands of white and black spruce, balsam fir, jackpine, white cedar, poplar, and white birch occur over the greater part, with increasing areas of muskeg to the north. The main forest product is black spruce pulpwood.

The District population is approximately 50,000, centered around the towns in the southern portion. The town of Cochrane, on the present trans-Canada highway and the junction of the east-west, north-south railway lines, is the administrative headquarters of the Cochrane Forest District.

Ontario: "Season 1955" on the Cochrane District[3]

George J. Wood, Forest Protection Technician
Cochrane District, Ontario Department of Lands and Forests

From the patrolling Beaver aircraft, the District appeared as flat as a western prairie and almost as vast (Figure 16.2). The yellow float-plane itself looked like a minute insect droning over a limitless dinner plate, the rim of which was lost in the haze of the earth's curvature. Below was an assorted salad of dark green spruce and balsam fir, garnished with shreds of lighter aspen where the drainage improved and seasoned with a sprinkling of tamarack in the wetter spots. Except for the yellow-brown of the open muskegs, colors disappeared in the mid-distance, leaving just the broad tones, blending into the flat, gray curve of James Bay. Sprinkled generously at first, but growing fewer toward the salt water, were the northern lakes, each one intriguing, most of them unnamed and unexplored, all

A

[3] Updated by W. G. Cleavely, Supervisor, Forest Protection Section, October 5, 1970.

B

Figure 16.2 Illustrations of the inaccessible country in Ontario. *A.*
Typical terrain in lake country of Canada where primary access for
fire fighting is by aircraft and motorboat, which limits the kinds of
fire-fighting equipment used. *(U.S. Forest Service photo.) B.* Typical problem fire in lake country of Ontario. Water surfaces improve
access by air, but lakes and rivers at times are more effective
barriers to ground transportation than to the spread of the fire by
spotting.

of them infinitely lonely. A silent country, a silence not of peace, but of unspoken
challenge.

Upstairs in the radio room of the Cochrane headquarters, the six-channel
receiver crackled with static as the operator checked the position report of the
aircraft far to the north. Burning index statements from the Divisions and
sub-Divisions were lying on the desk to be passed to the Protection Supervisor.
Behind these reports lay the story of the build-up: the ice that left the lakes so
early this year, the deep snow that had vanished so rapidly under the onslaught of
week after week of low humidity and drying winds, the lack of the long-expected
spring rains.

The cumulative burning index graph on the wall confirmed the warning of
the reports. For almost a month the trend had been upward, falling slightly here
and there under the influence of local showers, but rising again, each peak higher
than the last.

There had been forty fires so far this season, some of them bad ones, but
these were merely the prelude to the worst fire season the District and the
Province had experienced for years.

The operator turned as the telephone rang, glancing out of the window as he did so. For a moment he stared in disbelief at the billowing column of smoke that had appeared as if by magic just 10 miles to the west. He picked up the phone to clear the line. The urgent voice from the receiver didn't wait. "Glackmeyer Tower. Smoke report. Lot six, Concession three, Ottaway Township, looks like a slash fire the way it came up so suddenly."

And so it began: with a cigarette dropped on a strip road between the piles of peeled spruce pulpwood surrounded by the shredded bark as dry as tinder.

The initial crew had been dispatched with a power pump, 2,500 feet of hose, back-pumps, hand tools, and walkie-talkie radio. The aircraft, diverted from the patrol, had turned south to radio a fire report and to give details of access, proximity to water, and fuel types in relation to the head of the fire, so that the follow-up crews, in view of the lack of access roads, would be able to get to the place where they could be most effective with the minimum of bush walking.

Fanned by a 20 mile per hour wind, the fire had traveled over 3 miles within 3 hours of starting and had jumped the Buskegau River. The initial crew had traveled west along the highway, south down a transmission line as far as possible by truck, and then had progressed on foot to the logging camp near the start of the fire. The aircraft was circling overhead, and the crew, knowing that the follow-up crews would be directed to leave the highway farther east to get at the head of the fire, concentrated on saving a larger area of slash and cut wood near the pulp camp toward which the fire was backing steadily.

As the reports came in to headquarters from the aircraft, the fire was plotted on a large 4-inch to 1-mile fuel type map. It was obvious from the weather and fuel conditions that little work could be attempted at the head of the fire during the afternoon burning period. But by dawn the following morning, a bulldozer, power pumps, and fresh men were located ahead of the fire, and a line from a lake in the north to a clearing in front of the fire was being built. From the clearing, the line ran southward through second-growth aspen and patches of old slash overgrown with alder to another small lake. Part of the line was backfired, burning some 20 cords of cut wood in the process, and the fire was allowed to burn toward the rest of the line, which was controlled by power pumps. By the time conditions had reached the blowup stage on the second day, little fuel remained ahead and the line held. Meanwhile, crews were working on the long jagged flanks east from the transmission line and west from the head. Twenty days were to pass before the fire could safely be declared under control. Most of these days were spent digging out the long arms of fire that had burned deep into the dry peaty soil of the spruce stands on the flanks. The fire moved slowly underground, burning off the roots of the alder bushes and standing trees which would then fall, dry out, and burst into flame, causing the crews to rush back over the patrolled line and go to work again and again on areas which they thought they had made safe.

The Ottaway fire burned 2,800 acres and tied up many men and much equipment; men and equipment that were to be sorely needed on the bigger fires that were yet to come.

In the days that followed, practically all the District's eighteen detection towers were reporting lightning storms. The Regional Forester was receiving reports from the other two Districts within the Region, Kapuskasing District (20,000 square miles) in the west and Swastika District (5,389 square miles) to the south. The story was the same. Dry lightning. As the reports came in, storm paths were plotted on a small scale to give a total picture of the situation. The storm paths followed a similar pattern. Crossing the western boundary of the Region, the big cumulonimbus clouds with their destructive potential swung in a long curve to the south. Some, however, continued easterly crossing into Quebec and starting many fires there. Commercial aircraft servicing the Hudson Bay posts and settlements up the coasts reported large fires burning in the hinterland. Moosonee at the southern tip of James Bay was covered with a pall of smoke from fires burning in the scrub spruce and muskeg.

It seemed almost as if some evil military mind had planned this campaign of fire. The Ottaway fire was a feint at the heart of the District to immobilize the bulk of the immediately available equipment. Then the blitzkrieg with lightning strikes in vulnerable areas many miles away from roads or waterways. And all the time a "fifth column" of settlers' clearing fires burned uncontrolled throughout the settlement area, sometimes threatening the existence of the small communities. Some fires burned deep into the peaty soil demanding bulldozers, high-pressure pumps, and tankers. Others filled the air with smoke, reducing the efficiency of the tower and aircraft detection system: a series of concerted attacks which could have completely exhausted and disorganized the whole protection system.

The defense was planned on a Regional basis with the Regional Forester deciding priority of fresh equipment and aircraft to the three Districts. From the office of the Protection Chief in the Provincial capital of Toronto, word had gone to all other Districts by telephone and radio: " Mobilize all available help for the Northern Region."

Pumps, hose, tools, blankets, tents, cargo-chutes, water bombs, seasoned fire bosses and crew foremen poured in a seemingly unending stream through the headquarters at Cochrane. Seven of the Province's forty-four aircraft and two helicopters were in the Region. Three commercial planes were added to the air fleet. The far-northern fires constituted a difficult logistical problem. With the present air power, how many men could be put on the isolated fires way up in the northern bush? There had to be a margin of safety in case the situation deteriorated to the point where the men must be pulled out in a hurry. Sufficient planes must be available for that. Every extra man flown in added to the burden, being dependent on aircraft for every item of food and equipment. There seemed to be no immediate answer, unless the rest of the Province were to be denuded of aircraft. However, since the pressure showed no signs of letting up, some reserves had to be maintained.

Mobilization was quick and complete. Every available member of the staff, regardless of his normal job, was called in to implement the control organization. The Research Forester acted as commissary, and as new equipment arrived and was dispatched to the various fires, he estimated future needs and arranged for the servicing of returned equipment. Reforestation officers and game wardens worked as fire and line bosses, took their turn as loaders, checkers, mappers, and the many other jobs so necessary in big-fire organization. At headquarters, returned and serviced fire hose festooned every rack and prop that would assist drying. Extra fire fighters threaded their way to the employment office through a curtain of drying hose draped over the roof of the warehouse. Down in the basement, charcoal-grimed hose was being washed, tested, and repaired, ready to be sent to the next fire. Equipment and men from other parts of the Province were arriving by rail, road, and air. But still the crying need was for aircraft. This need was filled in a spectacular manner by the Royal Canadian Air Force. Early in July, a detachment of the Royal Canadian Air Force arrived in the Region. This detachment consisted of four De Havilland "Otter" aircraft equipped with pontoons and capable of carrying nine men besides the pilot; an S-55 Helicopter to support the District's hard-pressed Bell D-1; and the weird and wonderful twin rotored Piasecki H-21, looking like an immense flying banana.

The operation now took on a definitely military aspect. The organizational problems of forest fire control on a large scale are, in fact, similar to those of a military operation. The Department of Lands and Forests maintains a force sufficient to take care of normal fire situations. But under an emergency fire load, when one forest district may have up to a thousand men fighting at one time, the organization has to expand enormously, not in a period of months, but literally overnight.

In the conference room, a large operations blackboard was set up on which appeared the call sign of each aircraft and the name of the pilot. Details of the job were chalked opposite each call sign. Load to be carried, lake to land at, or camp at which to para-drop. This information was usually put on the board late at night or in the early morning hours after the operation conference broke up and reports on the fire situation and serviceability status of aircraft were in. The Regional Forester presided at operational conferences. Each fire was reviewed from the manpower and equipment situation, new priorities were established, and any necessary changes in plans were made. When new camps were required, instructions were passed to the equipment and manpower officers. Tactical changes in accordance with the latest weather forecasts were discussed. Finally, a nightly phone call was made to fire headquarters in Toronto, giving a rundown on each fire and requirements for the following day.

Pilots reported to the operations room in the early morning and took their instructions from the board. They then went to Lillabelle Lake—the float-plane base for headquarters—where extra docking and loading facilities had been hastily constructed. As aircraft space was at a premium, the exact weight was marked on each piece of freight. This enabled proper weight distribution of the load within the aircraft and assured that each aircraft was loaded to capacity without contravening air safety regulations. Particular attention was paid to the order in which cargo was placed in the aircraft, especially when it was to be para-dropped. A very reliable man is essential on a job of this kind. As a double check against any last minute changes, details of cargo, destination, names of men carried and time of take-off were also noted at the dock.

Parachute and cargo packers were taken along to assist in a drop whenever possible. This heightened the interest in the job and reduced packing failures. Eight-, eleven-, and sixteen-foot parachutes were used for dropping; special plywood containers were available for the pumps to be dropped. Canvas hose bags, cartons, and boxes, depending on the type of cargo, were also used as containers. The Otter aircraft with its 27-inch cargo hatch proved ideal for this method of camp supply. Approximately 200,000 pounds of food and quipment were para-dropped with relatively few failures. On one occasion, a case of eggs broke loose from the chute and fell into a small pothole lake by a fire camp. Observers in the next plane were mystified when they saw six naked Finnish lumberjacks disporting themselves in the water. The mystery was cleared up later when word got back that almost half the eggs had been recovered intact from where they had been scattered on the bottom of the lake.

Bush travel in Ontario is controlled by forest-travel permits. These permits are readily available and are issued without cost throughout the fire District. In times of extreme fire danger, and at the discretion of the Minister, permits may be canceled and certain areas closed to forest travel. This is a drastic step and one that is rarely taken, but it was found necessary within the Northern Region.

Public travel was still permitted on the highways and the larger lakes, but landings on shore away from point of entry were forbidden. For organized tourist operators and cottagers, it was business as usual, except that parties were told not to leave home waters. Thus, the risk of man-made fires was reduced.

Logging operations were allowed to continue as long as the men worked in the mornings only. During the afternoon men were standing by at the camps. As the fire load increased, work was stopped completely. Many of the woods operators, aware of the extreme danger, closed down their operations voluntarily. These operators offered their men and equipment to the Department unstintingly.

As the need for additional fire fighters arose, it was the practice to ask the logging camps to provide a given number of men, and to organize these men into crews as they reported to headquarters. Later, as known crew bosses became more scarce, the operator was asked to form the men into crews before they left camp. Thus, it was assured that the crew boss was of at least foreman caliber, and the embarrassing possibility of a wrong choice was avoided. The Region was indeed fortunate to be able to call on these lumberjacks and bush workers. Usually they brought their own axes and blankets, which cut down on equipment loss. They were all bush-hardened, and most of them, working under their own foremen, often with plenty of fire-fighting experience, formed highly efficient crews.

Every large fire seems to attract its share of free-loaders, men seeking free food and a few days' pay, but having no intention of working for it. The quicker these are weeded out, the better. But against these must be stacked the hundreds of temporary fire fighters who stuck to their jobs conscientiously and well.

Seven major fires were being fought in the District at one time. These were the ones that made the headlines. But of greater importance to the control organization were the many dangerous lightning fires which, in spite of the huge fire load, were extinguished at very small acreages. These were small routine actions where men used their common sense, their ingenuity, and experience; actions like the Laughton fire, a lightning strike picked up in the late evening by a patrolling aircraft while there was still only one tree smoldering. The bush was dense spruce and balsam fir, completely lacking topographical features that could be pin-pointed on a map. Three miles from the nearest logging camp, this fire, unless found quickly, promised to blow up and destroy not only the logging camp but the whole of the season's cut that still lay in its own slash to the west of the fire.

To reach the fire area at first light, eighteen men left the logging camp at 3:30 A.M., carrying flashlights, hand tools, smoke signals, and a walkie-talkie radio. As the sun rose, an aircraft was also trying to relocate the fire. As soon as the thin smoke plume was seen, the pilot radioed the ground crew to ignite their smoke signal so that he could find them in the dense trees. Then he flew low over the orange signal smoke directly toward the fire. These directional courses are standard procedure in such cases, and they were repeated until the ground party had obtained a new compass bearing. The eighteen men then spread out line abreast at right angles to their course and proceeded. One more smoke signal was ignited, and the course was again indicated by the pilot, together with the approximate distance the crews had to travel, which, by this time, was a few hundred feet.

Within two hours of daybreak, the fire had been extinguished at $1/8$ acre.

Then there was the lightning fire that occurred in the cutting area of a camp that several days before had been stripped of men to fight other fires. When discovered, the fire was $1/4$ acre of burning slash and peeled wood. Within an hour, three Royal Canadian Air Force Otters, carrying men and equipment, picked up from a stand-by camp, had landed in the lake adjacent to the fire. Control of the fast-moving fire was directed from the air by radio, and the fire, which could have very easily become a major one, burned only 45 acres and 800 cords of pulpwood.

At the end of the season, 106 fires had been fought within the District. Some of these were well over ten thousand acres in size. But many others that could have been just as big were extinguished at less than one acre.

Season 1955 had its headaches and its heartaches; it showed experienced fire fighters that there was still plenty to learn about fire behavior, and it turned inexperienced men into veterans.

Season 1955 exposed organization weaknesses and also unexpected strengths in many places. It turned military pilots into bush pilots and gave them greater confidence in the performance of their machines and in their own ability. It showed that some confusion is an almost inevitable by-product of sudden mass activity under stress, and it confirmed the axiom that a fire-fighting organization should be prepared for such confusion and bend every effort toward keeping it to a minimum.

The North is big. You have to look hard to find the scars of even the most spectacular fires, the scars of temporary defeat, or, at best, delayed victory. But the monument to the routine successes stretches mile after mile in the green and living trees.

Notes: This is an account of protracted emergency fire fighting in backcountry under the difficulties imposed by occurrence of a large number of lightning fires and very limited access by road. Bulldozers and other heavy equipment could be used only in buffer areas. The primary dependence was on aerial transportation, use of portable power pumps, and men with hand tools. Slow, tedious mop-up of fires due to the deep duff and organic soil of northern spruce and muskeg made it necessary to establish many fire camps and to maintain crews for long periods on each larger fire. The accumulated requirements for supplying so many back-country camps by aircraft soon exceeded provincial resources. This dilemma was relieved by the Royal Canadian Air Force which supplied both aircraft and pilots in the emergency. Decisions on priorities became crucial and were decided by conference rather than by a single individual.

Case 3
Fire Control in Michigan
By Michigan law, responsibility for prevention and control of nonurban fires is assumed by the state and is assigned to the Department of Natural Resources. Within the Department, fire prevention and control is handled by the Forest Fire Division. Close cooperative contacts are maintained with Law Enforcement, Parks, Forestry, and other Divisions of the Department as well as with the U.S. Forest Service on National Forests within the state.

The basic organizational framework in descending order of authority is as follows:

1 The Natural Resources Commission, the policymaking authority.

2 Department of Natural Resources, with a director in charge.

3 Deputy director in charge of all field operations and Forest Fire Division staff.

4 Forest Fire Division, with Chief responsible for all planning and policymaking.

5 Regions. Michigan is divided into three administrative regions with a regional manager in charge of all field operations and a regional fire supervisor in each directly responsible for fire.

6 Districts. There are 11 districts with a district supervisor in charge of each. These districts are further divided into zones, with several fire equipment stations in each zone. Initial fire dispatch is usually handled by the fire or zone officer at the station.

7 Local key men, responsible local citizens who have agreed to act on fires in their respective territories (usually within a county) and who are paid only when actually employed.

While decentralized in operation, the Michigan fire organization is completely integrated with full two-way radio communication. County fire officers can obtain help from district offices, which in turn can get support from the regional and state offices. There are no county or local barriers of any kind to the movement of men and equipment to fires; the resources of the entire statewide Department of Natural Resources can be mobilized for fire on exceedingly short notice.

Michigan: The Drain River Fire[4]

John A. Anguilm
Michigan Department of Natural Resources

The situation and setting were as follows: It was a Saturday in mid-August on the Bass Lake District in the state of Michigan. Paul Jones was the District Supervisor and fireman. The district was experiencing very high fire danger. It had reached this level six days before with high temperatures and had continued with no rain so that it was on the verge of extreme fire danger. At the same time fire risk was high with many recreationists and other users in the area. Two fires were caught at small size the previous Sunday, one in deep muck which was still burning, two more small ones were controlled on the previous Monday and Tuesday, and a fast-moving, 90-acre fire was controlled by emergency action on Wednesday but was still not entirely safe. On Friday eight more fires were controlled and one or more men were still working on each.

Besides the Bass Lake Headquarters, the District had six equipment stations or attack centers. Each station, lookout, and fire truck were equipped with two-way radio. Available equipment consisted of two bulldozers and five truck tankers besides a tractor plow unit, portable pumper, and a mounted tanker unit at each station.

Two regular fire officers were assigned to each station and a total of 15 conservation officers were attached to the district. In addition, a number of keymen (local resident cooperators) who were experienced and highly competent were available to serve as foremen or straw bosses.

Local officers besides Paul Jones were Jim Harrington, his alternate, Arne Kangas, the dispatcher, and Lyle Strom at the Sentry Equipment Station.

The Sentry area had a large area of logging slash from operations of the Hammer Lumber Company.

Description of action from this point follows:

"Sentry lookout to Sentry Station. I have a reading of 318 degrees on a smoke about 14 miles away. It's in logging slash on the Little Drain in Section 14, T.47 N.; R.16 W. I'll clear an exact description later, but by the looks of it you'll want to roll while I check."

Sentry Station: "OK, Sentry Tower, we'll push the tanker and tractor-plow

---

[4] Statement updated by Brian M. Ainsley, Forest Fire Supervisor, August 12, 1970.

unit now. Will advise Headquarters and suggest the big bulldozer. Have Super-intendent Collins of the Hammer Company send in the crew and foremen from Camp 16. We'll post direction signs at the entry road."

The three men listened while the lookout called Buck Knoll Tower and verified his location. The fire was accurately located by intersection of the readings in the NE-$\frac{1}{4}$ of SW-$\frac{1}{4}$ of Section 14. Arne called Sentry Station to advise that the big bulldozer would be sent immediately.

Paul knew the big "Cat" was loaded on the low-boy trailer outside ready to go, but he looked out to see, for the assurance that its massive bulk gave him. He walked to the garage where the operator, George Campbell, waited for the word that would put him on this snorting, crashing machine in heat and smoke for more hours than most men could take, with one purpose in mind—to create wide breaks free of forest fuel to halt the tremendous drive of fire loose in the woods. Campbell listened intently to Paul's instructions and then carefully maneuvered the big unit out onto the highway. The powerful transport motor roared as he straightened into the right lane and headed for the fire.

The planning of months and the experience of years was now to be tested. Everyone knew instinctively this could be a big one. Paul considered the experience and capabilities of the men already dispatched. He knew Lyle Strom, the Sentry zone officer, would quickly proceed to the fire. If it was caught quickly, maybe at 25 acres, he would have the experience to handle it. If not, well, it would be a job requiring the stuff that Jim had; know-how, command, and nerve, blended with care for men and machines. Also, he and Jim had long experience in working closely together. The next 15 minutes would tell if control might be at minus 100 or minus 500 acres. And 2 hours would tell if it would be worse.

Paul called Manisto Station and asked that the station tractor-tanker-plow unit proceed to Sentry Station, and Arne radioed Sentry Station concerning this movement. If Sentry needed a second tractor, the Manisto unit would be at their command. Dispatching for the fire would stay at the Sentry Station level until their resources were committed. Then District Headquarters would assume dispatch.

The flow of radio traffic was smooth. District radios not closely involved avoided all but essential transmission. Sentry lookout advised Sentry Station that Collins and his 25-man crew from Hammer Company would arrive at the fire at about 3:00 P.M.

The Sentry tractor-plow unit was to attempt to cut the head and east flank of the fire (Figure 16.3). The tanker was to attempt control on the west flank. Paul knew the tanker crew would make a stand along one of the logging roads running south from the main road which traversed the tract east and west.

He consulted the District slash map for the year of the cut; it was four years previous. The logging road map showed three southerly roads in Section 14. The fire probably had started along one of these. The roads were not currently being used and probably were blocked by down timber.

Lyle Strom, the Sentry zone officer, called District direct from his car as he approached the fire: "It's likely to be an extra period fire; smoke is rolling and it's heavy. Appears to have a fast start. We'll need power saws. Hammer Company can supply five from Camp 15. Will you call them?"

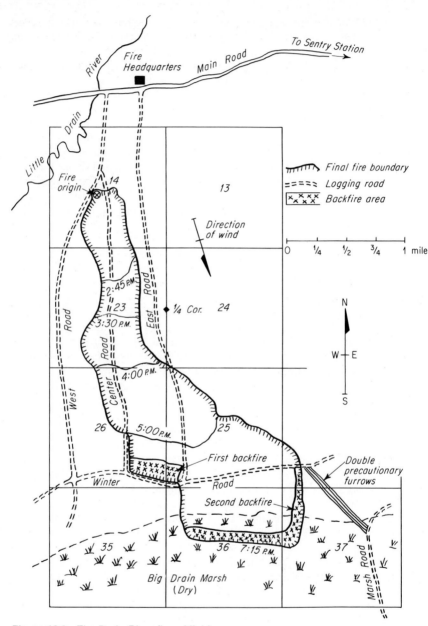

Figure 16.3   The Drain River fire—Michigan.

Arne called the Hammer Company office. It would take 'til 5:00 P.M. to get the sawyers from their cutting strips and on the fire. They would be given food en route. Hammer Company advised that their low-boy bulldozer trailer was 100 miles away at Stenson, bringing in a new shovel. If their bulldozers were needed, could District arrange transportation?

Arne radioed: "Unit 4-16 (Campbell), make low-boy trailer unit available to zone officer for use in bringing Hammer bulldozers if needed."

"Will do," was Campbell's immediate reply.

Strom advised the Manisto operator to proceed direct to the fire. The delay in the arrival of the Hammer bulldozers could be the big difference on this fire. At best, Campbell couldn't arrive at the fire before 3:15, and it would be near 5:00 before the first Hammer bulldozer could be in action. Dispatch of Keyman Jim Gerou's bulldozer from Bass Lake Headquarters would get a second machine in by 4:30. Paul called Gerou, who lived only 2 miles north of the station, and found him ready to go.

"I've been kind of expecting something today, Paul," Jim said. "The air just smelled like a fire day. I'll take a partner along, and between the two of us we can keep going quite a while."

Paul reported dispatch of Gerou on the radio, heard Lyle Strom acknowledge, and later sign out of radio service as he reached the fire.

Paul walked to his desk and pulled out a pad of paper. This was likely going to be a full-sized job and beyond Strom's experience. He listed the organization needed to carry on through the night if early efforts proved inadequate. First, he needed a fire boss to head up all the elements of procurement, supply, service, records, and action. This job was familiar to Jim Harrington, who had handled it all in the past. Paul was sure his organization support would permit Jim to stay at the fire location to direct activities. He listed as follows the men who would directly perform key functions for the next 12 hours if necessary.

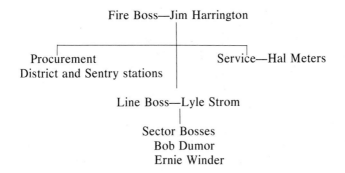

If the situation required more, each man knew the subordinate positions required fully to perform each function and would appoint assistants. Timekeepers, records officers, cooks, guides, messengers, equipment operators—all these might be required in expanding numbers if the fire was not controlled quickly.

2:35 P.M. Sentry lookout was relaying word in from the tanker unit. The fire was astraddle the center of the three south roads (Figure 16.3). They were able to control the fire on the north, but questioned the effectiveness of water on the flanks. The side movement was not rapid, but the fuel was heavy and it was difficult to extinguish the burning edge. They were using their winch to remove down trees across the west logging road.

The Sentry tractor-plow unit had begun work on the east flank after being unable to make a stand on the southeast, or head of the fire. It was tying its line into the rear section stopped by the tanker and was proceeding southeasterly.

Arne started a map as these reports came in and began to project the fire about as it appeared to be running. The fuel-type map showed the slashing to extend a bit more than $2^{1}/_{4}$ miles south before it was divided by a narrow belt of aspen and scattered jack pine from the currently dry and flammable Big Drain River Marsh and muck lands.

Paul and Jim discussed the merits of putting in a night crew and considered it necessary if the blaze continued to move in early evening. The wind might drop around 5:00 P.M. Paul would handle this phase from Headquarters, if necessary.

Jim checked the outline Paul had filled in on the scratch pad. Said Paul, "We'll set up a relief organization to take over line work at 6:00 A.M., Jim, if the fire is still loose then. Hal Meters can set up his transport plans, appoint a timekeeper, and secure such camp facilities as you think you'll need tonight and still catch a little sleep. We'll expect him to function tomorrow and need his close knowledge of labor and equipment dispatched today. I'll tell Strom you're taking over and notify the rest of your crew. She's yours."

As Jim's car turned from the driveway his rear wheels sprayed gravel and Paul knew he would waste no time in getting to the fire. By telephone and radio, Arne informed Meters, Dumor, and Winder of their assignments.

2:45 P.M. Sentry reported Campbell had passed with the big Cat.

Strom reported the rate of line construction on the east flank with the tractor-plow unit was slow because of slash. The Hammer crew had arrived and was working with the tractor-plow unit in holding line as it was constructed. Three men formed a work crew with the tanker. The fire was estimated to cover 45 acres with its head into Section 23. Rate of spread at head about 50 chains per hour. Strom was told that Jim Harrington was taking charge. Relieved of contact work, Strom could now do a better job of reporting fireline progress using radio.

The Sauk plane had reported Dodgeville fire as confined to present lines. Paul fought off a certain reluctance to commit District strength heavily in one place and requested Aubin Station to start the smaller low-boy trailer and bulldozer to Sentry, Mack Aine, operator. If other fires started and needed this equipment, radio contact would be kept for the next hour while it traveled the 45 miles to Sentry.

Arne's dispatch sheet was filling fast as he received information from Strom, the Sentry lookout, and Paul on the moves which were being made to converge men and machines on the junction of the east logging road with the main road (Figure 16.3) where Strom had set up fire headquarters. The Hammer Company's woods foreman had taken over line locating for Sentry tractor-plow unit, and a straw boss was keeping the line crew busy holding the constructed line. Paul and Arne heard an interchange of talk with the truck carrying the Manisto tanker-plow unit. Strom asked the operator to stop at Sentry Station and pick up lights and extra batteries. Fifty local laborers from Sentry Station were being sent in.

Passage Station reported another blaze. A mill crew was sent, as well as a plow unit. Manisto Station put out a small grass fire along the highway. Blueberry pickers set that one.

3:05 P.M. Harrington had seen Meters' car at Sentry Station as he passed. He intended to have Meters keep the low-boy hauler going all night if necessary to bring in more bulldozers. He heard Arne advise of the dispatch of Mack Aine with a bulldozer from Aubin.

Gerou and Aine would team up well for the west side. Campbell, he guessed, was already charging down the east side getting ahead of about as much fire edge as he figured the Sentry tractor-plow unit could safely build. Jim could see in his mind how Campbell would flare out his starting line to catch the side spread of the uncontrolled fire behind him until the tractor behind him could close the line at his starting point. Experience like Campbell's was important. He had been pushing the big Cats since the first of them were equipped with blades.

Strom's car was parked along the main road with its motor running to keep the battery up for the heavy drain occasioned by the use of the transmitter. The location was within sight of the fire. Jim Harrington pulled up, and as Strom explained the deployment, sector bosses Ernie Winder and Bob Dumor arrived. Harrington then proceeded to lay out work plans for the next few hours. He assigned Winder to the east sector and Dumor to the west sector. It was decided to request two more mobile water units.

Jim Harrington proposed to check the east side on foot with Winder and Strom, taking a portable radio along. Contact was established with Sentry Station and the two tankers requested from Bass Lake. Dumor was to await the arrival of the Gerou and Aine bulldozers at the Fire Headquarters. The first Hammer bulldozer was to unload on the west line and proceed to clear the west road of down trees. The fire hadn't crossed this road, and it was proposed to run the machines to the south edge of the slash area and attempt to cut the head after 5:00 P.M.

The fuel was heavy along the east line where the tractor-plow had made a narrow opening. The skidding trails, where the logging tractors had dragged the logs to the truck roads, were at right angles to the direction of the line, and this was a factor against speed. The tractor line extended about 1,600 feet, and Jim paused only briefly to see the activity about the plow unit as men with axes and saws were hacking and sawing into the heavy slash. He followed the track of Campbell's bulldozer as it had snaked around, picking the easiest places to go forward; not far ahead he heard the staccato beat of the motor. Campbell was just beginning to approach the fire edge, having completed a flare-out section to protect his rear. Jim waved in passing and proceeded on ahead. The Hammer Company cruiser was temporarily locating trail for Campbell. Harrington took a worn plat book from his pocket and with a stubby pencil pointed out the winter road (Figure 16.3) running along the south edge of the slash area and across the face of the fire. The present rate of spread would bring the fire to the aspen belt near the marsh before 6:00 P.M. The question Jim asked himself and expressed was, "What about tomorrow's wind? If it shifts more to the west, this east flank line will suddenly become 2¹/₄ miles of head. Even if we stop the fire at the aspen, we've still need to put this east line in before 10:00 A.M. tomorrow."

Strom had been on the winter road earlier in the season and expressed his opinion. "Jim, I believe we ought to keep Campbell on the east flank and have Gerou's bulldozer help him. Aine's and the Hammer bulldozers can run free down the west logging road to the junction with the winter road and a crew of 25 men under Dumor, and I will start backfiring from the road. If we can catch the spot fires, we'll stop the head. I don't believe we can get around it short of 500 acres anyhow, and this way will figure about 700 acres with less risk of the fire reaching the marsh. What do you think, Ernie?"

"Yes," Winder replied, "Gerou's bulldozer should work with Campbell, and we ought to be able to corral this east side tonight. If the fire does jump your backfire, we should be able to stop it in the marsh tonight with the truck tankers and booster units on trailers."

Jim answered, "OK, it sounds good. We'll backfire from the winter road." He then radioed to Dumor at Fire Headquarters to send Gerou's machine in with Campbell on the east line. Aine's and the Hammer bulldozers were directed to clear the west road south and get to the junction with the winter road as soon as possible.

Said Jim, "Lyle, you and Winder go back and pick up Dumor. I'll keep on around and meet you on the west side. If Meters is at the fire camp, ask him to have at least 25 sleeping bags available. We'll keep some of the local men here tonight."

Jim continued south on the east road, passing the front of the fire. Smoke was heavy, and he estimated the wind velocity, increased by the fire draft, was in excess of 25 miles per hour. Spot fires were starting 40 rods (1 rod = 16.5 feet) ahead of the fire perimeter. As Jim passed the fire head he found a marker indicating the center of Section 23. He made some calculations. The time was 3:30 P.M. The fire had covered about one mile in an hour and 25 minutes from a single flame at the starting point. It was a fair presumption that this speed would double. No more than an hour could be allowed to establish a line and backfire along the winter road and organize the crews to catch sparks in the marsh beyond. He hurried west to pick up the west logging road down which they planned to bring the equipment to the marsh area.

Forty-five minutes of fast walking had been used in making the reconnaissance. Strom met Harrington on the west road and reported the Sentry fire fighters were at the Fire Headquarters. The tanker from Bass Lake had just arrived. The second tanker was en route from Sauk Station and would arrive about 5:00 P.M. The Manisto tractor-tanker-plow unit operated by George Olds was coming down the west side. As Harrington drove back toward Fire Head-quarters, he passed the Sentry tanker unit, which was holding the fire as it backed toward the west logging road. About ¹/₄ mile of road edge was burned out and held.

Harrington called the District office and gave them the information as to fire size and plans. The plane was over the fire, and radio traffic was stilled while the pilot gave Jim his impression of the fire. The pilot advised he would refuel and then continue in flight over the area until dark.

The Bass Lake tanker and the Sentry laborers were assigned to Fire Officer Dumor and directed to the winter logging road which they were to begin clearing of down trees and brushing out. Strom, who would be in charge of backfiring, awaited the arrival of Aine and the Hammer bulldozers to lead them to the winter road.

At Bass Lake Headquarters, Paul listened to Harrington's report and the report of the pilot. He could get little comfort from the close planning which was involved in the proposed stand on the winter road. He weighed the possibilities of the units on the east side turning the head. As a guide, he figured the Sentry tractor-plow with its crew of men could do $1/4$ mile in one hour. Campbell's bulldozer would do about $3/8$ mile in the same time. It was obvious that they alone could not gain on the fire spread.

To prepare for worse trouble, calls were made to local cooperators within 50 miles of the fire, and arrangements made to place three additional tractor-plow units on the fire by nightfall. Three additional bulldozers were to report at 6:00 A.M. Relief crews of laborers were enlisted by calls to Keymen in the 50-mile area surrounding Sentry. Fifty men were to report at 6:00 P.M. More were engaged for 6:00 A.M. Sunday.

The location of Fire Officer George Olds and the Manisto tractor-tanker-plow unit on the west line along with the Sentry tanker was sufficient insurance that the fire would be held east of the west logging road down which men and equipment were to reach the fire head. Olds was to follow the fire edge as it quartered away from this road and to make burned-out line secure. The usefulness of the tractor equipped with tanks and pumps as well as a heavy plow was demonstrated in this operation. Concentrations of slash frequently needed to be cooled down with the high-pressure spray before Olds could work close enough to the fire edge to build safe line. When sparks started fires across his plowed furrow he turned and either drowned out the burn or put a new furrow around it.

4:00 P.M. A report from the Hammer Company cruiser who was locating line for Campbell's big bulldozer placed the fire on the south line of Section 23 approximately $1^1/2$ miles south of its starting point. It was still narrow and estimated to be 220 acres. A deep gully had slowed the fire progress only briefly.

Aine with the Aubin bulldozer had arrived and was being taken to the winter road. Dumor had cleared this road east nearly to the junction with the east road and pushed his crew steadily forward. As the fire was still a mile away, he hadn't set up a patrol.

Strom took over action on this sector as preparations were made to backfire along the winter road. Indications were the fire head would be near the east side of Section 26, and therefore the backfire was started at the junction with the east road and continued west to the junction with the center road. The possibility of it crossing the east road was accepted as a risk not important if the head could be held.

No lessening of the wind was apparent as the first fires were set. The tanker kept the fires from excessive flare-up near the road. The fury of the fire after it had spread out to areas of 20 feet diameter from ignition points indicated early the need for close patrol south of the road. Men with back-pack pumps and shovels were kept busy catching spot fires which sprang up as whirls of sparks were thrown across the line from large brush piles. The flames backed slowly to the north away from the road, and as soon as another stretch of line could be fired safely, Strom would set more fires. These quickly joined and another 20 to 25 rods of area would require close attention. The tanker was drowning out the larger spot fires south of the road while Aine's bulldozer turned soil around these and others the tanker could not reach. It was "touch and go" on occasions, but time was short, and if success was to be had the backfire must be completed across the front of the oncoming fire. Heat was intense from the heavy fuel, and the tanker crew was aware they could not waste much water cooling the backfire. Bob Dumor was keeping a moving patrol south of the road as far as 1/4 mile. His crew were kept so busy in the poplar and jackpine cover near the marsh, it was apparent a similar stand in the hardwood-hemlock slash, where fuel was much heavier, would have been futile.

Jim Harrington had been busy. The Hammer bulldozer had arrived, was unloaded and moving into position on the winter road at 4:30 P.M. Strom started it north up the east logging road to hold the backfire from easterly spread. The Gerou bulldozer was moving into position to help Campbell. Together they would remove the woody material while the tractor-plow unit turned the soil, thus increasing total rate of line production. The Sauk tanker was to increase the holding strength of this line, which, as it increased in length, was becoming more difficult to hold with hand tools only.

The plane was circling the fire, and aerial reports were giving Jim an up-to-the-minute picture of the fire. Correlated with the reports from Ernie Winder, Sector boss on the east side, the pilot's observations were providing needed information, on which plans and expectations were based.

The Forester of the District arrived shortly before 5:00 P.M. and was available for scouting and mapping. The backfire was being held along the winter road from the center to the east logging road. The point of greatest concern was the uncontrolled perimeter of fire moving toward the east logging road. The Manisto tractor-tanker-plow unit was pinching off fire perimeter along the west side at a satisfactory rate. Harrington dispatched the District Forester down the east line with orders to go through and meet Strom, who was to start north from the winter road, and advise of conditions.

Sentry Tower to Bass Lake Headquarters (Jones): "White smoke north of the center of Section 23 indicates control to this point. Heavy smoke south. Local crews prepared to go in at 6:00 P.M. for relief."

Things looked pretty good, and then came a break.

Fire Headquarters (Harrington) to Sentry Tower for relay to Bass Lake District Headquarters: "We're getting a 40° change in wind direction to the west, can cause trouble, will advise."

Paul Jones saw the risk of a sudden wind change to the west. The southeast section of the fire where no forces were yet applied could blow out, and by crossing the east logging road could create a head of free-running fire to the east of the backfire.

Airplane pilot to Fire Headquarters: "It's difficult to see the head, but I believe the fire is across the east road now, about $3/4$ mile north of the winter road."

Fire Headquarters to Strom: "Have Hammer unit go around the fire to tie into the east road on the north of the breakdown and work south. Have the Forester return to Campbell and tell him to run free to the breakthrough and work with Hammer unit. Attempt to hold the section across the road. A messenger will start from here with the same orders. We'll bring the Sentry tanker down the east road as soon as possible to support bulldozers."

The Sentry tanker crew had been maintaining patrol with little activity. The east line along the fire was not yet built through to the breakover across the east road, and it was unlikely the east road would be open. There was a sizable gap to plug, and the entire uncontrolled east perimeter was now dangerous. Clearing 2 miles of road to move equipment over it would be time-consuming.

Jim Harrington was meeting this problem. The power-saw crews had arrived in three pickup trucks and were being held at Fire Headquarters. Two were dispatched south on the east road to cut out wind-fallen trees. They were to go on through as rapidly as possible and join up with Campbell and the Hammer machines. If they could hand-spike the fallen trees they could drive through. If not, they were to proceed on foot. Meters would take them in.

Fire Headquarters (Jim Harrington) to Bass Lake Headquarters (Jones): "Action taken on the southeast break, expect head will reach marsh. Equipment and manpower plan for marsh area will be needed. Will District prepare?"

Jim reviewed his deployment. The Manisto tractor-plow-tanker unit, alone on the west flank, would progress more steadily with the wind change. This line was safe for a while. The Gerou bulldozer was halfway down the east line with the Sentry tractor-plow unit. Some progress would be made, but danger of breakover was increased with the wind shift and the uncontrolled perimeter south would move east all too fast. The Sauk tanker had a big holding job on the constructed line. Campbell and the Hammer bulldozer were assigned to the breakthrough and would try to circle the break and hold line built. A tanker was badly needed there, too. Hand labor, also, would be desirable as soon as Sentry crews came in at 6:00 P.M. Jim sent a scout out to intercept these crews and sent them south on the east road. The third saw crew was dispatched to Dumor, with orders to knock down stubs back 20 rods from the winter road east of the backfire.

Aine's bulldozer and the Bass Lake tanker were still having difficulty holding the backfire, which was now a separate problem. The main fire had sidestepped the backfired area and would now hit the winter road to the east.

Jim thought how often the glamorous backfire didn't work or itself backfired on fire officers. Time did not permit another attempt to backfire the winter road east of the backfire. He conceded a sizable acreage in the marsh. The action there now was largely up to Paul and the district organization. Jim strove to hold the east line particularly. The marsh was rapid-burn area, but it could be plowed and four-wheel drive equipment could be used there during the night, as it might be freed from patrol duty.

The west line was now relatively safe because of the wind change, and, by messenger, Jim ordered the Manisto unit to tie into the southeast corner of the backfire (junction of east and winter roads), plow south half a mile, east a mile, and then north to the winter road.

On receipt of Jim Harrington's last message, Paul Jones took over dispatch of forces needed in the marsh area ahead of the fire. He arranged for delivery, to Sentry, of three district-owned rubber-tired plows and three privately owned tractors from mills near Sentry. The ability quickly to supplement his equipment strength was due to written arrangements with the tractor owners and to the location of four sulky-type plows at Bass Lake. After several contacts with cooperators, he advised Arne of his plans and proceeded to the fire to direct action in the marsh in person.

Since the fire blocked the east road, access from the north was impractical. However, Paul knew of a marsh road, used by berrypickers, by which he could approach from the south and bring equipment within a mile of the winter road. His radio would keep him in touch with the whole district until he left the car, and he concluded that the lateness of the hour made a greater danger unlikely that day.

It was now 6:10 P.M., and the role of smoke as he approached the fire didn't lessen his anxiety. This fire was burning hard. The assembly of equipment at the Sentry Station was as promised. Paul gave word for its dispatch to the fire. He decided to begin burning out a strip in the marsh as soon as lines could be put in. He started two new plow units putting in a precautionary double line from the marsh road northwestly to the winter road where the Manisto unit had just tied into it after making a big rectangle of plowed line. He directed the Manisto unit to double the east line it had just made and ordered one plow unit to continue building line in the northwest. He sent the third new plow south along this east line into the marsh to plow a furrow west about 20 rods (330 feet) north of the east-west line south in the marsh the Manisto unit had just built. Keymen, with hand crews, were immediately put to firing along the east line and to burning out the south strip. Scurrying under the urgency of the moment, they lit the marsh grass, and amid blinding smoke, shovel men and pump men knocked down the flame, which reached out to ignite grasses across the furrow. Repeatedly, as the backfire increased in size, the Manisto tanker-plow unit on the east side turned back, to catch breakovers with water, and as the burnout backed away from the line, flames leaped 20 feet into the air.

The head of the main fire ran into the backfire, and as the two lines of fire met, eddying winds fanned great swirls of flame—but gradually the fire died out. The lines held, and the marsh fire was caught!

The breakthrough on the east wasn't yet circled, and the fire continued to burn hard on this side. The possibility of the fire flanking to the east was still present, but the bulldozers could be heard coming. They soon broke from the logging slash area into the poplar and jackpine fringe of the marsh and tied in to the plowed and burned line going south from the winter road. Standing on the road where the lines joined up, Paul grinned at Jim's calculation. He hadn't allowed a bit more ground to burn than necessary—he had probably figured it a bit too closely to be safe for sure.

Fire controlled at 7:15 P.M.—a fortunate time of day, Paul thought, as he considered the added difficulties which would have been encountered if the fire had hit the marsh at noon—or at any time before 4:00 P.M.

The night crew still had much to do, but lights on all vehicles would make it possible to line the fire completely by morning. Tomorrow the pressure would be put on to make safe a 100-foot strip around the entire perimeter. Shovel men, tankers, and men with back pumps would "mop up" aggressively from daylight on. Vigilant patrol would be maintained while crews put out every spark and cut all dangerous snags.

Paul Jones had respect for this fire. It was close to a blowup, and he had given it a lot of his district's strength. Close teamwork had paid off. Also, seven other fires had been successfully fought that day, and he hadn't required out-of-district help. Maybe he had taken a chance, but it is hard to justify leaving more than a bare minimum of experienced men and available equipment uncommitted if a going fire needs it, as this one surely did.

Notes: In reviewing the action on the Drain River Fire, several factors should be noted. First, there was good road access, and there was plenty of heavy equipment to build fire line. A strong, well-planned organization is pictured with seasoned officers in action. Note particularly the close calculation of the fire's spread and the manner of employment of backfiring techniques. Note, too, that the fire boss knows the capabilities of each officer intimately and uses a line boss to advantage in this instance. To follow each move more closely, a sketch map copy of Figure 16.3 may be used to advantage.

Case 4

Lassen National Forest

The Lassen National Forest is one of the 16 National Forests in California which make up the California Region of the Forest Service. It is in northern California, occupying wild-land areas of both sides of the north end of the Sierra Nevada Mountains. Prevailing fuels are those typical of ponderosa pine type and brush. Summers are longer and drier than area in Case 1 and fires spread faster but are more quickly mopped up. Each National Forest Region within the United States differs somewhat from its neighbors in its fire organization. Distinctive differences from Case 1 in dispatching and in use of aircraft are apparent in this account of the Cabin fire on the Lassen National Forest.

War on Forest Fires[5]

Merle S. Lowden, Director
Division of Fire Control, U.S. Forest Service

A small wisp of smoke slowly drifted up over Butte Creek Rim. Jo saw it first. Was it a fire? As dependable Forest Service lookouts, Jo and Jim Worthey must be sure before they reported it to the fire dispatcher. Once reported as a "fire," this smoke would become the focal point of the firefighting efforts of the more than 250 employees of the Lassen National Forest. And if it should grow bigger, there was always the backup help from hundreds more U.S. Forest Service firefighters in California as well as other States.

This time both Jo and Jim were sure. They immediately directed their firefinder on the smoke and started to fill out their report—degrees of azimuth, distance, type of topography, size of fire, and the type of smoke. Then they transmitted it to the dispatcher at the headquarters for the ranger district. Little did Jo and Jim realize when they started this report the many exciting events and grim tragedy that would take place the next few days, almost at their doorstep, in the mountains of northern California.

Before the Cabin fire was stopped, some 4,000 acres of beautiful pine forests would be burned and leave a graveyard of trees for many years to come.

Their actions started a "battle" that engaged more than 600 men, 16 tractors, 3 helicopters, and 9 airplanes. Before it was stopped, this fire cost $200,000 to put out and destroyed a million dollars worth of timber, recreation, watershed, and other resources. Although a detailed investigation was made, the Forest Service still is not sure who caused all this trouble, except that someone was careless with just a small "warming" fire.

This was but one of the 100,000 forest fires which are started by man's carelessness in the forests of the United States each year. However, there were double this number before the Smokey Bear program was launched 25 years ago by the Forest Service, the State forestry departments, and the Advertising Council. Every year the Forest Service spends nearly $50 million preparing for these fires and in fighting them.

To meet the threat of forest fires, it has become necessary to organize, train, and to have ready the largest fire department in the world. It can call up thousands of men who have had fire "battle" training at some time in their career.

There are available 400 smokejumpers, 800 ground tankers, 200 helicopters, 100 air tankers, and other airplanes forming an armada of more than 1,200 aircraft.

I first heard of the Cabin fire at Reno where we were completing a fire-training movie. It wasn't long before I was on my way to the scene of action. I don't "chase" fires, but I do like to know what goes on. By checking the firefighting, I get an excellent indication whether the months of training and preparation have accomplished their purpose.

---

[5] Taken from "Outdoors U.S.A." *Yearbook of Agriculture,* 1967, U.S. Department of Agriculture, pp 82–87.

It was only 9:16 A.M. on a Saturday morning when the Wortheys made their discovery. They had been up since 6 o'clock scanning their territory closely. Jo and Jim were two of the more than 2,000 lookouts that serve as sentinels to report any smoke they see on the 154 national forests in the United States. It had been a quiet year, and they were beginning to think they were to get by without any bad fires on the Lassen. Don Renton, the district ranger, Earl Nichols, the forest fire staffman, and Irv Bosworth, the forest supervisor, had all been thinking—and hoping—the same thing. Our record had been good all over the West, and the Forest Service fire leaders were hoping that their luck would hold.

Smoke Increases

The smoke began to increase even as Jim gave his report to the dispatcher at the ranger station. There was increasing tempo and excitement in his voice as he reported: Bearing, 153°20′; distance, 7 miles, area, flat; type, pine; size, about three campfires, and the smoke going straight up, light blue in color.

The Lassen uses a system of automatic dispatch which means that all fire forces within a given area converge on a fire as soon as it is reported. In less than five minutes, three "ground" tankers were speeding for the fire. Within 45 minutes, four men with pulaski tools and shovels were trying to put a fireline around the fire which had increased to one-fourth acre. The "pulaski"men were cutting brush and tree limbs with the ax side of their tools and digging a trench with the hoe side.

For a while it was a race between time and fire with the men feverishly building a fireline. They threw dirt on the flames where the fingers seemed to reach out. Then they tried desperately to clear the grass and needles to dig a trench. It was soon apparent it was going to be a nip-and-tuck affair if they "got" the fire. About 10 A.M., a "strong, erratic" wind came up and that decided the issue. Ed Cunningham, district fire control officer (and the fire boss at that time), saw several of the fellows "lose" their portions of the line. The fire spread across their trench in spite of all they could do.

By 10:30 Ed knew they needed more help so he radioed for more ground tankers and crews. It was clear to the men back at headquarters that there was much trouble ahead. It was time to call for air support and heavy equipment. Air tankers were ordered from the zone dispatcher in Redding, and tractors were requested from the local loggers.

Within a half hour the wind reached about 25 miles per hour, and the fire was spreading rapidly to the northeast. It was certain that the firefighters had a "project" fire on their hands. Preparations were proceeding rapidly back at forest headquarters in Susanville and at the Redding zone office to get the men and machinery to "handle" it. This meant getting firefighting overhead from other parts of the Lassen Forest and from other national forests. Word was spreading all through the region that a big fire was in the making on the Lassen.

The lead plane pilot, Ernie Gentry, was over the fire by 11:30 A.M. It was Ernie's job to direct the air tankers following him where to drop their loads of water and chemical mix. They must go just where the fire boss wants them. By now Earl Nichols had taken over as fire boss and was in a helicopter above the fire. He was directing the action on all fronts. The first job assigned the air tankers was to cut off the head of the blaze at the northeast corner and hopefully to keep it from getting as far as the Butte Creek Rim.

Once the fire had "hit" the rim, it was pretty sure to go over the top and to spread on across the plateau. That would mean practically having two fires—one above and one below the rim. Three drops were made upon the head, and momentarily it looked as if they might stop it sufficiently for the ground forces to rush in and hold it. This hope was short lived because two large "spot" fires showed up ahead of the cutoff point. Burning embers had blown ahead and were starting more fires. More air tankers were not immediately available, so the planned stand had to be given up.

Shifts Strategy

By noon the fire was burning hard on all fronts. The pickup in wind made the fire spread much faster. Fire Boss Nichols had to change his strategy. As he saw it, there was no use to hit the "head" of the fire directly. He decided to concentrate on the flanks and try to squeeze the head. The next few airdrops were helpful, but the fire outflanked the men. It was now a case of dropping back, redirecting the crews, and being sure to hold each flank.

It wasn't an easy thing to rustle up crews on this Saturday afternoon in the middle of the hunting season. Loggers were caught working in their gardens, painting their garages, doing the family shopping and dozens of other weekend chores. A number out hunting were not aware of the fire until they came home at night. Many crews came from State conservation camps. These are prison inmates placed in the camps to rehabilitate themselves and forest areas.

Camp for 500

Loggers had to find truckdrivers to haul in tractors. Drivers had to be found for these "dozers" and taken to the fire.

All this required time, and time was precious. Carefully arranged plans made months in advance paid off.

A camp must be set up and back-of-the-line forces made ready to support the men on the fireline. Perishables were added to the food caches, assembled tools were placed onto trucks and dispatched to the fire. A camp was set up at an old cabin in a clearing on the west side of the fire. This was out of the timber where the camp could be protected from the fire if it got away on that side. The camp boss got preparations underway to feed and sleep 500 men. He must be ready before the crews came in from the line at dark. Even the timekeepers were on their way to camp to start setting up time slips and checking men in and out. Many men were doing dozens of jobs in many locations to support firefighters both on the ground and in the air.

Back at the fire things weren't going so well. On the north and east sides it was burning hot, and smoke was blowing low. The west side was easiest to get to, and some progress was being made there. However, the fire had crossed the main road and spotted to the top of the rim, three-fourths of a mile ahead.

Airdrops were successful on the west side in the sagebrush flats, and this tended to "push" in that side.

However, once the fire was on top of the rim it spread very rapidly and soon burned across a powerline. This cut off the power in Susanville and much of the surrounding country at 3:39 P.M. Now local people who hadn't heard about the fire knew something was wrong. The important Black Mountain Experimental Forest was less than a mile to the northeast and real fear arose that the fire would get into it. This could mean loss of valuable study plots. A fire could destroy research findings in the making for years. Fire must be kept out of this experimental forest at all costs.

Air Tanker Aid

From 3 until 7 P.M., it was a hectic struggle on the northeast side. It would seem the crews were going to hold their line. Then a gust of wind would come and drive them back. Air tankers were making drops to knock down hotspots and help the ground crews. Bulldozers were busy widening lines, and crews were firing material inside the line to get the ground cover "burned out"—before a "run" got started farther inside. Everyone gave it all they had in this struggle. By night it seemed the crews might win.

The plans chief was making plans to complete the line and to stengthen it during the night. Crews and machines must be made ready for the wind that could be expected the next day. Orders went out to get a line as close to the fire as possible, around the perimeter, making sure all material was "burned out" inside the line. This would require more railroad flares and firing torches to do the burning during the night.

Some new crews came in about dark. They were fresh, and after a good meal were ready for the night shift. Other crews had to continue through the night despite the fact they had started work during the afternoon. It was not possible to man all the line and do the other jobs that must be done that night with fresh men. This sometimes happens on the first day on fires when men have to work extra long hours until enough help arrives. By 2 A.M., the 15-mile perimeter had been circled with a fireline and the fire was at least "contained."

Shortly after daybreak I made a helicopter reconnaissance with Nichols, to see how the "battle" had gone during the night. Reports from men coming off the line were good.

As we flew above the treetops, we inspected conditions on the ground through intermittent smoke. Wherever we could see there was a good "line" and men were hard at work.

They had a "black"line and had done a good job in using fire to fight fire.

This was most encouraging. The night crews had done the gigantic job assigned to them. How well it was done would be proven by whether or not the fire held through the day. Men were astir all along the line. Things must be well set to meet the predicted high wind at noon.

By 8 A.M. Sunday morning there were more than 600 men on the fire, 16 bulldozers, and 20 ground tankers. A temporary lookout was posted on a hill to the north to watch for sleeper spots from any brands that might have been blown ahead on Saturday and were yet to flare up. In fact, several fast-spreading spots were found on Saturday and some on Sunday. Crews were assigned especially to this spot fire search job. Smoke blowing close to the ground made the job a particularly difficult one.

It was a tough, hard job all day for the crews strung out along the line. Roads were built to get tankers and their precious water close for the mopup work. One flareup occurred on the east side. Three air tanker drops held it in check. A new 250-man camp was established near the northernmost point of the fire. The Weather Bureau meteorologist had set up his portable office-camper at the experimental forest and gave hourly reports over the air on local wind direction and speed, temperature, and humidity.

He studied the general area forecast carefully and gave Nichols detailed information on what wind, humidity, and temperature conditions we could expect around the fire for the balance of the day and for the following day.

The strongest effort Sunday was put on the east side since the forecast was for another west wind. On the third day when the wind shifted and came from the east, firefighters were shifted and concentrated on the west side.

The mop-up work continued for several days. Crews were gradually reduced as the work became more routine and hours of work became shorter. It was the time then for me to move on and perhaps get in on another fire battle someplace else. The only live fire was now far inside the perimeter. Because of the heavy timber in the fire area, there was often deep fire in trees or logs. It was not until October 10 that the mop-up was completed. Even then, occasional patrols continued for a whole month longer.

When the fire was all over it was hard to believe that one man failing to put out his "little" warming fire could be the cause of all this trouble. Blood, sweat, and grief put out by 600 men had done the job, but it all seemed such a waste. The 4,000 acres of beautiful pine forest wouldn't be replaced for a hundred years. Part of nature's wonderland and its beauty was gone. Must man always be so careless?

Notes: The 1967 account of the campaign to control the 1966 Cabin fire on the Lassen National Forest helps to update practices of the U.S. Forest Service and illustrates some problems peculiar to this fire as well. Efforts to control the fire at smaller size were evidently carefully drawn and executed and nearly succeeded at several stages. For that reason, no doubt, the fire has served as a case study in programs to improve practices and to train fire bosses. Nevertheless, the history of most blowup fires follows a familiar pattern. Though early efforts to control the fire were too little and too late to keep it small, it may not have been possible to stop it in any case since there are many situations where the best available fire-fighting methods are inadequate to check the head of the fire. This may have been true during most of the run of the Cabin fire.

Some of the features to note in this account are use of a married couple on the lookout, a degree of automatic or preplanned dispatching, backup by a "zone" dispatcher drawing from neighboring National Forests, dependence on air tankers and air drops to slow down the head of the fire, mobile forecasting service to enable better predicition of local winds, scouting by helicopter by the fire boss, attack on the flanks of the fire during the main run, and early assumption of the fire boss duties by the best qualified man available.

Part Three

Fire in Wild-land Management

Parts One and Two present the behavior and effects of forest fire as a phenomenon and the methods for bringing wildfire under control. Part Three utilizes this knowledge in two basic areas. One is use of fire under control in wild-land environments. This has proved to be a valuable tool in wild-land management. The second area concerns the difficult but essential problems of seeking economic balance in wildfire control. The relative cost and effort that should be devoted to forest fire control in competition with other public needs becomes an important matter of public policy.

Chapter 17

Uses of Fire in Wild-land Management

This chapter presents in broad terms the range or scope of beneficial use of fire in wild-land management. Techniques in using fire follow in Chapter 18, illustrated by descriptions of regional practices in several contrasting environments.

In previous chapters, several concepts that can be stated as premises were developed in respect to fire effects on wild lands. The first is that fire effects are potentially complex, since they represent changes in the local environment as well as direct effects on existing flora and fauna, and that their nature may be identified as long-range or short-range in terms of time and as tangible or intangible in terms of money (Chapter 4). All may come into play after a single fire on a relatively small area, though typically a specific effect tends to dominate in each plant community in which fuels are similar. Consequently, identification of the effects to be expected when fuel, cover types, and the level of fire danger are known in advance can be predicted with some confidence (Chapter 7). This is the primary premise on which use of fire by the wild-land manager is based.

A second premise is that fire effects over any considerable area are never totally destructive or totally beneficial. Consequently, in the use of fire, the realistic objective is to attain maximum *net* benefits after deducting offsetting damages and costs.

The influence of wildfire in the past in the evolution of American tree species and in the maintenance of the dominance of certain commercially valuable subclimax timber types is also a part of this background (Chapters 3 and 4). On the other hand, the almost overwhelming destructiveness of uncontrollable wildfire under conditions of very high or extreme fire danger or in abnormally hazardous fuels is clearly demonstrated nearly every year in the United States as well as by the historic conflagration fires of the past cited in Chapter 1. Clearly then, beneficial use of fire also means positive predetermination or control of its behavior. It is a more sophisticated form of control than the effort to control wildfires since it usually requires control of the fire's intensity as well as confinement of its spread to the area intended. It has the special advantage that it is not an emergency operation, as is usual in control of wildfires. Time, place, burning conditions, and techniques of the operation can be carefully selected in advance and the plan of action can be designed accordingly.

An analogy with medicine is in point. In the hands of a skilled physician, a powerful drug may be used with beneficial, often lifesaving results. Misused, the same drug may be a deadly poison. No one maintains that because a drug may be harmful it should not be used at all. Further, no physician will generalize very far in his treatment of patients. Each presents individual problems and needs, with separate clinical history, diagnosis, and treatment. So it is with fire. It is powerful medicine, and evidence is abundant that it can be extremely harmful. Yet, with accurate diagnosis and skillful application, it can be a good prescription in particular situations. It is because of this medical analogy and connotation that the term *prescribed burning* has been adopted and is applied generally to planned use of fire in wild-land management in the United States. This emphasizes planned use, carefully designed for specific situations.

Controversial Aspects

Though use of fire in wild-land management has won increasing acceptance in the United States for the purposes described in succeeding sections, broadcast burning of extensive wild-land areas has remained a controversial practice. Some of the reasons are:

1 The seeming contradiction between an active fire prevention

program which seeks to put a stop to all burning which fails to meet legal requirements of the locality, and a program for use of fire by the same agency, even though it is fully within all legal requirements. One reason is that inevitably not all illegal burning will be destructive and not all legal burning will yield the benefits intended. But the conflict is largely psychological. After one has preached and fought for wildfire control, caution in advocating use of fire is understandable.

2   Conflicts in use of wild-lands also makes the use of fire controversial. Burning that may improve pasture for cattle or browse for deer, or the water yield for irrigation may accelerate soil erosion or may be destructive of timber or recreation values.

3   Public concern about air pollution has entered as a potent new factor in the 1970s. Though diluted smoke from natural fuels is of low toxicity, incomplete combustion may result in a high yield of particulates associated with moisture particles. This adds to the density of any existing smog and reduces visibility wherever present. Such obvious effects make prescribed burning a natural target of antipollution campaigns (Murphy et al., 1970).

4   Conflicting ideas on the importance of net benefits obtained through prescribed burning also lead to much controversy, since a high proportion of benefits and damages is often intangible in nature.

5   Lack of knowledge, equipment, or manpower to control fire effectively induces fear of escape of prescribed fire. This is heightened by the feeling of ignominy on the part of a fire control officer who is unable to control a fire he started himself. At times such fears are well grounded. In California chaparral, a satisfactory burn requires a hot fire, which is difficult to control in the dry June to August period. This is often true also in heavy slash fuels in the conifer types.

6   Liability to damage suits is a strong inhibiting factor where mixed ownership occurs and some of the owners oppose use of fire. Such a liability becomes real whenever a set fire crosses the property line of such an owner, even though damage by the fire itself may be nominal.

7   Lack of appreciation of what can be accomplished by skillful use of fire, and lack of funds for carrying out such projects where and when needed, are also common negative reasons for not using prescribed fire.

These seven sources of inertia or controversy limit the prescribed use of fire to widely varying degrees in the various forest regions of the United States and Canada. Each has primary importance in some localities. In the past, the most prevalent opposition to use of fire in the United States relates to item 1. Overly simplified fire prevention propaganda which gave recognition only to the destructive effects of fire led also to a school of thought that all fire on wild-lands was bad and that even accepted uses of fire must be tolerated only as a matter of choosing the lesser of two evils. This was strengthened by the corollary belief on the part of many land managers that any acceptance of use of fire was sure to weaken the cause of fire prevention in the minds of the public. Fortunately these sources of opposition did not prevent continuing research and development in fire effects and in prescribed burning techniques. In time, the useful role of prescribed fire has become more generally accepted, as well as the need to give more depth and discrimination to education of the public in fire prevention.

The most prevalent recent source of opposition to prescribed burning relates to item 3. There are several reasons why prescribed burning practices are likely to result in significant even though temporary reduction of atmospheric visibility. First, when burning conditions are favorable for complete control of set fires, strong atmospheric circulation is lacking. Second, at least a part of the fuels are moist. Third, ideal fuel and weather conditions for prescribed burning are usually quite limited in time and duration, with the result that many burning projects may be initiated almost simultaneously in the same meteorological subregion. The potential result is the generation of a high level of particulates which produces a dense, highly obscuring drift smoke that may spread out under an inversion over a considerable area and linger for several days, with interference to the operation of aircraft and other activities.

Part of the solution is naturally in the field of public relations on the part of wild-land management agencies, but research under way gives considerable promise of reducing the problem as well through more refined techniques, such as identification of safe conditions when drift smoke will not accumulate, burning techniques which induce more complete combustion and less dense smoke, and through lengthening the season during which prescribed burning can be carried out. Such provisions will require that prescribed burning be carried out under somewhat more dangerous conditions and will demand more skill in execution. This can be attained.

It is to be expected that public opposition to drift smoke will curtail use of fire where its advantage is that of cost or convenience only. But as long as continuing research and development in this field is maintained, gradual extension of systematic use of fire to accomplish varied land-management objectives is to be expected.

USES IN SILVICULTURE

Natural Regeneration

Seeds of most forest tree species, conifers especially, germinate and grow best on mineral soil surfaces. Where it can be used, fire is often the most efficient means of seedbed preparation. It will consume surface litter and duff, exposing mineral soil, and will also reduce competition from grass and other subordinate vegetation. Fire is often used to aid natural regeneration in southern conifer types and in some western conifers, particularly ponderosa pine (Chapter 3). A practice in southern pines, longleaf especially, is to broadcast burn, normally not more than a year before expected seed fall. Good seed crops usually can be predicted a year in advance of cone maturation. In longleaf, a second fire is used one to six years after a seedling stand is established, and one such fire is preferable to repeated light burns (Bruce and Bickford, 1950). At this stage, in most of the range of longleaf pine, a burn accomplishes two objectives. It frees the seedlings from grass and other herbaceous competition and effectively checks the progress of brown-spot disease, which would otherwise greatly retard or kill most of the longleaf pine seedlings. Such early treatment is limited to longleaf, since it is the only tree species resistant to fire in the juvenile or "grass" stage (Chapter 2).

Following nature's method, fire is effective in aiding natural regeneration of lodgepole and jack pine through clearing the seedbed and opening cones that characteristically remain unopened in the crowns of these species. Broadcast burns in advance of cutting are seldom practicable, and slash fires are difficult to handle and likely to destroy the seed supply. However, it has been demonstrated in lodgepole pine that if logging slash is bunched in windrows during clear cutting so that it covers less than 20 percent of the surface, burning temperatures that would be lethal to the seed can be confined to the heavily burned strips under the windrows. Natural seeding then quickly restocks the remaining 80 percent of the area. Little or no supplemental planting is needed.

In addition to seedbed preparation and reduction of competition from weeds and grass, fire often gives a temporary growth stimulus because of the fertilizing effect of mineral nutrients released in the ashes (Chapter 3). The degree to which fire will destoy seeds on the ground at the time of burning is important in some situations. If all the organic mantle and surface litter is burned, seed accumulated in it will be killed. This requires a hot fire when heavy fuels are dry. This may or may not be desired. Such problems arise also in brushland and range types involving both desired and undesired species.

Cutting Methods

Fire is sometimes an essential tool in carrying out cutting methods. For example, in clear-cutting Douglas-fir, western white pine, and some other conifer types, the large volume of slash usually remaining after logging is not only a fire hazard but may prevent silvicultural completion of the method. The ground must be cleared to permit full natural or artificial regeneration.

Applied with skill, fire can be a means of thinning overdense stands in certain situations. It has produced silvicultural benefits of this kind in pine stands in the southern United States and offers some possibilities in the western United States in ponderosa pine (Weaver, 1947). Fire is, however, a tricky tool and is normally nonselective, from a silvicultural viewpoint, in the kind of thinning it produces. Consequently, it is seldom used in timber types where wood production is the primary value of the land.

Change or Modification of Cover Type

Based on observation of what wildfire can do, fire is often used as a means of maintaining or bringing about a desirable forest cover type or species composition from man's standpoint. It may be desired to convert non-productive and semipermanent brush areas, as found in California, the Pacific Northwest, and elsewhere, to productive timber types. In other situations, the need may be to maintain pine against hardwood encroach-ment or to convert hardwood types of low value to more valuable conifers; this kind of problem is often encountered in the eastern United States. Sometimes the aim is to convert mixed conifers of tolerant species to less tolerant but more valuable species. An example would be conversion of a western hemlock–grand fir type to one composed mainly of Douglas-fir or western white pine. Lodgepole, jack pine, and aspen can be favored over their competitors by judicious use of fire. In the majority of situations and in conifer-hardwood mixtures particularly, the aim is modification of species composition rather than outright type conversion. There is no hard and fast line between the two; what constitutes a forest type is a matter of essentially arbitrary definition. An example of burning to control low-value hardwoods is given in Chapter 18.

Type manipulation by fire should be based on a sound ecological knowledge of natural successional trends. Fire may accelerate or retard them; the latter effect is by far the most common. In other conifer types, some subclimax successional stage is frequently more valuable from a commercial standpoint.

USES IN FIRE PREVENTION AND CONTROL

Suppression

The expression "Fight fire with fire" is embedded in the folklore. As brought out in Chapters 7, 12, and 16, use of fire is often absolutely essential in suppression. It is commonly used in backfiring from prepared lines and in burning out dangerous fuel "islands" or other concentrations within control lines.

Prevention

Use of fire in hazard reduction is presented in Chapter 10. Fire is used in several ways:

    1 In the construction and maintenance of firebreaks or barriers constructed in advance of suppression action.
    2 In the disposal of slash and other forest debris by pile and burn, spot burning (usually following windrowing or bunching), and progressive methods.
    3 In broadcast burning of areas to reduce the total fuel hazard. This is practiced primarily in the southern United States.

Training

As noted in Chapter 15, the execution of prescribed burning provides invaluable opportunity to the participants to observe and understand fire behavior and to observe and practice basic methods of fire control. Often this may be the only opportunity for fire personnel to work directly with fire as prevention and control activities increase in efficiency.

USES IN RANGE MANAGEMENT

More acres have been and possibly are being burned for grazing purposes than for all other uses of fire put together. Both forest and nonforest land uses are involved; the subject goes far beyond the purview of the forester. The practice of burning to stimulate forage production is of long standing. Also, as pointed out in Chapter 9, this practice is of major importance in conditioning the attitudes of rural people about forest fires and their prevention. Principal uses of fire in relation to grazing are briefly sketched below.

Change of Plant Community

From a grazing standpoint, millions of acres of land in the United States support weed, brush, woodland, or forest types whose forage production can be greatly increased by conversion to grassland or some other more desirable forage cover. Large brushland areas of low forage productivity are utilized for grazing in California, the Intermountain Region of Utah and southern Idaho, the Southwest, and the Missouri Ozarks. Use of fire in California brushlands is described in Chapter 18. As might be expected, the ecological relationships vary widely in these diverse shrub communities, with consequent variation in the effects from fire. In many areas undesirable cover conditions were created by wildfires and unwise grazing practices. In such areas any benefits from fire depend on accompanying cultural and protective measures, in which prescribed burning comprises one step only.

Large areas of forested lands are grazed in the United States. On some of them timber and forage production conflict. While these uses often can be harmonized fairly well, they may also be incompatible, especially if recreation and watershed values are involved. This necessitates a choice. Under present management, many forest areas in the United States are unproductive of timber and forage as joint products but could be productively managed for one or the other. Grazing should usually be suppressed on high-quality hardwood timberlands, because forage production is low and timber production is seriously reduced by grazing. In contrast, in each of the mountain states of the western United States, there are large, privately owned woodland areas fringing the more productive agricultural lands of the valley bottoms. Most of these areas are grazed, but their forage production is low. In some of these situations, it is sound economics to convert second-rate forest into good forage areas through pasture-improvement programs. Fire is often employed as a tool in effecting such conversion. The same general situation prevails in parts of the Ozarks and in smaller dispersed areas in the eastern United States. Fire is similarly employed to convert sagebrush and some other nonforest types into grassland or other better grazing cover.

As in silviculture, successful use of fire in forage-type conversion requires sound and thorough ecological information, careful integration with other land-use objectives, understanding of fire effects, accurate knowledge of fire behavior, skill in its application, and good follow-up to ensure the beneficial effects of fire.

Improvement or Restoration of Existing Grazing Lands

In forested areas where timber is the principal crop, the aim in using fire for grazing purposes is essentially to improve forage production without changing the major cover type. The outstanding example of this is the practice of light burning in the South. While there is much misinformation, prejudice, and custom involved in the matter, it is an undeniable fact that burning does improve forage production in many situations. Grazing, burning, and forest relations have been most thoroughly studied in the coastal plain areas of the lower South. Here, burning improves grazing by increasing quality, productivity, and accessibility of forage, aiding distribution of cattle, and checking growth of shrubs (Hilman and Hughes, 1965).

An eight-year study of the effects of grazing and burning on a coastal plain pine-wood area near Alapaha, Georgia (Halls, Southwell, and Knox, 1952), as summarized by Shepherd (1953), gave the following results in terms of forage production and cattle weight gains:

> The effect of winter burning on forage quality was pronounced, but primarily limited to the spring months. Protein and phosphorus content of the important grasses were 2 to 3 times higher, and lignin content appreciably lower, on burned range during the early leaf stage of growth. But after the grasses reached full leaf—usually in June—forage from burned and unburned range was chemically similar. Cattle gains were likewise much greater on burned range than on unburned range during the spring, and 2 to 3 times higher for the entire season (Figure 17.1). Also, cattle showed a strong preference in the spring for fresh burn when available. Appreciable use of "rough" areas at this time occurred only after burns were closely utilized. Much of this palatability advantage, like the nutritional advantage, had disappeared by July and grazing of unburned areas increased in late summer. However, some effect carried over into the

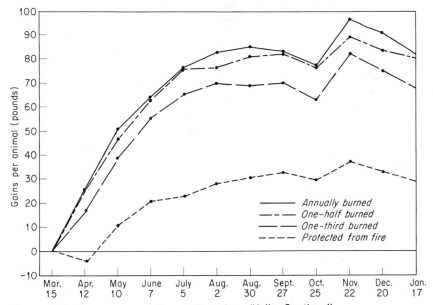

Figure 17.1 Average cumulative cattle gains. *(Halls, Southwell, and Knox, 1952.)*

second spring when, in the absence of adequate fresh burn, cattle preferred 1-year-rough over older rough.

Heavier utilization of the burned area, and lower cattle gains, resulted from burning only $1/3$, rather than $1/2$ or all of a range yearly. But these responses were more closely related to the amount of burn than to the frequency of burning. Over the 7-year period cattle gains showed no definite long-time trends, either upward or downward, attributable to the different burning practices. Vegetation responses under grazing also were similar for the three burning schedules; apparently the 2- or 3-year recovery period compensated for the more intense grazing which resulted when cattle concentrated on the burned $1/2$ or $1/3$ of the range.

Subsequent research has proved the advantages of rotational burning on a three-year cycle (Duvall and Whitaker, 1964).

Practically all understory species of Coastal Plain pinelands tolerate winter burning. Without grazing, burning increased the herbaceous ground cover, apparently by removing litter which had accumulated for 8 years on part of the experimental area, and held brush in check. But the combination of grazing and burning markedly decreased the two dominant bunch grasses (pineland threeawn and Curtiss dropseed) which are most important for summer and fall grazing. Without burning, the total herbaceous ground cover decreased and brush increased, whether grazed or not. An outstanding exception was Curtiss dropseed, the most important grass for winter grazing, which increased considerably under protection from burning and grazing.

The two principal shrubs in Coastal Plain forests, gallberry and saw palmetto, are well adapted to a fire subclimax. Both species sprout vigorously after fire. A number of these sprouts die the second year after a fire, but foliage cover per stem increases gradually with protection. After two or three years, number of stems and foliage cover return to about the same levels as before the fire (Hilman and Hughes, 1965).

When burning is carried out on a short rotation for forage improvement, it usually prevents establishment of new pine seedlings. It consequently maintains or increases the proportion of open area. This was the trend in this study. However other studies show that when longleaf pine seedlings are already present in the grass stage, many are sufficiently stimulated in height growth by a burn at this stage that they escape serious injury from subsequent prescribed burns at intervals as frequent as three years.

The study also showed significant reduction in accumulation of herbaceous fuels due to grazing and burning.

When the ungrazed, unburned ranges were taken as the normal condition, grazing alone reduced herbaceous fuel by 24 percent; burning alone, 42 percent; and burning and grazing, 72 percent. The intensity of grazing was moderate to heavy and the reduction in herbaceous fuel may have been more than normal for the average unfenced forest range.

From the standpoint of protection against wildfire, forest grazing may be desirable. On unburned range, the livestock gains would be small, but the advantage to be gained by reducing the amount of herbaceous fuel by moderate to heavy grazing may be enough to justify such practice (Halls, Southwell, and Knox, 1952).

In Australia, grazing by both sheep and cattle has been found to be very helpful in maintaining exterior firebreaks to forest plantations and in reducing fuel hazards in the plantations during the critical period after a plantation has become established but before the crowns have closed to form a crown canopy.

The problem in grazing forest lands is to harmonize timber and forage uses to give the best total result in accordance with the purposes of management, fundamentally an economic problem (Gregory, 1955). Recent trends, as toward wider spacings (12 by 12 feet and wider) of trees in coniferous plantations and selections of shade-tolerant grasses, assist the land manager significantly in overcoming obstacles to integrated management (Hughes et al., 1966). Exploration in depth of forestry-grazing relationships is beyond the scope of this book. Where fire is involved, it adds the further technical complication that its use must be coordinated with grazing needs, on the one hand, and forest needs on the other. Generalizations are unhelpful and often misleading. Careful prescriptions are needed. When carried out the term *prescribed burning* then becomes highly significant.

Regeneration

As with tree seeds, burning can improve seedbed conditions for range regeneration. Whether or not it destroys seed on the ground of both desired and undesired species is also important (Sampson, 1944). Burning can also stimulate seed production in some situations. An example of this is reported by Biswell and Lemon (1943) in the wire grass type of the Southwest.

Clumps of many native grasses will live for years without producing seed stalks; but if burned, they will produce in abundance. Many weeds respond in about the same way.

Fires in late spring and early summer, after seasonal growth is well started, seem to stimulate seeding more than fires in early winter or spring. Actual counts of seed stalks of six native grasses under three conditions in close proximity showed that medium-sized clumps that were unburned did not produce any seed stalks, whereas similar clumps burned in late winter averaged 25 stalks and those burned in early summer averaged 90 seed stalks per clump. Unless these grass clumps are burned again the next season, they do not produce stalks the following summer.

USES IN WILDLIFE MANAGEMENT

Fire and wildlife have had a long and intimate association both in and out of a forest environment. Fire, though rarely lethal to most forms of wildlife, does have profound effects, both detrimental and beneficial, on food and cover conditions. The latter are of concern here. Fire is an efficient and economical tool for improving food and cover conditions for certain wildlife species. In general, except in southern pine forests, these results in the United States are obtained at the expense of timber production. The use of fire primarily for wildlife purposes seldom fits in with silvicultural aims. The basic reason, and this applies with particular force in conifer forests, is that the more valuable wildlife populations from a hunting standpoint are, for the most part, favored by maintenance of forest cover types of low and irregular density. Such cover includes a good proportion of shrubby and other subordinate vegetation having greater food productivity and cover value than well-stocked forests of commercially valuable timber. Heavy stands of coniferous timber constitute a biological desert as far as most wildlife species are concerned.

Timber-production aims can, however, often be harmonized with wildlife needs. A well-managed forest, with a good mixture of age and size classes and active cutting operations in progress, can provide good food and cover conditions for a moderate population of wildlife species without major alteration of cutting practices. When much larger populations are desired to meet hunting pressure, the problem becomes a decision as to best use of the land. Certain areas or parts of areas may be dedicated to wildlife, and habitat conditions may be altered accordingly. Here is where fire use specifically for wildlife purposes enters the picture in forest land management.

The situation in Michigan provides an excellent illustration. As stated by Smith (1948), "Michigan's northern public hunting grounds and her public forests are one and the same." Hunting, fishing, and other recreation are a major industry of the state; one has to participate in the deer hunting to appreciate the tremendous pressure for public hunting opportunity. An important segment of forest lands owned by the state was purchased with money appropriated for game purposes. There is tremendous variation in site quality and cover conditions, ranging from fine-quality commercial timber and timberland to brushy and grassy areas of low timber productivity but often high wildlife value.

The land-management problem requires coordination of game and timber production. Under good fire protection, the cover gradually closes in to the exclusion of certain game species. In 1942, Smith estimated that, on about 10 million acres in Michigan classified as deforested or in a restocking condition and hence suitable for game, this closing-in process was proceeding at the rate of about 90,000 acres a year. Game needs are carefully considered in the selection and arrangement of planting sites and in the conduct of timber stand improvement and harvest cutting. Some areas are classified as more valuable for game than for timber production and are managed accordingly. It is here that prescribed fire is used for game purposes. The aim is to reduce brush and timber cover and to improve food conditions on areas primarily managed for upland game birds.

Use of fire for wildlife purposes may briefly be classified by major species and habitat groups as follows:

Big Game

The situation with big game is basically much the same as with domestic stock. Big game consisting of grazing and browsing animals, is favored by land-management practices that encourage creation of grass and low browse cover. There is a popular saying that "deer follow the ax." They do; and also the wildfires that so frequently have accompanied the ax. Cutting stimulates new shrub and sprout growth and creates openings and margins that favor big-game production, but past wildfires have done it on a much larger scale.

Although fire could be used rather extensively in timber and in some brushland areas to improve big-game conditions, it is rarely so used. The reasons are basically economic. Most such areas are considered more valuable for watershed timber or domestic forage production. Also, burning may run counter to recreational objectives. Any significant exception to this is likely to be on lands owned for big-game hunting by private hunting clubs or individuals. For the most part, however, and including lands privately owned for big-game purposes, game needs can be and are met by land-management practices not necessitating broadcast use of fire.

Upland Birds

Quail, grouse, partridge, prairie chickens, pheasants, turkeys, and other upland birds are in general favored by semiopen or open conditions that in part may be created by burning. The ruffed grouse is an exception; it is a forest species, whereas some grouse are not. As with all other wildlife, upland birds basically need suitable food and cover conditions. The use and place of fire in upland bird management, quail especially, has had special study by Stoddard (1931, 1935), Cushwa and Martin (1969), and others in the Southeastern states. Fire is also used to some extent to improve conditions for prairie chickens and sharp-tailed grouse in the Lake states. In general, the carrying capacity of the environment for upland birds is measured by the amount of edge between open grass and shrub or tree cover. To increase the amount of edge by use of fire, a very patchy type of burn is required.

Song Birds

The habitat for song birds is also strongly affected by fire. For example, it has been determined that Kirtland's warbler, a vanishing species in the state of Michigan, is dependent on the availability of semiopen areas of low brush and young jack pine for nesting sites. Such sites are created by recent burns. A program of prescribed burning on selected state and federal lands to ensure availability of nesting sites is the key provision in the plans to maintain this species (Mayfield, 1963; U.S. Department of Interior, 1968).

Marshland Birds and Animals

As brought out in Chapter 2, fire is no stranger to marshlands and wet areas in general. In times of drought, the large vegetative accumulation that is characteristic of such areas burns readily and often with decisive effects on the cover type. Burning has long been practiced in some marshland areas, particularly along the Gulf Coast. Marsh fires can be grouped into three classes (Lynch, 1941):

 1 Cover burns. These are fires burning over standing water in accumulated dead vegetative material. Properly directed and timed, they create better habitat for ducks and geese (the latter especially); accelerate the production of food for waterfowl, muskrats, and cattle; increase availability of food by making new growth more accessible; facilitate trapping and hunting operations; and give some protection against severe summer or fall wildfires. Since in cover burns the fire is above the basal parts of perennial plants, they do not affect the structure of the marsh but do affect species composition to some extent.

 2 Root burns. These fires are characteristic of peaty marsh types. If left unburned, a jungle of vegetation is formed and an organic layer builds up in which plant roots develop. The upper portion of this layer becomes dry periodically and burns readily. Root burns tend to kill climax vegetation and allow plants of lower successional groups to reappear. In some instances, subclimax species are better food producers. Shallow swales and pools are also formed that are desirable for wildlife.

3 Peat burns. These are deep burns that occur infrequently during periods of extended drought. They may burn down to mineral soil and completely change the character of the area. They commonly create large holes which subsequently fill with water. Such burns are very destructive but do have offsetting benefits. The water holes attract aquatic birds and animals, and production of food plants which they utilize is often improved. Although root and peat fires must be applied with much discretion and only at long intervals, they have a place in marshland management. Cover burns are much more extensively employed.

Fish

The effects of fire on fish populations are consistently adverse; prescribed use of fire seems to have no place.

CONTROL OF INSECTS AND DISEASES

A popular belief in the cleansing and sanitary effects of fire goes back to antiquity. In agriculture, fire is frequently used to control certain pests by burning their habitat and to destroy weed seeds, diseased plants, and crop residues. It is used as a sanitary measure in swampy and other areas harboring disease carriers such as the dreaded tsetse fly of Africa. Most of these uses are in nonforest environments.

While pathological and adverse entomological effects caused by fire are abundant, desirable effects justifying special use of fire in forest areas are relatively few. Fire is used successfully to control the brown-spot disease in longleaf pine. The danger of certain insect populations developing in slash and attacking green timber is an important factor promotiong slash disposal in some situations. Fire is often employed to dispose of insect- or disease-infested trees in control operations, including particularly heavy infestations by mistletoe in Western regions of the United States. The word *sanitation* with an antipathological implication is sometimes applied rather loosely to burning on areas supporting timber heavily infected with wood-rotting fungi. The actual antipathological benefit is probably of minor consequence.

USES IN LAND CLEARING

In pioneer times, land clearing was a major forest job and fire was the most powerful and economical tool available to the settler in wresting agricultural lands from the forest. It was almost universally used. Along with grazing, this use of fire has been an important factor conditioning the attitude of agricultural people toward the forest. Modern timber utilization, explosives, and power equipment have largely obviated the necessity for fire as a major tool in land clearing and have taken most of the backbreaking labor out of it. Also, relatively little forest land is being cleared at the present time. However, areas prepared for forest plantations in pulp company holdings in the South are commonly cleared of existing cover similar to clearings for agriculture. In Australia, complete clearing and burning of forested sites to enable the establishment of coniferous plantations is carried out. This is done on a systematic basis often involving the manipulation of mass fires of high intensity on several thousand acres.

In nearly all clearing of forest or brush cover for any purpose, fire is used to dispose of the resulting slash in piles or windrows, or by broadcast burning following the same general methods used in slash disposal. Wildfires from large planned projects are rare, but burning of forest debris following the cutting of one or a few trees continues to be an important cause of wildfires in the United States (Chapter 9).

USES IN WATERSHED MANAGEMENT

As brought out in Chapters 2 and 3, fire can have profound effects on soil and on vegetation in wild-land areas. The literature of forest-water-soil relationships is extensive and cannot be reviewed here. In general, wherever fire exposes bare mineral soil even for a few months, the effect is unfavorable from the watershed viewpoint. Runoff and soil erosion tend to increase and infiltration to decrease. The effects are naturally most marked on steep slopes and on clay soils of low organic content. Consequently, high-intensity wildfires are nearly always destructive to watershed values.

On the positive side, the yield of water from a watershed is strongly influenced by the type and density of vegetative cover it supports. To maintain maximum yields of clean water, various forms of manipulation of the cover have been found to be beneficial. This includes use of fire to reduce vegetation.

Except in critical areas where watershed values predominate, desired effects can be, and preferably are, brought about through coordination of the management of timber, recreation, grazing, and wildlife resources of forest land. In any event, use of fire under prescription must be closely correlated with these forest uses.

Chapter 18

Techniques and Application of Prescribed Burning

As brought out in Chapter 17, fire can be used to perform a wide range of useful tasks in the management of wildlands and is an effective tool when skillfully used. But it is always a potentially dangerous tool. To use it successfully, several exacting requirements must be met.

1 Most important is intimate knowledge of fire behavior in the particular environment in which fire is to be used.

2 Next is complete information on current and prospective burning conditions by such means as fire danger ratings and detailed fire weather forecasts.

3 There must be knowledge of burning techniques and how to use them safely to accomplish maximum net benefits at acceptable costs.

4 There must be careful advance planning of the prescribed burning operation, including the equipment and manpower needed and a time schedule for each phase of the operation and taking into account the safety provisions needed and the fire behavior to be expected.

The background for understanding fire behavior has been given in previous chapters. This includes the ways fire behavior responds to fuels and weather and how it may be predicted in advance. It is the purpose of this chapter to build on this knowledge to present techniques and planning methods that have been found effective in carrying out prescribed burning projects. These will be illustrated by a description of prescribed burning practices in a range of environmental situations.

PRESCRIBED BURNING TECHNIQUES

All prescribed burning techniques are based on utilizing one or more characteristics of fire behavior to accomplish the purpose intended. These are identified for each of the more common techniques of prescribed burning.

As set forth in Chapter 7, the typical free-burning fire spreads most rapidly at the head, most slowly at the foot or base, and at intermediate rates along the flanks. This assumes, as is usually true, that the spread is influenced by wind movement, significant slope, or some combination of both. These basic relationships are universally utilized in controlled or prescribed burning. Along with the increasing rates of spread go increased depths of the flame front and increased rates of release of heat energy. Consequently, control of the fire's perimeter becomes progressively more difficult from rear to flank to head. At the same time, burning conditions and fuels control the average level of fire intensity at any given time. The forward spread rate of a fire may increase ten times as fire danger increases. From this it is evident that the prescribed burner has several options. He can select the level of burning conditions to fit the fuels he wishes to treat, and he has the further choice of using such techniques as the backfire, the flank fire, or the head fire—whichever may best accomplish the intended purpose at that particular burning condition. Several such options or choices are illustrated in Figure 18.1 and will be briefly described.

Backfire Burns

Backfiring or back burning is typically done by setting a line of fire along a natural or artificial firebreak and permitting it to spread against the wind or down a moderate slope. On flat or gently sloping terrain, the line of fire is set at right angles to the wind direction. In steep topography, it is set along the ridgetop. An additional firebreak is required for each line of fire set. It is illustrated by Figure 18.1*A*, and is most commonly used on flatlands where rates of spread are high or when burning is done under hazardous conditions. It is considered further in relation to head fire burns.

Flank-fire Burns

The flank fire is illustrated by Figure 18.1*B*. It is set along a line parallel to the wind and allowed to spread at right angles to it. After a burned safety strip has been established along a firebreak, new fires or lines of fire in level terrain are set along short vertical lines into the wind. They are kept to equal length and are spaced at uniform intervals. The lateral spread of fire between these lines usually doubles the rate of spread of the backing fire and considerably increases the heat output. Flank firing is seldom employed over extensive areas but is often employed as a modification of back burning to speed up the job or to obtain a cleaner or hotter burn. When fire danger is low and it is difficult to maintain a satisfactory backing fire, this flank-fire technique becomes very useful and is frequently employed in the final stages of a back-burn project. However, flank firing has certain disadvantages and requires considerable skill to achieve uniform results. At the point where the flames meet by lateral spread from two parallel lines of fire, there is a strong tendency for turbulence or even fire whirls to develop. In a timber stand, this greatly increases the amount of scorch of green foliage and may result in crowning out a patch of trees. Such results are usually evidence of impatient or unskilled use of fire. Only a slight increase in wind speed or reduction in the moisture content of fuels can transform flank firing from a useful to a destructive technique. Irregularities in terrain and in fuels are usually sufficient to prevent a flank fire from traveling very far as a smooth flank. Sooner or later a point of fire gets in advance of the rest of the flank. When this happens, a slight gust of wind or a spot of hot fuels may convert it to a head fire. It is for this reason that new lines of fire are set at intervals, even though this creates some turbulence as they close together.

The Chevron Burn

The back-burn and flank-fire techniques are designed for flat or nearly flat topography. A modified backfire technique which is at times referred to as the chevron burn is commonly used where the prescribed burning area has definite ridges and valleys (Sackett, 1969). It consists of establishing the line of fire in a crescent or V-shaped pattern. Figure 18.1*C* illustrates the pattern where a backing fire is being brought down a small drainage. The same pattern may be used in bringing a backfire down a ridge or the face of a slope. In general, the chevron pattern is made to conform to that of the rear of a wildfire or to the mirror image of a natural head fire. This gives stability to the fire front of the backing fire. The technique may be supplemented by use of flank-fire or head-fire techniques, depending on circumstances.

Head-fire Burns

Head-fire burning consists of setting fire to run with the wind or upslope. It is the reverse of the back-burn technique, though the head fire is seldom permitted to run freely for any considerable distance in a prescribed burning project. Usually a broad safety strip or firebreak is burned out first, then a line of fire is set at a predetermined distance from it and parallel to it and permitted to burn into it with the wind. This creates a new burned strip. As soon as it has burned out, a new line of fire is set parallel to it and the process is continued until the entire area to be treated has been burned over (Figure 18.1D). One advantage of this method is that no interior firebreaks are required within a burning unit (as compared to the back-burning technique in strip burning), though such requirements may be relieved somewhat by use of flank fires.

The backfire produces shorter flames than a head fire and burns more slowly. Less energy is being released per minute so it is easier to control. But the low rate of spread under some fuel conditions becomes a handicap when applied in a timber stand to reduce fuels under living trees. Often the first 12- to 16-inch section of young tree stems above the ground is exposed to high heat for more minutes than by a more rapidly moving head fire. This is particularly true when there is little or no wind movement to dissipate the heat from the burning fuels. For this reason some minimum wind velocity is usually included in the prescription for back burning.

The greater heat developed by head fires gives them preference under poor burning conditions and at times when selective killing of underbrush and certain tree species is sought. For a given fuel the first control of the amount of heat is the burning condition at the time and the second is the length of run the head fire is permitted to make before it reaches burned-over area or is contained by firebreaks. At very low fire danger the length of run is not significant as the fire reaches a plateau in its rate of spread in a very short distance. But as burning conditions build up at moderate or high fire danger, the fire keeps on accelerating with time and distance traveled. By holding head fires to short runs, both the energy level and controllability can be kept within bounds.

The Area Grid Method

The primary difference between the behavior of the backfire, the flank fire, and the head fire is due to the differing angle of exposure of unburned fuels to the flames. The angle is determined by the geometry of slope and fuel arrangement and by air movement. The latter, in the form of prevailing wind near the ground surface, is the most prevalent determi-

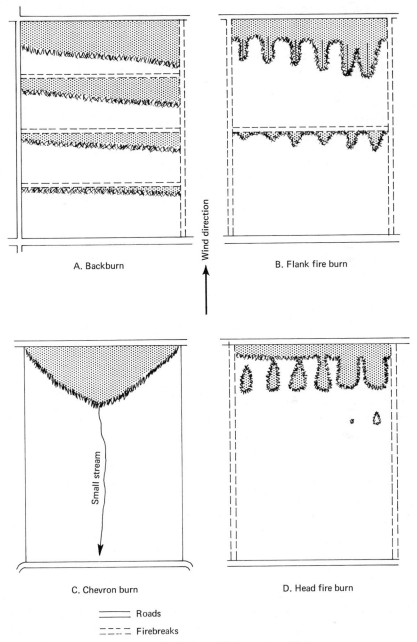

Figure 18.1 Burning techniques. In *A*, *B*, and *D*, the order of firing is from the right to the left. In *C*, it is from both sides to the center.

nant, though convective forces created by the fire itself often enter in. The techniques described in the preceeding sections depend for their success largely on avoidance of building up strong convective forces.

The area grid method consists of spacing set fires just far enough apart that they will not interact yet will cover the area intended by the end of the burning period. It is especially designed to avoid strong convective activity. The purpose is to reduce fuel hazards over large forest areas at low cost and minimum damage to the forest stand. It has been highly developed in Australia (Peet, 1965; Baxter, Pacham, and Peet, 1966). The technique depends on use of a carefully developed burning guide and fire weather forecasts to identify weather and fuel moisture conditions at which flash fuels will ignite and carry fire but the fire will spread slowly and will not develop enough heat to kindle heavier fuels. When such conditions have been identified and their continuance is forecast, the operation is carried out in a few hours. Ignition may be accomplished by either ground or aerial methods. When ground methods are used, torch men are spaced at predetermined distances apart and move along parallel routes. Each sets spot fires at the same interval along his route to create a grid pattern of ignitions.

Special aerial techniques for applying the area grid method to large inaccessible areas have been developed in Australia. These involve use of aircraft to dispense incendiaries in a grid pattern. This is accomplished by operating the aircraft along successive parallel courses, spaced at a predetermined distance apart, and dispensing incendiaries at the same intervals along each course. Usually the prescribed burn areas include rough terrain. Both the incendiaries, which are in capsule form, and the dispenser are especially designed for the purpose. The spacing between the incendiaries is adjusted so that no two set fires will stimulate each other. Instead, by selection of both burning conditions and time of ignition, they are scheduled to burn together after sunset near the end of the burning period. The rate of spread has then slowed down naturally and convective activity is at a low ebb. The minimum spacing of spot fires by aerial methods is approximately five chains.

The special advantage of this method is that carefully selected burning conditions can be utilized fully, even though they may occur infrequently. Where this kind of treatment is appropriate, a very large area can be covered in a few hours at low cost. Normally, the objective in Australia is to remove fuel on only 40 to 50 percent of the area. For this purpose burning conditions are selected when fire will spread only on exposed slopes and dry sites.

In the southern pine region of the United States, the area grid method is at times applied using ground ignition techniques. The purpose is usually to speed up the coverage of area and reduce costs. The method requires highly experienced personnel, but where a somewhat patchy burn is satisfactory, considerable area can be treated in a single burning period with little or no construction of interior firebreaks.

The disadvantage of the area grid method is that weather forecasts and evaluation of burning conditions must be accurate, since it is difficult to halt a large project once it has been initiated. If burning conditions exceed expectations, the set fires will burn together before the end of the burning period and may interact to create damaging hot spots. The method depends for its success to a considerable degree on the nature of the fuels present as well as their moisture content. It works best where there is a minimum of smoldering fuels and set fires can be expected to die out overnight. Where smoldering fires do persist adjacent to large unburned pockets of fuel, an increase in fire danger in the days following will result in damaging wildfires or in protracted commitment of men and equipment to ensure against such occurrences.

Simultaneous or Area Ignition Method

The simultaneous or area ignition method is a technique by which strong convective forces are induced and utilized to create a hotter fire and a stronger convection column than would otherwise occur. In the brush-lands of California, green and dead fuels may exceed 40 tons per acre. Fires will not spread in the brush during the season of rapid new growth, but they build quickly into high-intensity fires at other times. Mild, slow-moving fires are not feasible, consequently controlled burning is usually difficult and costly. A special technique of burning has been designed to made such projects more manageable by taking advantage of the convective forces underlying the firestorm, as described in Chapter 7.

Some weeks or months prior to burning, a bulldozer or other heavy equipment is used to mash down a portion of the standing brush throughout the area to be treated. This increases the proportion of dead material in the fuel. The same result is often produced by application of dessicants or herbicides to the area. On the day selected for the burning, fires are set simultaneously or in quick succession in a grid pattern close enough together that they will soon interact (Fenner, Arnold, and Buck, 1955). As the individual fires merge, violent convection with fire whirls and a firestormlike effect is created. In the absence of a strong wind, a strong, single convection column is formed with embers going to a great height. The fire burns clean with a blowtorchlike intensity but with little threat to adjoining areas. Three factors operate to hold the fire within bounds: first, most embers cool before reaching the ground; second, the moisture content of the natural complex of live and dead fuels will not support fire spread independently; third, convective forces minimize the exposure of outside fuels to the heat energy generated.

There are both advantages and disadvantages to the method. The chief advantages are already implied. Narrower firebreaks and less reserve manpower and equipment add up to lower costs for control of the burn area (as compared to the cost of the precautions necessary when fire will run freely in the brush cover). Of perhaps even greater importance, the threat to property outside the treated area is much reduced. Some of the disadvantages are that costs are generally high because careful pretreatment and planning, including special provision for simultaneous or near-simultaneous ignition, are necessary. As in the Australian method, accurate evaluation of burning conditions and reliable prediction of fire behavior are necessary.

Center Firing

Center firing consists of firing in such a way that a strong convection column is created at or near the center of the area to be burned. When heavy, high-energy fuels such as logging slash are burned, the convection column tends to stabilize once it is formed and to act as a chimney toward which ascending warm air in its vicinity is drawn. The burner can hasten the formation of the convection column and influence its location by the sequence and location of ignitions in the area to be treated. In fact, though convection is the primary force the burner seeks to direct in this technique, the chief means of doing so is through the timing and sequence of ignitions. This is significant as well in the strip and edge firing which follow in this section. All three might well be termed sequential methods of firing. Techniques of this kind are practiced when backfiring is skillfully employed as a fire control measure as well as in prescribed burning.

Center firing is commonly employed on level areas and on slopes up to 20 percent. A cluster of fires is started in the center of the prepared area and allowed to spread until the rapid release of heat energy induces an active convection column. In areas larger than about 10 acres, a second series of fires is then started 50 to 100 feet in from the outer edge. These fires merge, are drawn toward the hotter fire in the center, and slowly back out to the extreme outer edges of the area. Steps in the application of this method are diagrammatically illustrated in Figure 18.2. Through center firing, smoke, heat, and sparks are drawn toward the center. This makes it easier for men to work around the edges and also reduces the likelihood of spot fires occurring outside. Because of the strong convec-

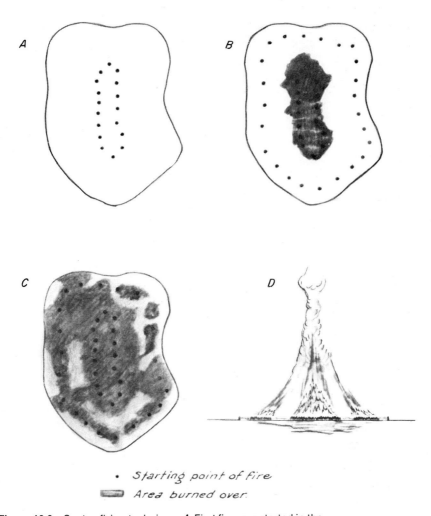

• *Starting point of fire*

▨ *Area burned over.*

Figure 18.2 Center-firing technique. *A.* First fires are started in the center of the area. *B.* Fires in the center are united, and a second series of fires is started near the outer edge. *C.* Inner and outer fires begin to merge, and fire slowly backs to outer edge of area. *D.* Cross-section view of *C* showing smoke and flame drawn toward center.

tion toward the center, fires will not run toward the outer edge. The column of rising hot air and gases in the center acts as a stabilizer, preventing rapid outward spread. Wind velocities toward the center of from 8 to 10 miles an hour caused entirely by the fire have been observed along the edges of center-fired areas.

Strip Firing

Firing in progressive strips is necessary on slopes greater than about 20 percent. The method is diagrammatically illustrated in Figure 18.3. The procedure closely parallels the technique in use of head fire illustrated in Figure 18.1D. The significant difference is that head-fire burning does not depend on using the convection column as a part of the control. Differences in topography, burning conditions, and the risks being taken further differentiate the methods. This will be discussed in the sections following on current burning practices in different forest regions. The first fires are set along the extreme upper edge. As soon as the upper edge is well burned out, a second strip or band of fires is started 100 to 200 feet down the slope, which burns up to and joins the upper strip. It is usually desirable to start the fires lower on the slope in the center of the area than near the edges, so the chevron pattern may be adopted. This is to help draw smoke and heat away from the sides. The process is successively repeated until the entire area is burned over, the last series of fires being set along the lower edge of the prepared area. Strip firing promotes even burning of the entire area and at the same time avoids release of too much heat energy at any one time, which might induce violent fire whirls or firestorm effects endangering outside areas.

Edge Firing

This consists of starting fires along the outer edge of an area and letting them spread toward the center. The method is applicable on small areas of an acre or two in light to moderate fuels or as an auxiliary to strip and center firing on larger areas. It may be partially used to fire small gulches that are included in larger areas separately. These gulches should be fired along their upper slopes on both sides in the chevron pattern, the fire backing down into the gulch on both sides simultaneously. This helps to prevent runs or fire whirls which might scatter embers outside the area to be treated. The firing of large areas or even small areas of high-energy fuels from the edges is unsafe, since dangerous runs against one side may develop. There is no strong central convection as in the case of center firing, or natural updraft as in the case of strip burning on slopes, to direct and stabilize fire spread. Smoke and sparks have a tendency to blow outside the broadcast-burned area, making fire control difficult. However, such difficulties are often met by use of the principle of center firing. Fires are set well inside the edge and permitted to build up strong convection before the edge is fired.

A combination of center-, strip-, and edge-firing methods involving both backfire and head-firing techniques can often be employed to

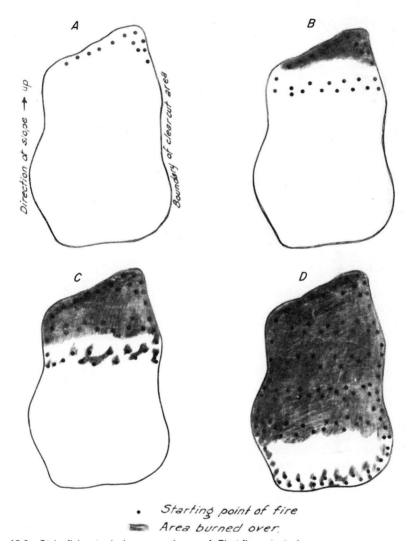

•   *Starting point of fire*

▬   *Area burned over.*

Figure 18.3 Strip-firing techniques on slopes. *A.* First fires started along extreme upper edge of area. *B.* Second series of fires started 100 to 200 feet down the slope as soon as the upper edge is well burned out. *C.* Third strip of fires started. *D.* Final fires started along lower edge of area.

advantage in a single area. Each gulch, knoll, slope, and change of fuel type presents an individual problem of technique that must be accurately appraised for burning. The sequence in which ignitions are made is always a very important determinant of how the prescribed fire behaves. The success of results depends heavily on the judgment of the man in charge of the burning.

PLANNING PRESCRIBED BURNING PROJECTS

Control of fire in prescribed burning has the advantage of being a planned rather than an emergency activity. It also offers full opportunity to take advantage of what is known about fire behavior and the changes to be expected from variations in fire weather or fire danger. Skillfully applied, it is a more carefully planned and more sophisticated activity than the control of unwanted fires. But to attain this status, at least three steps are always required. These are an evaluation of need, selection of areas to be treated, and preparation of areas selected for burning.

Evaluation of Need

Determining whether there is need to use fire is naturally the first step. This should consist of a clear and accurate appraisal of purposes and objectives and the degree to which they might be advanced by use of fire. To be conclusive, such an appraisal should be supported by the results of experimental burning in representative test areas. It should also include a comparison of benefits that might be expected from other possible procedures. If benefits appear favorable to use of fire, it is helpful if they can be related to possible offsetting damages in monetary terms. This enables determination of the net benefit it is reasonable to expect. Because some uncertainty is inherent to most use of fire, it should not be employed unless there is a clear showing of substantial benefits to be gained from it. This may well include the demonstration value of results on test areas.

In appraising benefits to forest land management, priorities in use of the land must be taken into account. Where multiple use policies apply, several uses must often be considered in relation to fire effects. Timber, water, grazing, wildlife, and recreation uses often must be harmonized one with another and in varying order of priority. There is also need for coordination within a given use. For example, if a broadcast burn to reduce fuel hazards is to be carried out, it should be so timed and managed that it will not destroy established seedlings that will be hard to replace and that it will create a favorable seedbed at the proper time for successful natural or artificial seeding or for scheduled planting. Similarly, there is no point in broadcast burning an area and planting it to western white pine without providing for adequate and continuing protection against blister rust that can destroy the pine. This problem is so costly to solve that much of the blister rust control program in Idaho white pine has been abandoned. Range-land burning should not be done without provision for reseeding or other treatment that may be needed.

Next comes the question of cost. Practically nothing can be accomplished by fire that could not be done with complete safety by other means if cost did not need to be considered. Slash and other forest debris can be reduced to chips to avoid air pollution or taken out of the forest and burned in some safe place to reduce hazardous fuel volumes; seedbed preparation can be accomplished by mechanical means; competing hardwood understories can be poisoned or cut from good pine stands by hand; and undesirable brush can be mechanically removed from range lands. In some situations fire can do or aid in doing such things much more cheaply; sometimes it is the only economically practicable means. The total cost of using fire must, however, be fully faced. When the added cost of subsequent reburns or other necessary follow-up treatments are taken into account, it is frequently much more than realized.

Selection of Areas

Areas chosen should be those that show promise of substantial net benefits based on all available information. For example, California brush fields consist largely of species that depend on fire for regeneration. If replacement of the brush by a more productive or less hazardous cover is sought, it is obvious that burning alone can produce only limited and temporary benefits. To establish a forest cover or permanent range grasses in place of the brush species, the rapidly developing brush seedlings and sprouts must be killed by chemical or other treatment, the area must be planted or artificially seeded, and considerable follow-up for some years must be feasible. Research has demonstrated that only on certain selected sites will forest plantings be successful and only on certain other sites will it be feasible to establish permanent range grasses. Except at exorbitant conversion cost, the remainder will support only the existing type of brush cover.

In the flatwoods of the South, there is a high potential for damage when hazard-reduction burning is done for the first time in young pine stands. Prescribed burning for control of hardwoods in young pine pulpwood stands and for brown-spot control in longleaf pine are almost equally hazardous. This places a high premium on careful selection of areas where such treatment will currently pay best returns. Without such a process, based on sound criteria and field examination, net benefits easily convert to fire-caused deficits.

Preparation of Areas

Once a decision is made to use fire in a particular area, the next step is careful preparatory planning on the ground. This is the job of a fire technician. Basically, the need is to get the intensity and duration of heat needed to produce the desired results and to restrict fire to designated areas. Principal factors involved are (1) the combustible fuels, (2) topography, (3) weather, (4) firebreaks and barriers, and (5) ignition techniques. Coordination of these things requires thorough and detailed planning. As in a military action, once the fires are started, there is little opportunity to change general plans and dispositions, and often there is no turning back.

Major items to consider in preparation are the following:

1   Area and boundary selection. Areas must be selected and boundaries defined not only in accordance with treatment needs but with an eye to burning problems. Prevailing winds, topography, and fuels in the area to be treated and nearby must be appraised as they bear on probable intensity, rate, and direction of fire spread within the area and the possibilities and consequences of spread to nearby areas. Irregular boundaries almost always lead to difficulties in burning. The size of the unit to be treated must also be gauged in terms of what can be handled during a given burning period.

2   Firebreaks and other barriers. Since one requirement of successful prescribed burning is that the fire be contained within a predetermined area, means of containment must be given careful appraisal. All natural barriers within or near the area to be burned, such as ridges, swamps, or cover types of low flammability, should be identified and evaluated. Artificial barriers such as roads, power lines, and other breaks should be utilized fully where available. Additional firebreaks must be constructed where needed and surplus breaks need also to be taken into account in setting up the burning plan. In some situations, as in grass or light fuel types, little preparatory work is needed. Firing is sometimes done without prepared lines, the outer edge of the fire being controlled by water or trenching as the burning progresses in the same way as in direct attack in wildfire suppression. In some situations, as in the flatlands of the South, a single plowed line suffices; in mountainous areas and with heavy fuels, a much wider firebreak is needed. Snag felling and other special hazard-reduction work may be necessary. The need for constructing containment barriers must be met on an individual area basis; few general rules can be given.

3   Preparation of fuels. Sometimes, as in the South, no special preparation of fuels may be needed. In other areas, brush must be grubbed or mashed or killed by a herbicide on most of the area to be treated. Live or dead timber may need to be felled; fuels close to

important containment barriers may need to be moved back. In some situations, fuels may need to be windrowed where a hot broadcast burn is not wanted, and fuels may be otherwise consolidated in various ways to ensure the desired intensity and spread of the set fire.

4 Burning plan. A major insurance of success and safety in prescribed burning is skill in firing. A specific firing plan should be prepared defining when, where, how, and in what sequence fires are to be set. Here is where accurate knowledge of fire behavior with a particular combination of fuel, topography, and weather factors is put to the test. Control of the burning process depends on the burning technique selected and on the sequence of application. Usually a combination of several techniques is applied. The application of these techniques in representative areas is described later in this chapter.

5 Men and equipment. Crews and firing equipment needed for the actual burning must be provided. Additional men and equipment often must be organized and kept in readiness either on or near the area on a standby basis. The operation as a whole is organized in the same general way as in wildfire suppression, with clear lines of organization and authority and a fire boss in full charge.

Determining When to Burn

Determining when to burn is nearly always crucial to the success of the undertaking. This may involve selection of the year to burn; selection of the proper stage in the growing cycle, which means the proper season of the year; and finally selection of the times when favorable weather and fuel moisture conditions prevail. Determination of the best year is usually accomplished through analysis of the need, as already described; selection of the best time of the year is usually resolved by use of trial burns. Selection of the most favorable burning conditions for carrying out the operation is highly exacting and can seldom be done very many days in advance. Usually weather and fuel moisture conditions within a narrow range are sought. This is often exceeded by the usual range of diurnal variation, so that each day becomes a distinct burning period during which a project or project unit must be completed.

Selection of burning conditions is complicated by the need to avoid creating or aggravating air pollution problems. Stable air conditions make it much easier to control a prescribed fire but may result in creating heavy and persistent drift smoke. As stated in Chapter 10, a skilled fire weather forecaster can identify and forecast local atmospheric conditions which do not favor erratic behavior of set fires but do favor the complete dissipation of the smoke they generate. Such service is so valuable that a mobile forecasting unit is well justified on all large or costly prescribed burning projects.

A very important corollary provision is that of determining any peculiarities of diurnal airflow at the burning site that result from local topography and cover or that are inherent in atmospheric conditions at a particular time. The fire weather forecaster can usually determine the latter to an acceptable degree of accuracy, but several days of observation and study at the site may be required to establish the local patterns of airflow created by topography and cover that need also to be taken into account (Shroeder and Buck, 1970). Advance observation and measurement of these local interrelationships is often very important to the success of prescribed burning projects in high-energy fuels.

Information on the state of fuel moisture may be assembled in several ways. Danger ratings (Chapter 8) are useful and are applied as a general guide as to when and where not to burn, but often they do not sufficiently define precisely when to burn. The moisture content of calibrated fuel moisture sticks continues to be valuable for this purpose. Use of daily weather forecasts is necessary to avoid unstable burning conditions and to take advantage of desirable burning periods. Prevailing wind direction and information on wind profiles is often especially important. One of the frustrations of prescribed burning is to be organized and ready to burn, with men and equipment on the ground, only to encounter unfavorable burning conditions because of an unexpected change in the weather. A danger of prescribed burning is the temptation, when all set to go, of starting the burning job when weather and fuel conditions are not suitable. This can result in an expensive fizzle if fuels are too wet or excessive damage and possible spread to adjacent areas if too dry or windy. Fluctuations in burning conditions further emphasize the need for localized fire weather forecasting and careful advance planning and organization; one must be ready to take advantage without delay of desirable burning periods, which often are all too few.

Execution of Burning

Good execution of prescribed burning is an art to a large degree. Sound planning and preparation will do much of the job, and if everything goes according to schedule, the actual burning operation is uneventful, even routine. But things often do not go according to schedule; fuel or weather conditions may not be quite right or may change during the course of burning. There are gradations and variations in fuel types and topographic situations that cannot be foreseen in planning but which must be appraised on the ground, often very quickly. There is no substitute for skill and experience in the execution of prescribed burning; the experienced judgment of dedicated personnel is an essential that cannot be imparted in any textbook or manual.

Not the least requirement is courage to wield the torch and stay with the job in the face of current setbacks or seeming danger. This requires confidence in men, equipment, preparation, and firing techniques combined with thorough knowledge of fire behavior. There have been instances where a successful job was not accomplished because the man in charge lost his nerve at seeing a temporary flareup and became excessively concerned with the suppression of a few spot fires and breakovers instead of going ahead with the burning schedule. Brash overconfidence and recklessness based on lack of experience and sound judgment are equally undesirable.

Follow-up after Burning

Follow-up to gain the benefits contemplated in the selection of each area is of the utmost importance but is frequently neglected in planning. Use of fire is usually only a step in a sequence of wild-land management operations. This must be kept in perspective. Further use of fire may be indicated, lands may have to be seeded or planted, and various cultural or other management practices may have to be applied to obtain the full benefit of a land-management program in which a prescribed burn may be only a beginning step. Use of fire is not an end in itself.

PRESCRIBED BURNING PRACTICES

Field practice as described more specifically in four different forest environments will serve to illustrate how varied purposes of prescribed burning may be served by selection of burning conditions, adaptation of burning techniques, and preparation of the area to be treated.

Western White Pine Type

Prescribed burning as developed and applied in the western white pine type of northern Idaho and western Montana is illustrative of use of fire in heavy fuels and on slopes (Beaufait, 1966). The area is mountainous and characterized by rather short, steep slopes with timber stands extending over the ridgetops. Timber stands are generally dense. Figure 18.4 portrays the nature of much of the country. Topographic and stand conditions are generally similar to those in the Douglas-fir type of the Pacific Northwest. What is said about white pine is generally applicable to Douglas-fir, in which considerable broadcast burning is done for essentially similar reasons.

Purposes of Burning   Prescribed burning has been employed in the western white pine type principally (1) to reduce excessive fuel volumes

Figure 18.4   Topography typical of the western white pine type of northern Idaho. Coeur d'Alene National Forest. *(Courtesy photo section Washington National Guard.)*

in timber stands killed by fire, and (2) to dispose of large quantities of slash and defective or otherwise unmerchantable timber remaining after logging in certain kinds of stands.

The first, it is hoped, is a transitory problem. As extensive and hazardous fuel types are broken up into smaller areas, fuel volumes are reduced, and further occurrence of large fires is prevented, the need for such work is correspondingly reduced. While extensive areas were burned for fuel reduction purposes in the past (Chapter 10), little of this kind of work has been done in recent years.

The second is also in part a transitory problem. In old-growth stands, there is often a substantial volume of defective and unmerchantable live timber which, if left standing after logging, will occupy the site and prevent the establishment and growth of trees of desired species and quality. Because of the large volume of this material and of logging slash, sometimes the only practical thing to do is remove everything merchantable, fell the rest, and broadcast-burn to clear the site and permit regeneration of the area either naturally or artificially. Most broadcast burning has been and is done in such situations. As old-growth stands are cut over and vigorous young stands established in their place, and as more intensive utilization is practiced, the need for such work will diminish accordingly. Clear cutting appears, however, to have a permanent place in western white pine silviculture, since the type is subclimax in nature (Chapter 2). Where clear cutting is practiced, prescribed burning has been a natural corollary. With increasing concern by the public for the esthetics of the forest environment, burning practices can be expected to come under increasing restraint. Alternative methods to use of fire need to be carefully considered in preliminary analysis and planning for that reason. Where prescribed burning appears to be essential, ways to minimize air pollution and other detrimental effects will continue to increase in importance.

Area Selection and Fire Barriers   Good selection and layout of the particular area to be treated contribute greatly toward the success of the project. The following items are important:

1   Though the blister-rust control program has largely been abandoned in Idaho white pine, preference may be given to areas that are a natural blister-rust control unit or logical portion of one.

2   Units need to be designed to be burned out completely in a single burning period. Formerly these might be as large as 200 acres. In more recent practice they are less than 100 acres.

3   The boundaries should be as regular as possible. Sharp turns, long fingers, and deep indentations always make for trouble in fire control and at the same time often cause an irregular burn and unsatisfactory combustion of fuels.

4   Where an area extends to the top of or near the top of a ridge, the burning area should be extended just over the top of the ridge. This avoids scorching timber and facilitates fire control. It is often necessary to bound an area only part way up a slope. This can be done but offers control difficulties. It must be kept in mind that fires have a strong propensity for running to the top of the ridge.

5   In treating one side only of a narrow canyon, it is best not to extend the treated area close to the bottom because hot fires are likely to spot across and run up the other side.

6   In laying out the area, full advantage should be taken of available fire barriers such as roads, streams, ridgetops, clearings, natural openings, and natural cover types of low flammability.

7   A firebreak approximately 20 feet wide, cleared of all logs and branches but not the natural duff, should be constructed around the area except where natural firebreaks are available. It should be emphasized, however, that control in burning is based more on good preparation,

favorable fuel and weather conditions, and skillful execution of firing techniques than on firebreaks. No comparatively narrow break, 20 or even 50 feet in width, will stop a fast-moving fire in heavy fuels. Firebreaks are best constructed by bulldozers.

8 A fire trench dug to mineral soil within the firebreak is seldom needed completely around the area. Fire trench should be constructed before burning only in areas where the need is definitely apparent, as in areas of heavy duff and rotten wood.

Preparation for Burning Attempts to burn standing timber are seldom successful except in special instances where an initial surface fire is allowed to sweep through an area to kill live timber, with a second and major cleanup fire following a few years later. Except in special circumstances, all standing timber, dead or alive, should be felled. The purpose of felling is to concentrate the material to be removed so that it will be consumed. Trees and snags should ordinarily be felled up and down the slope, and crossing of logs should be avoided. Felling is best accomplished by means of power chain saws. The cost of felling work by contract is usually substantially less than when crews are directly hired.

It is usually worthwhile to lop limbs from the top side of felled trees lying within about 50 feet of the outer edge of the area and to do some slash bunching along the edge. This makes fires easier to start and promotes consumption of fuels along the edges, where the greatest difficulty in getting a sufficiently hot fire is usually experienced. Lopping and occasionally some bunching of slash should also be done where a hot fire is not anticipated, as in moist bottoms and in areas of low fuel volume. Lopping and bunching is not necessary in areas with high fuel volume. More lopping and bunching is needed with hemlock fuels than with other species since hemlock is of relatively low flammability. Lopping is expensive and should not be done unless the need is manifest.

Snags standing outside the area within a distance of at least 75 to 100 feet should be felled. Where fire control difficulties are anticipated, as in saddles at the head of gulches or on exposed slopes, snag felling should be extended 200 feet, or sometimes an even greater distance, beyond the area to be burned. Standing snags outside the area are one of the principal hazards in burning; they are readily ignited by flying sparks even when ground fuels are too damp to ignite.

When to Burn Problems of timing the burn both in relation to cutting and in relation to the fire season need to be resolved. Formerly three to five years were permitted to elapse between felling the residual stand and burning. This was intended to ensure complete germination of

Ribes seed and maximum subsequent destruction of the resulting seedlings by burning. This practice caused undesirable delay in reducing extreme fuel hazards and has been largely discontinued.

The second problem is the particular time to burn within the season selected. This necessitates careful evaluation of weather, fuel, and safety factors. Hard and fast rules are not possible since much depends on judgment. Fire danger ratings and fire weather forecasts, including stability of the atmosphere, are indispensable (Chapter 5). The fall is normally the best season in which to burn, although it is also feasible at times to burn during the summer.

Burning in the spring is seldom successful or desirable. While the finer fuels and the outside of branch wood and logs may be dry, the interior of the heavier fuels is usually too wet to burn satisfactorily. It is consequently difficult to eliminate more than the finer fuels. Once a fire has covered an area and consumed these fuels, it is almost impossible to get a satisfactory fuel reduction by a second fire except during midsummer when burning may be too hazardous to be attempted. Another objection to spring burning is that deep duff is quite prevalent in this type in which fires may hang over for weeks and break out at an inopportune time during the summer.

The aim is to have a combination of weather and fuel conditions such that fire will spread readily and burn hard in the treated area while at the same time fuels outside are too damp to ignite from sparks. No wind at all is preferable, but winds up to about 5 miles per hour are tolerable. These conditions are most nearly realized during the latter part of the day and evening of a calm clear day, two or three days after the first fall rain of about 1 inch. At such a time, the concentrated and more or less compacted fuels in the treated area, which have been dried out during the summer, are still comparatively dry, while the moisture content of the duff and fine surface fuels outside the area is too high for them to be readily ignited by sparks and embers. Under such conditions, very hot fires can be permitted with almost complete safety. Special fire weather forecasts are of material aid. In general, firing should not be started in the morning hours since burning conditions during the day may change markedly.

The fuel volume also has an important bearing on the timing of burning. Heavy fuel concentrations will generate sufficient heat to burn satisfactorily even though they are partially green or damp from recent rains. Actually, the greater the fuel concentration, the more safely an area can be burned, since burning can be done when the burning index is low. Fine scattered fuels, on the contrary, must be burned when they are relatively dry and the burning index is consequently high, or else the fire will not spread and consume the fuels satisfactorily. Green timber can be felled in the spring and early summer and burned the same fall provided about 60 days of good drying weather elapses.

Protection problems must also be taken into account. If the surrounding area offers a high fuel hazard, conditions must be very favorable to get a satisfactory reduction of fuels and at the same time avoid the spread of fire outside the prepared area. Within limits of safety, however, the drier the better. It is much easier to direct the spread of fire when the fuels are dry since fires can be started readily and their direction of spread can be more accurately gauged.

Burning Methods Although good preparation, favorable weather, and suitable fuel conditions contribute greatly to the success and safety of controlled burning, much depends on skillful direction of the actual burning. For the most part, the sequential methods of firing are employed, starting with the leeward and ridgetop locations and then working downhill or into the wind. Much of the burning could be described as strip firing or back burning though it is more complex in execution, since the timing of each set in relation to those in other parts of the area is the critical factor. In an area of irregular topography of several hundred acres scheduled to be burned in one operation, the proper placement and timing of ignitions throughout the area becomes very much an art. The fire boss must have continuous radio contact with each crew and independent torch man and must be able to observe the progress of the burn. In basins and flats, center firing is commonly used. Edge firing in these fuels is considerably modified and begins well inside control lines to create convection that will tend to pull flames in, as in center firing. A detailed burning plan is necessary, with a planned sequence of ignitions based on fuels, topography, and expected fire behavior.

Figure 18.5*A* to *D*, illustrates the progression in this type when prescribed burning is employed. As described in the caption, a varying residual stand of old-growth defective trees, usually white fir and hemlock, often remains after all merchantable material has been removed. All must be felled in the area to be treated. This requires expensive preparation of the area for burning. But burning results in greatly reduced fire hazards and vigorous young growth on the area. This is closely paralleled by the patch cutting practices in old-growth Douglas-fir in the Pacific Northwest.

Pine Flatwoods of the Southern United States

Fire has had a long history in the piney woods of the South (Chapters 2, 9, 10, and 17). Wildfires have been a major factor in type formation, and fire

Figure 18.5 Prescribed burning in the western white pine type to dispose of slash and unmerchantable timber, Coeur d'Alene National Forest, Idaho. *A.* Stand before felling (unmerchantable at the time of treatment). *B.* After felling, ready to burn. *C.* After burning. *D.* Vigorous planted white pine 11 years after burning. *(U.S. Forest Service photos.)*

has been used deliberately for many years. Attention in this case is centered on prescribed use of fire in the longleaf–slash pine types, with some consideration given to loblolly pine intermixtures. The loblolly and shortleaf types offer somewhat different problems. Frequently both are in admixture with valuable hardwoods. Consequently they offer less net benefits from prescribed burning and are only partially considered here. Prescribed burning is done in relatively fine natural fuels. It was first accepted as a part of forest management in the flatwoods of the South only but has progressively extended into pine areas of the piedmont through use of the chevron burning technique. This is in contrast to the preceding discussion of burning practices in western white pine, which dealt with heavy volumes of felled timber and logging slash fuels mostly on steep slopes.

Purposes of Burning   In the southern pine region, use of fire by the landowner serves a variety of purposes which may be placed in two general categories. The first is to reduce the severity of the fire control problem; the second is to facilitate some phase of management of wildland resources. The first is usually referred to as hazard reduction or rough reduction.

Hazard Reduction   Natural surface and understory fuels consisting of living and dead herbaceous vegetation, forest litter, palmetto, brush species such as gallberry, and wax myrtle accumulate in pine stands and are collectively termed the *rough* (Chapter 4, Figure 4.4). As much as 25 tons of fine fuels may be accumulated per acre. Potential rates of spread are high in such stands, and very destructive wildfires often occur when this rough has been unburned for a number of years. Depending on stand conditions, the accumulations of rough become a serious threat after six to eight years and sometimes sooner. Rather than risk a destructive wildfire, it is often considered desirable to reduce this rough periodically during the winter by prescribing burning at times when a minimum of damage will result. The most frequent repetition is required in natural woodlands where palmetto, gallberry, and other flammable understory species are abundant. In pine plantations where the soil was not disturbed prior to planting, the rough may be almost equally troublesome. In many of the more recent pulpwood plantings, site preparation includes grubbing out the understory species. Where this is done, requirements for rough reduction are at a minimum. In addition to reduction of tree damage from wildfire, a particular purpose is sometimes to protect naval-stores operations. Trees with working faces are highly flammable, and wildfires easily kill or ruin such trees for gum production and entail much loss in installed equipment. The primary purpose of perhaps 80 percent of the prescribed burning in the flatwoods of the South is hazard reduction.

Wildland Management   The second category of purposes is that of using fire as a tool in facilitating resource management. More than one purpose may be served by a prescribed burn. The six given are not exclusive but illustrate the scope of potential uses in this particular environment.

   1   *Control of undesirable hardwoods and shrubs.* With increasingly effective protection from wildfires, there is a natural tendency for hardwood trees of low value and for shrubs and palmetto to invade pine stands or prevent the establishment of pine. The need for such control is highly variable. The hardwood problem is usually most pressing in loblolly mixtures, but there is also much brush encroachment in long-leaf–slash pine types. Fire is used primarily because of its low cost.
   2   Seedbed Preparation. Natural regeneration of all the southern pines, longleaf especially, is benefited by exposure of mineral soil. In many situations, reduction of vegetative cover is necessary to get satisfactory natural seeding. Fire can be a means of doing this cheaply. It is even more important in preparing seedbeds for broadcast seeding. Since successful methods of protecting the seed from birds and rodents have developed, it has become a part of the prescription for large broadcast seeding projects. It is commonly applied in advance of planting as well.
   3   Improving Forage for Livestock. As brought out in Chapter 17 (Hughes et al., 1966), burning can increase the abundance, availability, palatability, and nutrient content of spring forage in the woods and has been widely applied for this purpose. In one form of management, plantations are established with trees widely spaced. For the intervening years required for the trees to fully occupy the site, it is managed to produce maximum forage for livestock, including use of prescribed fire.
   4   Reducing Brown-spot Needle Disease. Applies mainly in long-leaf pine when seedlings are in the grass stage.
   5   Improving Access and Visibility. A factor in naval-stores production, hunting, timber marking, and logging.
   6   Improving Game Habitat. Food and cover conditions for upland game birds can be improved and hardwood sprouts for deer browse increased by prescribed burning (Cushwa, 1969).

   The first four are the main silvicultural purposes, their relative importance varying widely from area to area. The next is a general purpose that people often hold as a reason for setting fires but is seldom if ever a primary justification of fire use. Use of fire for game improvement is a limited application in timbered areas. It is, however, important for the reason that it has popular acceptance and is the excuse given by many for setting fires.

A single prescribed burn may serve two or more purposes. Any program of prescribed burning should be based on consideration of both fire control and silvicultural objectives and the total management needs of the stand or forest.

Area Selection and Fire Barriers Specific areas should be selected for treatment, with purposes, burning methods, and containment problems clearly in mind. If burning is to be done for hazard-reduction purposes, areas should be located so as to get the maximum protection benefit possible with respect to probable origin of wildfires, normal direction of spread, and age and volume of rough. Protection strategy of forest units as a whole should be considered. It is often possible to distribute areas to be burned in roughly a checkerboard fashion so that the areas treated will serve as wild barriers to protect the rest and avoid the necessity of burning large solid blocks. Where silvicultural purposes are involved, close attention to detail is necessary to identify which areas are in need of treatment and what kind of burning technique will best serve the purpose.

Whatever the purpose, care should be taken to identify and exclude areas that should not be burned. Full advantage should also be taken of existing barriers such as roads, swamps, and areas of low flammability such as fields, recent burns, and the like.

Firebreaks should be constructed as needed, with the burning techniques to be employed in mind. A single plowed line exposing from 4 to 6 feet of mineral soil, constructed by a fire plow without any supplemental clearing, is normally sufficient. These lines should be constructed as close to the time of burning as possible, usually within a week. Lines plowed three weeks, or sometimes even two weeks, before burning can become covered with needles or leaves to a degree that reduces their effectiveness. Lines should be so spaced that the area to be burned can be broken up into units, each of which can be covered in a seven- to eight-hour period. This is an application of the same principle stressed in white pine burning practice; do not leave unburned areas within a burning unit from one day to the next. The spacing of the lines depends on the method of burning and rate of spread expected. For example, if the fire is to be backed against the wind, is estimated to spread at the rate of about 85 feet an hour, and a seven-hour day is assumed, the lines should be spaced about 600 feet apart at right angles to the prevailing wind so that the distance can be covered in one burning day. The ends of the strips must be tied in to natural barriers or firebreaks.

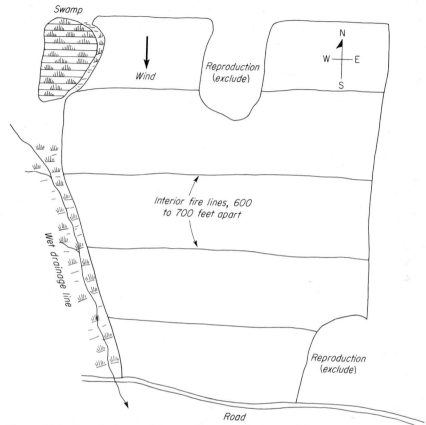

Figure 18.6 Sample firebreak layout for prescribed use of fire in southern pine.

A typical firebreak layout is shown in Figure 18.6. It is assumed here that the fire will be backed against the wind, and the parallel interior lines are spaced accordingly. In burning this area, the first strip of fires would be set along the road. When this edge is safe, fires would be set along the windward side of the interior lines, progressively working northward against the wind. If burning is to be done with the wind, the interior lines can be more widely spaced or even dispensed with, since the rate of spread is greater and firing is often done in progressive strips, each burning into the strip previously burned.

Special preparation of fuels for burning as in western slash areas, is not necessary. Southern pine burning is much simpler in this respect.

It is usually desirable practice to map areas for possible prescribed burning treatment in some detail. Depending on circumstances and need, such a map and written material keyed to it should show or include the following:

1   Roads and other means of access
2   Areas to be burned and those excluded from burning, the latter shown down to the smallest size it is economical to protect in burning
3   Age of rough and general fuel conditions for all areas to be burned and for associated areas
4   Purpose or purposes of burning by areas, that is, for hazard reduction, seedbed preparation, and so forth
5   Burning procedure recommended, including month and year to burn, weather conditions, and firing techniques
6   Existing firebreaks and layout of plowed firebreaks needed
7   Burning crew and equipment needs, especially if there are some special features or problems

When to Burn   As with western white pine slash, there are two separate problems of timing to meet in deciding when to burn. The first is selection of the proper year from the standpoint of the best time to accomplish the desired purposes. The second is selection of the specific season, day, and time of day.

Selection of Year   For hazard reduction, the work should be done when the fuels in the rough build up to what is adjudged to be a hazardous level. The probable sources of fires and the nature of control problems have to be appraised to determine probable damage to the stand from accidental burning. No consistent timetable can be given. Burning for fire control reasons may be done at three- to six-year intervals or longer. In practice, it is not usually done more than every four or five years for this purpose only.

For seedbed preparation, both the timing of seed crops and the need for natural regeneration must be considered and related to cutting schedules. Burning usually should precede seed fall or seeding as closely as possible. An exception is a situation in which seed consumption by birds may be excessive in exposed, freshly burned areas. A six- to eight-month growth of grass and other vegetation following burning may be desirable to help hide the seed. Germination and seedling establishment are best in a fresh burn or a one-year rough. The beneficial effect of burning diminishes rapidly after one year and is mostly gone after three years. Burning for regenerative purposes is not a recurrent need; once a new stand is established or stocking built up to a desirable density, no further effort in this direction should be needed for a considerable period of time.

For reduction of undesirable hardwoods or understory species, burning has to be timed both in relation to their treatment and to damage to the pines. Except for established longleaf seedlings in the grass stage, pine stands seldom can be burned without excessive damage if an important part consists of trees less than 6 to 8 feet in height. Hardwood trees and brushy stems up to about 2 inches in diameter can usually be killed without undue damage to pine which has attained 6 inches or more in diameter. Both killing and sprouting of hardwoods are also related to the season of the year; damage is normally greatest during the height of the growing season and least during dormancy. Tolerances between how much heat is necessary to reduce encroaching species and how much a given pine stand can endure are often close and require skilled judgment on the ground. No general rules can be given. From a timing standpoint, the need is to schedule burning at that stage of stand development when major benefits can be obtained with minimum damage.

For reduction of brown-spot disease on longleaf pine, it is necessary to select a time when the disease is seriously in need of checking and the trees can stand the treatment. This requires careful diagnosis on the ground.

Selection of Season and Specific Time   The second general problem of timing is to select the season of the year, specific days, and time of day when burning can best be done. This is a job for the fire technician.

Winter is the best time, the burning season extending from middle or early December to about March 1. Summer burning can and has been done to get a hotter fire to kill hardwoods (Riebold, 1955), but it is more dangerous and harder to handle than winter fires and is little practiced for this reason. Heavy accumulation of rough cannot safely be reduced by summer fires.

Specific weather conditions are sought. A steady, northerly wind of from 3 to 10 miles per hour is best. Burning is seldom done without a wind. A north winter wind is preferred because it is the least variable in the southern coastal plain area. These conditions are best realized one to three days after a rain. The combination of a steady wind and low enough fuel moisture for the fire to spread readily is a critical need. Another critical factor (Chapter 3) is internal temperatures of the cambium layer in tree stems. This may lag behind changes in air temperature. Optimum air temperature, relative humidity, and fuel moisture depend on the kind of fire desired. For fuel reduction using backfires, which is done in the winter, air temperature should be below 60°F, relative humidity above about 50 percent, and fuel moisture from eight up to about 20 percent. For hardwood reduction, a hotter fire, higher temperatures, and lower humidities and fuel moisture content are utilized. Optimum and acceptable temperatures, relative humidity, and fuel moisture can be defined only by specified areas, fuels, and burning objectives. Much remains to be learned.

Based on experience, there are from 45 to 60 possible burning days in an average winter season. Burning should not be attempted before an impending storm because of the likelihood of sudden and unpredictable changes in wind. Good daily local weather forecasts are indispensable. It is good practice to check burning conditions by use of small test fires.

Daylight burning is best, starting fires at about 10 A.M. and continuing operations until about 6 P.M. Night burning is more costly and not so reliable as daytime burning under good conditions. The wind may die down, resulting in high scorching, since the hot gases are not dissipated by the wind but rise upward. When dew falls, the fuel edge burns unevenly and parts of the fire go out; the fire may not burn to the control line, and conditions may be dangerous the following day. Supervision is also more difficult at night; men may lose direction and make mistakes (Hartman, 1949).

Burning Methods   The technical objective in burning is to get just enough heat to do the job. For fuel reduction, brown-spot disease control, seedbed preparation, and grazing improvement, the aim is to consume fuels. Fire intensity is kept as low as is consistent with desired fuel consumption. For hardwood control, the aim is to get enough heat to kill undesired living trees, not to consume them.

Factors controlling fuel consumption and heat are wind, fuels, fuel moisture, and kind of fire used. Fuel, fuel moisture, and wind can be regulated only by selecting the right season, day, and time of day as described above. The burner can, however, dictate the kind of fire used, which is his major immediate control. This is done through employment of the head fire, flank fire, backfire, or chevron burning techniques already described. Head fires spread more rapidly and are hotter at least 18 inches or more above the ground than backfires. Evidence by Lindenmuth and Byram (1948) suggests that head fires may, however, be cooler near the ground. Head fires are often set in progressive strips 25 to 100 feet in width, working against the wind. Each strip burns with the wind into the previously burned area (Riebold, 1955; Silker, 1955). Head fires are necessary where fuels are too light, scattered, or moist to spread against the wind and do the desired job. Backfires spread more slowly and the flames are kept nearer the ground, with a consequently lower scorch line on trees. They are the most frequently used; the major exception is in hardwood control, where greater heat and higher scorch is desired. Flank fires are intermediate in heat production but harder to apply.

Men and Equipment   Experienced and dependable men who know when and when not to burn are the prime requisite for successful burning. The work is done by small crews of three to five men, with a foreman in charge. This man must be thoroughly familiar with the purposes of burning, location of firebreaks, the firing plan, and fire behavior. It is desirable that he participate in planning and preparation.

In conducting the actual burning, the men do not work closely together but spread out, firing different strips according to the burning schedule. If things go right, the job is mainly setting fires. Close patrol must be given, however, to detect breakovers and spot fires; usually the foreman is primarily responsible for this. The work must be done at low cost per acre to be practicable. Five men can burn up to 1,500 acres a day if conditions are right, but normally they will burn between 500 and 1,000 acres.

Equipment needed is simple. Firing is usually done with drip backfiring torches. Fusees can also be used. A few backpack water pumps, rakes, or flaps should be on hand, and a plow unit or two should be readily available for emergencies.

Eastern Pine–Hardwoods

Past wildfires have had variable effects, good and bad, on the associations of pitch, shortleaf, pond, and loblolly pines, with hardwoods in the middle Atlantic area of the eastern United States. On the desirable side they have sometimes created conditions bringing about the establishment and maintenance of pine stands of good quality and stocking. Undesirably, and in conjunction with destructive cutting, they have created large areas supporting low-value mixtures of sprout oaks and stunted pitch and shortleaf pines. The so-called pitch pine plains of southern New Jersey (Lutz, 1934) are an outstanding example of an area reduced to almost total unproductivity, mostly by fire. With complete fire exclusion, ecological studies indicate that most of the present pine and pine-hardwood areas would eventually revert to hardwoods, of lower commercial value than the pines.

Economically feasible means of increasing the value of large areas of deteriorated pine and pine-hardwood stands in the general area of New Jersey has been the subject of much past research (Buell and Cantlon, 1953). This has demonstrated that prescribed burning offers such a means in selected areas, particularly in New Jersey and the eastern shore of

Maryland in the United States (Little, Allen, and Moore, 1948; Little, 1953; Little, Somes, and Allen, 1953; Little and Moore, 1953).

Purposes of Burning   As in the southern pine, purposes of burning fall into two groups, silvicultural and hazard reduction.

Silvicultural   Silvicultural purposes of burning center on regeneration and maintenance of seedling-origin pines. Pitch, shortleaf, and pond pines do not naturally reproduce satisfactorily on duff surfaces. Loblolly will reproduce in fairly heavy duff but also is favored by mineral soil surfaces. Duff accumulation in pine-hardwood mixtures greatly reduces the establishment of seedling pine. Fire is a cheap means of removing duff and exposing mineral soil. Planting without use of fire is also possible but more expensive and must be followed by aggressive hardwood control to free the pine.

Maintenance of pine in these stands can be strongly aided by fire. On swampy sites, a single but hot fire at the end of the rotation is sufficient to prepare a satisfactory seedbed for pine. If this fire is deep-burning, many of the competing hardwoods are eliminated. This requires burning during seasonal drought conditions of late summer or early fall. On dry sites, repeated light fires during the winter prepare seedbeds favoring natural reproduction of pine. They also check hardwood succession, but here they do so by consuming seed, eliminating small seedlings, and killing back larger hardwood stems that are usually less than 2 inches dbh. When properly used and timed, these light fires do not damage pines 3 inches dbh and larger. But where oaks or other hardwoods in mixture make up an important part of the future crop, much care must be exercised to avoid damaging fire scars on these trees.

In major outline, fire is useful in helping to check the succession to hardwoods and in preparing seedbeds for natural pine reproduction. Although one hot fire is adequate where it burns deep and destroys the dormant buds of hardwoods or where rapidly growing seedlings of loblolly pine are favored, periodic light fires are more effective on the drier sites. But both become complicated where a mixed pine-hardwood forest is to be maintained. Consequently, techniques must be planned in more detail and applied to much smaller units or subunits than in the pure pine stands of the South.

Hazard Reduction   These same periodic fires also reduce fuel accumulations and the chance of wildfire damage as well as facilitating the suppression of wildfires. As has been emphasized (Chapter 10), wildfires tend to breed more wildfires.

Periodic severe fires . . . promote a continuation of hazardous conditions by keeping the overwood open, while the stems killed from the last fire and the resulting sprouts of trees and shrubs accumulate. These in a few years build up a good vertical continuity of fuel leading to the tops of the tallest surviving pines . . . light winter fires, when properly used, reduce fuel continuity on the ground and favor a closed overwood. [Little, Allen, and Moore, 1948]

Several specific instances of fuel reduction accomplished by prescribed burning that were instrumental in controlling wildfire and in reducing damage are given by Moore, Smith, and Little (1955).

When to Burn As in the two previous discussions of regional practices, decision on when to burn must be based on proper selection of both the year and the specific season and time of day. The best year depends on the timing of desired regeneration, stand development, harvest-cutting practices, and fuel accumulations. Accurate knowledge of the silvicultural characteristics of individual pine and hardwood species, and of fire effects on them, is required, but this cannot be reviewed here. Here is where, as always, the prescription part of burning prominently enters the picture.

Prescribed burning is usually done in the winter, mostly from late December to the middle of March or a little later, depending on the season. Air temperatures below 50°F are desired. Burning is done with hardly any or with light steady winds (up to about 8 miles per hour under stands). Desirable fuel moisture content, which largely controls flammability, depends on the amount, arrangement, and composition of fuels and the heat intensity desired. Flammability should be just high enough for fires to spread readily and do the job prescribed (Little, Somes, and Allen, 1953). Burning index ratings (Chapter 8) are helpful in delimiting periods when burning can be safely and successfully done, but exactly when to burn depends on experienced judgment. Burning is done during daylight hours, or, under somewhat drier conditions, at night. Suitable burning days are all too few, about 20 to 40 occurring per season.

Burning Methods The same general principles of planning, area selection, and boundary determination used in the South also apply. Full use of natural boundaries is important to reduce the amount of control line that must be constructed.

Head fires are mostly employed on upland sites. The reasons are that they spread more rapidly, reduce cost by shorter burning time and less need for interior control lines, and cause less containment difficulty if the wind direction changes. They can also be used because surface fuels are mostly light and head fires are not too hot when properly timed. Backfires or flanking fires are sometimes employed where burning conditions are such that a head fire will be too severe or dangerous. Techniques of setting fires are much the same as in the South.

Burning must be done cheaply to be practicable, though burning units are usually small. Skill in tactical use of natural breaks, selection of the time to burn, and in application of burning techniques minimizes the chances of any wildfire developing. Nevertheless, good planning always ensures that sufficient men and equipment can be available to prevent escape of fire if it threatens to jump predetermined boundaries.

California Brushlands

Approximately 45 million acres of range land lies between the upper limits of the valley floor and the lower limits of commercial timber forests in the coast ranges and Sierra Nevada of California (Sampson and Burcham, 1954). These authors estimate that brush control may be needed and perhaps economically feasible on about 9 million acres of this area classified as follows:

Type of brush	Million acres
Woodland-grass	4.7
Woodland	1.4
Chaparral, minor conifer, and coastal sagebrush	3.3
Total	9.4

Soils are of all kinds, from deep and fertile to shallow and infertile. Slopes vary from level to very steep. "Brush" species occur in many associations, ranging from pure sagebrush to chaparral.

Existing brush cover is in part a natural stage in plant succession. On shallow, infertile soils, for example, foothill chaparral occurs as a pioneer species in soil development. In larger part, however—and no precise figures can be given—present abundance of brush is a result of past wildfires, timber cutting, and grazing practices. The brush problem of California is not limited to these range land areas. It is a critical problem in many conifer commercial timber areas, ponderosa pine especially.

Deliberate use of fire to improve range forage conditions in California brush lands is a practice of long standing. Before 1945 it was done with poorly defined legal sanction under a general fire permit statute and mostly on a haphazard "convenience" basis. State law specifically authorizing issuance of a burning permit for range improvement was enacted in 1945 and later amended. The present law (1957) is administered by the state forester and requires investigation on the ground. This is to enable the Division of Forestry to provide for additional fire protection for lands which may be endangered by brush-burning projects. It does not include supervision of the burning job or the supplying of fire control crews at the burning site. Since 1945, burning has been done on an increasingly systematic and scientific basis, and considerable research has been devoted to selection of area and burning problems. The work has been done mostly on privately owned lands on an expanding then diminishing scale. Area burned under permit totaled 50,424 acres in 1945, a high of 227,131 acres in 1954, then 149,043 acres in 1956, 128,430 acres in 1960, decreasing to 53,042 acres in 1968 (California Division of Forestry, 1968).

Purposes of Burning   As indicated, most brush-land burning is done to increase forage for domestic livestock. Big game, upland birds, and other wildlife are also benefited. In the northern coast ranges, about 18 percent of the permits and 12 percent of the area burned are primarily or wholly for game range improvement. There is increasing awareness among ranchers of hunting-right values. Controlled burning in brush and other areas is extensively practiced to reduce fuel hazards along highways. Hazard reduction employing fire has been applied on an area basis to a limited extent in brush-land areas to protect particular areas or improvements of high value, but it has not been extensively employed as a wild-land protection measure.

Legalized burning has substantially reduced the number of incendiary fires set for purposes of brush burning and the acreage so burned (Sampson and Burcham, 1954).

Selection of Areas   The underlying aim in selection of areas is to pick sites on which substantial and continuing range forage benefits can be obtained at reasonable cost without causing significant adverse effects to soil and water relationships. Further and essential conditions are that fire can be successfully applied and confined to the area to be treated.

Fulfilling these conditions is often difficult. It requires accurate plant, soil, and water data on relationships for a wide range of conditions, effectively integrated with knowledge of fire behavior and effects. Prescribed burning should not, and this fear is often expressed, be applied to gain a short-time forage gain at the expense of longer-range site deterioration. It must be remembered that the prevalence of brush, and especially on the better sites, is largely due to past wildfires as well as to ineffective or unwise timber-cutting and grazing practices. Further use of fire, under any name, should be aimed to rectify not aggravate any retrogression in resources.

Selection of the specific area is the responsibility of the land manager utilizing the best information available. The Soil-Vegetation Survey of the State of California is an excellent source of reliable information. The job is complex, and only the major considerations can be described.

Soil should be of sufficient depth and fertility to be capable of good forage production of desirable species. Good soils can be damaged by burning as much or more than poor soils. But on good soils the possibility of increased benefit is large enough that the cost of preventive measures can be borne and some short-term damage can be accepted. On sites with poor soils, the benefit potential is low and soil damage is likely to result in a long-term loss.

Degree of slope is especially important. On gentle slopes (0 to 30 percent), all methods of brush disposal, reseeding, and follow-up brush-control treatment can be applied. Erosion danger is low, and livestock are easier to control on the range. On steep slopes (30 to 50 percent), erosion becomes a severe hazard, often limiting use of mechanical clearing (as by bulldozer) because of soil disturbance, and stock distribution is more difficult unless the area is well watered. On very steep slopes (over 50 percent), damage from using fire usually exceeds any possible benefits, since the soil erosion hazard is high and stock handling and reseeding are difficult.

Much depends on the cover species present. On areas having a brush cover of less than about 50 percent density, there is usually sufficient seed from forage species in intermingled openings that reseeding the area is not necessary. Chaparral species that do not sprout readily may be satisfactorily controlled by systematic use of fire and chemicals. Freely sprouting species may require several treatments by fire or chemicals or complete grubbing of the entire plant. A surface fire may only aggravate the brush problem. Specific knowledge of the many associated species and of fire effects on them is essential. Despite study of many brush species, much more information is needed to guide their treatment by fire.

Preparation for Burning   As in the white pine region, considerable preparation for burning is usually necessary, including the establishment of boundaries and firebreaks and preparation of the fuels. Such work often constitutes the major cost of the burning job.

Boundaries and Firebreaks   The firebreaks and boundaries along which firing will be done become critical because of the intensity of the fire. It is necessary that the work be done by natural units, each of which can be burned in a single day. Boundaries should be as regular as possible.

Where possible, it is often desirable to locate boundaries to include grass or other fine fuels extending for a short distance from the control line into the area. This makes fire starting easier in areas where the brush fuels are difficult to ignite.

Studies by Sampson and Burcham (1954) show that the total-cost-per-acre curve (including cost to state of investigation, permit issuance, and standby protection) decreases sharply with increasing size of a tract (about 40 acres a minimum) and reaches a low point between 400 and 500 acres. Unit costs then increase somewhat up to about 640 acres, but thereafter they may decrease again, though insufficient data were available to be sure of trends. Statistically at that time, minimum cost was 60 cents per acre achieved at 440 acres, but the variation between individual cases was high.

Successful containment is a considerable problem, as evidenced by the fact that of the total area burned from 1945 to 1952, 12.8 percent was in "escapes" outside predetermined lines. Nearly 58 percent of these escapes were due to spot fires resulting from sudden spurts or shifts of wind, sparks blowing across the control line, and similar causes. Crowning accounted for about 9 percent of the escapes, and inadequate patrol and improper methods each about 8 percent. These brush fires are primarily flaming combustion and reach high intensities.

Control lines around the tract are necessary, making full use of existing barriers of roads, topography, fuel types of low flammability, and the like. Width of line depends on circumstances; the precise width is usually not as important as avoidance of situations that may permit development of hot fires near control lines. If a fire will spot at all, a few feet more or less in width of control line is seldom a decisive factor. For this reason, expected wind direction, thickets of trees that may crown near control lines, and other fuel accumulations must be appraised with care. If such fuels cannot be excluded from the area, special advance burning, or preburning, near boundaries may be necessary. A broad fireline, 100 to 200 feet wide, consisting of two parallel bulldozer or similar strips burned out in between, is used on the downwind side in some sagebrush burning (Pechanec, Stewart, and Blaisdell, 1954).

Preparation of Fuels   Fuel preparation may vary from none to complete smashing, grubbing, or windrowing of fuels or complete treatment with herbicides. It is determined by the need for fine, dry fuels to spread fire over the area and by the quantity of fuels that must be consumed to kill or remove the brush satisfactorily. A number of methods are employed.

If initial ignition is difficult for lack of fine dry fuels but the brush will burn satisfactorily once started, mashing or bunching of brush fuels near the boundaries or other ignition points may be necessary. "Walking" a tractor over brush, usually with a bulldozer blade kept raised, will breakdown enough of the cover so that it will ignite from the dead material as soon as it has dried out. In recent practice, herbicides have gained favor over use of heavy equipment in pretreatment of fuels, particularly in rough terrain, and they are used to some degree on nearly all brush control projects.

Where the brush cover is open on flats and gentle slopes, as is typical of large areas of sagebrush, a common practice is to mash and partially grub it by dragging a railroad steel behind a tractor ("railing") or by means of a cable or chain drawn between two tractors, sometimes with a heavy ball or other weight in the middle to hold the cable close to the ground. If an anchor chain is used, no other weight is needed and the brush is literally mowed down. Heavy brush—and tree cover as well— can be broken down by cable or chain if the terrain permits heavy tractor use.

In timberland brush fields which are to be planted to trees, heavy equipment may be used to grub out the rootstocks of sprouting brush. In some areas neither herbicides nor fire is used. In others the area is burned over as the first operation.

Where heavy equipment is not used, a prescribed burn is followed by application of herbicides to kill back the new brush sprouts and seedlings.

Where area ignition techniques are used, spraying with desicants such as pentachlorophenol was found effective as a means of quickly increasing the flammability of brush cover (Arnold et al., 1951) and this is sometimes done instead of using herbicides. Helicopters have been found very effective in applying chemicals from the air where access by ground equipment is limited.

Complete preparation for a high-intensity burn in dense brush cover requires accurate appraisal of the job as a whole and advance planning of each phase of the job. This includes determination of the intensity of fire needed to accomplish the purpose as well as decisions regarding the weather, the burning techniques, the firebreaks and barriers, and the men and equipment that will enable successful execution.

Execution of Burning   The success of all high-intensity burning projects depends strongly on good organization. A competent man must be in full charge, safety precautions must be taken, a specific ignition schedule must be prepared, and sufficient men and equipment must be on hand for the burning, with reserve forces quickly available for emergencies. Authorities and neighbors must be properly notified. California brush burning is often a cooperative neighborhood affair.

An analysis of 1,408 controlled burns showed the distribution by burning season, in percentage, to be as follows: July, 9.5; August, 31.2; September, 32.3; October and fall, 20.5; spring before July, 6.5. Desirable season varies widely by locality. For the most part, burning must be done when the fire danger is moderately high to get satisfactory fire spread and fuel consumption. Full use should be made of weather forecasts and danger rating techniques. As elsewhere, suitable days for burning are often few and the work must be well organized in advance to take advantage of good burning conditions when they occur. For this reason, it is difficult to set precise dates very far in advance, desirable as this is from a cost and organization standpoint.

Burning methods include simultaneous or area ignition and center, strip, and edge firing (pages 578–583). Center and strip firing are essentially head-fire tactics. Firing may be done by strips or blocks established by mashing lines through the brush. Backfires are little used except where there is plenty of fine fuel to carry the fire.

Satisfactory ignition is often a problem. This can sometimes be solved by fuel preparation, as described above. In addition to the usual firing equipment, flamethrowers are used where a hot kindling fire is needed. Grenades (Figure 13.2), either hand-thrown or dropped by helicopter, have been successfully used. Brush areas are often almost impenetrable and are dangerous to any personnel who undertake to work in them near a fire.

Because it produces effective results when burning conditions are such that a fire from a single ignition source spreads only slowly, an area-ignition burn can be scheduled for the less dangerous periods of the year. Therefore, fewer men are needed and less advance work around the area is required to assure control of the fire. The method can often be used for burning out wide fire-control lines during off seasons or at times of day when fire is not difficult to handle. Or area ignition can be used for burning out sections of planned burns during periods when control is easy; these burned out sections then minimize the threat of escape when the larger area is ignited.

Follow-up after Burning   Appraisal of the results of prescribed burning and need for continued treatment cannot be covered here since they are primarily a land-management rather than a fire matter, even though fire may be subsequently employed. It cannot be emphasized too strongly that the landowner should be prepared to follow up with subsequent brush cover treatment and forage plant reseeding where necessary and with continued good range-management practices. A single burn may be quite beneficial in terms of quick financial gain. But its effect is only temporary and without consistent follow-up may be achieved at the expense of long-time benefit either to the individual or to society as a whole. The brush problem of California is deeply rooted in the ecology and land-management practices of the region. It cannot be solved by any quick or easy means.

Chapter 19

Fire Control Policies
and Objectives

Preceding chapters have set forth the pragmatic approach to the control of fires and to the prescribed use of fire on wild lands. Collectively they integrate what has been learned through research and field experience. They share a common assumption that something needs to bc done about fire. How much should be done to be in balance with other public needs and what internal variations are justified can seldom be determined precisely. Yet analysis of such questions is highly important to sound policy toward wild-land fires and to efficient organization of fire-fighting forces.

BACKGROUND TO FIRE POLICY

Need for Fire Control

How much needs to be done about wildfire control depends on both measured and unmeasured factors. At times the unmeasured factors dominate. So it often becomes a question of decision with few guidelines.

In an undeveloped country, the damage done by fire and its

ecological effects are usually poorly recognized. Frequently use of fire to benefit some particular use of the land, such as grazing by domestic livestock, or shifting cultivation, is well entrenched in local custom but runs counter to the long-term national interest. This is true wherever wildfire causes deterioration in the environment or damage to other uses that exceeds the benefits sought. A program for controlling the use of fire then requires high priority and must usually be inaugurated before the question of how much protection can be resolved.

In the United States the progressive extension of systematic protection of forest lands over the last 60 years has resulted from positive decisions to give protection after weighing the factors believed most important. Areas under protection have increased in scope from National Forest lands and small autonomous associations of private holdings to countywide then statewide protection under both state and federal sponsorship.

The following are the most obvious factors in making such decisions:

1   Frequency of fires
2   Nature and severity of damage from fire
3   Who benefits from use or occurrence of fire
4   How fire affects use of the land
5   Emotional attitudes toward wildfire

Frequency of fires alone is an important factor. Where wildfires are so infrequent that they have not been experienced by most landowners or users in a particular locality, there is a natural tendency to give low priority to arrangements for control of fires or to question the need for any provision. At the other extreme, where fires occur with such frequency that surface fuels do not accumulate, they are usually mild, as was true in much of the southern United States at one time. This situation too may lead local residents to question the need for doing anything to prevent or to control fires.

The nature and severity of damage from fire is also important. Where the damage is slight or not obvious to the casual observer, there is little incentive to fight fire. But where human life, homes, public utilities, fences, livestock, and equipment are endangered by fire, much stronger incentives operate.

In a series of studies (Craig, Frank et al., 1946) in the southeastern United States, fire damages were considered in the following seven categories:

1 Timber values. Marketable and young growth including regeneration, effect on stand composition, insect and disease damage directly resulting from fire, deterioration or improvement of the site for timber growth
2 Watershed values. Flood erosion and sedimentation damage attributable to fire, reduction in groundwater reserves and in base streamflow
3 Wildlife values. Loss of game birds and animals, effect on their environment
4 Recreational values. Damage to established facilities and the effect on recreational use of forest land
5 Grazing values. Effect of fire on range values and use
6 Other property values. Loss of or damage to agricultural produce, farm buildings, fences, livestock, and other miscellaneous property
7 Socioeconomic values. Effect of loss of growing timber or a deterioration of the environment on the social and economic pattern or the area

Though the studies did not succeed in their purpose of determining justifiable protection costs and resulted in no formula for determining how much systematic fire control was necessary in a particular area, they helped to define values at stake in the use and control of fire and the areas of concern both to the individual and to various levels of government.

Subsequent changes in priorities in the minds of the public are well reflected by the rather scant attention given to deterioration of the environment in the 1946 publication. It was included in 7 above along with social and economic aspects. Although deterioration of the environment is difficult to measure and often difficult to recognize until well advanced, environmental aspects are now regarded as of overriding importance in determining public fire control policies. This attitude is common among urban residents.

But the self-interest of the local resident or user continues to be a strong factor as well. Benefits from use of fire, such as improved access by hunters and improved grazing by livestock, often mask the accompanying damage from prescribed fire that has been poorly controlled.

To what degree fires interfere with the use of the land is also important. Where recreational uses are dominant, almost any fire is considered detrimental. On the other hand, local livestock owners in some localities consider almost any fire beneficial.

Emotional attitudes toward fire also enter in and may dominate policies and practices. Fear of uncontrolled fire is a powerful force. It becomes an important factor wherever recent experience has demonstrated that fire is a threat to lives and property. It results in a demand for public security from fire that may far outweigh considerations based on loss of forest resources.

Development of Public Fire Control Policies

In Chapter 2, the history of organized protection against wildfire in the United States is outlined. This reflected a gradual shift in public land policy away from the laissez faire attitude accompanying the rapid settlement and physical development of the country prior to 1900 to one of increasing acceptance of public responsibility toward land resources.

The first serious public effort to control fires was in 1897, when the United States Congress provided for administering the federally owned Forest Reserves; but the first systematic fire control on federal lands is more nearly identified with the organization of the National Forests, beginning in 1907. Participation in the responsibility for control of wildfires by individual states began with the Weeks law of 1911 by which the Secretary of Agriculture was authorized "to cooperate in financing the organization and maintenance of a system of fire protection on any private or state forest lands—upon the watershed of a navigable river." This was broadened and strengthened by the Clark-McNary act of 1924, as mentioned in Chapter 2.

Prior to support by federal or state agencies, private forest landowners had begun to band together into mutual timber protective associations. The first was probably the Linn County Fire Patrol Association of Linn County, Oregon, organized in 1904. In 1906, a timberland owners' forest fire protective association was formed in Idaho. The idea spread quickly, and many similar associations developed in the states of Washington and Oregon. These associations soon became a strong force in the organization of forest fire control, but difficulties arose when not all landowners within a specific watershed were willing to cooperate financially or otherwise. The participating landowners were then compelled to protect the nonparticipating land in self-defense. This was eventually overcome in several Western states by the enactment of laws which compelled all owners to contribute to maintenance of the protection organization. Though private protective associations have become less numerous as state fire organizations have grown stronger and more efficient, wherever they have continued under good management they make a distinctive contribution. This consists of enabling more direct participation by the landowner in protecting his property and higher standards of protection in high-value areas. Throughout their history, private protective associations have been a strong force in shaping public policy in forest fire control.

Growth of the total area protected in the United States is a good indicator of the growth of public support for forest fire control as a public service. In 1917, for example, 176 million acres were under some form of organized protection, mostly federal. By 1930, the area had grown to approximately 400 million; by 1950, to 600 million; and by 1970, to well over 1,100 million acres. Most of this increasing coverage was privately owned forest land for which state agencies were assuming responsibility for protection.

By 1970, the total area of wild lands and rural areas in need of organized protection was estimated to be 1,592 million acres. This area is classified as follows (in millions af acres):

National Forests	186
Other federal	469
State and private	517
Rural areas	420
	1,592

Less than one-third of this area is classed as commercial forest land. By broad categories of cover type and use it is classified as follows:

Commercial forest	510
Other forest lands	251
Non-forest	411
Mixed rural areas	420
	1,592

This increased emphasis on nontimber values and public security from fire is significant in terms of public policy. Commercial forest land values, which were at first regarded as the primary justification for control of fire, now receive much less intensive protection than critical watershed areas, such as the brushlands of southern California, where fires directly threaten lives and property. Consequently values other than timber production now predominate on two-thirds of the area protected in the United States.

Problems of Financing

Equitable financing of forest fire control is always a problem. The landowner has a direct responsibility to protect his own property, but failure to do so may threaten other property and may have adverse effects on the tax base and the environment. So the public is also involved.

To what degree the public needs to share in this responsibility may be illustrated. The simplest case is that of the owner of a small woodland. If he has a Christmas tree plantation of several acres, he has a specific investment to protect from fire. He might cover his risk of loss by insurance if available. But since his own management greatly influences the chance of loss by fire, he may properly assume the full responsibility himself, as he probably does for personal property. If the plantation is surrounded by pasture lands or cultivated lands under his own control, it may be relatively easy for him to minimize the chance of fire by simple measures entirely within his own control. If loss does occur through his own negligence, he alone is affected.

If his plantation is surrounded by lands not under his own control, the problem becomes more complex. He may reduce the chance of fire spreading from his neighbors' lands by firebreaks, as described in Chapter 10, or he could enter into cooperative arrangements with his neighbors to set up a more logical and more easily protected fire unit.

As soon as considerable acreages are involved, it becomes impracticable fully to exclude risk of fire from public travel and use. Usually too, there are so few positive barriers to a spreading fire that a single fire threatens a large area both within and without the organized unit. The responsibility may then become too broad for one or a small group of landowners to assume.

In some situations of this sort, the banding together of private owners in a timber protective association offers a good solution. The circumstances most favorable to such a solution exist (1) when the lands involved form a reasonably autonomous geographic unit not materially threatened by outside fires and not very likely to generate fires that will seriously threaten outside arcas, (2) when the values protected are primarily commercial values common to all the lands in the unit, and (3) when the area is large enough that an assessment of a reasonable amount per acre per year from each owner is sufficient to provide supplemental prevention, and pay for presuppression and suppression services, sufficient to meet fire control standards in that locality.

As areas in need of protection increase in size and particularly as public security or noncommercial values become dominant, as in scenic or recreation areas or important watersheds, the purpose of protection and consequently its cost as well can no longer remain an affair concerning only the private landowner. Protection on this scale is independent of ownership of the land. The recognition of this principle is the basis on which public participation and sponsorship of wild-land protection has developed and has been gradually extended in the United States.

The problem of proper allocation of funds is never static and has a different aspect at each level of organization. This normally involves decisions on at least three different levels:

1 Distribution of funds in financing fire control functions within a single administrative unit
2 Allocation of fire control funds between units of a particular organization
3 Allocation of funds for fire control purposes in relation to financing other dissimilar needs

Obviously, the manager of a single administrative unit (first level) can decide only how to spend the funds allocated to his unit at the second level. Also at the second level, the head of an organization can decide on the allocation of funds only as they are made available to his agency by decisions at the third level. Competition for funds naturally operates at each of these levels.

The principle of joint financing and sharing the responsibility between private, state, and federal agencies has taken a variety of forms involving each of these levels. They range from minimal public support of private protective associations in fire prevention programs and in the acquisition of fire equipment to complete statewide assumption of responsibility for systematic protection by the state, financed by general tax revenues rather than by direct assessment of the landowners concerned. Equitable sharing of costs that should be assumed by the federal government under general formulas developed by the Clark-McNary law and other supporting legislation has been the subject of many detailed studies. The factors that enter into allocation of federal funds vary in importance among the states. Consequently, a distinctive cooperative program operates in each state of the United States. The evolution of the cooperative program in California has recently been described (Clar, 1969).

POLICY OBJECTIVES

The primary purpose of forest fire control is to protect wild-land resources from damage. It follows that the intensity of protection must bear some relation to the values being protected and more specifically to the damage fire is likely to cause. The fire control manager determines how much protection can be achieved for the funds available but not how much is needed. This is a policy decision on the part of the state in behalf of the public interest as well as that of the owner or manager of the land concerned.

In the early days of forestry in North America, justification for expenditures to control fires was obvious. When little or no organized fire control exists and disastrous losses from conflagration fires are recurrent, the need for better control of fires requires no analysis. As control becomes more effective and more costly, questions of desirable economic balance become correspondingly more important. With the tremendous growth in coverage and in intensity of fire control that has occurred in the United States in the 1917 to 1970 period, the forest fire control organization has become both highly complex and expensive in many areas. Protection standards believed unattainable in the 1930s and fire-fighting facilities formerly thought to be too costly are now commonplace in intensively protected areas. At the same time the environmental and social values of wild lands throughout the United States have grown with the population. Consequently the forest resource values damageable by fire and the property values threatened by fire have also increased tremendously, perhaps at a faster rate than fire control costs. As these resources become more valuable and their management intensifies, the importance of defining protection needs more precisely also increases.

Justifiable costs of fire control are related to the values being protected. These are often referred to as the values at stake. It should be recognized that the need for fire control does not necessarily rest on total values at stake but only to the degree to which they may be damaged by fire. This more restricted relationship is at times referred to as total destructible or damageable value. How much of it is threatened by fire depends on the kind of fire. For example, if hazardous fuels have been eliminated to the point that crown fires will not occur, the values threatened will be quite low compared to the situation where heavy mixed fuels will produce a high-intensity crown fire. To attain the same level of protection, fire control costs will naturally be much higher in the second instance.

Although it is customary in studies of the economics of fire control to treat fire control costs as increasing in a smooth curve from zero to some maximum point as fire control forces and facilities are increased, the fire control planner finds that local variations follow certain principles. To achieve even the most economical level of organized fire control, a certain minimum level of cost at some point considerably above zero is necessary. This may be regarded as the floor in cost determinations. As the fire organization is strengthened by adding mechanized equipment or fire crews, the level of cost may rise in stair-step fashion rather than in a smooth curve. The ceiling is set by total destructible values. Through control of hazards and risks, adequate fire control may be attained considerably below the ceiling.

The Least-cost-plus-damage Objective

Many attempts have been made to develop a formula for a desirable level of fire control that would permit valid comparison with other economic activities. They have mostly followed the so-called least-cost-plus-damage approach which has had a long history within the U.S. Forest Service (Show and Kotok, 1923; Sparhawk, 1925; Loveridge, 1944; Arnold, 1950). It was advocated especially by Roy Headley who was chief of fire control for the U.S. Forest Service for 20 years prior to 1945[1]. It is based on the concept that the total fire cost is the monetary sum of control cost plus losses (damage), and it assumes that there is some optimum level of activity in each aspect of fire control which, when used in combination, will bring damages to the point where total costs plus total damages will be at a minimum. The combination is thought of as the sum of costs for prevention + presuppression + suppression + damage. This is sometimes written as $P+P+S+D$ = Total fire cost. Or the first part may be more simply stated as $P+S+D$, where prevention and presuppression costs are combined. Different investigators have differed somewhat on just what each term includes. Basically it is expected that D will decrease as expenditures for prevention, presuppression, and suppression increase. The occasional conflagration fire which causes extraordinary suppression costs and very high losses as well is difficult to deal with in these determinations. Some investigators omit such fires for statistical reasons, others regard both costs and losses from such fires as items which properly belong in the damage column. This is based on the concept that the extraordinary costs as well as the losses from the conflagration were the result of the inadequacy of the existing organization to deal with large fires.

　　　The underlying assumption in the least-cost approach is that it is just as important to save a dollar in costs as to save a dollar in damages. The point of least total costs is close to where the two just balance. Beyond this point, each additional dollar spent buys progressively less reduction in damages until these reductions offset only a fraction of the money spent. Relationships are graphically shown in Figure 19.1.

　　　The approach places fire control on a general economic basis and focuses attention on the components of the cost-loss equation. Its working can be illustrated very simply, as in Table 19.1. The figures used can be units of any monetary magnitude desired. The assumption is that different combinations of prevention and preparedness have been tested in an area and can be compared with resultant changes in direct suppression costs

[1] As set forth in his unpublished manuscript *Rethinking Forest Fire Control*, 1944.

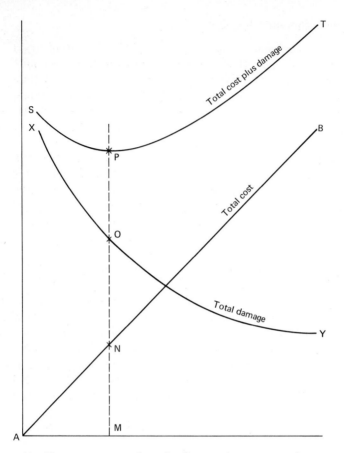

Line AB represents a range of complete fire control costs necessary for different degrees of fire control intensity on an assumed unit.

Line XY represents damage which would decrease as a result of increasing cost and intensity of fire control.

Line ST represents the sum of the values from the base line to AB and from the base line to XY. Thus MN+MO = ST at P.

N marks the point of fire control cost which will result in P, the lowest attainable total of all costs and damage.

Figure 19.1 Model diagram illustrating the effect of various levels of protection cost on the fire damage to expect and on the magnitude of the sum of costs plus damage. Adapted from early models of least-cost plus damage relationships *(Sparhawk, 1925).*

and damage. In the first case, nothing was spent for prevention and little for presuppression. The suppression bill and damage were high. In Case 2, some prevention work was done, preparedness was emphasized, and more vigorous action was taken in the suppression of slightly fewer fires.

Damage was sharply reduced, and the total was less. Prevention effort was increased sixfold in Case 3 and preparedness increased slightly. Direct suppression costs were approximately halved, and the cost-plus-damage total was further reduced. Encouraged by success in prevention, all-out prevention was attempted in Case 4, plus reasonably strong preparedness. The number of fires was sharply reduced, along with suppression and damage costs. But the total was higher than in Case 3. The conclusion is that Case 3 represents approximately the best combination in this situation.

It is possible to approximate the point of minimum cost plus damage without establishing the total for all the elements as done in Table 19.1. For example, if specific increases in control costs (such as occasioned by adding mechanized equipment or strengthening a fire crew) can be associated directly with a decrease in damage, then determination of the point where the increase is offset by a similar decrease in damage will come close to the point of minimum cost plus damage. This approach is commonly applied by fire agency managers.

The least-cost-plus-damage approach is soundly based in economics and provides a general guide for presuppression expenditures. Too great a sum spent for presuppression may not be warranted when considered in the light of destructible values protected. It also has the advantage of being applicable, at least in theory, to any administrative unit, state, or region. Perhaps its most important value has been in focusing attention on the nature of and need for economic balance in fire control systems.

For both technical and practical reasons, the least-cost approach has not been satisfactory either in defining planning objectives or in providing administrative guides to the fire control manager. Technical defects may be illustrated by Figure 19.2. If, instead of the array in Figure 19.1, the decreasing damage associated with increasing costs is plotted below the base line of Figure 19.1, then a vertical line from the damage curve to the cost curve will represent the sum of costs plus damages at any given

Table 19.1 Illustration of the Least-cost-plus-damage Approach to a Desirable Economic Level of Fire Control

Item	Case 1	Case 2	Case 3	Case 4
Prevention	0	200	1,200	3,000
Presuppression	500	1,800	2,000	1,800
Suppression	2,000	2,500	1,200	500
Damage	5,000	2,000	1,000	700
Total	7,500	6,500	5,400	6,000

Figures are monetary units of expenditure or damage.

point. When plotted in this way, it becomes apparent that a minimum total of costs plus damage is not a single well-defined point but rather a zone or segment of nearly identical totals. In most public fire control enterprises, the aim is to approach a 1:1 ratio as a general guide so that each dollar expended will save at least a dollar in damage. But probable damage is always an approximation, with a rather wide margin of possible error. So for practical purposes there is seldom a real question of public justification until costs substantially exceed the losses to be expected. In Figure 19.2 the point of least cost plus damage comes at *A* but is nearly identical through *B* and does not increase very fast until *C* is reached. The 1:1 ratio is close to *B*. This illustrates that the point of least cost is likely to be unstable, since it is on a rapidly changing part of the curve and may be only slightly less than still lower damage at a slightly higher cost farther along the curve. In fact, the operation of the law of diminishing returns (page 344) is not very apparent until *C* is reached. Beyond this point, relatively heavy expenditures are necessary to reduce damage by $1 or by some other unit. These relationships will vary somewhat with changes in the shape of the damage curve, which may be either flatter or steeper than that used in Figure 19.2. However, it is apparent that a policy objective based on least-cost computations might justifiably be located at any point from *A* to *C* on the damage curve depending on the policy adopted.

Besides the fact that "least cost" is not consistently a well-defined point, there are several practical obstacles to the useful application of this approach. The most important is the lack of accurate measurements or evaluations of fire damage. Early attempts were confined to conservative commercial timber values only. Water, recreation, and soil values were disregarded or valued at a nominal flat rate. Due to the growing concern for environmental protection, it is now recognized that noncommercial and so-called intangible values predominate in importance on most of the wild lands of the United States, but no satisfactory method of general application has yet been devised for evaluating—in monetary units— damage to such values. If the *D* in the least-cost formula is uncertain, the whole approach becomes equally so.

Another weakness is the necessity of basing curves on past history. If material changes have occurred, the "hindsight" represented by the curves may be inadequate for projections into the future.

Other practical difficulties in least-cost determinations arise from the fact that it is assumed that the levels of prevention, presuppression, and suppression systems can be varied at will and in relation to each other. It is also assumed that the effect on damage of each variation in the fire control system can be adequately measured. These things can be

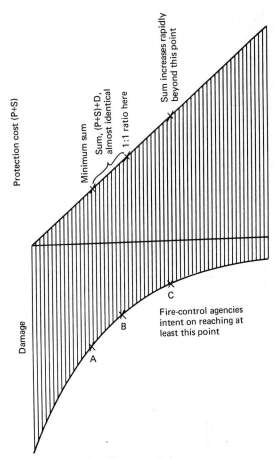

Figure 19.2 Figure 19.1 replotted to illustrate that "least cost" is not a well-defined point. The sum of protection costs plus expected fire damage is here represented by the total length of the vertical lines. Costs of protection consist of *P*, prevention and presuppression costs, plus *S*, suppression costs. *D* represents the fire damage experienced or anticipated. *A*, *B*, and *C* are selected totals of similar magnitude but differing ratios between cost and damage.

accomplished only in a most indirect manner with no assurance of accuracy.

For these reasons, the minimum cost and damage objective remains largely a theoretical approach. It is difficult to translate into operating policy and attempts to do so have failed. However, it has been useful in stimulating analysis of economic balance and of public objectives. In time, as methods for evaluating public values improve, the accuracy of least-cost determinations should also improve. In any case, the philosophy of least cost will no doubt continue to influence forest fire control policy at higher administrative levels.

Adequate Control

Instead of a specific economic formula, a more generalized approach may be used to achieve a desired level of fire control "equal or sufficient to the need." This is the precise meaning of *adequate*, which then becomes the key word. It places the emphasis on integrated planning but provides no formulas or precise guidelines for arriving at "adequate forest fire control." The adequate-control concept was first specifically formulated by Flint (1928), who defined it as "that degree of protection which will render the forest property as safe on the average from destruction by fire as are other forms of destructible property in which moderately conservative investors are willing to place their funds." A natural corollary is a degree of control that makes forest properties regularly insurable at reasonable premiums. Some degree of general acceptance is also implied by the definition.

Adequate control is consequently a business-social-political concept. It aims for practical reality with due consideration to time, place, and circumstances. Adequate control has about the same relation to the least-cost approach as do open-market prices to appraised values. The two are not antagonistic or necessarily even different. Market prices represent the integration of both buyer and seller interests that determine price at a particular time and place. Appraisal is based on the same factors, but it is an estimate of value, usually from the point of view of either buyer or seller, so often it does not conform to the accepted price at a given time.

What constitutes an adequate intensity of fire control in an area must be sought through careful analysis of fire control costs and effectiveness in relation to public and private interests and trends in resource use. It implies integrated planning, as defined in Chapter 14.

The central purpose is to bring fire control effort into balance with needs. An adequate control objective should not be regarded as merely an acceptance of what is. The level of control existing in an area may be insufficient to permit successful timber production. It may not be possible to convince the public and its representatives that a higher level is justified, in which case control may continue at an inadequate level from a timber growing standpoint. The level also may or may not be adequate from water conservation, soil erosion, or recreational standpoints. Many situations exist where such public values justify a higher intensity of control than private business interests can afford. Different points of view must be considered and reconciled. Understanding of what is adequate changes with time, and concepts and valuation of forest land resources change as well. Flint developed the idea of adequate control with the timber business primarily in mind, but the concept should not be so limited.

Many studies of fire control in an area have been made to determine what constitutes a reasonably adequate level from some point of view. For the most part, these studies follow a common pattern of (1) a statistical analysis of control costs, fire occurrence, and area burned; (2) estimates of damage; and (3) an attempt to define some justifiable level of control. These kinds of analyses have been made repeatedly in area-cost studies of cooperative fire control under the Clarke-McNary act. All public wild-land protection agencies make such studies. The problems involved are complex and ever-changing, and definitive answers are not possible. No matter how rigorously one attempts to define needs, qualifying adjectives like *adequate, acceptable,* or *desirable* creep in. It seems desirable to recognize frankly that this is so and to strive for the best solution currently attainable. Adequate control is a useful concept and a realistic approach, but it is manifestly not definable as an economic theory. In the final analysis it is a subjective approach, but that does not mean that it is established by subjective decisions alone. It is most successful when it is based on accurate data and systematic planning by fire control experts subject to the modifications needed to make it consistent with public policy and local interests.

For example, adequate protection of wild-land resources based on planned fire control systems may not show the need for totally excluding fire risk in certain areas, and it may contemplate use of prescribed burning to hold down fire control costs. But risks to personal property and local sentiment against all forms of air pollution may generate a strong demand for higher standards of prevention. With this goes acceptance of higher fuel hazards because of public willingness to accept the associated higher costs of protection than would otherwise be justified. Adequate fire control tends to focus on what is wanted on the ground. Fire control experts convert this into means, methods, and secondary standards to bring it about.

Fire control programs developed through such modifications of the adequate control concept and through application of the least-cost approach can greatly increase the validity of cost-benefit comparisons with other public service programs of all kinds. This enables the orderly development of priorities as expressed in budgets and apportionment of public funds.

PERFORMANCE OBJECTIVES

Performance objectives, like primary objectives, can be applied to fire control practice anywhere. But they are internal in nature so do not lend themselves to comparisons with nonfire activities. All are related in some way to the speed and adequacy of action taken or to the number of fires, area burned, damage suffered, or costs incurred.

Control During the First Work Period

Policy objectives and most performance objectives have one basic limitation in common: They are of little or no help to the fire dispatcher confronted with an immediate fire situation and decisions to make. They are actuarial sorts of approaches depending on past statistics. No dispatcher can say, "Our record is good, so we can ease off on fire suppression today." Neither can he balance the season's least-cost-plus-damage ledger in advance of taking action on a particular fire. He needs a definite operating guide.

What is termed the first-work-period control objective or 10 A.M. policy was developed to meet this need.[2] The aim is to achieve control before the beginning of the next day's burning period. Failing this, action is taken to dispatch sufficient force to control the fire before the advent of the burning period of the following day and, if still unsuccessful, for each succeeding day thereafter. Strictly speaking, control during the first work period is the specific objective, and strong initial attack is the governing policy. It is usually spoken of as a policy. In essence, the objective is strong first attack on all fires, vigorously followed up when necessary to obtain prompt control. In large protection units under adverse fuel or weather conditions, a few fires will escape from control by the first attack force, even with a highly efficient presuppression organization. Usually this happens in late afternoon. The fire makes a run of variable size but slows down at sunset and usually becomes quiescent during the night.

Most of the time the fire organization has an opportunity to completely control and mop up such a fire during the night if vigorous action is taken. At any rate, if no large fire exceeded the area of its first run, fire losses

---

[2] As restated by the U.S. Forest Service (1971), the first work period is the time between discovery of a fire and 10 A.M. of the following calendar day. Succeeding work periods are 24 hours beginning at 10 A.M. Within the Forest Service, it is commonly called the "10 A.M. policy."

would be kept well within acceptable limits. Failure to control a fire at the end of its first run often leads to a rapidly increasing fire front and a costly but losing fight to contain a conflagration.

The first-work-period objective was first specifically formulated and applied by the U.S. Forest Service in 1935 (Loveridge, 1944), and, though such an objective may be differently stated, is followed generally by all successful control organizations. Though it is highly important organizationally and is often spoken of as a policy or as a primary objective, it should be emphasized that it is primarily designed as an operating guide for day-to-day use. It is not antagonistic to primary objectives but is a specific means of carrying them out.

Consideration of the reasons that prompted adoption and continuance of the first-work-period objective will clarify its relationships.

1 The need for a definite, unequivocal action policy. It is impossible to administer an economic theory, adequate control, or area-burned objectives on a day-to-day basis no matter how logical and meaningful they may be as concepts.

2 Recognition of the fact that aggressive initial action is the cheapest in the long run. Fire suppression analyses have consistently supported this point. Many fires are overmanned under such a policy, but the costly experience of large fires shows that it is cheaper to do this than to risk losing control of some fires because the suppression force needed was underestimated. Increased accessibility and modern fire equipment greatly increase the feasibility of first-work-period control.

3 Frank recognition of the fact that damage to forest values is highly variable and difficult to determine. In any event, the evaluation of forest values is beyond the capacity of a suppression organization on a fire-by-fire action basis. A major criticism of the least-cost approach was (and is) that control action is weakened to reduce suppression costs because they are thought to be out of line with damage reduction. This has led to so-called "too little or too late," "take a chance," "herd 'em," or "let burn" practices (Loveridge, 1944).

4 The need to build and maintain morale in fire suppression. Protracted fire fighting on the same fire, besides being exhausting, is extremely discouraging and frustrating, especially when it is known or believed to be the consequence of "too little and too late" action to begin with. Many men have broken their hearts as well as their strength trying to suppress a fire with inadequate attack force and have had to witness destruction of forest resources in their charge notwithstanding. The first-work-period control plan is designed to gain a first-round knock-out.

While control in the first work period is in itself a purely arbitrary objective, it serves as an action guide toward attainment of the more general objectives and sets standards for fire control plans.

As an action guide, it gives emphasis to the speed and strength of attack that will give the organization at least a reasonable chance to limit the maximum size of the fire to its first burning period.

In practice, strict application of this policy to conflagration fires, which develop during high and extreme fire danger, may and has led to extravagant expenditures, since the firestorm type of behavior defies all existing methods of control. A more prudent course frequently applied is that of reanalysis of probabilities after failure to control a fire in the first work period. Then a special plan may be formulated that will provide for control on a time schedule designed to minimize the threat of the fire at a cost in keeping with the local values at stake. Under unfavorable conditions, it will stop short of the mobilization of forces theoretically necessary to control a temporarily uncontrollable firefront.

Number of Fires

The number of man-caused fires is often used as a measure of the success or lack of success of the fire prevention activity. To compare fire occurrence in different units, it is often converted to the rate per million acres. But the number of fires is strongly influenced by fuel moisture conditions as well as by the activity of fire starting agencies. For that reason, before a meaningful comparison can be made for this purpose, allowance must be made for differences in prevailing fire danger for the seasons being compared. This can be done by careful analysis of the relation between fire danger ratings and ignitions from different sources of fire risk. By such means a more discriminating objective can be formulated.

The number of fires by causes is similarly used. The same limitations apply, but differences in the number of fires from a particular cause, in one year compared to another, gain in significance for use in fire prevention if converted to percent of the total number for the years of interest. Characteristic association of causes is illustrated in Figure 9.1, Chapter 9, pages 268–269.

The number of fires by size classes has long been used as a general index of the success of the presuppression organization. The usual classification is as follows:

    Class A — 0.25 acre or less
    Class B — 0.26 to 9.99 acres
    Class C — 10.00 to 99.99 acres
    Class D — 100.00 to 299.99 acres
    Class E — 300.00 acres or larger

The success in keeping fires small is often gauged by computing the percentage of fires that reached size C or larger. Similarly, the number of E fires not controlled during the first period and the circumstances that lead to their development are often the subject of special review and analysis.

Area Burned

The area burned is commonly used as a general measure of accomplishment and as a basis for performance objectives. It is the most specific and measurable aspect of a fire after its control. Cause, cost, and damage may be uncertain, but the area burned is observable and can be measured. For this reason, definition of a control objective in terms of some maximum standard of average area burned is both obvious and logical. The term *allowable burn* is commonly used in this connection and is defined as "the maximum average loss in acreage burned for a given period of years that is considered acceptable under organized control for a given area" (U.S. Forest Service, 1956). The word *allowable* should not be construed to mean "permitted" or "desired," as no wildfire is "allowed" to burn. The term "tolerable" burn is more appropriate and is often substituted.

A great deal of thought has been given to the establishment of tolerable burn standards as general guides for control in various parts of the country. Much of this has been initiated by the U.S. Forest Service. Such standards have been established for groups of National Forests and for timber types by administrative regions. Annual or periodic area-burned figures, whether considered in relation to a stated standard or not, are widely used in making comparisons between local districts, states, or larger regional groupings of federal, state, or private forest lands.

What constitutes an acceptable tolerable burn figure is a matter of arbitrary determination. For example, 0.1 percent was at one time widely used as indicating a tolerable average annual burn. It was originally based on an assumption that timber management could stand about that much loss on the average and stay in business. A relationship to the adequate and least-cost control objectives is apparent; *tolerable burn* can be thought of as a translation of these general concepts into specific and directly measurable forest terms.

Area burned has the obvious disadvantage that it is often poorly correlated with either damage or control cost. The intensity of the fire as well as the amount and value of timber and other resources damaged or destroyed per unit of area can and does vary endlessly. For example, fire destroying valuable old-growth Douglas-fir timber is in no respect comparable in terms of damage per acre with a light surface fire in southern pine. Interregional comparisons of burned-area figures are consequently often misleading as well as meaningless.

Variation in the area burned from year to year for a specific protection unit is the most easily available and direct measure of the status of fire control in that area. Area burned can also have much comparative significance within a forest region, particularly if burned areas are segregated by major forest types and value categories. If meaningful tolerable burn standards are developed for each category, they can be applied to produce an overall measure of tolerable damage and are often so used. Although crude, such measures are specific and are useful for many purposes.

Fire Damage

Although the primary justification of all fire control activity is to prevent or reduce damage, it has not been feasible to base either policy or performance guidelines directly on damage. This is for the reasons discussed in the preceding section on least cost. Nevertheless, accurate estimates of damage are highly important in setting fire control standards and in measuring final accomplishment. Where commercial timber productivity values are high, so-called intangible damage from fire, such as damage to soil and site or deterioration of the local environment, is often minor. Where this is so, conventional methods of determining loss by computing the value of timber before and after a fire become useful. The accepted method of evaluating immature timber has been that of estimating the value of the timber at maturity, then discounting this value back to the present at some assumed rate of interest. A more realistic method of estimating damage to young stands which are a part of extensive holdings is that of calculating *growth loss* based on the growth to be expected per acre per year multiplied by the age of the stand and current values per unit. If the young stand is only partially killed, an appropriate percentage may be used instead.

Watershed damage may be long-term and may represent permanent deterioration of the environment. A distinctive feature is off-site damage downstream, which may be more critical than on the burned area. Systematic appraisal of watershed values and estimates of potential damage from fire on southern California National Forests (Buck, Fons, and Countryman, 1948) showed a range of potential damage per acre of burn exceeding 1,000 to 1.

Damage to recreation values also varies widely and may reach very high dollar values. Though no generally accepted methods of appraising such values have yet been established, increasing study is being given to this subject. Basically such values may be viewed as varying with variations in two primary factors. The first may be defined as the intrinsic worth and the second as the demand or use value. A campground in a rare and beautiful scenic area may have a high intrinsic value, but if it is so inaccessible that it is enjoyed by only a few people, associated values may be much less than those of a similar development in a very ordinary setting so located that it is utilized by a great many people. A closely related approach is that of gauging recreational values by the amount actually spent by recreationists in order to enjoy them.

Improved methods of evaluating each kind of fire damage should in time greatly increase the accuracy of damage estimates and of the values at stake on which expenditures need to be based.

Forest Fire Insurance Relationships

It is common to insure buildings and personal property against loss from fire. It is not so common to extend insurance against fire to wild-land resources. Such insurance has long been available in the Scandinavian countries but is employed to lesser degrees to protect private commercial forests in other European countries. It is also being systematically employed in New Zealand and in a more limited way in Australia.

In the United States, forest fire insurance has rarely been available. The subject has received considerable attention in the United States from associations of landowners, insurance companies, state and federal agencies, and others over a period of more than fifty years. Occasional insurance programs have been undertaken, but there has not been sufficiently widespread support to enable them to continue on a commercial basis.

Insurance serves to spread the economic impact of losses from forest fire but does not directly reduce the aggregate loss itself. Nevertheless, forest fire insurance has significance to the success of forest fire control in at least two ways. First, credits in the insurance rate are normally granted for specific measures which reduce the probability of fire damage. Both the fuels and the risks to which they are exposed are subject to at least partial control by the landowner, particularly if he enters into cooperation with other landowners. His incentive to exercise such control on his land then becomes a matter of reducing costs and of conforming to a set of fire prevention standards, just as the owner of a structure must conform to certain standards prescribed by fire underwriters. This process tends to develop built-in provisions against fire in day-to-day activities on the ground and to reduce losses indirectly. Second, it has been the universal experience that when capital has been committed to the payment of insured losses, insurance organizations engage in educational and loss prevention activities, including technical research, that also reduce fire loss.

A policy favorable to the development of forest fire insurance is not enough to bring about its successful application. A program of forest fire insurance requires a wide spread of risk if the law of large numbers (law of averages) upon which insurance is based is to operate. Such a spread of risk has not yet been established for the wide diversity of growing forests in the United States.

Usually insurance based on a wide spread of risk is available at lower cost than if it were based only on local factors. This may make insurance rates more attractive in the future. However, large numbers of forest owners must have an interest in obtaining forest fire insurance before any insurance program can succeed. The probabilities of fire and the severity of damage in the United States involve so many uncertainties that much further research in fire damage and in fire probabilities appears to be necessary before a sufficiently specific and sound base for computing insurance rates can emerge.

FIRE CONTROL POLICIES AND OBJECTIVES IN SUMMARY

The policy of instituting some control of fire on wild lands in the United States is no longer questioned, but the degree of control and the objectives to be served are subject to continuing study and appraisal.

It is clear that no single objective will suffice. General objectives such as adequate control at reasonable cost are above criticism as to purpose and are useful in policy and planning, but they are not very helpful to the fire control manager. It is also clear that fire damage that inflicts either long-term or permanent damage to the environment will not be regarded as tolerable by the American public, and systems or policies that permit such damage will be regarded as unacceptable.

It is also clear that the importance of so-called intangible values in undisturbed wild-land environments has been seriously underrated in the past and that they have greatly increased with rising population and use. This increase is of sufficient moment to call for a reevaluation of local fire control objectives place by place and item by item.

The concepts of adequate control and of maximum contribution to public needs at least cost are basic to such determinations. Fire control needs of all users of the land regardless of whether or not they pay directly for the privilege must be taken into account. Performance objectives, such as setting goals for fire prevention and first-work-period control in suppression, are positive in defining what is needed to attain what is regarded as an adequate level of control at a particular time.

Regardless of how carefully policies and objectives may be defined, they must remain flexible. In the final analysis, the level of public protection of wild lands is set by the taxpayer but will fluctuate depending on the interrelations with other public objectives. To provide security against fire for life and property and to avoid impairment of resources, the taxpayer is normally willing to pay far more than a dollar of fire control funds to prevent a dollar of loss. For that reason the taxpaying public at large may demand and be willing to pay for a higher level of protection than would the landowner himself to avoid direct financial loss. Problems arising from the need to revise local objectives from place to place demand continuing attention.

BIBLIOGRAPHY

Chapters 1, 2, and 3: Man and Fire and Its Effects on Forest Lands

Adams, F., P. A. Ewing, and M. R. Huberty 1947. Hydrologic aspects of burning brush and woodland-grass ranges in California. Calif. Dept. of Nat. Resources, Div. of Forestry.

Anderson, Hal E. 1968. Sundance fire, an analysis of fire phenomena. *U.S. Forest Serv. Res. Paper* Int-56.

Baker, F. S. 1929. The effect of excessively high temperatures on coniferous reproduction. *Jour. Forestry,* **27**:949–975.

———— 1950. Principles of silviculture, 2d ed. McGraw-Hill Book Company, Inc., New York.

Baker, J. 1968. Effects of slash burning on soil composition and seedling growth. *Rept.* B.C.-X-29. Forest Res. Lab., Canadian Dept. of Fisheries and Forestry, Victoria, B.C.

Barrows, J. S. 1969. Forest fire science. McGraw-Hill Yearbook of Science and Technology, pp. 46–57. McGraw-Hill Book Company, Inc., New York.

———— 1971. Forest fire research for environmental protection. *Jour. Forestry,* **69**(1):17–20.

Beadle, N. C. W. 1940. Soil temperatures during forest fires and their effect on the survival of vegetation. *Jour. Ecol.,* **28**:180–192.

Beaufait, Wm. R. 1960. Some effects of high temperatures on the cones and seeds of jack pine. *Forest Sci.,* **6**:194–199.

Bentley, Jay R. 1967. Conversion of chaparral areas to grassland. (Techniques used in Calif.) *Agr. Handbook no.* 328, USDA Forest Service.

Brown, A. A. 1964. Forest fire research in the Forest Service, U.S. Dept. of Agr. *Fire Res. Abstracts and Reviews,* **6**(3). N.A.S.-N.R.C.

Bruce, David 1947. Thirty-two years of annual burning in longleaf pine. *Jour. Forestry,* **45**:809–814.

———— 1951. Fire, site and longleaf height growth. *Jour. Forestry,* **49**:25–28.

———— 1951. Fire resistance of longleaf pine seedlings. *Jour. Forestry,* **49**:739–740.

Burns, P. Y. 1952. Effects of fire on forest soils in the pine barren region of New Jersey. *Yale Univ. School Forestry Bul.* 57.

———— 1955. Fire scars and decay in Missouri oaks. *Univ. Mo. Agr. Expt. Sta. Bul.* 642.

Byram, G. M., and R. M. Nelson, 1952. Lethal temperatures and fire injury. U.S. Forest Serv. Southeast. *Forest Expt. Sta. Res. Note 1.*

Chang, Ying-Pe 1954. Bark structure of North American conifers. *U.S. Dept. Agr. Tech. Bul.* 1095.

Clements, F. E. 1910. The life history of lodgepole burn forests. *U.S. Forest Serv. Bul.* 79.

Colman, E. A. 1953. Vegetation and watershed management. The Ronald Press Company, New York.

Corbett, E. S., and L. R. Green 1965. Emergency revegetation to rehabilitate burned watersheds in southern Calif. *USFS Res. Paper* PSW-22.

Crosby, John S. 1960. Forest and range fire problems of the Missouri Ozarks. *USFS Central States FRES Misc. Release* 32.

Cushwa, Charles G. 1968. Fire: A summary of literature in the U.S. from the mid-1920's to 1966. U.S. Forest Serv. Southeast. Forest Expt. Sta.

Daubenmire, R. F. 1947. Plants and environment: a textbook of plant autecology. John Wiley & Sons, Inc., New York.

Dyrness, C. T., C. T. Youngberg, and Robert H. Ruth 1957. Some effects of logging and slash burning on physical soil properties in the Corvallis watershed.

Eyre, F. H., and R. K. LeBarron 1944. Management of jack pine stands in the Lake States, *U.S. Dept. Agr. Tech. Bul.* 863.

Fowells, H. A., and R. E. Stephenson 1934. Effect of burning on forest soils. *Soil Sci.,* **38:**175–181.

Fritz, Emanuel 1932. The role of fire in the redwood region. *Univ. Calif. Agr. Expt. Sta. Cir.* 323.

Gisborne, H. T. 1942. "Milestones of Progress." Review of problems and accomplishments in fire control and fire research. *Fire Control Notes,* **6**(2):47–63.

Graham, S. A. 1952. Forest entomology, 3d ed., McGraw-Hill Book Company, Inc., New York.

Gruschow, G. F. 1952. Effect of winter burning on growth of slash pine in the flatwoods. *Jour. Forestry,* **50:**515–517.

Guthrie, J. D. n.d. Great forest fires of America. *U.S. Dept. Agr. Forest Serv. Bul.* (unnumbered).

Haig, I. T. 1936. Factors controlling initial establishment of western white pine and associated species. *Yale Univ. School Forestry Bul.* 41.

———, K. P. Davis, and R. H. Weidman 1941. Natural regeneration in the western white pine type. *U.S. Dept. Agr. Tech. Bul.* 767.

Haines, Donald A., and Rodney W. Sando 1969. Climatic conditions preceding historically great fires in the North-Central Region of the U.S. *USDA-FS Res. Paper* NC-34.

Hall, A. G. 1947. Four flaming days. *Amer. Forests,* **53:**540–542.

Hardy, Charles E., and J. W. Franks 1963. Forest Fires in Alaska. *USFS Res. Paper* Int-5.

Hare, Robert C. 1961. Heat effects on living plants. Occasional Paper 183, Southern Forest Expt. Sta., Forest Service, U.S.D.A.

Hepting, G. H. 1935. Decay following fire in young Mississippi Delta hardwoods. *U.S. Dept. Agr. Tech. Bul.* 494.

———, and G. G. Hedgcock 1937. Decay in merchantable oak, yellow poplar, and basswood in the Appalachian region. *U.S. Dept. Agr. Tech. Bul.* 570.

Heyward, Frank 1936. Soil changes associated with forest fires in the longleaf pine region of the South. *Amer. Soil Survey Assoc. Bul.* 17.

——— 1937. The effect of frequent fires on profile development of longleaf pine forest soils. *Jour. Forestry,* **35:**23–26.

——— 1938. Soil temperatures during forest fires in the longleaf pine region. *Jour. Forestry,* **36:**478–491.

—— 1939. Some moisture relations of soils from burned and unburned longleaf pine forests. *Soil Sci.,* **47:**313–324.

Holbrook, S. H. 1943. Burning an empire. The Macmillan Company, New York.

Isaac, L. A. 1943. Reproductive habits of Douglas-fir. Charles Lathrop Pack Forestry Foundation, Washington, D.C.

—— and H. G. Hopkins 1937. The forest soil of the Douglas-fir region, and changes wrought upon it by logging and slash burning. *Ecology,* **18:**264–279.

Jansson, J. R. 1949. Some effects of fire upon Douglas-fir soils in the Big Belt Mountains. *Proc. Mont. Acad. Sci.,* Missoula, **9:**17–21.

Jemison, G. M. 1943. Effect of single fires on the diameter growth of short leaf pine in the southern Appalachians. *Jour. Forestry,* **41:**574–576.

—— 1944. The effect of basal wounding by forest fires on the diameter growth of some southern Appalachian hardwoods. *Duke Univ. School Forestry Bul.* 9.

Kaufman, C. M., J. B. White, and R. J. Monroe 1954. Growth of pond pine in a pocosin area. *Jour. Forestry,* **52:**275–279.

Kimmey, J. W. 1955. Rate of deterioration of fire-killed timber in California. *U.S. Dept. Agr. Cir.* 962.

Kittredge, Joseph 1948. Forest Influences. McGraw-Hill Book Company, Inc., New York.

Kucera, Clair L., and John H. Ehrenreich 1962. Some effects of annual burning on central Missouri prairie. *Ecol. Soc. Amer. Bul.* **32**(2):334–336.

LeBarron, R. K. 1939. The role of forest fires in the reproduction of black spruce. *Minn. Acad. Sci. Proc.,* **7:**10–14.

Lindenmuth, A. W. Jr. 1961. Effects on fuels and trees of a large intentional burn in ponderosa pine. *Jour. Forestry,* **60**(11):804–810.

Lorenz, R. W. 1939. High temperature tolerance of forest trees. *Univ. Minn. Agr. Expt. Sta. Bul.* 141.

Lutz, H. J. 1956. Ecological effects of forest fires in the interior of Alaska. *U.S. Dept. Agr. Tech. Bul.* 1133.

—— 1960. Fire as an ecological factor in the boreal forest of Alaska. *Jour. Forestry,* **58:**454–460.

——, and R. F. Chandler, Jr. 1946. Forest soils. John Wiley & Sons, Inc., New York.

Maine, State of 1947–1948. The 1947 forest fire disaster (by A. H. Wilkins). Twenty-seventh Bien. Rept. Forest Commissioner, Augusta.

McArdle, R. E., W. H. Meyer, and Donald Bruce 1949. The yield of Douglas-fir in the Pacific Northwest. *U.S. Dept. Agr. Tech. Bul.* 201.

McCulley, R. D. 1950. Management of natural slash pine stands in the flatwoods of south Georgia and north Florida. *U.S. Dept. Agr. Cir.* 845.

Martin, R. E., 1963. Thermal properties of bark. *Forest Products Jour.* **13:**419–426.

Metz, Louis J., Thomas Lotti, and Ralph A. Klawitter 1961. Some effects of prescribed burning on coastal plains forest soil. *U.S. Forest Serv.-SE Sta. Res. Paper* 133.

Morris, William G. 1970. Effects of slash burning in overmature stands of the Douglas-fir region. *Forest Science,* **16**(3): 258–270.

Moss, V. D., and C. A. Wellner 1953. Aiding blister rust control by silvicultural measures in the western white pine type. *U.S. Dept. Agr. Cir.* 919.

Muntz, H. H. 1954. How to grow longleaf pine. *U.S. Dept. Agr. Farmers' Bul.* 2061.

Nelson, R. M. 1952. Observations on heat tolerance of southern pine needles. *U.S. Forest Serv. Southeast. Forest Expt. Sta. Paper* 14.

———, I. H. Sims, and M. S. Abell 1933. Basal fire wounds on some southern Appalachian hardwoods. *Jour. Forestry*, **31**:829–837.

Pearson, G. A. 1951. Management of ponderosa pine in the Southwest. *U.S. Dept. Agr. Agr. Monog.* 6.

Plummer, Fred G. 1912. Lightning in relation to forest fires. *U.S.D.A. Forest Service Bul. No.* 111.

Pogue, R. 1948. Effect of woods burning on lumber recovery. *Jour. Forestry*, **46**:689–690.

Putnam, J. A. 1951. Management of bottomland hardwoods. *U.S. Forest Serv. South. Forest Expt. Sta. Occas. Paper* 116.

Sampson, A. W. 1944. Plant succession on burned chaparral lands in northern California. *Univ. Cal. Agr. Expt. Sta. Bul.* 685.

——— 1952. Range management: principles and practice. John Wiley & Sons, Inc., New York.

Shantz, H. L. 1947. The use of fire as a tool in the management of the brush ranges of California. Dept. of Nat. Resources, Div. of Forestry, Calif.

——— 1948. An estimate of the shrinkage of Africa's tropical forests. *Unasylva*, **2**(2):66–67.

Shirley, H. L. 1936. Lethal high temperatures for conifers and the cooling effect of transpiration. *Jour. Agr. Res.*, **53**:239–258.

Show, S. B., and E. I. Kotok 1924. The role of fire in the California pine forests. *U.S. Dept. Agr. Bul.* 1294.

Skolko, A. J. 1947. Deterioration of fire-killed pulpwood stands in eastern Canada. *Forestry Chron.*, **23**:128–145.

Spalt, K. W. and W. E. Reifsnyder 1962. Bark characteristics and fire resistance: a literature review. *Yale School of Forestry and U.S. Forest Serv. South. Forest Expt. Sta. Occas. Paper* 193.

Spencer, Betty G. 1956. The big blowup. Caxton Printers, Ltd., Caldwell, Idaho.

Spurr, S. H. 1954. The forests of Itasca in the nineteenth century as related to fire. *Ecology*, **35**:21–25.

Stickel, P. W. 1940. The basal wounding of trees by fire. The effect of basal wounding by fire on trees in the northeast. *N E Forest Expt. Sta., Forest Serv. U.S.D.A., Technical Note No.* 30.

——— 1941. On the relation between bark thickness and resistance to fire. *U.S. Forest Serv. Northeast. Forest Expt. Sta. Tech. Note* 39.

Tarrant, R. F. 1954. Effect of slash burning on soil pH. *U.S. Forest Serv. Pacific Northwest Forest and Range Expt. Sta. Res. Note* 102.

——— 1954a. Soil reaction and germination of Douglas-fir seed. *U.S. Forest Serv. Pacific Northwest Forest and Range Expt. Sta. Res. Note* 105.

——— 1956. Changes in some physical soil properties after a prescribed burn in young ponderosa pine. *Jour. Forestry*, **54**:439–441.

Toole, E. R. 1959. Decay after fire injury to southern bottomland hardwoods. *U.S.D.A. Tech. Bul. 1189.*

Trimble, G. R., Jr., and N. R. Tripp 1949. Some effects of fire and cutting on forest soils in the lodgepole pine forests of the northern Rocky Mountains. *Jour. Forestry,* **46:**640–642.

U.S. Forest Serv. 1956. Glossary of terms used in forest fire control. *U.S. Dept. Agr. Handbook* 104.

Wahlenberg, W. G. 1946. Longleaf pine. Charles Lathrop Pack Forestry Foundation, Washington, D.C.

———, S. W. Greene, and H. R. Reed 1939. Effects of fire and cattle grazing on longleaf pine lands as studied at McNeill, Miss. *USDA Tech. Bul.* 683.

Wakeley, P. C., and H. H. Muntz 1947. Effect of prescribed burning on height growth of longleaf pine. *Jour. Forestry,* **45:**503–508.

Weaver, Harold 1951. Fire as an ecological factor in the southwestern ponderosa pine forests. *Jour. Forestry,* **49:**93–98.

——— 1955. Fire as an enemy, friend, and tool in forest management. *Jour. Forestry,* **53:**499–504.

Wells, B. W. 1942. Ecological problems of the southeastern United States coastal plain. *Bot. Rev.,* **8:**533–561.

Wexler, Harry 1950. The great smoke pall. *Weatherwise,* Sept. 24–30, 1950.

Wilkins, A. H. 1948. The story of the Maine forest fire disaster. *Jour. Forestry,* **46:**568–573.

Chapter 4: Forest Fuels

Anderson, Hal E., Arthur Brackebusch, Robert Mutch, and Richard Rothermel 1966. Mechanisms of fire spread. Research progress report no. 2. *U.S. Forest Serv. Res. Paper* Int-28.

Anonymous 1955. Measurement of fuel bed characteristics of grass and chaparral fuels. *Firestop, Calif. Div. Forestry and Coop. Agencies, Prog. Rept.* 5.

——— 1955a. Seasonal changes in chaparral moisture. *Firestop, Calif. Div. Forestry and Coop. Agencies, Prog. Rept.* 6.

Barrows, J. S. 1951. Fire behavior in northern Rocky Mountain forests. *U.S. Forest Serv. North. Rocky Mt. Forest and Range Expt. Sta. Paper* 29.

Bentley, Jay R., Donald W. Seegrist, and David A. Blakeman 1970. A technique for sampling low brush vegetation by crown volume classes. *U.S. Forest Serv. Res. Note* PSW–215.

Blackmarr, W. H., and Wm. B. Flanner 1968. Seasonal and diurnal variation in moisture content of six species of pocosin shrubs. *U.S. Forest Serv. Res. Paper* SE-33.

Blow, F. E. 1955. Quantity and hydrologic characteristics of litter under upland oak forests in eastern Tennessee. *Jour. Forestry,* **3:**190–195.

Boe, K. N. 1956. Regeneration and slash disposal in lodgepole pine clear cuttings. *Northwest Sci.,* **30:**1–11.

Brown, James K. 1965. Estimating crown fuel weights of red pine and jack pine. *U.S. Forest Serv. Res. Paper* LS–20.

——— 1970. Physical fuel properties of ponderosa pine forest floors and cheatgrass. *U.S. Forest Serv. Res. Paper* Int-74.

―――― 1970. Vertical distribution of fuel in spruce-fir logging slash. *U.S. Forest Serv. Res. Paper* Int-81.

Bruce, David 1951. Fuel weights on the Osceola National Forest. *Fire Control Notes,* **12**(3):20–23.

Buck, C. C. 1951. Inflammability of chaparral depends on how it grows. *U.S. Forest Serv. Calif. Forest and Range Expt. Sta. Misc. Paper* 2.

Byram, G. M., W. L. Fons, F. M. Sauer, and R. K. Arnold 1952. Thermal conductivity of some common forest fuels. Thermal properties of forest fuels. U.S. Forest Serv., Div. of Fire Res.

――――, and G. M. Jemison 1943. Solar radiation and forest fuel moisture. *Jour. Agr. Res.,* **67**:149–176.

Curry, J. R., and W. L. Fons 1938. Rate of spread of surface fires in the ponderosa pine type of California. *Jour. Agr. Res.,* **57**:239–267.

Davis, K. P. 1961. Fire and the folly of pattern thinking. Paper given at annual meeting Southern Pulpwood Conservation Assoc., New Orleans, La.

Davis, W. S. 1949. The rate of spread and fuel density relationship. *Fire Control Notes,* **10**(2):8–9.

Fahnestock, G. R. 1953. Inflammability of the current year's logging slash. *Res. Note* 124.

―――― 1953a. Chipping takes the hazard out of logging slash. *Res. Note* 125.

―――― 1953b. Relative humidity and fire behavior in logging slash. *U.S. Forest Serv. North. Rocky Mt. Forest and Range Expt. Sta. Res. Note* 126.

―――― 1970. Two keys for appraising forest fire fuels. *U.S. Forest Serv. Res. Paper* PNW-99.

――――, and William K. Key, 1971. Weight of brushy forest fire fuels from photographs. *Forest Sci.,* **17**(1) 119–124.

Fons, W. L. 1946. Analysis of fire spread in light forest fires. *Jour. Agr. Res.* **72**: 93–121.

Fosberg, Michael A. 1970. Drying rates of heartwood below fibre saturation. Fuel moisture response, drying relationships under standard and field conditions. *Forest Sci.,* **16**(1)57–63 and 121–128.

―――― 1971. Climatological influences on moisture characteristics of dead fuel: theoretical analysis. *Forest Sci.,* **17**(1)64–72.

Hornby, L. G. 1936. Fire control planning in the Northern Rocky Mountain Region. *U.S. Forest Serv. North. Rocky Mt. Forest and Range Expt. Sta. Prog. Rept.* 1.

Jemison, G. M. 1935. Influence of weather factors on moisture content of light fuels in forests of the northern Rocky Mt. *Jour. Agr. Res.,* **51**:885–906.

――――, and J. J. Keetch 1942. Rate of spread of fire and its resistance to control in the fuel types of eastern mountain forests. *U.S. Forest Serv. Appalachian Forest Exp. Sta. Tech. Note* 52.

Kiil, A. D. 1968. Weight of fuel complex in 70 year old lodgepole pine stands of different densities. *Canada Dept. of Forestry and Rural Develop. For. Br. Pub. No.* 1228.

Kittredge, Joseph 1944. Estimation of the amount of foliage in trees and stands. *Jour. Forestry,* **42**:905–912.

―――― 1948. Forest influences. McGraw-Hill Book Company, Inc., New York.

Kurucz, J. 1969. Component weights of D. fir, w. hemlock and western red cedar biomass for simulation of amount and distribution of forest fuels. *Univ. of Br. Columbia Pub. No.* 2649.

Lyman, C. K. 1947. Slash disposal as related to fire control on the national forests of western Montana and northern Idaho. *Jour. Forestry,* **45**:259–262.

McArthur, A. G. 1966. Weather and Grassland Fire Behavior. Forest Research Institute, Commonwealth of Australia. Leaflet No. 100.

Matthews, D. N. 1937. The small plot method of rating forest fuels. *Jour. Forestry,* **35**:929–931.

Morris, W. G. 1953. Fuel moisture indicator stick as guide for slash burning. *Timberman,* **54**(10):128.

——— 1954. Rate of spread on a Washington fern fire. *Fire Control Notes,* **15**(1):32–34.

Munger, T. T., and D. N. Matthews 1941. Slash disposal and forest management after clear-cutting in the Douglas-fir region. *U.S. Dept. Agr. Cir.* 586.

———, and R. H. Westveld 1931. Slash disposal in the western yellow pine forests of Oregon and Washington. *U.S. Dept. Agr. Tech. Bul.* 259.

Mutch, Robert W., and Charles W. Philpot 1970. Relationship of silica content to flammability in grasses. *Forest Sci.* **16**(1)64–64.

New Jersey Department of Conservation 1942. Forest fuel types of New Jersey. In cooperation with U.S. Forest Serv.

Olson, D. S. 1953. Preliminary tests on relative inflammability of logging slash by species in the western white pine type. *Univ. Idaho Forest, Wildlife, and Range Expt. Sta. Res. Note* 5.

——— 1953a. Solids and voids in logging slash. *Univ. Idaho Forest, Range, and Wildlife Expt. Sta. Res. Note* 8.

——— 1953b. Slash volume in relation to species and timber volume harvested. *Univ. Idaho Forest Range, and Wildlife Expt. Sta. Res. Note* 9.

———, and G. R. Fahnestock 1955. Logging slash: a study of the problem in Inland Empire forests. *Univ. Idaho Forest, Wildlife, and Range Expt. Sta. and U.S. Forest Serv. Intermtn. Forest and Range Expt. Sta. Bul.* 1.

Pearson, G. A., and A. C. McIntyre 1935. Slash disposal in ponderosa pine forests of the Southwest. *U.S. Dept. Agr. Cir.* 357.

Philpot, Charles W. 1965. Diurnal fluctuation in moisture content of ponderosa pine and whiteleaf manzanita leaves. *U.S. Forest Serv. Res. Note PSW* 67.

——— 1969. Seasonal changes in heat content and other extractive content of chamise. *U.S. Forest Serv. Res. Paper INT-61.*

Richards, L. W. 1940. Effect of certain chemical attributes of vegetation on forest inflammability. *Jour. Agr. Res.,* **60**:833–838.

Rothacher, J. S., F. E. Blow, and S. M. Potts 1954. Estimating the quantity of tree foliage in oak stands in the Tennessee Valley. *Jour. Forestry,* **52**:169–173.

Schroeder, George 1953. Analysis of the fire hazard: the fuels we work with. *West. Forestry and Conserv. Assoc. Proc.,* **44**:53–55.

Show, S. B. and E. I. Kotok 1930. The determination of hour control for adequate fire protection in the major cover types of the California pine region. *U.S. Dept. Agr. Tech. Bul.* 209.

Storey, T. C., W. L. Fons, and F. M. Sauer 1955. Crown characteristics of several coniferous tree species. *U.S. Forest Serv., Div. Fire Res., Interim Tech. Rept.* AFSWP-416.

Wendel, G. W., T. G. Storey, and G. M. Byram 1962. Forest fuels on organic and associated soils in the coastal plain of North Carolina. *U.S. Forest Serv. Southeastern Forest Expt. Sta. Paper* 144.

Williams, D. E. 1955. Fire hazard resulting from jackpine slash. *Canada Dept. North. Affairs and Nat. Resources, Forest Res. Div., Tech. Note* 22.

Chapter 5: Fire Weather

Advisory Committee on Weather Control 1957. Final report of the advisory committee on weather control. Library of Congress Card 58-60006, Government Printing Office.

Barrows, J. S. 1951. Forest fires in the northern Rocky Mountains. *U.S. Forest Serv. North. Rocky Mt. Forest and Range Expt. Sta. Paper* 28.

——— 1968. Preventing fire from the sky. Yearbook separate 3589, U.S. Dept. Agriculture, 1968. pp. 217–223.

Berry, F. A., Jr., Eugene Bollay, and N. R. Beers (Eds.) 1945. Handbook of meteorology. McGraw-Hill Book Company, Inc., New York.

Blakadar, A. K. 1957. Boundary layer wind maxima and their significance for the growth of nocturnal inversions. *Bul. Amer. Met. Soc.* **38**:283–290.

Buajiti, K., and A. K. Blakadar 1957. Theoretical studies of diurnal wind structure variations in the planetary boundary layer. *Quart. Jour. Royal Met. Soc.,* **83**:486–500.

Byers, H. R., and R. R. Braham 1949. The thunderstorm. U.S. Dept. of Commerce, Weather Bureau (unnumbered).

——— 1959. General meteorology. McGraw-Hill Book Company, Inc., New York.

Byram, Geo. M. 1954. Atmospheric conditions related to blowup fires. *U.S. Forest Serv. Southeast Forest Expt. Sta. Paper* 35.

Civil Aeronautics Adm. 1955. Pilots Weather Handbook. *U.S. Dept. of Commerce CAA Tech. Manual* 104.

Countryman, C. M. 1959. Fire environment and silvicultural practice. *Soc. Amer. Forest. Proceedings, 1959,* p. 22.

Defant, Friedrich 1951. Local winds, in Compendium of meteorology. American Meteorological Society, Waverly Press, Inc., Baltimore.

Fuquay, Donald M. 1967. Weather modification and forest fires. Reprinted from Ground level climatology. *Amer. Assoc. Adv. Sci.*

———A. R. Taylor, R. A. Howe, and C. W. Schmidt 1972. Lightning discharges that caused forest fires. *Jour. Geophys. Res.* **77** (12).

Gisborne, H. T. 1941. How the wind blows in the forests of northern Idaho. U.S. Forest Serv. North. Rocky Mt. Forest and Range Expt. Sta.

Gunn, Ross 1951. Precipitation electricity, in Compendium of meteorology. American Meteorological Society, Waverly Press, Inc., Baltimore.

Hagenguth, J. H. 1951. The lightning discharge, in Compendium of meteorology. American Meteorological Society, Waverly Press, Inc., Baltimore.

Jackson, A. W. 1968. The drought index, a fire weather forecast tool. *Canadian Dept. of Transport Met. Br. Tech. memo* 1740.

Klein, W. H. 1960. Storm tracks. *U.S.W.B. Paper* 40.

Krumm, W. R. 1954. On the causes of downdrafts from dry thunderstorms over the plateau area of the United States. *Bul. Amer. Met. Soc.*, **35**(3):122–125.

MacHattie, L. B. 1969. Modern meteorological services and forest fire control. *Pulp & Paper Mag. of Canada*, **70**(16), pp. 87–89. (also paper).

Petterssen, Sverre 1941. Introduction to meteorology. McGraw-Hill Book Company, Inc., New York.

———, P. A. Sheppard, C. H. B. Priestly, and K. R. Johonnessen 1944. An investigation of subsidence in the free atmosphere. NAVAER 50-IR-149. U.S. Navy, Aerology Section.

——— 1956. Weather analysis and forecasting. 2 vols. McGraw-Hill Book Company, Inc., New York.

Riehl, Herbert, M. A. Alaka, C. L. Jordan, and R. J. Renard 1954. The jet stream. *Amer. Met. Soc. Met, Monog.*, **2**(7).

Ryan, Bill C. 1969. A vertical perspective of Santa Ana winds in a canyon. *USDA-FS Res. Paper PSW*-52.

Schaefer, V. J. 1946. The production of ice crystals in a cloud of supercooled water droplets. *Science*, **104**:457–459.

——— 1949. The possibilities of modifying lightning storms in the northern Rockies. *U.S. Forest Serv. North. Rocky Mt. Forest and Range Expt. Sta. Paper* 19.

——— 1957. The relationship of jet streams to forest wildfires. *Jour. Forestry*, **55**:419–425.

Schroeder, M. J. 1950. The Hudson Bay high and the spring fire season in the Lake States. *Fire Control Notes*, **11**(1):1–8.

———, et al. 1964. Synoptic weather types associated with critical fire weather. U.S. For. Serv. Pacific S. W. For. Expt. Sta., Berkeley, Calif.

——— and Charles C. Buck 1970. Fire Weather. *USDA Forest Service, Agr. Handbook* 360.

Sinclair, J. G. 1922. Temperatures of the soil and air in a desert. *Monthly Weather Rev.*, **50**:142–144.

Taylor, Dee F., and Dansy T. Williams 1967. Meteorological conditions of the Hellgate Fire. *U.S. Forest Serv. S.E. Forest Expt. Sta. Res. Paper* SE-29.

Thiessen, A. H. 1945. Weather glossary. *U.S. Dept. Commerce, Weather Bureau*, no. 1445.

U. S. Forest Serv. 1956. Glossary of terms used in forest fire control. *U.S. Dept. Agr. Handbook* 104.

Vonnegut, B. 1947. The nucleation of ice formation by silver iodide. *Jour. Appl. Phys.*, **18**:593–595.

Williams, Dansy T. 1968. Fire behavior and the sea breeze front. Paper presented at A.M.S.-SAF conference on fire and forest meteorology.

——— 1970. Ten years of forest fire meteorology at the Southern Forest Fire Laboratory. *Proceedings of Southern States Fire Control and Information and Education Chiefs Meeting, Macon, Ga.* pp. 57–66.

Chapters 6 and 7: Combustion and Behavior of Fire

Abell, C. A. 1940. Rates of initial spread of free-burning fires on the national forests of California. *U.S. Forest Serv. Calif. Forest and Range Expt. Sta. Res. Note* 24.

Anderson, Hal E. 1968. Fire spread and flame shape. *Fire Technology*, 4(1)51–58.

――― 1969. Heat transfer and fire spread. *U.S. Forest Serv. Res. Paper* INT-69.

――― 1970. Forest fuel ignitibility. *Fire Technology*, 6(4)312–319.

―――, Arthur Brackebusch, Robt. Mutch, and Richard Rothermel 1966. Mechanisms of fire spread. Research progress report no. 2. *U.S. Forest Serv. Res. Paper Int-28.*

Arnold, R. K., and C. C. Buck 1954. Blow-up fires—silviculture or weather problems? *Jour. Forestry*, **52:**408–411.

Barrows, J. S. 1951. Fire behavior in northern Rocky Mountain forests. *U.S. Forest Serv., North. Rocky Mountain Forest and Range Expt. Sta. Paper* 29.

Bond, Horatio 1952. Fire safety in the atomic age. Leaflet—National Fire Protection Assn., Boston.

Brown, A. A. 1940. Lessons of the McVey fire, Black Hills National Forest. *Fire Control Notes*, 4(2):63–67.

Brown, James K. 1970. Ratios of surface area to volume for common fine fuels. *Forest Sci.*, 16(1):101–105.

Byram, Geo. M. 1954. Atmospheric conditions related to blowup fires. *U.S. Forest Serv. Southeast. Forest Expt. Sta. Paper* 35.

――― 1963. An analysis of the drying process in forest fuel material. Paper presented at International Symposium on Humidity and Moisture. Washington, D.C.

――― 1966. Scaling laws for modeling mass fires. Paper, Western States Section. The Combustion Institute, Denver, Colo.

―――, H. B. Clements, E. R. Elliott, and P. M. George 1963. An experimental study of model fires. *U.S. Forest Serv. S.E. For. Expt. Sta. Technical Report No. 3, Project Fire Model.*

―――, H. B. Clements, M. E. Bishop and R. M. Nelson, Jr. 1966. An experimental study of model fires. *U.S. For. Serv., S.E. For. Expt. Sta. Final report, Project Fire Model* OCD-PS-65-40.

―――, and G. M. Jemison 1943. Solar radiation and forest fuel moisture. *Jour. Agr. Res.*, **67:**149–176.

―――, and Robert Martin 1962. Fire whirlwinds in the Laboratory. *Fire Control Notes* 25(1).

―――, and Robert E. Martin 1970. The modeling of fire whirlwinds. *Forest Sci.*, 16(4):386–399.

―――, and R. M. Nelson 1951. The possible relation of air turbulence to erratic fire behavior in the Southeast. *Fire Control Notes*, 12(3):1–8.

―――, and Ralph M. Nelson, Jr. 1970. The modeling of pulsating fires. *Fire Technology*, 6(2):102–110.

Carmen, E. P. 1950. Kent's mechanical engineers' handbook. Power volume, sec. 2, Combustion and fuels, 12th ed., pp. 39–41. John Wiley & Sons, Inc., New York.

Committee on Fire Research, 1959. National Academy of Sciences. *International Symposium on the Use of Models in Fire Research.* Pub. 786, 1961. National Academy of Sciences, National Research Council, Washington, D.C. The Fire Research Conference.

Cooper, Robert W. 1965. Wind movement in pine stands. *U.S. Forest Service S.E. For. Expt. Sta., Georgia Forest Research Paper 33.*

Countryman, Clive M. 1964. Mass fires and fire behavior. *U.S. Forest Serv. Research Paper* P.S.W.-19.

———— 1969. Project Flambeau—an investigation of mass fire 1964–1967. Final Report. Vol. 1. *U.S. Forest Serv.* PSW F and R Expt. Sta. Berkeley, Calif.

————, and Craig C. Chandler 1966. Mass fire behavior research. *Proceedings of the 12th annual NATO Scientific Working Party,* Paris, France, May 10-13, 1966, pp. 163–172.

Fenner, R. L., R. K. Arnold, and C. C. Buok 1955. Area ignition for brush burning. *U.S. Forest Serv. Calif. Forest and Range Expt. Sta. Tech. Paper* 10.

Fons, W. L. 1946. Analysis of fire spread in light forest fuels. *Jour. Agr. Res.,* 72:93–121.

———— 1950. Heating and ignition of small wood cylinders. *Ind. and Engin. Chem.,* 42:2130–2133.

————, H. D. Bruce, and W. Y. Pong 1961. A steady state technique for studying the properties of free burning wood fires. *Fire Research Abstracts and Reviews,* 2(1):28–30. Reprinted from *NAS-NRC Pub.* 786, pp. 219–234, Washington, D.C.

Friedman, R., and J. B. Levy 1957. Survey of fundamental knowledge of mechanisms of actions of flame-extinguishing agents. *W.A.D.C. Tech. Rept.* 56-568. Wright-Patterson Air Force Base, Wright Air Development Center, Ohio.

Graham, H. E. 1957. Fire whirlwind formation as favored by topography and upper winds. *Fire Control Notes,* 18(1): 20–24.

Halpern, Y., and S. Patai 1969. Pyrolitic reactions of carbohydrates. *Israel Jour. Chem.,* Part V, 7:673–683; Part VI, 7:685–690; Part VII, 7:691–696.

Hissong, J. E. 1926. Whirlwinds at oil-tank fire, San Luis Obispo, Calif. *Monthly Weather Rev.,* 54:161–163.

Houminer, Y., and S. Patai 1969. Pyrolitic reactions of carbohydrates. Parts II and III, *Israel Jour. Chem.,* 7:513–524 and 7:525–534.

Jones, D. C., and Abe Broido 1971. Apparatus for determining glowing combustibility of thin fuels. *Jour. Fire Flammability,* 2:77–86.

McArthur, A. G. 1966. Weather and grassland fire behavior. Leaflet No. 100, Forest Res. Institute, Commonwealth of Australia.

Morton, B. R. (Monash Univ., Aus.) 1970. The physics of fire whirls. Nat. Acad. of Sciences. *Fire Research Abstracts and Reviews,* 12(1).

Murphy, Peter J., Wm. R. Beaufait, and Robt. W. Steele 1966. Fire spread in an artificial fuel. *Montana Forest and Conservation Expt. Sta. Bul. No.* 32, July 1966.

Musham, H. A. 1941. The great Chicago fire, October 8–10, 1871. Papers in Illinois history and transactions for 1940, pp. 68–189. Illinois State Historical Society, Springfield, Ill.

Mutch, R. W. 1965. Ignition delay of ponderosa pine needles and sphagnum moss. *Fire Research Abstracts and Reviews,* **7**(2):83–84.

Newman, L. L. 1950. Kent's mechanical engineers' handbook. Power volume, sec. 2, Combustion and fuels, 12th ed. John Wiley & Sons, Inc., New York. pp. 66–69.

Patai, S., and Y. Halpern 1970. Pyrolytic reactions of carbohydrates. Part IX. The effect of additives on the thermal behavior of cellulose samples of different chrystallinity. *Israel Jour. Chem.* **8**:662–665.

Rothermel, Richard C. 1969. Tailoring the fire spread rate model to the field. Spring Meeting, 1969. The Combustion Institute.

Scesa, S. and F. M. Sauer 1954. Possible effects of free convection on fire behavior—laminar and turbulent line and point sources of heat. *U.S. Forest Serv., Calif. Forest and Range Expt. Sta. Tech. Paper* 8.

—— 1957. Transfer of heat by forced convection from a line combustion source. U.S. Forest Serv., Div. of Fire Res.

Schaefer, V. J. 1957. The relationship of jet streams to forest wildfires. *Jour. Forestry,* **55**:419–425.

Shroeder, Mark J., and C. C. Buck 1970. Fire weather. *U.S. Dept. Agr. Forest Serv. Handbook.* 360.

Small, R. T. 1957. The relationship of weather factors to the rate of spread of the Robie Creek fire. *Monthly Weather Rev.* **85**:1–8.

Stamm, A. J. 1946. Passage of liquids, vapors, and dissolved materials through softwoods. *U.S. Dept. Agr. Tech. Bul.* 929.

——, and E. E. Harris 1953. Chemical processing of wood. Chemical Publishing Co., Inc., New York.

Taylor, Dee F., and Dansey T. Williams 1967. Meteorological conditions of the Hellgate Fire. *U.S. Forest Serv. S.E. For. Expt. Sta. Res. Paper* SE-29.

Vehrencamp, J. E. 1955. An investigation of fire behavior in a natural atmospheric environment. *Univ. Calif., Los Angeles, Dept. of Engin., Rept.* 55-50.

Chapter 8: Fire Danger Rating

Beall, H. W. 1947. Research in the measurement of forest fire danger. Dominion Forest Service, Ottawa. (5th British Empire Forestry Conference, Great Britain, 1947.)

—— 1948. Forest fire danger tables (provisional). Dominion Forest Serv., *Dept. Mines and Resources, Forest Fire Res. Note* 12.

Blackmarr, W. H., and William B. Flanner 1968. Seasonal and diurnal variation in moisture content of six species of pocosin shrubs. *U.S. Forest Serv. Res. Paper SE*-33.

—— 1971. Equilibrium moisture content of common fine fuels found in Southeastern forests. *U.S. Forest Serv. Res. Paper* SE-74.

Brown, A. A., and W. S. Davis 1939. A fire danger meter for the Rocky Mountain region. *Jour. Forestry,* **37**:552–558.

——, and A. D. Folweiler 1953. Fire in the forests of the United States. John S. Swift Co., Inc., St. Louis, Mo.

Chandler, W. G., and N. E. Westmore 1949. Assessment of fire danger conditions. *Austral. Forestry,* **13**:53–62.

Countryman, C. M. 1957. California fire weather severity in 1956. *U.S. Forest Serv. Calif. Forest and Range Expt. Sta. Res. Note* 118.

——, and P. H. Intorf 1953. A fire season severity index for California National Forests. *U.S. Forest Serv. PSW, Forest and Range Expt. Sta. Misc. Paper* 14.

Cromer, D. A. N. 1946. Hygrothermographic fire danger rating and forecasting. *Australian Forestry,* vol. 10, Canberra, A.C.T.

Crosby, J. S. 1949. Forest fire burning conditions in the Lake States. *U.S. Forest Serv. Lake States Forest Expt. Sta. Paper* 16.

—— 1954. Probability of fire occurrence can be predicted. *U.S. Forest Serv. Central States Forest Expt. Sta. Tech. Paper,* 143.

Deeming, John E., James W. Lancaster, and Michael A. Fosberg 1971. Instructions for the 1971 field trials of the NFDR System. *U.S. Forest Serv., Rocky Mountain Forest Expt. Sta. Misc. Pub.*

Dubois, Coert 1914. Systematic fire protection in the California forests. *U.S. Forest Serv. Bul.* (unnumbered).

Fahnestock, G. R. 1951. Correction of burning index for the effects of altitude, aspect, and time of day. *U.S. Forest Serv. North Rocky Mt. Forest and Range Expt. Sta. Res. Note* 100.

Fosberg, Michael A. 1970. Drying rates of heartwood below fibre saturation, under standard and field conditions. *Forest Sci.,* **16**(1):57–63 and 121–128.

Gisborne, H. T. 1928. Measuring forest fire danger in northern Idaho. *U.S. Dept. Agr. Misc. Pub.* 29.

—— 1936. Measuring fire weather and forest inflammability. *U.S. Dept. Agr. Cir.* 398.

—— 1936a. The principles of measuring forest fire danger. *Jour. Forestry,* **34**:786–793.

Hardy, Charles E., E. D. Syverson, and J. H. Dieterich 1955. Fire weather and fire danger station handbook. *U.S. Forest Serv. Intermtn. Forest and Range Expt. Sta. Misc. Pub.* 3.

——, and Arthur P. Brackebusch 1959. The intermountain fire danger rating system. *Soc. Amer. Foresters Proc.* 1959, 133–136.

Hayes, G. L. 1941. Influence of altitude and aspect on daily variations in factors of forest-fire danger. *U.S. Dept. Agr. Cir.* 591.

—— 1944. Where and when to measure forest fire danger. *Jour. Forestry,* **42**:744–751.

—— 1949. Forest fire danger. U.S. Dept. Agr. Yearbook.

Hood, F. C. 1954. Fuel-moisture forecasts. *Fire Control Notes,* **15**(1):35–38.

Jemison, G. M. 1944. Fire danger indexes. *Jour. Forestry,* **42**:261–263.

——, A. W. Lindenmuth, and J. J. Keetch 1949. Forest fire-danger measurement in the eastern United States. *U.S. Dept. Agr. Handbook* 1.

Keetch, John J. 1954. Instructions for using forest fire danger meter type 8. *U.S. Forest Serv. Southeast. Forest Expt. Sta. Paper* 33.

—— 1957. Occurrence rate as a measure of success in fire prevention. *Fire Control Notes,* **18**(1):41–45.

—— and G. M. Byram 1969. A drought index for forest fire control. *Station Paper* SE-38. SE FRES.

Lindenmuth, A. W., and J. J. Keetch 1949. Open method for measuring fire danger in hardwood forests. *U.S. Forest Serv. Southeast. Forest Expt. Sta. Tech. Note* 71.

——, and —— 1950. A new measure of the severity of fire seasons. *Fire Control Notes,* **11**(1):15–19.

——, and R. M. Nelson 1951. Forest fire damage appraisal procedures and tables for the Northeast. *U.S. Forest Serv. Southeast. Forest Expt. Sta. Paper* 11.

——, and —— 1951a. Forest fire danger measurement in the United States. *Unasylva,* **5**(2):67–70.

Luke, R. H. 1961. Bush fire control in Australia. Chap. 8, The measurement of fire danger. Hodder and Stoughton, Melbourne, Aust.

Mattsson, J. W. 1953. Region Four's flash fuel burning index. *Fire Control Notes,* **14**(2):7–9.

McArthur, A. G. 1963. Forest fire danger meter. Forest Res. Institute, M No. 3, Canberra, Australia.

—— 1966. The fire control problem and fire research in Australia. *Proceed. 6th World Forestry Congress,* Madrid, Spain, 1966.

Mitchell, J. A. 1953. Burning index ratings in fire control planning. *U.S. Forest Serv. Lake States Forest Expt. Sta. Paper* 28.

—— 1954. Rating the effectiveness of forest fire protection. *Jour. Forestry,* **52**:183–185.

Mutch, Robert. W., and Orval W. Gastineau 1970. Timelag and equilibrium moisture content of reindeer lichen. *U.S. Forest Serv. Res. Paper* INT-76.

Nelson, R. M. 1955. How to measure forest fire danger in the Southeast. *U.S. Forest Serv. Southeast. Forest Expt. Sta. Paper* 52.

—— 1969. Some factors affecting the moisture timelags of woody materials. *U.S. Forest Serv. Res. Paper* SE-44.

Peace, T. R. 1948. The estimation of fire hazard in Great Britain. *Forestry,* **22**:195–210.

Shank, H. M. 1935. A measure of forest fire hazard in central Idaho. *Jour. Forestry,* **33**:389–391.

Simard, A. J. 1968. The moisture content of forest fuels. Forest Fire Research Institute, Ottawa, Canada. Information Reports FFX-14, 15, 16.

Turner, J. A., S. J. Muraro, Gy Peck, and R. N. Russel 1969. Contributions on the development of a national fire danger rating system for Canada. (1) A drought index to simulate moisture content of the full organic layer. Also paper 1–12, 1968. (2) Muraro and Turner. Comparison of Petawawa Mark IV and B.C. Mark II drought indexes. Also Misc. Pub. J–4. (3) Muraro. A modular approach to a revised national fire danger rating system. Also Misc.

Pub. J–4. Dominion Forest Service, Ottawa, Canada, Dept. of Fisheries and Forestry, Forestry Branch.

Van Wagner, C. E. 1970. New developments in forest fire danger rating. Canada, Dept. of Fisheries and Forestry, For. Br., P.F.E.S., Chalk River, Ontario. PS-X-19.

Verret, M. 1947. L'Indice d'inflammabilité des forêts en rapport des incendies forestiers en 1946. (Index of inflammability of forests in relation to forest fires in 1946). *Serv. Protect. Quebec Bul.* 7.

Villeneuve, G. O. 1948. Méthode d'evaluation des dangers d'incendie forestier dans la province de Quebec. (Method of rating forest fire danger in the Province of Quebec). *Bur. Meteor. Quebec Bul.* 7.

—— 1949. Méthodes d'evaluation des dangers d'incendie forestier au Canada et aux Etats-Unis. (Methods of rating forest fire danger in Canada and the United States). *Bur. Meteor. Quebec Bul.* 13.

Williams. D. E. 1963. Forest Fire Danger Manual. Dominion of Canada. Dept. of Forestry Pub. No. 1027.

Wright, J. G. 1933. Forest fire hazard tables for mixed red and white pine forests eastern Ontario and western Quebec regions. Div. For. Protection Forest Service, Dept. Interior, Ottawa.

Chapter 9: Prevention of Man-caused Fires

American Forests 1956. Southern Fire Prevention Conference Issue. *Amer. Forests,* **62**(5):1–96.

Baird, A. W., J. W. Robinson, Jr., and A. R. Jones, Jr. 1969. Beliefs and practices of selected rural residents toward forest conservation and management. *Miss. State Univ. Soc. Sci. Res. Cent. Report* 28.

——, and M. L. Doolittle 1969. Rural Residents and Forest Fire Risk: guides to forest fire prevention. *Miss. State Univ. Soc. Sci. Res. Center Report* 29.

Barney, Richard J. 1969. Interior Alaska wildfires 1956–1965. USDA-FS PNW Institute of Northern Forestry Misc. Pub.

Barrows, J. S. 1968. Preventing fire from the sky. Yearbook of Agri. Separate No. 3589. Reprinted from pp. 217–223, 1968.

Bernardi, Gene C. 1970. Three fire prevention television films varying in "threat" content—their effectiveness in changing attitudes. *U.S. Forest Serv. Res. Paper* PSW-63.

Bertrand, Alvid L., Wm. D. Heffernan, Dale G. Welch, and John P. O'Carrol 1970. Attitudinal patterns prevalent in a forest area with high incendiarism. *Louisiana Agr. Expt. Sta. Bul.* 648.

Burns, Robt. 1970. Combatting special fire prevention problems in California. *Proc. National meeting Soc. of Amer. Foresters,* 1970.

Cobb, S. S. 1952. An answer to forest fire prevention and control in anthracite coal fields. *Jour. Forestry,* **50**:834–837.

Colvill, L. L., and A. B. Everts 1952. An informal study of power-saw fires. *Fire Control Notes,* **13**(1):1–5.

Davis, Clint 1951. Only you can prevent forest fires. *Amer. Forests,* **57**(4):6–10, 40–41.

—— 1952. Smokey—at point of sale. *Fire Control Notes,* **13**(2):41–46.

Davis, K. P. 1961. Fire and the folly of pattern thinking. Paper given at annual meeting, So. Pulpwood Cons. Assn., New Orleans, La.

Dickerson, B. E., and A. L. Bertrand 1969. Potential roles of local opinion leaders in the communication of forest fire prevention messages. *La. Agr. Expt. Sta. Bul.* 639.

Doyle, J. A. 1951. A survey of forest fire causes (in Canada) and suggested corrective measures. *Forest Chron.,* **27**:335–348.

Everts, A. B. 1953. Fire extinguishers for use with power saws. *Fire Control Notes,* **13**(1):6–7.

Folkman, Wm. S. 1965. Motorists knowledge of the "No Smoking" ordinance in southern California. *USFS Res. Note* PSW–72.

—— 1965. Residents of Butte County, Calif: their attitudes regarding forest fire prevention. *USFS Res. Paper* PSW–25.

Greeley, W. B. 1949. Keep Green pays off. *Amer. Forests,* **55**(10):6–9.

Haug Associates 1968. Public image of and attitudes toward Smokey the Bear and forest fires. Report from study by Haug Associates for Cooperative Forest Fire Prevention Program. U.S. Dept. Agr., Forest Service.

Huber, W. W. 1957. How to use CFFP material. *Fire Control Notes,* **18**(3):97–102.

Keetch, J. J. 1941. Smoker fires and fire brands. U.S. Forest Serv. Southeast. *Forest Expt. Sta. Tech. Note* 49.

Lehman, J. W., and R. A. Vogenberger 1955. The role of a regional agency in forest fire control. *Jour. Forestry,* **53**:430–435.

Lindenmuth, A. W., Jr., and J. J. Keetch 1953. Fire prevention efforts pay off in the Northeast. *Fire Control Notes,* **14**(1):14–16.

Lindh, A. G. 1940. Separating the good people from the careless. *Fire Control Notes,* **4**(2):68–70.

Marsh, S. H. 1949. West Virginia episode. *Fire Control Notes,* **10**(1):7–9.

Morris, W. G. 1955. Accidental fires in slash in western Oregon and Washington. *Fire Control Notes,* **16**(2):21–23.

Mullin, G. B. P. 1942. Fire prevention in the eastern region "hot spot." *Fire Control Notes,* **6**(1):6–8.

Murray, Edw. J. 1964. Motivation and emotion. Foundations of modern psychology series, Prentice-Hall, Inc., Englewood Cliffs, N.J.

Noyes, J. H. 1955. Prevention action correlated to fire danger rating. *Fire Control Notes,* **16**(3):25–26.

Prater, J. D. 1952. Coordinated fire prevention in logging operations. *West. Forest and Conserv. Assoc. Proc.,* **43**:38–43.

Priaux, A. W. 1950. The story of Keep Oregon Green. *Jour. Forestry,* **48**:87–91.

Reynolds, R. D. 1950. Fire protection law enforcement trends in California. *Jour. Forestry,* **48**:696–699.

Robinson, D. D. 1952. Gasoline power-saw operation fires. Loggers' Handbook, vol. 12, Pacific Logging Congress, Portland, Ore.

—— 1953. A study of power saw fires. *Jour. Forestry,* **51**:891–896.

Sarapata, Adam, and Wm. S. Folkman 1970. Fire prevention in the Calif. Division of Forestry—personnel and practices. *USDA-FS Res. Paper* PSW-65.

Shea, J. P. 1940. Getting at the roots of the man-caused forest fires. U.S. Forest Serv.

Siegelman, E. Y., and Wm. S. Folkman 1971. Youthful fire-setters—an exploratory study in personality and background. *USDA-FS, Res. Note* PSW-230.

Sipe, Henry 1949. Law enforcement in fire control on the Cumberland National Forest, *Fire Control Notes,* 10(3):33–40.

——— 1950. "Grass roots" fire prevention. *Fire Control Notes,* 11(4):1–3.

——— 1952. So you have too many fires! *Fire Control Notes,* 13(1):44–46.

Smith, L. F. 1955. Prevention pays off on the Toiyabe. *Fire Control Notes,* 16(1):21–23.

Stradt, G. H. 1950. Debris burning on the Ouachita. *Fire Control Notes,* 11(4):4–5.

Tennessee Dept. of Conservation, Div. of Forestry, and Tennessee Valley Authority 1954. How fires get started in Cumberland and Morgan Counties, Tennessee. Completion Report, Joint Project 19, Contract TV-84695 of above agencies.

Chapter 10: Hazard Reduction

Anonymous 1951. Fire control. *Forestry Dept. North. Rhodesia Rept.* 7.

——— 1952. Firebreaks in N. Rhodesia. *Forestry Dept. North. Rhodesia Rept.* 7.

Ash, L. W. 1951. Paper-covered piled slash. *Fire Control Notes,* 12(3):18–19.

Barrows, J. S. 1951. Forest fires in the northern Rocky Mountains. *U.S. Forest Serv. North. Rocky Mt. Forest and Range Expt. Sta. Paper* 28.

Bentley, Jay R., Craig Chandler, and Verdie E. White 1963. Guidelines for fuel breaks in southern California. *U.S. Forest Serv., Calif. Region. Fuel-break Report No.* 9.

Boe, K. N. 1956. Regeneration and slash disposal in lodgepole pine clear cuttings. *Northwest Sci.,* 30(1):1–11.

Chandrasekaran, R., and Ronald W. Shepard 1966. Optimal strategies of fire fighting by firebreaks. Univ. of Calif., Operations Res. Center, ORC-66-30.

Colvill, L. L. 1946. Development and use of forest service slash buncher teeth. *Jour. Forestry,* 44:89–91.

Crafts, A. S., H. D. Bruce, and R. N. Raynor 1941. Plot tests with chemical soil sterilants in California. *Univ. Calif. Agr. Expt. Sta. Bul.* 648.

Davis, K. P. 1961. Future problems in Lake States fire control. Paper given at Lake States Forest Fire Res. Conf. at Green Bay, Wisconsin.

——— 1967. Relation of forest fire, its control and use, to multiple use management. Paper given at annual meeting Western Forestry and Conservation Assn., Seattle, Wash.

Davis, L. S. 1965. The economics of wildfire protection with emphasis on fuel break systems. State of Calif. Res. Agency, Dept. of Conservation, Div. of Forestry.

Dell, John D., and Franklin R. Ward 1969. Reducing fire hazard in ponderosa pine thinning slash by mechanical crushing. *U.S. Forest Serv. Res. Paper* PSW-57.

Douglas, D. R. 1967. Fire control policy and practice in the forests of South Australia. F, A. O. Symposium on man-made forests.

Fahnestock, G. R. 1954. Roofing slash piles can save—or lose—you dollars. *Fire Control Notes,* **15**(3):22–26.

—— 1968. Fire hazard from precommercial thinning of ponderosa pine. *U.S. Forest Serv. Res. Paper* PNW-57.

——, and John H. Dieterich 1962. Logging slash flammability after five years. *U.S. Forest Serv. Int. Expt. Sta. Res. Paper* 70.

Gilbert, Richard, and J. Schmidt 1970. Ball and chain brush crushing. *Calif. State Div. Forestry, Range Improvement Studies No.* 19.

Gisborne, H. T. 1935. Shaded firebreaks. *Jour. Forestry,* **33**:87.

Green, Lisle R. 1970. An experimental prescribed burn to reduce fuel hazard in chaparral. *U.S. Forest Serv. Res. Note* PSW-216.

——, and Harry E. Schimke 1971. Guides for fuel-break in the Sierra Nevada mixed-conifer type. USFS PSW Handbook.

Harrison-Smith, J. L. 1948. Protective burning. *New Zeal. Jour. Forestry,* **5**:428–430.

Hughes, R. H., and J. L. Rea, Jr. 1951. Forage for fire protection: grazed firebreaks in the North Carolina coastal plain. *South. Lumberman,* **183**:157–160.

Ikenberry, G. H., H. D. Bruce, and J. R. Curry 1938. Experiments with chemicals in killing vegetation on firebreaks. *Jour. Forestry,* **36**:507–515.

Lindenmuth, A. W., and L. S. Gill 1959. Nature's slash "dispose-all." USFS RM Station Reprint—*The Timberman,* **60**:42–43.

Linstedt, K. W. 1950. The mounting Douglas-fir slash problem in western Oregon and Washington: what can we do about it? *Fire Control Notes,* **11**(3):22–24.

Loomis, R. M., and John S. Crosby 1970. Fuel hazard from breakup of dead hardwoods in Missouri. *Jour. Forestry,* **68**(8):490–493.

Lowden, M. S. 1947. Slash disposal in selective cut ponderosa pine stands. *Fire Control Notes,* **8**(4):35–40.

Lyman, C. K. 1945. Principles of fuel reduction for the northern Rocky Mountain region. *U.S. Forest Serv. North. Rocky Mt. Forest and Range Expt. Sta. Prog. Rept.* 1.

—— 1947. Slash disposal as related to fire control on the national forests of western Montana and northern Idaho. *Jour. Forestry,* **45**:259–262.

McArthur, A. G. 1966. The fire control problem and fire research in Australia. *Proc. Sixth World Forestry Congress,* Madrid, Spain.

Munger, T. T., and D. N. Matthews 1941. Slash disposal and forest management after clear-cutting in the Douglas-fir region. *U.S. Dept. Agr. Cir.* 586.

Murphy, J. L., Leo Frischen, and Owen Cramer 1970. Research looks at air quality and forest burning. *Jour. Forestry,* **68**(9):530–535.

——, Harry E. Schimke, Bernard Sweatt, and others 1967. Pre-attack planning for fuel breaks in northern Calif. timber areas—preliminary guide lines. U.S. Forest Serv. PSW.

Olson, D. S., and G. R. Fahnestock 1955. Logging slash: a study of the problem in Inland Empire forests. *Univ. of Idaho Forest Wildlife and Range Expt. Sta. and U.S. Forest Serv. Int. Expt. Sta. Bul.* 1.

Pearson, G. S., and A. C. McIntyre 1935. Slash disposal in the ponderosa pine forests of the southwest. *U.S. Dept. Agr. Cir.* 357.

Pech, Gy 1969. (No. 2123) The relevance of current hazard stick reading to the moisture content of logging slash. *The Forestry Chronicle,* April 1969. pp. 107–113.

Price, J. H. 1934. The ponderosa way. *Amer. Forests,* **40:**387.

Roberts, A. 1949. Slash piling by machine on the southern Idaho forest protective district. *Fire Control Notes,* **10**(2):1–4.

Schimke, Harry E., and Lyle R. Green 1971. Prescribed fire for maintaining fuel breaks in the Central Sierra Nevada. U.S. Forest Serv. PSW, Berkeley.

Steele, Robert W., and Wm. Beaufait 1969. Spring and autumn broadcast burning of interior Douglas-fir slash. *Montana Forest and Conservation Expt. Sta. School of Forestry, U. of Mont. Bul. No.* 36.

Weaver, Harold 1946. Slash disposal on the Colville Indian Reservation. *Jour. Forestry,* **44:**81–88.

White, Verdie E., and Lisle R. Green 1967. Fuel breaks in southern Calif., 1958–1965. U.S. Forest Serv. Pacific S. W. Forest and Range Expt. Sta.

Chapter 11: Forest Fire Detection

Abell, C. A., and R. M. Beeman 1936. Visible area mapping. U.S. Forest Serv., Appalachian Forest Expt. Sta.

———, and ——— 1937. Planning a lookout system. U.S. Forest Serv. Appalachian Forest Expt. Sta.

Barrows, J. S. 1954. Lightning fire research in the Rocky Mountains. *Jour. Forestry,* **52:**845–847.

Boyle, W. S., and J. D. Keys 1949. Proposal of a new approach to forest fire detection. Pulp and Paper Res. Inst. Canada.

Brown, A. A. 1935. Improving forest fire detection in California. *Jour. Forestry,* **33:**923.

Bruce, H.D. 1941. Theoretical analysis of smoke-column visibility. *Jour. Agr. Res.,* **62:**161–178.

——— 1944. Observations on the visibility of a small smoke. *Jour. Forestry,* **42:**426–434.

Buck, C. C. 1938. Factors influencing the discovery of forest fires by lookout observers. *Jour. Agr. Res.,* **56:**259–268.

———, and W. L. Fons 1935. The effect of direction of illumination upon the visibility of a smoke column. *Jour. Agr. Res.,* **51:**907–918.

Byram, G. M., and G. M. Jemison 1948. Some principles of visibility and their application to forest fire detection. *U.S. Dept. Agr. Tech. Bul.* 954.

Chorlton, R. W. 1951 (1958 reprint). Preparation of visible area maps by field sketching. *Canada Dept. of No. Affairs and Natural Resources, Forestry Br. Forest Res. Div., Res. Note* 16.

Curry, J. R. 1933. Binocular telescopes in forest fire detection. *Jour. Forestry* **31**:51.

Dieterich, J. H. 1967. Wildfire detection in the United States. *Proceedings XIV IUFRO Congress,* **5**:702–703.

Fielder, R. L. 1968. Window tinting of lookouts. *Prot. Div. B.C. Forest Service, Canada Plan. Res. Rept. No.* 5. Document No. 1773.

Goodman, J. F. 1966. An analysis of the results of the aerial detection projects Temegami and Kenona areas. *Ontario Dept. of Lands and Forests, document* No. 1861.

Graves, H. S. 1910. Protection of the forests from fire. *U.S. Dept. Agr. Forest Serv. Bul.* 82.

Haines, A. L. 1949. An investigation of photographic methods of mapping the areas visible from a fire patrol aircraft flying a predetermined course. Montana State Univ. Master's Thesis.

Hand, R. L., and H. K. Harris 1947. Preliminary report on aerial detection study. *Fire Control Notes,* **8**(1):28–32.

Harris, H. K., and G. R. Fahnestock 1954. Aerial observer versus lookout. *Fire Control Notes,* **15**(2):35–41.

Hirsch, Stanley N., Robert L. Bjornsen, Forrest H. Madden, and Ralph A. Wilson 1968. Project fire scan fire mapping final report Apr. 1962—Dec. 1966. *U.S. Forest Serv. Res. Paper* INT-48.

———, and Forrest H. Madden 1969. Airborne infrared line scanners for forest fire surveillance. *Society Photo-Optical Instrum., Eng. 14th annual technical symposium,* **2**:51–57.

Hornby, L. G. 1936. Fire Control planning in the northern Rocky Mountains. *U.S. Forest Serv. North. Rocky Mt. Forest and Range Expt. Sta. Prog. Rept.* 1.

Jemison, G. M. 1938. Relation of Byram haze meter readings to safe visibility distance of smoke from an eighth-acre fire. *U.S. Forest Serv. Appalachian Forest Expt. Sta. Tech. Note* 28.

——— 1939. The influence of locality, season and time of day on visibility distance. *U.S. Forest Serv. Appalachian Forest Expt. Sta. Tech. Note* 36.

——— 1940. The influence of locality, season, time of day, and year on the visibility of smoke columns. *Jour. Forestry,* **38**:435–437.

Kerr, E. 1954. Eyes that don't grow sleepy. *Pulp and Paper Mag. Canada,* **55**(12):152, 156.

Kourtz, P. H., and W. G. Regan 1968. A cost-effectiveness analysis of simulated forest fire detection systems. *Hilgardia* **39**(12):341–366.

McArdle, R. E. 1935. A visibility meter for forest fire lookouts. *Jour. Forestry,* **33**:385–388.

——— 1936. Some visibility factors controlling the efficient location and operation of forest fire lookout stations. *Jour. Forestry,* **34**:802–811.

MacLeod, J. C. 1966. Detection and control of forest fires (Canada). *Proc. Sixth World Forestry Congress,* Madrid, Spain.

Mays, L. K. 1938. Visibility mapping from panoramic photographs as used in Region 6. *Fire Control Notes* **2**(1):31–36.

Moessner, K. E. 1938. Seen area mapping: an improved technique. *Fire Control Notes,* **2**(1):18–25.

Morris, W. G. 1947. What is the time between ignition and discovery of lightning fires? *U.S. Forest Serv. Pacific Northwest Forest Expt. Sta. Res. Note* 40.

Shank, H. M. 1931. Visibility maps by field sketching. *Jour. Forestry,* **29**:526–532.

Show, S. B., and E. I. Kotok 1937. Principles of forest fire detection on the national forests of northern California. *U.S. Dept. Agr. Tech. Bul.* 574.

———, G. M. Gowen, J. R. Curry, and A. A. Brown 1937. Planning, constructing and operating forest-fire lookout systems in California. *U.S. Dept. Agr. Cir.* 449.

Stahelin, Rudolph 1932. Visibility maps constructed with the slide rule. *Jour. Forestry,* **30**:983–987.

Tyler, J., and C. H. Lewis 1953. Air patrol for better detection and protection in the South. *Jour. Forestry,* **51**:444–446.

U.S. Forest Serv. 1954. Planning, developing and operating a combination air-ground detection system. Region One.

——— 1970. National forest fire seminar on aircraft management. Division of Forest Fire Control, Washington, D.C., 12 papers.

Valenzuela, J. M., and P. H. Kourtz 1970. An analysis of the forest fire detection alternatives in a 7,000 sq. mi. area in Manitoba. (F.F.-14). Canadian Dept. of Fisheries & Forestry, Canadian F.S., F.F.R.I., Ottawa, Ont.

Worrell, A. C. 1955. Economics of fire detection in the South. *Jour. Forestry,* **53**:639–644.

Wright, J. G. 1942, 1953. A lightning protection system for forest lookout structures. *Canada Dept. of Resources and Develop. Forestry Br., Forest Res. Div. Research Note No.* 11.

Zimmerman, E. W. 1969. Forest fire detection. Div. Coop. Forest Fire Control, Forest Service, U.S. Dept. Agr., U.S. Gov't. Printing Office.

Chapters 12 and 13: Forest Fire Suppression and Fire Control Equipment

Aamodt, E. E. 1951. Jeep plow. *Fire Control Notes,* **12**(2):32–34.

Ames, F. G. 1953. Exploring the possible use of fireline plows in the West. *Fire Control Notes,* **14**(3):9–10.

——— 1953a. Planning for the use of fireline plows. *Fire Control Notes,* **14**(4):35–41.

Anderson, Hal E. 1968. Sundance Fire—an analysis of fire phenomena. *U.S. Forest Serv. Res. Paper* INT-56.

Anonymous 1948. The use of a bulldozer for fire-line construction. *Forestry Chron.,* **24**:315.

——— 1955. Aerial fire fighting: bulk water drop by fixed wing aircraft. *Firestop, Calif. Div. Forestry and Coop. Agencies, Prog. Rept.* 9.

——— 1955a. Aerial firefighting: the helitanker. *Firestop, Calif. Div. Forestry and Coop. Agencies, Prog. Rept.* 10.

——— 1955b. Fire Retardants, I. Firestop, Calif. *Div. Forestry and Coop. Agencies, Prog. Rept.* 4.

Arnold, R. Keith 1955. "Operation Firestop." *Fire Control Notes,* **16**(2).

Barrows, J. S. 1947. Aerial bombing of forest fires. *Proc. West. Forestry and Conserv. Assoc.,* **38**:20–21.

Campbell, J. F. 1938. Developments in the one lick method. *Fire Control Notes,* **2**(1):25–29.

Clepper, Henry 1969. First wings over the forest, Part 1. *American Forests,* June.

Cliff, E. P., and R. E. Anderson 1940. The 40-man crew: a report on the activities of an experimental 40-man suppression crew. *Fire Control Notes,* **40**(2):47–62.

Committee on Fire Research, Div. of Eng. National Res. Council 1971. Employment of air operations in the fire services. Proc. Symposium, June 9–10, 1971, Argonne Nat'l. Lab., Illinois National Academy of Sciences.

Cooper, J. W. 1955. Tractor-plow vs. 60 miles of incendiarism. *Fire Control Notes,* **16**(1):18–20.

Ely, J. B., and A. W. Jensen 1955. Air delivery of water helps control brush and grass fires. *USFS Calif. Forest and Range Expt. Sta. Res. Note* 99.

———, ———, L. R. Chatten, and H. W. Jori 1957. Air tankers: a new tool for forest fire fighting. *Fire Control Notes,* **18**(3):103–109.

Fenner, R. L. 1953. A safe, cheap, and effective forest fire grenade. *Fire Control Notes,* **14**(2):22–24.

Fielder, R. L. 1968. An infrared fire detector telescope. *Prot. Div. B.C. Forest Serv. Plan and Res. Rept. No.* 8. Document No. 1776.

Fons, W. L. 1950. Wet water for forest fire suppression. *U.S. Forest Serv. Calif. Forest and Range Expt. Sta. Res. Note* 71.

———, and R. S. McBride 1950. Wet water for pretreating litter fuels. *Fire Control Notes,* **11**(2):26–27.

Friedman, R. and J. B. Levy 1957. Survey of fundamental knowledge of mechanisms of actions of flame-extinguishing agents. *W.A.D.C. Tech. Rept.* 56–568. Wright-Patterson Air Force Base, Wright Air Dev. Center, Ohio.

George, Charles W., and Ronald A. Sussott 1971. Effects of ammonium phosphate and sulphate on the pyrolysis and combustion of cellulose. *USDA-FS Res. Paper* INT-90.

Grace, Harry 1948. Characteristics of certain fog nozzles. *U.S. Forest Serv. Equip. Devlpmt. Rept.* 11.

Hess, Q. F. 1952. Fighting forest fires with water bombs. *Pulp and Paper Mag. Canada,* **53**(6):146–148.

Hartman, A. W. 1948. Machines and fires in the South. *U.S. Dept. Agr. Yearbook.*

——— 1952. Recent developments in southern fire control. *Fire Control Notes,* **13**(2):25–29.

Hulett, H. C. 1940. Organizing natives to function as fire fighting units using the 10- to 15-foot method. *Fire Control Notes,* **4**(3):101–111.

Jones, Stuart E., and Jay Johnson 1968. Forest fire—the Devil's picnic. *National Geographic,* July 1968.

Luke, R. H. 1953. Tractor-plough units for constructing fire lines. *Austral. Timber Jour.,* **19**:576–577.

MacLeod, J. C. 1947. Effect of altitude, length of hose line, and head on performance of forest-fire pumping units. *Forest Serv. Canada, Forest Fire Res. Note* 13.

MacKay, R. N. 1948. Pumps challenge the forest fire meance. *Timber of Canada,* **8**(10):37, 78, 80, 82–83.

Mackey, T. E. 1954. Aerial water bombing. *Fireman,* **21**(3):19–20.

MacTavish, J. S. 1955. Slip-on tankers for forest fire suppression. *Dept. North. Affairs and Natl. Res., Forestry Branch, Tech. Note* 12, Ottawa.

McReynolds, K. P. 1936. Speeding up fire-line construction by the one-lick method. *Fire Control Notes* **1**(1):23–26.

Miller, H. R., and C. C. Wilson 1957. A chemical fire retardant. *U.S. Forest Serv. Calif. Forest and Range Expt. Sta. Tech. Paper* 15.

National Fire Protective Assoc. 1955. Standards for wetting agents. Ser. 10, no. 18, Boston.

———— 1956. Community equipment and organization for fighting forest, grass and brush fires. No. 259M, Boston.

———— 1967. Chemicals for forest fire fighting. National Fire Protection Association, Boston.

———— 1965. Revised 1972 Air operations for forest, brush, and grass fires. A report of the NFPA Forest Committee.

Neuns, A. G. 1950. Water versus fire. U.S. Forest Serv., Calif. Region.

Orell, B. L. 1944. Fire fighting with fog. *Jour. Forestry,* **42**:423–425.

Platt, C. F. 1969. The need for equipment development in forest fire control. *Pulp & Paper Mag. of Canada,* **70**(19):99–101.

Reynolds, G. L., G. E. White, and E. G. Madsen 1948. Comparative performance of D-6 and D-7 caterpillar tractors equipped with hydraulic angle dozers. *U.S. Forest Serv. Equip. Develop. Rept.* 13.

Stewart, G. I. 1934. The use of shallow wells in forest fire suppression. Mich. Dept. of Conserv., Lansing.

———— 1952. The field of engineering in forest protection. *Jour. Forestry,* **50**:379–383.

Stilling, F. I. 1951. Bulldozers for fire suppression in the mountainous terrain of the northern Rocky Mountain region. *Fire Control Notes,* **13**(2):18–21.

Storey, T. G. and R. W. Bower 1967. Comparative fireline production rates among U.S.F.S. regions for hand crews and bulldozers. *Fire Control Notes,* **27**(6): 1967.

Such, Steven 1952. Michigan power-wagon plow. *Fire Control Notes,* **13**(2):18–21.

———— 1956. The importance of design in equipment development. *Fire Control Notes,* **17**(2):1–3.

Tang, W. K., and H. W. Eikner 1968. Effect of inorganic salts on the pyrolysis of wood cellulose and lignin determined by differential thermal analysis. *U.S. Dept. Agr. Forest Serv. Res. Paper* F.PL-82.

Truax, T. R. 1939. Chemicals in forest fire control. *Jour. Forestry,* **37**:677–679.

U.S. Forest Serv. 1951. Ejection suction booster. *Fire Control Notes,* **12**(3):14–17.

———— 1955. A guide for judging fireline plows. Region Eight.

———— 1956. Improved fire hose dispensing tray for helicopters. *Equip. Develop.*

Rept. 44. USFS Equip. Develop. Center, San Dimas, Calif.

—— 1966. One-man flail trencher. *Equip. Develop. Rept.* 5100-14. U.S. Forest Serv. Equip. Develop. Center, Missoula, Mont.

—— 1966, 1972. Spark arrestor guide. San Dimas Develop. Center, San Dimas, Calif.

—— 1969. Water handling equipment guide. San Dimas Develop. Center, San Dimas, Calif.

—— 1971. Fireline handbook. USDA Forest Serv.

—— 1972. Fireman's handbook, USDA Forest Serv.

—— 1972. Investigations and tests of backfiring projectiles and protecting devices. San Dimas Develop. Center, San Dimas, Calif.

U.S. Forest Service, Missoula, Montana 1969. History of smoke jumping, 1925–1969. U.S. Dept. of Agr., Forest Serv., Northern Region.

——, and Calif. Div. of Forestry, 1970. Forest fire fighting fundamentals. Reprint 1970, Training book.

Webster, L. T. 1950. The use of mobile pumper units in fire suppression. *Proc. West. Forestry Conserv. Assoc.,* **41**:42–44.

Wood, William C. 1968. That forests may live—the smokejumpers. 1968 Yearbook of Agriculture, pp. 193–197.

Chapters 14 and 15: Designing and Operating Fire Control Systems

Alabama Department of Conservation and Tennessee Valley Authority 1952. Forest fire control. Tennessee Valley Counties of Alabama.

Barrows, J. S. 1951. Forest fires in the northern Rocky Mountains. *U.S. Forest Serv. North. Rocky Mt. Forest and Range Expt. Sta. Paper* 28.

Beall, H. W. 1951. Some modern aspects of forest fire control in Canada. *Proc. UNSUCCR, Lake Success, N.Y.,* **5**:40–43.

Brown, A. A. 1952. Mainstays of forest fire protection. *Fire Control Notes,* **13**(4):29–34.

——, and F. W. Funke 1936. Redesigning Plans of Communication for the National Forests of California. *Jour. Forestry,* **34**:798.

Chandler, C. C. 1956. Integrating prevention into fire control planning. *Fire Control Notes,* **17**(2):6–7.

Clar, C. R., and L. R. Chatten 1954. Principles of forest fire management. Calif. Dept. of Nat. Resources, Div. of Forestry.

—— 1969. Evolution of California's wildland fire protection system. Leaflet, State of Calif. Dept. of Conservation, Div. of Forestry.

Clepper, Henry 1969. Smokejumpers—the corps d'elite. First wings over the forest. Part II American Forests, July 1969.

Cobb, S. S. 1952. An answer to forest fire prevention and control in anthracite coal fields. *Jour. Forestry,* **50**:834–837.

Committee on Fire Research 1971. Div. of Eng. Nat'l. Res. Council. Employment of air operations in the fire services. *Proc. Symposium,* Argonne Nat'l. Lab, Illinois. National Academy of Sciences, U.S.A.

Crocker, C. S. 1949. Fighting fires from the air. *U.S. Dept. Agr. Yearbook,* pp. 508–516.

Dominion Forest Serv. 1948. Fire control plan for the Petawawa Forest Experiment Station, Chalk River, Ontario.

DuBois, Coert 1911. National forest fire-protection plans. U.S. Dept. Agr. Forest Serv.

——— 1914. Systematic fire protection in the California forests. U.S. Dept. Agr. Forest Serv.

Fielder, R. L. 1968. Smoke generators. *Prot. Div. B.C. Forest Serv. Plan. Res. Rept. No.* 6. Document No. 1774.

Fraser, D. G. 1964. Forest fire control aircraft in Canada. *Jour. Royal Aeronautical Soc.* **68:**546–552.

Gilbert, J. M. 1949. Fire control in Tasmania. *Austral. Forestry,* **13:**34–39.

Gisborne, H. T. 1939. Hornby's principles of fire control planning. *Jour. Forestry,* **37:**292–296.

Grace, H. D. 1951. Intensive pre-planning for fire suppression. *Fire Control Notes,* **12**(2):37–46.

Greeley, W. B. 1911. Better methods of fire control. *Proc. Soc. Amer. Foresters,* **5:**153–165.

Hall, R. L. 1951. The helicopter as a fire-fighting unit. Canadian Pulp and Paper Assoc., Woodlands Section.

Hand, R. L. 1953. Actuarial fire planning in the Northern Region. *Fire Control Notes,* **15**(3):1–8.

Hanson, P. D. and C. A. Abell 1941. Determining the desirable size of suppression crews for national forests of N. Calif. *Fire Control Notes,* **5**(3):156–160.

Harris, H. K. 1954. Helicopter use—fire suppression. *Fire Control Notes,* **15**(2): 7–12.

Holmes, C. F. 1948. Common errors in fire fighting. *Forestry Chron.,* **24:**135–140.

Hornby, L. G. 1936. Fire control planning in the northern Rocky Mountain region. *U.S. Forest Serv. North. Rocky Mt. Forest and Range Expt. Sta. Prog. Rept.* 1.

Jefferson, F. J. 1947. Fire control logistics. *Fire Control Notes,* **8**(2–3):5–7.

Lindquist, James L. 1970. Building firelines—how fast do crews work? *Fire Technology,* **6**(2):124–134.

Mackey, T. E. 1952. Forest fire protection in Ontario. Ontario Dept. of Lands and Forests, 6th British Commonwealth Forestry Conference, Canada.

MacLeod, J. C. 1964. Planning for forest fire control. *Canada Dept. of Forestry, Forest Research Branch, Pub. No.* 1048.

McMasters, A. W. 1963. Preliminary analysis of the influence of hand crews on fire growth. *Res. Rept.* ORC 63-7. Operations Res. Center, Univ. of Calif., Berkeley.

Mitchell, J. A. 1954. Rating the effectiveness of forest fire protection. *Jour. Forestry,* **52:**183–185.

Norcross, T. W., and R. F. Grefe 1931. Transportation planning to meet hour control requirements. *Jour. Forestry* **29:**1019.

Northeastern Forest Fire Protection Commission and U.S. Forest Service, Region Seven 1954. Manual for forest fire control. Northeast. Forest Fire Protection Commission, Chatham, N. Y.

Pierce, E. S., and C. A. Gustafson 1949. Building a fire organization. *U.S. Dept. Agr. Yearbook.*

Pirsco, Arthur R. 1961. Selecting fire control planning levels by burning index frequencies. *Misc. Paper* 55 PSW and *Fire Control Notes*, **22**(4):109–112.

Show, S. B., B. Clarke et al. 1953. Elements of forest fire control. *FAO Forestry and forest products studies No.* 5. United Nations.

————, and E. I. Kotok 1930. The determination of hour control for adequate fire protection in the major cover types of the California pine region. *U.S. Dept. Agr. Tech. Bul.* 209.

Simard, A. J., and D. E. Williams 1969–1970. Study of the feasibility of a Canada-wide air tanker fleet. *Pulp & Paper Magazine of Canada*, **70**(12).

Spaulding, A. E., 1952. U.S. Forest Service views fire protection plans for logging operations. *Fire Control Notes*, **13**(1):38–40.

Storey, Theodore G., D. Ross Garder, and Ernest T. Tolin 1969. INFORMAP—a computerized information system for fire planning and fire control. *U.S. Forest Serv. Res. Paper* PSW-54.

Strong, Clarence C., and Clyde S. Webb 1970. White Pine, King of Many Waters. Mountain Press Publishing Co., Missoula, Mont.

U.S. Forest Service Missoula, Montana, 1969. History of smoke-jumping, 1925–1969. *U.S. Forest Serv. Northern Region.*

———— 1966, Revised 1972. Fireman's Handbook, USDA Forest Service, 5125.3.

———— 1966, Glossary of terms used in forest fire control. *U.S. Dept. Agr. Handbook* 104.

———— 1970. National forest fire seminar on aircraft management. U.S. Forest Serv., Div. Forest Fire Control, Washington, D.C., 12 papers.

————, and State of California Division of Forestry, 1970. Forest fire fighting fundamentals.

———— 1972. Manual for forest fire fighters. Northeastern Area, Forest Fire Protection Compact. State and Private Forestry Division.

(Similar manuals for various other state and state compact groups).

Van Wagner, C. E. 1965 (1969 in French) (Pbn. No. 1127 and 1127F). Aids to forest fire control planning at Petawawa. Canada Dept. of Forestry, Forest Res. Branch.

Chapter 16: Control of Large Fires

American Forestry Association 1969. Disaster fires, why? and other fire subjects. *Amer. Forests.*

Anderson, Hal E. 1968. Sundance Fire: an analysis of fire phenomena. *USDA Forest Service Res. Paper* INT-56.

Brown, A. A. 1937. The factors and circumstances that led to the Blackwater Fire tragedy. *Fire Control Notes*, **1**:384.

———— 1940. Lessons of the McVey Fire, Black Hills, N. F. April 1940, *Fire Control Notes*, **4**(2):63–67.

————, and A. D. Folweiler 1953. Fire in the forests of the United States. Chapter XIII, Analysis of fires.

Countryman, Clive 1969. Project Flambeau—an investigation of mass fire 1964–
67. Final Rept., Vol. 1, USDA-FS, PSW F & R Expt. Sta., Berkeley,
Calif.
_____ 1969. Fire weather and fire behavior at the 1968 Canyon Fire. *USDA-FS
Res. Paper* PSW-55.
_____ and Craig Chandler 1963. The fire behavior team approach in fire control.
Fire Control Notes, **24**(3).
Davis, J. B. 1968. Forest fire control decision making under conditions of
uncertainty. *Jour. Forestry,* **66**(8):626–631.
Davis, M. H. 1954. Maintaining an effective organization to control the occasional
large fire. *Jour. Forestry,* **52**:750–755.
DeCoste, John H., Dale D. Wade and John E. Deeming 1968. The Gaston Fire.
U.S. Forest Serv. Res. Paper SE-43.
Douglas, D. R. 1965. The Clare fire—an assessment. *Jour. Agr., South Australia,*
69:102–8, 131–6.
Dunn, P. M. 1956. Organizing fire suppression forces. So. Pulpwood Cons. Assn.
The Unit, Newsletter, **61**:34–39.
Evans, R. M. 1950. Northeastern interstate forest fire protection compact. (Now
Northeastern Forest Fire Protection Commission). *Fire Control Notes,*
11(4):44–46.
Headley, Roy 1939. Lessons from larger fires, 1938. *Fire Control Notes,* **2**(4):7–17.
_____ 1940. Lessons from larger fires, 1939, taken from reports of fires over 300
acres. *Fire Control Notes,* **4**(1):29–36.
Jefferson, F. J. 1947. The fire on Cedar Creek. *U.S. Dept. Agr. Yearbook.*
Jones, Stuart E., and Jay Johnston 1968. Forest fire, the Devil's picnic. *National
Geographic,* July 1968, pp. 100–127.
Kiil, A. D., and J. E. Grigel 1969. (A-X-24) The May 1968 forest conflagrations in
Central Alberta—a review of fire weather, fuels and fire behavior. Canada,
Dept. of Fisheries and Forestry, Forestry Br., Forest Res. Lab., Edmonton,
Alta.
Lawson, E. L., Director, Div. of Forestry, Minnesota Dept. of Conservation 1959.
The Badoura Fire of May 1, 1959.
Lehman, J. W., and R. A. Vogenberger 1955. The role of a regional agency in
forest fire control. *Jour. Forestry,* **53**:430–435.
Loveridge, Earl W. 1944. The fire suppression policy of the U.S. Forest Service.
Jour. Forestry, **42**(8):549–564.
Lowden, Merle S. 1967. War on forest fires. Yearbook of Agriculture, "Outdoors
U.S.A." U.S.D.A., pp. 82–87.
MacKay, S., W. Girard, and E. Simard 1968. A board of review report on the
Riviere Dupont forest fire. The L.F.P.A., Ltd.
McArthur, A. G., D. R. Douglas, and L. R. Mitchell 1958. The Wandilo Fire, April
5, 1958. Fire behavior and associated meteorological and fuel conditions.
Leaflet No. 98, O.D.C. 431.6, Forest Research Inst., Australia.
_____, and N. P. Cheney 1968. Report on bush fires in Southern Tasmania of Feb.
7, 1967. Forest Res. Inst., Canberra, Australia.
Palmer, Thomas Y. 1969. Project Flambeau—an investigation of mass fire

1964–67. Final Rept., Vol. II, Catalog of Project Flambeau Fires. USDA-FS PSW Misc. pub.

Pyles, Hamilton K. et al. 1966. The Loop Fire Disaster, Nov. 1, 1966. A brief of the report of the group assigned by the Chief of the USFS to analyze the Loop fire accident—fire overran fire crew, killing 10, injuring 12.

Stewart, G. R. 1948. Fire (a novel). Random House, Inc., New York.

Storey, T. G. 1969. Project Flambeau—an investigation of mass fire, 1964–67. Final Rept., Vol. III. Appendixes—preparation of test plots using wildland fuels to simulate urban conditions; also tree weights and fuel size distribution.

Towell, William E. 1969. Disaster fires, why? *Amer. Forests,* **75**(6).

Whittingham, H. E. 1964. Meteorological conditions associated with the Dandenong bushfires of 14–16 January 1964. (Near Melbourne, Victoria.) From *Australian Meteorological Magazine,* no. 14, pp. 10–37.

Chapters 17 and 18: Uses and Techniques of Use of Fire on Wild Lands

Arnold, Keith, L. T. Burcham, R. L. Fenner, and R. F. Grah 1951. Use of fire in land clearing. Univ. Calif. Agr. Expt. Sta.

Baxter, J. R., D. R. Packham, and G. B. Peet 1966. Control burning from aircraft. Leaflet. CSIRO chemical research labs. Melbourne, Aust.

Beaufait, William R. 1966. Prescribed fire planning in the Intermountain West. *U.S. Forest Serv. Res. Paper* INT-26.

Bentley, Jay R. 1967. Conversion of chaparral areas to grasslands—techniques used in California. *U.S. Dept. Agr. Handbook* 328.

Bickford, C. A., and J. R. Curry 1943. The use of fire in the protection of longleaf and slash pine forests. *South. Forest Expt. Sta. Occas. Paper* 105.

——, and L. S. Newcomb 1947. Prescribed burning in the Florida flatwoods. *Fire Control Notes,* **8**(1):17–23.

——, and R. S. Campbell 1945. Better management on southern coastal forest ranges. *U.S. Dept. Agr.* AIS-17.

Biswell, H. H., and P. C. Lemon 1943. Effect of fire upon seedstalk production of range grasses. *Jour. Forestry,* **41**:844.

——, R. D. Taber, D. W. Hedrick, and A. M. Schultz 1952. Management of chamise brushlands for game in the north coast region of California. *Calif. Fish and Game,* **38**:453–484.

——, and A. M. Schultz 1957. Surface runoff and erosion as related to prescribed burning. *Jour. Forestry,* **55**:372–374.

Blaisdell, J. P. 1953. Ecological effects of planned burning of sagebrush-grass range on the upper Snake River plains. *U.S. Dept. Agr. Tech. Bul.* 1075.

Bruce, David 1947. Thirty-two years of annual burning in longleaf pine. *Jour. Forestry,* **45**:809–814.

——, and C. A. Bickford 1950. Use of fire in natural regeneration of longleaf pine. *Jour. Forestry,* **48**:114–117.

Buell, M. F., and J. E. Cantlon 1953. Effects of prescribed burning on ground cover in the New Jersey pine region. *Ecology,* **34**:520–528.

California Div. of Forestry 1968. Brushland range improvement. *State of Calif., Dept. of Conservation, Div. of Forestry, Annual Report.*

Carpenter, S. B., J. Bentley and C. Graham 1970. Moisture contents of brushland fuels dessicated for burning. *U.S. Forest Serv. Res. Note P.S.W.* 202.

Chaiken, L. E. 1949. The behavior and control of understory hardwoods in loblolly pine stands. *U.S. Forest Serv. Southeast. Forest Expt. Sta. Tech. Note* 72.

Chapman, H. H. 1942. Management of loblolly pine in the pine-hardwood region in Arkansas and Louisiana west of the Mississippi River. *Yale Univ., School Forestry, Bul.* 49.

―――― 1947. Prescribed burning vs. public forest fire services. *Jour. Forestry,* **45**:804–808.

――――, and W. L. Hall 1947. Prescribed burning in the loblolly pine type. *Jour. Forestry,* **45**:209–212.

Conarro, R. M. 1942. The place of fire in southern forestry. *Jour. Forestry,* **40**:129–131.

Cooper, R. W. 1953. Prescribed burning to regenerate sand pine. *U.S. Forest Serv. Southeast. Forest Expt. Sta. Res. Note* 22.

Cramer, Owen P., and James N. Westwood 1970. Potential impact of air quality restrictions on logging residue burning. *U.S. Forest Serv. Res. Paper* PSW-64.

Crosciewicz, Z. 1970. Regeneration of jack pine by burning and seeding treatments on clear-cut sites in Central Ontario. Canada, Dept. of Fisheries and Forestry, Canadian FS. For. Res. Lab., Ste. Marie, Ontario. O-X-138.

Cushwa, C. T. 1968. Use of fire: A summary of literature in the U.S. from the Mid-1920's to 1966. U.S. Forest Serv. Southeastern Expt. Sta.

――――, and R. E. Martin 1969. The status of prescribed burning for wildlife management in the Southeast. *Trans. thirty-fourth North Amer. Wildlife and Natural Resources Conf.,* pp. 419–428.

Davis, K. P., and K. A. Klehm 1939. Controlled burning in the western white pine type. *Jour. Forestry,* **37**:399–407.

Dell, John D., and Don E. Franks 1970. Slash smoke dispersal over western Oregon—a case study. *U.S. Forest Serv. Res. Paper* P.S.W-67.

Duvall, V. L., and L. B. Whitaker 1964. Rotational burning: A forage management system for longleaf pine-bluestem ranges. *Jour. Range Manag.,* **17**:322–326.

Dyer, C. D., and C. N. Brightwell 1955. Prescribed burning in slash and longleaf pine forests of Georgia. *Univ. Ga. Agr. Ext. Serv. Bul.* 594.

Fenner, R. L., R. K. Arnold, and C. C. Buck 1955. Area ignition for brush burning. *U.S. Forest Serv. Calif. Forest and Range Expt. Sta. Tech. Paper* 10.

Ferguson, E. R. 1961. Effects of prescribed fires on understory stems in pine-hardwood stands of Texas. *Jour. Forestry,* **59**(5):356–359.

Folweiler, A. D. 1952. The place of fire in southern silviculture. *Jour. Forestry,* **50**:187–190.

Fritschen, Leo J., H. H. Boree, Konrad Buettner et al., 1970. Slash fire atmospheric pollution. *U.S. Forest Serv. Res. Paper* P.N.W.-97.

———, S. G. Pickford, H. H. Boree, Leo E. Montieth, R. J. Charlson, and J. L. Murphy 1969. Prescribed burning and management of air quality. *Proc. Seminar on Prescribed Burning and Management Air Quality.* Southwest Interagency Fire Council, Tucson, Ariz.

Green, Lisle R. 1970. An experimental prescribed burn to reduce fuel hazard in chaparral. *U.S. Forest Serv. Res. Note* PSW-216.

Gregory, G. R. 1955. An economic approach to multiple use. *Forest Sci.,* 1:6–13.

Halls, L. K., B. L. Southwell, and F. E. Knox 1952. Burning and grazing in coastal plain forests. *Univ. Ga., College Agr., Bul.* 51.

Hartman, A. A. 1949. Fire as a tool in southern pine. *U.S. Dept. Agr. Yearbook,* pp. 517–527.

Hills, J. T. 1957. Prescribed burning techniques in loblolly and longleaf pine on the Francis Marion National Forest. *Fire Control Notes,* 18(3):112–113.

Hilmon, J. B., and R. H. Hughes 1965. Fire and forage in the wiregrass type. *Jour. Range Manag.,* 18:251–254.

———, and ——— 1965. Forest service research on the use of fire in livestock management in the South. *Proc. Fourth Ann. Tall Timbers Fire Ecology Conference,* 261–275.

Hodgson, A., and N. P. Cheney 1970. Aerial ignition for backburning. *Jour. Inst. Foresters Australia,* 33(4):268–274.

Hughes, R. H., J. B. Hilmon, and G. W. Burton 1966. Improving forage on southern pine woodlands. *Ninth International Grassland Congress Proc:* 1305–1307.

Jenkins, B. C. 1946. What about controlled burning? *Mich. Conserv.,* 15(4):12–14.

——— 1948. The role of fire in wildlife management. *Mich. Conserv.,* 17(4):10, 12.

Lemon, P. C. 1946. Cattle aid in fire hazard reduction. *Forest Farmer,* 5(6):8.

——— 1946a. Prescribed burning in relation to grazing in the longleaf-slash pine type. *Jour. Forestry,* 44:115–117.

Leonard, O. A., and C. E. Carlson 1957. Control of chamise and brush seedlings by aircraft spraying. *Cal. Div. of Forestry, Range Impr. Studies no.* 2.

Lindenmuth, A. W., Jr., and G. M. Byram 1948. Headfires are cooler near the ground than backfires. *Fire Control Notes,* 9(4):8–9.

Little, Silas, Jr. 1953. Prescribed burning as a tool of forest management in the northeastern states. *Jour. Forestry,* 51:496–500.

———, J. P. Allen, and E. B. Moore 1948. Controlled burning as a dual-purpose tool of forest management in New Jersey's pine region. *Jour. Forestry,* 46:810–819.

———, and E. B. Moore 1949. The ecological role of prescribed burns in the pine-oak forests of southern New Jersey. *Ecology,* 30:223–233.

———, and ——— 1953. Severe burning treatment tested on lowland pine sites. *U.S. Forest Serv., Northeast. Forest Expt. Sta. Paper* 64.

———, H. A. Somes, and J. P. Allen 1953. Choosing suitable times for prescribed burning in southern New Jersey. *Fire Control Notes,* 14(1):21–25.

———, and ——— 1961. Prescribed burning in the pine regions of southern New Jersey and eastern shore Maryland—a summary of present knowledge. *USDA FS Research Paper* NE-151.

Love, R. M., and B. L. Jones 1952. Improving California brush ranges. *Univ. Calif. Agr. Expt. Sta. Cir.* 371 (rev.).

Lynch, J. J. 1941. The place of burning in management of the Gulf Coast wildlife refuges. *Jour. Wildlife Mangt.,* **5:**454–457.

Martin, R. E., and L. S. Davis 1961. Temperatures near the ground during prescribed burning. *Mich. Acad. Science Arts and Letters, Papers* Vol. XLVI (1960 meeting).

Mayfield, Harold 1963. Establishment of preserves for the kirtlands warbler in the state and national forests of Michigan. *Wilson Bul.* **75:**216–220.

McArthur, A. G. 1962. Control burning in eucalypt forests. *Forest. and Timb. Bur. Leaf.* 80, Canberra, Aust.

McCulley, R. D. 1950. Management of natural slash pine stands in the flatwoods of south Georgia and north Florida. *U.S. Dept. Agr. Cir.* 845.

Moore, E. B., G. E. Smith, and S. Little 1955. Wildfire damage reduced on prescribed-burned area in New Jersey. *Jour. Forestry,* **53:**339–341.

Muraro, S. J. 1967. Methods and needs for evaluating performance of prescribed fires. Paper presented at the XIV Congress of the Int. Union of Forest Rs. Organizations, Munich, Germany, Sept. 4–9, 1967. Canada Dept. For., B.C. Region, Victoria, B.C. (Also Pb. No. 1231).

Murphy, J. L., Leo Frischen, and Owen Cramer 1970. Research looks at air quality and forest burning. *Jour. Forestry,* **68**(9):530–535.

Oettmier, W. M. 1956. The place of prescribed burning. *Forest Farmer,* **15**(8):6, 7, 18.

Pechanec, J. R., George Stewart, and J. P. Blaisdell 1954. Sagebrush burning: good and bad. *U.S. Dept. Agr. Farmers' Bul.* 1948 (rev.).

Peet, G. B. 1965. A fire danger rating and controlled burning guide for the northern Jarrah forest of western Australia. *Bul.* 74, Forests Dept., western Australia.

Pomeroy, K. B. 1948. Observations on four prescribed burns in the coastal plain of Virginia and North Carolina. *Fire Control Notes,* **9**(2–3):13–17.

Riebold, R. J. 1955. Summer burns for hardwood control in loblolly pine. *Fire Control Notes,* **16**(1):34–36.

Sackett, S. S. 1969. The chevron burn—a new prescribed firing technique for hilly terrain. *S. Lumberman,* **219**(2728):147.

Sampson, A. W. 1944. Plant succession on burned chaparral lands in northern California. Univ. Calif. *Agr. Expt. Sta. Bul.* 685.

_____ 1952. Range management: principles and practices. John Wiley & Sons, Inc., New York.

_____, and L. T. Burcham 1954. Costs and returns of controlled brush burning for range improvement in northern California. *Calif. Div. Forestry Range Improvement Studies* 1.

_____, and A. M. Schultz 1957. Control of brush and undesirable trees. Forestry Div., Food and Agr. Org. of the United Nations, Rome.

Schimke, Harry E., John D. Dell, and Franklin R. Ward 1969. Electrical ignition for prescribed burning. Forest Service, USDA, PSW Forest Expt. Sta., Berkeley, Calif.

_____, and Lisle Green 1970. Prescribed Fire for Maintaining Fuel Breaks in the Central Sierra Nevada. U.S. Forest Serv., Pacific S.W. Forest and Range

Expt. Sta., Berkeley, Calif.

Shantz, H. L. 1947. The use of fire as a tool in the management of the brush ranges of California. Calif. Dept. of Nat. Resources, Div. of Forestry.

Shepherd, W. O. 1953. Effects of burning and grazing flatwoods forest ranges. U.S. Forest Serv. Southeast. *Forest Expt. Sta. Tech. Note* 30.

Silker, T. H. 1955. Prescribed burning for the control of undesirable hardwoods in pine-hardwood stands and slash pine plantations. *Tex. Forest Serv. Bul.* 46.

Smith, N.F. 1948. Controlled burning in Michigan's forest and game management programs. *Soc. Amer. Foresters Proc.,* **1947:**200–205.

Squires, J. W. 1947. Prescribed burning in Florida. *Jour. Forestry,* **45:**815–819.

Stoddard, H. L. 1931. The bobwhite quail: its habits, preservation, and increase. Charles Scribner's Sons, New York.

―――― 1935. Use of controlled fire in southeastern upland game management. *Jour. Forestry,* **33:**346–351.

Tall Timbers Research Station, Tallahassee, Florida 1969. *Proceedings Tall Timbers Fire Ecology Conference.*

Trippensee, R. E. 1953. Wildlife management, vol. 2. McGraw-Hill Book Company, Inc., New York.

U.S. Dept. Int. 1968. Rare and endangered fish and wildlife of the United States. *U.S. Dept. Int. Bur. of Sport Fisheries and Wildlife sheet* B-57.

Vlamis, J., H. H. Biswell, and A. M. Schultz 1955. Effects of prescribed burning on soil fertility in second growth ponderosa pine. *Jour. Forestry,* **53:**905–909.

Weaver, Harold 1947. Fire: nature's thinning agent in ponderosa pine stands. *Jour. Forestry,* **45:**437–444.

―――― 1951. Observed effects of prescribed burning on perennial grasses in the ponderosa pine forests. *Jour. Forestry,* **49:**267–271.

―――― 1952. A preliminary report on prescribed burning in virgin ponderosa pine. *Jour. Forestry,* **50:**662–667.

Williams, D. E. 1960. Prescribed burning for seedbed preparation in jack pine types. *Pulp & Paper Mag. of Canada, Woodlands Review Section,* **61**(4):94–198.

Chapter 19: Fire Control Policies and Objectives

American Forestry Assn. 1969. Disaster fires, why? and other fire subjects. *American Forests,* June issue.

Arnold, R. K. 1950. Economic and social determinants of an adequate level of forest fire control. Dissertation, Univ. Mich., Ann Arbor.

Artman, J. O. 1954. Twenty years of fire records for state and private forest lands in the Tennessee Valley. T.V.A., Div. of Forestry Relations.

Beall, H. W. 1949. An outline of forest fire protection standards. *Forestry Chron.,* **25:**82–106.

Brown, A. A. 1947. Fire control in resource management. *Fire Control Notes,* **8**(2–3):1–4.

―――――, and A. D. Folweiler 1953. Fire in the forests of the United States. Chap. XIV, Forest Fire Economics. John S. Swift Co., St. Louis, Mo.

Buck, C. C., W. L. Fons, and C. M. Countryman 1948. Fire damage from increased run off and erosion on the Southern California National Forests. Forest Service, U.S. Dept. Agr.

Chapman, H. H. 1949. Local autonomy versus forest fire damage in New England. *Jour. Forestry,* **47**:101–106.

Clar, C. R. 1969. Evolution of California's wildland fire protection system. State of Calif., Dept. of Conservation, Div. of Forestry (monograph).

Craig, R. B., B. Frank, G. L. Hayes, and G. M. Jemison 1945. Fire losses and justifiable protection costs in southern piedmont of Virginia. U.S. Forest Serv. Southeast. Forest Expt. Sta.

——, ——, ——, and T. F. Marburg 1946. Fire losses and justifiable protection costs in the southwestern coal section of Virginia. U.S. Forest Serv. Southeast. Forest Expt. Sta.

——, T. F. Marburg, and G. L. Hayes 1946. Fire losses and justifiable protection costs in the coastal plain region of South Carolina. U.S. Forest Serv. Southeast. Forest Expt. Sta.

Davis, K. P. 1954. American forest management. McGraw-Hill Book Company, Inc., New York.

—— 1960. (Forest and Range Land Problems in Underdeveloped countries.) Extension of remarks on natural resources and development Panel G, Michigan Conference on International Development, Ann Arbor, Mich. May 16–17.

—— 1961. Future problems in Lake States fire control. Lake States Forest Fire Res. Conf., March 7–8, Green Bay, Wisc.

Demmon, E. L. 1955. The president's column. *Jour. Forestry,* **53**:464.

Dubois, Coert 1911. National forest fire-protection plans. U.S. Dept. Agr. Forest Serv.

—— 1914. Systematic fire protection in the California forests. U.S. Dept. Agr. Forest Serv.

Duerr, Wm. A., and Henry J. Vaux (eds.) 1953. Research in the economics of forestry. Charles Lathrop Pack Forestry Foundation, 1953.

Eden, L. T. E. 1967. Forest fire insurance. Congress of the IUFRO.

Flint, H. R. 1928. Adequate fire control. *Jour. Forestry,* **26**:624–638.

Gisborne, H. T. 1950. Forest protection. Chap. 2, Fifty years of forestry in the U.S.A., Soc. Amer. Foresters, Washington, D.C.

Graves, H. S. 1910. Protection of forests from fire. *U.S. Dept. Agr. Forest Serv. Bul.* 82.

Greeley, W. B. 1911. Better methods of fire control. *Proc. Soc. Amer. Foresters,* **5**:153–165.

Gustafson, C. A. 1950. Impact of destructive forest fires on the timber resource of a management unit. *Fire Control Notes,* **11**(2):18–23.

Kling, J. B. 1951. Cooperative forest fire control. State University of New York, College of Forestry.

Lehman, J. W., and R. A. Vogenberger 1955. The role of a regional agency in forest fire control. *Jour. Forestry,* **53**:430–435.

Loveridge, E. W. 1944. The fire suppression policy of the U.S. Forest Service. *Jour. Forestry,* **42**:549–554.

McLean, D. L. 1970. Economic determinants of an optimal level of forest fire protection. Canada Dept. of Fisheries and Forestry, Canadian FS, FFRI, Ottawa, Ontario, FF-13.

MacLeod, J. C. 1960. Research in forest fire control. Proceedings 5th World Forestry Congress, G.P./55/III/D. Canada. Aug. 29–Sept. 10, Seattle, Wash.

Matthews, D. N., and W. G. Morris 1940. Forest fire control in western Snohomish County, Washington, U.S. Forest Serv. Pacific Northwest Forest and Range Expt. Sta.

———, and ——— 1942. Adequate forest fire control based on a study of the Clackamas-Marion patrol unit in Oregon. U.S. Forest Serv. Pacific Northwest Forest and Range Expt. Sta.

Mitchell, J. A. and Neil LeMay 1952. Forest fires and forest fire control in Wisconsin. Wis. Conserv. Dept.

———, and Durward Robson 1950. Forest fires and forest fire control in Michigan. Mich. Dept. of Conserv., Lansing.

Shepard, H. B. 1937. Forest fire insurance in the Pacific Coast states. *U.S. Dept. Agr. Bul.* 551, 1937.

Murphy, James L. 1968. An evaluation of the forest fire problem in the Republic of Chile and of the national plan of protection against forest fire. *Univ. of Wash., College of Forest Resources, misc. pub.*

Show, S. B., B. Clarke, et al. 1953. Elements of forest fire control. *FAO Forestry and forest products studies No. 5 of the United Nations.*

———, and E. I. Kotok 1923. Forest fires in California, 1911–1920: an analytical study. *U.S. Dept. Agr. Cir.* 243.

———, and ——— 1929. Cover type and fire control in the national forests of California. *U.S. Dept. Agr. Dept. Bul.* 1495.

Sparhawk, W. N. 1925. The use of liability ratings in planning forest fire protection. *Jour. Agr. Res.,* **30:**693–762.

Stahl, W. J. 1954. Cooperative forest fire protection. *Fire Control Notes,* **15**(1):14–15.

U.S. Forest Serv. 1958. Timber resources for America's future.

Williams, D. E. 1969. Economics of forest fire control. Paper presented at the 6th National Fire Conference, Winnipeg, Manitoba, April 15–17. Canada Dept. Fisheries and Forestry, Forestry Br., F.R.I.

INDEX